GREAT BASIN KINGDOM

GREAT BASIN KINGDOM

An Economic History of the Latter-day Saints

1830–1900

LEONARD J. ARRINGTON

University of Utah Press
Copublished with the
Tanner Trust Fund
Salt Lake City

1993 Reprint by the University of Utah Press
Reprinted by arrangement with Harvard University Press

This edition printed on acid-free paper

Library of Congress Cataloging-in-Publication Data

Arrington, Leonard J.
Great Basin Kingdom : an economic history of the Latter-day Saints, 1830–1900 / Leonard J. Arrington.
p. cm.
Originally published: Cambridge : Harvard University Press, 1958, in series: Studies in economic history. With new pref.
Includes bibliographical references and index.
ISBN 0-87480-420-5 (pbk. : alk. paper)
1. Church of Jesus Christ of Latter-day Saints—Utah—History—19th century. 2. Mormon Church—Utah—History—19th century. 3. Utah—Economic conditions. 4. Economics—Religious aspects—Mormon Church. I. Title.
BX8611.A774 1993
330.9792′ 02—dc20 93-2943
CIP

To Grace

And it shall come to pass in the last days,
That the mountain of the Lord's house
Shall be established in the top of the mountains,
And shall be exalted above the hills;
And all nations shall flow unto it.

THE BIBLE (Isaiah 2:2)

Great things are done when men and mountains meet;
This is not done by jostling in the street.

WILLIAM BLAKE

CONTENTS

BIBLIOGRAPHY, NOTES AND REFERENCES

List of Illustrations and Maps

Maps

[Drawn by Herbert M. Fehmel]

Preface to the Reprint Edition

To mark the thirtieth anniversary of the publication of *Great Basin Kingdom,* Mormon and non-Mormon scholars gathered for an interdisciplinary symposium at Utah State University on May 4, 1988. Sponsored jointly by the Mountain West Center for Western Studies at Utah State University and the Charles Redd Center for Western Studies at Brigham Young University, the symposium featured participants representing the disciplines of history, economics, sociology, anthropology, and geography who reappraised the impact of this work on the economic history of the Latter-day Saints.

Regarding the book as one of the "truly outstanding books written in this century about the American Frontier," Donald Worster, environmental historian at the University of Kansas, described *Great Basin Kingdom* as "the work of an economic and social historian who was interested in how institutions took shape in one small part of the West and how they differed from those in other parts of the region and those back east." The author's "chief interest was how a vague, half-articulated set of ideas had migrated to Utah and taken shape there as a thriving, distinctive economic order." An unconscious theme of the book, declared Worster, was that "the work of redeeming the desert from its sterility was simultaneously a work of self-redemption for humanity."

Richard W. Etulain, a former Idahoan now a literary historian at the University of New Mexico, stated that the staying power of *Great Basin Kingdom* was its literary excellence. He compared the book with Perry Miller's *The New England Mind,* Edmund Morgan's *The Puritan Dilemma* and *The Birth of the Republic,* and Richard Bushman's *From Puritan to Yankee* and described it as a "well-researched, balanced account of the Saints. . . . The stress on change over time, on theory wrung from daily competition and community building broke new ground in western historical writing, which too often centered on the westward movement without attendant analysis of institution-making once pioneers settled in the West." The work was also one of the first to treat religious influences on western settlers, sketching out the interrelationships between religious and economic practices, and "signaled a new era in Mormon historiography with his [Arrington's] willingness to ask analytical questions based on thorough research and challenging conceptualizations." It is a work that asks probing questions about church leaders and points out failures, while avoiding filiopietistic and chauvinistic conclusions. Thomas Alexander, professor of history at Brigham Young University and editor of a book of the essays presented at the symposium, found the most significant contribution of *Great Basin Kingdom* to be that "it speaks both to those inside the Mormon community and to scholars and lay persons outside the community."

The many scholarly books and articles that have expanded on themes mentioned or developed in *Great Basin Kingdom* and follow-up works in Mormon history are listed in Thomas Alexander's *Great Basin Kingdom Revisited* (Logan: Utah State University Press, 1991), and in Davis Bitton and Maureen Ursenbach Beecher, eds., *New Views of Mormon History* (Salt Lake City: University of Utah Press, 1987). Some of these have provided new perspectives and challenging interpretations of Mormon history. My own subsequent publications have included biographies, business histories, articles and books about the activities of Mormon women, the nature and extent of cooperative endeavor, and the major role played by many "ordinary" Latter-day Saints who were not part of the top leadership of the church.

As the readers of *Great Basin Kingdom* have discovered, I made every attempt to relate Mormon history and institutions to the wider world of American thought and experience. The dream of the Mormons to build a kingdom of God was really only a manifestion of the hope of all Americans to build a more perfect society. The Mormon experiment in group economics—the trials, errors, and successes—can be viewed as a heightening, a more explicit formulation of the total American experience. A thorough description of the problems, policies, and institutions of the Mormons is thus a case study in American economic history, economic policy, and the economics of religion in the Far West.

After describing the establishment of new institutions, the impact of the gold rush, the organization of immigration, the system of public works, agricultural development, construction of railroads, and the establishment of cooperative mercantile and industrial institutions, *Great Basin Kingdom* moves on to describe and analyze the antipolygamy "raid" of the 1880s, the confiscation of church properties by the federal government, and the successful federal attempt to eliminate the most characteristic aspects of Mormon life. The Mormon community then merged into the national pattern.

Some persons have asserted that Mormon historians have tended to leave Mormon history outside the mainstream; as Charles Peterson alleged in *Great Basin Kingdom Revisited,* they have "sighted down the narrow gallery of internal examination." Some western historians, however, have been guilty of the same "exceptionalist" history. Studies of western women frequently leave out Mormon women. Studies of western treatment of Indians often leave out the

Mormon story. Studies of western business seldom mention Mormon cooperatives. If the Mormons do not fit the pattern of most westerners, there is a temptation to simply leave them out. Whatever the merits of Mormon "exceptionalism," *Great Basin Kingdom* represented an attempt to relate the Mormon story to the larger world and to connect it with the nourishing bloodstream of American scholarship. By discussing Mormon relationships with the environment, Native Americans, and the important role of Mormon women, it also anticipated some of the interests and concerns of the New Western History, as promulgated by Patricia Limerick, Richard White, Donald Worster, Peggy Pascoe, and other western scholars. Further studies of Mormon Country will continue to broaden the spectrum of Mormon studies, to "regionalize" and "generalize" its meaning.

Above all, scholars will need to build on the nineteenth-century Mormon experience in their studies of the American West in the twentieth century. To what extent has the Mormon experience been unique? What has been the impact of urbanization, internationalization, and the immigration of blacks, Hispanics, and Asians? What is the pattern of relationships with Native Americans? And what has been the Mormon response to environmental programs, feminism, and twentieth-century capitalism? In 1958 there were 1,500,000 members of the church, more than 80 percent of whom were in the western United States. In 1992 there are 8,400,000 members, almost half of whom are outside the boundaries of the United States, with only about one-fourth in the American West. What has the emergence of the Great Basin Zion into a worldwide church meant to Mormons, their beliefs, and institutions? At some point an energetic scholar must prepare a new synthesis of Mormon social history and church policy that will incorporate both the nineteenth- and twentieth-century experiences, thus providing a needed sequel to *Great Basin Kingdom.*

* * * * *

After more than three decades, the story of the writing of *Great Basin Kingdom* may deserve recounting. The narrative that follows also gives me an opportunity to credit several people influential in its creation.

It was my good fortune to do my graduate work at the University of North Carolina at Chapel Hill and North Carolina State University at Raleigh. During my stay from 1939–42, the South was experiencing a cultural renaissance, and North Carolina professors were leading the way. A group of poets, novelists, playwrights, and journalists—John Crowe Ransom, Allen Tate, Robert Penn Warren, Paul Green, Thomas Wolfe, W. J. Cash, W. T. Couch, and Jonathan Daniels—were reasserting the significance of the legends and historical incidents of the Old South. The scholarly concentration on regional studies was led by Howard W. Odum, Rupert Vance, Samuel H. Hobbs, C. Horace Hamilton, and other sociologists. Milton S. Heath, my graduate advisor in economics, always insisted that I become immersed in southern studies so that I could return to the West and undertake studies of the economics and history of my native region. The intellectual setting was exhilarating.

Then, in the spring of 1941, to my great surprise, I found a description of a Mormon village in T. Lynn Smith's *Sociology of Rural Life.* With mounting excitement I read similar commentaries about Mormon group experiences in works of other sociologists. Locating studies of Mormon communities in the 1920s by Lowry Nelson, I searched for other articles and books on the secular aspects of Mormon life, works by historians, economists, sociologists, and folklorists. I was particularly fascinated by Richard T. Ely's 1903 article in *Harper's* on "Economic Aspects of Mormonism." When I happened to meet Ely at the annual convention of the American Economic Association in Philadelphia in December 1941 and mentioned to him how much I enjoyed that article, he lectured me on the importance of the Mormons in American history and their significance as a people. The combination of his scholarly stature, his interest in Mormons, and his respect for their contribution was overwhelming for this Idaho Mormon chicken farmer—turned aspiring graduate student.

My education was interrupted by military service in North Africa and Italy during World War II. My assignments enabled me to visit local villages, particularly in Italy, where I was struck with the inability of local villagers to act together for their own good or for any end beyond the immediate material interest of their own family. This seemed so different from Mormon villages where the settlers had achieved, through cooperative activity, a highly organized improving society, even where natural resources were sparse. It would be interesting, I thought, to do a study of the self-sufficient Mormon economy: how it got that way, how it functioned, and how its institutions compared with those of other western communities such as mining, cattle, and lumber towns.

In July 1945, contemplating my approaching discharge and return to North Carolina to complete graduate work, I wrote to Dr. John A. Widtsoe, a Mormon apostle who was also a former president of Utah State University and the University of Utah, asking him if he thought a dissertation on the economic institutions and activities of the Mormons would be practical. He replied that such a study would be desirable, that there was ample source material, but that there was difficulty in gaining access to the materials in the church archives. With respect to the latter, he suggested that if, at the beginning of my research, I asked only for printed materials, and as the days and weeks went by, gradually progressed to theses, scrapbooks, ward records, diaries, and name files, and if I patronized the library regularly, worked quietly and professionally, he was sure that, in the end, they would give me access to everything I wanted to see. I later followed his advice and was able to examine a vast array of documents that had not previously been seen by any professional scholar.

With this encouragement, I planned upon my return from overseas to do a dissertation on some aspect of Mormon economics. My North Carolina graduate advisor approved and wrote letters of support to economics departments in western universities where I might teach and be close to research materials. I received a satisfactory appointment to Utah State University, where I continued as a professor for twenty-six happy and productive years.

I began research in the summer of 1946 and finished "Mormon Economic Policies and Their Implementation on the Western Frontier, 1847–1900" in the spring of 1952. My advisor, Dr. Milton S. Heath, suggested that I seriously consider expanding the dissertation for publication by the Committee on Research in Economic History, which had a Rockefeller grant to publish several volumes on American economic history through Harvard University Press. Upon Dr. Heath's recommendation, that committee gave me a grant to work on the manuscript, and I finished "Building the Kingdom: Mormon Economic Activities in the West, 1947–1900," in the summer of 1954. But the more I thought about it, the more convinced I became that the manuscript was, in the words of my colleague George Ellsworth, "a wonderful piece of research from which a splendid history could be written." Too detailed, it lacked a central theme; it was—to be honest—tedious and dull.

Having been granted a twelve-month fellowship to the Henry E. Huntington Library in California, which had an outstanding collection of Western Americana, I decided to use a sabbatical from Utah State University. At the rate of one chapter per month, I wrote *Great Basin Kingdom,* completing it in the fall of 1957. Accepted with few alterations, it was published by Harvard University Press in 1958. Lewis Atherton, reviewer for the press, reported: "Based on long study of voluminous materials, this book has the virtues of intensive research and mature deliberation. . . . All will have to recognize the scholarly, penetrating, and provocative nature of this important book."

My work on Mormon economics was enhanced by interviews with several Utah scholars and old-timers. I talked with William Wallace, often called the father of Utah irrigation, who was with his father in the 1870s when he had a private consultation with Brigham Young. Charles C. Richards, then 96, an Ogden banker and legislator, explained some of the financial dealings of the church that enlarged my understanding. So did LeRoi C. Snow, secretary to the church's First Presidency at the turn of the century. I talked with Ephraim Ericksen, Feramorz Y. Fox, Dale Morgan, Juanita Brooks, my Utah State department head Evan Murray, and other Mormon scholars. When I went East in 1949 I interviewed American history scholars, including Oscar and

Mary Flug Handlin, Frederick Merk, and Arthur H. Cole, each of whom stressed the importance of the Mormons in American history. My project received an extra boost in December 1950 when I met George Ellsworth, a recent addition to the Utah State University faculty in the Department of History. With a brillant mind, sound training in history at Berkeley, a precise writing style, and helpful manner, George tutored me in the intricacies of Mormon history, literature, and historiography and reviewed the drafts of each chapter. His comments were very helpful. Conversations with Thomas O'Dea, William Mulder, Austin and Alta Fife, Richard Poll, Eugene Campbell, Gustive Larson, Russell Mortensen, Everett Cooley, and Merle Wells also contributed to *Great Basin Kingdom*.

Great Basin Kingdom was well received. Letters from historians and graduate students complimented me on the book and then asked—ever so timidly, ever so obliquely—if I were a Mormon. They suggested that in reading the book they could not determine my religious affiliation. If I was a Mormon, why wasn't the treatment more faith-promoting? If I was a Gentile, how could it be so even-handed and fair? In that age of "objectivity" this was a high compliment.

Reviewers were particularly struck with the amount of research that preceded the writing of the book. Dale Morgan, in a review in the *Utah Historical Quarterly*, commended the "massive ordering of data . . . its notes and bibliography represent one of the broadest surveys of Utah historiography yet attempted, by no means limited in its viewpoint to economic history." Kimball Young wrote in the *American Sociological Review* that "Arrington's well-written book represents years of tedious plowing and searching among extensive and sometimes obscure original sources."

Although most reviewers thought the principal conclusions in the book were persuasively demonstrated, the prominent British authority on American history, P.A.M. Taylor, thought there was too much emphasis on assisted immigration. Taylor also thought that my insistence on the close connection between Mormonism and antebellum America, especially in the Age of Jackson, may have been overdrawn, and felt that one could not carry the idea of commonwealth to the point of the massive central direction that characterized Mormon society. The large measure of cooperative organization in farming, industry, and trade, and the minutely detailed supervision of individual behavior, the whole backed by spiritual and not merely worldly sanctions, was something beyond the practice in most antebellum American commonwealths.

Nevertheless, as Rodman Paul wrote in his review for the *Mississippi Valley Historical Review* (now *The Journal of American History*), Mormon Utah emerges from *Great Basin Kingdom* as "a highly conservative community that employed its theocratic control not only to create self-sufficiency from a world that was politically hostile to polygamy and religious eccentricity, but also to minimize such disturbing influences as economic inequality, economic monopoly in private hands, and the social confusion characteristic of boom towns. . . . Social attitudes and firmly held prejudices seem to have been rather more important than the unusual problems created by climate, soil, and distance."

* * * * *

I hope that this new reprint edition of *Great Basin Kingdom* will help students of western history not only to understand the experiences of the Mormons but also to develop further insights into the history of the American West in the nineteenth and twentieth centuries.

Preface to the First Edition

At a time when government is exercising a potent influence in molding the economy of all of us, and when "advanced" countries are sending billions of dollars, and some of their finest experts, to underdeveloped areas to stimulate economic growth and expansion, it does not seem out of place to discuss the role of the Church of Jesus Christ of Latter-day Saints in developing the economy of the Mountain West. While the general nature of the Mormon recipe for development has long been recognized to include systematic planning, organized cooperation, patient sacrifice of consumption in favor of investment, and pious devotion to the ideal of the Kingdom of God on earth, the economic institutions and policies of the church, though well-documented, have never been described in detail. This book attempts in some measure to fill that gap.

The economic development of Mormon Country is of particular significance for four reasons: (1) It illustrates the problems associated with the settlement and growth of an isolated, mountainous, and semi-arid region. (2) It dramatizes the strengths and weaknesses of attempting a comprehensive development program without outside capital. (3) It represents one of the few regional economies in modern history founded for a religious purpose, dominated by religious sentiments, and managed by religious leaders. (4) It offers an interesting case study of American pioneering experience generally. The present volume may be said to suggest the positive role which a government, whether secular or theocratic, if sufficiently strong, can play in the building of a commonwealth. It also bears out the contention of Max Weber and others that much can be learned by systematically observing the relationship between religion and economic life.

Great Basin Kingdom represents an attempt to give meaning to an American experience that often has been obscured by sectarian controversy. Despite their assertions of "peculiarity," much of what was done by the Mormons was truly American. To paraphrase Alfred Marshall, the Latter-day Saints were "a leading species of a larger genus." Just as Mormonism often has been regarded as a typically American religion, so Mormon economic experience, to use the words of Thomas O'Dea, presents a distillation, a heightening, a more explicit formulation, and a summation of American experience generally. As Ralph Barton Perry observed in *Characteristically American:* "Mormonism was a sort of Americanism in miniature; in its republicanism, its emphasis on compact in both church and polity, its association of piety with conquest and adventure, its sense of destiny, its resourcefulness and capacity for organization." It was not only a Mormon dream, but the dream of many Americans to build on this continent a Kingdom of God. It was the dream of all Americans, as Goethe said, to escape from the past of European man, and to build a new society. Thus, while the focus of this study is narrowed down to a region whose population even today is less than two million, and while the events here discussed have made no great splash in American, much less world, history, many of the problems confronted by the Mormons, many of the solutions hit upon, many of the policies and institutions, were representative of human experience generally.

Although the findings of other scholars have not been neglected, every attempt has been made in this work to use primary materials. The Mormon pioneers were avid diarists and record-keepers, and almost everything they left has been preserved. The necessity of using only the material of interest to the economic historian, however, does a certain amount of injustice to the originals, which often are replete with descriptions of religious experiences, discussions of theology, and evidences to the writers of divine favor. Because of the relative inaccessibility of much of the source material, quotations are used more frequently than usual in a work of this kind.

One reader of these pages has expressed his delight and fear that *Great Basin Kingdom* will be regarded and used as an economic history of Utah to 1900 — delight, because it introduces an important and neglected phase of Utah history; fear, because the work should not be considered as anything but a study of Mormon (as opposed to non-Mormon) economic policies, practices, and institutions. I do not pretend that this is an economic history of Utah in the same sense that, say, Frederick Merk's *Economic History of Wisconsin During the Civil War Decade* is a study of that interesting state. The critical omissions — e.g., Utah's mining history after 1869 — were made purposefully in order to make possible the detailed treatments of the more unique and lesser known economic activities, institutions, and responses of the Mormons. The book is largely a study of Mormon concepts, and of the efforts of church leadership to develop an economy in harmony with those concepts.

The approach to Mormonism in this book is that religion, as with all social institutions, must be judged according to its usefulness in attacking the ageless problems of humanity. That leaders of the Mormon Church throughout the nineteenth century attempted in a systematic way to improve the economic welfare of their followers as a group, seems undeniable. If, as the Mormons believe, Joseph Smith was personally commissioned by God to form the Church of Jesus Christ of Latter-day Saints, the best evidences in favor of the theory are the essential social usefulness of the church throughout its history, and the advanced theory of social action which Joseph Smith and his successors espoused during their lifetimes.

To be sure, much of what may be called "the Mormon myth" has been unacceptable to social theorists. The writer's view is that ultimate truths are often, if not always, presented artistically or imaginatively in a way suited to the needs and exigencies of the living community of persons. While the Mormon story may not appeal to the rational faculty of the majority as an objective picture of the world about us, there can be no doubt that, somehow or other, it tapped immense creative forces in those believing it, and that it inspired a whole commonwealth of converts to make the desert blossom as the rose.

Finally, a word to Mormon readers who will be troubled about my naturalistic treatment of certain historic themes sacred to the memories of the Latter-day Saints. The church holds, of course, that it is based on divine revelation. The body of revealed knowledge, however, at least to the Latter-day Saint, is not static, but constantly changing and expanding. Revelation is continuous and expedient — "suited to the people and the times." Moreover, it is impossible to separate revelation from the conditions under which it is received: "We have this treasure in earthen vessels." Or, as Brigham Young expressed it, "the revelations which I receive are all upon natural principles." The true essence of God's revealed will, if such it be, cannot be apprehended without an understanding of the conditions surrounding the prophetic vision, and the symbolism and verbiage in which it is couched. Surely God does not reveal His will except to those prepared, by intellectual and social experience and by spiritual insight and imagination, to grasp and convey it. A naturalistic discussion of "the people and the times" and of the mind and experience of Latter-day prophets is therefore a perfectly valid aspect of religious history, and, indeed, makes more plausible the truths they attempted to convey. While the discussion of naturalistic causes of revelations does not preclude its claim to be revealed or inspired of God, in practice it is difficult, if not impossible, to distinguish what is objectively "revealed" from what is subjectively "contributed" by those receiving the revelation.

Since the reasearch on which this book is based has taken place over a period of many years, I am indebted to many persons and institutions for assistance. The directors, librarians, and staff members of the L. D. S. Church Historian's Office and the Utah State Historical Society, in Salt Lake City; Institute of Religion and Utah State University, in Logan, Utah; Brigham Young University, Provo, Utah; University of Utah, Salt Lake City; Bancroft Library, Berkeley, California; Henry E. Huntington Library & Art Gallery, San Marino, California; Library of Congress; National

Archives; New York Public Library; the William Robertson Coe Collection at Yale University; and the Houghton and Widener libraries at Harvard University, have all been helpful and generous to a fault. Grants from the Committee on Research in Economic History, Utah State University, University of North Carolina and the subsidies of the the G. I. Bill of Rights (Public Law 342) made possible study of the various collections of Mormon, Utah, and Western materials throughout the nation. Above all, I am indebted to Director John E. Pomfret, Librarian Leslie E. Bliss, and the staff of the Huntington Library for a fellowship and pleasant year of research and writing while concluding the study.

Elder A. William Lund, Assistant Church Historian; those who directed my dissertation at the University of North Carolina, particularly Professors Milton S. Heath and D. H. Buchanan; Professor S. George Ellsworth, Utah State University; Professors Richard D. Poll and Eugene E. Campbell, Brigham Young University; Professor Lewis Atherton, University of Missouri; and those associated with the Committee on Research in Economic History, particularly Professors Arthur H. Cole, Thomas C. Cochran, Anne Bezanson, and Edward C. Kirkland, have read portions or all of the manuscript in various drafts and have made valuable suggestions. President Daryl Chase, Director D. Wynne Thorne, Dean M. R. Merrill, and Professor Evan B. Murray, of Utah State University, have provided continuous inspiration and encouragement, as have Professors William Mulder, University of Utah; Thomas F. O'Dea, Fordham University; Philip Taylor, University of Birmingham, England; Paul W. Gates, Cornell University; A. R. Mortensen and Everett L. Cooley, of the Utah State Historical Society; and my parents, Mr. and Mrs. N. W. Arrington, in Twin Falls, Idaho. While none of the above persons is to be held responsible for anything written herein, collectively they have given the book whatever scholarly merit it might have. The book is also dependent on the pioneering work of a host of scholars, including, particularly, Andrew Jenson, Dale L. Morgan, Nels Anderson, Juanita Brooks, Feramorz Y. Fox, Hamilton Gardner, B. H. Roberts, Gustive O. Larson, Joel E. Ricks, Joseph A. Geddes, Milton R. Hunter, Andrew Love Neff, Preston Nibley, and L. H. Creer. Mrs. Joan Wardle Bingham did most of the typing.

The editors and publishers of the *Utah Historical Quarterly, Pacific Historical Review, Western Humanities Review, Huntington Library Quarterly, Business History Review,* and *Journal of Economic History* have given permission to publish paragraphs from articles of mine which appeared in a different form in their journals. Mr. Herbert Fehmel, of Salt Lake City, drew the maps. Photographs were generously supplied by the L. D. S. Church Historian's Office, Henry E. Huntington Library, and Utah State Historical Society, out of their ample collections.

I am particularly grateful to the Committee on Research in Economic History, Dr. Arthur H. Cole, editor, for having made possible the completion and publication of the manuscript. Their continued interest and support has made this book possible.

Leonard J. Arrington

Utah State University
March 1, 1958

DESIGN OF THE KINGDOM

[1830–1846]

* I *

The burgeoning democracy of the Age of Jackson spawned many societies devoted to the improvement of social institutions. Destined to become one of the most permanent and successful of these societies, the Church of Jesus Christ of Latter-day Saints underwent a turbulent early history, characterized by forced migrations from New York, Ohio, Missouri, and Illinois, and culminating in a well-ordered removal to the Great Basin in 1847. The communitarian climate in which the church was conceived, and the early group experiences of the Mormons, produced a set of ideals which were to find permanent embodiment in institutions uniquely suited to the geography and economics of the Great Basin.

CHAPTER I

Early Economic Experiences of the Latter-day Saints

The history of Mormonism reaches back to the fervor of religious enthusiasm which engulfed western New York during the first half of the nineteenth century. During the 1820's Joseph Smith, an uneducated but sensitive Vermont-born farm youth, purportedly received visitations from heavenly beings and translated from gold plates a six-hundred-page record of the ancient inhabitants of the Americas called the *Book of Mormon*. His prophetic powers were accepted by a small group of relatives and friends and, on April 6, 1830, in Fayette, Seneca County, New York, the Church of Jesus Christ of Latter-day Saints was organized.[1] Some notable conversions were made, the church grew, communities were built in Ohio, Missouri, and Illinois, and a systematic theology was developed.

The Mormon Church claimed to be a restoration of Primitive Christianity, and its religious beliefs included worship of a personal God, acceptance of the Bible and *Book of Mormon* as divine scriptures, emphasis upon education and group progress, and conviction that divine authority had been granted to Joseph Smith and his associates to establish "the one true church." Mormonism thus had a particularly strong appeal to the descendants of the New England Puritans. Its comprehensive theology, Old Testament literalism, militant faith, and providential interpretation of history, coupled with the "chosen people of God" concept, attracted particularly the sons and daughters of New England who were discontented with the theology and polity of contemporary Calvinism. The closeness of the Mormons to their fatherly God, His believed interest in their daily affairs, and the direct and complete influence of church over their spiritual and temporal lives indicate a considerable and significant reaction against contemporary Calvinist absolutism and deistic secularism. Most of the early members, and virtually all of the early leaders who shaped the faith, including Brigham Young, were born in New England or were of New England parentage. On the whole, the creed and practices of the Mormons were relatively conservative and unemotional, although contemporary observers sometimes stressed the exceptions.[2]

As a social movement, Mormonism reflected early American experience and polity. The patriarchal family, the union of church and community, the value of cooperative endeavor, and progressive movement toward the great unsettled West — these and other early Americanisms were part and parcel of early Mormon thought and practice. The Mormons also had a strong belief in the destiny of America — it was a "land choice above all other lands."[3] Because of its fundamentally democratic character, the federal Constitution was regarded as inspired of God and well-nigh sacred.[4] If Americans lived up to their "promise," their land would never be ruled by a monarch, but would always be a government of, by, and for the people.

Thus, as with Americanism itself, Mormonism represented the coalescence of those two widely differing philosophies — Puritanism and democracy. From their Puritan grandfathers, the Mormons inherited a strong sense of duty, a passionate yearning for righteousness, and an unshakable confidence in their own high destiny. From the contemporary philosophy of democracy the Mormons inherited its optimism, equalitarianism, progressivism, strong self-assertion, and a belief in the dignity and worth of the individual. It was no doubt these characteristics of Mormonism which led Count Leo Tolstoi to tell Ambassador Andrew White that "the Mormon people taught the American religion."[5]

Perhaps the most significant environmental influence on early Mormonism, however, was that of the so-called "Protestant Ethic." Those habits of mind and patterns of collective behavior to which early capitalism owed so much were carried over into Mormonism and proved to be invaluable in meeting the problems encountered in settling the arid West. "The Mormon ethic" included a this-worldly approach to the problem of life, a capacity for rational calculation, hatred of mendicancy, emphasis on the righteous pursuit and development of an earthly calling, the practice of abstemiousness and self-discipline, and, above all, the conviction of the Mormons that they were immediately and specifically invested by God with the task of preparing the earth for the Second Coming of Christ. This task required action rather than contemplation. It required extensive social organization and effective group action. And it profited from implementation of the principle of continuing revelation, which facilitated change and adjustment, made possible an instrumental approach to social and economic problems, and stimulated a social inventiveness that is rare in the history of religion.

PLACE OF ECONOMICS IN MORMON THEOLOGY

As with their Puritan ancestors, the early Mormons gave first allegiance to religious ideas and sentiments. Of the Mormons it could be said, as it was of the Puritans, that there was a constant "tendency to carry inferences from dogma into secular life." [6] This was perhaps inevitable. If the basic goal of the individual religionist was salvation, it was to be achieved only in and through the church. The church's task, however, did not end with the conversion of individual souls. As the germ of the Kingdom of God, the church must gather God's people, settle them, organize them, and assist them in building an advanced social order. Ultimately, according to Mormon theology, the church must usher in the literal and earthly Kingdom of God ("Zion") over which Christ would one day rule. Man would "work out his salvation" in preparing for this Kingdom; the church would exercise leadership in fostering it. All individuals who participated in this divine and awesome task would be specially blessed and protected. One day, when the Kingdom was finally achieved, there would be no more wars or pestilences, no more poverty or contention.

The establishment of God's Kingdom on earth, according to Mormon belief, required equal attention to the temporal and spiritual needs of man. Preaching and production, work and worship, contemplation and cultivation — all were indispensable in the realization of the Kingdom. Indeed, the religious and economic aspects and problems of the individual and the group were viewed as incapable of disassociation. This was not a rationalized interpretation of the Bible, but a specific element in the early theology of Mormonism. As early as September 1830, six months after the organization of the church, a revelation was announced stating: "Verily I say unto you, that all things unto me are spiritual, and not at any time have I given unto you a law which was temporal." [7] Brigham Young interpreted this revelation for the Latter-day Saints as follows:

> We cannot talk about spiritual things without connecting with them temporal things, neither can we talk about temporal things without connecting spiritual things with them. They are inseparably connected. . . . We, as Latter-day Saints, really expect, look for and we will not be satisfied with anything short of being governed and controlled by the word of the Lord in all our acts, both spiritual and temporal. If we do not live for this, we do not live to be one with Christ.[8]

Economics, and secular policy in general, were thus placed on a par with — or incorporated in — religion. Indeed, a considerable part, if not the bulk, of the "revealed" scripture of the Mormons dealt with temporalities.[9] Of the one hundred and twelve revelations announced by Joseph Smith, eighty-eight dealt partly or entirely with matters that were economic in nature.[10] Out of 9,614 printed lines in Smith's revelations, 2,618 lines, by actual count, treated "definitely and directly of economic matters." As one scholar noted, "Mormonism, though a religion, is largely, if not primarily, an economic movement, at least insofar as it offers to the world anything that is new." [11] While the Mormons probably would not have subscribed to this view, there is no doubt of the Mormon teaching that religion was concerned with the everyday duties and realities of life, and that church leaders were expected to minister not only to the spiritual wants of people, but to their social, economic, and political wants as well. Indeed, this preoccupation with the things of this world was one of the grounds for sectarian opposition to Mormonism. The editor of a Pittsburgh Universalist publication, for example, visited the Mormon community of Kirtland, Ohio, in 1837 and wrote that it was his impression that the Mormons had "too much worldly wisdom connected with their religion — too great a desire for the perishable riches of this world — holding out the idea that the kingdom of Christ is to be composed of 'real estate, herds, flocks, silver, gold,' &c. as well as of human beings." [12]

Joseph Smith and other early Mormon leaders seem to have seen every part of life, and every problem put to them, as part of an integrated universe in which materialities and immaterialities were of equal standing, or indistinguishable, in God's kingdom. Religion was relevant to economics, politics, art, and science. If Christianity was "the most avowedly materialist of all the great religions," as asserted by William Temple, the Archbishop of Canterbury,[13] Mormonism came near to being the most avowedly materialist of all the Christian religions.[14] Mormonism, and the social milieu which produced it, thus attempted to reverse the trend in the Western world which separated the church from the daily life of mankind.[15] Religion, the Mormons believed, was not only "a matter of sentiment, good for Sunday contemplation and intended for the sanctuary and the soul," but also had to do with "dollars and cents, with trade and barter, with the body and the daily doings of ordinary life." [16]

EARLY MORMON ECONOMIC EXPERIENCES

The particular organizational procedures and social thought-patterns which characterized Mormon responses throughout the nineteenth century developed out of the early experiences of the sect, of which there were five phases. In each of these phases various types of group action were resorted to, out of choice or necessity, and their relative strengths and weaknesses were noted. The net result was the formulation of an economic creed which was at once distinctive, yet peculiarly American.

Jackson County, Missouri. In January 1831, less than a year after the founding of the Mormon Church, its headquarters were moved from New York to Kirtland, in the Western Reserve of northern Ohio. New York adherents to the faith were counseled to "gather" there temporarily while a permanent place for settlement was found. When some missionaries to the Indians returned from western Missouri in the summer of 1831 and reported the land to be rich and abundant, Joseph Smith and other leading elders journeyed to the region and dedicated Jackson County, in western Missouri (the region around present-day Kansas City and Independence), as "Zion," the gathering place of the Saints:

> Wherefore I the Lord have said gather ye out from the eastern lands, assemble ye yourselves together ye Elders of my Church; go ye forth into the western countries, . . . build up churches unto me; and with one heart and with one mind, gather up your riches that ye may purchase an inheritance which shall hereafter be appointed unto you, and it shall be called the New Jerusalem, a land of peace, a city of refuge, a place of safety for the saints of the most high God; and the glory of the Lord shall be there, and the terror of the Lord also shall be there.[17]

Within a year, between three and four hundred converts had migrated to Jackson County, and within two years, almost 1,200. They built the first of several Mormon communities in the Midwest. A printing concern and general store were established, and several thousand acres of land were placed in cultivation.

The public land on which the Mormons settled could be had for $1.25 an acre, but supplying farms to all the new citizens was somewhat of a problem because the church had no funds and most of the migrants had used up their resources in getting to the western Zion. Moreover, in order to build a compact community some land had to be purchased from local settlers and speculators at what were then considered to be "high prices." A plan to facilitate the collective purchase of land and to institute "the Lord's law" of economic relations was announced in February 1831, shortly before the Missouri migration. Known variously as the "United Order," "Order of Enoch," and the "Law of Consecration and Stewardship," this supposedly divine system was intended to produce economic equality and assure the socialization of surplus incomes. It was also designed in such a way as to retain a large measure of freedom of enterprise.[18]

Upon the basic principle that the earth and everything on it belonged to the Lord, members of the church were asked to "consecrate" or deed all their property, both real and personal, to a church leader called the "Presiding Bishop of the Church." The bishop would then grant an "inheritance" or "stewardship" to each family out of the properties so received, the

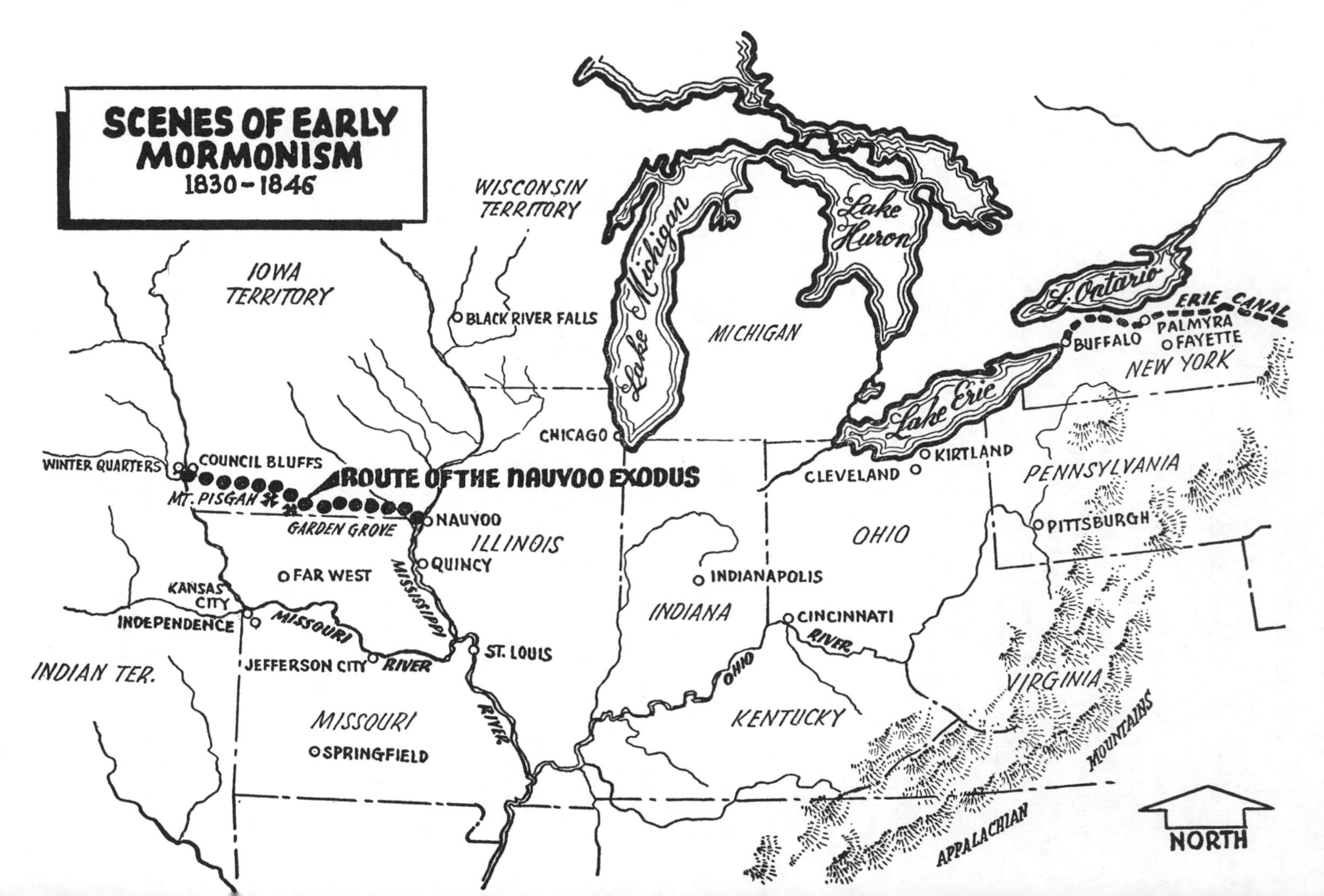

SCENES OF EARLY MORMONISM
1830–1846
WISCONSIN TERRITORY
IOWA TERRITORY
BLACK RIVER FALLS
Lake Michigan
Lake Huron
MICHIGAN
L. Ontario
ERIE CANAL
PALMYRA
BUFFALO
FAYETTE
NEW YORK
Lake Erie
CHICAGO
KIRTLAND
CLEVELAND
PENNSYLVANIA
WINTER QUARTERS
COUNCIL BLUFFS
ROUTE OF THE NAUVOO EXODUS
MT. PISGAH
GARDEN GROVE
NAUVOO
ILLINOIS
OHIO
PITTSBURGH
QUINCY
FAR WEST
MISSISSIPPI
INDIANAPOLIS
KANSAS CITY
INDEPENDENCE
MISSOURI
INDIANA
CINCINNATI
RIVER
ST. LOUIS
JEFFERSON CITY
RIVER
INDIAN TER.
OHIO
VIRGINIA
KENTUCKY
MISSOURI
SPRINGFIELD
RIVER
MOUNTAINS
APPALACHIAN
NORTH

amount depending on the wants and needs of the family, as determined jointly by the bishop and the prospective steward. The stewardship might be a farm, building lot, store, workshop, or mill, or simply an appointment to serve the community as a teacher or doctor. It was expected that in some cases the consecrations would considerably exceed the stewardships. Out of the surplus thus made possible the bishop would grant stewardships to the poorer and younger members of the church who had no property to consecrate or too little to procure an adequate "inheritance." The words of the basic revelation were as follows:

Behold, thou shalt consecrate all thy properties, that which thou hast unto me, with a covenant and a deed which cannot be broken; and they shall be laid before the bishop of my church, and two of the elders, such as he shall appoint and set apart for that purpose. . . . The bishop of my church, after that he has received the properties of my church, that it cannot be taken from the church, he shall appoint every man a steward over his own property, or that which he has received, inasmuch as shall be sufficient for himself and family.[19]

This redistribution of wealth placed all family heads on an equal economic footing, considering their respective family obligations, circumstances, needs, and "just wants"; for, according to another 1831 doctrine, "it is not given that one man should possess that which is above another, wherefore the world lieth in sin."[20]

In addition to the consecration of properties, family heads were asked to consecrate annually all their surplus production to the storehouse provided by the bishop for this purpose. This surplus, or "residue," was to be used primarily to distribute to those who for one reason or another—perhaps unseasonal arrival, illness, improvidence, or misfortune—failed to produce sufficiently to provide for the needs and just wants of their families. The surplus was also to be used to provide for such church expenditures as publications, land purchases, temples and meetinghouses, education, and granting credit to the stewards who needed funds for improvement and expansion.

While the collection, administration, and investment of the initial and annual consecrations were to be under the supervision of the Presiding Bishop and his advisers, there was to be freedom of enterprise in production and in the management of properties held as stewardships. There was no provision for the minute and intimate regulation of economic activity which prevailed in some contemporary communitarian societies. Nevertheless, group interests were exalted. John Corrill, an early bishop who later apostatized, emphasized the role of the law of consecration and stewardship in Jackson County as follows:

It is believed by them [the Latter-day Saints] that the Church ought to act in concert, and feel one general interest in building up the "great cause"; and that every man ought to consider his property as consecrated to the Lord for that purpose.[21]

Another phase of the idealism surrounding the settlement of Jackson County was the attempt to follow a new and "ideal" settlement pattern worked out by Joseph Smith in the early 1830's, called the "Plat of the City of Zion." The village plot was to be one mile square, with each block or square containing ten acres. With twenty lots to the block, each lot would be a half acre in size. Moreover, the lots were laid off alternately in such a way that no house would be exactly opposite another house. Uniform regulations would assure that there would be only one house to a lot, and that each house would be located at least twenty-five feet from the street. A large block in the center was set aside for such public buildings as the bishop's storehouse, meetinghouses, temples, and schools. Streets would run north-south and east-west and would be wide. The city would contain about 1,000 family units, each with a respectable garden space and grove, lawn, or orchard. Outside the city would be the farms. And when this city is filled up, wrote Joseph Smith, "lay off another in the same way, and so fill up the world in these last days." [22]

While the enthusiastic converts were wending their way to Jackson County to assign their consecrations, receive their inheritances, and live in the "City of Joseph," others served as missionaries and agents, in the East and elsewhere, soliciting funds for the purchase of land and the building of Zion. The Jackson County bishop found it necessary to caution those intending to migrate to Zion that they should pay their debts, husband their property and savings carefully, and secure improved breeds of cattle, sheep, and hogs, and pure varieties of seeds to bring with them.

For the disciples to suppose [he wrote] that they can come to this land without ought to eat, or to drink, or to wear, or any thing to purchase these necessaries with, is a vain thought. For them to suppose that the Lord will open the windows of heaven, and rain down angel's food for them by the way, when their whole journey lies through a fertile country, stored with the blessings of life from his own hand for them to subsist upon, is also vain. . . .

And notwithstanding the fulness of the earth is for the saints, they can never expect it unless they use the means put into their hands to obtain the same in the manner provided by our Lord. When you flee to Zion, we enjoin the word, prepare all things, that you may be ready to labor for a living, for the Lord has promised to take the curse off the land of Zion . . . , and the willing and the obedient, will eat the good of the same: not the idle.[23]

The results of this frontier communitarianism are difficult to assess. Official communications mention that the "disciples" were "in good health and spirits" and "doing well." They also mention that the burden of migrating, of purchasing land, of establishing the printing office and store, and, above all, of transforming a "wilderness and desert," into a "garden of the Lord," was greater than most had anticipated.[24] By and large, those who participated and left recollections wrote of their experience with pronounced nostalgia:

There was a spirit of peace and union, and love and good will manifested in this little Church in the wilderness, the memory of which will be ever dear to my heart. . . . Peace and plenty crowned their labors, and the wilderness became a fruitful field, and the solitary place began to bud and blossom as the rose. . . . In short, there has seldom, if ever, been a happier people upon the earth than the Church of the Saints now were.[25]

One of the principal administrative problems had to do with the nature of the property rights to be granted to the stewards. Initially, title to the property rested with the church and the stewards were given a life-lease subject to cancellation if the convert left the community, did not work his land, or otherwise became a "trouble-maker."[26] Because of legal and other difficulties this policy was changed in 1833 to provide that all stewardships be given out as deeds in fee simple.[27] A second administrative problem concerned the size of the inheritance to be given each steward. Who was to decide the all-important question of what was "sufficient" for a man and his family? In case the prospective steward and the bishop could not agree on this matter, it was finally determined that it should be submitted to a group of twelve men that "harmony and good will" might be preserved in Zion.[28]

These arrangements, however, did not obviate such fundamental problems as the transferral of consecrated properties from the relatively well-to-do to the poor, when the latter were incapable of wise management of property; and the diminution of incentive which might be brought about by the requirement that stewards were to consecrate all their surplus income. Even these difficulties might have been successfully surmounted, as they were in many contemporary American idealistic communities, had not the Mormons been driven out of their half-built Zion in 1833. In July of that year the Mormon printing establishment was wrecked and the Presiding Bishop and his companion were tarred and feathered. On July 23, 1833, the "Missouri Mob" reassembled, thoroughly armed and bearing a red flag, and required the Latter-day Saints to leave the county within a fixed time. The Mormons were finally driven from Jackson County in November. Most of them crossed the Missouri River into Clay County, north of Jackson County.

According to contemporary testimony, most of the homes and other improvements of the Mormons were burned or otherwise destroyed. Virtually nothing was obtained in the way of remuneration or payment for their investment of labor and capital in "building up Zion."[29] Attempts were made in the courts to get damages and freedom of access to the land, but to no avail. At one point, church leaders in Ohio organized a group called "Zion's Camp" to march to Missouri to "redeem Zion." [30] The one hundred and thirty men led by Joseph Smith, who comprised this little army, practiced their own law of consecration by living out of a common treasury built up by their several consecrations. An outbreak of cholera took a heavy toll, however, and the group did not succeed in its purposes. Nevertheless, church officials were able to bring some order out of the chaos produced by the Jackson County evacuation, and a common treasury was established to support the needy in Clay County.

Kirtland, Ohio. With the expulsion of the Mormons from Jackson County, attention was centered on the Mormon headquarters at Kirtland. Kirtland was a rural trading center with about a thousand people when the New York Mormons first arrived in 1831. Most of the original settlers joined the church at this time. Within five years Mormon migration to Kirtland had caused the population to rise to more than 3,000. Albert Gallatin Riddle described the settlement process as follows:

> One almost wondered if the whole world were centering at Kirtland. They came, men, women, and children, in every conceivable manner, some with horses, oxen, and vehicles rough and rude, while others had walked all or part of the distance. The future "City of the Saints" appeared like one besieged. Every available house, shop, hut, or barn was filled to its utmost capacity. Even boxes were roughly extemporized and used for shelter until something more permanent could be secured.[31]

The problem of providing for the new settlers was the same as in Missouri, and similar devices were applied. A bishop was appointed, a storehouse was erected, consecrations were received, and each person was given a stewardship over his own property. In this way the older settlers divided their land and possessions to some extent with the newcomers, and the more prosperous divided with the poor. Each person was held to account for the use of his stewardship. A plan of settlement similar to the Plat for the City of Zion was worked out and rural and urban real estate were collectively acquired. A general store, tannery, printing shop, and steam sawmill were also established, by the method of joint stewardships of leaders. The operation of these enterprises was coordinated by church and business leaders in what were called the "United Firm" and the "Central Board of the United Order." All of them proved to be failures from a financial point of view, primarily because they could not be operated on a strictly profit-making basis in that religious community. As one early Mormon recalled:

> In those days there was a tendency of feeling that each should share alike in everything, so much so that it was impossible for any man to do business in the

mercantile line. A good brother who was needy would think it was selfish if he could not go to a store and get what he wanted without paying the money for it. . . . Let a brother commence the mercantile business, and the first thing he knew his whole capital stock was credited out to the brethren. He could not refuse to credit a brother. O, no! If he did it was said at once that he was selfish and was no friend to the poor.[32]

The most important cooperative endeavor of the Mormons in Kirtland was the building of a temple. This $40,000 structure served as meetinghouse and schoolhouse, and required three years (1833–1836) to complete. It represented a kind of public works enterprise which encouraged consecrations from the wealthy and at the same time provided employment for the needy. Men quarried stone, hauled it to the building site, cut and dressed it, and laid the walls, while women fed the workers and made clothing. Workers drew necessities from Mormon stores, while the merchants used consecrations and credit in purchasing supplies. The temple was thus an essential support to a deficit economy.

The completion of the temple, however, and the continued influx of new members, largely the poor, made necessary the establishment of a stronger economic base. It has been estimated that by 1836 as much as $150,000 may have been owed by the Mormons of Kirtland to merchants, banks, and capitalists in Cleveland, Pittsburgh, New York, and Buffalo.[33] The one big asset of the church was real estate — an asset which would almost assuredly rise in value with the increase in population and wealth. To take advantage of this asset in paying debts, to keep money in the town, and to make credit available to the mercantile establishments and shops in the community, the church decided to establish a bank.

On November 2, 1836, the Kirtland Safety Society was organized, with a stated capitalization of $4,000,000.[34] Sidney Rigdon was president, and Joseph Smith, cashier. The capitalization consisted almost entirely of real estate, accepted at inflated values, and pledged by the stockholders for the redemption of notes issued by the bank.[35] One church authority was delegated to make application for a charter with the legislature, while another was dispatched to Philadelphia to obtain a supply of bank notes. Apparently, both officials returned to Kirtland the same day, January 1, 1837 — the one with news that the legislature had refused to entertain the request for a bank charter, the other with $200,000 in beautifully engraved new bank notes of various denominations, procured at "great expense." [36] Believing the bank to be an essential support for the burgeoning and strained economy of Kirtland, church leaders organized, on January 2, 1837, the Kirtland Safety Society Anti-Banking Company, with Sidney Rigdon, secretary, and Joseph Smith, treasurer.[37] The previously engraved notes were overstamped with "anti-" in front of Bank, and "ing co." after Bank so that the notes would conform to the new name of the society.[38] If a bank was illegal, they reasoned, an anti-bank was not! The bank proceeded to issue its notes in payment of church obligations, and general, if artificial, prosperity was stimulated in Kirtland.

We were very much grieved [wrote Heber C. Kimball] on our arrival in Kirtland, to see the spirit of speculation that was prevailing in the Church. Trade and traffic seemed to engross the time and attention of the Saints. When we left Kirtland [a short time before] a city lot was worth about $150; but on our return, to our astonishment, the same lot was said to be worth from $500. to $1000., according to location; and some men, who, when I left, could hardly get food to eat, I found on my return to be men of supposed great wealth; in fact, everything in the place seemed to be moving in great prosperity, and all seemed determined to become rich; in my feelings they were artificial or imaginary riches.[39]

For a month or two the notes circulated without difficulty. Local citizens wishing to redeem the notes were quite willing to accept real estate in lieu of specie. Since the charter refusal made it impossible for currency holders to demand payment, the bills were not acceptable to many creditors of the church. According to Cyrus Smalling, a determined effort was made to exchange the notes for other currency that would pay debts, even to the extent of selling them for as low as twelve and one-half cents to the dollar.[40] As the notes thus got farther into circulation, the problem of redemption became serious. Outside merchants, banks, and capitalists, in presenting notes for redemption, insisted upon specie. Yet, according to two contemporary reports, not more than $6,000 in specie was ever paid into the bank—an obviously inadequate sum, considering that an estimated $50,000 to $100,000 in notes were issued.[41] When the spread of the Panic of 1837 forced the larger banks of the country to collect specie, and ultimately caused most of them to close their doors, the Kirtland bank also ceased payment.[42] In August 1837 Joseph Smith formally renounced the bank; in November of the same year the bank (or anti-bank) closed its doors.

Individuals both in and out of the church, caught with large sums of the notes, complained bitterly of their losses, and the church's connection with the enterprise gave it (the church) an uncertain future.[43] Joseph Smith was wracked with law suits. Considering the law suits, the dissension within the church, and the lack of faith in his enterprises by businessmen in the region, the Mormon prophet finally left Kirtland in the dead of night, in January 1838, never to return. His destination was the new Zion of the Mormons—Far West, Missouri. When the corps of five hundred faithful Mormons left Kirtland for Far West later in 1838, virtually all their fixed property—farms, homes, stores, and industries, and their temple, were paid on indebtedness or lost by foreclosure.[44] It would be many years before church leaders would have the courage to initiate another bank or currency scheme, and then the reserves of specie would provide almost 100 per cent backing.

Far West, Missouri. In 1837, considering the failures in Kirtland and the growing strength of the church in Missouri, Far West, in newly created Caldwell County, was proclaimed as the new gathering place for the Mormons. From eight to ten thousand Mormons gathered at this point in 1837–1838, including those expelled from Jackson County, and perhaps a thousand from the Kirtland area. Under organizations set up by the church the leadership collected consecrations, bought land, dedicated a lot for a temple, and commenced to arrange for a large community. The Saints were instructed to operate under the law of consecration and stewardship, with each person required to consecrate all his surplus property, and with each family given in return a stewardship with deeds in fee simple. A new proviso was added: In place of church members contributing their surplus incomes each year, they were asked to pay "one tenth of all their interest annually."[45] The consecrations were used in buying land, paying church debts, and supporting the priesthood in their manifold enterprises of a spiritual and temporal nature.

Under these arrangements the Mormons began once more to build a "Kingdom of God in the wilderness." According to one contemporary observer, the Mormons, "by persevering industry soon opened extensive farms and it seemed by magic that the wild prairies over a large tract were converted into cultivated fields. Persons visiting the county remarked, 'that no other people of the same number could build a town like Far West and accomplish as much in the agricultural line in five years as the Mormons had in one.'" There were six Mormon stores in Far West in 1837, "and all doing very good business. . . . Land was entered at one dollar and twenty five cents per acre and nearly every family was in possession of a farm."[46]

The form of agricultural cooperation is of particular interest because of its use later in the Great Basin. Voluntary cooperative enterprises, called "United Firms," were organized to consolidate property holdings. These were known as the Western, Eastern, and Southern Agricultural Companies.[47] In the case of one of these companies, at least, a decision was reached to enclose a field of twelve sections, containing 7,680 acres of land, for the growing of grain. Overseers were elected to direct the work of the men and draft animals.

According to other accounts, plans were underway to organize, in addition to the agricultural companies, three other "corporations" uniting mechanics, shopkeepers, and laborers. One participant described them as follows:

All kinds of necessary articles will soon be manufactured by these firms that we may be under no necessity of purchasing of our enemies. The firms furnish constant employ for all who join them and pay $1.00 per day for a man's work. Any surplus that may remain after paying the demands of the firm is to be divided according to the needs and wants (Not according to the property invested) to each family, annually or oftener if needed. . . . The operations of these firms enables a man to get a comfortable house in a very few days when he gets about it. 1st by working for the firm 70 or 80 days then the firm turn out stone cutters, teams, carpenters, masons, &c., to complete the house and nearly every thing (save the land) is paid for by a man's own labor day after day. . . .

Arrangements will soon be made that a person can get every necessary to eat, drink, live in, on & to wear, at the store house of the firms, and the best part of it all is that they want no better pay than labor. Arrangements are making that no person shall have the excuse for not laboring, nothing to do, nor shall the idle eat the bread of industry.[48]

John Corrill, who was a leading participant in these plans, wrote of them:

Every man was to put in all his property by leasing it to the firm for a term of years; overseers or managers were to be chosen from time to time, by the members of the firm, to manage the concerns of the same, and the rest were to labor under their direction. . . . Many joined these firms, while many others were much dissatisfied with them, which caused considerable feeling and excitement in the Church. Smith [Joseph] said every man must act his own feelings, whether to join or not.[49]

All these arrangements, however, were never completely worked out. Once more, the Mormons were driven from their homes and forced to leave Missouri and all their cooperative undertakings and hopes behind. From twelve to fifteen thousand Latter-day Saints were involved in the expulsion, and, according to one report, more than $300,000 worth of property was abandoned.[50]

Profiting from their experiences in leaving Jackson County and Kirtland, the church and its leaders assumed responsibility for the removal of the poor among their number. On January 29, 1839, a "covenant" or agreement was entered into whereby church members signed a pledge "to stand by and assist each other to the utmost of our abilities" in removing from Missouri. They contracted as follows:

We do hereby acknowledge ourselves firmly bound to the extent of all our available property, to be disposed of by a committee who shall be appointed for the purpose of providing means for the removing from this state of the poor and destitute who shall be considered worthy.[51]

In this way, the entire group was mobilized to move across the Mississippi to Quincy, Illinois, where citizens organized a relief fund to aid them until they found a permanent home.

Nauvoo, Illinois. The area eventually settled by the Mormons in Illinois was the swampy village on the banks of the Mississippi named "Commerce." Here Joseph Smith and his followers purchased a large tract of land, rechristened it "Nauvoo" (said to mean "Beautiful Place" in Hebrew), obtained a liberal charter for an "independent principality," and commenced to build what became, next to St. Louis, the most important city of the Upper Mississippi. By 1844, an estimated 25,000 Mormons resided in Nauvoo and nearby villages.[52]

Nauvoo represents, in Mormon history, a phase of what might be called nation-building. The scale of the planning, the exclusiveness and self-sufficiency, the emphasis on "productive powers" or "spiritual capital" — all these bespeak a high degree of Mormon nationalism. The formation of an independent city militia of three to four thousand Mormons, called the "Nauvoo Legion," also lends support to this view. Joseph Smith's forceful leadership in military, political, economic, and religious affairs also reflected and magnified the self-confidence of the Nauvoo Mormons in their ultimate mission and destiny.

In planning their model city, Mormon leaders used a modified form of the Plat of the City of Zion. A large agricultural hinterland provided food, while hundreds of shops and "factories" were established with the intention of making it the "workshop of the Middle West." Missionaries were sent to England, with immense success, and several thousand English converts migrated to the city to add their skills. Sporting the varied industries and occupations of easterners, southerners, Englishmen, and frontiersmen, Nauvoo was largely a self-contained commonwealth. Farmer converts without the means of purchasing land were allowed to raise crops on a huge community farm just outside the city.[53] Laborers and skilled craftsmen who lacked employment worked on a huge temple, which was financed by voluntary contributions of labor and materials.[54] Work on the temple was supplemented by the construction of a $150,000 church-sponsored hotel, the Nauvoo House.

Joseph Smith's economic policy emphasized the importance of manufactures, and the necessity of local production of the raw materials for a manufacturing industry.[55] Under his stimulus, the church organized the Nauvoo Agricultural and Manufacturing Society, with a capital stock of $100,000. This marked the beginning of a drive to replace the old stewardship principle with a joint-stock system of ownership. The society made plans to build a railroad and construct a dam to generate power. In other ways it sought to stimulate and coordinate Mormon economic activity. Within two years the city had steam sawmills at Nauvoo and Black River Falls, Wisconsin, a steam flour mill, a tool factory, a foundry, and a factory for chinaware. The city also owned a steamboat.[56]

It was in Nauvoo that the church first systematized its revenues and collections by establishing a Tithing Office. This office, which became a familiar sight in the Great Basin, replaced the bishops' storehouses which had existed in Kirtland and Missouri. With the establishment of the tithing office also came a revision of the consecration principle: Church members were expected to contribute one-tenth of their possessions and one-tenth of their annual increase. Those who had no property, and therefore no annual increase, were expected to labor one day in ten for the church.[57] The tithed properties, it was explained by church officials, would "furnish a steady public fund for all sacred purposes, and save the leaders from constant debt and embarrassment." In addition to tithing their property and income, members were also advised to hold themselves "in readiness to be advised in such manner as shall be for the good of themselves and the whole society." [58]

Once more, however, the Mormons and their leaders ran into conflicts with citizens in surrounding towns and with public officials. Joseph Smith and his brother, Hyrum, were assassinated in 1844, and Brigham Young succeeded to the leadership of the church. Various enterprises, particularly the temple, were kept alive supporting Mormon workmen, but an exodus from Nauvoo was inevitable. In the fall of 1845 citizen committees demanded the removal of the Mormons from Illinois by the spring of 1846. The Mormons agreed to go, but complained of difficulty in selling their property. The pressure continued, armed mobs threatened the lives of the people, and finally, in February 1846, while it was still winter, some 16,000 Mormons evacuated the "City of Joseph," crossing the Mississippi River on the ice and in ferries. They went in 3,000 wagons, and took with them 30,000 head of cattle, a "great number" of horses and mules, and "an immense number" of sheep.[59]

Exodus to the West. The migration of the Mormons from Nauvoo across Iowa to the Missouri River, and from the Missouri to the Great Basin, was a particularly important phase of early Mormon economic experience because it was in that phase that the organization which the Mormons used in colonizing the Great Basin was perfected.

The problem of supporting the "Camp of Israel," as it was called, was not a simple one. The Mormons were able to realize very little from sales of their Nauvoo property. This applied particularly to church property. The million-dollar temple which they had hoped to sell for $200,000, was burned shortly after their departure; and the Nauvoo House apparently became the property of Joseph Smith's widow. The industrial enterprises were worth much more as going concerns than as isolated physical properties awaiting use, and the farming lands were worth less to isolated individual farmers than to the Mormons who valued them as a compact unit. Moreover, the rush of leaving forced the abandonment of much property, both real and personal. John Taylor, a church official, estimated that the Mormons did not obtain a third of the value of their farms, houses, lots, and other property.[60] Benjamin Brown's personal experience must have been typical:

> My property [he wrote] was rather more pleasantly situated than many others, and I succeeded in getting the munificent sum of 250 dollars for my house and orchard, the nursery to which contained six thousand grafted young fruit trees, and was worth three thousand dollars, at least. Many of the Saints would have been glad to have got off with no greater sacrifice than myself, but as the time drew near, the prices offered for our property fell in proportion. Some of the Saints did not get half as much as I did, for property equally valuable. Others got nothing at all, but had to leave their houses just as they were, and those living in the outskirts of the city were saved the sacrifice of *selling* their houses for less than their worth, for the mob burned about three hundred of them down, and destroyed the property of the owners.[61]

The Mormons attempted to make up through superior organization what they lacked in economic assets. Four months before their hurried departure, on October 6, 1845, the assembled Saints met and adopted the Nauvoo Covenant. Patterned after the Missouri Covenant, the Nauvoo Covenant was an agreement, solemnly entered into in the sacred Nauvoo Temple, "that we take all the saints with us, to the extent of our ability, that is, our influence and property."[62] The combined means of all the Saints was thus voluntarily placed at the disposal of a committee of the "Camp of Israel," of which Brigham Young was the chairman. Brigham Young, who was regarded as their spiritual as well as temporal leader, interpreted his delegated powers under this covenant very broadly, and men, supplies, and monies were commandeered for the accomplishment of the common goal.

The first task was the establishment of a temporary camp at Sugar Creek, Iowa, nine miles from the Mississippi. At this point the entire "Camp of Israel," as it was called, was organized for the overland journey. The organization was patterned after the abortive Zion's Camp expedition which Joseph Smith had led to "redeem Zion" in 1834.[63] Families were organized into groups of one hundred. Each hundred was divided into two groups of fifty each. And each fifty was subdivided into groups of ten each. Over each of these groups was a captain, appointed by church officials subject to the approval of the group concerned. In this way, responsibility for each family and each wagon was definitely assigned. Brigham Young was commander in chief or president of the entire camp. Others served as blacksmiths, wagonmakers, clerks, commissary agents, historians, and guards of the camp as a whole and of the smaller units as needed.

> Each family was . . . required to take a due proportion of seed grain and agricultural implements. Every wagon, load and team was inspected by a committee, and none were allowed to start on the plains without the required outfit. A strict guard was kept over the cattle by night and day, also in the camps, which were formed in an oval shape, the inside making a corral for the stock. Pigs and poultry were carried in coops attached to the wagons.[64]

Certain rules were adopted for the entire camp; others were adopted for each group. These pertained to such matters as (1) time to arise, pray, commence traveling; (2) manner of travel and care of guns; (3) length of noon hour; (4) manner of circling wagons at night; (5) manner and responsibility of guarding the stock; (6) time for evening prayer and retirement; (7) punishment for cursing, swearing, and beating animals; and so on.[65]

The movement of the entire body was planned in such a way as to get maximum benefit from "living off the land." Since much of the land in Iowa was unsurveyed, groups called "Pioneers" were assigned to go in advance to plow and plant patches of ground to be harvested by those coming along later. Others were assigned to work for farmers or shopkeepers along the route and earn money to be placed into a common fund to assist the poor. Some were detailed to build bridges, clear brush, and search out supplies of food and livestock.

Camps were established in Iowa at intervals along the route, the principal ones being Garden Grove, 135 miles from Sugar Creek; Mount Pisgah, 30 miles farther west; Kanesville (now Council Bluffs), on the eastern bank of the Missouri River; and Winter Quarters (now Florence, a suburb of Omaha), on the western bank of the Missouri. The activities of these camps were characterized by an advanced degree of organized cooperation. At Garden Grove, for example, some 715 acres were broken up, planted, and fenced cooperatively, for harvest by later groups. Of the 359 laboring men in this advance group, 100 were selected to make rails, 10 to build fences, 48 to build houses, 12 to dig wells, 10 to build bridges, and others to plow and plant. Houses were built along the sides of the field. For those remaining more or less permanently at the camp, the land was assigned in proportion to the size of the family. In no instance was a man permitted to regard land as his if he did not till it.[66] Neglected crops were placed in the common storehouse or tithing office.

These cooperative procedures were also followed at other camps. At Mount Pisgah 1400 acres were enclosed and planted, and the land was divided into five, ten, and twenty acre portions and distributed to the "permanent" settlers by casting lots. At Winter Quarters, where the Latter-day Saints remained until the exodus to the Salt Lake Valley, an immense area was laid out in uniform blocks, much as Nauvoo had been and the "city" of 3,200 families was divided into twenty-two wards, each with its own officials and policy. Many collective enterprises provided the basis of support.

Brigham Young planned to send an advance company to the Great Basin, or Upper California, in the summer of 1846, to explore for a new gathering place. These plans had to be postponed by the completion of arrangements to send a battalion of 500 young Mormons to participate in the war with Mexico.

The dispatching of the Mormon Battalion indicates the magnitude and detail involved in planning the exodus of the Mormons to the West. A committee had been sent to Washington, to seek government help in making a move to the West. Oregon, California, Texas, and Vancouver Island had all been considered as possible places of refuge. All Mormon proposals to the government were rejected, but President James K. Polk and his secretary of war worked out an arrangement with Jesse C. Little, the Mormon representative, whereby the U. S. Army would recruit 500 young Mormons to march to Santa Fe in support of the operations of General Stephen Watts Kearny.[67] They would have certain privileges with respect to their own officers, discipline, pay, and so on.

The value of this arrangement to the church was that each recruit would receive an advance payment of $42 for his year's expenditure of clothing. This amounted to $21,000 for the entire group. Most of it was immediately paid by the Battalion members into the common fund of the church.[68] In addition, arrangements were made by the church to pick up their pay at intervals and this money was used to support their wives and children, and to assist in the general removal of Saints.[69] The total amount of these payments was apparently well in excess of $50,000, a considerable amount of which was used for such group purposes as the purchase of supplies and provisions and the erection of a gristmill on the Missouri River. Some of the money was used to buy supplies in St. Louis, where prices were much cheaper than in the Indian trading posts on the Missouri, and these were subsequently retailed in the Missouri River camps.[70]

Thus, does Brigham Young say that "the Mormon Battalion was organized from our camp to allay the prejudices of the people, prove our loyalty to the government of the United States, and for the present and temporal salvation of Israel."[71] While the agreement with the government took away 500 "pioneers" who had been expected to constitute an advance party to explore Upper California in 1846, it brought advantages which more than compensated for the delay in moving West.

> It meant [wrote Golder] that five hundred of their men would be taken to California at government expense, that they would have the opportunity to explore the land, that their pay would help to fill the empty treasury, that the Mormons as a body would be protected and allowed to occupy Indian lands in their march across the country. . . . The awkward squads which left Council Bluffs entered Salt Lake as trained, disciplined soldiers, fully equipped. This equipment and training were of great service to them later in their Indian troubles.[72]

It being considered impractical to send a company further west in 1846, the 16,000 Saints on both banks of the Missouri were organized to prepare for the journey the following and succeeding years. With the permission of the Indians (and the Indian Agent) on whose lands they were camped, they laid out a town site, established a water supply system, and proceeded to work collectively in building a city according to plan. By December 1846 they had erected 621 houses, mostly of logs, a gristmill, a council house, and several thousand wagons.[73] The houses were formed close together, and the space between them filled with pickets, so as to form a kind of fort or stockade. Although observers found their general condition to be pitiful, their mutual dependence made it far from hopeless.

During the winter of 1846–1847 preparations were made and companies organized for the long trek west. On January 14, 1847, Brigham Young announced "The Word and Will of the Lord," which contained instructions for the westward journey.[74] The following April, an advance company of 143 men, 3 women, and 2 children departed for the west. Three months later, in July, what is sometimes called "the first emigration," consisting of 1553 persons, 566 wagons, 2213 oxen, 124 horses, 887 cows, 358 sheep, 35 hogs, and 716 chickens followed in their path. The organization of these camps was virtually the same as had been arranged in the exodus from Nauvoo, and the technique of collective support also applied. The advance company explored the country, blazed a trail, made careful notes on everything they observed, built ferries, and even earned cash by ferrying emigrants bound for Oregon across the rivers in their path. They reached the Salt Lake Valley in July 1847, and the larger company arrived there in September and October of the same year.

EARLY MORMON ECONOMIC IDEALS: A SUMMARY

Out of the experiences of Jackson County, Kirtland, Far West, Nauvoo, and the exodus emerged the common economic ideals of the Mormons. These beliefs and practices — a unique coalescence of Jacksonian communitarianism — are of special importance because they were the foundation stones upon which the Kingdom was built in the Great Basin, and because

THE MORMON
MIGRATION TO THE WEST
MORMON TRAIL
MORMON BATTALION TRAIL
SOUTHERN ROAD
Columbia Riv.
OBOISE
FORT HALL
Snake Riv.
Great Salt Lake
Bear L.
SOUTH PASS
FT. LARAMIE
WINTER QUARTERS
Missouri River
FT. BRIDGER
CHEYENNE
Platte Riv.
FT. KEARNEY
SALT LAKE CITY
Humboldt Riv.
GREAT SALT LAKE DESERT
FT. LEAVENWORTH
Utah L.
Green Riv.
DENVER
INDEPENDENCE
CARSON CITY
SUTTER'S FORT (SACRAMENTO)
YERBA BUENA (SAN FRANCISCO)
Sevier L.
Sevier Riv.
Colorado Riv.
ROCKY MTS.
Arkansas Riv.
MOJAVE DESERT
LAS VEGAS
SANTA FE
LOS ANGELES
PACIFIC OCEAN
SAN DIEGO
PHOENIX
Gila Riv.
TUCSON
Rio Grande
U.S.A.
MEXICO

they became the basis for conflict with businessmen and politicians whose views would become more and more hostile to such communitarian principles and institutions. Above all, the ideals which came out of the laboratory of early experience were incorporated into Mormon dogma as a permanent aspect of religious belief. That is, they were established and supported by revelations which were believed to be proclamations of the Deity, and their constant reiteration in sermons and their frequent publication in church books and periodicals established them officially as an inherent part of Mormon theology and church government. The problems faced by the early Mormons dictated certain expedients; these expedients were an integral part of the early revelations; and the content of the revelations came to be accepted, officially and otherwise, as Mormon belief and practice.[75]

These ideals — that is, the content of these revelations — can be summarized in terms of the following seven basic principles.[76]

1. *The Gathering.* The earliest principle, as developed in New York, Kirtland, and Jackson County, counseled the "pure in heart" to "gather" out of "Babylon" (the sinful world) to a place called "Zion," where "God's people" would build the Kingdom, dwell together in righteousness, and prepare for the Millennium. "Ye are called to bring to pass the gathering of mine elect," ran the revelation; "the decree hath gone forth from the Father that they shall be gathered in unto one place, upon the face of this land." [77] Eventually, the concept of gathering was included in the Articles of Faith of the church: "We believe in the literal gathering of Israel . . . [to] this (the American) continent." [78] The promulgation of this doctrine led to the development in the 1830's of a large and highly effective missionary system, an overseas emigration service, and the establishment of a series of "Zions" or gathering places.

2. *The Mormon Village.* Once gathered, the Latter-day Saints were to be settled, as suggested in the Plat of the City of Zion, in a network of villages consisting of a cluster of homes on lots laid out "four square with the world," and with wide streets intersecting at right angles. The uniform home lots were to be large enough to permit the production of fruits and vegetables, poultry, and livestock. Farmers were to live in the town and drive out to their fields every day for work. The village would not necessarily be an agricultural village — usually it would include mining and manufacturing enterprises as well — but it would be a self-sufficient village.

The Mormon village concept, which in some respects resembled the New England village, was used as a guide in the settlement of Far West, Nauvoo, Salt Lake City, and almost every other Mormon community in the West; indeed, it proved peculiarly adapted to the conditions required for colonizing the Great Basin. It provided security against Indians; facilitated cooperative efficiency by placing the members of the community in ready touch with directing officers of the group; made possible the maintenance of religious, educational, and other social institutions; permitted effective irrigation culture; and assured, in general, a highly organized community life. By separating the residence area from the arable lands, it also made possible a more advantageous utilization of the lands, especially common pasturing of the fields after harvest.[79]

3. *Property as a Stewardship*. The property rights and holdings of Mormon villagers were to be allocated and regulated by the church in accordance with the principle of "stewardship." "The earth is the Lord's," and man must consider his rights to land as derived and subject to church disposition. This principle assured primacy of group interest over individual interest, and every man was to consider his property as consecrated to the Lord for the building of the Kingdom.

The "true principle," as Brigham Young summarized it later, was "to hold emphatically everything we possessed upon the altar for the use and benefit of the Kingdom of God, and men shall be as stewards over that which they possess, not that everything shall be common or that all men shall be made equal in all things, for to one is given one talent, to another two, and to another five, according to their capacity." [80]

4. *Redeeming the Earth*. After the settlement of villages and the determination of property rights, the Saints were to proceed with the orderly development of local resources. This was a sacred assignment and was to be regarded as a religious as well as a secular function. One of the Articles of Faith of the church read: "We believe . . . that the earth will be renewed and receive its paradisiacal glory." [81] As explained by a leading apostle in an authoritative work, Latter-day Saints believed that the earth was under a curse and that it was to be regenerated and purified, after which war and social conflict generally would be eliminated and the earth would "yield bounteously to the husbandman." The City of God would then be realized at last.[82]

This purification was not to be accomplished by any mechanistic process nor by any instantaneous cleansing by fire and/or water.[83] It was to be performed by God's chosen; it involved subduing the earth and making it teem with living plants and animals. Man must assist God in this process of regeneration and make the earth a more fitting abode for himself and for the Redeemer of Man. The earth must be turned into a Garden of Eden where God's people would never again know want and suffering. The Kingdom of God, in other words, was to be realized by a thoroughly pragmatic mastery of the forces of nature. An important early admonition to be industrious, and not idle, was supplementary to this belief.[84]

Making the waste places blossom as the rose, and the earth to yield abundantly of its diverse fruits, was more than an economic necessity; it was a form of religious worship. As one early leader later wrote, the construction of water ditches was as much a part of the Mormon religion as water baptism. The redemption of man's home (the earth) was considered to be as important as the redemption of his soul. The earth, as the future abiding place of God's people, had to be made productive and fruitful. This would be accomplished "by the blessing and power of God, and . . . by the labors and sacrifices of its inhabitants, under the light of the Gospel and the direction of the authorized servants of God." [85]

When the Mormons reached the Great Basin this concept stimulated tremendous exertion. "The Lord has done his share of the work," Brigham Young told them; "he has surrounded us with the elements containing wheat, meat, flax, wool, silk, fruit, and everything with which to build up, beautify and glorify the Zion of the last days." "It is [now] our business," he concluded, "to mould these elements to our wants and necessities, according to the knowledge we now have and the wisdom we can obtain from the Heavens through our faithfulness. In this way will the Lord bring again Zion upon the earth, and in no other." [86]

The acceptance of the principle of resource development explains the passionate and devoted efforts of the Mormon people to develop the resources of the Great Basin to the full extent of their potentiality. While it was a sacred duty of Latter-day Saints to purify their hearts, it was an equally sacred duy for them to devote labor and talent to the task of "removing the curse from the earth," and making it yield an abundance of things needed by man. Devices for converting arid wastes into green fields thus assumed an almost sacramental character; they served to promote an important spiritual end.[87]

5. *Frugality and Economic Independence.* The goal of colonization, of the settled village, and of resource development was complete regional economic independence. The Latter-day Saint commonwealth was to be financially and economically self-sufficient. A "law" of the church established this principle in 1830: "Let all thy garments be plain, and their beauty the beauty of the work of thine own hands, . . . contract no debts with the world." [88] This rule occasionally had been departed from, particularly in the Kirtland Bank episode, with disastrous effects, and the frustration of these entanglements with "the world" undoubtedly served to reinforce its standing as a principle of faith. By the time the Great Basin was reached the revelation was given wide application. The Mormon people were asked to manufacture their own iron, produce their own cotton, spin their own silk, and grind their own grain. And they must do this without borrowing from "outsiders." Self-sufficiency was a practical policy, they believed, because God had blessed each region with all of the resources which were necessary for the use of the people and the development of the region.

6. *Unity and Cooperation.* The one quality required to successfully execute the economic program of the church, as often learned by its absence, was unity. Unity, as first enjoined in a revelation given in January 1831, was a high Christian virtue: "I say unto you, be one; and if ye are not one, ye are not mine." [89] The symbols of unity were a strong central organization and self-forgetting group solidarity: The participants in the sublime task of building the Kingdom were to submit themselves to the direction of God's leaders and to display a spirit of willing cooperation. Cooperation, as a technique of organization by which migrations were effected, forts erected, ditches dug, and mills constructed, came to be an integral part of this principle. Cooperation meant that everyman's labor was subject to call by church authority to work under supervised direction in a cause deemed essential to the prosperity of the Kingdom.

While unity and cooperation characterized the early church, it remained for Brigham Young to develop the technique of unified action and combined endeavor to its fullest extent. It was his aim that the church come to represent one great patriarchal family:

> I will give you a text: Except I am one with my good brethren, do not say that I am a Latter-day Saint. We must be one. Our faith must be concentrated in one great work — the building up of the kingdom of God on the earth, and our works must aim to the accomplishment of that great purpose.[90]

> I have looked upon the community of Latter-day Saints in vision and beheld them organized as one great family of heaven, each person performing his several duties in his line of industry, working for the good of the whole more than for individual aggrandizement; and in this I have beheld the most beautiful order that the mind of man can contemplate, and the grandest results for the upbuilding of the kingdom of God and the spread of righteousness upon the earth. . . . Why can we not so live in this world? [91]

His deeds matched his words. He instituted countless programs to achieve unity and facilitate cooperation. These included cooperative arrangements for migration, colonization, construction, agriculture, mining, manufacturing, merchandising — and, in fact, for every realm of economic activity.

The Mormon passion for unity and solidarity, strengthened and tempered as it was by years of suffering and persecution, at once provided both the means and the motive for regional economic planning by church authorities in the Great Basin. The means was provided by the willingness of church members to submit to the "counsel" of their leaders and to respond to every call, spiritual and temporal. The motive was provided by the principle of oneness itself, which was regarded as of divine origin, and whose attainment required planning and control by those in authority.

7. *Equality*. One final aspect of the church's economic program was that which pertained to justice in distribution. It should be obvious that developmental principles, such as those previously discussed, were the major emphasis of Mormon economic policy. In "working out the temporal salvation of Zion," to use a contemporary expression, the formulators of church policy centered primary attention on production and the better management of the human and natural resources under their jurisdiction. Nevertheless, early Mormonism, influenced by its own necessities and the democratic concepts of the Age of Jackson, was distinctly equalitarian in theology and economics, and this had significant influences on church policies and practices in the Great Basin.

The Latter-day Saint doctrine on equality was pronounced within a few months after the founding of the church: "If ye are not equal in earthly things, ye cannot be equal in obtaining heavenly things."[92] There was an earnest and immediate attempt to comply with the spirit of this revelation. In May 1831, when the New York converts to the infant church began to arrive at the newly established gathering place of Kirtland, Ohio, the Lord is reported to have inspired Joseph Smith to instruct that land and other properties be allotted "equal according to their families, according to their circumstances, and their wants and needs."[93] The revelation went on further to say: "And let every man . . . be alike among this people, and receive alike, that ye may be one." In a subsequent revelation to the Saints in Ohio the Prophet instructed: "In your temporal things you shall be equal, and this not grudgingly, otherwise the abundance of the manifestations of the Spirit shall be withheld."[94] When the stewardship system was tried in Jackson County, Missouri, similar instructions were given: "And you are to be equal, or in other words, you are to have equal claims on the properties, for the benefit of managing . . . your stewardships, every man according to his wants and needs, inasmuch as his wants are just."[95]

Although the goal of equality seemed to become less important with advances in material well-being, the core of the policy was reflected in the system of immigration, the construction of public works, the allotment of land and water, and the many cooperative village stores and industries.

THE KINGDOM OF GOD

It would, of course, be futile to attempt to determine whether the ideals just described were an outgrowth of early Mormon experiences, or whether the experiences were, to a considerable extent, a product of the ideals — whether, that is, the Mormon value system was essentially an idealization of the real, or whether the experiences were encountered in the process of attempting to realize the ideals. But it must be recognized that the Mormon response to these ideals was active rather than passive, collective rather than individual. Ideals were translated into action programs by means of organizational instrumentalities specifically developed to implement them. The strength, effectiveness, and lasting influence of the ideals, in early Mormonism and in the Great Basin, are seen in the recurrent efforts to embody them in concrete organizations, procedures, and institutions.

The most basic of these organizational devices for the realization of economic ideals, of course, was the "Kingdom of God"; that is, "Zion"—a *place,* a *community* of Latter-day Saints, and a *quality* of heart and mind.[96] In the first few years of Mormonism the government of the church was also the government for the Kingdom. This was handled by organizing the bulk of the male members into two lay "priesthoods" or governing bodies: the Melchizedek and the Aaronic. The Melchizedek priesthood, consisting of High Priests, Seventies, and Elders, governed the church in spiritual matters; the Aaronic, consisting of Priests, Teachers, and Deacons, supervised the temporal.[97] Each was divided into local groups or "quorums," with leaders appointed by general church authorities, with the consent of the quorum.

Mormon church government, thus equipped to govern the church both spiritually and temporally, is said to have been "theo-democratic" in nature.[98] All church officials, local and general, line or staff, were nominated by superiors, supposedly as the result of divine inspiration, with the consent or "sustaining vote" of the group or congregation concerned. Also, all officers were expected to serve without pay, and continue to make a living in the usual way, whether it be farming, medicine, or merchandising. Any person (that is, any male) might hold any line office in the church, depending on his personal qualifications and the whisperings of the Spirit to the superiors whose business it was to nominate him. This absence of a professional priesthood tended to prevent a spirit of world-negation, facilitated the contact of church leadership with daily life, and made virtually certain an intimate connection between religion and economics.[99] It gave the local priesthood meetings the appearance, if not the substance, of the New England town meetings.[100] Certainly the richest and most fascinating sources of material relating to the impact of church economic policy on local communities are the minutes of local priesthood meetings.

During the early years of the church, the priesthood not only had an interest in temporal affairs, but claimed the right to command in temporal affairs, and this tendency prevailed after the Mormons arrived in the Great Basin. As one bishop expressed it, "the Priesthood [has the right] to dictate to the people all kinds of duties to perform. The Lord spoke to Brigham, Brigham to the Bishops, and the Bishops to the people."[101] In obedience to ecclesiastical authority men established new settlements, set up sawmills, opened general stores, operated ferries, and transported immigrants. And if the call involved selling all their possessions and moving their families to a new and perhaps inhospitable location, the vast majority of them accepted the call as a command.[102]

At the head of all of the priesthood of the church was the president or "Prophet, Seer, and Revelator." He had two personally chosen "counselors," or assistants, who, with him, comprised the "First Presidency of the Church." As God's official spokesmen on earth, the president administered chastisement, revealed new items of doctrine, and directed the building of the Kingdom. By his authority regulations were established, subsidiary appointments made, and funds appropriated. He was also the legal trustee-in-trust over the real and personal properties of the church.[103] So far as the Latter-day Saints were concerned, their president was supreme in religious, political, and economic fields. His were the words of the Lord.

The presidents of the church were appointed by a group of twelve men called the "Quorum (or Council) of the Twelve Apostles." When a vacancy existed in the presidency of the church, the senior member of this Council succeeded to the position. The Quorum of the Twelve was a continuing body, each member serving for life or until he apostatized. When a vacancy was created by the death or removal of one member, his place was taken by a person appointed by the president of the church. Within the framework of policies established by the First Presidency, the Quorum of the Twelve made decisions with respect to church government, finance, the missions, colonization, and other phases of church activity.

The strictly financial affairs of the church, such as the collection of tithing, authorization of expenditures, record-keeping, and active management of church properties, were in the hands of a "Presiding Bishop of the Church," assisted by two counselors. They were, of course, under the supervision of the First Presidency and Council of the Twelve. The Presiding Bishop maintained close, continuing contact with local bishops. The members of the First Presidency, Quorum of the Twelve Apostles, and Presiding Bishopric were known collectively as "the general authorities" of the church.[104]

The geographical units of church government were also determined at an early stage. Local church congregations, or congregations in one part of a city, were called "wards." In charge of each ward was a resident "bishop," who was appointed by the general authorities of the church for an unspecified term of office. The bishop was the "father of the ward," and was expected to be particularly zealous in caring for the temporal needs of his congregation. He maintained contact with his flock by means of "block teachers" or simply "teachers," who were appointed to visit all family units in a designated area at least once a month. Their duties were various: to give religious instruction, to give spiritual and temporal advice, to ascertain the religious and economic condition of the family, to carry messages from the bishop, to collect special assessments, and to see that there was no "iniquity or ill-feeling" in the ward. The bishop also appointed a "Deacon's Quorum," often including teen-agers, to help in taking care of the poor, the aged, and the infirm. The deacons obtained and chopped wood for widows, milked cows for the aged, carried food to the sick, and in general ministered to the material wants of the needy. In Nauvoo, there also existed an organization of women called the "Female Relief Society," which played an important role in church welfare.

Several wards comprised a "stake of Zion." A stake might be a city-wide organization, as in Nauvoo, or it might be a group of country wards organized on a valley-wide basis. Presiding over a stake was a stake president whose duties were primarily spiritual rather than temporal. He might be an apostle or other high church official. Assisting him in the administration of the stake was a group of twelve men chosen by him and the general authorities called the High Council. The High Council arbitrated disputes between the wards and their members, and served as a kind of cabinet for the stake president.

Three special institutions of the early period had a particularly significant effect upon church government and economic development after the removal of the Mormons to the Great Basin. These were the Council of Fifty, the general conference, and economic missions.

The *Council of Fifty* was a specific outgrowth of the early Mormon belief that the church was separate from the Kingdom of God.[105] The Kingdom of God, it was recognized, must include within its bounds many persons who were not members of the church. The Kingdom of God also entailed the performance of many governmental functions not appropriate to the church. In the spring of 1844, during the unsettled period in Nauvoo, Joseph Smith secretly organized the government of the Kingdom of God.[106] This government was in the hands of a group of Mormons and friendly non-Mormons called the "Council of Fifty," or "General Council." Composed of persons "whose influence was needed in establishing order and securing consensus to regulations and ordinances that might not be legally effective, but would nevertheless be effective in regulating affairs within the Mormon Community," the Council of Fifty was intended "to bring a semblance of order into the civil affairs of that city [Nauvoo]. . . . Whenever anything of importance was on foot this Council was called to deliberate upon it."[107] Joseph Smith is said to have called it the "Living Constitution."

The Council of Fifty more or less directed the temporal or civil affairs of the Latter-day Saints from the time of its organization in 1844 until the State of Deseret was established in the Great Basin in 1849. According to the testimony of members, the Council of Fifty engaged in the following activities: (1) Directed memorials to Congress for redress of grievances and for self-government; (2) campaigned for the election of Joseph Smith as president of the United States; (3) sent a delegate to the Republic of Texas offering to collaborate with them in achieving nationhood in return for a large section of Mexican Territory; (4) organized the civil government in the Missouri River camps of the Mormons; (5) sent a group of some twenty-five young men to explore Oregon, Upper California, Lower California and "find a suitable place for the Saints to move"; (6) adopted Brigham Young's "Word and Will of the Lord" as the basis for organizing and directing the trek to the Great Basin.[108]

The organization through which most of the decisions of the general authorities and the Council of Fifty were communicated and voted upon by the church was the *general conference.* All of the quorums, all of the stakes of Zion, all of the members of the church, wherever located, were invited twice each year, usually in April and October, to attend the general conference of the church. Conducted by the general authorities of the church, the general conference consisted of a series of meetings devoted to the common spiritual and temporal interests of the Latter-day Saints. The proceedings of the meetings were usually published verbatim and are the richest source of early Latter-day Saint doctrine and practice. The conference was developed to a high point of effectiveness in the Great Basin where it served as the cement which held together the Mormon Commonwealth. If bishops, stake presidents, and those in charge of church enterprises throughout the region had problems to discuss with church leaders, these were usually saved until personal interviews could be had at conference. Missionaries, both temporal and spiritual, received their official "calls" at these gatherings.

It was through the instrumentality of the conference that church leaders were able to effect the central planning and direction of the manifold temporal and spiritual interests of their followers. It was in the conference that Latter-day Saints experienced most keenly the sense of belonging to a whole — a worshipping, building, expanding Kingdom. Other pioneering groups in the West studied the Bible, prayed, formed local institutions to solve their many problems, such as churches, schools, and associations, and developed many collective instrumentalities and enterprises, but for lack of an institution resembling the general conference, few that were scattered over such a wide territory achieved the militant strength and social cohesion of the Mormons. During the theocratic period of Utah history, the general conference was virtually legislature, town hall, and Chautauqua in its secular aspects, and preaching service and revival on the spiritual side. Or, as a correspondent for *Harper's Weekly* reported, the Mormon general conference was "the post-office, newspaper, legislature, Bible, almanac, temporal, spiritual, and social director of the people." [109]

One other institution of the early church which had great continuing influence in the Great Basin was the *economic mission.* The earliest "missions" were voluntary free lance efforts by newly made converts who, usually on their own initiative, visited friends, relatives, and neighbors to explain "the restored Gospel of Christ." As the church expanded and built up its central organization, a system of appointed missions evolved in which the missionaries selected were permitted to use their own judgment in the areas worked and in the methods used. After the body of the church moved to the Great Basin, the isolation of the region and the distance from the States compelled the discontinuance of free lance missionary activity. Individuals were "called" to go on missions; these calls specified the country or region; the missionaries were expected to remain on the mission until given an official "release." The duration of the mission usually varied from two to five years. Every male member of the church in good standing was subject to one of these "calls." "Personal conveniences were not a primary consideration. A man's farm, crops, flocks, business, whatever it might be, was left for another to tend and care for. . . . No church fund existed to defray his expenses. He took little or no money with him. He left what he had to provide the wants of his family." [110] The calls were usually made in one of the general conferences of the church, and usually were made without prior consultation or notice. After their call, the missionaries chosen had a few days in which to get their affairs in order; then they were given a blessing and a farewell.

It is of great importance to the development of the West that the institution of the mission was applied after 1848 to colonization and economic activity. At the same conferences at which persons were called to foreign and United States gospel missions, others were called, in the same spirit, to mine gold, manufacture iron, raise silk, settle a disagreeable country, and teach Indians the arts of agriculture. The zeal and enthusiasm which naturally came from telling the "good news" to neighbor and friend was thus transferred, in large measure, to the tasks of building the Kingdom. The same onus was attached to spurning the call; the same persistent application required until the date of the official release. The performance of economic activity, under church direction, thus came to occupy a position of honor alongside of evangelization. While some looked upon this adaptation as a materialization of the religion, the Mormons were proud to regard it as the spiritualization of temporal activity.

ROLE OF THE CHURCH IN ECONOMIC DEVELOPMENT

It should be emphasized that, in theory as well as in practice, the Mormon Church was expected to play the central role in erecting and maintaining an improved economic system for its members. Just as the economic role of government in ante-bellum New England was not neutral, neither did the Mormons nor their leaders expect the Mormon people to provide for themselves according to the principles of laissez-faire. They might expect government to play a laissez-faire role, but they did not expect their church to do so. The church's prime obligation was to forward the building of the Kingdom, and that meant it had positive functions to perform in increasing the production of goods and services. In line with this basic orientation, church funds were used to promote many types of new enterprises, ecclesiastical officials regulated many phases of economic activity, and positive measures were taken to counteract panic and depression and to improve the welfare of the church and its members. The role of the church, as interpreted by its founder, and as inherited by his Great Basin successors, was succinctly stated by President Joseph F. Smith as follows:

> Under the first president of the Church, the prophet Joseph Smith, tithes [church revenues] were used for all purposes which in the opinion of those who employed them could be of advantage to the whole church or a part of it, either spiritually or temporally. The tithes supported the poor; they served to build and maintain holy structures and to liquidate debts which the leaders had made. They served to procure houses and lands; tithing penetrated into the channels of trading and manufacturing; it covered the cost of printing of books and newspapers, steamerfares, cattle-raising, the preparation of exploring parties, education, the founding of cities and settlements, the holding of meetings of saints. . . . In short, it served for anything on earth that was attainable at the time for the furtherance of the temporal or spiritual advancement of Zion.[111]

The enactment and support of economic action programs by the church tended to place the stamp of religious dogma upon many of these programs. This tended to render church economic policy incomparably more effective than ordinary secular policy.[112] The acceptance of the various facets of the church's economic program, which was almost a condition of membership in the society, explains the extraordinary tenacity of the Mormons in colonizing and developing areas generally regarded as uninhabitable and uncultivatable.[113] It was a part of the building of the Kingdom. It also explains the state of mind which refused to be defeated by stubborn nature and stubborn foe.

The successful application of a church program — or, rather, of a series of church programs — in the Great Basin raises the founder, Joseph Smith, to the status of a social theorist of no mean ability.[114] Smith's youth — he was less than thirty when the basic economic goals and the organizational structure for implementing them were first outlined and put into operation — gives even greater significance to the intellectual crosscurrents in the ante-bellum America which gave birth to Mormonism. Mormon economic policies could have sprung from nowhere but America — that fruitful, bubbling, inventive America of the 1830's. Each phase of the Mormon system was "in the air." A sister movement, communitarianism, drew inspiration from the same sources. The form of state action (that is, church action) envisioned by Joseph Smith was part and parcel of the Puritan democratic theory concretely expressed in the Commonwealth of Massachusetts. The policies bear remarkable similarity to those applied by the original Georgia Trustees. One is tempted to conclude that, while the Mormons boasted of being a "peculiar people," their economic program was definitely "unpeculiar" in the America of its birth. Central planning, organized cooperation, and the partial socialization of investment implicit in Mormon theory would seem to have been a part of the democratic theory of the Founding Fathers.[115] Unquestionably, traditional American thought and practice sanctioned the positive use of public agencies to attain given group objectives, and this was, of course, the Mormon formula.

BUILDING THE KINGDOM

[1847–1868]

* II *

The basic declared goal of Mormon leaders was the establishment of the Kingdom of God on earth. Essentially, this meant providing the basis of support, in the Great Basin and contiguous valleys, for the ever-growing membership of the church at home and abroad. While the Mormons were inclined to regard the Great Basin as specially ordained by God to become their home, the physical conditions were not favorable for concentrated settlement. The aridity, the mountainous terrain, the severe winters, and the repeated invasions of grasshoppers and crickets militated against large agricultural production. The isolated character of the region prevented extensive commerce, even if Mormon theology had encouraged it. Difficulties with Indians and with the federal government siphoned away energies into defense. Only a high degree of religious devotion and discipline, and superb organization and planning, made survival possible. As the Kingdom grew, many of its shortcomings were converted into advantages. Mountain streams were diverted to water the desert soil; the oasis became a favored stopping place for overland emigrants; the spending of overlanders and of occupation troops was utilized in building the region's economy; and the rugged mountains adjacent to the Salt Lake Valley were discovered to contain rich stores of minerals. The building of the Kingdom was partly a process of turning disasters into windfalls, and partly a matter of hewing to the goals of the early church.

CHAPTER II

A New World

Mormon planning during the first formative years in the Great Basin provides a basis for explaining why the spirit of free enterprise characteristic of New Englanders and frontiersmen generally did not produce in Mormondom the kind of individualistic economy which was typical of the West. In the selection of the Salt Lake Valley as their ultimate resting place, in the establishment of their basic social and economic institutions, and in seeking solutions to the many problems which arose during the first years after settlement, the Mormons demonstrated the intimate relationship between economics and religion. Nothing was above the dictation of religion — nothing too trivial for its watchful care. This predominance of religious interest — this willingness of the individual pioneer to subordinate himself to the church — this subservience of every interest to the maintenance and perpetuation of basic ideals — explains the indestructibility of the solid phalanx of unity in Mormon thought and action in the face of the normal centrifugal forces of the frontier. It explains the singular mingling of work and worship, dancing and devotion, planning and piety, in Mormon group life.

CHOOSING A LOCATION FOR SETTLEMENT

There is every reason to believe that the Mormons who fled their Nauvoo homes in February 1846 fully intended to settle in the Valley of the Great Salt Lake. As early as 1842 Joseph Smith had written in his diary:

> I prophesied that the Saints would continue to suffer much affliction, and would be driven to the Rocky Mountains. Many would apostatize; others would be put to death by our persecutors, or lose their lives in consequence of exposure or disease; and some would live to go and assist in making settlements and building cities, and see the Saints become a mighty people in the midst of the Rocky Mountains.[1]

In 1844 and 1845, when removal from Illinois seemed more certain and necessary, church officials, particularly Joseph Smith and the Council of

Fifty, advanced a number of proposals to facilitate and finance the inevitable westward movement. One proposal was the dispatching of a group of young men to explore "California and Oregon and all that mountain country" to "hunt out a good location" for settlement.[2] Although several meetings were held to organize and prepare such an expedition, the many conflicts and disturbances associated with the assassination of the Prophet prevented consummation of the project.

A second proposal was contained in a memorial to Congress by Joseph Smith and his followers, requesting permission to raise 100,000 troops, independent of the army of the United States. The purposes of the expedition were:

> To open the vast regions of the unpeopled west and south to our enlightened and enterprising yeomanry . . . to secure them in their locations, and thus strengthen the government and enlarge her borders . . . to settle all existing difficulties among those not organized into an acknowledged government bordering upon the United States, and territories . . . to supersede the necessity of a standing army on our western and southern frontiers . . . to explore the unexplored regions of our continent . . . to search out the antiquities of the land . . . to extend the arm of deliverance to Texas; to protect the inhabitants of Oregon from foreign aggressions and domestic broils . . . to break down tyranny and oppression, and exalt the standard of universal peace.[3]

Needless to say, this ambitious plan did not receive congressional approval. Nor did a subsequent petition to the War Department, asking assistance to build blockhouses and forts on the route to Oregon, receive executive sanction. Also abortive were the negotiations between a Mormon "ambassador" and officials of the Republic of Texas to grant the Mormons a large chunk of modern Texas, New Mexico, Oklahoma, Kansas, Colorado, and Wyoming, in return for Mormon military and diplomatic action on behalf of Texan independence from Mexico.[4] Consideration was even given to the settlement of Vancouver Island, either on behalf of the United States or England.[5]

Failing in all these avenues of assistance, Mormon leaders were left to their own devices. Oregon and Texas were ruled out as being too full of "Missouri mobocrats."[6] California was not sufficiently isolated, and was too much under Mexican influence. A large area over which there would be little dispute or difficulty was the Great Basin. Nobody would envy the Mormons their possession of it; they would be remarkably isolated from their old "enemies"; primitive Indian tribes would offer little resistance; and, above all, the region seemed to be divinely ordained, for in the Bible it was written that the Zion of the last days would be built "in the tops of the mountains." Joseph Smith's last words to his friends, as he fled Nauvoo in June 1844, were: "Be ready to start for the Great Basin in the Rocky Mountains." [7]

A major preoccupation of church leaders after Joseph Smith's death was the determination of the suitability of the Great Basin for settlement. Through their representative in Washington the Mormons had acquired Fremont's report, detailing his first journey to the Rocky Mountains, and had published extensive extracts in the Nauvoo *Neighbor* and the *Latter-day Saints' Millennial Star.*[8] Brigham Young and the Twelve Apostles spent many hours studying maps and reading travelers' accounts. The invaluable Fremont report was read orally before the entire Quorum.[9] The Quorum even went so far in its deliberations as to include the subject of irrigation techniques. On September 9, 1845, church officials formally decided to send a company of 1,500 men to the Great Salt Lake Valley, and a committee of five was appointed to "gather information relative to emigration" and to supervise the arrangements for the expedition.[10] This plan was not actually carried out because of the stepped-up attacks on Nauvoo, but the information gathered was of great value when the exodus began the following year.

Thus, when the Mormons left Nauvoo it was with the full intention of proceeding forward as soon as feasible to some point in the Great Basin. It was, they felt, "a point where a good living will require hard labor"; but it would "be coveted by no other people"; it was "fertile"; and it was "unpopulous." [11] Discussions along the way with Father De Smet, Jim Bridger, and Moses Harris increased their confidence in the wisdom of their decision.[12] Before the advance party departed in the spring of 1847, therefore, Brigham Young announced that he and the Twelve had decided that their destination was the Salt Lake or Bear River Valley, in the Great Basin, and that a "Stake of Zion" would be located there.[13] We have gone, wrote the camp clerk of the advance company, "to find a home where the Saints can live in peace and enjoy the fruits of their labors, and where . . . the kingdom of God [shall] flourish." [14]

The Great Basin, of course, was Mexican territory at the time of the Mormon decision to move west, and there has been a disposition on the part of some writers to believe that the Mormons looked upon this as an advantage, hoping to establish an independent nation. While there is some evidence in support of this view,[15] there is more evidence that the Saints fully intended to claim the area for the United States and petition for statehood. In August 1846, for example, Brigham Young and other Mormon leaders, with the "unanimous sanction" of their followers, directed a letter to President Polk, containing the following resolution:

Resolved, that as soon as we are settled in the Great Basin we design to petition the United States for a territorial government, bounded on the north by the British and south by the Mexican dominions, and east and west by the summits of the Rocky and Cascade Mountains.[16]

The Mormons carried an American flag with them, as they journeyed west, and planted it in their Salt Lake Valley fort shortly after their arrival. Moreover, church officials in Kanesville, who appear to have been unaware of the Mexican Treaty, petitioned Congress in July 1848 for a Mormon territorial government.[17] As Apostle Orson Hyde said, the Latter-day Saints might not feel like celebrating Independence Day as they moved west in 1847, for, after all, they were being driven from the boundaries of the United States by some of its citizens. But as soon as they had houses to live in and some peace and hope, they would be ready to sing "Hail, Columbia!" as loudly as the best.[18] Mormon pioneers were, after all, American pioneers, and their struggle for "home rule" did not necessarily mean separatism.

EXPLORING THE GREAT BASIN

When they reached the Salt Lake Valley in the summer of 1847, members of the advance company "dedicated the land unto the Lord" and commenced a systematic program of exploration. Brigham Young said he intended to have "every hole and corner from the Bay of San Francisco to the Hudson Bay known to us."[19] Parties were sent north, south, and west, with instructions to keep a written record of their discoveries, and to look out for farming land, sources of water, timber, mill sites, grazing lands, minerals, and other resources essential to large-scale settlement.[20] Explorations were made immediately in Weber and Cache Valleys north of Salt Lake, in Utah Valley and Cedar Valley south, and in Tooele Valley to the west. During the same period, members of the Mormon Battalion, who had completed their march to San Diego, arrived in the Salt Lake Valley from California with reports on conditions along the northern route from Sacramento across the Sierra Nevada to the Great Salt Lake. Some members of this group were commissioned to return to California via what is now southern Utah and the Old Spanish Trail to explore the southern site, and to buy livestock and seed.

By the end of 1847 Mormon parties had explored the country along both the southern and northern routes to California, and had explored the valleys west of the Wasatch Mountains from Cache Valley, Utah-Idaho, on the north, to San Bernardino Valley, California, on the south. Apostle-professor Orson Pratt and Albert Carrington, two members of the company, had also surveyed the area to determine latitude and longitude, the heights of the mountains and valleys, and other features important to the laying out of a city. All of this research, in the minds of the Mormons, had confirmed the wisdom of the original intention to locate in the Salt Lake Valley. Cache Valley was too cold; Utah Valley was inhabited by Indians. Other valleys were too dry.[21]

The Great Basin region which these and later parties explored, as depicted by Fremont and others, was the region between the Rocky Mountains on the east, the Colorado River on the south, the Sierra Nevada Mountains to the west, and the watershed of the Columbia River to the north. Its boundaries included almost the whole of present-day Nevada, the western half of Utah, the southwestern corner of Wyoming, the southeastern corner of Idaho, a large area in southeastern Oregon, much of southern California, and a strip along the eastern border of California. Although about 210,000 square miles in area, the immense basin had no outlet to the sea. The most characteristic features were the Great Salt Lake in the north and Grand Canyon of the Colorado in the south. The important rivers — the Jordan, Weber, Bear, Sevier, and Humboldt — flowed respectively into Great Salt Lake, Bear Lake, Sevier Lake, and the Carson Sink.

In the center, as if to split the Basin in two parts, was the Wasatch Range of the Rockies, running north and south, which dwindled in its southern end into a series of high, wide, undulating mountain plateaus. The Wasatch was one of the dominant ranges of America, with snow-clad peaks varying from 10,000 to 12,000 feet above sea level. West of the Wasatch was the salty, dry, unyielding Great Basin desert land, broken by isolated ranges, and rich in minerals. To the east were the towering Uinta Mountains and the Uintah Basin, drained by the Colorado, which were too wild and canyonated to be traversed or cultivated. The outstanding characteristics were its isolation — Missouri Valley trading posts were 1,200 miles away — the difficulty of transportation to and within the region, the aridity — rainfall varied from eight to fifteen inches per year — and the scarcity of timber and game.

The Great Basin region would seem to have been singularly uninviting to people fresh from the verdant hills and lush countryside of western Illinois. Ninety-five per cent of the land was either mountainous or desert. The horizon was broken by naked, flat-topped mountains, rugged and full of unearthly color and beauty. Between the few arable patches were vast stretches of sagebrush and bunch grass, populated with coyotes, jackrabbits, and rattlesnakes. The atmosphere was one of loneliness and "empty immensity." Even after twenty years of development and improvement, Samuel Bowles still viewed the Great Basin as "a region whose uses are unimaginable, unless to hold the rest of the globe together, or to teach patience to travelers, or to keep close-locked in its mountain ranges those rich mineral treasures that the world did not need or was not ready for until now."[22] Travelers and explorers had avoided attempting to cross it; the Spaniards had refrained from settling it. Even the few Indians in the region were unbelievably primitive as regards food, clothing, and shelter. A few trappers and Mountain Men had camped, for a time, in its mountain valleys; but the entire region was, for all practical purposes, barren of civilized habitation at the time the Mormons arrived to establish their advance camp.

As Fremont pointed out, however, the region did contain a number of valleys at the western base of the Wasatch where colonies could be planted. While these appeared to be hopelessly dry, for the most part, they could be irrigated with a magnificent array of mountain streams which flowed from the Wasatch and distending plateaus further south. The well-drained alluvial soil in the valleys was fertile, and the valley plains were sufficiently broad to support a considerable population.

> The bottoms of this river, (Bear,) and of some of the creeks which I saw [wrote Fremont on September 12, 1843], form a natural resting and recruiting station for travellers, now, and in all time to come. The bottoms are extensive; water excellent; timber sufficient; the soil good, and well adapted to the grains and grasses suited to such an elevated region. . . . A civilized settlement, would be of great value here; and cattle and horses would do well where grass and salt so much abound. . . . All the mountain sides here are covered with a valuable nutritious grass, called bunch grass. . . . The beasts of the Indians were fat upon it; our own found it a good subsistence; and its quantity will sustain any amount of cattle, and make this truly a bucolic region.[23]

These qualities, along with others, were immediately noted by the advance company in July and August 1847. The Valley of the Great Salt Lake was found to be a level strip of land between Great Salt Lake and the Oquirrh Mountains, on the west, and the Wasatch Mountains on the east, which was from fifteen to twenty miles wide and from twenty to forty miles long. It occupied the center of what is now called the Wasatch or Salt Lake Oasis — an irrigable strip of land from two to twenty miles wide and some two hundred miles long, lying at the western base of the Wasatch. The western half of the Salt Lake Valley — that is, the section west of the Jordan River, which flowed from Utah Lake into Great Salt Lake — was not suited for farming, and thus primary attention was directed toward the immense amphitheater, some twenty to thirty miles square, east of the Jordan. Among the characteristics noted by the advance company were: the almost complete absence of trees, a plentiful supply of potential irrigating water in the mountain creeks and streams, a number of excellent mill sites, the ample facilities for grazing, the fertility of the land as evidenced by the size of the grass and brush, the abundance of "loathesome" large black crickets, and the large number of rattlesnakes.

THE FIRST YEAR IN THE VALLEY

The manner in which the advance company was organized to prepare the valley for occupation by the church is of special interest because of the pattern set for future Mormon colonizing activity. That this pattern of central planning and collective labor was ideally designed for the geography and conditions of settlement in the Great Basin was something which came to be appreciated later: It confirmed to the Mormons that their way was God's way. But before this was recognized — indeed, in the first camp meeting held in the Salt Lake Valley — leaders and followers reached a consensus that they would not "scatter" their labors — that they would combine and concentrate their efforts and work cooperatively — that a Kingdom built in any other way was a fraud — a "Kingdom of the world." As one of the pioneers expressed it, they formally agreed to put their "'mites' together for that which is the best for every man, woman and child."[24] In line with this decision, many of the early sermons were devoted to the theme of working for the common good and rooting out selfishness.

Consciously, then, but effortlessly — as if by force of habit — the advance company was divided into cadres or "committees" for work. One group staked off, plowed, harrowed, and irrigated thirty-five acres of land, which was planted in potatoes, corn, oats, buckwheat, beans, turnips, and garden seeds. Another party located a site for a temple and laid out a city of 135 ten-acre blocks, with the Temple Block in the center. Each block was divided into eight home lots of an acre and one-fourth each. The streets — uniformly eight rods wide — ran east-west and north-south, and were named, starting from the Temple Block, First East, Second East; First South, Second South; First West, Second West, and so on. The city was named "Great Salt Lake City, Great Basin, North America," and names were given to various creeks and streams in the valley, and to some of the peaks surrounding it. Regulations were adopted that the sidewalks be twenty feet wide, that the houses be built twenty feet back from the sidewalks, and that the houses be constructed of sun-dried, clay adobes, after the manner of the Spanish. Lots around Temple Block were apportioned to members of the Quorum of the Twelve (the First Presidency was not selected until December 1847), and other lots were distributed by lot. One of the blocks was selected for a fort or stockade of log cabins within which the pioneers would live until permanent structures could be erected on the city lots.

A large group was then assigned to build log cabins and a wall around the fort: "Sixty to hoke, twelve to mould and twenty to put up walls."[25] Within a month, twenty-nine log houses had been built in the fort, each eight or nine feet high, sixteen feet long, and fourteen feet wide. A block was set aside for a public adobe yard, and an adobe wall was constructed around the three open sides of the fort.

Another committee of the advanced party located timber in a nearby canyon, constructed a road, extracted logs for the cabins, and dug a pit for a whipsaw. A boat was made for use in the creeks, a blacksmith shop was set up, corrals were built, and a community storehouse was erected. Others were assigned to hunt for wild game, try their luck at fishing, and extract salt from Great Salt Lake. In eight days the hunters had been able to bag only "one hare, one badger, one white wolf, and three sage hens"; the fishing expedition had netted "only four fish"; and the salt committee had made 125 bushels of "coarse white salt," and one barrel of "fine white table salt."[26]

Other parties were sent on "missions": One group to California to establish contact with members of the church there; another to Fort Hall, Northwest Territory, to obtain provisions — at the rate of $20.00 per hundred for flour, and ten cents per pound for beef. Still another group went back on the trail to meet and assist the large company which had followed the advance party from Winter Quarters.

Religious services were held each Sunday in a man-made shelter of brush and boughs, called the "Bowery," built on Temple Block by returning members of the Mormon Battalion. One of the creeks was dammed to form a pool, and most of the camp members were rebaptized. This was done, wrote Erastus Snow, "because we had, as it were, entered a new world, and wished to renew our covenants and commence a newness of life."[27]

It was in "free and open discussions" in these services that all basic decisions were made. The earliest of these was that none should hunt or fish or work on Sunday. Another placed the government of the colony, for the next year at least, in the hands of a stake presidency of three and a high council of twelve. These men were to be appointed by the members of the Quorum of Twelve Apostles, with the approval of the congregation. Other officials included a clerk, watermaster, surveyor, and marshal. In another decision, the members of the camp agreed to fence in the city as a guard against livestock, and to establish a farming area south of the city, called the Big Field, where common farming practices would be followed.

Finally, in these meetings the group expressed approval of Brigham Young's proclamations with respect to land ownership and mercantile policy:

> No man will be suffered to cut up his lot and sell a part to speculate out of his brethren. Each man must keep his lot whole, for the Lord has given it to us without price. . . . Every man should have his land measured off to him for city and farming purposes, what he could till. He might till as he pleased, but he should be industrious and take care of it.[28]

We do not intend to have any trade or commerce with the gentile [non-Mormon] world, for so long as we buy of them we are in a degree dependent upon them. The Kingdom of God cannot rise independent of the gentile nations until we produce, manufacture, and make every article of use, convenience, or necessity among our own people. We shall have Elders abroad among all nations, and until we can obtain and collect the raw material for our manufactures it will be their business to gather in such things as are, or may be, needed. So we shall need no commerce with the nations. I am determined to cut every thread of this kind and live free and independent, untrammeled by any of their detestable customs and practices.[29]

These tasks being accomplished, and these policies being agreed upon, Brigham Young and Heber C. Kimball, who had more or less directed the group during its first month in the valley, left on August 26 with most of the men to return to Winter Quarters to report their labors and to prepare the great bulk of the 16,000 persons located there for migration to the valley in 1848 and succeeding years. The major party was preceded by a group especially assigned to hunt for game to sustain them on the return journey.

In September, the main body of emigrants, consisting of some 1540 persons, arrived in the valley to join the remnant of the advance company. Counting the influx from California and other groups, there were some 1681 persons who spent the winter of 1847–48 in the Salt Lake Valley.[30] This large group was organized for public labor by the Salt Lake Stake Presidency and High Council, a group which constituted what was referred to as "the municipal council." They were obligated to respect the authority of the members of the Twelve Apostles, as a kind of Supreme Court, and they were expected to exercise the government of the Mormon colony until after the return of Brigham Young and others in the fall of 1848.

Under the leadership of this ecclesiastical municipal council, two additional ten-acre blocks were added to the fort and some 450 log cabins were constructed; the adobe wall around the fort was completed; an eleven-mile pole and ditch fence was constructed around the city to control the movement of livestock; and a number of roads and bridges were built. A Big Field of some 5133 acres of farming land was "taken up" and prepared for planting. Some 872 acres of the field were planted in winter wheat. When Captain James Brown came from California with $5000 in Mormon Battalion pay, the Council appointed a group of persons to take some of the money to California to purchase "cows, mules, mares, wheat, and seeds of different kinds."[31] They returned in the spring with 200 cows (less forty lost in Nevada), purchased at $6.00 per head, and with grain and fruit cuttings of various kinds. The Council also appointed Captain Brown to use $1950 of the money in buying the Miles Goodyear ranch and trading post in Weber Valley.[32] This purchase removed a possible obstacle to the settlement of that large and productive area.

This "public labor" was largely accomplished through the tens, fifties, and hundreds which had been organized for crossing the Plains. The organization is illustrated by this notation in the church's Journal History for November 28, 1847:

> It was decided that Pres. John Smith and his Counselors should locate a road east of the fort and also one south, and build a bridge over the third creek from City Creek, and call on his hundred to do the necessary labor. Pres. Roundy and his Counselors were appointed to locate a road to the north canyon, and call on his hundred to work it.[33]

The High Council also allocated and regulated economic rights and privileges. Charles Crismon was asked to build immediately a small gristmill (with no bolt) on City Creek. He was to be "sustained" with "labor, good pay and as much grain as the people could be persuaded to spare." [34] When the mill began to operate in November, the stake presidency and High Council took under advisement "the regulation of the price of grinding and all things worthy of note," and on December 2 decided "that Bro. Charles Crismon be allowed twenty cents per bushel for grinding and that he keep an account of the number of bushels, who the grinding was done for and the time occupied in grinding, and if the payment agreed upon did not suffice, then the Council would reconsider the matter." [35] Later, John Neff was authorized to erect "a good flouring mill" before the next harvest.[36] Four sawmills were built or authorized; a carding mill frame was erected; and a water-powered threshing machine was placed in operation that would thresh and clean 200 bushels per day. Regulations were adopted with respect to the conservation of wood and timber: No person was allowed to build with logs without permission; no person was entitled to cut more than he could use quickly; and only dead timber could be used as fuel.[37]

While the colony seems to have been admirably organized to accomplish as much as possible with the limited supply of labor and equipment, it would appear that, under the circumstances, too many persons had been allowed to join the second contingent which left Winter Quarters in 1847. A food problem emerged. In the fall, the cattle and horses had gotten into the planted acreage and destroyed everything but the potatoes. Later in the winter, the Indians, wolves, and other "destroyers" and "wasters" made away with much of the livestock. A special committee was appointed by the High Council "to act in behalf of the destitute and to receive donations, buy, sell, exchange and distribute, according to circumstances, for that purpose." [38] Controls were placed on the prices of necessities,[39] and a voluntary rationing system was instituted limiting each person to about one-half pound of flour per day.[40] The people tried eating crows, thistle tops, bark, roots, and Sego Lily bulbs — anything that might offer nutriment or fill the empty stomach. One or two persons were poisoned by eating wild parsnip roots.[41] A typical experience was that of Priddy Meeks, who had been through many trials in his life and found this to be one of the worst:

> My family went several months without a satisfying meal of victuals. I went sometimes a mile up Jordan to a patch of wild roses to get the berries to eat which I would eat as rapidly as a hog, stems and all. I shot hawks and crows and they ate well. I would go and search the mire holes and find cattle dead and fleece off what meat I could and eat it. We used wolf meat, which I thought was good. I made some wooden spades to dig seagoes [Sego Lily] with, but we could not supply our wants.
>
> We had to exert ourselves to get something to eat. I would take a grubbing-hoe and a sack and start by sunrise in the morning and go, I thought six miles before coming to where the thistle roots grew, and in time to get home I would have a bushel and sometimes more thistle roots. And we would eat them raw. I would dig until I grew weak and faint and sit down and eat a root, and then begin again. I continued this until the roots began to fail.[42]

All looked forward to the spring harvest. But when the winter wheat and garden vegetables began to show their heads, late frosts injured a considerable proportion. And then, in May and June, hordes of hungry crickets moved upon the land and seemed certain to rob the settlers of the last vestige of food.

> Wingless, dumpy, black, swollen-headed, with bulging eyes in cases like goggles, mounted upon legs of steel wire and clock-spring, and with a general personal appearance that justified the Mormons in comparing him to a cross of the spider on the buffalo, the Deseret cricket comes down from the mountains at a certain season of the year, in voracious and desolating myriads. It was just at this season, that the first crops of the new settlers were in the full glory of their youthful green. The assailants could not be repulsed. The Mormons, after their fashion, prayed and fought, and fought and prayed, but to no purpose. The "Black Philistines" mowed their way even with the ground, leaving it as if touched with an acid or burnt by fire.[43]

Men and women alike fought the crickets with sticks, shovels, and brooms, with gunny sacks and trenches, but with little avail.

Finally, just before the entire crop had been eaten clean, came the announcement from the president of the High Council: "Brethren, we do not want you to part with your wagons and teams for we might need them," intimating that they were considering moving on to California or some other gathering place. But at the moment this announcement was being delivered, seagulls providentially moved in and began to devour the crickets, "sweeping them up as they went along." "I guess," wrote Priddy Meeks, "this circumstance changed our feeling considerable for the better."[44]

Nevertheless, the combination of disasters discouraged many. One of the settlers, a brother of Brigham Young, wanted to send an express to Brigham, telling him not to bring any more people to the valley, for "they would all starve to death." John Neff, who was building a large gristmill, "left off . . . for a while, as many expected there would be no grain to grind."[45] A few of the colonists went on to California and others returned to the Missouri Valley. Still others went to meet the incoming migration from Winter Quarters. When a partial harvest was reaped in July and August, the pioneers were so grateful for a substitute for green peas, roots, and berries that they held a special Thanksgiving "feast," with prayer, music, dancing, firing of cannon, and shouts of Hosannah.

ECONOMIC REGULATION DURING THE SECOND YEAR

Brigham Young and Heber C. Kimball, who had become the President and First Counselor respectively of the church in a general conference held in Winter Quarters in December 1847, arrived in the Salt Lake Valley with a group of approximately 2400 Saints in September 1848. With those already in the valley, this left approximately 4200 persons to be fed with whatever provisions they brought and the product of the partial harvest in the valley.

The problem of hunger, which became even more acute than it had been the preceding winter, was tackled by the new church presidency and Twelve Apostles, the Salt Lake High Council, and the Council of Fifty, the three being composed essentially of the same men. The Salt Lake High Council continued to govern in a municipal capacity until January 6, 1849, but with a diminished scope. The Council of Fifty, which had more or less governed affairs in Winter Quarters and Kanesville, operated in a significant behind-the-scenes capacity in the Salt Lake Valley from November 1848 to January 1850.[46] According to John D. Lee, this Council constituted "the Municipal department of the Kingdom of God set up on the Earth, and from which all Law eminates . . . to council, deliberate & plan for the general good & upbuilding of the Kingdom of God on the earth."[47] Perhaps its most significant action was the formation of a provisional state government in March 1849 called "The State of Deseret."[48] This political instrumentality served as the effective government until the establishment of territorial government in the spring of 1851. It continued to function as a "ghost government" until the 1870's.[49]

Apparently, the basic decisions relating to economic affairs in the second year were made in the Council of Fifty and then announced and executed, as seemed best, by the High Council, the First Presidency, the general conference, or citizens' mass meetings. The Council of Fifty was essentially an arrangement whereby the "leading citizens" would freely discuss and agree upon policies and procedures, and these men would then bend their efforts to achieve these results in the various civic and church groups in which they participated. Its regulations — or, rather, the combined regulations of the High Council, the bishops, and the church — centered primarily around the distribution of land, the control over natural resources, the construction of public works, the provision of a circulating medium, and the prevention of hunger and want. They are of particular interest because of their resemblance, in the economic sphere, to the regulations of local and state governments in the ante-bellum New England from whence most of the membership of the governing groups came.

The distribution of land. Although provisional distribution of some land had been made in August 1847, the general distribution of the primary lots in the city began in September 1848. On September 24, Brigham Young and Heber C. Kimball were appointed to apportion the city lots to applicants, and permission was granted to build on these lots during the fall and winter.[50] The distribution of these "inheritances," primarily by means of lotteries, followed the law of stewardship: "equal according to circumstances, wants and needs." A person was appointed to keep a "land record," and $1.50 was to be paid for each lot, $1.00 of it to the surveyor, and 50 cents to the clerk for recording. The original allocations, and subsequent deeds and transfers were written out by hand on small bits of paper, two by three inches. Unmarried men were not entitled to lots, but polygamists were entitled to one for each separate family. Since the city lots in the original plat were all taken up within a month, a new plat was surveyed to the east and additional lots were provided those whose applications were late. The plats were then divided into nineteen ecclesiastical wards and a bishop was appointed in charge of each. Under the supervision of the bishops, fences were constructed around each ward, a network of ditches was constructed to water the lots, and trees were planted around each block along the ditchbanks. Bridges were built at the crossings.

The plan to distribute farming lands was also worked out in September 1848.[51] This plan provided for an irrigation canal to run from Big Cottonwood Creek, a common enclosure of all the lands under this ditch, and the division of these lands among those who wanted them by casting lots. All those wanting farming acreages were asked to register with a clerk, indicating the number of acres wanted. Almost nine hundred applicants applied for the more than 11,000 acres of land.[52] Brigham Young explained how these lands were to be distributed so as to secure maximum effectiveness:

> It is our intention to have the five acre lots next to the city accommodate the mechanics and artisans, the ten acres next, then the twenty acres, followed by the forty and eighty acre lots, where farmers can build and reside. All these lots will be enclosed in one common fence, which will be seventeen miles and fifty-three rods long, eight feet high; and to the end that every man may be satisfied with his lot and prevent any hardness that might occur by any method of dividing the land, we have proposed that it shall all be done by ballot, or casting lots, as Israel did in days of old.[53]

Actually, the demand for the land in the "Big Field" was such that only five- and ten-acre tracts were included. Outside of the Big Field animals were free to graze. As the city increased in population and the demand for farming lands increased, lots outside the Big Field were surveyed and allotted, but the Council assigned each property owner the responsibility of fencing his land as protection against animal trespass.

The main principles underlying the distribution of land, then, were equality, productive use, and the small holding. The small holding, in turn, represented the only way of distributing lands fairly; made possible the distribution of the scarce water supply over the largest number of property owners; made the cooperative fencing arrangements practical; and rendered the city sufficiently compact to intensify social contact and facilitate defense against the Indians.

The control over natural resources. In line with the stewardship principle adopted with respect to the ownership of land, an early decision decreed that basic natural resources were subject to public rather than to private ownership. As expressed by Brigham Young, this policy was as follows: "There shall be no private ownership of the streams that come out of the canyons, nor the timber that grows on the hills. These belong to the people: all the people."[54] The same principle was applied to mineral resources.

The decision with respect to water was particularly crucial. Although water was first turned on the land on July 23, 1847, it took the Mormons at least three years to learn the importance and effective use of irrigation. In this they had little precedent to guide them. Anglo-Saxon law, as adopted generally in the East, provided that water must not be taken from the streams unless it could be returned undiminished in volume.[55] Known as the doctrine of riparian rights, this principle of law protected streams for use as sources of power and as channels of transportation. It also tended to restrict the establishment of homes to the banks of streams and gave privileged protection to the few who could profitably utilize the water.

The public ownership and management of water in the Great Basin prevented the application of this principle in curtailing irrigation, for obviously every use of water for irrigation robbed a stream of part of its water supply. Under the arrangement worked out by the Mormons in 1847–1849, dams and ditches were constructed on a community basis, rights to use the water were associated with the utilization of land, and a public authority was appointed to supervise the appropriation of water for culinary, industrial, and agricultural purposes. The avowed goal of this supervision was equitable division and maximum use of available water supplies.[56] In 1847–1848, for example, a community ditch furnished water primarily for culinary purposes, and its distribution was under the control of a "watermaster" appointed by the high council.[57]

It was during the next two years, however, when water matters were in the hands of the bishops of the various wards, that the Mormons developed the well-known principles by which canals and ditches were to be constructed and the waters divided. When a group of families found themselves in need of water (or additional water) to irrigate their farms and gardens, the bishop arranged for a survey and organized the men into a construction crew. Each man was required to furnish labor in proportion to the amount of land he had to water. Upon completion of the project the water would be distributed by a ward watermaster in proportion to this labor. The labor necessary to keep the canal in good repair was handled in the same way, in accordance with assignments made in regular Sunday services or priesthood meetings.

On this cooperative nonpecuniary basis, then, water was diverted from a natural source into a general canal, and from that into "laterals" and ditches which carried the water to the individual plots of ground needing it. "Corrugates" were dug next to each row to carry water to the crops. "Waste ditches" carried the water from one watered field to the next one below it.

When Utah became a territory this system of public ownership was confirmed by the legislature and placed under the legal supervision of the county courts. The territorial government gave additional recognition to this system of cooperative construction and ownership in 1865 by providing for the creation of irrigation districts, resembling Western mining districts, with a large degree of local autonomy. Even today, farmer-owned "mutual" companies control virtually all the irrigation canals in Mormon communities in the West. The vast majority of Utah's canals, as Thomas states, "were built by the farmers, owned by the farmers, and operated by the farmers. In fact they constitute one of the greatest and most successful community or cooperative undertakings in the history of America."[58]

A similar principle governed the allocation of timber. Timber was located only in the canyons adjacent the settlements, and the timber could not be procured until suitable access roads had been constructed. Under the direction of the bishops all turned out to build the road, and then all were permitted to use the timber in return for a token payment for upkeep of the road. As in the case of water, the territorial legislature confirmed the paramount public interest in timber supplies and in 1852 conferred the jurisdiction for its management on the county courts. The language of the act gives explicit recognition to the stewardship principle which had guided all Mormon property arrangements:

> The county courts shall . . . have control of all timber, water privileges, or any watercourse or creek, to grant mill sites, and exercise such powers as in their judgment shall best preserve the timber and subserve the interests of the settlements in the distribution of water for irrigation or other purposes.[59]

Occasionally, the legislature made exclusive grants to prominent Mormons, but in doing so it did not confer monopolistic privilege of use, but rather, "the exclusive right to orderly regulation and apportionment of water usage in accordance with socially desired ends . . . the legislative body resorted to the device of centralizing responsibility as a means of averting interminable controversies over this prime essential in food and crop production under arid conditions."[60] The general rule, as often expressed was: "In water [as in other] disputes, let the Priesthood rule."[61]

The erection of public works. The same type of informal cooperation which saw to the completion of canals and canyon roads, also characterized the erection of public buildings and the construction of roads and bridges. "The particular assignment and the units that were to do it were officially announced each Sunday in meeting," and in response to these calls a prodigious amount of work was accomplished.[62]

The first tasks were outlined in a church conference held in October 1848, in which the community voted to build a wall around the Temple Block and to build a Council House by tithing produce and labor; that is, by laboring one day in ten, and donating one-tenth of their production.[63] Pending the commencement of this work the next summer, a church appointee supervised the use of tithing labor in building a small adobe church-office building, a public bathhouse at Warm Springs, and an armory. A new bowery was also constructed, and this served as the central meeting place of the Mormons from 1849 to 1851. This shedlike structure was 100 feet long, 60 feet wide, had 100 posts to support a roof of boughs and dirt, and was large enough to shelter an audience of more than 3,000 persons.[64] One other public activity was the clearing and planting of 800 acres in what was known as the Church Farm.[65] This enterprise was intended to utilize labor and livestock tithing in producing food for the poor.

During the second year there were also a number of what might be called "mixed" enterprises; that is, partly private and partly public. Among these were the mills constructed in 1847–1848, a tannery and leather manufacturing establishment, additional gristmills and sawmills, and a foundry.

In some cases, the motivating force in the establishment of these was private, in others it came from the church. For example, on January 6, 1849, the Council of Fifty resolved "that Alanson and Ira Eldredge engage in the business of tanning and manufacturing leather, and that the Council exert its influence to sustain them therein."[66] The same Council resolved to "approbate Joel Johnson in his journey to the States to buy sheep." In another instance, Henry G. Sherwood was ordered to "build a glass factory as soon as circumstances would permit."[67] In harmony with the same philosophy the Council appointed a committee to do the community's trading with the Indians, and "that all other persons should be prohibited [from such trading] under fine."[68] As will be seen, the public works were organized on a more formal basis in 1850.

The provision of a circulating medium. Although the initial settlers of the Salt Lake Valley were acutely short of cash,[69] quantities of it were brought into the valley almost immediately from California. Reference has already been made to the $5,000 Mormon Battalion payroll, most of which was expended outside the valley. Some of the Mormon Battalion members who had remained in California during the winter of 1847–1848 were in the company which discovered gold at Sutter's Mill in January 1848. These persons brought several thousand dollars worth of gold dust into the Valley in the fall of 1848. The church aided in the circulation of this dust by setting up an office in which Willard Richards, trusted member of the First Presidency, weighed the gold dust and did it up in paper packages containing from one to twenty dollars of money.[70]

Because of the waste and inconvenience involved in circulating this medium church officials decided to convert the dust into coins of uniform weight, fineness, and value. Mormon leaders were particularly interested in doing this because they thought the coins could be used to advantage in trading with Mountain Men and overland travelers and traders. It was practical for the church to do this because much of the dust went into the coffers of the church in the form of tithing and other donations.[71] In November, a church mechanic who had had some experience in England was commissioned to make arrangements to coin the dust. Church officials worked out the inscriptions and appropriate stamps and dies were prepared. On one side the phrase "Holiness to the Lord" encircled the emblem of the priesthood, which was a three-point Phrygian crown over the All-seeing Eye of Jehovah. On the other side, the words "Pure Gold" and the denomination encircled clasped hands, the emblem of friendship.[72]

Persons holding dust were invited to leave their dust for coinage, beginning December 10, 1848. The first deposit made on that day was by William T. Follett, a Battalion member, whose 14½ ounces of gold dust were credited at $232, or $16.00 an ounce.[73] Within a few days, John Kay had minted forty-six $10.00 gold pieces, which were paid out at par or a slight premium.[74]

This effort at coinage, however, proved a failure. The crucibles were broken for all of the dies by December 22, 1848. It was impossible to make any more coins until materials were ordered from the East. The Journal History for December 22 records that "Many of the brethren came to the office to exchange gold dust for hard money, but no business was done on account of President Young not having any coin."

Realizing the continued need for a circulating medium superior to gold dust, and particularly anxious to keep the gold supply centralized in the church treasury, Brigham Young called a meeting on December 28 "to regulate the currency." [75] Brigham Young reported the results of the meeting as follows: "I offered the gold-dust back to the people, but they did not want it. I then told them we would issue paper till the gold could be coined. The municipal council agreed to have such a currency and appointed myself and Heber C. Kimball and Bishop Newel K. Whitney to issue it." [76]

Immediately, plans were made to issue paper currency bearing the date January 2, 1849. On that date 830 notes, with a total value of $1,365, were issued. Denominations of 50 cents, $1.00, $2.00, $3.00, and $5.00 were distributed, most of them being of the $1.00 denomination.[77] The bills were written out by hand on plain white paper with pen and ink, and were about two inches wide and four inches long. Each bore the signatures of Brigham Young and Heber C. Kimball, of the First Presidency, Newel K. Whitney, the Presiding Bishop, and of Secretary Thomas Bullock.[78] The notes were stamped with the private seal of the Twelve Apostles, which consisted of the emblem of the Priesthood encircled by sixteen letters: P.S.T.A.P.C.J.-C.L.D.S.L.D.A.O.W., which was an abbreviation for "Private Seal of the Twelve Apostles, Priests of the Church of Jesus Christ of Latter Day Saints, in the Last Dispensation All Over the World."

When this first issue of handwritten bills was exhausted a second issue was prepared bearing the date January 5, 1849.[79] This issue consisted of 735 separate bills with a face value of $1,217.50. Fifty-cent and one-dollar notes constituted the bulk of this issue. In addition, 256 notes of the Kirtland Safety Society Bank, with a face value of $1,331, were placed in circulation, in order "to fulfill a prophecy of Joseph [Smith] that one day they would be as good as gold." [80] Already signed by Joseph Smith and Sidney Rigdon, they were countersigned by Brigham Young, Heber C. Kimball and Newel K. Whitney. They represented denominations of $1.00, $3.00, and $5.00, mostly the latter.[81]

In the meantime, some type had been made by Truman Angell, the church architect, who also made a press with which to print paper currency.

This press made possible the printing of a third series of paper currency modeled after the handwritten ones. The third series was intended to consist of 1,000 each of 50 cent, $1.00, $2.00, and $3.00 bills and was dated January 20, 1849. Not quite a thousand of any of the four denominations was distributed, however, because of the discovery of flaws in some of them. This was the first printing done in the Great Basin.[82] A total of 3,329 bills were in this printed issue, with a value of $5,529.50. All told, a total of 5,150 notes, with a value of $9,443, was issued between January and April 1849.

The notes seem to have been generally acceptable, although not universally so. Some stock owners are reported to have refused to sell their beef for paper currency. This prompted Brigham Young to lash out at the "many who have beef to sell and will not take paper money." He told the butchers to "go & kill fat cattle any how and pay the owners a fair price for it." Two days later, Hosea Stout noted the result in his diary: "There is again beef in the market to be had for paper money so salutary was the sermon of the president on sunday on that subject. The market had stopped for several days because men would not sell for any thing but gold dust or coined money."[83]

According to one student, the notes were secured by at least an eighty per cent reserve of gold. "By April 2, 1849 notes had actually been paid out in excess of gold deposits by an amount of about $1,700. But the excess was amply secured by anticipated receipts on Church account."[84] Because of its gold dust basis, the currency may be variously described as "goldbacked treasury notes" or "warehouse receipts for gold dust." On the whole, church leaders were pleased with the experiment; the "General Epistle of the First Presidency," signed March 9, 1849, read: "Money is very abundant, owing principally to the gold dust accumulating here from the coast, upon the deposit of which bills have been issued by the presidency."[85]

The prevention of hunger and want. While the distribution of land, the digging of ditches, the construction of public works, and the provision of a circulating medium were important phases of church activity in the second year, the leading problem of the Council of Fifty and other governing groups was the prevention of hunger and want. Actually, of course, the method of distributing land and water was calculated to promote concentrated agricultural production. Public works activity also was organized so as to provide those employed with food, clothing, and firewood out of the church storehouse in return for their time. Even the technique followed in setting up a circulating medium was related to the problem of food supply, for it served to concentrate the cash resources of the community in the hands of the church which could use it in purchasing supplies and equipment which would add to the productive power of the community.

In attacking the problem of hunger and want the Council of Fifty and other groups acted first to increase the supply of available consumers goods. Mormon companies coming west in the summer of 1848 were instructed to bring enough provisions to supply themselves and others. Their own lack of means and the need of those still in Winter Quarters, however, militated against any large importation. Certainly none had expected the harvest of '48 to be so scanty. In November 1848, at the request of the church, Captain Grant, manager of the Hudson's Bay Company's post at Fort Hall, arrived in the valley with some pack horses, "laden with skins, groceries and other goods." [86] At least three attempts were made to get pack trains through to Fort Bridger to purchase supplemental provisions there, but the severity of the winter made each of these expeditions unsuccessful.

The food problem was related to the severity of the winter of 1848–49 as well as to the poor harvest. The winter of 1847–48 had been mild, grass had been abundant, the earth was tillable most of the time, and the inadequate housing caused no problems. The winter of 1848–49, however, was "more like a severe New England winter." According to a contemporary report:

> Excessive cold commenced on the 1st of December, and continued till the latter part of February. Snow storms were frequent, and though there were several thaws, the earth was not without snow during that period, varying from one to three feet in depth, both in time and places. The coldest day of the past winter was the 5th of February, the mercury falling 33 degrees below freezing point, and the warmest day was Sunday, the 25th of February, mercury rising to 21 degrees above freezing point, Fahrenheit. Violent and contrary winds have been frequent. The snow on the surrounding mountains has been much deeper, which has made the wood very difficult of access; while the cattle have become so poor, through fasting and scanty fare, that it has been difficult to draw the necessary fuel, and many have had to suffer, more or less from the want thereof. The winter commenced at an unusual and unexpected moment, and found many of the brethren without houses or fuel.[87]

Diaries emphasize the high degree to which the rigorous winter debilitated and decimated the cattle herd, affecting both the supply of meat and the potential draft power the ensuing spring and summer. Prospects were so dim in this respect that harsh measures were taken to oversee and shepherd the cattle and horses. The Council, for example, instituted a cattle and horse roundup and community herd, to protect animals from Indians and wolves. When some persons objected that they did not want their animals included in the herd, Brigham Young is reported to have said: "Natural feelings would say let them & their cattle go to Hell, but duty says if they will not take care of their cattle, we must do it for them. We are to be saviours of men in these last days. Then don't be bluffed off by insults or abuse." [88] The Council also sponsored a contest to kill off the "wasters and destroyers."

About 800 wolves, 400 foxes, 2 wolverines, 2 bears, 2 wildcats, 37 minx, and several thousand hawks, owls, eagles, and crows were killed in this hunt.[89] One dollar in tithing was offered on a continuing basis for each wolf and fox skin.[90]

As the winter wore on the food problem became critical. On February 9, 1849, a committee appointed to investigate the food supply reported that there was on hand a little over three-quarters of a pound of breadstuffs per head per day for the next five months — that is, until harvest. A large proportion of the people were having to satiate their hunger, as during the previous year, with rawhides, sego roots, and thistles.[91] None, however, had followed the Indians in eating grasshoppers and crickets. A number of measures were adopted to cope with the situation. The Council of Fifty instituted a regulation prohibiting the use of corn in making whiskey, and any intended for such use was to be "taken and given to the poor." [92] Church officials also wrote to leaders in Winter Quarters not to send companies west during the summer of 1849 unless they could depend entirely on their own resources, and unless they could bring with them enough provisions to last the winter of 1849–1850.[93] Finally, consideration was given to the plight of the poor in the matter of taxes for public improvements. The Council appointed Albert Carrington as assessor, collector, and treasurer, "with . . . discretionary power, to pin down upon the rich & penurious, and when he comes to a Poor man or widow that is honest, instead of taxing them, give them a few dollars." [94]

More important than these measures, however, was the institution of a voluntary rationing and community storehouse system. The city was divided into nineteen ecclesiastical wards, a bishop was appointed for each, and the bishops were instructed to provide for the poor in their wards. In subsequent meetings of these bishops there were reports of "many calls for assistance." Each person with a surplus was asked to turn it over to his bishop to be divided among the needy. Vigorous preaching and strong moral suasion were applied to insure the success of this voluntary share-the-surplus program. A journal entry for January 6, 1849, gives the following summary of a discussion on the subject in the Council of Fifty:

The principle of extortion among the Saints was talked of, especially in the article of Beef, which is selling from 5 to 7 cts. lb., tallow 15 cts. lb. & in fact, everything in proportion. Those that have fat cattle were grinding the face of the Poor. Some of the council were in favour of passing a law regulating the prices of Eatables, but Pres. B. Young objected & said, Let trade seek its own level and let every man of the Council use his influence to put down extortion by reasoning with the People & getting up Prayer meetings & preaching to the People & thereby draw their attention from fidling, dancing & fudling [drinking].[95]

At a meeting of the Council a month later, "the cries & sufferings of the Poor were [once more] called up in question":

The council were of the opinion that a sufficiency of Breadstuff was in the valley to sustain all the inhabitants, till more could be raised, could it be equally distributed. . . . Pres. B. Young said . . . if those that have do not sell to those that have not, we will just take it & distribute among the Poors, & those that have & will not divide willingly may be thankful that their Heads are not found wallowing in the Snow. . . . If the day should [be] fine next Sabbath, I will talk to the people in public. I know the strongest side are willing to do right.[96]

The following Sunday the president did, indeed, speak to the people on "the oppression of the poor. Said to those that [have] corn to spare, to let it go on reasonable terms; said to those that had to buy, not to be particular about what they had to pay, for it would be Salvation to them but Death to the Seller that extortioned . . . The remarks of Pres. B. Y. [added the diarist-reporter] greatly ameliorated the condition of the Poor, for every man that could be touched was Stirred by way of remembrance & began to let corn go. . . . Thus the reader may see the effect of the Preaching of the man of God." [97]

One colonist, however, did not heed the advice. He was called before the High Council and tried for "taking advantage of the people in the sale of his corn &c." He was judged guilty and ordered "to make restitution to all he has injured," presumably on forfeit of his fellowship.[98] Despite such measures, it would seem that the voluntary giving program was more successful than the stabilization of prices. Wheat commonly sold for four to five dollars per bushel, corn from two to three dollars, and potatoes from six to twenty dollars per bushel.[99] A major problem was that of assuring sufficient seed for summer planting.

The severity of the winter, the constant hunger, the poverty of the harvest the preceding autumn, and the pull of what was called "the California fever," caused some of the settlers to become discontented with the Great Basin as "the gathering-place of the Saints." A number openly declared that California was superior in every way and that the Saints ought to move there before they all starved or froze to death. James Brown, who lived through these events and kept a journal of them, described the crisis as follows:

In February and March there began to be some uneasiness over the prospects, and as the days grew warmer the gold fever attacked many so that they prepared to go to California. Some said they would go only to have a place for the rest of us; for they thought Brigham Young too smart a man to try to establish a civilized colony in such a "God-forsaken country," as they called the valley. They further said that California was the natural country for the Saints; some had brought choice fruit pips and seed, but said they would not waste them by planting in a country like the Great Salt Lake Valley; others stated that they would not build a house in the valley, but would remain in their wagons, for certainly our leaders knew better than to attempt to make a stand in such a dry, worthless locality, and would be going on to California, Oregon or Vancouver's Island; still others said they would wait awhile before planting choice fruits, as it would not be long before they would return to Jackson County, Missouri.

This discouraging talk was not alone by persons who had no experience in farming and manufacturing, but by men who had made a success at their various avocations where they had been permitted to work in peace, before coming west. Good farmers said: "Why the wheat we grew here last year was so short that we had to pull it; the heads were not more than two inches long. Frost falls here every month in the year—enough to cut down all tender vegetation.[100]

This was not just talk. One church chronicle reports that in March "about a dozen wagons and families moved, or prepared to move, off to the California gold mines."[101] Another report states that "quite a number" had gone, while an April letter declares with good humor that "Many of the tares have gone to the gold mines, and some of the wheat is probably gone with them."[102] Many of those already in California, elected to remain rather than join their brethren. And the great majority of the Saints in Winter Quarters and Kanesville, if we can believe diary entries and letters, were skeptical of the future of the Great Basin colony. There is no doubt that it was, all in all, a dark winter and spring.

Brigham Young, however, could not be swayed. In trying to hold the church together he stubbornly clung to the original decision to locate the Saints in the Great Basin. "God has appointed this place for the gathering of His Saints," Young declared, "and you will do better right here than you will by going to the gold mines. . . . Those who stop here and are faithful to God and His people will make more money and get richer than you that run after the god of this world." He continued:

We have been kicked out of the frying-pan into the fire, out of the fire into the middle of the floor, and here we are and here we will stay. God . . . will temper the elements for the good of His Saints; He will rebuke the frost and the sterility of the soil, and the land shall become fruitful. Brethren, go to, now, and plant out your fruit seeds. . . . We have the finest climate, the best water, and the purest air that can be found on the earth; there is no healthier climate anywhere. As for gold and silver, and the rich minerals of the earth, there is no other country that equals this; but let them alone; let others seek them, and we will cultivate the soil. . . . Then, brethren, plow your land and sow wheat, plant your potatoes. . . .[103]

The witness of these proceedings concludes his account with the second thoughts of a proven pioneer:

As the writer walked away from meeting that day, in company with some old and tried men, who had been mobbed and robbed, and driven from their homes, and whom he looked upon almost as pillars of the Church, one of them said he had passed through such and such trials in the past, but that that day, 1849, was the darkest he ever had seen in the Church. The thought of trying to settle this barren land, he said, was one of the greatest trials he had met.[104]

Thus poised, uncertain of their future, on the balance between success and failure, the pioneer settlers of the Great Basin planted their seeds, improved their homes, established their "State of Deseret," and awaited the outcome of the crucial harvest of 1849.

SIGNIFICANCE OF THE INITIAL MORMON ENCOUNTER WITH THE GREAT BASIN

It should be obvious that in establishing their institutions and in meeting their first problems in the Great Basin the Mormons relied primarily on their own early ideals and experiences. The careful planning which preceded the development of their great city, the patriarchal husbanding of resources and sharing of burdens, the pooling of productive efforts, the nature of their property institutions — all these might have been predicted long before the Mormons reached the Great Basin. The pattern had been foreshadowed in Jackson County, Kirtland, Far West, and Winter Quarters, and it had been formally incorporated in Mormon theology. Moreover, in acknowledging, as the first colonists in the Salt Lake Valley acknowledged, the social responsibility of government (in this case a theocracy) to arrange and supervise their economic life, the Mormons were recalling the policies and practices of early Americans in Massachusetts, where many of their ancestors were born; in Pennsylvania, where their first prophet was baptized and given the priesthood; and in Missouri, where their first economic experiments were tried.[105] Far from being unique, the spirit and technique of Mormon colonization and organized activity were common, if not typical, in the age which produced Mormonism.

Yet, Mormon economic institutions *were* unique in the contemporary American West. To be sure, there was the same hunger, the same improvisation, the same struggle for success, as in all Western settlements. But the unity, homogeneity, joint action, and group planning all stamped the Mormon frontier as unique — as a contrast with the scattered, specialized, exploitative, "wide open" mining, cattle, lumber, and homestead frontiers with which historians have familiarized us.

Hardly enough has been said in the present chapter to explain the cause of this uniqueness, which historians have variously attributed to the geography, early Mormon experiences, and/or Mormon religious beliefs. But the character of Mormon economic organization, as early as 1847–1849, and more certainly in the succeeding half-century, suggests the feasibility of regarding Mormon institutions as the more typically early American, and the individualistic institutions of other Westerners as the more divergent. The Mormon response to the problems imposed by the settlement of the Great Basin — a response which becomes ever clearer in succeeding decades — suggests that Mormon economic policies bore a greater resemblance to those of the ante-bellum northeast than did the economic policies of the West during the years when the West was won. Isolated as they were from American thought-currents after 1847, and under the necessity of continued group action to solve the many problems which plagued them, the Mormons were not affected by the growing accommodation to the private corporation, rugged individualism, Social Darwinism, and other concepts which account for the rise of laissez-faire after 1850. It may yet be conceded that the well-publicized conflicts and differences between the Mormons and other Westerners and Americans were not so much a matter of plural marriage and other reprehensible peculiarities and superstitions as of the conflicting economic patterns of two generations of Americans, one of which was fashioned after the communitarian concepts of the age of Jackson, and the other of which was shaped by the dream of bonanza and the individualistic sentiments of the age of laissez-faire.

If the Mormon pattern was reminiscent, it was also prophetic. For it was precisely this pattern of central direction, cooperation, and long-run planning which, as the result of the failure of individuals, the success of large corporations, and the impositions of government, came to characterize national policy with respect to the West in the twentieth century.[106]

In the years which followed the initial settlement in the Salt Lake Valley, the Mormons would demonstrate some of the advantages of their collective institutions. In 1849–1850 they gathered enough "seed corn" to finance a whole decade of growth.

CHAPTER III

The Harvest of '49

The effect of the Gold Rush upon the Mormon economy of 1849 and succeeding years is clear and unmistakable. Faced with hunger, inadequate clothing, poor housing, and a gross insufficiency of tools and equipment, the Mormon colonists would most likely have had to give up — or at least postpone — their dreams of a Great Basin empire had not the Argonauts passed through, strewing their many and varied benefits. As the result of the discovery of gold in California the Mormons were able to provide themselves with a convenient circulating medium, and, in addition, they were able to acquire the wherewithal with which to launch giant immigration, colonization, and other programs essential to the growth and development of their projected Kingdom.

THE MORMONS AND THE GOLD RUSH

The most important preliminary question is why the Mormons themselves did not join the Gold Rush, when, obviously, they were in a position to get in on the ground floor. Six members of the church who had been discharged from the Mormon Battalion were working with James Marshall when the gold discovery was made, and they, with some of their companions, discovered other rich deposits, including the fabulous Mormon Island. More than sixty of their comrades were working for John A. Sutter in the immediate vicinity, while another hundred were working in the San Francisco Bay region, and were among the first to reach the gold fields. Sam Brannan, who announced the discovery in San Francisco, had been a Mormon leader in New York and had taken a group of about 230 Mormons on the ship *Brooklyn* around Cape Horn at the time of the exodus in 1846. A considerable number of the *Brooklyn* Saints had established an agricultural settlement at what was called New Hope, not far from the gold fields. Elder Brannan had called the *Brooklyn* Saints together before making the "Gold Discovered" announcement and had advised them to go to the gold areas.[1] More than 300 Mormons were at work on Mormon Island in July 1848, according to William Tecumseh Sherman, who accompanied the governor of California on a tour of the gold fields at that time.[2]

In addition to these advantages, Brannan, a man of spirited enterprise, was in possession of a store at Sutter's Fort, a river launch, a large stock of supplies brought on the *Brooklyn,* a considerable sum of church money (tithing) with which he could obtain more supplies, and a large fenced-in farm at New Hope. If Brigham Young had chosen to send a messenger to Brannan to prepare to receive the body of the church in California, it would have been an easier task to lead his people there than it had been to get them to settle and remain in the desolate valley of the Great Salt Lake. With a strong nucleus of church members already in California, and with upwards of 20,000 more on their way westward, equipped with the necessary things to make the trip to California, the Saints could have acquired a giant's share of the precious metal.

The reaction of the Mormons in the Salt Lake Valley to the favorable situation created by the California discoveries, however, serves to illustrate their cohesiveness as a social body and the strength of the Kingdom concept in the thinking of the leaders. "We are gathered here," wrote the First Presidency, "not to scatter around and go off to the mines, or any other place, but to build up the Kingdom of God."[3] The Salt Lake Valley, Brigham Young added, was "a good place to make Saints, and it is a good place for Saints to live; it is the place that the Lord has appointed, and we shall stay here, until He tells us to go somewhere else."[4] Moreover, he said, the Sacramento Valley was an unhealthy place, morally and physically, in which to live: "If you Elders of Israel want to go to the gold mines, go and be damned."[5] Finally, he said, the average person would be better off economically by remaining in the Great Basin. He told those who wanted to go to the mines that he would remain in Salt Lake, mind his own business, help to build up the Kingdom of God, and when they returned from the mines he would agree to count dollars with them:[6]

I will commence at the north and go to the south settlements, and pick out twenty-five of our inhabitants as they average, and another man may take fifty of the gold diggers, off hand, and they cannot buy out the twenty-five men who tarried at home. Before I had been one year in this place, the wealthiest man who came from the mines, Father Rhodes, with $17,000, could he buy the possessions I had made in one year? It will not begin to do it: and I will take twenty-five men in the United States, who have staid at home and paid attention to their own business, and they will weigh down fifty others from the same place, who went to the gold regions; and again, look at the widows that have been made, and see the bones that lie bleaching and scattered over the prairies.[7]

These sentiments reflected the view of the vast majority of the Saints in the Salt Lake Valley and were repeatedly "sustained" in the general conferences of 1848–1851. Nevertheless, members of the Mormon Battalion were encouraged to remain in California to earn money, by prospecting and otherwise, before returning to Salt Lake; some of the Saints did go to California with the permission of the Salt Lake group; and two apostles, Charles C. Rich and Amasa Lyman, were called to go to California to minister to the Mormons who were there, to establish a "gathering-place," and to collect tithing and other donations. Moreover, upon the mere rumor of gold being discovered at South Pass, a group was called to go to the site and examine the reported find.[8] Nothing was earned at South Pass, of course, but the earnings of Mormons in California which were contributed to the church in the form of gold dust or coin probably amounted to more than $60,000 during the period 1848–1851.[9] It is probable that at least that much more came into the Valley from California on private account.

In spite of the refusal of the Mormons to participate in the Gold Rush, one cannot look at the events of 1849 and 1850 without seeing the tremendous influence they exerted upon the questionable economy of Zion. The immigrating program, the church's investment program, the colonization of habitable areas in the Great Basin, the initiation of important enterprises — all of these might have had a different history had not the Gold Rush occurred — or had not it occurred when it did. The agricultural harvest of the fall of 1849 was large enough to support the 4,200 souls in the Valley, the 1,400 Mormons who emigrated overland in 1849, the 200 or more who drifted in from California, and an additional 500 or so who wintered in Deseret in 1849–1850.[10] Moreover, the harvest of 1850 was sufficiently abundant to permit cancellation of the food rationing program, despite the necessity of feeding some 8,000 persons in the Salt Lake Valley and 3,000 persons in other Mormon settlements in the West.[11] In fact, a church epistle mailed in the fall of 1850 boasted that enough grain had been raised in Deseret to sustain thirty thousand persons.[12] When a farm was located in 1850 for the poor, and several houses were erected, church officials located only two persons who would admit their inability to provide for themselves, and the contemplated farm was converted into a church pasture.[13] Nevertheless, contemporary records leave no doubt that the most important crop of 1849–1851 was harvested, not in the Salt Lake Valley, but at Sutter's Mill, near Coloma, California.

Perhaps the best account of the Gold Rush and its effect upon the Mormons is told in a rare pamphlet published in Liverpool, England, in 1853, by Benjamin Brown, a Mormon missionary who had been bishop of the Salt Lake City Fourth Ward in 1849. Brown's narrative begins with a survey of the condition of the Saints before the Gold Rush occurred. They were living on roots, work cattle, and a small ration of cracked grain. Their clothes were wearing out; their agricultural implements were "getting used up, broken, or destroyed." Many of their wagons had broken down, and there was neither timber nor iron for repairing them. "There we were, completely shut out from the world . . . the first shop was a thousand miles off." And then the "miracle" of 1849:

Information of the great discovery of gold in California had reached the States, and large companies were formed for the purpose of supplying the gold diggers with food and clothing, and implements of every kind for digging, &c. As these companies expected a most tremendous profit on their goods, no expense or outlay of any kind was spared. Numbers of substantial waggons were prepared, stored with wholesale quantities of clothing of every kind; spades, picks, shovels, and chests of carpenters' tools, were also provided to overflowing, and, to complete the list, tea, coffee, sugar, flour, fruits, &c., on the same scale. In fact, these persons procured just the things they would have done, had they been forming companies purposely for relieving the Saints, and had they determined to do it as handsomely as unlimited wealth would allow.[14]

When these companies, after crossing the plains, arrived within a short distance of Salt Lake city, news reached them that ships had been despatched from many parts of the world, fitted out with goods for California. This threatened to flood the market. The companies feared that the sale of their goods would not repay the expense of conveyance. Here was a "fix" — the companies were too far from the States to take their goods back, and they would not pay to carry them through, and when to this was added the fact, that the companies were half crazy to leave trading, and turn gold diggers themselves, it will easily be seen how naturally the difficulty solved itself into the decision which they actually came to — "Oh here are these Mormons, let us sell the goods to them." Accordingly they brought them into the Valley, and disposed of them for just what could be got — provisions, waggons, clothes, tools, almost for the taking away, at least at half the price for which the goods could have been purchased in the States.

Many disposed of their waggons, because the teams gave out, and could not get on any further. Such sold almost all they had to purchase a mule or a horse to pack through with. Thus were the Saints amply provided, even to overflowing, with every one of the necessaries and many of the luxuries of which they had been so destitute. . . .

One of the worst deficiencies we had experienced was with respect to iron to manufacture or repair with, but as many of the "diggers" left their waggons on the other side of the ferries, or sold them to the ferrymen [Mormons] to burn up as fuel, or had done so themselves, tons and tons of iron, used in the manufacture of waggons, were brought into the Valley, and used up for every variety of purpose.[15]

It is estimated that from 40,000 to 50,000 persons journeyed overland to California in 1849, and an equal number in 1850, of which an estimated ten to fifteen thousand went by way of the Salt Lake Valley each year.[16] The effect of this horde of overloaded gold seekers upon Salt Lake markets was, of course, immediate and profound. Since the emigrants needed fresh teams and supplies, Latter-day Saints were able to get $200 each for fresh horses and mules normally worth $25 to $30. The scarce supply of Mormon flour sold at $10 to $15 per hundred, and vegetables commanded "a first-rate price."[17] At the same time, the Mormons were able to buy surplus wagons from emigrants at $15 to $25, compared to the $50 to $125 to which they had been accustomed. Harness could be had for $2 to $15 per set — less than one-third previously ruling prices. Coffee and sugar, which had been selling in the Salt Lake Valley at $1.00 per pint, now sold at from 10 to 15 cents. "Indeed," according to Almon W. Babbitt, "almost every article, except sugar and coffee, is selling on an average, fifty per cent below wholesale prices in eastern cities."[18]

Each pioneer diary reflects the influence of the Gold Rush on individual and family fortunes, and thus on the whole economy. Priddy Meeks, for example, recalled that just about the time his potatoes were "in condition to grabble, the gold diggers came in nearly perished for vegetables . . . and they having plenty of groceries, did not care for the price." Meeks "tried to deal gentlemanly with them," but managed to lay in "goods, bacon, tea, coffee and sugar, besides many other articles which I needed." He got a good scythe for 75 cents, and many other things proportionately low. As the result of the Gold Rush, Meeks wrote, the valley "was full of everything that was needed by the poor Saints especially clothing." Meeks had a splendid but lazy Indian pony which one emigrant wanted to use as a pack mare. Meeks describes the subsequent transaction as follows:

"What is your price?" says the man. I said, "I have no price but I want clothing for my family," which was five in number. I believe his heart was softened for he handed out goods, some readymade, and some not, until we all had two suits each from top to toe, both shoes and stockings and everything that was needed. He said, "How much more?" I said, "Hand out and I will tell you when to stop." He handed out factory and calico until I was almost ashamed; even my conscience reminded me of stopping. I said, "Here is a great coat and a high pair of boots for winter," and he handed them out without a word. . . .

Among the emigrants I made money enough to buy a stable horse and the best wagon I thought I ever saw, paying $60 for both.[19]

What the forty-niners did, in essence, was to trade their heavy wagons, worn-out cattle, and merchandise for a horse or mule outfit to carry them quickly to their California destination. A contemporary church chronicle reveals this to have been quite as true in 1850 as in 1849:

> The emigration across the Continent for California, more numerous this year [1850] than ever, caused provisions to be very high. Flour ran up to a dollar a pound. After harvest, which commenced on the first of July, it fell to twenty-five dollars a hundred. The four mills were crowded with work, grinding for the emigrants, who hung around, begging for enough to feed them to the gold mines. Beef was ten cents a pound. Horses, harness, carriages, wagons, etc., were bought of eager emigrants at one-fifth of their cost in the States.[20]

There is a suggestion in contemporary newspapers and diaries that Mormon leadership, fully cognizant of the necessitous condition of the emigrants — and the equally hazardous position of the Salt Lake economy — encouraged the Latter-day Saints to sell their supplies and equipment dearly. "What!" said Brigham Young, "sell bread to the man who is going to earn his one hundred and fifty dollars a day, at the same price as you do to the poor laborer, who works hard here for one dollar a day? I say, you men who are going to get gold to make golden images . . . pay for your flour!"[21] Not all overland emigrants agreed with this view, of course, but most of them appear to have been grateful for the few needed items they could get the Mormons to part with, regardless of price. When Jonas Olson traveled west in 1850, for example, his company stopped in Salt Lake City to buy provisions. Since the fall harvest had not yet come on to the market, flour was selling at $1.50 per pound. Nevertheless, "Those who had enough money and horses, as well as coffee and tea and even dried apples, could soon get what they needed and be on their way again."[22] By the end of the harvest, flour was down to $6.00 a hundred and potatoes sold at $1.00 a bushel.[23]

It was not only that the Mormons were able to buy cheaply and sell dearly. The servicing and re-outfitting of the overland emigrants furnished employment to Mormon blacksmiths, wagonsmiths, teamsters, laundresses, and millers, many of whom organized to take fullest advantage of this demand for their services.[24] They also had thoughtfully established ferries on the upper crossing of the North Platte, and on the Green and Bear rivers, which, though intended primarily to serve Mormon companies, were also used by the overland trains. In August 1849, John D. Lee met a Mormon company which had gone out from the Salt Lake Valley in the spring to man one of these ferries and reported that they had "met with Good success, having made about $10,000."[25] While this sum may have been exaggerated, the Mormons unquestionably bolstered their balance of payments position in this way, particularly in 1849 and 1850 when they had a virtual monopoly of this traffic. Usual charges were $4.00 per wagon.[26]

The Mormons also improved their exchange position by "wintering" the emigrants in the Salt Lake Valley, particularly in 1850 and succeeding years. (In 1849 the local food supply was still so short that overland parties were deliberately discouraged from remaining any length of time in the Salt Lake Valley.)[27] An estimated 1,000 emigrants, for example, wintered in the Salt Lake Valley during the winter of 1850–51.[28] In return for food and housing, most of these emigrants assisted with farm work, paid taxes, and in other ways contributed to the Salt Lake economy. The Mormons are said to have accommodated these "winter Saints" by establishing "a great many grog shops," and selling a locally brewed whiskey at $6.00 a gallon, a "valley tan" rum made from molasses and green tea at $8.00 a gallon, and "a very light and wholesome beer."[29] It is probable that the inferior bargaining position of the emigrants left them poorer, and the Mormons richer, than when they entered the Valley. Some of them accused the Mormons of conspiring to pay them exclusively in kind in order to prevent the drain of currency to California.[30]

One final source of Mormon profit from the Gold Rush was the windfall of commodities left along the route, which was picked up by Mormon parties journeying west and by gleaning parties dispatched from the Salt Lake Valley. Howard Stansbury, who undertook an exploration of the Salt Lake Valley for the Corps of Topographical Engineers in 1849, found the trail west from Fort Laramie to be literally lined with abandoned goods:

> Before halting at noon, we passed eleven wagons that had been broken up, the spokes of the wheels taken to make pack-saddles, and the rest burned or otherwise destroyed. The road has been literally strewn with articles that have been thrown away. Bar-iron and steel, large blacksmiths' anvils and bellows, crowbars, drills, augers, gold-washers, chisels, axes, lead, trunks, spades, ploughs, large grindstones, baking-ovens, cooking-stoves without number, kegs, barrels, harness, clothing, bacon, and beans, were found along the road in pretty much the order in which they have been here enumerated. . . . In the course of this one day [July 27, 1849] the relics of seventeen wagons and the carcasses of twenty-seven dead oxen have been seen.[31]

On the other days, similar sights greeted his expedition. Many Mormon diaries verify the generality of this picture and the richness of the Mormon harvest. For example,

> [August 6, 1849] Found an Excellent Premeum stove No. 3 worth about $50 dollars in the vally.

> [August 8, 1849] Commenced loading up with Powder, lead, cooking utensils, Tobacco, Nails, Sacks, Tools, Bacon, coffee, sugar, clothing, Smawl Irons, some Trunks, Boot legs, axes, Harness, &c.[32]

Again, in the spring of 1850, the church historian noted that some Chicago overlanders had abandoned thirty wagon loads of grain, which, presumably, the Mormons picked up.[33]

All told, while it is impossible to measure the precise economic advantage of the Gold Rush trade in terms of dollars and cents, it provided exactly the kind of leverage needed to avoid disaster and hasten progress. If there were 10,000 overlanders in each of the years 1849–1850, and another 5,000 in 1851, and if each party of ten contributed as much as $100 in exchange value to the Mormon economy, the total exchange value of the Mormons would have been enhanced $250,000 as the result of the Gold Rush trade. This sum appears to have represented precisely the margin needed to catapult a struggling valley economy, in three short years, into a burgeoning, confident, regional commonwealth. Or, to put it in the words of a contemporary Mormon, the overland trade not only cured "the California fever," but "enabled the brethren to furnish themselves with . . . every (almost) needful variety of necessary needful thing for the Saints to make use of":

> And thus in a few years in this desolated part of the mountains we were beginning to enjoy to some degree that which might have taken years had not the Lord provided for the poor saints by His providence in opening up the gold mines in California and inspiring the Gentiles with a lust for gold.[34]

THE GOLD RUSH AND CHURCH FINANCE

Coinage of gold. The abundance of California gold in the Salt Lake Valley, and the prospect of earning still more, led to two little-known phases of Mormon finance directly related to the Gold Rush: the coinage of gold and the Gold Mission.

It will be recalled that the church had attempted to mint Mormon Battalion gold dust into coin in December 1848. The lack of satisfactory equipment had forced the substitution of a paper currency. With continual accretions of gold from California, and with the increased need for a circulating medium in the Valley acceptable to the overland trade, church officials withdrew the currency and commenced once more to mint dust into coin. Dies were prepared for $2.50, $5.00, $10.00 and $20.00 gold pieces, and crucibles, acids, and other equipment were ordered from the church agent at St. Louis.[35] Coinage began at the Church Mint on September 12, 1849, and continued until early in 1851, during which time approximately $75,000 in gold pieces were coined. These coins resembled those designed in 1848 except that the words "Pure Gold" were represented by the initials P.G. and the letters G.S.L.C., for Great Salt Lake City, were added.[36] The coins were minted at first without any alloy, but a percentage of silver was later added to increase hardness.

The minting of these coins introduced a semblance of "prosperity" into the Salt Lake community, as indicated in diary notations and letters written during the months the mint was in operation. A month after coinage began, for example, William Appleby wrote: "Money, gold in particular, is quite plentiful." [37] When a reporter for the church newspaper, the *Deseret News,* visited the mint in 1850, he wrote in a similar vein: "We stepped into the mint, the other day, and saw two or three men rolling out the golden bars like waggon tires ready for the dies. This is what makes trade brisk." [38]

Mormon gold coins circulated principally in the Salt Lake Valley, but also in California and the Missouri Valley.[39] Mormon mechanics apparently did not understand the importance of relative fineness, and considered only the weight in making up and stamping the coins. Thus, what they intended to be full-bodied coins actually were worth from ten to fifteen per cent less, on the average, than the face value. The $10.00 gold pieces, for example, were worth approximately $8.70.[40] This overvaluing, although not unusual, gave the Mormon coins somewhat of a bad name, particularly in California, where they were considered to be "debased," "spurious," and "vile falsehoods." [41] As their overvalued nature came to be more widely known, Mormon coins circulated at a ten to tweny-five per cent discount in most places except the Great Basin, where there were strong social pressures to compel acceptance of the coin at face value.[42]

Ultimately, as the supply of gold brought into the Valley dwindled, and as the reputation of the coins began to affect the credit of the church, Brigham Young ordered the mint to close and allowed the coins to disappear from circulation. This was probably in 1852. Virtually all of the coins which had been minted up to that time were sold by their owners for their value as bullion. Church tithing scrip and wheat became the principal circulating media in Mormon communities throughout most of the 1850's. The coins had, however, performed a useful function, from the viewpoint of the church, in serving as a temporarily acceptable medium in the overland trade. At the conclusion of the issues in 1851 Brigham Young wrote:

> The Saints generally have been attending to the business of raising grain, building homes, planting vineyards and orchards, preparing to receive their brethren and friends when they arrive, while the money has gone to foreign markets to procure such things as we have not time and means to manufacture here.[43]

The Gold Mission. Shortly after the mint was reopened, church officials instituted a secret and little-known program to increase the local supply of California gold dust.[44] This was an attempt on the part of the church to allow some of its loyal members to participate in the Gold Rush without formally and publicly involving the church in its sanction. The abrupt change of policy from virtual exclusion of members who "deserted" to California to actually requesting a certain few to go suggests a growing confidence in the favorable aspects of the location of the church in the Salt Lake Valley. Church officials apparently reasoned that it would now be "safe" to call certain faithful members to go to California to mine for gold. If the missionaries succeeded, they would funnel more gold into Deseret and build the church treasury, without enticing many to leave. If they failed, it would bear out the wisdom of the church advice to "stay here and raise grain."

The Gold Mission consisted of two independently organized companies of young Latter-day Saint men, and a few others who were counseled to go as teamsters for overland emigrants. Most of them had previously been in California as members of the Mormon Battalion. Henry W. Bigler, a thirty-four-year-old convert and Battalionist, described his own unusual call in his diary as follows:

Sunday, 7th, October, 1849. This afternoon I was informed that President Young had told Father John Smith that as he had been kicked and cuffed about and driven out of the United States because of his Religion and had become poor, it was His counsil that Father Smith fit out some person and send him to California or to the gold mines and get some of the treasures of the earth to make himself comfortable in his old age, and the old Gentleman has called on me to go, saying that he could trust me because as he said he had confidance in me that I would do right. He wishes me to go with Brother Charles C. Rich who will leave with a company in a few days for the Gold mines. This intelligence was unexpectedly received by me. I was not looking for any such mission. Indeed it had been the Presidents counsil not to go to the gold mines and those who went after such counsil had been given was looked upon as "jack Mormons" as they were called. . . .

When word came to me that Father Smith wished me to go, I hesitated, however as he had sent for me I went and seen him when he explained to me what the president had said and the counsil president Young had given to him in relation to sending a man to the mines etc. After I had consented to go I could not help feeling sorrowful and a reluctance to go for I feel attached to this place and to this people for they are my brethren and dear friends and it was with some strugle with my feelings that I consented to go.[45]

Two days later, Bigler records that he had sold his wheat, paid all his debts, and was making preparations as fast as he could to leave with Apostle Rich. The bargain between him and "Father" Smith, he said, was that the latter was "to be all the expense of fitting me out for the gold mines, and after arriving there I am to be saving and prudent and after all the expenses was paid I am to have half the gold."[46]

Other loyal members were similarly called, and their arrangements with the leading church officials who sponsored them were also similar. Each of the selectees who left a record went with misgivings, and did so only because of his loyalty to the church. As one of them wrote, "There was no place that I would not rather have gone to at that time than California. I heartily despised the work of digging gold. I thought it poor business for men to be running over the country for gold. . . . There is no honorable occupation that I would not rather follow than hunting and digging gold."[47]

Two companies of gold missionaries left the Great Basin in the fall of 1849. The first, consisting of about twenty young men, with James M. Flake as captain, left Salt Lake City on October 11 to join Apostle Charles C. Rich, who, it will be recalled, had been appointed by Brigham Young to join Apostle Amasa Lyman in San Francisco and look after the affairs of the church in California. They traveled horseback with pack animals. They were joined by "some few [non-Mormons] whose only motive in going was to enrich themselves by digging gold,"[48] and reached Williams Ranch, near present-day San Bernardino, California, in December 1849. While recuperating there from a harrowing desert experience, they received a communication from Apostles George A. Smith and Ezra T. Benson in Salt Lake Valley asking "the brethren who are now on their mission to get Gold" to raise $5,000 for them "in order that their hands may be liberated and be enabled to return to their field of labour [missionary work]." Smith and Benson added that they would "pray the Lord to lead the brethren into some nook or corner where it [gold] lies."[49] Bigler probably expressed the typical response of the missionaries when he wrote: "as for my part I certainly would be pleased to be instrumental in helping to raise that amount of means and get their blessings." They left Williams Ranch overland for the mines in January 1850, and soon afterward the company split up, some of them stopping off to work in the Mariposa mines, and others going on to "Slap Jack Bar" on the Middle Fork of the American River, not far from Sacramento.

The second company, consisting of about thirty young Latter-day Saint men, with Simpson D. Huffaker as captain, left Salt Lake City on November 12, 1849, just a month after the first company. This group traveled by ox-team to southern Utah and thence over the Old Spanish Trail to Grape Vines, near San Bernardino. Expecting the trip to last eight weeks, the company was enroute three months and five days. To add to their trials, the missionaries found it necessary to divide their rations with some famished Forty-niners encountered on the trail. Met by Apostle Amasa Lyman and Jared Hunter at Los Angeles about March 1, 1850, the company went on to San Pedro where they took passage on a schooner to San Francisco. At Sacramento the missionaries were fitted out for mining. They worked prospects at Lewisville, Otter Creek, "the north fork of the middle of the American River," and elsewhere. They were notably unsuccessful, however, and most of them returned to the Great Basin in August 1850 with Apostle Lyman.

As with other Forty-niners, the Mormon missionary-prospectors labored under conditions of privation that seem almost unbelievable. Writing in September, Henry Bigler tried to describe the experiences of the preceding seven months:

> We arrived in the mines sometime dureing the latter part of last Feb. and ever since that time I have been at work trying as the miners say, "to make a raise," exposing myself to the rains and snows in the mountains, traveling here and there prospecting, building and repairing dams, working in water for weeks up to my arms and neck and have made but little, the expenses have been greater than gains or incomes. In August I sent Father Smith one hundred dollars in gold dust by Brother Amasa Lyman. . . . Some of my companions have sickened and died and we have had to lay them away in the silent grave far away from their dear friends at home and it is only a few days since I recovered from a severe spell of sickness. . . .
>
> I kept an exact account of the amount of gold dust I got and paid the tithing of all I made or got, amounting to eighty three dollars and 60 cents. this of course shows how much I have taken from the earth \$836.$\frac{00}{100}$, this would appear as though I aught to have some money by me, but I may say I have none! and it fairly makes the hair on my head stand erect when I think how little I have and I have been as Saveing and lived as equinomical as I knew how . . . I am tired of mineing and long to be at home in the vallies of the mountains among the Saints.[50]

The principal problem of one group of twelve missionaries appears to have been the erection of a diversion dam across the river to force the water through a previously dug ditch. They labored most of the summer on this dam, which spanned the river at a point sixty yards across. At one time, when the dam was nearly completed, a freshet "swepted it all away";[51] and at another time the dam washed away. By October 3, however, the dam was completed and the group commenced to take gold from their claim. During the first three days, they took \$2,400 worth of gold; another \$5,328 was taken out the next week; and three days later they were able to divide another \$1,104. To the chagrin of all, the claim failed on October 15, after less than two weeks of working! Less than $20,000 had been taken from it —this amount to be divided among twelve persons.[52] Bigler records the failure as follows:

> *Tuesday 15th,* today our claim refused to let us have any more of its precious metals. O what a pity! and yet it no doubt is all right [,] for our eyes might be so filled with gold dust that we might not be able to see.[53]

All in all, Bigler sent to Father Smith less than $500. Apparently, none of his associates did any better by their Great Basin sponsors.

Albert Thurber and some others in the second company mined at Green Woods, near Lewisville, for about a month, doing surprisingly well. "The gold was beautiful," wrote Thurber, "and we were very free to exhibit it to anyone, supposing that we could do better anywhere else than there, as it had been all prospected over by old miners."[54] Before they knew it, however, "the creek bed was nearly claimed and the place was alive with miners, leaving us small claims." Although they tried several other locations, none paid for the working and the men grew "weary and sick."

After four months of prospecting, Thurber ended up with "two mules, an old pair of boots, hat, a pair of pants and flannel shirt, $4.50 in gold dust."[55] These were the "earnings" he took to the Salt Lake Valley in the fall of 1850. He had been counseled by Apostles Lyman and Rich, with other unsuccessful missionaries who "had not good claims or found a chance to make a lot of money in a few days . . . to go home." Most of them were happy to take the advice. Thurber's close associate, Jacob Burnham, decided to stay and prospect a little longer. "He took sick and died two weeks later."

One of the more successful missionaries invested his earnings in a string of twenty-one pack mules and loaded them with provisions and supplies and trailed them across the Sierra into Carson Valley, Nevada, then part of Deseret. Here he sold provisions to overland emigrants for "a very high price." He sold flour for $1.25 a tin cup full; pork for $1.25 per pound, and sugar, coffee, tea, hard tack, and other things proportionately high. Among other transactions, he bought a Chicago wagon and two sets of harness complete for ten pounds of flour.[56]

The fifty men who returned with Apostle Lyman to the Salt Lake Valley in August 1850 and thereafter were good advertisements of the folly of "chasing after gold." Thurber relates that when he met Brigham Young, shortly after his return, the president asked, "Did you get rich?" Thurber detailed his lack of success. Asked if he was disappointed in returning with so little, Thurber replied, "I never felt better [than] when I got over the mountain." This attitude pleased the president, who replied: "You have [now] entered into a good work, the work of the Lord Almighty . . . be faithful. . . . Be a good boy."[57]

THE GOLD RUSH AND CHURCH PLANNING

The Church Mint and the Gold Mission have a certain curiosity about them, but the permanent effect of the Gold Rush upon the Mormon economy is seen in the initiation of important enterprises in the fields of immigration, freighting, and colonization. Accessions of gold from California, exchanges with overland companies, and profits from other activities connected with the Gold Rush supplied the economic wherewithal for a mammoth (to them) program of expansion. The rich harvests of '49 and '50 seem to have given Mormon leaders sufficient confidence in the economic strength and future of their Kingdom to plan for the reception of the 10,000 Mormons in the Missouri Valley and the 30,000 Mormons in England, to send missionaries to many parts of the world for the purpose of converting others, to establish new and distant colonies, and to initiate a large program of development. Not all of these enterprises and institutions were successful, of course, but all reflected the large scale and detail of Mormon planning. Essentially, the objectives and the means used in attaining those objectives represented an extension or magnification of the economic program developed in the early years of Mormondom.

The Perpetual Emigrating Company. The first of the great enterprises launched in the fall of 1849 was the Perpetual Emigrating Fund. This fund was instituted as a means of accomplishing the gathering, and fulfilling the pledge made in the Nauvoo Covenant to assist the poor in emigrating. It was also a means by which the earnings from the Gold Rush could be utilized in transporting the body of the church to the Great Basin.

On September 9, 1849, a committee of five was appointed to gather contributions "to bring the poor" from Kanesville and Winter Quarters.[58] Some $6,000 was raised that fall, mostly from California returnees,[59] and a Salt Lake bishop was appointed as agent to carry that sum east to expend in the purchase of wagons, livestock, and provisions, and also "such things as will improve in value by being transferred to this place [the Salt Lake Valley]."[60] With this help, some 2,500 persons and an undisclosed value of goods were brought to the Valley from Missouri River camps in the summer of 1850.

The satisfactory nature of the first season's experience with the Fund led church leaders to organize and incorporate a company. On September 11, 1850, the assembly of the State of Deseret passed an act incorporating the "Perpetual Emigrating Company."[61] Under the terms of the charter the company was to consist of at least thirteen men, chosen by a general or special conference of the church, of whom one was to be designated president and the other twelve were to be assistants. The general business of the company, including appointment of officers to fill vacancies, was to be "under the direction and supervision of the First Presidency of the Church, to promote, facilitate, and accomplish the Emigration of the Poor." The charter provided that "All persons receiving assistance from the Perpetual Emigrating Fund for the Poor, shall reimburse the same in labor or otherwise, as soon as their circumstances will admit." The company was empowered to own and manage property of all kinds, to carry on banking operations, and all other activities deemed "necessary and proper for the interest, protection, convenience, or benefit of said Company." The company was specifically authorized to procure wagons, cattle, mules, horses, etc., and to receive and hold donations, insurance, deposits, exchange, and engage in similar transactions. The islands of the Great Salt Lake — known as Stansbury's Island and Antelope Island — were "reserved and appropriated for the exclusive use and benefit of said Company, for the keeping of stock, etc."

Brigham Young served as president of the company throughout his lifetime, and the "assistant presidents" were largely members of the First Presidency and Quorum of the Twelve. The treasurer was the Presiding Bishop of the church, and the company agents were largely members of the church official family. All officers and agents appear to have served without pay or remuneration, except for subsistence while they were "on the job." The company did not sell capital stock. As a chartered company, it was a unique combination of business and welfare in the kind of undertaking which was often abused.

The theory of the P.E.F. was that voluntary donations would be secured from church members wherever located, and those benefited by the fund would continually replenish it after their arrival in the Valley:

> When the Saints thus helped arrive here, they will give their obligations to the Church to refund to the amount of what they have received, as soon as circumstances will permit; and labor will be furnished, to such as wish, on the public works, and good pay, and as fast as they can procure the necessaries of life, and a surplus, that surplus will be applied to liquidating their debt, and thereby increasing the Perpetual Fund.
>
> By this it will readily be discovered, that the funds are to be appropriated in the form of a loan, rather than a gift; and this will make the honest in heart rejoice, for they love to labor, and be independent by their labor, and not live on the charity of their friends, while the lazy idlers, if any such there be, will find fault, and want every luxury furnished them for their journey, and in the end pay nothing. The Perpetual Fund will help no such idlers; we have no use

for them in the Valley, they had better stay where they are . . . these funds are designed to increase until Israel is gathered from all nations, and the poor can sit under their own vine, and inhabit their own house, and worship God in Zion.[62]

The P.E. Company assisted some 2,500 persons to journey to Zion in 1851. This still left approximately 8,000 Saints in Iowa and Missouri, plus several hundred others on their way to those points from Britain and the East. The task of clearing out these camps was completed in 1852. Two apostles, Ezra T. Benson and Jedediah M. Grant, were specially appointed in the fall of 1851 to wind up the emigration the following season. "Urge on the emigration with all your might," their instructions read:

Tell the people not to be afraid of the plains, but to encounter them with any kind of conveyance that they can procure, with their handcarts, their wheel barrows, and come on foot, pack and animal, if they have one, and no other way to come. . . . We wish you to evacuate Pottawattamie [lands around Kanesville] and the states and next fall be with us.[63]

The First Presidency also issued a general call to the Saints to "come home to Zion" and complete the "American gathering":

Finally, brethren, fear God; work righteousness; and come home speedily. Prepare, against another season, to come by tens of thousands; and think not that your way is going to be opened to come in chariots, feasting on the fat of all lands. We have been willing to live on bread and water, and many times very little bread too, for years, that we might search out and plant the Saints in a goodly land. This we have accomplished, through the blessing of our Heavenly Father; and we now invite you to a feast of fat things, to a land that will supply all your wants, with reasonable labor; therefore, let all who can procure a bit of bread, and one garment on their back, be assured there is water plenty and pure by the way, and doubt no longer, but come next year to the place of gathering, even in flocks, as doves fly to their windows before a storm.[64]

The result was that some twenty-one companies, averaging over sixty wagons to the company, migrated to the Great Basin in 1852. This represented about 10,000 settlers and cleared out all the Mormon Missouri Valley camps except a skeleton force left to handle subsequent emigration.[65]

Great Salt Lake Valley Carrying Company. The second of the great Mormon enterprises launched in the fall of 1849 was a short-lived express and carrying company. In the same October general conference which approved the Perpetual Emigrating Company, a resolution was passed authorizing the formation of a company to carry freight and passengers from the Missouri River to Great Salt Lake Valley and California.[66] In pursuance of this purpose the Great Salt Lake Valley Carrying Company, also called the "Swiftsure Line," was organized in December 1849.[67] The company's prospectus, which was published in a number of Missouri Valley newspapers, stated that passengers would be carried from the Missouri River to Sutter's Fort in the spring of 1850 for $300, and that freight would be carried to the Salt Lake Valley for 12½ cents per pound, or $250 per ton.

Agents were placed in Kanesville, Salt Lake Valley, and at Sutter's Fort to handle the traffic expected to be carried.[68] Light wagons were to be used, each of which would accommodate a driver and three passengers with 150 pounds of baggage. Each wagon was to be drawn by four horses or mules, "with a sufficient number of loose animals as a reserve in cases of accident or failure." Wagons with merchandise would be drawn by oxen. Passenger caravans or trains destined for California would be restocked with horses and mules in the Salt Lake Valley. Passengers were also assured that they would be able to resupply in the Salt Lake Valley with everything except groceries. "Every exertion" would be made to render passengers comfortable, but "we do not wish any one to think that it is a play spell to cross the mountains."

In general, the company pledged a more "cheap, speedy and safe conveyance to and from the diggins than any company that could be organized on this side of the plains." And, indeed, the freight of 12½ cents per pound was somewhat less than the average of 17 cents per pound which was typical of overland rates during the period 1849 to 1869.[69] The company had been organized, the notice concluded, under the direction of "the highest authorities of the State of Deseret"—meaning, presumably, the Council of Fifty—and from them it looked for "strength, influence and support to aid us in our arduous undertaking . . . until the Great National Railroad shall supersede its necessity."[70]

Activities were initiated on a number of fronts during the winter of 1849–1850. A ferry was established, emigration from the Missouri Valley was started partly under the company's auspices in the spring of 1850, and the leaders of the company conducted a train of merchandise to the Valley to supply the local market. These goods, several thousand dollars' worth, were retailed in a "Church Store" in Salt Lake City.[71]

Despite the auspicious and timely beginning, however, the enterprise was dropped without carrying a single Gold Rusher to California. Considering the magnificence of the opportunities before it, this seems like surprisingly faint-hearted entrepreneurship. One explanation of the company's discontinuance was made many years later by A. O. Smoot: "A certain elder down east at the time [Orson Hyde?], killed and opposed the scheme."[72] What reason or reasons this "elder" had for killing and opposing it, despite wholehearted support of the company in the Salt Lake Valley, are not known. The most telling effect of the company's disappearance was that it removed a church-backed competitor and left to Gentile freighters and merchants the opportunity of supplying the Salt Lake market. In default of a major Mormon supply house, the bulk of the coin which Mormons earned as the result of the gold discovery, magnified as it was by collective effort, was carted out of the territory by non-Mormon merchants. "In came Livingston [the first of these merchants]," complained Smoot, "and took our gold by the bushel." Then came Ben Holladay who took even more.[73] Surely, Smoot would have agreed, the Kingdom would not be built in this way.

Merchandising. The failure — or, rather, the discontinuance — of the express and carrying company highlights the principal weakness of the Mormon economic program contemporary with the Gold Rush. The difference between what the Mormons took from the Gold Rush trade, in the way of cash, and what they paid out, appears to have been used primarily in the purchase of supplies brought to the Valley by non-Mormon merchant-freighters. In addition to the large supply of goods sold in the fall of 1849 by overland merchants, particularly the Pomeroy brothers, there were four merchants who brought goods to Salt Lake in 1849–1851 expressly for the Mormon market. Louis Vasquez, partner of Jim Bridger, brought a small quantity of goods in November 1849, including some sugar, which he sold at the rate of three pounds for two dollars.[74] John and Enoch Reese, the only continuing Mormon merchants, were more important, but they were never close competitors with two highly successful non-Mormon firms: Holladay & Warner and Livingston & Kinkead.

Ben Holladay, who bought Mexican War surplus oxen and wagons and took $70,000 worth of merchandise to Utah in 1849, built the foundation of the fortune which made him "Stagecoach King of the West" out of the earnings of his Salt Lake store. He profitably disposed of $150,000 worth in 1850, and still larger supplies in succeeding years. As the supply of gold in Utah dwindled, he traded for cattle and trailed them to California at enormous profits.[75]

Livingston & Kinkead, whose activities after they quit the Mormon trade in 1858 are not known, probably did even better.[76] They took their first train to the Salt Lake Valley in the late fall of 1849, after having purchased some $20,000 worth of goods in the East.[77] So eager were the Mormons to obtain these goods, according to Livingston, that those who were unable to enter the store, "thrust their money through the windows."[78] From two to three thousand dollars in gold was taken in every day until the supply was exhausted.[79] "You would have thought," wrote John Taylor, that "the ladies were bees and their stores the hives — though unlike in one respect, for the bee goes in full and comes out empty, but in this case it was reversed." "As the yellow stream continues to flow from the Pacific coast to the Valley," Taylor added, "the cry of the people is, goods! Goods!! GOODS!!!" [80] So plentiful was the local supply of gold, and so much in demand were the particular items which the firm had to sell, that the only guide to his prices was "charging as much as his conscience would allow." [81]

Livingston & Kinkead apparently did as well in subsequent years. Addison Crane, an overland emigrant in 1852, reported: "There are 5 large stores well supplied [in Salt Lake City] — Goods sell at enormous profits — and merchants must be getting rich . . . all kinds of goods are sold at over 100 per cent advance." [82] James H. Martineau recalled that Livingston & Kinkead had to ration such staple items as "factory" cloth, sugar, and coffee: "They must make their stock of staples 'go round' among all their customers." He continued:

> When the new goods did arrive — what a rush! The store was densely packed with would-be buyers, all anxious to get near the counter; there stands a man in the back holding above his head a big roll of money calling out, "don't forget me! you know you promised me!" and others are doing the same, almost crazing the twenty-five or thirty clerks behind the counters. There is a big crowd outside the doors and upon the sidewalk, all fearful the goods will be gone before they can get in.[83]

Brigham Young visited the store on one of these occasions and chanced to go behind the counter. "I saw," he said,

> several brass kettles under it [the counter], full of gold pieces — sovereigns, eagles, half-eagles, etc. One of the men shouted, "Bring another brass kettle!" They did so and set it down, and the gold was thrown into it, clink, clink, clink, until in a short time, it was filled. I saw this: the whole drift of the people was to get rid of their money! [84]

The total amount paid out to merchants by the Salt Lake community between 1849 and 1852 was estimated by Brigham Young to have been $500,000.[85] When Livingston & Kinkead had completed their 1850 sale and were preparing to load their wagons to return East, Brigham Young and the church historian went down to see how much gold they were carrying out of the territory. Their wagons were loaded, reported the historian, "with more gold dust than had come to the [church] mint that fall. In one box there was as much gold as a man could carry and there was a box of silver that required three men to lift it into the wagon." [86]

Much of these earnings, of course, were directly expended on the purchase and freighting of the goods sold. The total freight bill for the 505 tons imported by the five leading Salt Lake merchants in 1855, for example, was approximately $172,000.[87] Unquestionably, the Mormon economy would have gained if Mormon entrepreneurs had been willing and able to handle at least this phase of the trade. The church, which was best equipped to do so, contented itself with the importation of a number of wagon loads each year, and with the operation of a "church store." [88] Its supply was disposed of largely to church enterprises, church employees, and members of the church's official family.

That the church did not go into the business more extensively was due partly to a desire to emphasize local manufacture, rather than importation; and partly to its disastrous early experiences with merchandising. Church officials apparently viewed the mercantile drain as a temporary one which would be abolished as soon as home manufactures got a good start. It was also viewed as "unsaintly" to patronize the merchants.[89] The bearing of early church merchandising experience on the policy of the 1850's was explained with characteristic hyperbole by Brigham Young in 1852:

> "Why does not our Church keep a store here?" Many can answer that question who have lived . . . in Nauvoo, in Missouri, [and] in Kirtland, Ohio. . . . Let me just give you a few reasons . . . why Joseph [that is, the church] could not keep a store, and be a merchant. . . . Joseph goes to New York and buys 20,000 dollars' worth of goods, comes into Kirtland and commences to trade. In comes one of the brethren, "Brother Joseph, let me have a frock pattern for my wife." What if Joseph says, "No, I cannot without the money." The consequence would be, "He is no Prophet." . . . Pretty soon Thomas walks in. "Brother Joseph, will you trust me for a pair of boots?" "No, I cannot let them go without the money." "Well," says Thomas, "Brother Joseph is no Prophet; I have found *that* out, and I am glad of it." After a while, in comes Bill and sister Susan. Says Bill, "Brother Joseph, I want a shawl, I have not got the money, but I wish you to trust me a week or a fortnight." Well, brother Joseph thinks the others have gone and apostatized, and he don't know but these goods will make the whole Church do the same, so he lets Bill have a shawl. Bill walks off with it and meets a brother. "Well," says he, "what do you think of brother Joseph?" "O he is a first-rate man, and I fully believe he is a Prophet. See here, he has trusted me this shawl." Richard says, "I think I will go down and see if he won't trust me some." In walks Richard. "Brother Joseph, I want to trade about 20 dollars." "Well," says Joseph, "these goods will make the people apostatize; so over they go, they are of less value than the people." Richard gets his goods. Another comes in the same way to make a trade of 25 dollars, and so it goes. Joseph was a first-rate fellow with them all the time, provided he never would ask them to pay him.[90]

That, agreed Brigham Young, was why the church did not freight goods in sufficient quantities to supply the Mormon market. People were perfectly willing to pay cash to the Gentiles, but they insisted upon credit from "the brethren." The president explained:

If I had 100,000 dollars worth of goods in that store [pointing to a Gentile establishment], owned by myself, or held by a "Mormon" company, in six months the goods would be gone, and we should not have 100 dollars to pay the debt. But let an infernal mobocrat come into our midst, though he brands Joseph Smith with the epithet of "false prophet," and calls the "Mormons" a damned set of thieves, and would see all Israel in Tophet, you would give him the last picayune you could raise. . . . Suppose you owe that store across the road there 1500 dollars, would you try to pay it? Yes, you would lie awake at nights to think how to pay those merchants that do not belong to the kingdom of God; you would offer them horses, and wagons, and oxen, to liquidate that debt.[91]

But when it came to dealing with the tithing store, he said, members did not want to buy; they wanted to *borrow* — money, cattle, and grain — not only for family support but to pay debts to Gentile stores. "You trade with the Almighty worse than you do with the devil," he concluded.

MORMON COLONIZATION IN THE WAKE OF THE GOLD RUSH

If the lack of a giant supply concern was a weakness in Mormon planning for the Kingdom, Mormon colonizing efforts were a strength. Here, again, the influence of the Gold Rush is clear and unmistakable — in the choice of locations for settlement and in financing exploring expeditions and new colonies. The pattern of this colonization, as compared with Western colonization generally, also exhibits some of the superiorities of Mormon social organization.

Mormon colonization during the years 1847–57 went through two phases. The first phase was the founding of what has been called "the inner cordon of settlements."[92] In addition to the settlement of the Salt Lake and Weber valleys in 1847 and 1848, colonies were founded in Utah, Tooele, and Sanpete valleys in 1849; Box Elder, Pahvant, Juab, and Parowan valleys in 1851; and Cache Valley in 1856. Settlements in all of these "valleys" multiplied with additional immigration throughout the 1850's. The second phase was an expansion beyond the immediately available cultivatable valleys with a view to ringing the commonwealth with colonies located at strategic points of interception — all of them far distant from the central bastion. Carson Valley, Nevada, was settled during the years 1849–1851; San Bernardino, California, in 1851; Las Vegas, Nevada, in 1855; Moab, in southeastern Utah, in 1855; Fort Supply and Fort Bridger, Wyoming, in 1853 and 1856; and Lemhi, on the Salmon River in northern Idaho, in 1855. The area encompassed within this outer cordon embraced almost a sixth of the present area of the United States. It was 1,000 miles from north to south, and 800 miles from east to west.

Carson Valley, Nevada. From the standpoint of immediate economic policy, the most important of these efforts were the Carson Valley colony and the string of settlements known as the "Mormon Corridor." During the dark days of April 1849, when the future of the Salt Lake colony was in doubt, a group of fifteen Mormons joined a company of non-Mormons traveling westward to Humboldt Springs, the Sierra, and northern California. Upon reaching Carson Valley, near the California border, seven of them decided to remain and establish a supply station. Supplies were purchased in California and sold to passing emigrants at lucrative prices. According to the leader,

> Flour at that time [summer of 1849] was worth $2.00 a pound, fresh beef $1.00, bacon $2.00. A friend of mine went over the mountains and left a yoke of cattle with me, and one day I got a thousand dollars for one of those oxen in the shape of beef. . . . One time a captain of a train of emigrants came along and wanted to buy five hundred pounds of flour at $2.00 a pound, but I refused

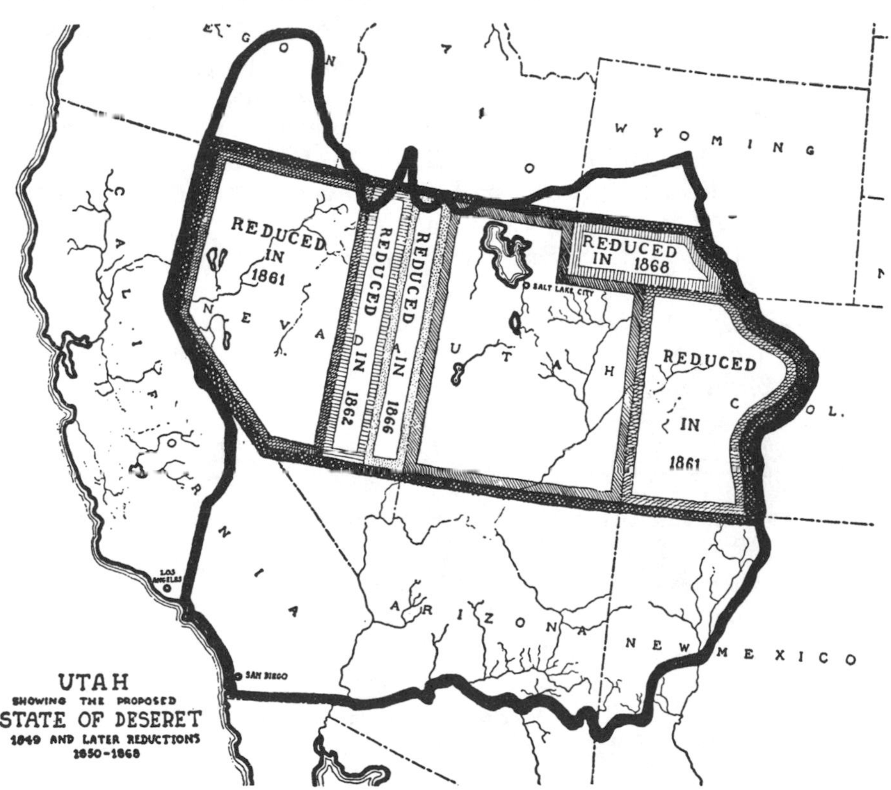

him, not having sufficient to deal out in such large amounts. . . . For a few loaves of bread I could get a good horse.[93]

The men returned to the Salt Lake Valley in the fall of 1849 with about one hundred head of horses, and with coin and other valuables. The station was operated only by returnees from the Gold Mission in 1850, but in 1851 Colonel Reese, the Salt Lake merchant, took a company, developed a profitable business, and established industries. In 1856, "Mormon Station" became an officially supported and strategic colony in the Mormon network around the Great Basin.

The Mormon Corridor. Much more important was the founding of a string of settlements stretching south from Salt Lake City to San Pedro and San Diego, California, in a great geopolitical scheme called the "Mormon Corridor."[94] The first in this chain of settlements was Utah Valley, immediately south of Salt Lake Valley, which was settled by thirty families in the spring of 1849. Within a year the population had grown to 2,026, and the foundation had been laid for a settlement on each of the eight streams in the valley. Later in 1849, fifty families were called to settle Sanpete Valley, south of Utah Valley, where a nucleus for many other settlements was also established. Still later in the year, an exploring party of fifty persons was outfitted under the direction of the Council of Fifty to determine locations for settlement between the Salt Lake Valley and what is now the northern border of Arizona, some 300 miles south. The ultimate goal, it was announced, was to "establish a chain of forts from Great Salt Lake City to the Pacific Ocean."[95] The region had been explored during the preceding two years, of course, by Mormon parties going to and returning from California, but this new official party, under the command of Parley P. Pratt, was charged with conducting a systematic exploration of the region. Over a three-month period the expedition covered approximately 800 miles, keeping a detailed written record in which were noted the topography, facilities for grazing, water, vegetation, supplies of timber, and, in general, favorable locations for settlements and forts.[96]

The expedition's report was quickly put to use. Additional settlements were made in Utah and Sanpete valleys during the fall of 1850, and in November of the same year a large group was sent to colonize the Little Salt Lake Valley in southern Utah. During the next year settlements were made in Juab and Pahvant valleys, and still other settlements in Utah, Sanpete, and Little Salt Lake valleys. Within three years after the exploring party's return, Brigham Young had sent colonists to virtually every site recommended by the expedition. By that time, the church had also supervised the exploration and "practically developed" the entire corridor route from Salt Lake to San Diego.[97] By 1855, some twenty-seven separate communities had been founded along the route.

The two most important colonies along the route were those in Little Salt Lake Valley at Parowan (Utah) and in San Bernardino, California. The Parowan settlement served the dual purpose of providing a half-way station between southern California and the Salt Lake Valley and of producing agricultural products to support an "iron mission." Near present-day Cedar City, Utah, the exploring company had found "a hill of the richest iron ore [Iron Mountain]," in close juxtaposition with "thousands of acres of cedar," constituting an almost "inexhaustible supply of fuel which makes excellent coal."[98] Following a call in July 1850, a company of 167 persons was constituted in December and sent, complete with equipment and supplies, to Parowan to plant crops and prepare to work with the pioneer iron mission established at Cedar City later in the year. Ultimately, the colony was the nucleus of at least a dozen settlements made in the region in the early 1850's.

The San Bernardino colony was also settled under official appointment in 1851. The considerations were recorded in Brigham Young's official journal, as follows:

> Elders Amasa M. Lyman and C. C. Rich . . . were instructed by letter to select a site for a city or station, as a nucleus for a settlement, near the Cajon Pass, in the vicinity of the sea coast, for a continuation of the route already commenced from this to the Pacific; to gather around them the Saints in California, to search out on their route and establish, as far as possible, the best location for stations between Iron county and California, in view of a mail route to the Pacific; to cultivate the olive and manufacture olive oil, and also to cultivate grapes, sugar cane, cotton and any other desirable fruits and products; to obtain information concerning the 'Tehuantepec route,' or any other across the Isthmus, or the passage around Cape Horn with a view to the gathering of the saints from Europe; to plant the standard of salvation in every county and kingdom, city and village, on the Pacific and the world over, as fast as God should give the ability.[99]

Lyman and Rich had wanted at first to purchase the large Chino Ranch, in San Bernardino Valley near Los Angeles, which belonged to Colonel Isaac Williams. Some members of the Mormon Battalion had been assigned there on detached service in 1847 and at that time Williams had reportedly offered to sell the twenty-four square miles of land, 8,000 head of cattle, and a large number of horses, for "five hundred dollars down, and taking our time to pay the remainder."[100] Jefferson Hunt, captain in the Battalion, who continued to advocate purchase of the ranch, thought that the cattle alone would pay for the ranch in two months.[101] Companies of Mormons going from Salt Lake Valley to southern California in 1848 and 1849 also stayed at the ranch and reported favorably on its value. When Lyman and Rich tried to buy the ranch in 1850–1851, however, the colonel became more reluctant and asked $150,000 for his ranch and 8,000 to 10,000 cattle. The Mormons balked at what seemed an exorbitant price.

Not far away was the Rancho del San Bernardino, belonging to the Lugo brothers, who were related by marriage to Williams. An agreement was finally reached in 1851 to purchase this 35,500-acre ranch for $77,500.[102] Money for the down payment and for sufficient supplies to put the colony on a working basis was obtained by soliciting donations from Mormons in the San Francisco and Sacramento regions. By the end of 1851, some $25,000 had been raised in California toward the purchase of the ranch, and a deed was executed. Subsequently, some money was raised by sending 100 of the colonists to work in the gold mines, by sending others to preach and solicit for money, and by solicitations in Mormon settlements in Utah.[103]

The colony itself was founded by some 450 church members from the Salt Lake Valley who arrived in California in June 1851. Within a year, a mile-square townsite had been laid out, a fort erected, wheat planted, and mills erected. By 1855 there were 1400 Mormon inhabitants, 4,000 acres of irrigated land had been planted to grain, and the hard-working colonists had set out 50,000 vines, many acres of fruit trees, and were fattening more than 15,000 oxen.[104] Their butter, cheese, eggs, and flour were sold throughout southern California. Another item which enjoyed wide sale was lumber, which was marketed in large quantities after the colonists had cooperatively hewn a sixteen-mile road into the San Bernardino mountains and set up a sawmill. The colony served as a port of entry for converts coming from the Pacific missions; as a gathering place for California Mormons generally; and as a rest and supply station for church missionaries going to and from California and Pacific missions.[105] Had the colony lasted longer, it would have served as a gathering place for converts from the Pacific Isles.

THE COLONIZING PROCESS

Approximately ninety-six colonies or "settlements," including those along the Mormon Corridor, were founded by the Mormons during the first ten years after the occupation of the Salt Lake Valley, and at least five hundred were founded during the nineteenth century.[106] The process by which these colonies were planted and nurtured demonstrates the manner in which the Mormons attempted to translate their early ideals into concrete institutions and patterns of social organization, both during the Gold Rush period and later. A three-phase sequence was involved: (1) Preliminary exploration was undertaken by companies appointed, equipped, and supported by the church; (2) a colonizing company was appointed to found the settlement; and (3) the company was expected to pattern its community institutions after those of Salt Lake City—which, in turn, were patterned after those of Winter Quarters, Nauvoo, Far West, and Jackson County. Mormon colonization, in contrast with much contemporary colonization of the far western frontier, was the directed movement of an entire new community according to plans carefully worked out by church authorities, rather than the result of the spontaneous and independent movement of individuals.

Calls to participate in the founding of new colonies, from Fort Lemhi in the north to San Bernardino in the south, were usually issued from the pulpit in a session of the general conference. In most cases, the names of the leaders and all other colonizers were specified. Each company was carefully selected to include men with the skills and equipment needed to subdue the wilderness and establish a workable community life. If dispatched from Salt Lake City, as was the usual thing, the colonizing company was usually called together for a meeting with the president of the church at which advice and counsel were given, questions answered, and prayers were offered for the success of the undertaking. In the case of some of the more difficult colonization projects, church leaders gave them a special sanctity by designating them as "missions" and referring to the company as a group of "missionaries." This clothed the project with special purpose and determination, and implied that none should leave the assignment without a specific "release." While there were occasional "backsliders," most selectees honored their call. "I have learned," said one, "that it was profitable to accept all calls made of me by the authority of the Church."[107] Failure to carry out an assigned responsibility would have thrust one into the limbo of community disesteem and religious nonrecognition. For many of them, the call was a test of their faith, and few Mormons shrank before such a challenge.

Once constituted and ready to depart, each company was organized in traditional Mormon military fashion — that is, into groups of ten, fifty, and one hundred — with the captains of hundreds responsible to the apostle or company president appointed by the church. As had been true in crossing the Plains, each company adopted certain rules for the regulation of travel. Difficulties between members were settled by the group captain, or, under an appeal system, by the company president.

Upon reaching their destination the colonists retained the same military organization while preparing the basis for community life. After the land had been suitably dedicated by prayer "for the settling of the Saints and the glorification of God," a fort or stockade was cooperatively erected which would serve as a temporary home and community center, as well as a protection against Indians. From this fort colonists went forth each day in organized groups to perform their "public works" — that is, to dig canals, erect fences, plant crops, build roads, construct homes, and otherwise prepare the groundwork for subsequent village life. This day-to-day work was usually planned in meetings of all the male heads of families — "priesthood meetings" — and each colonist was given specific assignments. These meetings, of course, were conducted under the direction of the president who, if not an apostle, was usually appointed to be bishop when community life commenced.

During this period of preparation the settlement area was surveyed and divided into blocks by an appointed church engineer who was assigned to the company. The blocks were separated by wide streets, and varied from five to ten acres in size. A large block in the center was reserved for public buildings, and an important early task was the construction of a combination meetinghouse-schoolhouse on this lot. Each block in the village was divided into equal lots of an acre or more each, which were distributed among the colonists in a community drawing in which each family was to receive one lot. On these lots the colonists built their homes, planted their orchards, raised their vegetables and flowers, and erected their livestock and poultry sheds.

Outside the village the surveyor located an area that could be conveniently irrigated called the Big Field, which was divided into lots ranging from five to twenty acres each, depending on the amount of irrigable land and the number of colonists. One of these farming lots was assigned to each family, again by a community drawing. In the case of the founding of Parowan, for example, each family head was entitled to a town lot and a five or ten acre lot in the Big Field. After the town lots were distributed, officials numbered each farming lot: No. 1, No. 2, and so on. Slips with the names of the colonists desiring these plots were then placed in a hat. The first name drawn by the bishop was entitled to lot No. 1, the second was given No. 2, and so on. The same procedure was followed in apportioning the ten-acre plots.[108] In the case of another colony, the settlers agreed in public meeting that farming land should be cut into ten-acre tracts, classified as first-class and second-class. Three drawings were therefore held, each family drawing for a city lot, a ten-acre tract of first-class land, and a ten-acre tract of second-class land.[109]

In all cases, no family was permitted to draw more than one lot, thus eliminating land monopolization and inequality. Lots not taken were reserved for newcomers, who were almost invariably admitted to the community on the same terms as the original settlers. In several communities the first settlers agreed to give up equal portions of their original twenty-acre allotments in order to provide farms for newly arrived immigrants.[110]

The survival and growth of each community obviously depended upon the maximum use of available land and water resources, and therefore speculative withholding of land from use was prohibited by common consent. An example of ecclesiastical enforcement of this policy was related by Marriner W. Merrill, who later became an apostle. Young Merrill had hired out as a laborer in the Salt Lake Valley until 1854, when he located some land outside the margin of irrigation. It developed that the land was claimed by Goudy Hogan, one of the early Norwegian converts to Mormonism. Merrill then related the sequence, as follows:

I applied to Brother Hogan to buy his claim as he had plenty of land without it, and as it had cost him nothing I thought I was entitled to a portion of the public domain to build a home upon. Brother Hogan refused to sell or let me have the land or any portion of it, and I felt that he was selfish and did not love his brother as the precepts of the Gospel require. So I applied to the Bishop, John Stoker, but did not get any encouragement from him, he letting me think there was no water for the land and that it was worthless to me. But I did not view things in that light exactly, although I was not at that time acquainted fully with the importance of irrigation to mature crops. So I applied to the Territorial Surveyor, Jesse W. Fox, who was very kind to me and gave me all the information he could about the land, and even took me up to President Young's office to talk to him about it. President Young did not favor the policy of one man claiming so much land and directed the surveyor, Brother Fox, to make me out a plot of the land for the 100 acres and also to give me a surveyor's certificate for it. This was done, and on presenting my claim to Brother Hogan he was very angry and said many hard things to me. But he surrendered his claim and I was the lawful claimant of 100 acres of land by the then rules of the country.[111]

In another instance, one James Robbins acquired a town lot in a central Utah town which he was not farming. One day passing by it he found a fellow church member working on it. "What are you doing here?" asked Robbins. "Making me a house and home," was the reply. "But what right have you to build on my land?" was the next query, to which he replied that it was now his lot because the bishop had given it to him. Robbins then went to the bishop and asked, "By what authority, Bishop, do you give away my property?" The bishop solemnly and devastatingly replied, "By the authority of the Priesthood of God!"[112] By such procedures, priority of occupation was not allowed to play, among the Mormons, the role which it had played elsewhere in America.

As in the case of the Salt Lake City example, farming lands in the Mormon villages throughout the west were occasionally farmed cooperatively, but the usual rule was individual farming of each plot. However, all farming land was usually fenced in by cooperative effort, in order to secure crops against livestock. The area outside the fenced portion was given over to common pasture. Stock were bedded down for the night in barns constructed by owners on their town lots. Early in the morning "herd boys" would walk down village streets, pick up the stock of each owner, and drive them outside the Big Field for daytime grazing. In the evening, the herd boys would drive the stock back to the village, and down the streets once more. The stock of individual owners would be singled out at each lot and driven in to be milked and/or bedded down for the night. Stock were allowed to graze in the Big Field after the fall harvest, and for that reason, every farmer was required to complete his harvest by a specified time.

When the town of Ephraim, in Sanpete Valley, was founded in 1854, there was a large natural meadow near the town, which was the principal source of hay. In the first few years there was more than ample to supply the wants of everyone, and each person used it as he wished. But as the demand for hay increased due to the increase in population, it became necessary to apportion this hay land. The apportionment for Ephraim was determined as follows:

> The ruling was made that no one should cut hay from the meadow until after midnight on the 25th day of July. As the individuals arrived at the meadow, each one would seek out the particular patch of forage he desired and with his scythe would mow a swath around it. This provision was made to restrain the gluttonous one: No man should cut a swath around a larger piece than he could mow with a scythe, single-handed, in one day. If he should overestimate his capacity, that which remained standing at the close of the day could be appropriated by anyone who wished it. . . .
>
> Later it became advisable to settle private ownership on this land, and it was done in this unique manner. The meadow was two miles in length, and instead of dividing it along section lines as is customary, it was decided that all would share more justly if it were sliced into two-mile strips. The width of the meadow was measured and divided by the number of family heads, and it was found that each would be entitled to a three-rod strip two miles in length. No fences were erected, only pegs driven at intervals of three rods across the "top" of the field. The strips were numbered and each individual drew lots for his portion. Pasture land was similarly divided so that each individual drew lots for his portion [and] shared equally with his neighbors.[113]

In the case of each village, the grazing lands were bounded by the mountains and canyons, with available timber. Roadways to the timber were constructed by collective effort, and community regulation prevented wasteful cutting and use of the timber. As in the Salt Lake Valley, the timber, grasslands, minerals, and water of each village were community property, and their use was dependent on community policy and the cooperative construction of facilities. In the 1850's, as previously noted, these resources were sometimes assigned to church officials as community stewardships, and in such cases religious sanctions were invoked to prevent their use for private advantage.[114]

Mormon colonization was strongly influenced by the desire to people the region with as many families as could make a living. This, rather than natural conditions, was undoubtedly at the root of the Mormon insistence on the small intensively farmed holdings. As the result of this emphasis, the limited amount of irrigable land was made to support as many people as possible. A member of the First Presidency who had witnessed the application of this early policy, later stated that he thought the Mormons had proved that "large tracts of land are not necessary for the public good," even in a semi-arid region. There was no doubt in his mind, he said, but that "small holdings are the best for the people." [115]

Whatever the reasons for the Latter-day Saint land policy, its application and enforcement in a legal sense were possible because Congress did not pass laws under which the land in Utah could be privately acquired until 1869.[116] Except in California, therefore, where the Mormon system was given a legal basis at San Bernardino, the burden of allocating and regulating property rights rested primarily upon the church. The nature of the property institutions, and the fact that land was "free" in a financial sense, in turn, made a market for land practically nonexistent in Mormon communities until after 1869. This partly explains the tardiness of banking development among the Mormons. Until, say, the 1880's, a man could obtain the means of a livelihood (that is, land) simply by going to the bishop and asking where he could settle. He "paid" for the land merely by laboring on a cooperative canal. Hence, there was no need of land banks, which played such an important role in other parts of the West.[117]

What was true of land was true, although to a more limited extent, of other property and means of livelihood. After the colony had been firmly established, for example, and the first joint undertakings were completed, settlers chosen in advance for the purpose were encouraged to establish shops and mills. The community often was asked to help these enterprisers when additional labor and materials were required. In return, the owners of sawmills, gristmills, tanneries, and such specialists as blacksmiths and carpenters, were expected to hold themselves ready to serve the entire community at reasonable rates, much as public utilities are expected to do today. When larger ventures beyond the means of local citizens were needed, the church, with its wide command of labor and other resources, was prepared to assist.

It should be added that when the conditions under which the colony was established were particularly difficult, the church was prepared to assist with grain and flour, livestock, seeds, tools and equipment, and with other supplies. The first settlers of Sanpete Valley, for example, were given ten wagon loads of grain to enable them to survive the first severe winter, while the early residents of Utah Valley were provided from the tithing office with "2500 pounds of flour, meat, etc., and all the hats and caps that can be obtained besides ammunition." [118] The church also assisted in financing the Little Salt Lake Valley and San Bernardino colonies.

To summarize, the Mormon colonization which followed in the wake of the Gold Rush of '49 was characterized by the confident and effusive ecclesiastical mobilization of human, capital, and natural resources for the greater benefit of Zion. In some instances, virtually all early enterprises were communal; in others, only a few. But the matter of property rights was in every case incidental to the common purpose. The pattern laid for the growth and expansion of the 1850's was shaped, not by forces of the market, but by the planning and decisions of administrators bent on building the Kingdom of God.

It is perhaps this ideological principle of group stewardship which most clearly differentiated the Mormons from other frontiersmen. While it was the ultimate view of many contemporary Americans, including some of the so-called "Robber Barons," that men were accountable to God for the use of the property under their care, there is a vast difference between the individual stewardship views of such men as John D. Rockefeller and Daniel Drew, and the collective principles and procedures of the Mormons, in which each member looked to the church to establish the conditions which would assure the use of all labor and property in building the Kingdom. That the Mormon concept of time and property as a collective trust, to be used "for the glory of God and the relief of men's estate," [119] should have continued throughout the half-century in American economic life when property rights were generally regarded as private, absolute, and unconditioned is, once again, a symbol of the difference between two generations of Americans. For, in the expanding economy of the 1860's, '70's and '80's resources appeared to be so abundant that what was appropriated or "wasted" by one would cause no hardship to others. America was bonanza — a land of limitless resources and opportunities. In such an environment it was perhaps inevitable that the obligations of property ownership should be relaxed — that property would no longer be contingent upon the performance of services to society. Property could mean, without obvious social disadvantage, the exclusive use, enjoyment, and control of resources, both natural and man-made.

That this conception of property as a right to which no corresponding obligation was attached should not have characterized Mormon thought and practice, even on the frontier, is partly the result of the niggardliness of nature in the Great Basin, and partly the effect of the social and intellectual origins of Mormonism. Having originated, socially speaking, in the poor New York-New England village, rather than on the lush frontier; and forced by dint of persecution and hardship to exalt the welfare of the group above individual freedom and license, when throughout the nation generally individualistic institutions were being strengthened, it is not surprising that the institutions of the Mormons should have been significantly different from those which were becoming increasingly typical of the age of the "Great Barbecue."

CHAPTER IV

Organization for Growth and Development

The two recurring themes in the history of the Mormon social economy during the first two decades after 1847 are the stimulus provided by such economic windfalls as the Gold Rush and the mining trade, and the triumph of superb organization over the many obstacles presented by desert colonization. The latter theme is particularly characteristic of the decade of the 1850's, during which the Gold Rush slowed down to a mere trickle and subsequent windfalls had not yet arrived. Virtually every traveler in Utah who left a commentary remarked of the effectiveness and cohesion of Mormon organization. When the late Professor Richard T. Ely wrote that "the organization of the Mormons is the most nearly perfect piece of social mechanism with which I have ever, in any way, come in contact," [1] he was echoing a point which had been made many times before — a point which could have been applied with particular accuracy to the Mormonism of the 1850's. The region which the Mormons had settled had plagues without number and hardships without end, but the facility with which the Mormons organized their labor and mobilized their capital for the accomplishment of common goals was sufficient to transform their struggling community into the thronging headquarters of a growing, diffuse, and self-confident Kingdom.

In all this activity, the primary goal of the church was to provide the basis of support for an ever larger number of people. Just as the Japanese government of the Meiji restoration sought to bring greatness to that island economy by deliberate industrialization, so the Mormon Church contrived to develop the Great Basin to the full extent of its potentiality. The building of the Kingdom might require a hundred years, but that was only an hour in the day of God. The building of the Kingdom might also necessitate holding back increases in individual incomes, but individuals had only one life to contribute to the great cause. Through church programs and group activity, it was thought, each man's labor could be made to count for the most.

THE ORGANIZATION OF IMMIGRATION

The first great task to which the Mormons devoted themselves in the 1850's was the build-up of population through the Perpetual Emigrating Company. As the result of the initial operations of that company, the Mormon population in the Great Basin had soared from some 6,000 persons in the spring of 1849 to approximately 20,000 persons in 1852.[2] The new task to which it now turned was the emigration of approximately 30,000 Latter-day Saints in England.[3] The primary motive of this emigration, of course, was the theological principle of the gathering, but there is no question that economic goals also were important. From one point of view, the P.E. Company was simply an organizational device for recruiting and supplying the laborers needed in building the Kingdom.

The preamble to the legislative act which incorporated the Perpetual Emigrating Company gave explicit statement to this economic objective:

> Labor, industry, and economy is wealth, and all kinds of mechanics and laborers are requisite for building up and attending the benefits of civilized society, subduing the soil, and otherwise developing the resources of a new country.[4]

Every attempt seems to have been made by the emigration agent in Liverpool to comply with this important objective. One of the agents stated that in the selection of those to be emigrated with P.E. funds, occupation was an important consideration, second only to "integrity and moral worth."[5] The instructions to the emigrants, given in the *Millennial Star* and in circulars issued by the Liverpool office, urged capitalists to take machinery, mechanics and professional men to take tools, treatises, and blueprints, and farmers to take seeds.[6] Mormon emigrant companies were noted for their heavy luggage.

In the spring of 1849, when so many plans were made for the development of the Great Basin, the First Presidency and Twelve discussed ways and means of "bringing companies of mechanics and artisans from the British Isles to the Valley."[7] Specifically wanted were iron manufacturers, metal workers, textile manufacturers, and potters. Church missionaries and agents were requested to "search out" such persons, band those of similar trades together, and have them "emigrate immediately . . . in preference to anyone else." Each company should be equipped with "machinery, tools, and materials for operating in all useful branches of industry . . . that a good foundation should be laid against the time that others of the poor shall go."

> Let not the presiding elders be slothful upon this subject until it is accomplished. When you find mechanics of the above description use every effort to get them

off to the Salt Lake Valley. . . . Our true policy is, to do our own work, make our own goods as soon as possible, therefore do all you can to further the emigration of artisans and mechanics of all kinds. . . .

We hope soon to see the time when this territory will be able to turn out the finest, most beautiful, and substantial articles of every kind now made in England.

When we can see the Saints from Europe come in this manner, prepared to stick together, and come through and establish employment . . . it will cheer our hearts to behold them by thousands, as doves flocking to their windows.[8]

The pages of contemporary Mormon periodicals in Europe are replete with appeals to mechanics and artisans and manufacturers to make immediate plans to emigrate to the Salt Lake Valley.

As an example of the skills added to the Mormon commonwealth by immigration, James Linforth gave a contemporary compilation of the skills of the emigrants leaving Liverpool during the years 1850 to 1854. Their skills run alphabetically from accountant to yeoman, and include 96 boot and shoe makers, 10 boiler makers, 12 cabinet makers, 46 engineers, 2 ironmongers, 226 miners, 73 masons, 8 printers, 22 spinners, 9 weavers, and some three hundred other specialized skills and occupations.[9]

The organization of European members for emigration is indicative of what was, in the estimate of Katherine Coman, "the most successful example of regulated immigration in United States history."[10] Agents and offices were located in Liverpool, at American ports of debarkation, at St. Louis, at an outfitting post on the Missouri River, and in Salt Lake City. Instructions were relayed to prospective emigrants by means of church missionaries in the various localities in Scandinavia, the British Isles, and on the Continent, and also by means of such missionary journals as the *Latter-day Saints' Millennial Star* (Liverpool), *Skandinaviens Stjerne* (Copenhagen), *Etoile Du Deseret* (Paris), *Zion's Panier* (Hamburg), and *Der Darsteller* (Geneva). The most important of these, the *Millennial Star,* had a weekly circulation of 20,000. Each prospective emigrant or head of family filed a formal application with the Liverpool (or local) agent, giving the name, age, occupation, and birthplace of the applicant and his family, accompanied by a deposit of one pound sterling. Emigrants were expected to provide their own bedding and cooking utensils, but food was arranged by the P.E.F.

Three kinds of "companies" were organized to make the long voyage from England to the States, and from the States to the Salt Lake Valley. These were the P.E. companies, the Ten Pound companies, and the cash emigrant companies. P.E. companies were composed of those who were too poor to pay any of their way from Europe to the Salt Lake Valley. Their transportation was completely financed by donations to the P.E. Fund. They were expected, of course, to contribute to the Fund in the form of labor and otherwise after they reached the Valley. The Ten Pound companies were composed of persons and families who were not poor enough to qualify for the P.E. companies, but were not wealthy enough to afford the usual expenses involved in transatlantic and transcontinental travel. The P.E.F. found that it could send emigrants from Liverpool to Salt Lake City for an out-of-pocket expense of ten pounds. Under the Ten Pound Plan, the P.E.F. bore all costs, but made a charge amounting to £10 per adult and £5 for those under one year of age. The cash emigrant companies were also organized and dispatched by the P.E. agents, but paid the full cost of their transportation to Utah.

The relative importance of the three kinds of emigrant companies is illustrated in 1853 when 2,312 persons emigrated to Utah under P.E.F. auspices. Some 400 of these were in P.E. companies; another 1,000 went in the Ten Pound companies; and 955 paid their own way. The entire expense to the Fund of the emigration of 1853 was £30,000, or an average of over £20 for those receiving assistance from the Fund. The Ten Pound Plan was converted into a Thirteen Pound Plan in 1854, and a Fifteen Pound Plan in 1855.[11] By the end of 1855, 21,911 European emigrants had been transported to Zion, of whom 15,585 had gone in the years 1849–1855.[12] An estimated £125,000 were expended by the P.E. Company during the four years from 1852 to 1855 in emigrating the "poor saints" from Europe to the Salt Lake Valley.[13] By 1870, when the completion of the transcontinental railroad greatly altered the pattern of emigration, more than 51,000 Mormon emigrants had been assisted to America, of whom more than 38,000 were British, and over 13,000 were from the Continent and Scandinavia.

For those who paid part or all of their way to Utah, the European Mission of the church encouraged systematic saving by sponsoring an Emigration Deposit Fund, Individual Emigration Account, and the Penny Emigration Fund.[14] Most, if not all, of the European tithing receipt sales went into the Fund, as did donations from wealthy European converts. During the season of 1855 the agency had deposits as high as £30,000 in the banks of London and Liverpool.[15] Some of the overhead expense was borne by the commissions received by P.E.F. Agents from lines on which Mormon emigrants and freight were shipped.[16] The principal source of revenue, however, consisted of the contributions of labor, produce, cash, livestock, and equipment by church members already established in the Great Basin. The assistant church historian at the turn of the century estimated this total to have been approximately $8,000,000.[17] Almost all of these contributions were "in kind," and were usually collected in the fall of each year. They were collected by or delivered to block teachers, bishops, and tithing offices throughout the territory and converted into cash wherever possible.

The nature of the contributions is illustrated by those made in a special drive in one community in northern Utah. After the block teachers had visited each family in the ward, the report shows contributions to the P.E.F. to have included $66.00 in cash, $58.00 in produce, $50.00 in "store pay," $2.50 in corn, 26 bushels of wheat, 10 dozen eggs, and 3¾ pounds of butter. Four families would give nothing, of which two were "too poor," and two were "too mean." [18]

Another local P.E.F. account shows the receipts divided into stock, labor, and current. The stock receipts included heifers, steers, cows, and bulls of various varieties, valued at $240.00; the labor account credits two persons with $50.00 each for having gone East to assist the immigrants westward; and the current account shows cash receipts on immigrants' indebtedness of $30.00, divorce receipts of 4 bushels of wheat, and receipts from the sale of stray stock amounting to $373.25 in wheat, $15.00 in barley, and $52.00 in cash.[19] Brigham Young had provided that all church receipts from divorce proceedings — usually $10.00 each — would go into the Fund. Similarly, many miscellaneous fines found their way into the Fund. In the late 'fifties, for example, the P.E.F. received a $100.00 fine from a man whose son had been convicted of starting a fight.[20]

Two other sources of funds for the P.E.F. illustrate the union of church and state in supporting the immigration activities. In 1849 an ordinance was passed by the High Council, providing that cattle left in the Estray Pound one month should be sold for the benefit of the "perpetual poor emigrating fund." [21] This provision was ratified and amplified by the State of Deseret, which gave an owner six months in which to appear, prove property, and pay damages and costs, after which the avails were to be paid "into the Perpetual Emigrating Fund for the Poor." These pounds were to be located by each county road commissioner in each precinct of his county. The law was ratified by the Utah legislature and remained in effect throughout most of the half century. The total amount collected from this source was upwards of a thousand dollars per year, amounting to $2,152 in the year 1859 alone.[22] The revenue from this source was supplemented with funds from the law of January 20, 1854, which instructed the judges of the probate courts to turn over to the P.E. Fund all unclaimed property of "deceased or absconded" persons, whether Mormon or Gentile.

The most remarkable thing about these contributions is not the size of them, but the miracle by which they were transformed into cash and effective supplies and equipment for the use of the emigration agents in Liverpool and at the frontier outfitting point. The writer knows of one case in which a Latter-day Saint deposited 100 bushels of wheat in his local tithing office and in return the P.E.F. agreed to emigrate his wife and three children from Shropshire, England. The church apparently made liberal use of what might be called sight drafts. That is, the Liverpool office was largely financed by European contributions, but occasionally drew on church deposits in New York. The New York office drew on church deposits in St. Louis, and the St. Louis office in turn was financed by contributions of westering emigrants and by drafts on the church treasury in Salt Lake City. The usual procedure was to ask European emigrants to leave all their money in the Liverpool office in exchange for a draft on the church. Similarly, all emigrants having liquid funds at the frontier were asked to exchange it for drafts good in Salt Lake. When the emigrants reached Salt Lake City these drafts were satisfied with oxen, horses, wagons, flour, and other equipment useful in settling in the West. These properties had been donated locally by the Fund, or purchased by the Fund in the Midwest.[23]

Occasionally, Brigham Young did not have sufficient tithing and other resources to redeem all the drafts upon sight. When he was caught short, the pulpit of the Bowery or Tabernacle was certain to resound with strong pleas to "renew your covenants and help emigrate the poor." The following excerpt from an 1855 sermon shows the financial problems involved:

> When br. Erastus Snow arrived on the first of this month, he came in the morning and informed me that he had run me [*i.e.*, the church] in debt nearly fifty thousand dollars to strangers, merchants, cattle dealers, and our brethren who are coming here; he said, "Prest. Young's name is as good as the bank." . . .
>
> I will pay you when I can, and not before. . . . It is the poor who have got your money, and if you have any complaints to make, make them against the Almighty for having so many poor. . . . I cannot chew paper and spit out bank bills that will pass in payment of those debts, neither shall I undertake to do it.[24]

Apparently, P.E.F. officials were allowed to assist so many each year, regardless of the European, American, and Salt Lake contributions to the Fund, and when the revenue was insufficient, the difference was made up out of tithing revenues. As an example, the amount of tithing used to support the P.E.F. amounted to $54,070 in 1859–1860.[25]

Theoretically, of course, the Fund was to have been perpetual. Every expense was to be repaid and the Fund was to grow ever larger. As a means of guaranteeing compliance with this charter requirement, the P.E. Company drew up a contract, signed by each emigrant of the first and all subsequent companies, in which the emigrants agreed as follows:

> On our arrival in the Great Salt Lake valley, we will hold ourselves, our time and our labor, subject to the appropriation of the Perpetual Emigration Fund Company, until the full cost of our emigration is paid, with interest if required.[26]

Actually, the Fund realized very little from repayments. The P.E.F. itself had little opportunity in which to use the labor of immigrants after their arrival, and so a scheme was devised by which the immigrants could work for the church, principally on the Public Works, and receive half a salary in tithing orders and the other half in the form of cancellation of their indebtedness. The church, in turn, placed tithing resources at the disposition of the P.E.F. to cancel its obligation in the arrangement.

The failure of many of the immigrants to make an honest attempt to repay the indebtedness was a constant source of irritation with Brigham Young. He reminded immigrant-debtors of their obligations at almost every annual and semi-annual church conference. When the indebtedness had reached $56,000 by 1855, Brigham declared,

> I want you to understand fully, that I intend to put the screws upon you, and you who have owed for years, and if you do not pay up now and help us we will levy on your property and take every farthing you have on earth.[27]

This was, of course, a mere rhetorical threat, for it was impossible to "put the screws" upon them. Most of the immigrant-debtors found it hard to accumulate a surplus in the Great Basin, and most of them had plenty to do to keep them busy. Usually one of the duties of the block teachers, once a year, was to list the outstanding indebtedness to the P.E.F. among the families in their districts, and to report whether they were prepared to repay and in what form. But there is no evidence that the debtors were abused or that the indebtedness was held *in terrorem* over them. The best evidence that there was little rigor in pressing for repayment is the constant mounting of these obligations, which totaled over $100,000 in 1856, reached $700,000 by 1872, and exceeded $1,000,000 in 1877.[28]

The ocean voyage. When the P.E.F. shipping agent received a sufficient number of applications for passage, he chartered a vessel and notified the passengers by printed circulars of the time of embarkation, price of passage, amount of provisions allowed, and other procedural instructions. Usually passengers were placed on board ship the day of their arrival in Liverpool in order to save the expense of lodging ashore and to prevent loss from sharpers who appear to have frequented the Liverpool port area. In almost every case, the agent chartered an entire ship for the voyage. When this was impossible, he made arrangements with the ship's captain to build a partition to separate the Mormons from other travelers. Many of the vessels were of large tonnage, some of them carrying as many as a thousand passengers. Vessels could frequently be chartered at low rates as they could seldom obtain return freight from England.

When a given company was taken on board the chartered vessel, the P.E.F. Shipping Agent appointed a president to preside over the entire company. Then the agent and president together chose two counselors. Generally all three of this "presidency" were missionaries from Utah who were returning from their "fields of labor." These three were then presented to the assembled company for a sustaining vote. The company was then divided into wards or branches, each with its bishop or branch president and two counselors. Each ward was assigned a part of the ship. In one instance, at least, the center of the ship was occupied by married couples; single men were placed in the bow; and single women were placed in the stern.

Strict discipline prevailed during the voyage. The companies arose at an early hour, made their beds, cleaned their assigned portion of the ship, and threw the refuse overboard. At seven they assembled for prayer, after which breakfast was had. All were required to be in their berths ready for retirement at eight o'clock. Church services were held morning and evening of each day, weather permitting. Many of the companies had excellent choirs which sang for the services. During the time of passage, which occupied something like a month, concerts, dances, contests, and entertainments of various types were held. Schools were held almost daily for both adults and children. The classes were particularly popular with Scandinavians who learned English *en route*.

The food was reported to be simple, although many declared it to be superior to what they had been accustomed in England during the 'fifties. Contemporary observers stated that the parliamentary minimum of oatmeal, flour, rice, sugar, tea, and salt was supplemented by the agent with meat, butter, cheese, and additional bread as needed.[29]

The measures taken by Mormon officers to preserve order, decency, and cleanliness on board made the Mormon companies favorites of ships' captains and managers of packet lines.[30] Charles Mackay contrasted the Mormon companies with "the slovenly and dirty habits of other classes of emigrants," who, if they had adopted "similar regulations" would have traveled in greater "comfort and health."[31] That peripatetic observer of Victorian England, Charles Dickens, devoted an entire chapter of his *The Uncommercial Traveller* to the P.E.F. He called the eight hundred emigrants he saw departing on *The Amazon* "the pick and flower of England." Wrote Dickens,

> They had not been a couple of hours on board when they established their own police, made their own regulations, and set their own watches at all the hatchways. Before nine o'clock the ship was as orderly and as quiet as a man of war . . . there was no disorder, hurry, or difficulty. . . . I afterwards learned that a Despatch was sent home by the captain, before he struck out into the wide Atlantic, highly extolling the behavior of these Emigrants, and the perfect order and propriety of all their social arrangements.[32]

Dickens concluded his comment by observing, "I went over the Amazon's side feeling it impossible to deny that, so far, some remarkable influence had produced a remarkable result, which better known influences have often missed." He appended a footnote mentioning that a Select Committee of the House of Commons on emigrant ships for 1854 had studied the activities of the Mormon agents and had come to the conclusion "that no ships under the provisions of the 'Passengers Act' could be depended upon for comfort and security in the same degree as those under his [the Mormon Agent's] administration. The Mormon ship is a Family under strong and accepted discipline, with every provision for comfort, decorum, and internal peace." [33] A London correspondent of the *Cambridge Independent Press,* after attending the hearing, is reported to have written:

> There is one thing which, in the opinion of the Emigration Committee of the House of Commons, they [the Mormons] can do, viz.—teach Christian shipowners how to send poor people decently, cheaply, and healthfully across the Atlantic.[34]

The journey inland. Mormon converts who set sail from Liverpool faced a long journey to Salt Lake City. Before 1854 emigrant ships landed at New Orleans. From there they took a 700-mile trip by river steamer up the Mississippi to St. Louis. This trip usually took a week. From St. Louis they took a river boat some 500 miles to Kanesville, Iowa, or whatever point was selected for outfitting.[35] This trip took two weeks and more. In 1852 and 1853 "river diseases," such as malaria and cholera, took such a toll of the traveling emigrants that in 1854 the port of entry was shifted to eastern ports, usually New York, from which they went overland via rail to St. Louis and beyond.

At each point the emigrant companies were met by an agent who had chartered boats, purchased supplies and equipment, and provided for their well-being. Housing had to be provided for those who remained at each stopping place on account of sickness or other reasons; also housing for the entire company in case of unexpected delay.

Obviously, the long trip from Liverpool was expensive and provocative of delay. Converts leaving England in January did well to reach Salt Lake City by the first of September. Attempts were made to route the emigrants around Cape Horn or across the Isthmus of Panama to San Pedro and San Bernardino, California, thence overland to Utah, but these attempts were unsuccessful.

When the emigrant companies arrived at the frontier camp their outfit had been purchased by the Emigration Agent and was waiting for them. An "outfit" consisted of one wagon, two yoke of oxen, two cows, and a tent, the total cost of which varied from $250 to $500 in the 1850's.[36] This outfit served ten emigrants. As an example of the efficiency of planning and organization, the agents worked out a method by which the cost of wagon covers and tents could be greatly economized. Twilled cotton was purchased in England and distributed to the converts at the time of their embarkation. The emigrants then sewed their own tents and wagon covers during the voyage under the instruction of their "presidency." Thus, tent and cover were brought down to a cost of about ten dollars per wagon.

Food, of course, had to be purchased and provided by the frontier agent. The P.E.F. allowances of food for each wagon of ten emigrants in 1853 were as follows:[37]

1,000 pounds of flour
50 pounds of sugar
50 pounds of bacon
50 pounds of rice
30 pounds of beans
20 pounds of dried apples and peaches
5 pounds of tea
1 gallon of vinegar
10 bars of soap
25 pounds of salt

Some supplementation in this diet was obtained with milk from cows and with wild game. Each wagon was carefully inspected by captains so as to insure ample provisioning, proper equipment, and necessary ammunition.

The magnitude of the task of the P.E.F. agent at St. Louis is not difficult to appreciate. Horace S. Eldredge, who served as emigration agent and church purchasing agent at St. Louis during the 1853 and 1854 seasons, wrote that in 1853 he purchased over 400 wagons and 2,000 head of oxen, at a total cost in excess of $120,000, in addition to a sufficient quantity of provisions and supplies to take care of 4,000 people during the three-month journey to the Salt Lake Valley.[38] During the 1854 season he had approximately the same number of cattle, wagons, and provisions to buy, and, in addition, received orders from the church in Salt Lake City to purchase and send along with the trains "a large quantity of merchandise, machinery, agricultural implements, and to provide wagons, teams, teamsters, etc. for their transportation." The frontier agent also supervised the emigrants in using any liquid capital they might have on their persons to buy supplies which were scarce in Utah. A Norwegian emigrant, for example, was advised to buy "a plow, a stove, a keg of nails, a box of window lights, and a few other small things, all of which proved to be very useful indeed."[39]

One difficulty confronting the emigrant companies as they moved West was the crossing of each of the several considerable streams. Within the territory controlled by Mormons there were two rivers — the Green and the Bear — whose crossing was necessary and difficult. In 1853, the territorial legislature granted ferry rights to Daniel H. Wells (on the Green) and an association of individuals (on the Bear), authorizing them to charge from three to six dollars per vehicle, depending on the weight, and stipulated sums for livestock, and stipulating that ten per cent of all the proceeds were to be paid into the Perpetual Emigrating Company.[40] Obviously, this ten per cent was levied on the tolls paid by non-Mormon emigrants as well as by Mormons. "Thus," wrote Nels Anderson, "the emigrants to California and Oregon were taxed indirectly to help Mormon emigrants reach Zion."[41]

The length of time involved in crossing the Plains — some eighty days as a rule — and the problems involved in carrying enough provisions to last the emigrants this long, prompted church authorities in Salt Lake to inaugurate a regular schedule of "relief trains." These were a continuation of a practice which began in 1847, of sending trains with provisions, fresh teams, and spare equipment to meet the westward emigration as it went through present-day Wyoming. In 1852, for example, 200 volunteer wagon teams went from the Salt Lake Valley to the assistance of that year's immigration companies, and these carried to the various camps "some 50,000 pounds of flour and large supplies of vegetables, which enabled them to come in, in safety."[42] Brigham Young's view of this voluntary help was that it represented the essence of Christianity. "I care not what you believe about the resurrection, if I can only get religion enough in the people to accomplish that [the dispatching of sufficient relief trains], it will satisfy me for the present."[43] This problem was partly resolved in 1853 when the church purchased and improved Fort Bridger and built a large new way station at Fort Supply, in western Wyoming. These forts involved an investment of approximately $60,000 in cash, labor, and materials, and also made it possible for the church to guard the Mormon ferries on the Green River.[44]

Arrival in Utah. The care bestowed on immigrant companies after their arrival in Utah testifies to the importance which church leaders and members attached to the coming of these groups and to the manner in which they planned to use them. The first English company of P.E.F. immigrants arriving in the Salt Lake Valley was met at the mouth of Emigration Canyon, east of Salt Lake City, by President Young, several members of the Quorum of the Twelve, a large delegation of leading citizens of Salt Lake City, and by a brass band. Melons and cakes were distributed and everybody is reported to have danced and sung. As the company passed Temple Square it was saluted by the firing of cannons, after which the immigrants were camped on Emigration Square and treated to a welcoming address by Brigham Young:

> First I will say, may the Lord God of Israel bless you, and comfort your hearts. (The company and bystanders responded AMEN.) . . .

With regard to your obtaining habitations to shelter you in the coming winter — all of you will be able to obtain work, and by your industry, you can make yourselves tolerably comfortable in this respect, before the winter sets in. All the improvements that you see around you, have been made in the short space of four years. . . . All this that you now see, has been accomplished by the industry of the people. . . .

We shall want some of the brethren to repair to some of the other settlements, such as mechanics and farmers. . . .

Again, with regard to labour — don't imagine unto yourselves that you are going to get rich, at once, by it. As for the poor, there are none here, neither are there any who may be called rich, but all obtain the essential comforts of life. . . .

Do not any of you suffer the thought to enter your minds, that you must go to the gold mines, in search of riches. That is no place for the Saints. . . . You must live here; this is the gathering place for the Saints.[45]

In general the immigrants were accorded the same kind of treatment by the Salt Lake community that country homes typically accord visiting relatives and friends. The following report of the arrival of one 1864 company may be considered typical:

The Bishops and their assistants have had a stirring time since Captain Hyde's train got in, enormous quantities of meat, pies, bread, potatoes, and other consumables having been "taken up" through the wards and "put down" with considerable gusto by the arrivals on emigration square.[46]

These receptions were under the charge of the Presiding Bishop's Office. After the immediate needs of the immigrants were met the Presiding Bishop attempted to place the families in the various wards of the city until they received a "call" to settle in some outlying region. The bishops were instructed in advance to be prepared to receive these families. For example, the following instruction "To the Bishops," was issued by the First Presidency on June 28, 1854:

You are hereby instructed to proceed forthwith, and make diligent inquiry, to ascertain who in your ward can take into their families, or houses, some of the brethren, or members of their families, who are now on their road to this land, and give them employment and food until the harvest of 1855, and furnish those who need it, transportation from this city to their several places of destination. . . . Bishop Hunter will see that all the Bishops alluded to, make the desired reports by the 15th of August, that we may know how much we can assist, and where we can send the coming emigration.[47]

After the arrival of the immigrants, a "placement meeting" was held at which the immigrants and their families were definitely assigned to bishop's wards for their first winter. William Hepworth Dixon, on the occasion of a visit to Salt Lake City, described one of these meetings as follows:

> Last Sunday, after service at the Tabernacle, Brigham Young sent for us to the raised dais on which he and the dignitaries had been seated, to see a private meeting of the bishops, and to hear what kind of work these reverend fathers had met to do. . . . The old men gathered in a ring; and Edward Hunter, their presiding bishop, questioned each and all, as to the work going on in his ward, the building, painting, draining, gardening; also as to what this man needed, and that man needed, in the way of help. An emigrant train had just come in, and the bishops had to put six hundred persons in the way of growing their cabbages and building their homes. One bishop said he could take five bricklayers, another two carpenters, a third a tinman, a fourth seven or eight farm-servants, and so on through the whole bench. In a few minutes I saw that two hundred of these poor emigrants had been placed in the way of earning their daily bread.[48]

Once these families were situated in a ward, it was the bishop's responsibility to see that they were taken care of, and in this respect church leaders constantly stressed the importance of providing employment rather than handouts:

> Bishops, we have a word of counsel to you. You are the fathers of the poor, and stewards in Israel. . . . True charity to a poor family or person consists in placing them in a situation in which they can support themselves. In this country there is no person possessing an ordinary degree of health and strength, but can earn a support for himself and family. But many of our brethren have been raised at some particular trade or employment in the old country, and have not tact and ingenuity to turn their hand to anything, which forms a strong feature in American character. It therefore becomes our duty to teach them how to live. They are generally good citizens of industrious habits, and with a little teaching will soon be able to support themselves. We desire bishops to give them employment which they can perform, and exercise a little patience in instructing them; and it will soon be found that they will no longer prove a burden upon the public funds.[49]

Eventually most of these immigrants found land or labor in one of the many villages in the territory, or, as happened in many cases, they were called, individually or collectively, to colonize a new area or strengthen a growing settlement. A careful record was made of their occupations and an attempt was made to utilize their skill to advantage in the economic life of the region.

THE ORGANIZATION OF PUBLIC WORKS

The transformation of a Welsh coal miner into a seasoned desert colonizer required some intermediate period of adjustment and training. Moreover, the building of the Kingdom required the construction of buildings and the establishment of enterprises which individuals or private sectors of the economy could not be depended upon to provide. Church public works thus served the dual purpose of building the Kingdom and of providing gainful employment to the newly arrived immigrants while they were becoming adjusted to the problems of the frontier.

The first permanent organization for the construction of public works in the Great Basin was established January 26, 1850 when the Office of the Superintendent of Public Works was created. Daniel H. Wells, a leading military and civic figure, was appointed superintendent and served until the office was transferred to the Presiding Bishop in 1870. The office was a church appointment and Superintendent Wells was considered to be one of the "general authorities" of the church. A church architect was also appointed. Under orders from Brigham Young and the Council of Twelve, the architect drew up lists of materials and labor needed in the construction of various works, and the superintendent saw to it that such materials and labor were donated as tithing, purchased on the local market, or imported from the East.[50] Most of the labor was recruited by the superintendent from the various wards in the Salt Lake Valley. The procedure is illustrated by the following announcement, dated September 28, 1850, issued from the Office of the Superintendent of Public Works and published in the *Deseret News* of that date:

> The bishops are requested to come with the brethren of the respective wards, to work on the public works the coming week as follows: Bishop C. Williams of the 3rd; J. Reese of the 4th, and Wm. N. Nickenlooper of the 6th Ward on Monday.—Bishop S. Taft of the 9th and A. F. Farr of the 17th on Tuesday.—Bishop D. Pettigrew of the 10th and J. Lytle of the 11th on Wednesday.—Bishop B. Covey of the 12th on Thursday.—Bishop T. Lewis of the 13th Ward on Friday, and Bishop J. Murdock of the 14th on Saturday.
>
> —D. H. Wells, Superintendent

Although he often paid with nothing but "tithing credit," the superintendent became the largest employer of labor and the most important purchasing agent in the territory. At the peak, he probably employed as many as two thousand workmen and expended up to a quarter of a million dollars a year in cash, labor, and commodities. From 200 to 500 men were employed on the average on these works in the 1850's.

With the establishment of the Public Works Department in 1850, the various mechanics and tradesmen in the Salt Lake Valley were "classified" according to skills and preparations were made for each to render tithing labor in the field of his specialization. Full-time foremen were appointed to supervise the work of carpenters, joiners, masons, and the "tithing hands." Carpenters and joiners were initially paid or credited with $2.00 per day, masons drew $2.50 per day, and blacksmiths were hired at salaries ranging from $2.50 to $3.00.[51] Headquarters for the various types of work were established on the northeast corner of Temple Block. These included a carpenter shop, paint shop, stone-cutting shop, and blacksmith shop. A lime kiln was built at the entrance to one of the canyons near Salt Lake City, and a public adobe yard was located not far away from Temple Square. These shops functioned not only in connection with public works but also did a sizeable private business as well, for which full-time employees were hired. Carpenters, for example, built a number of homes for church officials, missionaries, and others.[52] The stone shop cut millstones for gristmills, and the blacksmith shop, in addition to providing tools and materials for public works projects, shod horses, cast wheels, and fashioned many types of machinery and equipment.

As the public works department became larger, and as its activities became more complex and involved, three additional shops were established which constituted the first light industry in the region. These were the machine shop (1852–1864), the foundry (1854–1864), and the nail factory (1859–1865). The machine shop, which included machinery for wood and metal work, was established in the winter of 1852–1853. The machinery was powered by a large water wheel made possible by running a channel from City Creek down the north side of North Temple Street. This shop was operated partly for the benefit of public works projects and partly as a service to the community and church-at-large. In the former capacity it manufactured, repaired, and sharpened tools of many types, and manufactured wheels, cranks, flanges, locks, and other equipment useful in construction. In the latter capacity the shop made a fire engine, a carding machine, threshing machines, and two large lifeboats for the use of the church president. The cutlery manufactured at the shop, which attained wide popularity among Mormon officials, included Congress knives, swords, saws, currier's tools, and pruning hooks.

The foundry was erected adjoining the blacksmith shop in 1854. In this shop were cast iron, brass, copper and lead materials in many patterns, including such useful items as cog wheels, cranks, mill gearing, water wheels, trip hammers, and anvils.

The expensiveness of nails, due to the length and difficulty of haul by ox-team from St. Louis, hampered Mormon construction activities until the coming of the railroad in 1869. Church leaders continually experimented with construction materials and devices which would economize in the use of nails. Some buildings, as for instance the famous Mormon Tabernacle which still stands, were tied together with rawhide thongs and required few or no nails. The widespread use of rocks and adobe cut down the use of nails as well as of timber. As early as 1850, a mission was dispatched to Iron Mountain, in southern Utah, to develop an iron industry which would make possible homemade nails. While this Mission was struggling to produce home-mined iron, one of its skilled members produced nails from wagon tires and other iron articles which had been transported into the Great Basin. A quantity of these cut nails were sent to Salt Lake City in 1851, and again in 1855, but the quantity which could thus be fashioned was severely limited.[53] When federal troops occupied Utah during the years 1857–1861, iron supplies once more became abundant, causing Brigham Young, as trustee-in-trust of the church, to order machinery for manufacturing nails and screws.[54] The machinery arrived in Salt Lake City with the first Church Train in 1859, and was installed in a factory constructed on Big Canyon Creek. By April 1861, public works employees were turning out nails by the ton.[55] The supply of iron left by the army was exhausted by 1865, however, and the "Old Nail Factory" closed down.

The establishment of the so-called "Temple Block Public Works" in 1850 represented the first employment of a group of skilled mechanics in the construction of permanent buildings and improvements for the use and benefit of the community. It also provided the first organization prepared to provide labor for any person not otherwise engaged. For immigrants, it could provide the start in life — the buffer — which would assure food and clothing, when gainful employment might be unobtainable in the private sector of the economy. It was also a means by which the community would benefit from the skill of immigrant mechanics and artists which might otherwise have been lost or wasted for lack of such a bureau.

Among the earliest construction projects to which public works specialists devoted their time were: the Council House, a $45,000 two-story sandstone structure, completed in 1855, which was used by church, city, county, and territorial officials until its destruction by fire in 1883; the Old Tabernacle, a large adobe meetinghouse built in 1851–1852; a two-story adobe Social Hall, built in 1852; a two-story adobe Endowment House, erected in 1855 for use in performing sacred ordinances; a Bath House and connecting fixtures, completed in 1850 on the site now occupied by the municipally operated Wasatch Springs; a Tithing Store and Storehouse, built in 1850–1852, which contained the offices of the Presiding Bishops and rooms and facilities for the reception and disbursement of tithing; and a store for Livingston and Kinkead, the first mercantile building in the territory. The public works also built in the 1850's an arsenal, a wall around part of the lands allocated to the University of Deseret (now University of Utah), a wall around Temple Block, an official residence for Brigham Young, a church office building, a few private residences for church officials, and schoolhouses in some of the wards.

The public works department also commenced construction of the mammoth Salt Lake Temple in the 1850's. As it was originally contemplated to build the structure of red sandstone from buttes several miles east of Salt Lake City, the public works commenced to build a wooden railway to run from Red Butte Canyon to the Temple Block. The road was graded and most of the timber and rails were secured, but a decision was made in 1855 to build the temple of granite from quarries in the Little Cottonwood Canyon twenty miles southeast of Salt Lake City.[56] Using tithing labor, the public works devoted two years to building a canal from a point near the canyon to the Temple Block. This canal was intended to augment the supply of water for irrigation and for the operation of mills, as well as for boating granite rocks to the temple. The canal proved to be impractical as a means of transportation, however, and was largely abandoned as the wooden railroad had been before it.[57]

Partly to furnish labor during the winter for incoming immigrants, and partly to furnish a "good example" to other communities near the Indians, the public works undertook to build a wall around Salt Lake City in 1853–1854. Twelve feet high, six feet thick on the bottom, and two and a half feet thick on a rounded top, this wall was built of mud, mixed with straw or hay and gravel. Less than half the twenty-mile wall was completed when construction was dropped, but it did serve "to keep the English and Danes at work." An estimated $34,000 was spent on the project.[58]

PROGRAMS OF INDUSTRIAL DEVELOPMENT

In harmony with its immigration and public works program the church began a systematic campaign of industrial development in 1851–1852. Many sermons were delivered on the subject in church meetings; a series of editorials were published in the *Deseret News;* individuals were called to establish various kinds of home industries; "epistles" were directed to European members to bring designs and tools; and the legislature made appropriations and gave other kinds of encouragement to the "home industry" program.[59]

The reasons given for inaugurating the program were both theologic and economic. Theological arguments stressed the revelation to Joseph Smith that the Latter-day Saints should wear only the garments of their own make, and the belief of the Mormons that "Babylon" would become involved in wars, strifes, and contentions, and thus prove to be undependable as a source of supply. Material independence, in short, was divinely ordained. Economic arguments stressed the abundance of skilled artisans in Zion, the necessity of providing employment for the large anticipated immigration, the huge cost of importing items from the East, and the desirability of "keeping money at home." Governor Brigham Young emphasized these arguments in a strongly worded message to the legislative assembly in January 1852, in which he said:

I have no hesitation in saying that our true interest is, and will be most wisely consulted in domestic manufacturing, to the exclusion of almost every article of imported goods. Our clothing, of every description, sugar, candles, soap, leather, crockery, paper, glass, nails, much of the hardware, castings, steel, and many other articles, for which our merchants continually drain the country of money, might be manufactured just as well at home, within our own limits, thereby furnishing lucrative employment to the many artisans of every description, who are constantly flocking hither, and form the basis of a free and independent State, that can in no other way be accomplished. . . . I do therefore most earnestly and sincerely hope, that all needful and necessary encouragement may be given in protective legislation, as well as in appropriations, as shall be conducive to the accomplishment of such desirable results. . . . Produce what you consume; draw from the native element, the necessaries of life; permit no vitiated taste to lead you into the indulgence of expensive luxuries, which can only be obtained by involving yourselves in debt; let home industry produce every article of *home* consumption.[60]

In subsequent sermons and official addresses throughout the year he hammered home the same point with increasing emphasis. Pointing out that almost $300,000 worth of goods had been imported from the States in 1852 since the home industry campaign had begun, he said:

If all the people of the Territory, would dispense with every article of manufactured goods, except such as were manufactured in their own families, until they could be produced by Manufactories established among themselves within the Territory; even if it had to be done at the sacrifice of a few comforts in the first instance, and at the expense of raising a little less grain, or cultivating a few less acres of land, they would in my opinion find their own interest materially advanced, and the circulating medium would soon find its home in the Territory, instead of traveling to Eastern cities, to defray the expense of imported goods.[61]

Of course, this argument would not have had as much effect if the profits of the Gold Rush trade had continued at the usual rate.

In some cases, of course, private enterprise could be relied upon to provide the requisite industry, and a number of letters were dispatched to interested individuals encouraging them to establish branches of manufacture in which they had had experience. But this was not typical. Pottery, paper, and sugar manufactories were established or operated by the church public works department; companies for the manufacture of wool and iron were organized under church and territorial auspices; and "missions" were called to mine coal, iron, and lead. All of these industries were promoted by the church for reasons of self-sufficiency. Tithing resources were used when necessary to initiate them and to insure their continued operation until failure was obvious.

Pottery. Two converts to the church from Staffordshire, England, were encouraged to establish a "Deseret Pottery." Although some yellow earthenware was produced in 1851, the difficulty of obtaining wood for burning the ware led to the absorption of the enterprise into the public works. In January 1852, the proprietors announced:

> We are pleased that the Church has taken hold of this branch of business, and wish that all others were under the finger of the Priesthood, for under that director this Territory would in three years be in a more flourishing condition, than it otherwise would be in five.[62]

Perhaps church authorities felt the pottery plant could use the lumber leftovers from construction projects. Or perhaps it was necessary to support out of tithing resources the men engaged in developing the industry until they were able to support themselves. The Deseret Pottery continued to be unsuccessful, however, and was abandoned in 1853, after some $12,000 in labor and materials had been expended on the enterprise.[63] The eventual establishment of a successful pottery business in 1856 was accomplished without direct church sponsorship.

Paper Mill. The first edition of the *Deseret News,* the official organ of the church and the first newspaper established in the Mountain West, came out June 15, 1850. Because of the prohibitory cost of transporting paper from St. Louis to Salt Lake City, the profitability of this pioneer newspaper, and other frontier publications, depended upon the ability of the church to develop a successful local paper industry. When Thomas Howard, a skilled paper maker from Buckinghamshire, England, joined the church in 1850, emigration officials rushed him to Utah. Upon reaching church headquarters in 1851, Howard was appointed by Brigham Young to supervise the construction of a paper mill as part of the church public works. A machinist was appointed to assist him and the two went to work immediately. By October 1851, a draft of the machinery was prepared and the construction of the mill commenced.

In the meantime, the *Deseret News,* under the direction of church officials, sponsored a campaign to collect rags for Howard's use. Howard and his machinist also solicited the aid of the bishops and others in facilitating the gathering of rags and other materials with which to make paper. These were to be turned into the Tithing Office in Salt Lake City. However, the plant was constructed of makeshift materials and was unsatisfactory. The paper manufactured was coarse in texture and was typically a dull, gray color.

In an attempt to improve the quality of his product, Howard prevailed upon the trustee-in-trust to import a paper machine, which was brought to the valley in 1853 at a cost of $8,500. Howard also obtained permission from

President Young to use for paper making some of the machinery that had been brought to the valley for the manufacture of beet sugar. This water-powered plant was in operation for four years, and represented the first effective paper mill west of the Mississippi.[64] Partly as a consequence of the Utah War, the plant was dismantled in 1857, and the engine and some of the machinery were sent to Cedar City for use in the iron works there.

Later, the trustee-in-trust sent his agent on a mission east to purchase, among other things, a new paper mill. Two paper engines and a 36-inch Gavite cylinder machine, valued at from $20,000 to $25,000, were carried by Church Train to the valley in 1860.[65] The mill remained under the direction of the Public Works Department until 1868, when the management was transferred to the Deseret News Company—also a church concern. The mill continued in operation until 1883 when it was moved to the Granite Paper Mill in Cottonwood Canyon and used as a "spare" until the destruction of that mill by fire in 1893.

The successful production of paper by these mills required a continuous flow of rags to the Tithing Office. Church officials, the *Deseret News,* and the public works department carried on a joint campaign to "get out the rags." Bishops were instructed to sponsor rag drives in their local wards and settlements, and to give credit on the tithing books for the value of the rags contributed. In 1861, after the completion of the new plant, a church stalwart by the name of George Goddard was called on a "Rag Mission." Goddard was asked to "visit every town and settlement" in Salt Lake and adjoining counties, "for the purpose of gathering up whatever might be obtained convertible into printing paper."[66] This mission lasted for three years, during which time Goddard seems to have been supported out of tithing resources. Wrote Goddard:

> [This calling] was a severe blow to my native pride. . . . But after being known in the community for years, as a merchant and auctioneer, and then to be seen on the streets going from door to door with a basket on one arm and an empty sack on the other, enquiring for rags at every house. Oh, what a change in the aspect of affairs. . . . When President Young first made the proposition, the humiliating prospect almost stunned me, but a few moments' reflection reminded me that I came to these valleys of the mountains from my native country, England, for the purpose of doing the will of my Heavenly Father, my time and means must be at His disposal. I therefore answered President Young in the affirmative, and for over three years, from Franklin, Idaho, in the north, and Sanpete in the south, my labors extended, not only visiting many hundreds of houses during the week days, but preaching rag sermons on Sunday. The first time I ever spoke in the Tabernacle, Salt Lake City, . . . was a rag discourse, and Presidents Brigham Young and Heber C. Kimball backed it up with their testimony and enlarged upon it.[67]

At the end of ten months Goddard had collected 20,000 pounds of rags, and by the end of his three-year mission, he had collected more than 100,000 pounds of rags for the paper project.[68] In 1867 the task of rag collection was assigned to the Women's Relief Society.

Sugar. The expense of importing sugar into the territory led to early attention to the production of a local substitute. The need for sugar, which would, of course, become greater as the population grew, was estimated to be 300 tons annually in 1851.[69] Except for the brief respite provided by the Gold Rush trade, sugar sold at upwards of 40 cents per pound, which meant a total drain on the territory, if all needs were supplied from outside the Great Basin, of approximately $240,000 per year.[70] Those without purchasing power, of course, resorted to such devices as boiling parsnips, carrots, beets, watermelons, and even squeezing juice from cornstalks.

Church leaders placed greatest reliance for a successful local product on the sugar beet, which had attained prominence in France during the Napoleonic wars. Some desultory experiments had been made with sugar beets in America, but none of them had attained their object, largely because of the flourishing sugar trade with the West Indies. In March 1850, the Mormon delegate to Congress obtained enough sugar beet seed to plant two acres of ground.[71] This was speeded to the Salt Lake Valley, and a satisfactory crop of both seed and beets was raised. This preliminary success led church officials to announce later in the year that attempts would be made to "relieve the sugar market" by cultivating and refining sugar beets. In his message to the legislature in December of the same year, Brigham Young discussed the need for a sugar beet industry and pointed out that at prevailing freight rates a factory to process the beets could be built for the price of one year's importation of sugar. It would be "suicidal," Young said, for the territory "to be dependent upon other than" its own resources for sugar.[72]

Although some individual efforts were made to set up sugar processing plants, these were too small to solve the problem which must inevitably be faced with large-scale immigration and population growth.[73] Shortly after the delivery of his gubernatorial message, President Young wrote to Apostle John Taylor, who was serving a mission for the church in France and elsewhere, asking him "to get ideas and machinery if necessary to send to 'Deseret' to further and build up her industries."[74] In company with the brilliant young engineer-convert, Phillip De LaMare, Taylor went to Arras, in Pas-De-Calais, France, where the sole sugar beet factory surviving the Napoleonic defeat was still in operation.[75] Their investigations seemed to confirm Brigham Young's hope that sugar beet culture was practicable in Utah. They immediately organized a company, apparently in August 1851, called the Deseret Manufacturing Company, with a capital of £12,000

($58,080).[76] Only £6,645.9.1, worth $32,173.08, was actually paid into the company treasury in cash.[77]

The new company purchased 1,200 pounds of "the best French Beet seed," and ordered £2,500 ($12,100) worth of carefully specified machinery from Faucett, Preston & Co., of Liverpool.[78] French machinery had been made of cast iron, but this was regarded as too heavy for transportation to Utah, and the specifications therefore called for wrought iron. The machinery was designed to produce 300 tons of sugar per season. Other preparations included the searching out of European "brethren" who knew something of the mechanics and chemistry of beet sugar manufacturing.[79]

The fabrication was completed in February 1852, and the machinery was shipped, along with several operatives, from Liverpool on the *Rockaway* on March 6, 1852, arriving in New Orleans after a seven weeks' voyage across the Atlantic. It was at New Orleans that the company experienced its first embarrassment when it was forced to pay a $4,056.10 duty on the machinery.[80] The church absorbed this obligation, making it possible for the company to proceed up the Mississippi River by boat to St. Louis, and thence down the Missouri River to the outfitting point at Fort Leavenworth, Kansas.

Meanwhile, the sugar beet seed, carefully sealed in large tin boxes, had been shipped to the Salt Lake Valley, and a crop was being grown there preparatory to the arrival of the factory.[81] Much of it was planted on the Church Farm, south of the city. De LaMare and Russell had also left early to prepare for the transportation of the machinery across the Plains — De LaMare to purchase the requisite number of ox-teams, and Russell to manufacture the wagons. Both men were untrained in the problems of the frontier and ran into unlooked-for obstacles. Russell's wagons, fifty-two in all, were too light to bear the great weight of the machinery, and had to be given to a number of "poor Saints" accompanying the Sugar Train. The church was forced to buy, at great expense, forty great Santa Fe prairie schooners. De LaMare had $6,000 in gold with which to buy four hundred head of cattle, and he literally scoured the countryside before he found them. Many of them were wild and untamed to the yoke. He also purchased a large amount of flour on credit which proved to be "worthless, filled with worms, and heavily mixed with 'plaster of paris,' and had to be thrown away, and replaced by another purchase on credit."[82] To add to his worries, his eldest child died with cholera.

The expedition carrying the first sugar beet machinery west of the Mississippi left Fort Leavenworth on July 4, 1852, and finally arrived in the Salt Lake Valley on November 10. The journey, in itself, was a major enterprise, with individual tales of heroism, hardship, and instances of near-disaster.[83] It was during the more than four months on the Plains that individuals in the company decided that the large letters D.M.C. on its equipment stood for "Damn Miserable Company." After arrival in Salt Lake City, the company had still to go fifty miles to Provo where, because of the excellent facilities for power, it had been decided to erect the factory. Because of snow and inclement weather, an additional three weeks elapsed before they finally reached their destination.

Before a factory to house the machinery was built in Provo, the company experimented in order to test the technical efficiency of the machinery in separating the sugar from the beets that had been grown in Utah. Although the company had hoped that it could produce 100 tons before the spring of 1853, this became increasingly doubtful.[84] It was clear that there would be no easy solution to the chemical and mechanical problems involved. The company had expended all of its resources and had no other recourse but to fall back on the church, which had already come to its rescue in New Orleans, Fort Leavenworth, and Fort Bridger.[85] As trustee-in-trust, Brigham Young was favorable to a plan to assist the company in seeing the enterprise carried through to success, but felt that the problems could best be solved by the Public Works Department of the church which, alone in the territory, had the equipment and men needed to construct the factory and put it into operation. As the result of Young's counsel therefore, the machinery was returned by tithing hands to Salt Lake City in December 1852, and set up on the northeast corner of the Temple Block.[86] The little "village" which the company had erected in Provo for its employees was disposed of to private interests.[87]

After two months of further trials the experimenters succeeded in producing only a quantity of inedible molasses.[88] With their eastern creditors pressing them for payment, the company arranged with Brigham Young to assume its obligations and take over its properties. The Deseret Manufacturing Company had failed. Beginning in February 1853, therefore, the Sugar Works was a church public works enterprise, and Apostle Orson Hyde was appointed to superintend its operations.[89] In the following April the public works began the erection of a factory on the Church Farm, four miles south of Salt Lake City, in what is now Sugar House. Brigham Young's statement in taking over the enterprise was as follows:

> I for one . . . would have been glad to have had other men engaged in the manufacture of sugar from the beet, and not have troubled us with it at all; but so it is in the all wise providence of God, and he does all things right.[90]

Its history after the assumption of responsibility by the church is one of continuing disappointment. Taylor and company had no plan for the building in which to house the Sugar Works. Nor were the plans of the machinery and equipment in sufficient detail to ascertain how all of it fitted together. It seems doubtful that individual items were numbered and classified. Church Architect, Truman O. Angell, unfamiliar with this type of enterprise, had a Herculean task fitting together the pieces of the giant jigsaw.[91] Some of the "experts" imported by Taylor and De LaMare were of great help, but even they were unable to solve many of the construction problems as they arose. The foundation was not completed until September 1854, and the machinery was not put into working order until February 1855. The three-story adobe factory was 103 feet by 40 feet, with two additional machine houses.

As with all public works projects, the construction was performed by crews of workmen from the various wards in the Salt Lake Valley who adopted this manner of paying their tithing labor. The men were allowed $1.50 per day for this work — or $3.00 per day when they came with teams. Flour, feed, and other supplies were furnished these men out of tithing storehouses. A daily account of all tithing resources devoted to the construction of the factory indicates that approximately $45,000 worth of labor, produce, and supplies, thus modestly valued, went into the Sugar House factory. An additional $5,000 in tithing resources were expended on other than construction aspects of the enterprise.[92]

While the construction was being undertaken, two seasons had gone by in which farmers had been urged to plant beets in the expectation of exchanging them for sugar. The anticipated completion of the factory was used as a talking point to get farmers to continue, possibly against their better judgment, to devote their energies to beet production. The planting, thinning, weeding, and harvesting of beets required a great deal of labor. That farmers continued, year after year, to plant beets only to find the factory unable to process them, is a measure of their faith and obedience. Brigham Young attempted to sustain this faith by such statements as the following:

> There is not the least doubt we can make the Sugar from the Beet; we shall never give it up, nor cease our operations, until we manufacture everything we can eat, drink, or wear, from the native element, and make the earth itself, like the garden of Eden.[93]

Beet seed was distributed by the tithing offices, the *Deseret News* carried editorials and feature articles on the cultivation of the beet, and other devices were resorted to for encouraging farmers to persevere. In 1855, when the factory was completed, about three hundred acres of beets were planted, which would have meant a production of roughly three thousand tons of beets to refine.

But the factory was a failure. Over a seven-week period more than 22,000 bushels of beets were ground into molasses, but the production of sugar was "a complete failure."[94] To add to the difficulties, the sugar beet crop failed in 1855 and 1856 because of drouth and grasshopper destruction of the seed. While the First Presidency sought "the blessing of the Lord, that no failure of the kind will again thwart our wishes, and that we shall soon be able to furnish, from the beet, sugar sufficient for home consumption,"[95] they eventually became convinced that Utah's beets were too alkaline to refine into sugar, or that the enterprise was not worth the effort required to establish it. The factory seems not to have been operated after the fall of 1856. The direct loss to the church and the investors was about $100,000,[96] while the losses of those who had based their private expectations on the success of the enterprise must have amounted to an additional $50,000. The only salvage — the equipment — came to be used for such varied purposes as the manufacture of linseed oil, paper, iron, and wool. The factory building housed, in turn, wool carding machines, a machine shop, and a paper factory.

The reasons for the failure of the Sugar Works appear to have been many. M. Mollenhauer, the "expert sugar maker" imported to superintend the operations, blamed the lack of success on the failure of the company to order "retorts." Retorts were the cast-iron ovens in which bones were burned to make the animal charcoal needed to clarify and purify the beet juice before it could be made into sugar. Retorts were not ordered later, according to Mr. De LaMare, because "The company received such opposition from quarters not expected, it was broken up and disheartened." Architect Angell said the greatest need was "a set of strangers to run said factory."[97]

Whatever the reasons for failure — chemical, mechanical, financial, or administrative — the enterprise demonstrated that beets could be produced in Utah, and that near-success could be obtained in carrying out a major manufacturing enterprise. The venture also demonstrated what Roberts has called "the spirit of daring enterprise" of early church leaders.

In abandoning the goal of a territorial sugar industry based on beets, Brigham Young continued his campaign for self-sufficiency by advocating the culture of sorghum cane. He implemented the spoken word by distributing free seed to farmers. He also directed the organization, by the Deseret Agricultural and Manufacturing Society, of a company of prominent men to raise enough cane to supply the Utah market with sweets.[98] This cane, which was grown throughout the territory, furnished a creditable molasses. Scores of horse- and water-powered molasses roller mills were established by private individuals and by communities throughout the territory to crush the corn and squeeze out the juice. The juice was then boiled down until it became a thick golden syrup. Molasses remained the principal source of sweet in the territory until the successful establishment of the beet sugar factory at Lehi in the 1890's.

Wool. The importation of machinery to manufacture woolen yarn from locally produced wool was encouraged by both church and territory. During the outpouring of enthusiastic planning in the fall of 1849 the First Presidency wrote to the church president in England requesting that he send, "if possible," woolen and cotton machinery, together with a company each of woolen and cotton manufacturers, the following spring.[99] In February 1851, at the request of Brigham Young, the General Assembly of the State of Deseret passed a resolution appropriating $2,000 "to encourage the manufacture of wool in Great Salt Lake County." [100] The resolution also included a pledge by the legislators "to use for ourselves and in our families, only Domestic manufactured clothing as soon as a sufficient quantity of it can be furnished to supply the market." Whether this money was spent — and if so how — is not ascertainable. The territorial legislature approved a similar resolution in 1852.[101] The funds may have been spent by the Perpetual Emigrating Company in Europe, which had received orders from Brigham Young to organize a company of woolen manufacturers, purchase sheep and machinery, and establish a woolen factory in Salt Lake City. The company was organized in Paris by Apostle John Taylor in March 1851, and plans were made for its exportation later that year.[102]

While some of the personnel went to Utah in 1852, some operatives and the machinery appear to have been transported to St. Louis, Missouri, in 1853. It is doubtful that the sheep were included. In February 1853, Brigham Young wrote to the church's agent in St. Louis that the church had acquired the properties of the company and wished it looked after:

> We understand that there is now on the way from the old country considerable amount of property belonging to the company, principally invested in machinery for a woolen factory . . . we do not expect to be able to bring that property across the plains this season. . . . The operators, we are informed, who design to work in the factory, and assist in putting it into operation are with this machinery, and will probably wish to come through this season; if so, and they need assistance to come through, you will assist them with the emigrating funds.[103]

During succeeding seasons, one difficulty or another prevented the transportation of the machinery to the Salt Lake Valley, and it was not until 1862 that a long train of mule teams — part of the Church Teams dispatched under the auspices of the Perpetual Emigrating Fund in that year — finally took the machinery to Salt Lake City.[104] The factory was established on Big Kanyon Creek, near Salt Lake City, and referred to as "Brigham Young's Woolen and Cotton Factory." [105] The factory, with 240 spindles, was assembled and put in motion in 1863, thus providing the first commercial market for wool in the territory. Although Matthew Gaunt and Shadrach Holdaway operated small private mills in Salt Lake City and Provo during the early 1850's, it may also have been the first woolen factory of its size to be operated in the West.

The lack of success in establishing a large-scale territorial wool manufacturing industry was apparently due to the insufficiency of sheep, and the heavy losses due to the severity of winters, wolves, and disease; and also the inability of the population to make wool manufacturing worthwhile, considering the fact that the work could be done in the home.[106] One of the "shepherd boys with Scotch collies" brought to Utah in the P.E.F. woolen company in 1852 later reported that the church sheep had been "devoured by wolves and coyotes," and so he was employed on "Brigham Young's farm" during the remainder of the 1850's.[107]

Iron. It will be recalled that a colony had been planted at Parowan in 1850–1851 to serve as a supply base on the Salt Lake to California route and to initiate an iron industry. This colony was largely made up of farmers and frontiersmen, but it included a number of persons who were experienced in mining coal and working with iron. The first year's efforts were devoted to the construction of roads, bridges, canals, and a fort, and to the planting of crops. In November 1851, after the harvest had been completed, a group of thirty-five men skilled in mining and manufacturing were called to found the "pioneer iron mission" at Cedar City, some twenty miles south of Parowan. Committees of these "iron missionaries" were appointed to lay out a village, erect a fort, dig a canal, plant a cooperative farm, construct a road to the coal deposits, build a road to the timber, and locate materials with which to build a small blast furnace. On September 29, 1852, less than a year after the mission had been founded, the blast was put to the furnace, and "a small quantity of Iron run out, which caused the hearts of all to rejoice."[108] The iron was used in making horseshoe nails and a pair of andirons (called dog-irons).[109]

Meanwhile, Brigham Young and other church officials were taking steps to enlarge the Iron Mission and give it a strong financial and technical base by instructing leading missionaries in Europe to send qualified men and necessary equipment to Utah. In September 1851, while the advance company of Iron County colonists was harvesting their first crop, President Young wrote to leaders of the church in Europe, asking them to search out "brethren who could make different kinds of iron from magnetic iron ore" and send them to the Salt Lake Valley:

> If a company of the brethren could be formed in England, Wales, Sweden, or any other country, to come and make Iron from ore (magnetic ore of the best quality) and machinery for rolling, slitting, and cutting nails, and drawing off wire, it would be one of the greatest auxiliaries for advancement in building up the vallies of the mountains; and the presiding elders in those

countries are instructed to examine this subject, and forward such a company with the least possible delay.[110]

In obedience to the instructions in the Epistle, Franklin D. Richards and Erastus Snow, presidents of the British and Scandinavian missions, discussed the matter in a number of church assemblies in England, and finally held a special European conference of the church in London, at which they presented before the assembled thousands the necessity of helping to establish an iron manufacturing industry in Utah.[111] Richards and Snow obtained from the presiding elders of the various Mormon congregations in Europe the names and addresses of the "wealthier brethren" and spent most of the next month in visiting them. They "laboured" with these brethren and reported finding "a general readiness on their part to receive our counsel, and employ their funds as we thought best for the making of iron in these valleys."[112] They also visited various iron works in England, Wales, Ireland, and Scotland and obtained general information "on the subject of making iron from magnetic and other ores."

On April 28 and 29, 1852, Snow and Richards held a meeting in London with the ironmasters and men of means who expressed an interest in the project. The "Deseret Iron Company" was organized with a capitalization of £1,000,000 ($4,840,000), of which eight shares, valued at £4,000 ($19,360), were subscribed at this initial meeting. The officers included Erastus Snow, president; Franklin D. Richards, secretary; and Thomas Tennant, treasurer. All subscribers were Mormon convert-capitalists. The "articles of compact" shows the mixture of religious sentiment and business procedure which was typical of most Mormon enterprises of the period, and includes the following:

> For as much as we invoke the blessing of our Heavenly Father upon our Capital and Business. Therefore, Resolved that each member of the Deseret Iron Company shall hallow his Stock vested in the company unto the Lord by paying tithes thereon, and that the company regularly tithe their increase ever after.[113]

Snow and Richards, with the assistance of some experienced ironmasters, arranged for the purchase and transportation of various kinds of iron-making machinery, and then hurriedly embarked for the new world. They arrived in the Salt Lake Valley in August, 1852, in time to be present when the Iron County delegation took the first supply of precious molten iron to Brigham Young. Warmly complimented by the First Presidency for their success in organizing a company and securing Old World capital, Snow and Richards were advised to establish works in Iron County as rapidly as possible.[114]

Upon their arrival in Cedar City in November 1852 Snow and Richards suggested that the newly formed Deseret Iron Company buy out the Pioneer Iron Company by exchanging its stock for the investment of the latter.[115] This was done, and President Snow reported the results of the visit of himself and Franklin D. Richards as follows:

> Considerable excitement prevailed through the County on the subject of Iron at the time of our arrival [in November 1852], much heightened by the arrival of those whom we had recently sent there who had been operators in the Iron business in Wales and in Pennsylvania, and we found a Scotch party, a Welch party, an English party, and an American party, and we turned Iron Masters and undertook to put all these parties through the furnace, and run out a party of Saints for building up the Kingdom of God.[116]

The consolidated Deseret Iron Company, with a paid-up capital of nearly $40,000, now made plans to employ regularly half of the seventy men in the colony. As one of them wrote: "All that is wanted is Mormon Capital: Bone and Sinew."[117] When one of the workers, in examining the Pioneer blast furnace, discovered a four hundred pound lump of "superior quality pure malleable iron," the stockholders (which now included all workers) and church leaders found it difficult to suppress their excitement and enthusiasm, despite the onset of a severe winter which made it impossible to use the water in Coal Creek or use the road to the coal mines. The territorial legislature caught the contagion of this enthusiasm, and not only approved the incorporation of the Deseret Iron Company with substantially the same charter as that drawn up in London, but also appropriated $5,000 "to advance the Iron interests in Iron County."[118]

The bulk of the territorial appropriations was expended in the spring of 1853 on explorations for a superior vein of coal and the construction of a suitable wagon road to it. A long vein, seven feet thick, was located on the precipitous side of a mountain about seven miles east of Cedar City, a quantity of coal was dug, and the road completed at the reasonable cost of $6,000. For a time, this mine produced coal at the rate of 100 tons per week.[119] The company also employed a Mr. J. James of the Victoria Iron Works, Wales, to construct a small air furnace in which to try the experiment of fluxing the richer ores without the blast. This furnace, completed in the summer of 1853, was built of adobe and rock and had a funnel 300 feet long through which smoke was conveyed to a chimney stack forty feet high. A casting house was also completed. An average of about seventy men worked more or less regularly on company assignments.[120]

Despite the enthusiastic and hopeful labor of the missionaries, however, a number of circumstances delayed the work. When active preparations were on foot for putting the blast to the furnace near the end of July, news reached the southern settlements that an Indian war had commenced. The iron work was suspended and the colonists were instructed to devote their now-famous "persevering industry" to the erection of extensive fortifications and securing grain, hay, and wood for the winter.[121] On September 3, the community was visited again by "a terrible flood" which "swept down Coal Creek, carrying before it all bridges and dams, completely inundating the site of the works, and sweeping off much of the Company's property."[122] Twenty and thirty ton boulders were deposited with the debris. The remainder of the year was required to rebuild the dam and repair the breaches. The year 1853 passed without tangible result, though the company had expended more than $18,000 in "cash," of which $10,000 was expended in Utah for labor, food, and equipment, and $8,000 in England on machinery and transportation.[123]

The First Presidency of the church, however, continued to support the colony and took measures to nurse it along. They called Isaac C. Haight, recently returned from a mission to England, to go to Cedar City and "take charge of the iron works."[124] They also denied the petition of a number of the colonists asking for release from the Iron County mission:

> If you were now on a mission to France or England or any other part of the earth, you would not sit down and counsel together about going to get your families, or about going home till your mission was ended. This is of quite as much importance as preaching the Gospel. The time is now come when it is required of us to make the wilderness blossom as the rose. Our mission is now to build up stakes of Zion and fill these mountains with cities, and when your mission is ended you are at liberty to go.[125]

During the spring of 1854, after the completion of the fort, coal was hauled on sleds and the furnace was again put into operation. Some iron was made, but repeated experimentation had impaired the workability of the furnace, and it was necessary to construct a new one. This task occupied the attention of the iron company during most of the year. The red sandstone furnace, built under the direction of Elias Morris, foremost Mormon carpenter and building contractor, was twenty-one feet square and thirty feet high, and required 650 tons of rock. Estimated to cost $4,000 in labor and materials, the new furnace had a capacity of ten tons per day. The blast was made by a new large blowing apparatus powered by a waterwheel. Six coke ovens were also built, in order to supply the furnace with good coke.[126]

Recognizing the many unexpected obstacles the company had to contend with, Utah's territorial and church leaders were not yet discouraged. After all, they reasoned, the experience gained in the first two years augured well for future success.[127] Responding to the suggestion of Brigham Young, the legislature advanced the company another $4,840 on January 19, 1855, by authorizing the governor to purchase on behalf of the territory two shares of stock.[128] As trustee-in-trust of the church Brigham Young advanced another $4,840 by subscribing for two shares. Both subscriptions were probably paid "in kind," that is, in the form of food, clothing, materials and supplies, livestock, and labor.[129]

In anticipation of Brigham Young's visit to Cedar City in the spring of 1855, every effort was made to institute a successful run. In order to keep the furnace burning a large quantity of sage brush was pulled and piled before the flue. On the first twenty-four hour run, 1,700 pounds of "good iron" were produced. By constant effort, another ten tons were manufactured in April. It was from some of the iron made in this run that the company made the only casting which survives — a bell cast by the public works department in 1855, whose ringing called the colonists to church.[130]

Having solved, as they thought, the technical problem of producing iron, the next step was to acquire more workers. A call was made in May 1855 for 150 wagoners, miners, colliers, lime burners, lumbermen, quarrymen, brick and stone masons, carpenters, machinists, charcoal burners, and furnace men, besides fifty teams to haul fuel and ore.[131] Virtually all of these responded. By the fall of 1855, the iron works were reported to be "progressing first-rate," with a "hot blast, which operates complete," and "several tons of castings of various descriptions," and with other "good iron" manufactured in November. The uncertainty of the waterpower, however, hampered operations during the winter of 1855–1856 when the stream was frozen for three months. Coal was also inaccessible during the same period.[132]

An attempt was made to overcome this dependence on waterpower by the installation of two thirty-horsepower steam engines. At least one of these engines seems to have been supplied by the church.[133] While this gave a more dependable source of power, the problem of obtaining suitable coking coal remained. Coke made from the Cedar City coal was very weak and friable; in addition to this weakness, it is said to have carried about five per cent sulphur.[134] Brigham Young thought for a while to solve this difficulty by moving the iron smelting operations to Wales in Sanpete County, where a large bed of coal, ideal for foundry work, had been located. The iron ore was to have been taken to Wales by team from Iron Mountain.[135] This project was never carried out.

Other accidental factors hampered operations in 1856. When the furnace was started up in June, for example, the hot blast pipes accidentally burned out, chilled the furnace, and they had to "blow out" without producing any iron. Everything was in order by the first week of August, and the furnace started up once more, but an untimely drouth caused a failure in the water supply and they had to "blow out" once more. Finally, the grasshopper plague of 1856, which devastated virtually the entire territory, forced the iron colonists to devote most of their efforts to securing enough food to keep their families from starving.[136]

Other difficulties operated in 1857. The danger of floods forced them to move the scene of their operations to higher ground. A new site was laid out, complete with lots for homes, public buildings, and iron works. This relocation occupied the colonists several weeks. When they were ready to resume manufacturing operations, they received word from Brigham Young "to suspend all business and take care of the grain as the United States were sending troops into the Territory to oppress the Saints, and force officers upon us contrary to our wishes and the constitution."[137] Convinced that the "Utah Expedition" was seeking to repeat the kind of "persecution" to which the Mormons had long been subject, the iron missionaries, along with other Mormons, immediately began a series of military drills and exercises.

Almost a year was devoted to various kinds of service connected with the Utah War. When that question was settled, in 1858, the company built a new furnace, but "for the want of fuel and the lining giving way" they had to blow out.[138] Two more unsuccessful trial runs were made in September and October 1858, after which the experiment was finally given up and the works were officially closed.[139] Almost ten years of labor, and the direct expenditure of approximately $150,000, had resulted in nothing more than a few andirons, kitchen utensils, flat irons, wagon wheels, molasses rolls, and machine castings. Small, volunteer, cooperative industry was simply unable to cope with the problems associated with developing a major resource.

Lead. In June 1855, a group of thirty men was called by the church to go to Las Vegas Springs, in what is now southern Nevada, to serve as "Indian missionaries." During one of their exploring expeditions outcroppings of lead were discovered at Cottonwood Springs, near the Colorado River, thirty miles southwest of Las Vegas. Some specimens of this ore were taken to Brigham Young during the winter of 1855–1856. He was sufficiently interested to call Nathaniel V. Jones, in February 1856, with a group of thirty others, to go to Las Vegas to search for ore and "go into the lead business."[140] Jones left in April 1856 with a letter from Brigham Young asking bishops and branch presidents to give him every assistance on this mission:[141]

> Beloved Brethren: — You are hereby authorized and required to use all reasonable exertions to furnish the bearer, Bishop Nathaniel V. Jones, with such men, animals, tools, etc., as he may call upon you for, to enable him to safely, diligently, and successfully accomplish the purpose of the mission upon which he is now sent, viz: to search for and examine into the location, quality and quantity of different ores and metals, as specimens of rich lead ore have already been brought to me from that region, and it is highly desirable that we be able to make our lead, copper, etc., at the earliest practicable date.
>
> Your brother in the gospel,
> Brigham Young

According to Jones' statement the settlers in the southern towns "responded promptly and cheerfully" to his requests. The Cedar City Iron Mission furnished provisions and means of transportation, and the Cedar City bishop accompanied Jones to Las Vegas.

After two months of intensive exploration, Jones' party returned to Salt Lake City and reported the prospect to be "exceedingly flattering," although the nearest running water was twelve miles away, and there was an almost complete lack of grass to feed the animals. Immediately, preparations were made to send a company to work the mine.[142] On July 9, 1856, Jones left with three companions, two four-mule teams, and necessary tools and supplies. The company carried a letter instructing bishops of the southern settlements to respond to Jones' calls for men and other assistance in prosecuting the work.[143]

Supplied with food, feed, and equipment by the Indian missionaries, and also by tithing houses in Utah, the lead missionaries first constructed a road to the top of the high mountain where the lead was situated. While some of them were locating materials for a furnace as far as seven miles away and painstakingly hauling the materials to the mine, others were hauling several tons of lead ore to Cedar City, Provo, and Salt Lake City. When the furnace was finally put to the blast in September, they found to their disappointment that the local materials would not withstand the fire.[144] Rather than waste time experimenting with local materials with possible risk of failure, Jones left most of his co-workers in Las Vegas and returned to Salt Lake City — more than five hundred miles distant — to secure the construction of a bellows, blast furnace, and hearth by the church public works employees. Jones and others returned from Salt Lake in December 1856, loaded with the necessary supplies and equipment. They began smelting on Christmas Day, and within two weeks, about 9,000 pounds of lead were produced, most of which was taken to Salt Lake City with teams previously dispatched by Brigham Young. Most of this lead was made into bullets by the church public works.[145]

Despite this seeming success, Jones and company decided to abandon the mine as unprofitable late in January 1857. The ore was yielding only twenty to thirty per cent lead; there were many impurities which caused much of the lead to burn up during the smelting, and washing was impractical since the nearest stream was twelve difficult miles away; provisions and forage for the animals had to be hauled 230 miles over a difficult road; and the Indians were giving trouble. The group returned to Salt Lake City in March 1857, after a mineral survey along the way. The property was abandoned, with only sixty tons of ore having been mined.[146]

As with the Iron Mission, which failed on a mountain of 200,000,000 tons of fifty-two per cent iron ore, the Las Vegas Lead Mission failed on a rich silver-bearing galena. Very near the mine from which Jones and company obtained lead the fabulous Potosí silver mines were "discovered" by non-Mormons in 1861.[147]

CHARACTER OF MORMON ENTERPRISE

It should be noted that the enterprises planned by the Mormons in the 1850's were financed by contributions from the legislature, the church, and private individuals, and thus were "mixed" enterprises, typical of many chartered corporations in ante bellum America. Representing an attempt to utilize the skill of European converts, the goal of every enterprise was that of building the Kingdom and achieving economic independence. The boldness of the church's design in attempting to provide the economic foundations for a commonwealth is clearly evident. That in each case the church eventually assumed responsibility and control was due partly to the lack of private capital, and partly to the belief that all institutions in Mormondom ought to be under the influence of the Priesthood. While this assured a concentration of efforts in building the Kingdom, it also involved the danger of tying the hands of the "experts" who were engaged in the active management of these enterprises. Brigham Young and his appointed lay leaders were outstanding colonizers, and there can be no doubt that they were dedicated to the Kingdom, but the more the specialists depended on them for leadership, the more the specialized industries were apt to suffer from inexpert direction. Brigham Young himself admitted, in 1855, that he had just learned why the iron company had to build a new furnace every time a "blow out" occurred. Up to that time, he had thought that the iron workers were merely "dilatory." [148] Even after the iron enterprise was abandoned, he attributed the failure, not to the lack of suitable coal, not to the lack of capital, not to the lack of technical prowess, but to the spirit of self-seeking among the iron missionaries.[149] It is quite possible that the sugar, iron, and lead enterprises, and perhaps others, would have been more successful if knowledgeable private interests had been allowed a freer hand in the day-to-day direction, and a stronger voice in the making of basic decisions.

Whatever the efficacy of the Mormon way of doing business, there can be no question that the Mormon concept of enterprise was a product of — or in harmony with — early American thought. The Handlins characterized the relationship of government to economic growth in ante-bellum Massachusetts, as follows: "All looked to the Commonwealth, the guardian of the common interest, to breathe life into the productive system. From the growth of the economy would the state's own stature grow, and, growing, suffuse the entire community with well-being." [150] By substituting "church" for "Commonwealth," and "Kingdom" for "state," the characterization applies equally well to Mormon Deseret. The Mormons emphatically believed that the responsibility for the successful establishment and operation of the Kingdom rested with the church. In a philosophical, if not in a practical sense, the firm — the enterprise — was a creation of the church. As with most governments, the church was content to delegate a large share of its responsibility for the organization and management of resources to private interests. But enterprises were never "private" in a functioning sense — they were instruments of the church with limited jurisdiction over a portion of the economic activity of the Kingdom. The church initiated projects, suggested the organization of companies, supplied tithing labor and produce, and assigned to each a role to play in building the Kingdom.

As with property owners, therefore, businessmen possessed no inviolable rights in the Mormon commonwealth. The consideration of who "owned" enterprises, or who had "invested" in them, was secondary. As Brigham Young vividly expressed it:

> In reality, we should have only one mess chest, one place of deposit, one store-house, one "pile," and that is the kingdom of God upon the earth; it is the only store-house there is for Saints, it is the only "pile," the only safe place of deposit, the only place to invest our capital. This is rational to me; and all who contend for an individual interest, a personal "pile," independent of the kingdom of God, will be destroyed. . . . The gold, the silver, the wheat, the fine flour, buffalo, the deer, and the cattle on a thousand hills, are all His, and He turns them whithersoever He will.[151]

The Mormon idea of a businessman, in short, was not a capitalistic profit-calculator, but an appointed overseer of a part of the Kingdom.

It was this concept of collective entrepreneurship and administration which saved the Great Basin Kingdom from the oblivion which seemed inevitable when so many of its major projects fell through. But it was also this unity and cooperation of church and business which ran counter to the individualistic and laissez-faire tendencies of the nation during the post-Civil War period, and which thus created the basis for the conflict with other business and political interests which led to the eventual undoing of Mormon economic separatism.

CHAPTER V

Ways and Means

The extensive Mormon program of economic development obviously required fiscal activities of considerable magnitude. Church fiscal arrangements were particularly important in the 1850's because of the heavy investment in immigration, colonization, public works, and industry, and because repeated agricultural and industrial failures made capital formation progressively more difficult. Thus, despite the planning and the intimate direction of activities, the church's program of development in the 1850's did not contribute substantially toward contemporary prosperity or future greatness. The pottery, paper, sugar, wool, iron, and lead enterprises all failed or marked time, with consequent waste of human and capital resources; and agricultural production was never quite sufficient to support the new enterprises which were initiated. Natural disasters, such as grasshopper invasions, hard winters, and late-season drouths, as detailed later, were important causes of agricultural failure, as were Indian depredations and preparations for defense. But a further cause usually has been overlooked; namely, that in emphasizing industrialization the Mormons gave inadequate attention to agricultural improvement. It seems likely that the labor and capital expended on the development projects of the 1850's could have been used to better advantage in the construction of additional irrigation works, barns, corrals, and the purchase of farm equipment. Or, to put it in another way, the development projects required tremendous investment in industrial machinery, equipment, supplies, and transportation, which absorbed most of the exchange potential of the Mormons without adding anything to it, thus creating an unfavorable balance of trade which grew ever greater as the Gold Rush traffic declined. If there had been no iron, sugar, and similarly ill-fated programs, the States-wide exchange acquired by the Mormons could have been used to import blooded livestock, agricultural machinery, nails, and tools.

But, of course, Mormon leaders did not know their development programs would fail. What they wanted was to make their own machinery and equipment. In seeking to strengthen capital formation in the Great

Basin, the Mormons suffered, as many communities and nations have suffered, from preoccupation with the big project, the spectacular project, to the neglect of the hundreds of small, uneventful, atomistic ventures which had far greater prospect (it would seem) of coming off successfully.

Nevertheless, the fiscal institutions of the Mormons were well-designed to induce saving and produce a social surplus for investment. They might have become even more important if the movement to restore the law of consecration and stewardship in the middle 'fifties had been successful. They were also designed to cope with such emergencies as those produced by the agricultural disasters of 1855–1856. Finally, as calamity followed upon calamity, Mormon policy was modified in accordance with the deteriorating fiscal situation produced by a decade of failures, and the handcart companies and Brigham Young Express and Carrying Company were the issue. The constant adjustment of Mormon strategy and tactics to the caprice of nature and to the exigencies of a barter economy is a major theme of the middle 'fifties, as indeed it was a major theme throughout the nineteenth century.

Before discussing the course of Mormon financial policy in the 1850's, however, a word should be said about the means and ends of church fiscal administration. Mormon officials were well aware of the fact that the ambitious immigration program, the large volume of imports required in carrying out the church's development program, and the impossibility of achieving a substantial volume of exports, were involving the Great Basin economy in a chronic shortage of cash. Given the religious goals of the church, the solution to this balance-of-payments difficulty lay in: (1) obtaining "free" imports by encouraging immigrants to bring with them many articles in excess of personal need; (2) cutting down on the need for commercial imports by encouraging local industry; (3) taking maximum advantage of the opportunities for "invisible" exports; and (4) perfecting organizational devices for creating and capturing the social surplus and converting it into means suitable for local investment and outside expenditure.

Since economic progress depended on the magnitude of well-invested savings, and since these savings in a cashless economy had to take the form of devoting commodities and labor to the expansion of facilities which would magnify the productive power of labor and the land, the handling of the social surplus was of crucial importance. Thus, if an investment in manufacturing was called for, the church must provide the machinery by which the people could contribute the materials and labor needed in erecting, equipping, and operating a factory. In contrast with the monetary arrangements which surround the investment process in Western countries today, the Mormons saved and invested by clearing land, digging canals, constructing roads, building schoolhouses, and inaugurating semipublic industrial enterprises.

THE ORGANIZATION OF TITHING

The pivotal organization in early Utah for requisitioning and handling surpluses, and financing economic growth by cooperative saving and investment "in kind" was the tithing office. Tithing collections were made in the Salt Lake Valley as early as November 1848, but the elaborate network of tithing houses, and the establishment of a General Tithing Office in Salt Lake City, were products of the 1850's.

In each ward and settlement a tithing house or bishop's storehouse was erected, with a lot on which were constructed granaries, barns, corrals, lumber yards, and other facilities for handling and storing tithing. These facilities were in the charge of the local bishop or presiding elder. A district tithing office and storehouse, under the management of a regional presiding bishop, was similarly established in each valley, with a full-time clerk or manager. A central tithing office and storehouse, occupying half a block, and variously known as the General Tithing Office and Bishop's General Storehouse, was set up in Salt Lake City in 1850 to serve the entire church. This was under the direction of the Presiding Bishop of the church. Throughout the territory were also located, at strategic points, church farms on which herds of tithing horses, cattle, sheep, and their offspring could graze and be quartered.

The administration of this extensive system of church finance was in the hands of the trustee-in-trust. Brigham Young was appointed trustee-in-trust by a general conference vote in 1848, and his legal position in the territory was established by legislative action in 1851. In the charter by which the Church of Jesus Christ of Latter-day Saints was incorporated, the power of the church to acquire and hold real and personal property was limited only by "the principles of righteousness or the rules of justice."[1] Stipulation was made that such property "shall be used, managed, or disposed of for the benefit, improvement, erection of houses for public worship and instruction, and the well being of said church." The corporation was authorized "at a general or special conference," to elect one "trustee-in-trust, and not to exceed twelve assistant trustees, to receive, hold, buy, sell, manage, use and control the real and personal property of said church." With the exception of two brief periods (1873–1875 and 1887–1897) the trustee-in-trust was invariably the president of the church.[2] All the church property, real and personal, in all Mormon settlements from the time of its incorporation until 1862 was held in the name of the trustee-in-trust. After 1862 much of the church property was held in private trusts, usually by the trustee-in-trust in a private capacity.[3]

The funds and properties at the disposal of the trustee-in-trust consisted of tithing donations, donations for the Perpetual Emigrating Fund and other special purposes, and income from the administration of church properties. Approximately three-fourths of these receipts — and probably the greatest single source of saving in the economy — was in the form of tithing donations. Tithing, it will be recalled, was based upon the belief of the typical Latter-day Saint that he should contribute to the church one-tenth of all his property at the time of his conversion, and thereafter, one-tenth of all his "increase"; that is, one-tenth of the production of his land, one-tenth of the production and time of his livestock, and one-tenth of his own time and wages.[4] In general, it could be said that many faithful church members paid one-tenth of their gross income rather than one-tenth of their net. Basically, five types of tithing were involved:

1. *Property tithing* consisted of the ten per cent capital levy on property owned by the individual at the time he began to pay tithing. This tithing was usually paid in the form of cash or livestock. Because of the lack of a satisfactory tithing system in Winter Quarters and in the first four years in the Salt Lake Valley, and because of the need for additional revenue to finance the church's public works and other development programs, a special resolution was adopted by the September 1851 general conference requiring each member to pay a tenth of the value of all the assessed property in his possession at that time, whether or not he had previously paid a faithful tithe.[5]

2. *Labor tithing* consisted of donations of every tenth day toward various church projects such as the construction of forts, meetinghouses, irrigation canals, roads, and other public enterprises. The bishop was in charge of these projects when they were local in character. When they assumed regional or church-wide importance, the trustee-in-trust, or the superintendent of public works, assumed direction. Several hundred men with teams were regularly employed in this manner in the Salt Lake Valley, and proportionately fewer in the smaller settlements. In some cases the men were expected to furnish their own board and feed their own teams; in other cases provisions were furnished out of the tithing office. The former arrangement, of course, was preferred by the church. Said Brigham Young:

> We do not want men to come here and say, "Here is a horse," or "I will turn out an ox," or "Brother Wells, I will send a team, if you will support it and hire a man to drive it." We do not want any such proffered blessings, but we want them proffered upon the principle that you hire your own board and bring it with you; and bring your horse-feed and maintain yourselves, just as you do at home about your own work, and come and do the labour necessary to be done. We do not wish any man to say, "Here I am; I want you to board me, and I want some horse-feed, stable room, reins, whippletree and everything else." We want men to stay at home, unless they come to do the clean work and provide for themselves and animals.[6]

Very often, the more well-to-do members paid their labor tithing by hiring others to work on their behalf. Brigham Young, for example, is said to have paid his labor tithing by hiring two men, each with a mule team, and "two good common laborers," to work on the Salt Lake Temple. He fed, clothed, and paid the men, fed the teams, and kept the wagons in repair. On occasion, he also kept two or three teams with drivers traveling to and from the country settlements to gather and bring in butter, cheese, eggs, and vegetables to feed church public works employees.[7] Some artisans (for example, shoemakers) were encouraged to render their tithing in their own merchandise, which, in turn, was used to support the hands on the public works. "We would not wish our tradesmen," Superintendent Wells said, "to leave their shops to work out their labor tithing in common labor with the shovel, the pick, &c. . . . We want them to pay their tithing in the kind of labor they are constantly employed at, and the products of this we can place to an excellent use."[8]

3. *Produce and stock tithing* was a tenth of the yield of household, farm, ranch, factory, or mine. Usually, the church preferred that members follow the custom of paying the tenth as it was produced, in the form in which it was produced. Bishops were urged to keep close watch on the yields of their ward members to be certain that the church was not cheated:

> And we recommend to the bishops throughout these vallies, to keep their ears open, and when they hear their neighbor's pigs squeal, just step over and see how many have died, and what they weigh, and what proportion arrives at the tithing office; for many tons of pork went out of sight last year, and the bishops made no record of it, and many more will this year, if the bishops don't attend to their duty, and the Lord will require the cost at the bishop's hands.[9]

Of course, this was not strictly enforced, and considerable leeway was allowed individuals in the form in which they paid their tenth. The majority allowed their tithing to run into arrears, and then paid it up in a lump in some staple article, such as wheat or a calf, that could be conveniently spared. A tithing shipment from Sanpete Valley in 1857, for example, consisted of 848 bushels of wheat, 1,196 bushels of oats, 21 bushels of barley, 1,970 bushels of flour, and 1,562 pounds of lead.[10]

Livestock tithing and/or stock in the church herds was the usual medium of satisfying church obligations to merchants. Thus, 300 head of cattle were paid to Livingston & Kinkead in 1857 in satisfaction of a $12,000 debt.[11] Occasionally, cattle and horses were driven to California and converted into gold for expenditure in the East. Particularly large stock drives were those of the summers of 1852, 1853, and 1857, all of which were intended to provide cash for the purchase of materials for church public works. Public announcement was made of these drives in church gatherings, and individuals throughout the territory were invited to contribute animals to the drive, either on their own or on church account. The 1853 drive is said to have consisted of some 2,300 work steers, which were trailed to California and sold for $100 to $125 each. This would have grossed from $200,000 to $300,000.[12] The 1857 drive consisted of about 625 head of cattle and several wagon-loads of flour, and probably grossed between $75,000 and $100,000.[13] Cattle and horses appear to have been Utah's only significant visible export in the 1850's.

Produce tithing, such as dairy and poultry products, was usually used to support laborers on church public works. For example, an announcement was made in the *Deseret News,* on July 24, 1852, that a total of 5,046 pounds of butter, 2,254 pounds of cheese, and 1,151 dozen eggs had been received during the preceding fifteen weeks at the General Tithing Office in Salt Lake City. All of this had been given to the families of 320 laborers. The amount of butter tithing would have been greater, it was said, but the merchants had been paying higher prices for butter than those allowed at the tithing office, and thus the Saints had sold their butter to the merchants and paid their tithing in other forms, "forcing the public hands to eat dry bread." [14] This system of collecting butter and other produce for the purpose of building public works caused widespread comment in areas blessed with better circulating media. Even in Hong Kong, an English newspaper commented on the "curiosity" of building temples with butter.[15]

A few weeks after the above announcement the Superintendent of Church Public Works published an appeal urging the brethren to "bring in Leather, Cloth, Hats, and Shoes, to clothe the men, and Glass, Nails, Paints, Oils, Lumber, Timber, Shingles, Iron, Steel, Tools for workmen, Meat, Butter, Cheese, Groceries, and vegetables, for them to eat, and every other article necessary for the support of the men and the prosecution of the works. . . ." [16] Similarly, in August 1854, the First Presidency issued a call to the Saints to bring in grain tithing "that the hands laboring on those Public Works . . . may not go hungry to work, as they have often had to do." [17] By 1857, 14,000 pounds of flour were being dealt out weekly by the public works offices to part- and full-time employees.[18]

4. *Cash tithing* included donations of U. S. coin and currency; local coin, currency, and scrip; and gold dust. It represented a minor part of total tithing revenue, but was particularly sought after by the church. Cash receipts of tithing houses were almost invariably forwarded to Salt Lake for expenditure by the trustee-in-trust in the East or on the Coast. Summarizing his experiences in trying to get cash to "financier" for the church in the 1850's, the president said:

At times it seems as though all hell and earth are combined to keep money out of my hands. A great many people would give me millions if they had it; but most of those who have it will not part with it. . . . Scarcely a man comes into this church, having much of an amount of money, but what spends his money before he gathers with the Saints. . . . If you think that you can keep the money from me, you will be mistaken, for I shall have what is necessary to carry on this work; and those who take a course to hedge up my way in business transactions, pertaining to carrying on this work [that is, the work of the church], will go to the Devil. . . . I do not curse people, but I bless that class with a plenty of devils.[19]

Brigham Young's stress on cash tithing led him to assert that he considered it an obligation upon members to contribute to the church one-tenth of their cash receipts, regardless of their position vis-à-vis natural increase. In 1860, for example, he stated that throughout the 1850's some $5,000,000 had been spent by Mormons on goods imported into Utah Territory. If the Saints had done right, he said, they would have paid $500,000 of that to the tithing office.[20]

5. *Institutional tithing* was a levy on the profits of stores, shops, and factories, and was thus a kind of forerunner of the modern corporate profits tax. These revenues did not bulk large in church revenues until the 1870's and '80's when most cooperative establishments tithed their net incomes.

Tithes were not compulsory, but they were strongly emphasized.[21] A person must pay a full tenth, or he was not considered to be a tithepayer. A study of tithing in one valley disclosed that more than ninety per cent of the potential tithepayers paid a full tithe—or at least satisfied the bishop that they had done so. This does not include a considerable number of people who were officially "excused" from paying tithes on the ground of poverty. In the first few years, when most contributions were in the form of labor, tithing receipts averaged $48 per person per year. In the later 1850's and 1860's, when the receipts consisted largely of highly priced farm products, tithing averaged about the same. After the Panic of 1873, when farm prices went into a secular decline, tithing dropped to an average of $20 to $30 per person per year.[22] The tithing records of Cache Valley, in northern Utah-southern Idaho, show that an average of 2,500 tithepayers donated a total of $2,613,081 during the period 1863–1900, for an average of $29.58 tithing per tithepayer per year. These contributions were classified as follows: Property and miscellaneous, $708,504; labor, $403,409; wheat and other grains, $832,409; livestock, dairy, and poultry products, $333,594; and cash, $335,165. The property tithing, of course, was usually contributed in livestock or cash. Institutional totals were not separately reported. The gradual advance of the monetary economy is symbolized in the rise in cash tithing from approximately one per cent of all tithing in the 1860's to more than thirty per cent of all tithing in the 1890's. Labor tithing, on the other hand, represented a very large proportion of all tithing in the 1860's and declined rapidly toward the end of the century.[23]

Although each person was expected to pay his tithing regularly throughout the year as the increase came, the crucial accounting occurred on December 31 of each year in a transaction known as "tithing settlement." On that date, each tithepayer was asked to report to the bishop and the tithing clerk for an examination of his credits and debits. If his net credits did not amount to a full ten per cent of his annual increase for the year, he would then indicate the manner in which he would make up the deficit. If his net credit was more than his yearly tithing obligation, he would receive a credit for "overpayment," and pay correspondingly less the next year. The tithing settlement procedure is illustrated by notations made on December 31, 1854 in the account of Ira Allen:[24]

Tithing he should pay		*Tithing he did pay*	
Oats	$ 3.00	Oats	$ 1.25
Potatoes	10.25	Potatoes	10.50
Vegetables	1.65	Vegetables	1.05
Chickens	.25	Chickens	.25
Pork	7.65	Pork	7.62
Wheat	28.00	Wheat	28.00
Labor	48.00	Labor	29.00
Corn	2.09	Butter	1.00
		Hay	9.60
Total	$100.89	Wolf skin	5.25
		Cash	1.00
		Credit (evidently for overpayment of previous year)	25.85
			$122.37 [$120.37]

No similar composite table for the entire territory for any year in the 1850's appears to be available. But the nature of tithing receipts is well illustrated by the table on the next page summarizing receipts for a year in the 1860's.[25]

Since the report gives only the tithing receipts of the General Tithing Office, and since not all receipts of local tithing offices were forwarded to Salt Lake City, it is quite possible that total tithing receipts of the church in the year indicated were well in excess of the $143,000 figure given here — possibly exceeding $275,000. Receipts other than tithing may have pushed total church revenues over the $300,000 mark in that year. Whatever the total in 1868, it is certain that church receipts were considerably less in the 1850's. The only published report of receipts in the 1850's covers the period November 1848 to March 1852. During that three and one-half year period, tithing receipts were given as $244,747, and total receipts of all kinds as

TITHING RECEIPTS OF THE GENERAL TITHING OFFICE, SALT LAKE CITY, 1868

Cash	$25,114.12
Due bills and orders on retail stores	21,000.00
Merchandise and home manufactures	11,690.26
Labor	2,758.40
Wheat (10,092 bushels at $2.00)	20,183.80
Flour (15,562 pounds at $6.00 cwt.)	933.74
Oats (759 bushels at $1.00)	758.88
Barley (543 bushels at $1.50)	814.40
Rye	80.84
Corn (1544 bushels at $1.50)	2,316.71
Hay (83 tons at $15.00)	1,242.01
Fodder	175.00
Livestock	19,892.93
Increase in value of livestock (est.)	$5,000.00
Meat	5,859.37
Dairy products	6,953.34
Molasses (3072 gallons at $2.00)	6,143.78
Potatoes and other vegetables	7,334.61
Fruit	4,022.87
Wood	319.60
Coal	53.20
Building material	455.01
Store utensils	269.90
Total tithing receipts of all kinds	$143,372.77

$390,261.[26] It was specifically stated that during this period little had been received in the form of cash.

The point which can hardly be overemphasized is that in the 1850's—and, indeed, throughout the half-century—tithing receipts were almost entirely "in kind." Most of the Gold Rush earnings had ceased by the early 'fifties, and there were virtually no other opportunities for the Mormons to earn cash until the 1870's. What little was earned in the way of cash was sent East promptly to purchase consumer goods, pay the transportation of immigrants, and buy supplies and equipment for farm and shop. This is the real cause of the money scarcity in Utah in the 1850's and succeeding years, and was recognized to be so by Mormon officials and writers.[27]

Because of the nature of church receipts, the task of receiving, storing, and handling the tithing, and of expending it and converting it into a form suitable to church creditors, was an exceedingly involved one. To use Brigham Young's term for it, it required "financiering" of a very high order. Some idea of the financial problems of the trustee-in-trust can be had by imagining what it would be like if the receipts of the federal government consisted of wheat, steel, laminated clapboards, pullet eggs, volunteer labor, soft drink bottles, molasses, castoff clothing, wool, magazines, pumpkins, and do-it-yourself kits. And if it be remembered that Mormons, as with all peoples, were inclined to apply Gresham's Law by passing off the cheap and keeping the dear, the improvisation task of Mormon empire builders is appreciated even more.

In chastising his followers for their failure to live up to their collective responsibility in providing the wherewithal to carry out the various charitable and economic programs of the church, Brigham Young left some classic descriptions of tithing receipts. For example, the following in 1852:

> Walk into the storehouse, and examine for yourselves. To be sure there was an old silk dress put in for $40, that had been lying for years rotting in the chest: this is a specimen of the rest. What are such things worth to our workmen? Why, nothing at all. We wish you to put in strong and substantial clothing. Good, strong, homemade stuffs make the most suitable clothing for those who are building up the public works.[28]

Or this in 1855:

> Some were disposed to do right with their surplus property, and once in a while you would find a man who had a cow which he considered surplus, but generally she was of the class that would kick a person's hat off, or eyes out, or the wolves had eaten off her teats. You would once in a while find a man who had a horse that he considered surplus, but at the same time he had the ring-bone, was broken-winded, spavined in both legs, and had the pole evil at one end of the neck and a fistula at the other, and both knees sprung.[29]

As one might guess, in this amalgam of humanity there were occasionally found bishops and tithing clerks who were not entirely honest in handling the tithing. The hams and eggs which came in as tithing would end up on their dinner tables instead of in the storehouse for payment to those on the public works. Brigham Young said he had discovered a number of such cases:

> When a good, handsome cow has been turned in on tithing, she has been smuggled, and an old three-titted cow — one that would kick the tobacco out of the mouth of a man who went to milk her — would be turned into the General Tithing Office, instead of the good cow. If one hundred dollars in cash are paid into the hands of a Bishop, in many instances he will smuggle it, and turn into the General Tithing-Office old, ring-boned, spavined horses, instead of the money. I am inquiring after such conduct, and will continue until I cleanse the inside of the platter.[30]

This was surely not the rule, but it was common enough to evoke an occasional sermon on the subject. Fitz Hugh Ludlow, who visited Utah during this early period, described the General Tithing Office as a place where the "shelves and the deep ware-rooms of the all-devouring theocracy groan and bulge with everything which it is conceivable that mankind should sell and buy on this side of the Rocky Mountains."

Here are piles of rawhide, both cow and mustang, or even pig-skin; bins of shelled corn, and cribs full of corn in the ear; wheat and rye, oats and barley; casks of salt provisions; wool, homespun, yarn, and home-woven cloth in hanks and bales; indigo; cocoons and raw silk; butter, cheese, and all manner of farm produce; even the most destructible of vegetable growths, — not only potatoes, turnips, and other root crops, but green pease [sic] and beans; fruit, and young cabbages; hay, carpenters' work, boys' caps, slop-shop overalls; hemp-rope, preserves, tinware, stogies, confectionery, adobe bricks and tiles, moss and gramma mattresses; buckskin leggins, gloves, moccasins, hunting-shirts, and complete suits. . . . These are but a minute fraction of the contents of the Church Tithing Stores.[31]

The tasks of the tithing offices, to put it briefly, were to serve as agents of the church in receiving and distributing contributions in kind; and to convert such items as were received into acceptable means of payment wherever the church made purchases. On church order resources were used in the upkeep and operation of church enterprises, including the tithing office itself, or they were expended on the poor, the Indians, and local construction projects. Approximately one-third of the tithing went for such purposes in the communities in which it was collected. The other two-thirds was transported to Salt Lake City for disbursement by the General Tithing Office on general church projects. The following instructions in the disposition of tithing in Parowan in 1851 is typical of the rest:

Your labor tithing you may apply in building a stone house for this year; your grain tithing we expect to dispose of to the poor brethren who are going into the iron business. Your cattle tithing we shall require to be driven at a proper time to Salt Lake.[32]

Similarly, the first settlers of Sanpete Valley were instructed in 1850 to devote their labor tithing to making "a good state road north across the swamp, ditching it well on each side, and building a bridge across the river." [33]

The disbursements of the trustee-in-trusts through the tithing offices seem not to have been made on the basis of systematic budgets. Nor did they render an accounting to the church, except in the most general way, of their actions in disposing of the tithing. Brigham Young once remarked, "It is my business to control the disbursements of the Tithing paid by the Saints, and not the business of every Elder in the kingdom who thinks the Tithing belongs to him." [34] Many contemporary observers charged Brigham

Young with being particularly arbitrary in his use of church funds, but there seems to have been remarkably little objection registered by church members themselves. Most of them seem to have felt, as Young himself undoubtedly did, that he was simply doing what the inexorable logic of his position dictated. A popular contemporary expression reflects this view: "He is a Prophet, because he is of Profit to the people." The president's attitude throughout thirty years of service as trustee-in-trust was that it was the duty of the Saints to pay tithing, and his responsibility to see that it was spent in the interests of the Kingdom:

> If the Lord requires one-tenth of my ability to be devoted to building temples, meeting-houses, school houses, to schooling our children, gathering the poor from the nations of the earth, bringing home the aged, lame, halt and blind, and building houses for them to live in, that they may be comfortable when they reach Zion, and to sustaining the Priesthood, it is not my prerogative to question the authority of the Almighty in this, nor of his servants who have charge of it. If I am required to pay my Tithing, it is my duty to pay it.[35]

In addition to serving as agents of the trustee-in-trust, the tithing houses also served conveniently as fiscal agents for the county and territorial governments. On territorial order they collected taxes and other payments in kind and disbursed the same in the construction of walls, roads, bridges, schoolhouses, and other secular enterprises. All of the receipts and disbursements of the State of Deseret were made through the General Tithing Office and most of those of Utah Territory and Salt Lake City and County in the 1850's were made through the same office.[36] An attempt was made to get the taxpayers to pay all taxes in wheat, and for this purpose public announcements were made each year of the price which would be allowed for wheat turned in on taxes. Tithing houses also received subscriptions and contributions to various public and semipublic enterprises in which the church and/or community had an interest; and tithing houses served as "banks" or receiving agencies for many local shops and stores.

In devising schemes for converting tithing receipts into readily acceptable means the tithing houses became completely immersed in the economic activities of the communities and valleys in which they were located. The "Deseret Store" maintained by the General Tithing Office, for example, was probably the important retail and wholesale institution in the territory in the 1850's. Local and valley tithing houses served as community warehouses, general stores, banks, weighing stations, relief and employment agencies, and communication centers. By regulating the prices at which goods and services would be received they standardized prices. Throughout most of the 1850's the tithing houses also served as the postal system of the territory and received and forwarded mail by tithing labor.

The records of local tithing houses indicate a heavy trade in what were known as "exchanges." Persons would bring in wolf skins and take out eggs; drive in a yearling and take out hay; unload a wagonload of wheat and get credit on the books which could be used in paying hired help. One individual's account for one year, to take an example, covers five pages of daily entries, about evenly divided between credits and debits. The accounts may be recapitulated as follows:[37]

Credits

Deliveries of tithing produce — includes specified amounts of potatoes, soap, oats, wheat, barley, onions, beans, pork, and tallow	$504.75	
Credit for tithing labor — includes hauling for the tithing office, furnishing a team to go East for immigrants and goods, and helping to drive church livestock	121.14	
Other credits — includes cash donations of $50.00 and purchase of materials on behalf of the tithing office	220.00	
Total credits		$845.89

Debits

Items obtained from tithing office — includes several dozen entries for such items as butter, salt, potatoes, peas, yearlings, lard, cheese, steers, pigs, chickens, eggs, squash, oats, and barley	$436.03	
Payments to laborers made through the tithing office — includes the part-time wages of four individuals	102.00	
Payments of cash by the tithing office to tithepayer — in return for cash purchases made by tithepayer on behalf of tithing office	150.00	
Total debits		$688.03
Net credit balance		$157.86

The latter figure is presumably this faithful churchman's tithing for the year. His account demonstrates the extent to which church tithing offices provided community accounting and exchange facilities, particularly before the advent of the general store and local banks in the 1870's and 1880's.

The tithing offices also extended consumer and producer credit by permitting individuals and institutions to withdraw tithing produce in excess of book credits. In other instances, individuals and businesses "saved" by accumulating credits which could be withdrawn at a later date. These accumulated credits could be transferred to others by a written order on the tithing office resembling in every respect the modern check. Transfers were also made from one tithing house to another in the same manner. One man in northern Utah supported his father in Arizona by depositing produce in his local tithing office and obtaining an order on the General Tithing Office in Salt Lake City which would allow his father to withdraw an equivalent value from the Arizona tithing office.[38] In another instance, a group of northern Utah Mormons went to southern California to get some milling machinery. They took grain to the General Tithing Office in Salt Lake City, which then gave them an order on local tithing offices along their route. In this manner they were furnished with hay, grain, and other provisions at American Fork, Springville, Payson, Fillmore, Beaver, and Cedar City, and were thus able to save their cash for necessary purchases in California.[39]

The instrument developed to facilitate transfers between individuals and between tithing houses was known as "tithing scrip." The General Tithing Office and most of the local tithing offices issued scrip. In the early 1850's the scrip was simply a handwritten notation like the following:[40]

Bro. E. Bingham [Bishop of Ogden North Ward]

Newton Goodale has deposited at this office [General Tithing Office] sixteen and a half bushels of wheat. Please pay him the same amount out of the Tithing in your charge, and we will a/c when you return this Order.

Wm. Clayton

G. S. L. City
Feby 10, 1852

As the tithing system grew and was used more widely, standard due bills were printed or engraved. These were variously redeemable in meat, produce, or in any other commodity which the tithing office happened to have that the bearer might want. As a matter of regular practice, this scrip was issued to church employees, welfare recipients, and to church creditors generally. It was usually accepted by Mormon business institutions, although sometimes at a discount, and usually by Gentile businesses at a greater discount. Made out "to the bearer," they enjoyed wide circulation throughout the half-century, particularly after the disappearance of church coins in the early 1850's.

While due bills were not an uncommon part of the contemporary American scene, many travelers throughout Utah were struck by their widespread use. One of the most amusing stories, undoubtedly apocryphal, was told by the humorist, Bill Nye:

In these days if you wanted to go to the theatre you took butter, eggs, chickens, potatoes, wheat, anything like that to a tithing house, and they would give you script for it. Then you took the script to the theatre or to any store and bought what you wanted with it.

On one occasion, I took a big fat turkey up to the tithing yard to sell for script and the tithing clerk had gone to supper. I waited and he did not return, so I had to go and get the young lady I had invited to go with me, and I carried the turkey into the window of the box office and asked for two balcony seats.

That clerk at the window handed out the two tickets and two spring chickens for change and I had to sit there all through the performance with a chicken under each arm and the young lady I was with was quite peeved that I paid so little attention to her. I was never so embarrassed and uncomfortable in all my life.[41]

Perhaps a more telling (and more truthful!) illustration of Utah's barter economy was told by John Codman in the 1870's. The tithing office at Lehi, he wrote, needed an account book, and finally located one in the hands of an Englishman. The price demanded for it was fifty cents, and that in coin. The bishop offered tithing scrip, eggs, potatoes, chickens, flour — items almost universally acceptable — but to no avail. Ten cents was all the "ready money" that could be collected. It was many months before the Lehi tithing office could get possession of the fifty cents necessary to buy the account book.[42]

CONSECRATION MOVEMENT OF THE 1850'S

The original law of consecration, as announced in 1831, required members of the church to place everything on the altar for the use and benefit of "the Kingdom of God." Although this early commandment had been replaced by the law of tithing, it was still held up as the ideal — as "the higher law." Brigham Young often remarked that there would be no necessity of restoring the higher law if everyone would pay tithing; that is, if everyone paid an honest tithe all church programs could be financed without the necessity of anyone contributing more than a tithe.[43] Apparently, either the receipts were too disappointing or the programs too ambitious, for continuous difficulty was experienced in making budgets balance. The failure of the federal government to bear its share of territorial expense no doubt contributed to these deficits, as Mormon leaders alleged.[44] At any rate, the necessity of paying more tithing to meet prospective deficits was a recurring theme of sermons in the early 1850's. At first, considerable hope was held out that those who were prospering in California would make heavy consecrations for the benefit of the church. The following letter, written in 1852, is typical of several dispatched in that direction in the early 1850's:

Our anxiety to promote every kind of domestic manufacture has induced us to encourage by all the means in our power every branch of home industry at no inconsiderable expense, which when added to the sums devoted to the emigration of poor saints, assisting the establishing of distant locations in the valleys, applying means to promote the cause of education and many other things in addition to the public works, and sending the gospel to all nations, forms in the aggregate, no inconsiderable sum and requires the most liberal exertions of the saints, as well as the munificent blessings of our Father in Heaven. . . . You should also consider that we have received nothing from the general government to sustain our state or territory and that has come upon this people and the public funds. Not one dime have the government of the United States paid to sustain peaceful relations with the Indians of this territory, etc. . . . we naturally look in that direction [California] for considerable amounts in money.[45]

These letters brought in some revenue, but not in the quantities expected. Brigham Young stated in 1852 that "the brethren in California" had made "no less than $100,000," and that he had not received anywhere near $10,000 in tithing from them.[46]

The failure of this source—and it dwindled continuously throughout the 'fifties—and no doubt other considerations, led the church to revive in 1854 the original law of consecration. Those desiring to comply "fully and frankly" with that law were asked to deed over to the trustee-in-trust all of their property. The trustee-in-trust would then assign them an inheritance according to their needs.[47] Although an 1854 epistle boasted that members were flocking "by hundreds and thousands to give in their names, devoting and deeding all and every thing which they possess, unto the Church,"[48] the movement was delayed until 1855 when a proper legal form was drawn up and printed.[49] The standard printed form on which the consecrations were listed read as follows:

Be it known by these presents that I, ——, of ——, in the County of ——, and Territory of Utah; for and in consideration of the good will which I have to the Church of Jesus Christ of Latter Day Saints, give and convey unto Brigham Young, Trustee-in-Trust for said Church, his successors in office and assigns, all my claim to, and ownership of the following described property. . . .[50]

During the period 1855–1856 about forty per cent of the 7,000 heads of families in the territory deeded all of their property to the church on such forms.[51] The thousands of forms, duly signed, witnessed, and acknowledged, were recorded by the various counties in the territory. They run the gamut from the short form of Soren Andersen of Manti, who consecrated his gun, sword, tools, and household furniture, to the amount of $36.00, to that of Brigham Young, who consecrated to himself as trustee-in-trust a long list of real and personal property valued at $199,625.[52] With the exception of the last item, the following consecration is typical:[53]

Property and improvements of real estate	$775.00
Cattle, wagon, and pigs	541.00
Farming tools and rifle	105.00
Household furniture, bedding, etc.	150.00
Twelve sheep and two pistols	72.00
Silver watch and cooking stove	55.00
Sixty bushels wheat	120.00
Corn, vegetables, etc.	145.50
Sundries	75.00
African servant girl	1,000.00
Total	$3,038.50

Feramorz Fox has suggested that the ultimate purposes of the consecration movement of the 1850's included a negative and a positive side.[54] Negatively, the concentration of property in the hands of the trustee-in-trust was expected to checkmate certain disintegrating tendencies that were defeating the major objectives of the church, such as inequality, the spread of unfriendly economic interest, and the removal of property from the territory by speculators, apostates, and deserters. Positively, the uniting of means — the pooling of capital — would further the work of building the Kingdom: immigration, colonization, public works, and the development of agriculture and industry. At the very least, church officials may have reasoned, the emphasis upon consecrating everything to the church ought to increase the willingness of most members to contribute at least a tenth. Unquestionably, the movement served to build up sentiment for making greater contributions to the public purse.

Nevertheless, the consecration movement never culminated in the assumption of control by the church over any of the properties consecrated nor in the assignment of any inheritances. While to the Latter-day Saints the making of deeds was accompanied by an outpouring of religious enthusiasm, visitors, Gentiles, and apostates saw it as simply another extension of the theocratic despotism which was snuffing out all prospect of free enterprise and private property in Utah.[55] Since the Congress had not yet passed laws permitting land ownership in Utah, the Mormon consecration movement was a good reason to postpone it still further. Considering the laissez-faire sentiments of many national leaders, it is doubtful that Congress would ever have permitted or legalized by land law legislation the acquisition and ownership by the church of substantial blocks of property in Utah. This seems to be borne out in the periodic reports of the General Land Office. Taking note of the consecration movement in 1857, the Commissioner of the General Land Office formally suggested that the proceeding was "incompatible with our system [whatever that was]," and suggested a congressional investigation.[56] In 1862, as we shall see, Congress specifically prohibited the church from owning more than $50,000 worth of property.

In the face of widespread adverse comment in the national press, therefore, not to mention the advance of the federal troops on the territory to insure federal supremacy in all such matters, the church dropped the plan in the summer of 1857. A few consecrations were made after that date, but they appear to have been intended only as expressions of support and good will. Once more, resort was had to "the lesser law" of tithing.

AGRICULTURAL DISASTERS OF 1855–1856

Despite continuous attempts to improve the organization of resources through the tithing houses, the office of the trustee-in-trust, and other agencies and programs, church assistance to needy projects was always on the verge of being too little and too late. This was primarily due to the inadequacy of the agricultural surplus — for the one area in which the Mormon economy failed to live up to its promise in the 1850's was agriculture. This might have been expected, considering the niggardliness of the Great Basin homeland. The harvest of 1850 had been "abundant," and the harvest had increased each year thereafter for four straight years.[57] The winter of 1854–1855, when the consecration movement was inaugurated, was particularly prosperous because of the market provided by the presence in Salt Lake City of Lieutenant Colonel Edward J. Steptoe and some 400 federal troops and civilian employees, together with their 750 horses and mules.[58] Among other things, Colonel Steptoe expended approximately $25,000 in federal funds in the territory on the improvement of roads. This was a rare windfall since, as Turrentine Jackson has pointed out, Congress was "less generous with Utah than with other western territories in granting money for internal improvements" because of "the Mormon Question."[59]

This is not to say that the Mormon economy of the middle 'fifties was characterized by abundance. Sugar varied from 40 to 75 cents per pound and coffee a little less; white shirts were $4.00 each; and men's clothing was so scarce that an invited guest to a grand ball held by Brigham Young was not able to purchase in the entire city of Salt Lake a pair of black pants or a broadcloth coat.[60] At the same time, a seventeen-year-old boy worked three months for a pair of buckskin pants that "came half way between my ankles and knees" in dry weather, and "in wet weather would flippity flop on the side walk every step I took."[61] Nevertheless, the public works and colonization programs, and the paternalistic overseership of the church in general, enabled most everyone, as they expressed it, to "make a live of it."

Beginning in the summer of 1855, however, occurred a series of natural disasters which, in one year, wiped out the entire social surplus and placed the 35,000 persons in the territory in the same position of semistarvation in which the early Salt Lake colonists found themselves before the Gold

Rush.[62] These tragedies underwrote the impotence of humanity when confronted with malignant nature. What the church did about them is a story of desperate survival mitigated by supreme confidence in the outcome.

The first blow was the grasshopper visitation in the summer of 1855. Grasshoppers, or Rocky Mountain locusts, had permanent breeding grounds in eastern Idaho and Nevada, and had given intermittent trouble to local Mormon settlements in Utah since 1849. In Weber Valley, the crops were said to have been "destroyed five years in succession" by invasions of grasshoppers and crickets.[63] Coming up like a cloud, they fell on the land like a plague or blight, and stripped it of everything green. With "powerful jaws, an efficient digestive system, and phenomenal reproductive powers," they were insignificant individually but mighty collectively, in their destructiveness.[64] As an early Utah merchant described it:

> They would come suddenly, millions of them and eat every green thing in their way; even shawls or sheets thrown over plants or trees to protect them, would be quickly destroyed. They would be found among the shirts, under a muslin dress, eating and destroying anything. . . . They devastated hundreds of acres, and as they would rise and fly high in the air, the air would be darkened with them. They seemed to be massed together and to take but one direction, flying not more than 8 or 10 miles perhaps and then settling upon another field of action.[65]

No previous grasshopper infestation had borne any comparison in destructiveness to that of 1855. In the Salt Lake Valley they gathered "like snow flakes in a storm," and filled the air over the city "as far as the eye can reach." In many places in the valley they destroyed entirely, "not only the first, but second and third sowings, also some corn, and even buckwheat." The sound of the locusts was "continually in the ears of the husbandmen."[66] In Davis County, the same story is told:

> Everything was literally covered with them by night and from 10 o'clock in the forenoon till the sun an hour high at night. The air was full so that it appeared like a snow storm even to somewhat obscuring the rays of the sun at times. They destroyed the most of the crop taking in one night the heads of oats, the blades of corn, beans and almost every green thing eating up the grass, etc.[67]

Similar visits were made in Utah, Juab, and Millard Counties, with equal destructiveness.

Attempts were made to fight the grasshoppers, but with little success. The settlers used sticks and sacks to drive them into ditches to drown or be buried; straw was placed on concentrations of them and burned; gunny sack traps were laid; pits were dug and covered over; farmers and housewives even attempted to knock them out with boards and brooms. Whole fields were burned to protect others from the hungry horde, but to little avail. Crop after crop was planted as each was eaten off until the end of the season made further planting futile.

Considering that the immigration of 1855 was the heaviest since 1852—some 4,225 persons in that season—this destruction would have been serious enough, but it was accompanied by a hot, dry summer and a light runoff from the mountains, causing late-season drouth. This affected not only the supply of irrigation water, but also the facilities for grazing. In recording these events as they occurred, the church historian wrote at the end of June, 1855, that the weather had been "oppressively hot," that there had been "no rain of any amount," that the streams were uncommonly low, and that the water had already failed in many places:

> At Fillmore the wheat is entirely destroyed, Chalk Creek being very low. . . .
>
> The fields in Juab County present the appearance of a desert.
>
> About two-thirds of the grain in Utah County is destroyed, and a large black bug is devouring the potatoes.
>
> All the farms south of this city [Salt Lake City] are nearly a desert; the northern counties and Tooele have fared considerably better, but within the last few days the latter have had a visit from the enemy, and the result is that wheat stalks have lost their heads; and, moreover, as the farms have been located on small streams, a large quantity of wheat has been burned up for the want of water. This is rather a dark picture, but I regret to say it is not *overdrawn*.[68]

Counting the damage of both grasshoppers and the drouth, the harvest of the fall of 1855 was estimated to have been reduced by from one-third to two-thirds, depending upon the locality.[69] In Bountiful, Joseph Holbrook harvested only 500 bushels of wheat in 1855 compared to 1,700 bushels in the previous year.[70] In Salt Lake City, Heber C. Kimball did not raise "one spoonful," and the amount of grain taken to his large gristmill for grinding did not yield him "one bushel of toll per day."[71]

With the destruction of the grass supplies by the grasshoppers and by the drouth, the next step was the moving of cattle high up on the mountains or to new and distant locations with virgin grass.[72] This brought a new danger. The place to which the church and most of the large cattle owners decided to send their cattle was Cache Valley, in northern Utah and southern Idaho, which had not been grazed previously because of the fear that it was too cold. Now necessity required it. First, the legislature granted Cache Valley as a herding ground to Brigham Young, as trustee-in-trust for the church.[73] Next, a drive was instituted, a company of twenty-five persons was organized, cabins and corrals were built, and a church ranch with about 2,000 church cattle and about 1,000 privately owned cattle was established. Some 200 tons of wild hay was cut and stacked for winter use.[74]

None could have foreseen the severity of the winter that followed. It was said to have been easily the most severe winter experienced by the colonists since settlement began in 1847. If the grasshoppers and drouth had destroyed their crops, the bitter cold was now to destroy the greater part of their herds.

A heavy snow came early in November and continued for a number of days. The ranchers . . . became fearful that many of the cattle would die of starvation before spring, since they had only a little hay for such a large herd. The forage was scarce and difficult to locate. The herders began at once to round up the stock and drive them into the Salt Lake Valley by way of Sardine Canyon. The snow fell so fast that it was more than two-feet deep on the level and much deeper in the canyon. The herders were forced to drive the cattle almost night and day to keep the trail open. Only those in good condition were started over the trail, and many of these perished before they reached the winter range at the mouth of the Weber River. The poorer cattle were left behind at the ranch [where herders made trails to brush patches and cut willows which they fed to the cattle]. Of the 2,000 head of church cattle, only 420 survived the hard winter.[75]

The experience in Cache Valley was not unique. Wilford Woodruff estimated that "four out of every five head of cattle in the northern counties" had been killed:

Many persons are nearly ruined. The Church had lost, last October, over 2600 head in Weber and Cache Counties; now they can count nearly 500. Gilbert and Gerrish [merchants] had nearly 700 head when they started from the Missouri River; now they have 95. Mess and Kerr [merchants] lost their entire herd, valued at $60,000, and all the citizens in proportion. Hundreds of persons have lived on dead cattle when they could not be got at for snow, and now it has disappeared; they are living on weeds, roots, and greens.[76]

Heber C. Kimball stated that about half of all the cattle in the territory had died as the result of the winter. Moreover, he wrote, the Indians, confronted with starvation for the same reasons as the Mormons, had stolen over 100 head of cattle by February 1856, and by July had taken many more.[77] Chandless wrote that every single one of the 400 head of cattle in the train in which he came west died before the winter was over.[78] Joseph Holbrook, who lived in Bountiful, wrote that he had sent 45 head of his own cattle along with those of his ward to Bear River Valley, "on account of the scarcity of feed," and that "nearly one half of the stock perished on the range during the winter."[79] To complete his year of woe, Holbrook fed one and one-half tons of hay previously infested with grasshoppers to his sheep and thirty-five of them died because of "the infection left on the grass by the grasshoppers."

The destruction of both crops and livestock brought on a near-famine.

Every journal of the period, and virtually every available letter, records the seriousness of the problem with which they were confronted. Heber C. Kimball wrote in February 1856 that there was "scarcely any grain in the country, and there are thousands that have none at all scarcely." [80] Kimball, who had gone through the hunger of 1848–1849, called this winter, the winter of 1855–1856, "more close" than any yet experienced; and this, he wrote, was "universal through all the settlements."

There are not more than one half the people that have bread, and they have not more than one half or one quarter of a pound a day to a person. A great portion of the people are digging roots, and hundreds and thousands, their teams being dead, are under the necessity of spading their ground to put in their grain. There is not any settlement or people, in any part of the Territory, but what feel the scarcity of food, money, cattle, horses, &c.; and there is a pretty universal break with our merchants, as there is no one to buy their goods, and their stock are mostly dead.[81]

Many resorted, as in 1848–1849, to pigweeds, thistle roots, mustard leaves, and to mixtures of vegetables with bran or shorts.[82] The economic indicators provide some measure of the scarcity. A pound of butter, which had averaged 35 cents a pound before the famine, now exchanged for a pound of tea, which had traditionally sold at $1.50 to $2.00 a pound.[83] Flour was unobtainable commercially because of church prohibition, but is said to have sold undercover for as much as a dollar a pound in an instance or two.[84]

The first response of the church to the famine was the distribution of a circular signed by the First Presidency, suggesting a number of measures that could be taken by individuals to shore up food supplies and prevent waste. The circular suggested that all fences be improved to prevent trespass on fields and gardens by livestock; that mechanics and artisans forsake their customary employment "for three or four months" while they attempt to raise a sustenance for their family on their home lots, and that farmers share their shovels and hoes and seed with these persons; that more intensive agriculture be practiced: "let every inch of field and garden be put in the highest state of cultivation"; that every effort be made to keep out weeds from growing crops; and "let those who have impart liberally to those who have not." [85] A later circular advised bishops to supervise closely the consumption of food in the wards and to organize parties of gleaners to comb the fields for additional kernels of grain and possible leftovers of other crops.[86] In fact, wrote John E. Booth of Provo, Brigham Young did everything that could be done short of marrying all the gleaners! [87] Church authorities also may have encouraged a number of the more well-to-do members to add plural wives to their households. At least, this would seem to be a plausible economic explanation of the very large number of plural marriages which took place in 1856–1857.[88]

To encourage and permit the 200 or 300 church employees to devote the spring to planting and working their garden and farming plots, as well as to conserve the small supply of church grain and other provisions for the most needy, the church public works were closed throughout the spring and summer of 1856. However, fifteen men were employed making seed drills which were distributed among the larger farmers for the purpose of cutting down the amount of wheat that would be needed for seeding. It was estimated by the First Presidency that the use of drills would cut down by two-thirds the amount of grain that would have been used by the traditional method of sowing broadcast.[89]

Two kinds of share-the-wealth (or share-the-poverty) programs were established. The first was a device called "fast-day offerings." Members of the church, from the time of the early 1830's, had followed a practice of devoting certain days to fasting and prayer in order to purify the soul and lead the mind to communion with God. During the winter of 1855–1856 this institution was adapted to the economic situation by asking each member of the church to fast for a twenty-four hour period on the first Thursday in each month and donate the food thus saved to the bishop for distribution to the poor.[90] Instructions were sent to the bishops directing the use of fast offerings solely for the benefit of the poor and needy. So close did the community come to starvation, and so impressed were the leaders with the thought that only the sharing of the more well-to-do with the poor averted this disaster, that the institution of fast offerings, and the philosophy of grain-saving in general, became an integral part of Mormonism. It is still a basic belief and practice of the church.

The other phase of the voluntary rationing program was patriarchal in nature. Each head of family (or families) was asked to place all of his household on a ration of one-half pound of breadstuff per day, and to use his surplus supply in feeding additional persons in his employ or in his ward. In introducing this program, Brigham Young said:

> If you do not pursue a righteous course, we will separate you from the Church. Is that all? No. If necessary we will take your grain from your bin and distribute it among the poor and needy, and they shall be fed and supplied with work, and you shall receive what your grain is worth.[91]

The methods are illustrated by those followed in the Heber C. Kimball family, as related by Elder Kimball in letters to his son in England:

> I have been under the necessity of rationing my family, and also yours, to two thirds of a pound of bread stuff per day each; as the last week is up to day, we shall commence on half-a-pound each. . . . Brother Brigham [Young] told me to-day that he had put his family on half-a-pound each. . . . My family, at this time, consists of about one hundred souls, and I suppose that I feed about as

many as one hundred besides. . . . When this drouth came on, I had about seven hundred bushels of wheat, and it is now reduced to about one hundred and twenty-five bushels, and I have only about twenty-five bushels of corn, which will not provide for my own family until harvest . . . ; still, we are altogether better off than the most of the people in these valleys of the mountains. There are several wards in this City [Salt Lake City] who have not over two weeks provisions on hand. . . . Moreover, there is not a settlement in the Territory, but is also in the same fix that we are. Some settlements can go two months, some three, and some can, probably, at the rate of half-a-pound per day, till harvest. . . . Money will not buy flour or meal. . . . Dollars and cents do not count now, in these times, for they are the tightest that I have ever seen in the Territory of Utah.[92]

Other families with a grain or flour surplus, after the half-pound-per-day ration had been calculated, followed similar measures. Brigham Young is said to have fed more than two hundred persons per day from his provisions, in addition to the members of his own family which must have numbered over sixty, and the workers he employed.[93] The president employed a considerable number of extra persons in building a large dwelling and barn. When these were finished, they were put to work in building a wall around his own estate and the grounds of the General Tithing Office.[94] Built of cobblestone and lime mortar, the walls were approximately eight feet high. In defending the make-work construction of these walls, and the Salt Lake City wall of 1853, the president made the following statement:

Some have wished me to explain why we built an adobe wall around this city. Are there any Saints who stumble at such things? Oh, slow of heart to understand and believe, I build walls, dig ditches, make bridges, and do a great amount and variety of labor that is of but little consequence only to provide ways and means for sustaining and preserving the destitute. I annually expend hundreds and thousands of dollars almost solely to furnish employment to those in want of labor. Why? I have potatoes, flour, beef, and other articles of food, which I wish my brethren to have; and it is better for them to labor for those articles, so far as they are able and have opportunity, than to have them given to them. They work, and I deal out provisions, often when the work does not profit me.

I say to all grunters, grumblers, whiners, hypocrites and sycophants, who snivel, crouch and crawl around the most contemptible of all creatures for a slight favor, should it enter my mind to dig down the Twin Peaks, and I set men to work to do so, it is none of your business, neither is it the business of all earth and hell, provided I pay the laborers their wages. I am not to be called in question as to what I do with my funds, whether I build high walls or low walls, garden walls or city walls, and if I please, it is my right to pull down my walls tomorrow. If any one wishes to apostatize upon such grounds, the quicker he does so the better; and if he wishes to leave the territory, but is too poor to do so, I will assist him to go. We are much better off without such characters.[95]

The church also attempted to prevent, so far as possible, the exploitation of its members who were in need. Brigham Young reported that a man was stopped by his bishop from building a house because "he got first rate mechanics to work for five pounds of flour a day"; which was considered to be too little pay. "The bishop told him that he could not build a house in his ward upon any such principle." [96]

One other church program of the period was calculated to mitigate the suffering and need, namely a stepped-up colonization and missionary program. When large numbers of men were seen to congregate in Salt Lake City, without employment, and apparently resigned to their unemployed condition, Brigham Young began to call groups of them to go to outlying areas where, regardless of income, they could be kept busy and would build the Kingdom at the same time. Some two hundred men were called in this fashion in the spring of 1856. Heber C. Kimball may have overemphasized the relationship of the calls to the circumstances of the moment, but his description of it is nevertheless interesting:

There has been Courts in session here for weeks and weeks, and I suppose that one hundred and fifty or two hundred of the brethren have been hanging round, with the Council House filled to the brim. This scenery continuing for a long time, one day brother Brigham [Young] sent Thomas Bullock [his secretary] to take their names, for the purpose of giving them missions, if they had not anything to do of any more importance. So brother Brigham counseled me to make a selection — for Los Vegas some thirty, who are ordered to sell their possessions and go with their families as soon as the weather will permit, for the purpose of going down on to the Rio Virgin to raise cotton; another company of forty-eight to go to Green River to strengthen up that settlement, make farms, build mills, &c.; and some thirty-five or forty to go north to Salmon River, where Thomas J. Smith is, to strengthen up that post; some thirty to go to Carson Valley to strengthen that post; some thirty to go into the lead business near the Los Vegas; eight to go to the East Indies. . . . There are [also] eighteen called to Europe, and seven to Australia. . . . These are all good men but they need to learn a lesson.[97]

Kimball adds that another one hundred men were selected "to go back with ox teams to fetch on the Church goods that lie in Missouri and St. Louis, if there are cattle enough left alive to do so." All told, about 300 missionaries were called to different missions in the spring of 1856. Most of them would expect to be provided with their sustenance in 1856 from what was produced in the Salt Lake Valley, but they might very well be independent of that source in future years if their efforts were a success.[98]

The upshot of all these measures was that, while all suffered, none died of starvation. And this is somewhat remarkable since the summer of 1856, which followed on the heels of the disasters of 1855 and 1855–1856, was also a bad "grasshopper year," with a harvest which was, if anything, less than in 1855.[99]

THE HANDCART COMPANIES

The terrible events of 1855–1856 had brought the Mormon community so close to starvation that tithing receipts dropped sharply, and donations to the Perpetual Emigrating Fund were almost negligible. It was clear to church officials that some phases of the church's development program would have to be severely curtailed or abandoned. The most expensive of these, in terms of cash, was "the gathering of the poor." The principal source of revenue for the immigration program, as previously related, was to have been the repayments of those who had been assisted to Utah in prior years, but their dire economic condition — and perhaps some disinclination — made it virtually impossible for them to meet these obligations. By April 1856, some 872 of the "Lord's poor" who had been emigrated during the period 1849–1855 owed more than $100,000 to the Fund.[100] Moreover, the winter having killed nearly all of the P.E. cattle, it was quite impossible for the company to finance operations by selling, as it had sometimes done, the livestock which had been purchased in previous years and driven to Utah.

Some raised the question of the advisability of attempting to bring companies west in 1856. Brigham Young expressed the prevailing view when he said that while they must be careful "and not permit that fund to swallow up all our available resources,"[101] the gathering should not be stopped because "the cry from our poor brethren in foreign countries for deliverance is great, the hand of the oppressor is heavy upon them, and they have no other prospect on earth through which they can hope for assistance."[102] What he proposed was that "the poor" be immigrated by handcart:

> I have been thinking how we should operate another year. We cannot afford to purchase wagons and teams as in times past, I am consequently thrown back upon my old plan — to make hand-carts, and let the emigration foot it, and draw upon them [the carts] the necessary supplies, having a cow or two for every ten. They can come just as quick, if not quicker, and much cheaper — can start earlier and escape the prevailing sickness which annually lays so many of our brethren in the dust. A great majority of them walk now, even with the teams which are provided, and have a great deal more care and perplexity than they would have if they came without them. They will need 90 days' rations from the time of their leaving the Missouri river, and as the settlements extend up the Platte, not that much. The carts can be made without a particle of iron,

with wheels hooped, made strong and light, and one, or if the family be large, two of them will bring all they will need upon the plains.

If it is once tried, you will find that it will become the favorite method of crossing the plains. . . . I do know that they can beat any ox train crossing the plains. I want to see it fairly tried and tested, at all events, and I think we might as well begin another year as any time, and save this enormous expense of purchasing wagons and teams — indeed, we will be obliged to pursue this course, or suspend operations, for aught that I can see at the present.[103]

Preparations were immediately begun in England, on the Missouri River, and in Salt Lake City to carry out the new plan. The First Presidency issued a General Epistle, explaining the reasons for adopting this method of immigration and in a general way stating the procedure to be followed. The idealism which accompanied the experiment is illustrated by the following:

The P.E. Fund is designed to deliver the honest poor, the pauper, if you please, from the thraldom of ages, from localities where poverty is a crime and beggary an offence against the law, where every avenue to rise in the scale of being to any degree of respectable joyous existence is forever closed, and place them in a land where honest labor and industry meet a suitable reward, where the higher walks of the life are open to the humblest and poorest, . . . Let them come on foot, with hand-carts or wheelbarrows; let them gird up their loins and walk through, and nothing shall hinder or stay them.[104]

Handcarts would save the enormous expense of purchasing wagons and teams; they would decrease the food bill; they could make the journey more quickly. Every company would be followed by a number of freight wagons which would carry the heavy baggage and supplies. In 1855, under the old plan, the expense had grown to £15 per capita; now the British agent could fix the rate at £9 per capita.[105]

Some nineteen hundred European Saints signed up to cross the Plains with handcarts in 1856. From Liverpool they sailed to New York and Boston, thence by railroad to Iowa City, Iowa, which was chosen as the frontier outfitting point. The handcarts, which were made at Iowa City, were designed to serve four or five persons each, with a burden of perhaps one hundred pounds of food, clothing, and equipment.[106] At Iowa City the emigrants were organized into companies of about 100 wagons each (400 to 500 persons), with "twenty persons to a large round tent, and one wagon and ox team to twenty carts."[107] Pushing and pulling, they traveled across Iowa to Florence (old Winter Quarters), Nebraska, where they recuperated and then started out on the long journey to the Salt Lake Valley. When the first two companies reached the Salt Lake Valley in September 1856, ostensibly in good condition and spirits, church officials were jubilant. Apostle Wilford Woodruff wrote:

I must say my feelings were inexpressible to behold a company of men, women, and children, many of them aged and infirm, enter the City of the Great Salt Lake, drawing 100 hand-carts . . . with which they had travelled some 1,400 miles in nine weeks, and to see them dance with joy as they travelled through the streets, complaining of nothing, only that they had been detained by the ox teams that carried some of their provisions, . . . Yes, our hearts swelled until we were speechless with joy, and not with sorrow. As I gazed upon the scene, meditating upon the future result, it looked to me like the first hoisting of the floodgates of deliverance to the oppressed millions. We can now say to the poor and honest in heart, come home to Zion, for the way is prepared.[108]

A third company was equally successful, but the last two of the five companies which left Florence in 1856 were delayed until late in the season. Due to a misunderstanding between the Liverpool and American agents, the handcarts for these companies had not been built, and they had to wait until this could be done.[109] The fourth company — that in the charge of James G. Willie — did not leave Iowa City until July 15, and the fifth company — that of Edward Martin — did not leave until July 28. Further delays were experienced at the Winter Quarters staging area. The few seasoned frontiersmen thought that it was too risky to attempt the crossing so late in the season, but fired by the enthusiasm which had brought them in the first place, the majority voted to leave, trusting to God that they would have no trouble. The Willie company left the Missouri River point on August 17; the Martin company ten days later.

When an express group of immigration officials arrived in Salt Lake in October to report that more than a thousand handcart immigrants were still on the way, Brigham Young immediately organized relief parties to carry food, clothing, and wagons to the belated companies. The published list of donations in this cause indicate both the grave concern over their fate by Salt Lake residents, and the rather considerable sharing of wealth, approaching, in all likelihood, the fast offerings and redistributions in Utah of 1855–1856.[110]

Once more, however, nature dealt a cruel blow. The winter on the Plains was uncommonly early, and the further the handcart companies went the slower and more difficult their progress became. A severe snowstorm, freezing weather, lack of food, and other incidents were disastrous. Sixty-seven of the 500 persons in the Willie company, and 135 of the 576 in the Martin contingent, died.[111] Only heroic action by the volunteer "rescue parties" saved the remainder. With more than 200 dead, it was a far worse disaster than the oft-publicized Donner Party.

The last company did not reach the Salt Lake Valley until November

30. On that date, Brigham Young was conducting a worship service in the Salt Lake Tabernacle. Upon hearing of the arrival of the immigrants, the president arose, gave instructions to the bishops and others present to distribute the newcomers among those with the best houses, and then added the following classic expression of Mormon religious philosophy:

The afternoon meeting will be omitted, for I wish the sisters to go home and prepare to give those who have just arrived a mouthful of something to eat, and to wash them and nurse them up. . . . Were I in the situation of those persons who have just come in, . . . I would give more for a dish of pudding and milk or a baked potato and salt, . . . than I would for all your prayers, though you were to stay there all afternoon and pray. Prayer is good, but when baked potatoes and milk are needed, prayer will not supply their place.[112]

As a device for mass migration, the handcart scheme had certain obvious advantages, but there were also limitations. All of the physically able had to walk the entire distance; the supplies and provisions were strictly limited to what they could cart; they had inadequate protection against the elements; and defense against the Indians was hampered by the lack of riding animals.[113] Nevertheless, the scheme was not abandoned immediately. As a matter of fact, the perfection of the handcart technique was one of the objectives of the gigantic church enterprise of 1857, known as the Brigham Young Express and Carrying Company, the story of which is reserved for the next chapter.

The point is that Brigham Young and his associates did not consider the handcart experiment to be a failure,[114] and the financial condition which had prompted its adoption in the fall of 1855 was not improved in the fall of 1856. "I admit that the gathering is one of the most important items," wrote Brigham Young, "and feel willing, and even anxious, to promote that interest in preference to many others; but while we emigrate, we must also build up and provide a Zion to live in, as well as gather people to it."[115] He therefore concluded that the "worthy poor" who wished to migrate in 1857 should do so by handcart, as others had done in 1856. What little funds there were in the church's hands would be used "to nurse our General Church business for a while."[116]

In order to demonstrate that the handcart scheme was both practical and efficient, when conducted under proper conditions, the president sent a company of seventy missionaries from Salt Lake City to Florence with handcarts, unaccompanied by wagons. They made the trip in forty-eight days, and averaged twenty-seven miles per day after they left the mountains. Nevertheless, the unfavorable publicity attending the Willie and Martin disasters, and the small amount of money which was available for financing immigration, led to a marked decline in immigration to Utah during the next four years. Only 480 persons crossed the Plains by handcart in 1857, and the Utah War prevented immigration in 1858. Even under the improved conditions of 1859 and 1860, only three handcart companies, composed of a total of 584 Saints, came with handcarts. They were the last. All told, during the period 1856 to 1860, approximately 3,000 persons walked the full distance from Iowa City to Salt Lake City, pushing or pulling a total of 662 handcarts. During the same period, approximately 5,200 migrated to Utah by wagon team.[117] A last resort prompted by the undependability of nature in the Great Basin and the depleted condition of the church's treasury resulting therefrom, the handcart scheme was dealt a ruinous blow by the early winter on the Plains in the late fall of 1856. A different method of immigrating the poor — one which would also save "foreign" exchange — would have to be adopted in the 1860's.

ROLE OF THE TRUSTEE-IN-TRUST

Despite the many problems which faced the church in the 1850's and later years — or perhaps because of these problems — the activities of the trustee-in-trust in collecting and disbursing tithing and other donations were used in implementing the traditional goals of Mormon economic history. In eras of growth and in time of famine, the trustee-in-trust was the agent through which the thousands of church members, in the Great Basin and elsewhere, were able to combine their savings and labor to develop the resources and increase the production of their deficit economy. In directing and financing the construction of canals, roads, sugar factories, iron works, and public buildings; in working with private enterprise to further the economic development of the Great Basin; in sheltering fledgling enterprises and communities from the storms of economic misfortune; and in devising schemes for immigrating the poor from Babylon, the trustee-in-trust functioned as the church's steward. To many contemporary Americans, particularly in the so-called "heroic" age of capitalism, the Mormon Church was just another trust, and the title "trustee-in-trust" merely assisted in the identification. But to the Latter-day Saints, the trustee-in-trust was the agent by which group savings and group investment were attempting to convert, under great natural obstacles, a lonely and unwanted desert waste into a prosperous, beautiful, and cooperative Kingdom of God.

CHAPTER VI

Mobilization, 1856–1858

The resiliency — the rebound power — of the Mormon people was perhaps their greatest asset in attempting to develop the pockets of agricultural and mineral wealth in the Great Basin. Natural catastrophe, weaknesses in organization, and failures in human judgment did not discourage them or bring about any retrenchment in their activity on behalf of the Kingdom. Whether it was a grasshopper plague, prolonged drouth, a winter of attrition, an Indian war, or "invasion" by hostile troops, the Mormons always seemed to rise from their "bed of affliction" to meet the almost overwhelming challenge. There is even a suggestion in some diaries and contemporary sermons of a kind of grim satisfaction, if not outright pleasure, with the favorable disciplining effects wrought by the hardship, destitution, and sacrifice. Indeed, the year 1856 has gone down in most Utah histories, not as the year of famine, nor even as the year of the handcart disaster, but as the year of the "Reformation," when moral principles were urged with great intensity, and when individual members searched their souls to discover and cast out sources of evil doing and evil thinking. The Willie and Martin handcart tragedies seemed to make the misfortunes of those already in Utah pale into insignificance. Their below-average harvest of 1856 suddenly became a cause for thanksgiving — a staff on which to lean while doing something great and unforgettable.

Three great ventures sprouted in rapid succession after the disasters of 1856: The Brigham Young Express and Carrying Company, the Utah War, and the Move South. Involving, as they did, large sections of the population of the territory, these three ventures represented a three-phased mobilization during the period 1856–1858: Mobilization to get the mail through, to transport immigrants, and to carry the immense volume of freight needed by the commonwealth; mobilization to delay, and, if possible, to prevent the occupation of the territory by federal troops; and mobilization to transform defeat into victory by migrating from northern Utah to central and southern Utah during the occupation of the territory by hostile federal troops.

THE BRIGHAM YOUNG EXPRESS AND CARRYING COMPANY

The first of these ventures was the Brigham Young Express and Carrying Company, more commonly known by contemporaries as the Y.X. Company. As the largest single venture yet tackled by the Mormons in the Great Basin, the Y.X. Company was a bold and well-conceived enterprise, which, if "war" had not been its outcome, would undoubtedly have changed the whole structure of Mormon, and perhaps Western, economic development. Designed to provide way stations for handcart companies and other immigration, to carry the United States mail between the Missouri Valley and Salt Lake City, and to facilitate the movement of passengers and freight between Utah and the East, the Y.X. Company anticipated the Pony Express, the Ben Holladay Stagecoach line, and the Russell, Majors and Waddell freight trains of the late '50's and early '60's.

Several factors prompted the formation of such a company.[1] First, there was a need for way stations and supply depots to accommodate the handcart companies and other overland migration of Latter-day Saints. The suffering of the Willie and Martin companies could have been avoided if a series of stations had been established along the way to provide food, clothing, lodging, equipment, and repair and other services. Second, an overland passenger line was needed to provide speedy and comfortable transportation of Mormon immigrants who were able to pay their own way, and to garner income from the regular overland-to-California traffic. The establishment of a passenger route would also induce "Priests, Editors, and the great ones of the earth who are so much concerned about the affairs of Utah," to travel to Mormon Country to "learn the truth relative to the Latter-day Saints and their institutions." [2] Third, since the failure of the Great Salt Lake Valley Carrying Company, an overland freight line was needed to provide the expanding Kingdom with an increasing supply of merchandise, machinery, tools, and equipment at reasonable rates. The smaller merchants would welcome a specialized freighting line, and the larger consumers and business houses could avoid the "excessive charges" of merchants by placing orders with a carrying company which could easily deliver merchandise, it was believed, for one-third less than the typical charge by such firms as Livingston & Kinkead. If this eliminated the big wholesale merchant, the Mormons reasoned, so much the better. Something needed to be done to correct the situation in which "so many" of the brethren were "working so hard for a bare pittance and spending their strength to enrich a set of ostentatious, proud and epicurean gentiles." [3]

Finally, there was need for a regular and dependable mail service. Utah had received poor mail service throughout the 1850's, and the Mormons became more and more convinced that they could carry the mail for Utah and the West at substantially less than the government was paying and with substantially better service. A four-year contract to carry a monthly mail between Independence, Missouri, and Salt Lake City had been awarded by federal authorities to W. M. F. Magraw (and J. M. Hockaday, a partner) in 1854 for $14,440 a year, later increased by Congress to $36,000. Upon further application by Magraw, Congress granted an additional $17,750 indemnity, but directed the Postmaster General to cancel the contract in August 1856.[4] The contract was finally annulled in October 1856, giving the Mormons the opportunity of bidding on the new mail contract.

Plans for the establishment of an overland express and carrying service began in November 1855, when Brigham Young proposed the establishment of a water freight line up the Missouri to Fort Union, in Dakota Territory, and down the Yellowstone River to present-day Yellowstone Park, from whence goods could be freighted to some point along the Mormon Trail, perhaps Fort Bridger.[5] Young estimated that the 1855 commercial freight from Council Bluffs to Salt Lake City amounted to 513 tons, which, at the rate of seventeen cents a pound, amounted to $174,420. Involved in this traffic were 304 wagons and 3,210 oxen. In addition, he pointed out, there was "the large amount annually required by the Trustee in Trust" which was not included in the commercial statistics. If a steamboat concern would agree to undertake the business, Young said, Utah interests would build a fort and warehouse at the head of navigation to receive the goods.

When it appeared that nothing would come of this proposal, the president then advanced a new land-freighting proposal to the territorial legislature, which was holding its sessions in Fillmore (the official capitol of Utah, 1851–1856). William Chandless, who was in Fillmore at the time, wrote that the chief topic of discussion was a proposal to establish a daily line of stages from the Missouri River, through Salt Lake City to California; the journey to be made in fifteen days — three or four days quicker from New York than by the Panama route:

The difficulties of the plan, the vast expense of providing animals for nearly 2000 miles' coaching, the necessity of establishing inns of some kind every ten or fifteen miles, the danger from Indians, and the clear impossibility of continuing the line through the winter, were set forth by one party; others demonstrated the certain profit from the scheme as a business, the advantages to the country of an influx of wealth, the probability of their carrying the United States mails, and receiving a good fat sum for the work, &c.[6]

On January 17, 1856, the territorial assembly passed an act incorporating the Deseret Express and Road Company, which was assigned the responsibility of constructing a road from South Pass on the eastern border of the territory to Carson Valley on the California border.[7] A number of mass meetings were held, and the legislature memorialized Congress for $200,000 with which to construct the road and asked for a daily mail. Brigham Young, presumably as trustee-in-trust, offered to furnish 300 miles of the route if a daily express were provided.[8] Although men were appointed to study and make plans to forward the enterprise, the appropriation was not forthcoming, and it was clear that the Mormons would be left to their own devices.

The principal problem was to obtain the United States mail contract. Brigham Young recognized that the government would never give the contract to himself or to the Mormon Church; therefore, when bids were called for, an application was submitted in the name of Hiram Kimball.[9] The Mormon bid was for $23,000 — considered to be a low price, and explainable by the fact that the church expected to engage in the passenger and freight business using the same employees, stations, animals, and equipment. A four-year contract for a monthly mail between Independence and Salt Lake City was awarded to Kimball on October 9, 1856, to cover the period December 1, 1856 to November 30, 1860.[10] When unofficial reports reached Utah in February 1857 that the contract had been awarded to Kimball, Brigham Young quickly got Kimball to agree to transfer the contract to the trustee-in-trust, or, at least, to hold it subject to his "orders and counsel."[11] This furnished precisely the opportunity desired. The Brigham Young Express and Carrying Company was organized, and the first mail carried by the company left Salt Lake City for the east on February 8, 1857, and arrived in Independence twenty-six days later. The Independence mail was picked up on May 1 and delivered to Salt Lake City in twenty-eight days.[12] Regular deliveries took place thereafter. Mail service between Independence and Fort Laramie was placed under the direction of John Murdock and William A. Hickman; that between Laramie and Salt Lake City was under the charge of Porter Rockwell.

The plan of the Y.X. Company was to institute immediately what was called a "swift pony express" to carry the mail; to prepare a wagon line to haul freight by the summer of 1857; and to establish a stage coach line to carry passengers by the fall of the same year. The pony express mail line was expected to deliver mail between Independence and Salt Lake City regularly in less than twenty days; freight and passengers might require a few days longer, but service was regularly planned for winter as well as summer, and would be available by "express" at higher rates.[13]

The stations which the Mormons had already established at Fort Supply and Fort Bridger in 1854 and 1856, were to be strengthened. Additional stations were to be established at the head of the Sweetwater River, near Rocky Ridge; at Devil's Gate, east of South Pass; at La Bonte; at Deer Creek in the Black Hills; at Horseshoe Creek, thirty miles west of Fort Laramie; and at Beaver Creek (Genoa), 100 miles west of Florence, Nebraska, not far from the juncture of the trails west from Florence and north from Independence. (Most of these stations were subsequently maintained by the Pony Express.) At each of these stations a mile-square village settlement was to be laid out, grain and vegetables were to be planted, and each settlement was to be equipped with mills and shops, storehouses, corrals, and other requirements of village life. In addition, supplies of food were to be freighted from Utah to supply the workmen and immigrants until the first crop could be produced. Ultimately, stations were to be established every fifty miles or so, in order that there would be a station for every day's travel. The proximity of stations would also permit emigrants to walk from station to station and "have [their] supplies renewed at every such place." Remembering the needs of the handcart pioneers, the company (or the church, through the company) hoped to make it unnecessary for walking emigrants to carry all the supplies they would need on their journey across the Plains.[14]

As for freight, Brigham Young offered to carry all the freight wanted by Salt Lake City merchants at the rate of 12½ cents per pound. "Eventually," Young ventured to hope, "this may destroy the merchants' trade, for who will give 40 cents per pound for sugar and coffee, when they can send on their means and orders, and have it delivered here for 25 or 26 cents, and other things in proportion."[15] Indeed, company agents J. M. Groesbeck, in Independence, and Horace S. Eldredge, in St. Louis, were advised to "keep a clear eye upon the markets, and when Sugar is abundant in the markets, and but few purchasers, and prices in consequence fall, then take advantage and purchase at the lowest figures, and so with other staple commodities that we need."[16] A warehouse was to be built in Independence for the storage of these commodities until convenient to ship.

The Y.X. enterprise obviously required a large investment in labor and property. The building of the many stations, the fencing of yards and pastures, the manning of each station, the horses and mules and wagons, feed for the animals, and, above all, provisions and supplies for employees and passengers — the supplying of all these constituted a major undertaking. This was within the realm of financial possibility, however, since most of these items were to be found within the territory and could be obtained from consecrations.[17] Feramorz Little was directed to go east to buy harness and carriages; Horace Eldredge was instructed to buy scythes, grindstones, mill irons, and materials for blacksmith and machine shops for each of the stations; and William A. Hickman and Lewis Robison were authorized to buy animals from the previous contractors, Magraw and Hockaday.[18] Other

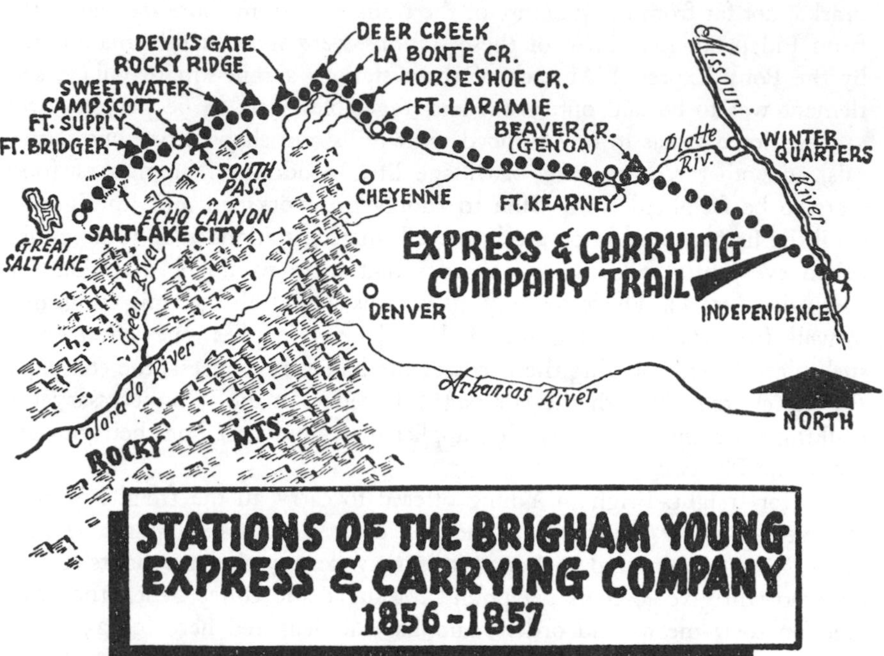

animals, equipment, provisions, and labor were supplied by Utahans, or by Mormon immigrants on their way to the West. The church's technique was to induce individuals in the territory to contribute labor, animals, and equipment as a matter of duty to the church and Kingdom, but to handle the enterprise on a partial business basis so that if and when profits accrued, those who participated would share in the dividends according to the investment made. Participating church members were told that none should ask, "how much shall I have for my labor?" Nor should those donating animals, wagons, flour, and other property expect immediate payment, although an arrangement was made with two merchants, Levi Stewart and W. H. Hooper, whereby they would "pay a fair price, in merchandize, for horses and mules that will fill the requirements," [19]

The ledger book of the company reflects the mammoth nature of the project. In response to the appeals of apostles and other appointed solicitors, an estimated four hundred persons contributed labor, livestock, provisions, and supplies.[20] Wealthier Mormons donated horses, wagons, and, in some cases, complete outfits. The leather makers in the territory, Jennings and Winder, Golden and Raleigh, and Philip Pugsley, were engaged to furnish boots and shoes, harness leather, saddles, and cushions. Butchers, blacksmiths, flour mill operators, and others devoted their efforts during the late winter and spring of 1857 to furnishing the company. "Aunt" Laura Kimball contributed "1 pair socks" for some grateful driver, while Joseph Busby furnished "2 old bridles." A $6.00 quilt by Sister Elizabeth Foss, a $75.00 grey horse by John Bagley, a $20.00 revolver by Heber C. Kimball, a wagon cover by Marriner W. Merrill worth $3.50, and $50.00 worth of "tithing office pay" by Joseph Horne are representative items, all of which were strictly accounted for on the company's ledger. Likewise, the major merchants of the territory contributed supplies and equipment in exchange for donations of butter, eggs, grain, and other produce by workers in the Kingdom or in exchange for "tithing pay" by the church. Virtually all the available resources in the territory were tapped to make the enterprise a going concern within a matter of a few weeks. The total value of all contributions to the Y.X. Company between February and July 1857 amounted, by actual count, to approximately $107,000.

The church's own financial involvement is indicated in a steadily mounting debt during the first half of 1857. Some $12,000 in credit, for example, was obtained from the firm of Livingston & Kinkead, through which eastern accounts were settled. A frantic call was made in June 1857 for donations of cattle to redeem the debt and to replenish that part of the church's public works stock which had been applied on the debt. The call was "liberally" met — some 200 head of cattle were collected — and the church's public works and other activities were continued, despite the strain imposed by the operations connected with the Carrying Company.[21]

Nearly all Mormon villages sent men to assist with the enterprise. The vast majority of these were called to the work as missionaries. Each man called to build and maintain the stations was told that he would be expected to stay "until his place can be conveniently supplied by a suitable person from the East on his way to Utah, or otherwise."[22] Ira N. Hinckley, who was called to go as a company blacksmith, was told by Brigham Young, "I want you to go for nothing, board yourself and turn something in." He was "set apart" or blessed for the mission by the "laying on of hands" in a religious ceremony, and fulfilled his six-month mission with "characteristic willingness and promptness."[23] Many of the "express missionaries" were outfitted and supplied by wealthier and older members who were similarly promised only partial returns on their investments.[24]

The principal activity of these men, of course, was concerned with the establishment of settlements. By April 6, 1857, three companies of up to a hundred men each had been dispatched from Salt Lake City to build stations in the mountains and on the prairies.[25] Each company took long wagon trains of food, feed, and equipment, "sufficient . . . to enable several hundred persons to winter . . . in case of such emergency as occurred last fall [that is, the handcart episode]."[26] With literally hundreds of men arriving and departing on Express Company business, Salt Lake City was said to be "teeming with life and activity to an unusual extent."[27]

It is to be emphasized that these were not to be way stations in the sense of those used by Ben Holladay and Wells Fargo in the 1860's. They were to be settlements. In a matter of a few weeks, for example, one company proceeding west from the Missouri River established a station called Genoa, on the Beaver River, approximately 100 miles west of Omaha. Two farms, of 750 and 100 acres respectively, were bound with sod fences, and planted to corn, potatoes, buckwheat, and garden greens. A saw mill was set in operation and a quantity of housing lumber was prepared. A brick yard was also operating "full blast." The number of available hands led company officers to boast that they would "build a city not a whit behind any other in Nebraska." The city itself was 400 acres in size with the Mormon village plan of settlement. Like a miniature Salt Lake City, the blocks were ten acres in size, with eight lots in a block, and the wide streets ran due east-west and north-south. By July 1, the colony numbered 162 persons, largely men, and a great variety of livestock, including 42 yoke of oxen.[28]

Similarly, a settlement was established at Deer Creek, about 100 miles west of Laramie, Wyoming, under the direction of Nathaniel V. Jones. By July 1857, a corps of 76 men had erected a log corral 150 feet square, stocked it with 76 mules and horses, nearly completed a stockade enclosing 42 houses, and constructed a large stockyard filled with cattle. Some 123 cattle were used in building the station. A large store of provisions, including 10 tons of flour, was stored there, and another 50 tons were on the way. In addition to establishing the settlement and station, they had fenced, broken, and planted fifteen acres, constructed irrigation facilities, and put up enough hay to last the winter.[29]

Other stations at Horseshoe Creek, La Bonte, Devil's Gate, and Rocky Ridge were in various stages of completion by July 1857. The interests of private parties at Rocky Ridge ("Markham's Fort") and at Devil's Gate ("Fort Simone") were purchased and 640 acres were claimed at each place.

Each plot was surveyed during the summer by a church surveyor.[30] On July 4, 1857, Brigham Young reported that the Y.X. Company was sending out "from 40 to 65 animals every mail," and that this would be continued "until we get the road stocked with 1,800 horses and mules."[31]

It is to be noted that these settlements were made upon Indian lands and that the Mormons did not seek or receive formal approval from the Indians or the government for establishing the way stations. This was an admitted weakness in the enterprise, but Brigham Young felt that the mail contract gave a kind of *ad hoc* blessing to the endeavor. Writing to the company's agent in St. Louis, he said:

> I learn from Dr. Bernhisel [Utah's congressional delegate] and others, that the Hon Manypenny [Commissioner of Indian Affairs] and other functionaries are very much opposed to the settling of any portion of the Indian lands, because the Indian lands are not yet bartered for and they cannot give away even by mail contract what they have neither bo't nor paid for! If we should defer our wayside settlements till they had arranged these matters righteously with the "natives," how long should we wait? We do not mean to put it into the power of Gov't. to refuse our making settlements, neither do we design to make much noise in our ceaseless labors to benefit the human family, and ourselves. How long should we have waited here for a home, had we waited until U. S. extinguished the Indian claim here?[32]

THREATENING CLOUDS

Just as the Mormons were well along toward realizing their goal of establishing the requisite number of settlements and equipping and stocking the route, the entire structure was demolished as if in one blow by the sudden and secret action of the government canceling the mail contract. Operatives of the Y.X. Company first got wind of this action about July 1, 1857, when the postmaster at Independence refused to hand over the mail to the company's representative. Shortly afterward they learned that the order to cancel the Mormon contract was dated June 10, and that the annulment coincided with the decision to send a large consignment of federal troops to Utah.[33]

Abraham O. Smoot, the mayor of Salt Lake City, was in charge of the mail going east from Salt Lake in June, and it was he who first learned of these actions and hurried back to Utah to tell Brigham Young. Fully recognizing the urgency of the situation facing the company and the church, Smoot and other Y.X. agents ordered the company's stock and station outfits all along the route east of Fort Laramie returned to Utah. At Fort

Laramie he and Porter Rockwell "hitched up two spans of our best animals to a small spring wagon" on July 18, and reached Salt Lake City on July 23, averaging more than 100 miles per day.[34] Brigham Young and several thousand associates and followers happened to be in Big Cottonwood Canyon, east of Salt Lake City, celebrating the tenth anniversary of the entrance of the pioneers into the Salt Lake Valley. It was there that public announcement was made of the government designs.[35]

Many urgent meetings of church authorities were held, and as reports continued to come in of the boasts of some of the soldiers on the expedition, the Mormons feared a repetition of their experiences in Missouri and Illinois. With the expectation of having to fight for their lives, and certainly with the assurance that the Y.X. Company could no longer operate, Brigham Young, on August 12, 1857, issued an order confirming Smoot's action in breaking up all Mormon stations between Fort Laramie and the Missouri River. He also ordered all stations between Salt Lake City and Fort Laramie closed. The forts and farms were abandoned, all movable property was taken to Utah, and the enormous outlay of labor and materials was almost a complete loss.[36] As these companies made their way back to Zion, the *Deseret News* bitterly reported that their return had "saved our enemies the trouble of clearing the road of American citizens lawfully occupying American soil." [37]

A settlement with those who had furnished horses, mules, wagons, harness, and other property was made in December 1857, after which Brigham Young estimated the total loss at "probably nigh $200,000." [38] While some of the stations were later used as stations on the overland telegraph line, and others were used by Holladay and others connected with the overland mail and express, the Mormons realized nothing financially from these uses. A gigantic enterprise — one which, as Stenhouse wrote, might have been the means of placing Utah in daily intercourse with the rest of the world a full decade before that desired end was accomplished by the railroad — died a-borning.[39]

THE UTAH WAR

While the Brigham Young Express and Carrying Company was engaged in dismantling its stations in July 1857, the United States Army was on the march to Utah. Originally named to head the expedition was Brevet-Brigadier General W. S. Harney, commander at Fort Leavenworth. But when it appeared that Harney was "indispensable" in Kansas, and perhaps a little too anxious to "put down the Mormon rebellion," he was replaced by Colonel Albert Sidney Johnston.[40] The first of 2,500 troops left Fort Leavenworth on July 18, 1857, and the entire force was on the way within two months. Including civilian teamsters, wagonmasters, suppliers, and other employees and hangers-on, the total expeditionary force totaled about 5,000 men.

These troops had been ordered to Utah by John B. Floyd, Secretary of War in the administration of President James Buchanan. The order to Harney from the Commanding General of the Army, dated June 29, 1857, explained the move as follows:

> The community and, in part, the civil government of Utah Territory are in a state of substantial rebellion against the laws and authority of the United States. A new civil governor is about to be designated, and to be charged with the establishment and maintenance of law and order. Your able and energetic aid, with that of the troops to be placed under your command, is relied upon to insure the success of his mission.[41]

This explanation was similar to that given the Congress by President Buchanan in December of the same year. Utah Territory, he said, was under the personal despotism of Brigham Young. "As Chief Executive Magistrate," he stated, "I was bound to restore the supremacy of the Constitution and laws within its limits." To effect this purpose he had appointed a new governor and other officials and "sent with them a military force for their protection, and to aid as a *posse comitatus,* in case of need, in the execution of the laws."[42] Alfred Cumming of Georgia, who had served as Superintendent of Indian Affairs on the Upper Missouri, was named in June to replace Brigham Young as governor.

Pressed by Congress, the Buchanan administration was able to produce three documents on the basis of which it had concluded that the Mormons were "in a state of substantial rebellion." These were letters from: the displaced mail contractor, W. M. F. Magraw; an appointed Associate Justice of the Utah Supreme Court, W. W. Drummond; and Thomas S. Twiss, Indian Agent on the Upper Platte. Each of the letters characterized the territory as being tyrannically governed by Brigham Young, with no respect for the United States or its laws and institutions, and with no protection for the rights of non-Mormon minorities. Federal appointees, they alleged, were impotent in discharging the obligations of office.[43] The administration admitted, however, that no investigation had been made of the various specific and general charges contained in the letters, and no attention was paid to the Mormon refutations. The troops were hurried off to Utah, it appears, over the objections of the Commanding General, Winfield Scott, who thought that the proposed force was too small and too late in the season to reach its destination before winter.[44]

The "real" or underlying reasons for the Utah Expedition have never been agreed upon. Although Buchanan was active in pressing and defending the expedition, the prime mover would appear to have been Secretary Floyd, who kept the letter of General Scott advising against the immediate expedition secret from the president.[45] Was Floyd, a Virginian and southern-sympathizer, trying to put the army out of action and deplete the federal treasury as the secession movement was gaining momentum?[46] Were Floyd and other administration leaders unduly influenced by businessmen and patronage-hungry politicians who expected to profit from the large contracts?[47] Or were the president and secretary really interested in demonstrating federal supremacy to the obstreperous Kansans and others, like the Mormons, who were giving "popular sovereignty" a bad name?[48] At a time when rumblings of secessionism were being heard, in other words, was the anxious dispatching of the Utah Expedition intended to serve as a vivid demonstration of the resolution that would be shown in putting down any states-rights rebellion?

Probably the weight of the various motives can never be determined. A recent study is inclined to reject the "conspiracy" theory and accept Buchanan's simple explanation that he wanted "to restore constitutional government" in Utah, and to register his party's disapproval of the Mormons at a time when it was politically desirable to do so.[49] One conclusion is inescapable, the $15,000,000 expedition accomplished "nothing that could not have been accomplished by tactful negotiation."[50] It was one of the few occasions in American history in which raw federal power, rather than the voluntary processes of reason, was depended upon to force conformity of social viewpoint and political submission.

Whatever the immediate and ultimate motives for appointing a new and non-Mormon governor and sending the Utah Expedition, three facts emerge as being of particular significance. The first is that, ironically enough, the activities of the Brigham Young Express and Carrying Company in carrying out the mail contract and in performing other economic chores for the church figured prominently among the factors which led to the actions taken. The letter of W.M.F. Magraw, for example, would appear to have been almost exclusively an outgrowth of his determination to wreak vengeance on his Mormon competitors. Indeed, the next government mail contract after the cancellation of the Kimball contract, was awarded in May 1858 to Magraw's erstwhile partner, John M. Hockaday and company, and provided for a weekly service between Salt Lake City and Independence paying $190,000 a year. Moreover, Magraw was a principal subcontractor in supplying the Utah Expedition.[51]

In the same vein, the letter of Thomas Twiss alleged that the stations established by the Y.X. Company in Nebraska Territory were upsetting Indian relations on the Plains, and that the ultimate intention of the church was "to monopolize all the trade with the Indians and whites within, or passing through, the Indian country." This view was seconded by Twiss' superior, George Manypenny, who reported that the Mormons had "studiously endeavored to impress on the minds of the Indians" that there was a difference between the Mormons, on the one hand, and the "citizens of the United States," on the other. The Mormons tried to convince the Indians, the federal commissioner said, that the "Mormonee" were their friends and that the "Mericats" were their enemies.[52] Thus, the bold design of the Y. X. Company itself, and the suspicion of Mormon aims and methods in relation thereto, had much to do with the cancellation of the contract, of the Utah Expedition, and it also compelled the abandonment of the enterprise.

The second significant fact in relation to the Expedition is the role played by the Gentile businessmen in Salt Lake City. While these firms did not lobby for the Expedition, neither did they lobby against it. As one Mormon stated before a Salt Lake congregation in 1857: "Like blood-suckers, all they want is our money; they have never written a letter to the States to rebut a single falsehood or misrepresentation."[53] When War Department and army officials were still doubtful of the practicability of sending the army in the fall of 1857, advice was sought from men who had done business in Utah. These are reported to have represented that "the season was not too late for moving troops across the Plains to Utah."[54] Whether or not these businessmen did give support to the Expedition, out of selfish or patriotic motives, the point is that the Mormons interpreted their actions as signifying approval of the government's action.[55] And, according to Mormon history, the merchants did not attempt to deny this. This led to a distrust of Gentile businessmen in general, and of merchants in particular, which influenced Mormon mercantile policy for the next forty years. The impact on Mormon attitudes and policies is perhaps most cogently illustrated by the following statement made by Brigham Young in the course of an interview with one merchant in October 1857:

> Mr. Ray I will tell you the truth, the Gentile merchants with yourself have been the means of bringing on this present war. You have been selling my blood and the blood of my brethren for gold; this I shall not put up with any longer, I shall not permit any Gentile merchant to do business in this territory after this year in the way they have been doing. We have been kind to them and I have been their friend, and our people have paid them promptly, and they should have been our friends and told the truth about us; but they have not realized what they were doing.[56]

The third significant fact in relation to Buchanan's action is that it represents the commencement of a theme which would be repeated with increasing virulence throughout the remainder of the nineteenth century: National institutions and customs must be made to prevail in Utah. Plural marriage, openly practiced since 1849 and openly advocated since 1852, was, of course, one of the "peculiarities" in the Utah social system which most adherents in the Republican Party, and some in the Democratic Party, believed should be brought into harmony with general American beliefs and practices. Equally objectionable to the "outsider" were the customs, regulations, and requirements which, in effect, subordinated business to religion. To free-enterprising Gentile businessmen like Magraw and the Livingstons, the rigid personal and business code of Mormonism was a symbol of puritanical superstition and an invitation to open resistance. Despite sincere efforts on the part of certain church leaders, including Brigham Young, to gain the support of Gentile capitalists and "rugged individualists" for Mormon social objectives throughout the 1850's, most of them seem to have felt that Mormon policy and practice, at least in its economic phases, was directed against *them*. The church would not permit the freedom of enterprise to which they had been accustomed and which would make possible the profits they sought; therefore, the church was dictatorial and the Prophet was a tyrant. The church frequently interfered to prevent the uninterrupted operation of free markets; therefore, the church was a combination in restraint of trade. The church encouraged its members to consecrate all their property to the trustee-in-trust; therefore, the church was a monopoly whose power and economic interests were growing stronger and stronger. The church expected extensive donations for community projects and cooperation in their completion and maintenance; therefore, the church was coercive.

Magraw, that "personal and political friend" of Buchanan who is said to have played a role in attempting to fasten slavery upon Kansas, struck out at the "helplessness" of those Gentile businessmen who tried honorably "to improve their fortunes" by dealing with the Mormons.[57] How could they penetrate that self-contained community unless federal authority loosened the cords which tied the Mormons together? How could the territory escape becoming the private preserve of a few well-entrenched church officials if the consecrations of 1856 and 1857 concentrated property in the hands of the trustee-in-trust? The "restoration of national sovereignty" by means of the Utah Expedition represented the first in a long series of federal attempts to secure the abolition of Utah's potent theocratic and cooperative social and economic institutions which were interfering with the spread of private capitalism throughout the West. The campaign against Mormonism was part and parcel of the rising national campaign for private property, the free market, competition, and unrestrained enterprise.

THE "INVASION" OF UTAH

Since Brigham Young was not given any official notification of his displacement as governor or of the assignment of federal troops to the territory, he chose to regard the troops as an hostile mob.[58] Two months after the troops had started from Leavenworth, the commanding general had sent Captain James Van Vliet, Assistant Quartermaster and Commissary of the army, to Salt Lake City to investigate the possibility of obtaining supplies from the Mormons and to assure Mormon leaders of their peaceful intentions. But Mormon spies could plainly see that the troops were "itching for a fight." Army troops, according to a typical report, were "anticipating fine times here this winter while walking over our people, hanging up our rulers and prostituting our women." [59]

The sequence of events illustrates with what importance and gravity the coming "invasion" was viewed by Mormon leaders. As governor, Brigham Young issued a proclamation declaring martial law: "*Citizens of Utah* — We are invaded by a hostile force." [60] If the army advanced into the territory, said the governor, the Mormons would "make a Moscow of every settlement, and a Potter's Field of every cañon." [61] Coincident with the proclamation, church and territory were mobilized to meet the oncoming threat. In order to conserve their food supply, orders were issued prohibiting persons from disposing of grain "to any Gentile merchant or temporary sojourner," or suffering it to go to waste.[62] The territorial militia, the Nauvoo Legion, was mustered into full-time service under the generalship of Daniel H. Wells. This force, consisting of about 3,000 men, was the kind of citizen army that younger officers were inclined to belittle, but which the old professionals never took lightly. As a later observer wrote, it was an "uncouth, undisciplined, and ragged set of men," with "every variety of weapon known to civilized nations," but it was a group, which in its own habitat, fighting for homes and families, could be ferocious and deadly.[63]

From this group a Corps of Observation, consisting of seventy-five men, was sent immediately to scout the army, protect and aid the Mormon immigration of 1857, and locate strategic points along the route for the interception of the federal troops. Another force of about fifty, known as the Blackfoot Fork Mission, was sent to scout the northern route of the Expedition. Finally, a company of a hundred or more was sent to harass the movement of federal troops and supplies. Part of the instructions of the latter reads as follows:

> On ascertaining the locality or route of the troops, proceed at once to annoy them in every possible way. Use every exertion to stampede their animals, and set fire to their trains. Burn the whole country before them and on their flanks.

Keep them from sleeping by night surprises. Blockade the road by felling trees, or destroying the fords when you can. Watch for opportunities to set fire to the grass on their windward, so as, if possible, to envelop their trains. Leave no grass before them that can be burned. . . . Take no life, but destroy their trains, and stampede or drive away their animals, at every opportunity.[64]

One early action of these raiders was to burn two prize and expensive Mormon outposts in eastern Utah, Fort Bridger and Fort Supply, which government forces had expected to occupy. The total loss to the Mormons in this "scorched earth" policy was in excess of $52,000.[65] Many of the personnel in these task forces had been employed by the Brigham Young Express and Carrying Company and thus were retained in the service of church and community. The sending of the task forces was followed by the movement into Echo Canyon of a defensive force of approximately 1,100 men known as the Eastern Expedition. The outfitting and provisioning of the first of these men to leave, as well as of the task forces, appears to have been done primarily with properties of the Y.X. Company which had been returned to Salt Lake City.[66]

Most of the men in the Eastern Expedition, however, were provisioned and outfitted by the local communities from which they came. In some cases the communities requested donations of cattle with which to pay commercial houses for supplies and equipment. The city of Provo, for example, outfitted fifty men by donating more than $480 worth of cattle, most of which were exchanged at the store of William H. Hooper for clothing and other supplies. Six head of cattle were used in the purchase of twenty cans of powder and 2,000 caps.[67] Whatever method of finance was followed, each community held a special drive to collect donations for "the brethren who were out for the defense of Zion against U. S. troops in the mountains." Representative of these contributions were those collected on October 25, 1857 in the little village of Manti:[68]

2 blankets	7 shirts
6 quilts	6 pairs of mittens
1 buffalo robe	3 pairs of gloves
21 pairs of stockings	1 set of undergarments
1 pair of breaches	1 handkerchief

1 pair of drawers

In addition, the village furnished ten men with horses and rations for fifteen days. Members of the militia who remained at their homes mustered with pitchforks and teams to harvest the crops of their brethren who had gone "out on the road."[69]

Outlying communities, such as San Bernardino and Carson Valley, were called upon to furnish ammunition and arms. One shipment from San Bernardino included 500 revolvers, while Carson Valley sent 2,700 pounds of church ammunition and a great deal of private ammunition "and a large amount of arms," besides another $800 worth purchased in San Francisco after the emergency broke. By the end of September 800 Mormons were "in the mountains," and another 400 were on the way. By October 15, 1100 men were in the mountains and another 700 camped on the public square in Salt Lake City "ready to leave at a moment's notice." When word reached Salt Lake City from the "front" on November 8 that Colonel Johnston would likely "want to push in" to the Salt Lake Valley immediately, another 1300 men were ordered to the mountains and many of these were on the way within two days. They were described as marching "towards the mountains of snow," with "wet feet, poor shoes, and straw hats, without tents or fire at night." Yet, church chronicles noted, "it shows the willingness the saints have to maintain the kingdom of God, and defend themselves against their enemies."[70]

While the expeditionary force was being prepared, the church public works, which had been more or less idle during the famine of 1856, and whose activities had been geared primarily to Y.X. operations in the spring of 1857, resumed full-scale activity, this time in the interests of defense. Large numbers of volunteer and employed workers labored "from sunrise to sunset," making guns, bullets, cannon balls, and canister shots. On the site of the old sugar works a chemical laboratory was erected, gunpowder was successfully manufactured, and a large supply of ammunition was produced. On Temple Square, at a new shop erected for the purpose, public hands made revolvers. According to one observer, they turned out revolvers resembling Colts at the rate of twenty per week.[71]

The final step in the Mormon mobilization process was the order to all the "outposts of Zion" and the missionaries located throughout the world to abandon their missions and "come home to Zion." This drastic act—sometimes called the "Big Move"—was made in the heat of preparations for the defense of the Kingdom and involved the definite abandonment of the Salmon River Mission, the Elk Mountain Mission, the Mormon Station in Carson Valley, the settlement at San Bernardino, and the recall of several hundred missionaries stationed throughout the world.[72]

Whether Brigham Young and his associates felt that this personnel was actually needed to protect the Kingdom, or whether he regarded the outposts as no longer tenable in view of the difficulties between the Mormons and the government, is difficult to determine. While the church gained several hundred "fighting men" with extensive arms and ammunition, the property sacrificed, particularly at Carson Valley and San Bernardino, shortly became worth millions. Within a year of the abandonment of Carson Valley the discovery of the Comstock and other mines made it, to use Stenhouse's phrase, "immensely valuable." [73] For all the property on both sides of the Carson River in Eagle Valley, for Carson City, and for other choice locations, the 450 Mormon settlers received less than $50,000. More than 500 Latter-day Saints left San Bernardino for Utah, with a similar sacrifice of economic property.[74]

The return migration was organized in Mormon military order, as in the case of the initial movements to colonize the settlements now being abandoned. Teams were sent from Salt Lake City to bring the personnel and their property to Utah. Two hundred men, for example, went to Fort Lemhi to bring the settlers in the Salmon River Mission back to Salt Lake City.[75]

With so many persons and families rolling into Zion from "abroad" it was fortunate that the harvest in the fall of '57 was as generous as it was. Wilford Woodruff called it the largest harvest "ever known in these valleys." [76] Not only was the supply of food sufficient to feed the incoming immigrants with no diminution in Utah living standards, but it was also quite sufficient to feed the Mormon standing army. This was another evidence to the Mormons that God was helping them to fight their battle.

The Mormon task force did succeed in slowing down the advance of federal troops. Major Lot Smith's "Mormon Raiders" managed to burn three freight trains, out of a total of forty-one, comprising seventy-four large freight wagons. The supplies destroyed included 68,832 rations of dessicated vegetables, 4 tons of bread, 4 tons of coffee, 84 tons of flour, 46 tons of bacon, 3,000 gallons of vinegar, and 7 tons of soap — enough to last the entire expedition three months.[77] The Mormons also captured 1,400 of the 2,000 head of cattle which accompanied the expedition.[78] These cattle were driven to Salt Lake City and pastured on a church herd ground until returned to the army the following summer. One of the federal soldiers recalled the harassment as follows:

> Every day when coming to camp they [the Mormons] would set the grass on fire, using long torches, and riding swift horses, so that before pitching tents we always had to fight fire. They destroyed so much of it that the animals had to be driven some distance to get feed. One morning, just before daybreak, they rushed through the camp, firing guns and yelling like Indians, driving off all our mules and horses, numbering about a thousand, and before we could get into line they were safely out of reach of our rifles. It was ten o'clock before we recovered our animals. They hovered around daily, watching and taking every advantage of us, feeling safe in their tactics, knowing our inability to cope with them, as we had no cavalry, while they had the fleetest of horses.[79]

As a result of such "raids," the army animals became poor, many of them died, and it became difficult for the army to move its supplies.[80] Eugene

Bandel, who was in a force that followed the army in the spring of 1858, said that hundreds of the government animals died for lack of pasturage. "During one night alone, not far from camp, almost five hundred animals perished." He described the advance of the army as comparable only "to the retreat of the French army from Russia." [81] The winter, the lack of supplies, the delay of troops, plus a general fear that the Mormon antagonist would prove to be tougher than originally feared, caused army officials to "hole up for the winter" near charred Fort Bridger at a place called Camp Scott. When this decision became evident to the Mormons, on November 29, 1857, all Mormon troops were withdrawn from Echo Canyon except a "guard of fifty men."

The government, of course, was not intimidated, and no doubt contractors worked sedulously to maintain interest in the Utah campaign. Buchanan was authorized to call an additional 3,018 officers and men, bringing the total number of men composing the Utah Expedition to 5,606.[82] General Harney was appointed to command the second expedition, which reached the ford of the South Platte River before a part of it was turned back. Each company was followed by "an immense drove of six or seven hundred horned cattle, to furnish their daily food." [83] New contracts provided for the expenditure of about $6,000,000 on about 4,500 wagons, 50,000 oxen, 4,000 mules, and to employ about 5,000 teamsters, blacksmiths, and others.[84] It was the magnitude of the contracts let in the spring of 1858 that led administration opponents to refer to the Utah Expedition as a "Contractors' War." The contract for the transportation of all the supplies to Utah, aggregating about 8,000 tons, was granted "without advertisement or subdivision" to the firm of Russell, Majors and Waddell, one of whose members was said to have compromised the Secretary of War.[85] The Quartermaster-General calculated that the whole supply train en route to Utah in the spring of 1858, if bunched together, "would make a line of about fifty miles." [86]

While these preparations for a new and larger onslaught were being made, the Mormons responded by strengthening their own defensive force, and at the same time sought to achieve a peaceful settlement. The Utah legislature, meeting in January, voted that delinquent taxes be collected to apply on the debts incurred by the hostilities; that all public finance and business, including the delivery of mail, be handled by the tithing offices; and that a standing army of 1,000 mounted riflemen be raised and supported out of tithing.[87] The cost of raising this force was estimated at $1,000,000. By and large the method of finance was to ask local men of means to outfit one or more of these "guards." The method is illustrated by Joseph Holbrook, of Bountiful, who explained his own obligation as follows:[88]

It fell to my lot to fit two men for the expidition after the following manner:

Two good horses, valued at ($125.00 each)	$250.00
1 good pack animal	100.00
2 good rifles	50.00
2 good revolvérs and scabbards	75.00
2 bridles and saddles	90.00
2 canteens and cups	2.50
1 camp kettle	3.00
4 good blankets ($20.00 each)	80.00
2 pair pants ($10.00 each)	20.00
1 pack saddle and rope	15.00
2 over shirts	10.00
4 over shirts [undershirts?]	10.00
Together with other needful clothing, for groceries, flour, meat, beans, etc., for one year	294.50
Total	$1,000.00

The Ogden First Ward, called to outfit fifteen men for this army on February 1, 1858, responded as follows:[89]

Item contributed	*Donor*
$25.00 cash	John Shaw
1 horse and saddle	Thomas B. Faye
2 bushels wheat, 3 bushels oats, 3 bushels corn	George Tomlin
100 lbs. pork, 10 bushels corn	William Chapman
1 two-year-old steer	William Jones
1 revolver and shirt and Minnie rifle	Charles De Saul
1 saddle	John Tuilson
1 rifle and 1 horse	Thomas Thomas
100 lbs. flour	Henry Manning
1 rifle	Mathew Fifield
1 Yauger, 2 blankets, 2 one-year-old steers	George Stranger
One-fourth of a man and outfit	John Hart
One-half of man and outfit	John Harris
One-fourth of man and outfit	William Eixon
$100	John Shawl

This thousand-man army was raised in February, and completely fitted and "ready for action," with a riding horse and pack animal for each man, and with a complete complement of revolvers, rifles, and other equipment, by March 22, 1858. Other defensive preparations included the establishment of a church bank to finance the defense, the manufacture of gunpowder by the church public works at Cedar City and Provo, and the organization of civilians to cache food and other property, burn their homes and fields, and "retreat to the mountain fastnesses" in case of sudden invasion.[90] The seriousness of the situation, from the Mormon point of view, is indicated by the fact that the general authorities of the church and many others fasted and prayed for three days and nights, soliciting God's help and favor.[91]

Brigham Young made many statements pledging that the army would not be allowed to set foot in Utah,[92] but his considered judgment was that a peaceful solution must be sought and that no untoward Mormon activities must be allowed to hamper that effort:

> There is . . . a hope prevailing among the Mormons that the Administration will yet call off the army. Their leaders had great difficulty to keep some down who were restive and panting for a fight. Brigham told them that "he would exercise faith that the troops should be kept away, and he wished all to do the same, instead of wishing them to advance." His orders were imperative not to shed blood; so that if another course should be adopted by the Administration towards them the feeling of revenge should not hinder the establishment of peace.[93]

Buchanan, hurt by adverse criticism of his precipitate action, likewise was in a mood to compromise. When that good friend of the Mormons, Thomas L. Kane, solicited permission to arrange a compromise solution, he was given the president's blessing.[94] Traveling incognito as "Dr. Osborne," and at great personal sacrifice, Kane met with Brigham Young and other church officials, and later with Colonel, now General, Johnston, and Governor Cumming. In February and March 1858, an agreement was reached for Cumming to go to Salt Lake City and assume the governorship without a military escort. After a leisurely trip through Echo Canyon during which Mormon forces sought to impress him with their strength, the new governor arrived in Salt Lake City on April 12. After satisfying himself that he would be recognized as governor, and that many of the charges against the Mormons were false, he returned to Camp Scott to get his wife and to order the federal army to march through, but not remain in, the Salt Lake Valley. News was likewise received from the administration in Washington that the president had issued a proclamation granting amnesty to the Mormon "rebels," and appointing an investigating committee. Clearly, the Mormons had won half of their battle.

This turn of events was not at all to the liking of the army, which thirsted for complete suppression of the Mormons after their trying experiences on the trail and at Camp Scott.[95] "We are all disgusted," wrote Lieutenant Du Bois. "If the Mormons are rebels, they should sue for pardon instead of its being given to them unasked. If they are not rebels this campaign is unjust."[96] "The best commissioners for Brigham Young and his insolent following," wrote another officer, "would have been eighteen pounders, backed by plenty of good rifles."[97] The peace arrangements were fully supported by Governor Cumming, however, and War Department instructions had placed the army at the governor's disposal.

Nor was the solution a happy one for the church. The Saints had lost some face, considering their extravagant boasts in the white heat of defense preparations in the fall of 1857. And the army would occupy the territory, with whatever lessened sovereignty that might bring. Brigham Young and his associates finally hit upon a scheme to turn the tide of world opinion in their favor. They would present to the world a picture of a long-suffering people, completely misunderstood, who, having been persecuted in Missouri and Illinois, were once more being harassed by a hostile government without any attempt at investigation and conciliation. All of the Saints in northern Utah would prepare their homes for the torch, migrate to central and southern Utah, and hold themselves ready to "flee to the desert" in case the army or the governor did not live up to the pledge of peaceful passage and inoffensive occupation. Any intimation of army plunder, occupation of Mormon soil, or hostile action of any kind would set in motion plans to destroy the Mormon countryside, as Forts Bridger and Supply had been destroyed, and retreat "to the mountains in the desert."

THE MOVE SOUTH

The decision to make the Move South was made at a "Council of War" held in Salt Lake City on March 18, 1858. At this meeting, Brigham Young announced his plan "to go into the desert and not war with the people [of the United States], but let them destroy themselves."[98] The most complete account of this important decision, and the reasons for it, is contained in the diary of Hosea Stout:

Thursday 18 March 1858: Attended a general Council at the Historians office of the first Presidency, Twelve [Apostles], and officers of the [Nauvoo] Legion. The object of which was to take into consideration the enemies, whether to attact them before they come near us or wait untill they come near, or whether it is yet best to fight at all only in unavoidable self defense or in case a large force is sent against us this spring [;] whether to fight or burn our houses & destroy every thing in and around us and flee to the mountains & deserts &c &c &c

It appears that the course pursued hitherto by Gov Young in baffelling the oppressive purposes of Prest Buckhannan has redounded to the honor of Gov Young and the Saints and equally to the disgrace of the President & his cabinet [.]

Mormonism is on the ascendancy and now what is the best policy to maintain that ascendency. If we whip out and use up the few troops at Bridger will not the excitement and sympathy which is now raising in our favor in the states, be turned against us. Whereas if we only anoy and impede their progress while we "Burn up" and flee, the folly, and meanness of the President will be the more apparrant and he and his measures more unpopular.

Three days later, in the regular Sunday Tabernacle service in Salt Lake City, the meeting was resolved into a special conference of the church to consider what was called the "Sebastopol Plan," referring to the Russian evacuation of Sebastopol during the Crimean War two years before.[99] Brigham Young "presented the policy which he intended to pursue, which was to remove the grain and the women and children from the city and then, if needs be, burn it and lay the country waste."[100] In the exceedingly rare published proceedings, Brigham Young said, among other things:

We are in duty bound to preserve life — to preserve ourselves on earth — consequently we must use policy and follow in the counsel given us, in order to preserve our lives. Shall we take a course to whip our enemies? or one to let them whip themselves? or shall we go out and slay them now? We have been preparing to use up our enemies by fighting them, and if we take that course and shed the blood of our enemies, we will see the time, and that too not far from this very morning, when we will have to flee from our homes and leave the spoil to them.[101]

The next day the president wrote:

We are now preparing to remove our men, women and children to the deserts and mountains, that our enemies may come in and complete their instructions to establish a military post at or near Salt Lake City, if that is their only alternative. . . . Will our enemies keep off and let us alone while we are removing, or are they so bloodthirsty that they will not be satisfied short of doing their utmost to destroy our lives?

So far as we have information, their present instructions only reach to establishing a "post" in this city and acting as a "posse" when called upon; and if they come here and find neither people nor city, what will be their next move?[102]

Although there was not unanimous church support for the Move, the great majority agreed with a local leader in Sanpete Valley who said, "We must destroy our property joyfully to disappoint our enemies."[103] "The prospect of ancient 'Mormonism' — of again leaving our homes," said Brigham Young, "gives a spring to our feelings, especially since we for the first time have the privilege of laying waste our improvements, and are not obliged to leave our inheritances to strangers to enjoy and revel in the fruits of our labors."[104]

I have been driven from Missouri, where I left a good property and planted fruit trees for somebody else to eat. I passed through the same ordeal in Illinois. I preferred leaving my homes to renouncing my religion. . . . I can go again and again, until death shall furnish me a quiet resting place, should our insane countrymen continue to trample the sacred rights of freemen, guaranteed by the institutions and blood of their fathers, under their feet with impunity.[105]

The government has "ordered large reinforcements to Utah for the extermination of the faithful," wrote another, "[and the latter] will be found, probably, (if found at all,) in rocks and deserts, or, like the ancient Saints, hid in dens and caves of the earth."[106]

The economic organization involved in the Move South had three phases: (1) the organization of parties to search out a new gathering place, should necessity require it; (2) the organization of the Move itself; and (3) the arrangements for finance and credit, including the husbanding of the food supply.

It is clear from the proceedings of the special conference that Brigham Young was convinced that the southwestern part of Utah Territory (now southern Nevada) possessed a large number of oases which were isolated from each other and from other habitable valleys by large strips of desert. These oases were thought to be capable of sustaining a population of half a million people (!), and were more or less free from Indians.[107] Brigham Young reasoned that once this place of refuge was found, it would be impregnable: "While small parties might be able to cross such a thirsty waste with comparative safety, an army would find it impassable, and the larger the force the more impracticable it would be; that while few men might find enough water in a small seap or water-hole to allay their thirst, a thousand men and animals would find it totally inadequate; and that such a desert would be a more formidable barrier than an army of forty thousand men."[108]

A church party under the leadership of Bishop David Evans, of Lehi, had been sent to explore this fierce and unfriendly region in 1854, but had failed to find the succession of watered areas which Brigham Young had imagined existed there. The president now assigned the responsibility of finding the valley or valleys to two parties of trusted frontiersmen.[109] One party of 104 persons, under the leadership of George W. Bean, moved south from Utah Valley down the Sevier River and westward to the White River Valley in present-day Nevada. The company was fully equipped with agricultural implements, seeds, teams, and wagons, and actually left forty-five of its number in what was called Meadow Valley (present-day Panacca) to open a settlement. The remainder explored northwest and southwest but found no such place as the president had described. In all, the Bean party covered about 800 miles, crossed seven ranges of mountains and as many valleys, and returned to Salt Lake City in the latter part of April with a negative report. "The difficulty was to find soil, timber and water together."[110] The bleak Meadow Valley settlement had to be abandoned at a later date.

The second party consisted of about sixty men from the southern Utah settlements under the leadership of W. H. Dame. This party, also equipped for colonization, explored the wild unbroken country north of the Colorado River for several weeks and ultimately joined forces with Bean's party to strengthen the "Desert Camp" at Meadow Valley. The report of the Dame party was also unfavorable.[111]

Some consideration was given to an offer by some representatives of the celebrated adventurer "General" William Walker and Colonel Kinney to sell to the church 30,000,000 acres of land on the Mosquito Coast in Central America, and to another proposition to settle Sonora, in northern Mexico. Despite the fact that some officials in Washington seemed to regard the proposition as offering means of disposing once and for all of America's "Mormon question"—and were prepared to recommend that financial inducements be offered the Mormons to accept—Brigham Young was determined to remain in Utah Territory, and did not carry the negotiations for these properties to an advanced stage.[112]

While Mormon parties were "searching out the desert fastnesses" and church officials were considering moves outside the country, the wards and settlements in northern Utah were organizing for the Move South. The organization for the Move was sketched in the special conference of March 21 which first approved the Sebastopol Plan. The Move was to be spearheaded by 500 families from Salt Lake City who had never before been driven from their homes. These persons were to be selected by Salt Lake bishops from "the poorest and most helpless" and their migration was to be "an ensample" to other wards and settlements throughout the territory. These people were to be assisted in moving by men, teams, and wagons donated by other members of their own and nearby wards. Within a week after the Move had been announced, they had been organized and had begun their hegira, at the rate of about forty families per day.[113]

The First Presidency, the Apostles, and the Presiding Bishopric supervised the organization of the remainder of the Saints. In general, the church was divided into three groups: (1) Those living in southern Utah who would not move, but who were instructed to send wagons, teams, and teamsters to northern Utah to assist in the Move. (2) Those living in northern Utah who were young, brave, and vigorous, and who would remain behind to irrigate crops and gardens, guard property, and set fire to the homes in case the Sebastopol treatment was ordered. Approximately a thousand "valiant men" would be in this group, and they were instructed to be ready to "fly at a moment's warning to meet the enemy" if he showed signs of hostility.[114] (3) Some thirty thousand persons living north of Utah Valley who would make the Move. Each ward and settlement was allotted a strip of land in Utah, Juab, Millard, or Iron County, as the immediate objective or resting place. The ultimate destination, of course, would depend upon moves made by federal officials or the army. Settlers north of Weber Valley, such as in Box Elder and Cache Valley, were to assemble in Ogden; Weber Valley settlers were to assemble in Salt Lake City; and Salt Lake, Davis, and Tooele County residents were to assemble in assigned places in Utah Valley.[115] The people of Tooele, for example, were directed to settle at Dry Creek (Lehi). Those wards being carried by southern Utah teams were to go farthest south. The grain was to be moved first and then the families.

The Move was to be carried out in strict Mormon military order, each ward being organized into tens, fifties, and hundreds, with a captain over each.[116] Each family was expected to transport furniture, in addition to food and clothing, so that personal and family possessions would not be burned, if that tactic were decided upon. Shavings, kindling, and dried grass were to be left in the entrances of homes to make the scorched-earth policy more effective. The housing when they reached their destination would have to consist of the bodies of their heavy covered wagons, or canvas tents. Inevitably, some would live in dugouts and temporary board shanties and cabins. Whatever the shelter, the regular work of making a living — making butter and cheese, raising stock and poultry, spinning and weaving — would be continued as if in their former homes. Several dozen southern Utah wagons, complete with oxen, horses, and mules, came north to assist with the Move.[117]

While bishops were organizing their wards for the Move the church public works was preparing for the transportation of church properties southward. The initial destination was Parowan, later changed to Fillmore, finally changed to Provo. One group cached all the stone which had been cut for the Salt Lake Temple, and leveled and covered over the foundations of this sacred edifice so that it would resemble a plowed field and remain unmolested by "desecrating maurauders." Another group boxed all of the tithing grain in bins holding seventy-three bushels each, and transported it south to granaries especially erected for its reception in Provo.[118] More than 20,000 bushels of wheat were said to have been hauled in this manner. Additional wagon trains carried machinery and equipment to be housed in specially built warehouses and sheds. Still another group hauled the public machine shop, the *Deseret News* print shop, and other machinery and equipment to Fillmore and Parowan. All the church records, papers and books were also packed in boxes and shipped to Provo.[119] Temporary public works mills and shops were set up in the principal settlements in central and southern Utah to grind wheat, repair equipment, manufacture armaments and munitions, and perform other public services.

The Move occupied a period of about two months, being virtually completed by the middle of May. This meant that several hundred wagons were constantly on the move during this period. One report states that an average of about 600 wagons had passed through Salt Lake City daily during the first two weeks of May.[120] Utah's new governor, Alfred Cumming, who was in Utah during part of this period, made several journeys along the line of moving caravans pleading with the people to return to their homes. On one trip he met 800 wagons. "Is there not some way to stop the moving?" he asked Brigham Young, to which the president replied that "if the troops were withdrawn from the Territory, the people would stop moving, but that ninety-nine out of every hundred of the people would rather live out their lives in the mountains than endure the oppression the Federal Government was now heaping upon them."[121] The president is also reported to have told some advance leaders of the Utah Expedition: "Our necks shall not be given to the halter. . . . I'm tired of this city."[122] As late as May 24, when the Move had been completed, Brigham Young and other church officials were giving serious consideration to burning Salt Lake City and all settlements north of it.[123]

The sight of an estimated 30,000 people on the move must have been one never to forget. John R. Young, who was returning to Utah from a mission in Hawaii, described the sight as follows:

> At Parowan, two hundred miles south of Salt Lake City, we encountered a scene that I shall never forget. I remember distinctly, the "Exodus," as it was called, from Nauvoo, when sixteen thousand souls left their homes and commenced that marvelous journey of fourteen hundred miles to the unknown valley of the Salt Lake. But that exodus was like a small rivulet by the side of a mighty river when compared with the seventy-five thousand [possibly 30,000] men, women, and children that we now met in one continuous line of travel.
>
> Horses, oxen, and cows were harnessed or yoked to wagons and carts; and one family by the name of Syphus, was moving their effects on a handcart drawn by a pair of yearling steers. Mothers and children walked along as merrily as if going to a corn husking; each family moving its little bunch of cows and flock of sheep, and all starting on the journey (that was never completed) to Sonora, in Mexico, or some other place.
>
> At times we were compelled to drive our wagon for miles outside the beaten road, everywhere hearing and seeing evidences that increased my gentile companions' wonderment of the marvelous power held by Brigham Young over his people.[124]

George Brimhall called it "a complete exodus beyond any human conception. The mother with her groups of little ones, and the more matured young folks, were walking, helping, shoeing, driving, going somewhere, but where nobody knew." "One thing is certain," he concluded, "it was done by us in perfect peace and harmony, reminding me of the grey squirrels in their migrations from the oak and beach woods in the State of Indiana to the Cumberland mountains in Tennessee, Virginia and Kentucky."[125] Perhaps the most expressive of the Move, however, is the following description from the pen of a pioneer teen-ager:

> We packed all we had into father's one wagon and waited for the command to leave. At night we lay down to sleep, not knowing when word would come of the army which we thought was coming to destroy us. . . . There were seven of us children in the family.
>
> We put away all our playthings, for the days found us so frightened that all we did was to follow father and mother from place to place, looking into their faces for a word of comfort and a look of cheer. One morning father told us that we should leave with a large company in the evening. He said little more. There were packing and the making of bread.
>
> Along in the middle of the day father scattered leaves and straw in all the rooms and I heard him say: "Never mind, little daughter, this house has sheltered us, it shall never shelter them." . . .
>
> That night we camped on Willow Creek in the south end of the valley, and at ten o'clock every soul with bowed head knelt in prayer to God. As I dropped to sleep I heard my mother whispering that the Lord had heard our prayers and that our homes should not be burned. I cried and cried, but at last I dropped to sleep.[126]

FINANCING THE MOVE SOUTH

The financial and economic problems involved in the Move South have never been fully understood or explained by Mormon historians. There are, first of all, the problems created by the departure from the territory in the fall of 1857 of all the large merchants. Not only would they be unlikely to supply the territory with imported commodities during the summer and fall of 1858, but their services as community bankers and bookkeepers would not be available. Some local substitute for the latter was necessary, as was also an alternative to the former. The second group of problems relate more directly to the Move itself: How would the church finance its own part in the Move? Above all, what provision could be made for the employment of the vast body of men concentrated in Utah Valley. Finally, assuming that tithing receipts in 1858 would be very low because of the Move, how would the church handle the burden of debt with which it would inevitably be saddled as the result of the war and the Move?

The church's economic program, as distinct from its military operations, during the period from July 1857 to July 1858, consisted of the encouragement of home manufacture, combined with grain conservation, to meet the problem of the absent merchants; the creation of an organization called the "Deseret Currency Association" to provide banking services and a circulating medium; and the expansion of church public works in Utah Valley to provide employment.

The home manufacture program was largely hortatory. Discourses were delivered by church officials on the subject in church conferences and in meetings of the legislature. Not only was home manufacture essential to self-preservation, the people were told, but the Lord had visited this "persecution" upon His people in order to teach them that they must sustain themselves from the elements about them.[127]

The Deseret Currency Association was an outgrowth of discussions in the legislature in regard to providing a circulating medium "for the convenience of the citizens of this Territory."[128] These discussions took place during the week of January 11–19, 1858, at a time when it was not settled whether there would be war, peace, or abandonment. At an important meeting on January 19, the legislature decided to abolish the territorial tax and carry out all public works with tithing labor under the direction of the bishops. The standing army of mounted guards, also appointed in the same meeting, was to be sustained by the wards and counties from which they were raised.[129] It was thus consistent that the new "bank" be chartered under church auspices, which was done at a public "mass meeting" on the night of January 19. Some persons referred to it as the "Bank of Deseret" in their diaries, but the official name adopted by the new association, recalling the unfortunate experience with the Mormon bank at Kirtland, was the "Deseret Currency Association." Brigham Young was elected president; Daniel H. Wells, treasurer; Hiram B. Clawson, secretary; and Heber C. Kimball, Daniel H. Wells, Albert Carrington, and W. H. Hooper, directors. The capital stock seems to have consisted of church property, and the notes of the association were to be made redeemable in livestock. "The people passed the act of incorporation with great enthusiasm and unanimity," after which the bank was discussed in the various wards and settlements.[130] All members of the church were asked to sign their names "to sustain" the currency expected to be issued by the bank.[131]

Since the church had no gold — that having been spent on the Brigham Young Express and Carrying Company — and since there was no intercourse with the United States by which state bank notes could be obtained, the territory was almost completely devoid of a circulating medium. Tithing scrip was not a satisfactory medium because its redemption depended upon full supplies of needed commodities in the tithing offices throughout the territory. The unsettled conditions of the preceding months had depleted those supplies and upset the regular deliveries of tithing. Merchants were no longer on hand to accumulate the tithing scrip and "make deals" with the tithing office for their redemption in bulk. The Deseret Currency Association, therefore, represented an attempt to meet the need for currency and credit by using the one type of commodity which was generally acceptable and at the same time generally available — livestock. Although most of the church cattle had been killed during the winter of 1855–1856, or bartered off to the merchants, the church had 3,000 horses in its herd on Antelope Island in the Great Salt Lake in 1856, and these had been augmented by the dissolution of the Y.X. Company. Most of the horses had been given to the Eastern Expedition, but they were still available. A total of 600 horses were in the church herd on Antelope Island in August 1858.[132] The church also had possession of the large herd of army cattle which had been "captured" by the Mormon Raiders. These cattle would not be touched, of course, but neither is the gold in Fort Knox! By the time cattle were needed for redemption purposes, a new supply would be coming in through tithing.

The plan was, then, to issue credit instruments and currency backed by livestock. Arrangements were made with the two leading Mormon mercantile firms, W. H. Hooper and Andrew and Levi Stewart, to accept the currency and redeem them in horses or other livestock. All other persons, as we have seen, were asked to pledge their support of the currency. John D. Lee wrote that when the subject of the "Bank of the Kingdom of God" was presented in Harmony, "The vote was in the affirmative, that every man hold it Eaqueal to gold, & that any person attempting to shave or impair it should forfeit the amount in Question besides his fellowship & standing in the church."[133]

The first series of notes issued by the Association was printed "in common type" in February and March 1858. During the five-week period from February 19 to March 27, approximately 8,000 separate notes, bearing a total value of more than $40,000 were printed in denominations of one, two, three, five, ten, twenty, fifty, and one hundred dollars.[134] Signed by Brigham Young and Secretary Clawson, these notes were paid out by the church to merchants and public works suppliers, and were also loaned to enterprisers who found no other source of credit.[135] The credit instruments used for the purpose of securing loans were in the form of printed promissory notes on which the borrower agreed to pay to the association a specified number of dollars, with interest at ten per cent. By means of this credit the currency played a role in stimulating domestic production, as was fully intended.[136] One of the church employees reported in April that the currency was already "working well for the good of all classes."

Its beneficial effects are already realized, and trade is more brisk than usual at this season of the year. Specie being very scarce, on account of no exportations, and the importations of the merchants having drained the country dry and Uncle Sam refusing to pay the ex-officials' drafts, something was necessary to keep trade alive; and this association was instituted in time to spread faith and confidence among the men of business who experience its salutary results.[137]

When the Move South commenced, a second series was issued from presses located in Salt Lake City and Fillmore. During the period March 31 to July 17, more than 15,000 pieces, with a total value of not quite $40,000, rolled from these presses. This series bore the same denominations as the previous one and the bills were used partly in meeting the expenses involved in the Move, and partly in financing the public works program during the summer.

The most important public works project was the employment of several hundred men in the construction of a road through Provo Canyon to connect Utah Valley and Round Valley (Heber City), and to open up Provo River Valley for settlement. Previous to the opening of this road, persons could pass from Utah Valley through this narrow but magnificent canyon only on horseback along an Indian trail. By dint of great labor, a large group of "Move Southers" cut through the promontories and rocky sidehills, built up the washes and hollows, and constructed an excellent fourteen-mile mountain road.[138] The road, which was chartered by the legislature as a toll road, enabled the people of Utah Valley, whose timber supply was limited, to carry away the wood found in the canyon. The toll arrangement made it legally possible for the road company — largely owned by Brigham Young as trustee-in-trust — to collect toll on the thousands of freight wagons which used the road in supplying federal troops at Camp Floyd. Approximately $20,000 was spent in making the road, which was approximately half of the second issue of the Deseret Currency Association.[139]

In general, the Deseret currency appears to have circulated at par until the return from the Move South. One or two Indian traders did not accept it, but Mormon traders were able to do so as long as the leading merchants would receive it. David Seeley, who had been a leader in the San Bernardino colony, was reported to have sold goods in Battle Creek (Pleasant Grove), and insisted on U. S. coin. When Brigham Young discovered this, he instructed the bishop "to tell him [Seeley] to clear out; he had gone to California to get gold and he ought to be contented with the gold there, and not come here to take the gold and silver from this community."[140] Brigham Young afterward told Seeley that "he [Brigham] could make this people rich if speculators would keep away with their rags and traps and the people would sustain the currency." Those who would not take "the currency of the Saints" ought to be told to "go and leave the territory."[141]

With the re-establishment of large Gentile merchandising houses in the territory in the summer of 1858, the most pressing need for the currency was obviated, and a call to turn in the currency was issued in August 1858. One diarist wrote that it was necessary to call in the Deseret currency because Gentile merchants were buying the currency at a 60 per cent discount and then attempting to exchange it in Salt Lake City for livestock, thus draining the church of its horses and cattle.[142] Most of the currency returned in the form of tithing and donations to the Perpetual Emigrating Fund and other church causes. In this way, most of the livestock in the church herds became the property of the P.E.F. and thus provided the basis for the Church Teams of the 1860's.[143] The Currency Association printed about $17,000 worth of engraved notes in denominations of one, two, three, and five dollars, in September and October 1858, to redeem the printed notes, held in small quantities. These circulated for a year until the plates were confiscated and damaged by the territorial marshal.[144] They were eventually redeemed with horses or with other tithing receipts.[145]

THE RETURN

When the Move had been completed, and when the Mormon metropolis was deserted except for the "home guard," Governor Cumming, supported by Buchanan's peace commissioners, declared, on June 14, that President Buchanan's "free and full pardon" had been unconditionally accepted and that "peace is restored to our Territory."[146] Under the leadership of General Johnston, the United States Army commenced its triumphal march from Camp Scott. Approximately 5,500 men were involved.[147] Passing by the abandoned and burned Mormon fortifications, huts, and breastworks in Echo Canyon, they followed the same route as that taken by the advance company of Mormon migrants in 1847. As the army marched through Salt Lake City on June 26, 1858, a correspondent accompanying the troops regarded the scene as "one of the most extraordinary" in American history. All day long, he wrote, from dawn till after sunset, the troops and trains poured through the city, the utter silence of the streets being broken only by the music of the military bands, the monotonous tramp of the regiments, and the rattle of baggage wagons.[148] "With the exception of a picked few of his 'destroyers' of decidedly rough and sinister aspect, left as policy, and with orders to fire the city in case we offered to occupy it," wrote an officer, "every man, women, and child, had, under the direction of the prophet departed — fled! . . . It was substantially a city of the dead, and might have been depopulated by a pest or famine."[149] One observer spoke of the "death-like silence" which characterized the "march through the deserted streets of the dead city." A few of the officers, he wrote, marched "with uncovered heads, as if attending a funeral." [150] And yet the city was beautiful — perhaps more beautiful than if the people had not fled:

> The city is beyond my power of description. It is beautiful — even magnificent. Every street is bordered by large trees beneath which & on either side run murmuring brooks with pebbly bottoms. Not a sign of dirt of any kind to be seen. The houses are surrounded by large gardens now green with summer foliage. All the houses are built of adobe nicely washed with some brown earth, the public buildings large & handsomely ornamented surrounded by walls of stone. . . .
>
> But oh how beautiful is this city, not unlike the foliage of plants nourished by corruption. A whitened sepulchre, "A den of thieves & murders," the emigrants say, but to our eyes alone it would seem to be an abode of purity and happiness, a going back to the Golden Age. I say to myself, "Can it be true?" this story of their crime & in spite of the evidence I am dissatisfied. I know it is true but feel that it cannot be. Grey hairs & venerable forms walk the streets — are they too chief of sinners? [151]

The army made no revelry in its "victory." "Our delights," wrote Captain Tracy, "were of comparatively short duration; for in place of halting soon, and beside the city, we were marched out westward miles away wholly without its limits, across the bridge of the Jordan and thence southward along the banks of that river." [152] After a few days delay, the army established its permanent headquarters in Cedar Valley, forty miles southwest of Salt Lake City, and named it Camp Floyd.

All Mormon observers spoke of the strict discipline attending the movement of government troops. Officers were scrupulous to see that no person was mistreated or property trespassed. This pleased church officials, and four days after the march, on June 30, 1858, the announcement was made in Provo: "All who wish to return to their homes in Great Salt Lake City are at liberty to do so." [153] Brigham Young himself led the return, and within two months upwards of thirty thousand Mormons were back in their homes in northern Utah.

All those who witnessed the return commented on the destitute appearance of returning companies. The grasshopper visitations of '55 and '56, the sacrifices for the Y.X. enterprise and expeditionary companies of '57 and '58, and the Move South had left them literally threadbare. One soldier who saw a group of returnees on July 6, said it was a "sad" sight: "Old women driving cows, feet bare, scanty dress, scarcely enough to hide nakedness; bleary-eyed women holding sickly looking children to their breasts and men with vice & hate mingled in their faces." [154] Still another wrote:

> [They] were wretched-looking beings, — men, women, boys, and girls, old and young, halt and blind, without shoes or stockings, ragged and dirty, though

some of the young girls had endeavored to make as respectable an appearance as possible, by making garments out of corn sacks. They were driving a number of animals, consisting of cows, sheep, and pigs. They were very demure, and manifested no resentment at our jeers.[155]

Whether or not these descriptions are exaggerated—and the Mormons described themselves in much the same way[156]—it was clear that a decade and more of achievement and social independence, in the face of hostile nature and hostile humanity, had ended in poverty and disappointment. The picture of 30,000 pioneers trudging back to their hard-won homes, farms, and orchards, with their skimpy and ragged suits and dresses, driving their pigs and family cows, to the accompaniment of jeers from "the cream of the United States Army" would live long in the hearts and minds of pioneer leaders. None would have dreamed that within three years Babylon itself would be engulfed in a terrible fratricide as the result of which the tables would be reversed: Soldiers would be pulled out of Utah leaving to the Saints the spoils.

CHAPTER VII

A Decade of Planning for Self-Sufficiency and Growth

A country which has gone through total war — that is, a war involving the majority of the whole population and most of the productive resources — commonly renews its determination to achieve complete economic self-sufficiency, even at the expense of efficiency and progress. In the Utah of 1858 and succeeding years this tendency was sharpened by the fact that self-sufficiency was already a well-established element of religious faith. The lack of clothing — the destitution and want — were often attributed, not to natural disaster and federal "persecutions," but to the failure of the people to do what they had been commanded; namely, cease to patronize the merchants and establish home industries. The struggle for self-sufficiency which characterized the decade from 1858 to 1868 is all the more remarkable because it was a struggle against "normal" economic accommodation. Despite the built-in market offered by the federal army and its suppliers; despite the opening of mines and markets in neighboring Colorado, Nevada, Idaho, and Montana; and despite the contracts to construct the transcontinental telegraph line and other windfalls, Mormon leaders uncompromisingly held to self-sufficiency as the official policy of the church. They did not expect absolute economic independence, of course, but they did seek such a high degree of autarchy as to prevent closer ties with the outside world from producing changes in the essential character of their economy. When the Civil War broke out, leaders and members felt that the self-sufficiency policy had been divinely inspired. But when that conflict ended, and the rational justification for self-sufficiency was much weaker, the official policy remained the same. Even the approach of the transcontinental railroad in the late 1860's brought no relaxation in the drive for independence from the economy of Babylon.

Brigham Young viewed all traffic with the Gentile world with misgivings. During the Utah War he declared that the government could never conquer the Mormons by sending in armies; armies can destroy but they cannot build. The easiest way to conquer the Mormons, he said, would be for the government to pay Gentiles to carry in merchandise, year after year, until the people had come to depend upon it. The Saints would then have lost their individuality and collective loyalty.[1]

> Let the calicoes be on the shelves and rot. I would rather build buildings every day and burn them down at night, than have traders here communing with our enemies outside and keeping up a hell all the time and raising devils to keep it going. . . . We can have enough [hell] of our own, without their help. . . . We sincerely hope that the time is not far distant when the people will supply their own wants and manufacture their own supplies; then and not until then will we become independent of our enemies.[2]

There is also some evidence that Brigham Young and his associates regarded purposeful adherence to the independent barter economy as the best insurance of high investment. With their earnings largely in goods and property, it was said, the Mormons could not dispose of them as easily as in a money economy, with the result that they spent less and accumulated more.[3]

Nevertheless, in the face of Mormon resistance, Salt Lake City did become the entrepôt of the Mountain West. Its central location, the abundance of skilled and professional labor, and, above all, its supply of raw materials and consumer goods, all contributed to that end. In the face of the new environment created by the discovery of minerals in the western mountains in the 1860's, Mormon leaders found it increasingly difficult to maintain distinctive Mormon institutions. It is somewhat ironic that the Mormon struggle for self-sufficiency in the 1860's was largely financed and supported by earnings from such economic windfalls (and destroyers of self-sufficiency) as the forces of occupation, the Overland Mail, and the booming trade with the newly opened mines in Utah and its neighboring territories.

WINDFALLS OF OCCUPATION

Camp Floyd. Just as the trade with Forty-niners had rescued the Great Basin colony from imminent starvation and collapse in 1849–1850, so the trade with Johnston's Army improved the gradually deteriorating condition of Mormon settlers during the fall and winter of 1858 and succeeding years. An estimated 4,000 federal troops were at first located at Camp Floyd. To these must be added an estimated 3,000 non-Mormon suppliers, employees, and camp followers, located at a place called "Dobietown," or "Frogtown" (now Fairfield). This, wrote Horace Greeley, was "the largest regular force ever concentrated upon the soil of our country in a time of peace."[4] Utah, of course, was not required to pay any of the costs of maintaining this large force. Under arrangements between the army and the freighting firm of Russell, Majors and Waddell, thousands of large freight wagons left annually from the Missouri River carrying food, clothing, and other supplies to the troops.[5] Thus, the initial fear of the Mormons that the army would attempt to supply most of its needs locally and bring danger of famine proved to be unwarranted. This forced a change in church policy. Whereas the wards and settlements had been counseled in July 1858 to save their grain and not sell it,[6] a member of the First Presidency three months later announced: "There is no sin in selling grain to the army, but the sin is in disposing of it for less than it is worth, and depriving the poor of obtaining sufficient for their wants."[7] Although most Mormon farmers had left their fields for the Move South, the Utah harvest of 1858 was a good one. Many took hope in the fact that the army was prepared to pay for everything it could get, and there was widespread satisfaction when it became clear that the army did not intend to plunder "as they had done in the states in our former persecution."[8]

The liberal government supply policy made it possible for the troops to bargain on an individual basis for such items as the Mormons could spare. A flourishing trade was built up, with Mormon villagers bartering dried fish, buttermilk, pies, vegetables, butter, eggs, and "Valley Tan" whiskey for such items as money, clothing, tea and coffee, pieces of iron, and stoves.[9] The rates of exchange were regarded by the Mormons as tempting and remunerative. One army group paid 25 cents a pound for potatoes, 75 cents for a dozen green onions, $1.25 for a dozen eggs, and $1.25 for a pound of butter.[10] Various church organizations, of course, drew up resolutions condemning this trade as being "trade with the enemy," but the advantages of it were so immediate and obvious, and the plight of those who could profit from it so pitiable, that a boycott was not placed in effect. However, to avoid competition and undercutting, all wards and settlements were advised to trade through officially recognized associations, committees, and agents. These committees were to insist upon a schedule of prices drawn up by the Presiding Bishop's Office, and published in the *Deseret News*. This schedule listed grain at $3.00 a bushel, flour at $10.00 a hundred, and equivalent high prices for meats, dairy and poultry products, and vegetables. Even cucumbers were given a price — 40 cents a dozen. In this way, the "poor and confiding" Saints were discouraged from "crowding wheat upon the army quartermaster at 95 cents a bushel," and other things proportionately low, when the quartermaster was perfectly willing to give up to $5.00 for it rather than not get it.[11]

In addition to this petty barter of consumer goods, and the markets provided for larger quantities of Mormon-produced hay, straw, grain, and meat, several hundred Mormons found employment about the camp in manufacturing adobe brick, assisting in the construction of quarters, and performing such specialized services as blacksmithing and watch repairing.[12] The greatest gains to the church, however, were from official contracts to supply grain and lumber, and from sales of army surplus. The church contracted to supply 150,000 bushels of grain for animals in 1859, at a price varying from $2.00 to $2.50 per bushel, and this amount was parceled out to the various wards and settlements so that all could profit from the favorable price.[13] The Big Cottonwood Lumber Company, which operated a chain of sawmills in the canyons south and east of Salt Lake City, and in which the church had a predominant interest, also supplied the timber used in the construction of the camp. Supplying timber at a price of $70 per thousand feet delivered, the church is said to have netted $200,000 on these sales. Much of the cash expended by the church during the years of occupation came from this source.[14] It will also be recalled that the church had constructed the Provo Canyon Road during the Move South. Since this toll road was regularly used by the supply trains of Russell, Majors and Waddell, several thousand dollars in toll were paid to the church each year. To the freighters the idea was slightly ludicrous:

> Here a saintly keeper, slate in hand, kept tally of our wagons as they lumbered past, the toll being one dollar per ton, or $1,250 for our train. The road belonged to the Mormon Church — otherwise Brigham Young. Paying an enemy toll to enter his conquered territory was the height of absurdity.[15]

The Mormon view was that God had "overruled" things for the benefit of His Saints.[16] The church made no toll charge for the use of the road by the army itself.

Both the church and its individual members profited from the occasional sales of army surplus. Periodic auctions of condemned food and surplus animals and equipment offered bargains in such wanted items as mules, bacon, boots, and doubletrees. One of the largest of these sales was the disposal of some 3,500 large freight wagons by Russell, Majors and Waddell, for $10 each. The wagons had cost the firm $150 to $175 apiece in the Midwest.[17] Many of these wagons were used as granaries, while the iron was removed and used in making nails. Large numbers of oxen and mules were also sold by the firm in the territory, for as little as $25 to $50 per yoke. If losses were sustained in these sales, they were partly recouped on lucrative army contracts.

The benefits of the unintentional helping hand of the potentially hostile forces of occupation continued until the summer of 1860, when the size of the army garrison was reduced to ten companies (about 1,500 men). In July 1861, upon the outbreak of the Civil War, the post (now named Camp Crittenden) was evacuated.

The abandonment of the post in 1861 led to what was probably the largest government surplus property sale yet held in the history of the nation. At one large auction, which commenced on July 16, 1861, the army sold an estimated $4,000,000 worth of property for approximately $100,000. Approximately two-fifths of this property was purchased in the name of Brigham Young for the bargain price of $40,000. This included iron, tools and equipment, livestock, stock feed, and a large supply of beans, flour, and other food.[18] Most of these acquisitions were turned over to the Department of Public Works. Flour, which had cost the government $28.40 per hundred pounds to purchase and transport to Utah, was acquired for as little as 50 cents per hundred. Meat was obtained for one cent a pound, sugar at 12½ cents per pound, while "whole wagonloads of musket barrels, after the breeches were burned," were purchased for $10.00. Scores of big government wagons, complete with all necessary fixtures and equipment, were acquired for $6.50 each.[19] Additional wagons, tents, harness, tools, mules, and overcoats went to Utah Valley farmers. John C. Naegle is said to have purchased the fort headquarters for $75 and supplied families with building lumber for years.[20]

Considering the obvious Mormon gains from these sales and from the occupation generally, there is a certain justice in the epitaph written by William Clayton. Thus ended, wrote Clayton, "the great Buchanan Utah Expedition, costing the Government millions, and accomplishing nothing, except making many of the Saints comparatively rich, and improving the circumstances of most of the people of Utah."[21]

Overland Mail and Telegraph. Before the "great Buchanan Expedition" had completely evacuated Utah, other windfalls presented the Mormons with opportunities for labor and supply. These were connected with the provision of improved transportation and communication services for the widely scattered but rapidly expanding settlements of the West. The firm of Russell, Majors and Waddell, which had secured the Fort Leavenworth-to-Camp Floyd freighting contracts, attempted to set up a more permanent freighting arrangement similar to the Brigham Young Express and Carrying Company. The Overland California and Pike's Peak Express Company was formed, and in April 1860 the firm initiated the Pony Express. The purpose of the Pony Express was to prove the feasibility of the central overland route and thus induce Congress to award them the mail contract. This well-known, short-lived venture lost about $500,000, but not without providing a substantial market for Mormon produce and labor.[22]

The construction by Western Union interests of the transcontinental telegraph line (1861) was also partly a Mormon project. Salt Lake City was recognized as the junction between the eastern (Pacific Telegraph Company) and western (Overland Telegraph Company) divisions of the line.

The superintendents of both divisions, Edward Creighton and James Gamble, respectively, let contracts to Brigham Young, and through him to other Mormons, to supply poles, subsistence, and transportation in connection with the construction of approximately 500 miles of the line.[23] Church records indicate that after the completion of the line in October 1861 Brigham Young received $11,000 in gold for his participation in the project. Said the president: "I did not touch that gold with my fingers or flesh until it was all paid in. I then put it in a vessel of water, cleansed it and said what words I wished over it; I then delivered every dime of it over for tithing."[24] The president also received a gift of $10,000 in stock in the Overland Telegraph Company from its president, H. W. Carpenter. "This was done to secure President Young's interest in the protection of said line."[25]

The completion of the transcontinental telegraph led to the discontinuance of the Pony Express and the assumption by Ben Holladay of control over the Central Overland California and Pike's Peak Express Company, later renamed the Holladay Overland Mail and Express Company. From 1864 to 1866 this company virtually reigned supreme between the Missouri River and Salt Lake City. The magnitude of the operations can be gauged from the fact that in 1864 Holladay hired no less than 15,000 men, used 20,000 wagons and 150,000 animals, and transported 100,000,000 pounds of freight between St. Joseph, Missouri, and Salt Lake City. This huge concern purchased much of its feed, and hired many of its teamsters and other employees in Utah. Hiram Rumfield, the Salt Lake agent of the company, reported that during an eleven-month period in 1861–1862 the company had purchased the principal part of "several hundred thousand dollars" worth of supplies in the Salt Lake Valley, and that this was "paid for in glittering gold!"[26] Brigham Young, as president of the church, contracted with the company in 1862 to furnish 50,000 bushels of oats and barley at $1.00 in gold and New York drafts per bushel, plus $1.25 for hauling each 100 pounds 100 miles from Salt Lake City. This contract was entered into, according to Brigham Young, "solely with a view to afford the brethren as good a chance as I could, under present circumstances, to turn some grain and labor into money."

In filling this contract, all classes can be accommodated, for the man who has but a few bushels surplus, can turn it in with those who have hundreds of bushels, and receive his share of the money; and those who have no grain can furnish a wagon or a yoke of cattle, or a span of horses or mules for hauling; while those who have neither grain, wagon, nor work animals, can drive teams.

I would suggest that it would be much the best for all, to the fullest extent they can afford to do so, to keep the money they earn on this contract, to pay their cash taxes and to send to the States next year for necessary machinery for manufacturing, etc., and for factory and such other staple articles as we do not yet produce in sufficient quantity and cannot well do without.[27]

Presumably other contracts were made with the company until the company began to raise its own feed in 1865. In a similar manner, the church furnished men, supplies, and transportation to parties surveying for the transcontinental railroad in 1864.[28]

Third California Volunteers. The protection of the overland mail and telegraph during the Civil War had an important long-run influence on the struggling economy of the Great Basin with the decision of the War Department to quarter troops in Utah. In 1862 the Third California Volunteers, comprising between 750 and 1,500 troops, were ordered to establish a camp (Camp Douglas) on the east bench overlooking the Salt Lake Valley. Commanded by Colonel (later General) Patrick Connor, these Union troops were instructed to prevent Indian hostilities and "keep an eye on the Mormons." The supplying of these troops during the period 1862–1866 served to continue the lucrative business begun at Camp Floyd. There was only one thing which infuriated the Mormons. Superpatriot Colonel Connor required that all those furnishing supplies to his troops repeat an oath of allegiance to the Union. "Those of doubtful loyalty need not apply." To Brigham Young and most of his followers this was an insult to Mormon integrity and hardly provocative of friendly relations. "What, take an oath to sell a few miserable potatoes? I would see them in Hell first." [29]

But there was another more far-reaching effect of Connor's occupation on the isolated Mormon economy. The Third California Volunteers were largely veterans of the California and Nevada gold fields, and made no secret of their desire to do a little prospecting in the mountains around Salt Lake City. When argentiferous ore was discovered twenty-five miles southwest of Salt Lake City in September 1863, Connor, who had developed an increasing disgust for the Mormons, their leaders, and their religion, delightedly planned to solve "the Mormon problem" by starting a mining boom. "I have no reason to doubt," Connor wrote his superiors, "that the Mormon question will at an early date be finally settled by peaceable means, without the increased expenditure of a dollar by Government, or, still more important, without the loss of a single soldier in conflict." [30]

Colonel Conner organized a mining company, framed laws for the government of mining districts, promised military "protection" for miners in dispute with the Mormons, encouraged his officers and enlisted men to prospect by granting indefinite furloughs and furnishing provisions and equipment, and, above all, distributed exaggerated releases to the eastern press advertising "rich veins of gold, silver, copper and other minerals" in Utah.[31] The Colonel himself discovered the first silver-bearing rock in Little

Cottonwood Canyon and erected a smelting furnace. He also founded an anti-Mormon newspaper, the *Daily Union Vedette,* the purpose of which was "to educate the Mormon people up to American views." His policy, clearly stated in public and in private, is best expressed in his own words:

> As set forth in former communications, my policy in this Territory has been to invite hither a large Gentile and loyal population, sufficient by peaceful means and through the ballot-box to overwhelm the Mormons by mere force of numbers, and thus wrest from the church — disloyal and traitorous to the core — the absolute and tyrannical control of temporal and civic affairs. . . . I have bent every energy and means of which I was possessed, both personal and official, towards the discovery and development of the mining resources of the Territory, using without stint the soldiers of my command. . . . These exertions have, in a remarkably short period, been productive of the happiest results. . . . Mines of undoubted richness have been discovered, their fame is spreading east and west . . . and the number of miners of the Territory steadily and rapidly increasing. With them, and to supply their wants, merchants, and traders are flocking into Great Salt Lake City, which, by its activity, increased number of Gentile stores and workshops, and the appearance of its thronged and busy streets, presents a most remarkable contrast to the Salt Lake of one year ago.[32]

Three factors prevented a full-scale miners' rush into Utah. First, contemporary mining prospects in other western states were even richer than those in Utah. Mines had been opened up in the years 1859–1863 in Colorado, Nevada, Idaho, and Montana, some with fabulous yields and fantastic profits.[33] Second, the distance of Utah from the Missouri River and the Pacific Coast made the exploitation of Utah's mines uneconomic. Indeed, although Connor sunk his own private fortune of $80,000 on mining ventures in Utah, and although eastern capitalists, attracted by Connor's flamboyant assurances and lavish press releases, expended up to a million dollars on Utah mining development, there is not a single instance of profitable exploitation of Volunteer discoveries until the completion of the railroad in 1869.[34] Finally, the church used its own devices to prevent the kind of subversion the Colonel intended.

The church's response was conditioned by the assumed unprofitability of mining development as well as by the desire to prevent a miners' stampede.[35] Agreeing with Adam Smith's dictum that mining was "perhaps the most disadvantageous lottery in the world, or the one in which the gain of those who draw the prizes bears the least proportion to the loss of those who draw the blanks,"[36] Brigham Young said that "the people have spent twenty dollars for every one they have obtained from the mines."[37] Sermon after sermon and editorial after editorial were directed at Mormon farmers and mechanics, urging them not to "take to the hills," but to let the Gentiles "roam over the hills and make holes in the ground." [38] The following expressions of Brigham Young are typical:

> On the bare report that gold was discovered over in these West Mountains, men left their thrashing machines, and their horses at large to eat up and trample down and destroy the precious bounties of the earth. They at once sacrificed all at the glittering shrine of the popular idol, declaring they were now going to be rich, and would raise wheat no more. Should this feeling become universal on the discovery of gold mines in our immediate vicinity, nakedness, starvation, utter destitution and annihilation would be the inevitable lot of this people.[39]

> Instead of hunting gold we ought to pray the Lord to hide it up. Gold is not wealth, wealth consists in the multiplication of the necessaries and comforts of life. Instead of hunting gold, go and raise wheat, barley, oats, get your bread and make gardens and orchards and raise vegetables and fruits that you may have something to sustain yourselves and something to give to the poor and the needy.[40]

> Can you not see that gold and silver rank among the things that we are the least in want of? We want an abundance of wheat and fine flour, of wine and oil, and of every choice fruit that will grow in our climate; we want silk, wool, cotton, flax and other textile substances of which cloth can be made; we want vegetables of various kinds to suit our constitutions and tastes, and the products of flocks and herds; we want the coal and the iron that are concealed in these ancient mountains, the lumber from our sawmills, and the rock from our quarries; these are some of the great staples to which kingdoms owe their existence, continuance, wealth, magnificence, splendor, glory and power; in which gold and silver serve as mere tinsel to give the finishing touch to all this greatness. The colossal wealth of the world is founded upon and sustained by the common staples of life.[41]

Apparently, this kind of preaching, combined with more subtle social pressures,[42] was effective, because only a handful of Mormons joined the Volunteers in the hunt for gold. The great majority were content to till their fields, anticipating improved prices for their produce.[43] When there was a sudden upsurge of interest in mining prospects in some valley, the president attempted to quiet the more restless spirits by dispatching telegrams urging all to "stay home and attend to your farms and do not think of gold mining." [44] The president also took a paternalistic attitude toward the "gold-crazy" Volunteers. When the short harvest and unprecedented demand of 1863–1864 forced the Mormons to ration their grain, the president directed the tithing offices to supply limited quantities of grain to the Volunteers — at the rate of $3.00 per bushel.[45] The Volunteers also were allowed to purchase approximately five tons of flour per week, as well as beef and vegetables, though at what Connor regarded as "enormous and unreasonable prices." [46]

TRADE WITH MINING COMMUNITIES

The combined effect of the simulated mining boom in Utah, and the working of mines in neighboring territories, was to open a large cash market for Mormon produce. Utah was the most economical source of food for nearly all the mines between the Rockies and the Sierra. Attracted by the generous prices offered at the mining camps for flour, salt, dried fruits, and butter, merchants and traders — both Mormon and Gentile — scoured the countryside for wanted products. Much gold and silver, and many of the newly issued greenbacks or "Lincoln skins," flowed into Mormon pockets as the result of this trade. In 1860, after the Pike's Peak discoveries, more than a hundred large wagons of Utah flour, grain, and other farm produce were freighted to Colorado. A representative of Russell, Majors and Waddell stated that more than 10,000 sacks of Utah flour were shipped out in September 1860.[47] Perhaps equal amounts were shipped from Utah to Colorado in 1861 and 1862. A much larger exportation went from northern Utah to Idaho and Montana in 1863 and succeeding years, as did a substantial exportation from southern Utah to Nevada.

The church did not encourage this trade, of course, because of the dangers of depleting the food supply and because of general objections to building a trading economy. But the trade took place, nevertheless, and the church's chief function was to organize the farmers in such a way as to assure them the highest possible price for their produce. Leading farmers and mechanics were invited to a "Price Convention" after the general conferences in April and October of each year, and prices were established which all pledged to support. In assuming the chairmanship of the Price Convention, Brigham Young stated that he "appeared as the representative of God in this convention as much as yesterday at conference." He added that the convention was not organized to aggrandize anyone. "It is not whether flour be $6 or $12 per hundred," he declared, "the main object is to get the people united in doing right in temporal things." [48] The prices agreed upon were approximately double those of the premine period, wheat being priced at $5.00 per bushel, corn at $4.00, and flour at $12.00 per hundred. The list of commodities and services whose prices were elevated by this action included all the grains, meats, dairy products, many vegetables, dried fruit, hay, and freighting.[49] There is no doubt that the priesthood-controlled conventions increased the bargaining power of Utah farmers generally and made it possible for them to furnish their families with many comforts which would have been beyond their reach had there not been this united effort to keep prices up.[50] As a single item illustrating its influence, Samuel Bowles reported that 200,000 pounds of dried peaches alone were sold by Mormons in Idaho and Montana in 1864. The price received at the farm for these peaches was fixed at 75 cents a pound by the Convention.[51] While the prices charged seem high, even by modern standards, there seems to have been no complaint of the Mormon action from buyers in the mining areas. Due to freighting delays and difficulties prices at the mines often reached as high as a dollar a pound for flour, and there was usually rejoicing when the food trains came in.[52]

The Price Convention was replaced in 1866 with the Utah Produce Company, a church-promoted, privately financed company which attempted organized disposal of Utah's domestic surplus at remunerative prices. This company disappeared with the advent of the transcontinental railroad in 1868–1869.[53]

DEVICES OF SELF-SUFFICIENCY: THE CHURCH TRAINS

All of these windfalls bolstered and cushioned the Mormon economy in the 1860's. They supplied cash and capital equipment for many colonies, manufacturing establishments, and for agricultural improvement. But they did not lead to the abandonment of self-sufficiency as the goal of economic life. The strength of the self-sufficiency motive is found in the discouragement of mining by the Mormons themselves, in the deprecation of trade with mining communities, and in the uses to which the Mormons put the money which they earned from the various windfalls. Far from easing the adjustment to the opportunities presented by the opening of markets around them, the Mormons as a group sought to withdraw themselves—to prevent the development of a specialized, market-oriented economy. While Babylon fought in the War Between the States, while eager prospectors were erecting the "Miners' Frontier" in the remainder of the West, while Gentile merchant-freighters were accumulating fortunes, the Mormons stubbornly struggled to build their Kingdom without outside help and without ties to outside economies.

The church's utilization of its own resources and of the gains from unhallowed windfalls in building the self-sufficient Kingdom is really the central story of the 1860's. The group struggle for self-sufficiency manifested itself in immigration, public works, communications, colonization, agriculture, industry, transportation, and in the church's investment policy generally. In each case one sees an attempt to develop an economy with few entangling alliances, and yet with a capacity for growth and expansion through superior organization. If group achievement was somewhat less than expected, it was due to the failure of Great Basin agriculture to produce bounteous harvests. If the new visitors brought to Utah by the transcontinental railroad in 1869 found an economy humming with industry, but not thriving in wealth, it could be blamed on the niggardliness of nature and the difficulties with Indians. Considering the obstacles presented by nature, Mormon production did well to keep up with the increase in population, for through effective immigration procedures and natural increase the population rose from less than 40,000 in 1858 to more than 80,000 in 1869. The support of this expanding population and of various non-Mormon communities and interests throughout the Mountain West are the most telling achievements of the Mormon economy in the 1860's.

Strange as it may seem, the new circumstances encountered in the occupied economy served only to strengthen the church's emphasis upon the gathering. No immigration had taken place in 1858, but the resumption of "normality" in 1859 saw the revival of immigration on as large a scale as during the 1850's. As the resources of the Perpetual Emigrating Fund Company were largely exhausted, those who did not have the wherewithal to procure teams were advised to cross the Plains by handcart.[54] However, only one company, consisting of 235 souls, with 60 handcarts and 6 wagons, made the trek in that manner in that year.[55] Total immigration was much more in 1860, but only two companies of 349 persons went by handcart. The handcart was clearly not a popular scheme, although mule trains were sent from the Salt Lake Valley to meet each of the companies as they reached Fort Laramie.

Before the immigration of 1860 was completed, church leaders had decided to abandon the handcart system in favor of dispatching companies of teams from Utah to bring back immigrants and merchandise. This would seem to have been a natural step, although it had been thought impossible to drive a yoke of oxen so far in one season. The P.E.F. inherited most of the animals and properties of the ill-fated Brigham Young Express and Carrying Company.[56] The supply of oxen, horses, mules, and wagons in the hands of private citizens, the church, and the P.E.F. had been greatly augmented by sales of the army and of the firm of Russell, Majors and Waddell in 1858–1860. At the same time, the rush of miners to Colorado and elsewhere was forcing the price of wagons and animals higher and higher in the Missouri Valley markets where they were sold. These tendencies were reinforced by the outbreak of the Civil War, which threatened commercial intercourse between the East and the Far West. The Mormons, who had striven twice before to do their own importing and exporting, now seized upon the organization of Mormon teams to carry back to their outfitting centers in the Missouri Valley provisions for immigrants and other exports, and to return to Utah with immigrants and their supplies, manufactured goods, machinery, staple imports, and other goods for church and private use. The "down and back" trips, as they were called, were to be made in one season. By transporting their own flour, beans, and bacon to supply the immigrants, the Mormons could reserve their cash to buy machinery and thus contribute to the success of the self-sufficiency campaign.

Merchants and church agents had experimented with round-trip freighting between the Salt Lake Valley and the Missouri Valley in 1859.[57] These experiments proved that oxen could make the 2,200 mile round-trip in approximately six months if they were properly cared for. The success of these experimental trains prompted a number of others to use the down-and-back scheme in 1860. One of these was Joseph W. Young, a nephew of Brigham, who captained an ox-team company of thirty wagons which left Utah in the spring of 1860 and returned the same fall with newly-purchased machinery and merchandise. Upon his return, Young was invited to deliver a sermon on "the science of Ox-teamology" before the October 1860 general conference.[58] His proposals were favorably received and preparations were made immediately to try out the scheme on a large scale in 1861.

The procedure to be followed was outlined by the First Presidency and distributed in printed form to all bishops and other local officials. "We are rich in cattle, but do not abound in money, either at home or abroad," said the circular, "and we desire to so plan and operate as to use our small amount of money and large number of cattle in the best possible manner for accomplishing the best good."[59] First, the number of men, teams, equipment, and provisions needed to transport immigrants and machinery would be determined. These would then be apportioned to each ward and settlement on a pro rata basis. On a specified date in April, all of the requested men, teams, and supplies were to be in Salt Lake City, ready for the trip East. In Salt Lake City they would be inspected and loaded under the direction of the Presiding Bishop, and organized into companies of approximately fifty each. The captain of each company was given complete authority to "see the train through."

Each wagon was to be pulled by four yoke of oxen, or its equivalent in mules, and should carry 1,000 pounds of flour. The teams would also take as many loose oxen as the year's immigration that came independent of church aid might want to purchase for their outfits, thus providing a market for Utah oxen, and keeping within the church family from $10,000 to $30,000 per year which had been paid out yearly in the Missouri Valley for cattle and wagons. Other Utah products which could be sold in the Midwest could also be carried along. In addition to the teamsters, a mounted man was required for each group of four wagons to look after the cattle and hunt for game.

The teams would be expected to reach the Missouri River in July and return with from ten to twenty immigrants per wagon. Some of the wagons would return with church freight, and each community was free to send additional persons and facilities for freighting machinery and other imported merchandise wanted by individuals or settlements. In case the teams sent from Utah were insufficient to transport all the immigrants and freight, the P.E.F. was prepared to augment the returning caravan by purchasing the necessary facilities.

The individuals who were called or who volunteered to take part in these expeditions were to be regarded as "missionaries," but they were credited on the tithing books with the value of the service rendered. Those who loaned teams, and who contributed flour and other produce, were also given tithing credit for their donations. In 1864 the amounts credited for these services in one valley were as follows: service as mounted guard, $300; mules, wagon, and teamster, $250; two yoke of oxen and wagon, $140; yoke of oxen, $60; wagon, $50; use of saddle, $5.[60] It was not uncommon for unmarried men to volunteer as teamsters in the hope that they would meet a prospective bride among the incoming immigrants. Many romances blossomed on these journeys.

The table summarizes the essential facts with respect to the Church Trains of 1861–1868.

CHURCH TEAMS SENT FROM SALT LAKE CITY TO THE MISSOURI VALLEY, 1861–1868

Year	Number of wagons	Number of men	Number of oxen	Amount of flour (in lbs.)	Destination	Estimated number of immigrants to Utah
1861	200	260[a]	2,200[a]	150,000	Florence, Nebr.	2,556
1862	262	293	2,880	143,315	Florence, Nebr.	3,000
1863	384	488	3,604	235,969	Florence, Nebr.	3,646
1864	170	277	1,717	150,000[a]	Wyoming, Nebr.	2,697
1865	(no teams sent)					1,301
1866	397[b]	515	3,042[c]	250,000[a]	Wyoming, Nebr.	3,335
1867	(no teams sent)					660
1868	543	650[a]	4,000[a]	156,000[d]	Benton, Nebr.[e]	3,232
Total	1,956	2,483	17,443	1,279,284		20,427

[a] Estimated.

[b] In addition to the complement sent from Utah in 1866, 62 wagons, 50 oxen, and 61 mules were purchased in the Midwest.

[c] And 89 horses, 134 mules.

[d] The 1868 teams also carried 120,500 pounds of meat.

[e] Later, Laramie, Wyoming.

Source: Compiled from Andrew Jenson, *Church Chronology,* pp. 65–78; Roberts, *Comprehensive History,* V, 109–110; "1866 and 1868 Emigration Team Accounts," MS., Church Historian's Office; Andrew Jenson, ed., "Latter-day Saints Emigration from Wyoming, Nebraska — 1864–1866," *Nebraska History Magazine,* XVII (1936), 113–127; and yearly notations in the *Deseret News* and HBY, 1861–1867.

During the six years that Church Trains were organized, approximately 2,000 wagons were sent east to receive the immigrants and these employed approximately 2,500 men and 17,500 oxen. As the result of these efforts, more than 20,000 European immigrants were assisted to Utah, of whom 16,226 went by Church Train, 229 were listed as P.E. immigrants (way completely paid), 726 purchased their own teams, and the remainder came in independent companies.[61] The "P.E." and "own teams" immigrants came only at the beginning of the period and then dropped out completely. These figures do not include immigrants from the United States. The total expenditures by the church for this immigration varied from $300,000 to $500,000 annually, or a total of about $2,400,000 for the Church Train period.[62] Almost all of this cost was borne by voluntary donations of labor, teams, supplies, and provisions. Very little money was involved in the whole operation.

The one item of interest which the table does not show is the kind and amount of machinery freighted by church teams. An exact accounting of this aspect of the Church Trains must await further study. It is known that the purchase and transportation of machinery was a major phase of church team activity in some of the years. The 1862 Church Train, for example, purchased and transported twenty-five carding machines, one hundred cotton gins and spinning jennies, a number of nail-making machines, several circular saws, and many boxes of "millfixings."[63] It should also be of interest that the east-bound trains of 1863 carried a cargo of 4,300 pounds of Utah-raised cotton. This was exchanged in St. Louis for cotton cloth.[64]

The manner in which each settlement met its quota for the yearly train is of some interest, as it reflects the informal cooperative endeavor which was characteristic of Mormon enterprise in the 1860's. In 1862, the stakes of Parowan, Beaver, and St. George, comprising the Southern Utah Mission, were asked to send fifty-seven wagons with three yoke of good cattle for each, and with provisions for a six months' journey for the teamsters and "the Lord's poor" they would bring back. They were also to furnish fifty-seven teamsters for these wagons and fourteen mounted men. Upon receipt of this call, the officers of the Southern Mission issued calls to each ward and settlement. The town of Harmony, for example, with less than a hundred people, was asked to furnish three outfits of wagons, with four yoke of cattle and 1,000 pounds of flour for each wagon. These outfits were raised in one day—the individual contributions (all in kind) ranged from that of Sister Susan Hill who "made a mat and pillow and night cap," and furnished a plate, spoon, cup, needles and thread, to that of John D. Lee who furnished "a good Chicago wagon and cover, one pair of pants, one pair of shoes, three overshirts, and flour, bacon and molasses, rifle and ammunition to the amount of $122.50." Three young men volunteered as teamsters. In

Sunday meeting the teamsters were presented to the congregation and "sustained by vote to make the trip and were formally blessed and set apart for this mission. Benjamin J. Redd requested a dance before leaving which was granted and a good time had." [65] These men had a trip of almost 500 miles before they could join their brethren in Salt Lake City for the journey east.

In larger, more commercialized, communities contributions sometimes took the form of money for the hire of a span of mules or a yoke of oxen or the purchase of provisions. Provisions in such communities were sometimes assessed against merchants. The widespread participation of all Latter-day Saints in the project is indicated in the following excerpt from the minutes of the Logan, Utah, High Priests — a group of perhaps twenty-five men:

> *February 9, 1861.* Br. Blair explained that the meeting was called to see what the quorum will do in regard to furnishing teames wagons &c to go to Florence next spring and wished to hear from the brethren present. . . .
>
> Br. Crockett sayes he will furnish one good ox wagon & cover compleate and probably some cooking utensils
>
> Wm Ballard will furnish a yoke of oxen and if that will not do 2 yoke wich is all he has
>
> J Goodwin will furnish a Chicago Wagon with cover &c
>
> John Nelson said all his oxen are ready if needed will give us one yoke with Chains.
>
> Thos Davidson will put in one yoke of oxen
>
> Charles Cowley will put in one yoke or all if required
>
> William Steele will furnish one wagon & bow complete
>
> Joseph Moffat has only one yoke of oxen but they are on hand if needed
>
> O J Beach has but two yoke but they are on hand gave 1 ox
>
> L Mallory has but one yoke of steers but will do something
>
> William Earl has a yoke of old cattle if needed
>
> William Austin has but one yoke of oxen but they are ready
>
> E Landers has two yoke can go with them if needed put in one yoke
>
> D B Dille will furnish one yoke
>
> L M Blair one yoke a span of $600 mules if needed
>
> John E. Jones will furnish one yoke of oxen
>
> J H Martineau has no oxen but will help all he can will sell his carriage if needed
>
> J P Wright had no oxen but would do all he could
>
> Br Gell Blair blessed the quorum for their liberal spirit manifested and hoped we would soon outgrow the name of old fogies[.] we can fitt out 3 teams and wagons wich is all that it was thought the whole town would furnish[;] prophisied that those who had agreed to furnish the teams and wagons should be blessed tenfold.

A notation was made in the minutes that two days later, Joel Ricks and T. E. Ricks, who were absent from the above meeting, subscribed 1 yoke of oxen and one wagon each. The minutes also contain a list of donations from the same people and others of sacks of flour, beans, butter, pork, mittens, coats, guns, lead, cash, quilts, molasses, vinegar, and potatoes to sustain the teamsters and the immigrants on the return trip.[66]

The contributions of the Church Trains to the building of the Kingdom were not negligible. Primarily, they were a voluntary, cooperative, community investment in people; that is, in immigrants. They also made possible the importation of needed machinery and merchandise, facilitated the marketing of an unknown quantity of surplus cattle and cotton, and made it unnecessary for the P.E.F. to make large purchases of cattle and wagons during the 'sixties. The Church Train phase of immigration and freighting, of course, ended with the completion of the transcontinental railroad in 1869.

CHURCH PUBLIC WORKS

As during the 1850's, the immigrants who were transported to Utah arrived in the Salt Lake Valley in the fall of the year and were apportioned out among the various wards of the city for "wintering." The largest share of them were employed on the church public works, which took advantage of their skills and of native materials to erect structures of improvised but undoubted magnificence. In addition to foundries, machine shops, and carpentry and paint shops, the public works also operated "factories" which supplied the territory with paper, nails, buttons, wooden buckets, carding machines, and milling machinery. The public works department also occasionally constructed roads, bridges, dams, and canals. The largest projects undertaken by the church public works in the decade of the 'sixties were the Salt Lake Theatre, the Salt Lake Tabernacle, and the Salt Lake Temple.

The Salt Lake Theatre. Constructed in 1861–1862, the Salt Lake Theatre represented a community investment of upwards of $100,000.[67] With a seating capacity of 3,000 persons, the theater was said to have been a close duplicate outside and inside of the famous Drury Lane Theatre of London. The auditorium had a parquet, dress circle, and three balconies. Samuel Bowles, who saw it in 1865, wrote of it:

> The building is itself a rare triumph of art and enterprise. No eastern city of one hundred thousand inhabitants — remember Salt Lake City has less than twenty thousand — possesses so fine a theatrical structure. It ranks, alike in capacity and elegance of structure and finish, along with the opera houses and academies of music of Boston, New York, Philadelphia, Chicago and Cincinnati.[68]

The construction of this building utilized nails made by a public works factory out of the iron left behind by Johnston's Army in 1861. "Judged from the present period," wrote a contemporary, "one would almost be led to believe that Johnston's Army was sent to Utah to assist the Saints in their recreational activities."[69] The construction also provided labor for scores of European architects, artists, masons, and carpenters. In August 1861, for example, sixteen stone masons, eight stone cutters, sixteen diggers, three millwrights, and fifteen carpenters were at work on the building.[70] After the roof timbers were placed, some three dozen carpenters were put to work on the interior.[71] Most of these laborers were paid with tithing orders, and in some cases with written promises of future theater tickets. One person recalled that Brigham Young specifically desired sailors to work on the new building because they were used to working on high levels.[72] One of these sailors of whom we have knowledge was George Jarvis, a one-eyed Englishman, who obtained food and clothing for his family of six in this way during the crucial winter of 1861–1862. By spring Jarvis had also earned enough credit with the president to obtain a "steady" yoke of oxen with which he took his family to settle in St. George. There Jarvis used the experience gained from working on the theater in helping to build the St. George Tabernacle and, later, the St. George Temple.[73]

The theater was a triumph of immigrant skill, frontier engineering, and cooperative effort. A sixteen-foot water wheel, formerly in use at the sugar works, was placed in a branch of City Creek near the building and connected with a drive shaft and gearing, and used in elevating the rock and massive timber used in its construction. F. H. Ludlow visited the theater shortly after it was built and wrote an interesting account of it, including another example of pioneer improvisation:

> I was greatly astonished to find in the desert heart of the continent a place of public amusement, which regarding comfort, capacity, and beauty has but two or three superiors in the United States. . . . My greatest surprise was excited by the remarkable artistic beauty of the gilt and painted decorations on the great arch over the stage, the cornices, and the moulding about the proscenium boxes. President Young, with a proper pride, assured me that every particle of the ornamental work was done by indigenous and Saintly hands.
>
> "But you don't know yet," he added, "how independent we are of you at the East. Where do you think we got that central chandelier, and how much d'ye suppose we paid for it?"
>
> It was a piece of work which would have been creditable to any New York firm, apparently a richly carven circle, twined with gilt vines, leaves and tendrils, blossoming all over with flaming wax-lights, and suspended by a massive chain of golden lustre. So I replied that he probably paid a thousand dollars for it in New York. "Capital!" exclaimed Brigham; "I made it myself! That circle is a cart-wheel, the wheel of one of our common Utah oxcarts. I had it waxed, and gilded it with my own hands. It hangs by a pair of ox-chains which I also gilded;

and the gilt ornaments of the candlesticks were all cut after my patterns out of sheet tin." [74]

As the theater was a church enterprise until its lease to a company of young Mormon artists in 1873, performers in the theater were often "called," much as missionaries and settlers were. One young lady was "requisitioned" with the following: "Dear Brother and Sister Colebrook: Would you allow your daughter Nellie to act upon the stage. It would very much please me. Your Brother, Brigham Young." [75] During these years admission was commonly paid by receipt for the delivery of a quantity of produce, poultry, or livestock to the General Tithing Office, and performers were also paid with "tithing pay."

The Salt Lake Theatre was the first theater of importance west of the Mississippi, and for the number and quality of its theatrical productions, it maintained pre-eminence throughout the remainder of the nineteenth century. During its heyday the best actors and actresses in the nation performed on its stage. Indeed, this product of public works represents a rare example of sponsorship by a Christian church of this type of recreation and amusement.[76]

The Salt Lake Tabernacle. The famous Mormon Tabernacle on Temple Square, about which so many visitors to Salt Lake City have remarked, was constructed during the years 1863–1870 and was finally dedicated in 1875. In use since October 1867, the tabernacle is an immense, elliptical, turtle-backed auditorium, 250 feet long, 150 feet wide, and 80 feet in height, which will seat 10,000 people. The most interesting feature of the building is the self-supporting, wooden roof, the lattice arches for which were put together with wooden thole pins rather than with nails.[77] The rounded dome was made of rawhide tied together with leather thongs. No nails were used in the construction of the building, although it required more than a million and a half feet of lumber. The architect boasted that it was "the largest Hall in the world unsupported by columns." [78] Especially notable have been the acoustical properties of the building, particularly since the completion of the gallery in 1870.[79] The church has always taken special pride in the large organ which was built of native materials by Mormon mechanics and which was thought to be unrivaled for tone elsewhere in the nation at the time of its completion. Exclusive of the cost of the organ, the building cost the equivalent of about $300,000.

An average of more than 150 men worked for approximately two years to complete the exterior. Much of the labor, again, was done by immigrants, particularly in the year 1867, which was a poor year financially. One newly arrived immigrant who found work on the building proudly reported that, despite the general slump, he could earn enough in two days to last him a whole week; and enough in fourteen days to "provide for the whole winter."[80] Typical wages, or credits as the case may be, were $2.00, $3.00, and $3.50 per day, depending on the nature of the work performed.[81]

The Salt Lake Temple. Perhaps the greatest effort of the public works throughout the frontier period was directed toward the building of the Salt Lake Temple, which cost an estimated $4,000,000. The site for this temple had been located in July 1847, four days after the first contingent of Mormons arrived in the Salt Lake Valley. Actual work on the construction, however, did not begin until 1853, when the ground was surveyed, dedicated, and broken. A foundation was built of sandstone during the next two years, but this was torn up when a large granite quarry was located in Little Cottonwood Canyon, twenty miles southeast of Salt Lake City.[82] Thereafter, with the exception of interruption by the Utah War, several hundred tithing hands were steadily at work getting out stone, hauling it, and dressing it. Other hands were getting out lumber from a sawmill in Big Cottonwood Canyon and sawing it preparatory for use on the temple.

About fifty teams from the various wards in the Salt Lake Valley were engaged more or less continually in hauling rock from the quarry to the temple site, where from fifty to one hundred and fifty stone-cutters were more or less constantly at work dressing the large stones. Three or four yoke of oxen were required for each load, which consisted of one huge block and two smaller blocks. Some of the larger granite blocks weighed as much as five tons, while three-ton blocks were common. Cattle yards of lumber, sufficient to take care of three hundred head of cattle, were constructed near the Little Cottonwood quarry to care for the ox-teams, most of which were the property of the church. Hay was furnished by the public works, and each ward was asked to furnish grain for the animals of its teamsters. The drivers lodged near the corral in tents resembling Indian wickiups. With good luck, it was possible for teams to go from Salt Lake City to the quarry and return with a load to the temple site in two days.[83]

Each ward in the Salt Lake region was given a quota of teamsters to supply each week. The instructions given to the wards in this matter are of interest:

> Send men to drive the teams and not boys; men who will have some interest in the work they are sent to do; men who will not sell the grain sent to feed the teams to buy whisky with; men who will not take their teams to haul wood with instead of rock for the Temple. Let the teamsters be fitted out with at least one spare shirt; that they may not be placed under the necessity of wearing one shirt five or six weeks, and then leave the work to go home if they are not supplied with more; this same remark will apply to shoes also. Either send men who do not use tobacco, or send them with a supply, that they may not come to me and tell me they will have to leave the work if they are not supplied with

tobacco. Some of the Bishops sent word if I would find the men from the Wards tobacco they would pay for it, which they have not done, and you may expect that in the future we shall not find them this article.[84]

The heavy amount of team hauling required the building of a good road system from the Canyon to Salt Lake City. While this road was officially under the jurisdiction of the territorial government, it was always, as one church leader reported, in such "miserable condition" that the church "took the matter in hand," and concentrated large gangs of tithing labor on the road to improve it, provide a drainage system, and keep it in shape for the steady traffic of granite-hauling ox-teams.[85]

Some of this hauling was done by regularly employed church hands, but most of it was done by tithing labor, volunteer donation, and by men hired by the various priesthood groups in the Salt Lake Valley and elsewhere in the territory.[86] In general, church leaders tried to restrict the use of tithing funds to the purchase of imported machinery and supplies and, after the construction of a railroad to the quarry in 1873, to the payment of freight. The construction of the railway, of course, made it possible for whole trainloads of granite blocks to be rolled on to the temple grounds every few days, as needed.

Threatened famine from grasshopper visitations and other natural crises interrupted the work many times. Work was also suspended in 1868–1869 during the time of the construction of the transcontinental railway, when all available strength was called to aid in completing the Mormon contracts on that road. This "Chartres of the desert," as Aldous Huxley once appropriately called it, was not completed until 1893, forty years after it had been commenced.

COLONIZATION

The problem of colonization in the 1860's was particularly important because of the large number of people called in during the Utah War, for whom homes and farms had to be provided in the inner cordon of settlements; and also because of the two to four thousand immigrants who were brought into the territory each year by the Church Trains. During the ten years after the end of the Utah War, approximately 150 new towns were founded.[87] New areas opened up for settlement included Bear Lake Valley and Cache Valley, in the north; Pahvant Valley and part of Sanpete Valley in the center; and the Sevier River Valley, Virgin River Valley, and Muddy River Valley in the south. Expansion within these and older settlements in the inner cordon continued until the 1890's. No attempt was made to resettle the colonies in the outer cordon either because they had not been particularly successful in the first place, or because some of the property had since been occupied by Gentiles, or because the borders of Utah Territory were greatly reduced by federal authority in 1861.

Much attention was paid, in establishing new settlements, to the contributions each could make toward territorial self-sufficiency. "So far as we have learned the resources of the country," said Brigham Young in 1863, "we are satisfied that we need not depend upon our neighbors abroad for any single necessity of life, for in the elements around us exists every ingredient of food and raiment." [88]

The role of economic independence in Mormon colonization in the 1860's is perhaps most strikingly illustrated in the Cotton Mission. A number of parties had been sent out from Parowan and Cedar City in the early 1850's to explore the Santa Clara and Virgin River basins and to determine their suitability for producing specialized agricultural products. The reports of these parties seemed to confirm the hope of Mormon leaders that the new region would be able to produce cotton, grapes, figs, flax, hemp, rice, sugar cane, and other much-needed semitropical products. Small colonies were sent to the area in 1857 and 1858, with the result that cotton was grown successfully on a small scale. Total production in 1860 was 155 bales.[89]

The self-sufficiency program which followed the Utah War and the outbreak of the Civil War in 1861 led Mormon leaders to greatly expand the southern colonies. In October 1861, 309 families were called to go south immediately to settle in what would now be called "Utah's Dixie." [90] They represented a variety of occupations and were instructed to go in an organized group and "cheerfully contribute their efforts to supply the Territory with cotton, sugar, grapes, tobacco, figs, almonds, olive oil, and such other useful articles as the Lord has given us, the places for garden spots in the south to produce." [91] Brigham Young specifically desired them to produce the territorial supply of tobacco — so as to eliminate "paying to outsiders from sixty to eighty thousand dollars annually for that one article" — and also wine: for the Holy Sacrament, for medicine, and for sale to "outsiders." [92]

The 309 families of Utah settlers were joined the same year by approximately thirty families of Swiss converts, most of whom had been transported to Utah in the Church Teams of 1861. The church provided this "poor company" with teams and wagons; tithing houses along the way furnished provisions and shelter; and upon their arrival in Dixie, they were given the "Big Bend" land at what is now Santa Clara, Utah. This colony was expected to raise grapes and fruit to supply the cotton producers.

At the October general conference of the church, held in Salt Lake City in 1862, the 339 were strengthened by the calling of 200 additional families. These were told that the mission of the previous year had been a "decided success," for "God was inspiring the mission," and that it was their privilege and duty to be associated with the others in this "great work."[93] The 200 men were chosen for their skills and capital equipment so as to balance out the economic structure of the community.

Two years later, in October 1864, another large group—some fifty or sixty families—was called to Dixie to settle on the Muddy River, approximately 100 miles southwest of St. George, in an area now partly inundated by Lake Mead. These were also instructed to raise cotton and other semitropical products. This group was later reinforced with 163 additional families called in October 1867. All told, nearly 800 families, representing about 3,000 persons, were called to Dixie in the early 1860's. At least 300 additional families—upwards of 1,000 persons—were called in the late 1860's and 1870's.

These persons were all selected with a view to the contributions they could make to the new community. A wide range of occupational training and experience was represented. Each man was expected to have the tools and implements of his skill, artistry, or profession to take with him to his new home. Under the direction of their leader, Apostle Erastus Snow, arrangements were also made to furnish them with a carding machine, threshing machine, sugar mill, and equipment for a sawmill. Presumably, these would be community property held as stewardships by men appointed to operate them. A herd of cattle also was taken along to be driven down the Old Spanish Trail to southern California to exchange for hives of bees, choice varieties of fruit seeds and fruit trees, and various types of agricultural equipment and textile machinery. To all of the missionaries the instructions were: Grow Cotton. They were told that the Cotton Mission should be considered as important to them as if they were called to preach the gospel among the nations.[94]

Arriving in Dixie during the winter of 1861–1862, the first company of cotton missionaries, 400 heavily loaded wagons strong, surveyed the new capital city of St. George, apportioned lots, and began the double task of making the families comfortable and the soil productive.[95] The land was cleared of rocks and chaparral, dams were constructed, and a series of canals and ditches were dug to carry the water to the soil. Their task was not an easy one. The river bottom and banks were sandy, and dam after dam was washed out by the uncertain river. When progress was finally made toward getting water on the soil, they discovered that the soil was heavily impregnated with minerals which precipitated to the surface with irrigation and formed a hard crust which prevented growth. Cotton was finally planted on June 1, 1862, and the first year's yield was 100,000 pounds of seed cotton.[96]

Some of this cotton was made up into clothing in the region, some was sold in Salt Lake City for grain and other supplies, some was freighted to the Missouri River, but the bulk of it could not be disposed of because of the lack of a factory. Some of the cotton was spun in Parowan by a small mill set up by Ebenezer Hanks at the specific request of President Young. Seventy-two spindles had been put in motion in this "factory" in April 1862, and by September it was reported to be making thirty-five pounds of serviceable yarn per day.[97] Powered by water, the carding and drawing frames were tended by one man and the roving and throstle frames by three girls and an Indian boy.[98] Other settlements also made arrangements for machinery to assist in working up the cotton on a local basis. John R. Young, who had been appointed to settle at Santa Clara, was called by the Santa Clara bishop in the spring of 1862 to drive an ox team to Omaha to get some cotton gins and spinning jennies for the benefit of the settlers. Leaving his own family encamped in a tent, he drove his own team of four yoke of oxen to Omaha and returned with the machinery late in the fall of 1862.[99]

Cotton which was freighted east, by Salt Lake jobbers and the growers themselves, was made into clothing on shares. Brigham Young encouraged this arrangement. "By exporting one load of cotton to the East," he said, "a man can make cloth enough to clothe his family many years."[100] Within eighteen months after the settlement of Washington County by the cotton missionaries of 1861, about 74,000 pounds of cotton were freighted east by independent haulers and church teams. This was sold for approximately a dollar a pound. Some of the cotton was traded for machinery needed to manufacture the cotton. Several dozen bales were also sold in California.[101]

After 1862 there was a decline in the cotton acreage. Acute shortages of food and feed, sickness, and back-breaking labor affected all of the settlers. The combination of poor soil, unruly rivers, distance from source of supply and market, and dreary landscape was enough to try the faith of the staunchest. Church leaders understood these difficulties and responded by remitting tithing, by granting credits at church institutions, by calling additional missionaries to strengthen the settlements, and by arranging for expanded facilities for manufacture. An added encouragement was the increase in the price of cotton in the East, and therefore in Utah. The production of 1863 consisted of 56,094 pounds of ginned cotton, priced at upwards of fifty cents a pound.[102] The 1864 production, while uncertain in amount, was reported to be larger, and was valued at up to $1.25 per pound in Utah.[103] The rising price led to a larger planting in 1864, and the introduction of several small carding and spinning machines improved the local market.[104]

As with all other produce, one-tenth of the cotton yield was hauled to the General Tithing Office in Salt Lake City as tithing, and was worked up into clothing by Salt Lake mills or transported to St. Louis for sale on the national market.

Despite the fact that cotton and other desirables were produced, the colony was not on a sure economic footing. It was clear that the mission would not be a success until a major factory, which could produce cotton goods of quality, was constructed. It was equally clear that the missionaries themselves would never be able to erect such a factory and purchase the necessary machinery with their own savings. Life was too precarious to venture on such a large investment without outside assistance. The assumption on which the mission was based was that the colonists should concentrate on the production of cotton and other specialties and exchange these elsewhere in the territory for their food and feed. Because of the natural disabilities of the region and the lack of lucrative local markets, however, the missionaries were never able to produce a sufficient supply of these specialties to obtain an adequate subsistence by exchange. In order to obtain even a bare minimum for subsistence, therefore, the cotton farmers were forced to devote more and more of their efforts in the direction of producing their own food, thus nullifying the very reason for the establishment of the colony.

The disadvantages of specialization in cotton production had become evident as early as 1864 when Erastus Snow, in general conference in Salt Lake City, asserted that there were "over a thousand persons in St. George, one-half of whom would have to leave unless something was done to relieve the mission and help the poor man to continue his labors on the fences and canals that were in progress there."[105] Upon the recommendation of church leaders, the conference unanimously passed a resolution to assist the Cotton Mission. More than one hundred of the wealthier church members in northern Utah were designated "to furnish the needful and substantial requisites to enable the laboring and willing poor" of the Cotton Mission "to accomplish the work designed by the Priesthood and inspiration that sent them there."[106] As the result of this call, many thousands of dollars worth of cash, merchandise, implements, and equipment were furnished the southern settlers.[107] Nature was eating away at the settlers' basis for existence, however, for the grasshoppers and "worms" destroyed most of the crops in Dixie in 1865, and additional assistance was needed.[108]

In the meantime, church officials promoted the establishment of an adequate cotton factory. The church agent at St. Louis had been asked in 1863 to buy enough machinery to stock a cotton and woolen factory with 240 spindles. This machinery was freighted west by church trains that year, together with some machinery previously purchased by church agents in England. A building was erected in Parley's Canyon near Salt Lake City to receive the machinery, and it operated there for two years.[109] Faced with a deteriorating economy in the cotton country, Brigham Young volunteered to have the machinery dismantled and sent to Washington, an agricultural settlement near St. George. The missionaries were requested to donate labor and materials toward the erection of a factory, and calls were made in 1866 and succeeding years. When one story and the millrace were finished, teams and wagons were sent to Salt Lake City to obtain and transport the spinning and weaving machinery to Dixie.

With the promised completion of the factory, and with additional agricultural and processing equipment, plantings were heavier in 1866 than in any previous year, amounting to a reported 466½ acres.[110] Indian troubles forced the colonists to neglect their crops, however, and the smaller settlements were ordered to abandon their homes and farms and move to the larger settlements. The crop actually harvested in 1866 was but three-fourths that of the previous year. To make matters worse, the end of the Civil War caused the price of cotton to drop fifty cents per pound.[111] Despite the erection of the factory, therefore, many church officials began to give up hope that the cotton acreage would ever be built up to assure territorial self-sufficiency. Only 300 acres were planted to cotton in 1867. "The great expense of irrigating the land in the cotton-growing districts," reported Apostle George A. Smith to the Assessor of Internal Revenue, "is very likely to cause the abandonment of the cultivation of cotton when the market is again supplied at its former reasonable price." [112] "So far as raising cotton is concerned," added a local correspondent, "it does not bring any price to justify the raising . . . many of the people are poor, and some quite discouraged." [113]

This discouragement did not spread to Brigham Young. He had set what he thought was a realistic goal of complete self-sufficiency with respect to cotton, and he regarded the difficulties, not as inevitable strokes of fate, but as obstacles which could be overcome with faith, energy, and persistence. Far from being deterred, he called an additional group of 163 young men from northern Utah in 1867 and instructed them "to marry and take wives with them." [114] Additional cotton missionaries were called in 1868.[115] The president even took steps to convert St. George into an entrepôt. This was to be achieved by constructing a warehouse at Call's Landing, fifteen miles above the present location of Hoover Dam. At that point immigrants and freight would be landed by ships steaming up the Colorado, and freighted north, via colonies on the Muddy River, to St. George and thence to Salt Lake City.[116] Missionaries were actually called to accomplish this task and church funds were appropriated. The warehouse was built, the Deseret Mercantile Association was founded to handle the freight, and, indeed, some business was done. But it is inconceivable that the president could have regarded this scheme as more than a work project and temporary encouragement to the cotton missionaries. The Pacific Railroad was under construction, as he well knew, and the navigation of the Colorado gave no promise of profitability after that road was completed.

Another device by which the church assisted the Dixians to "hang on" was the granting of subsidies out of tithing resources to construct a tabernacle in St. George. All of the necessary church tithing from south of Cedar City was ordered appropriated, year after year, for the building of this splendid New England-style community church. Construction was commenced in 1867, and it was completed eight years later, at a cost of approximately $110,000 in labor, materials, and supplies. It was a public works project by means of which many missionary families were supported or assisted. This project was followed by the construction of the St. George Temple, also a public works project, which was finally completed in 1877.

Several factors curtailed the production of cotton and other products during the late 1860's and early 1870's. The factory was not placed in operation until 1869, and much new machinery was required for quality production. Skilled help was difficult to obtain to run it. The mines at Pioche, Nevada, provided lucrative markets for wine, molasses, and dried fruits. Trading in these products, while not in harmony with the self-sufficiency policy, flourished enough to further shift the emphasis away from cotton.

Above all problems for the settlers, however, were those of physical survival under circumstances almost unbelievably adverse. It seemed to the colonists as though all earth and hell had conspired to render the Cotton Mission a failure. Year after year, calamity after calamity forced the colonists to their knees. Alkali soil, alternating flood and drouth, grasshopper and cricket infestation, Indian troubles, and backbreaking toil under a broiling sun—these and other conditions caused the less hardy to pull up stakes and try their luck elsewhere. Those who remained frequently had cause to doubt the wisdom of their call.

The cotton yields of the late 1860's and early 1870's, amounting to hardly 100 bales per year, were not enough to furnish the settlers with clothing, let alone make the operation of the factory profitable. Improved seed cotton from Georgia was introduced; epistolary letters urged increased acreages and buoyed hopes; favorable prices were paid by tithing offices and by the factory; and work in nearby mining camps was discouraged. But results were disappointing, and cruel jests were made by visiting travelers about the poverty of these loyal missionaries.

An added predicament forced the discontinuance of the Muddy colonies, which had furnished most of Dixie's cotton during the period 1866–1870. An official survey disclosed them to be located in Nevada, rather than in Utah. Nevada, whose officials at that time had no love for the Mormons, promptly assessed back taxes, which had already been paid in good faith to Utah, and required them to be paid in specie. In consideration of the tax situation, an outbreak of malaria, and the poverty of the settlers, Brigham Young advised them to abandon their settlements in 1871. Most of them moved to Long Valley, Utah, some seventy miles northeast of St. George, where they established a communal society at Orderville.[117]

The cotton industry was revived briefly during the depressions of 1873–1876 and 1893–1896. By the end of the century the amount of land in cotton was almost negligible. The factory was finally closed in 1910.

The ultimate fate of Dixie's other specialty crops is similar to that of cotton. Tobacco was never grown on an extensive scale. Church leaders after Brigham Young preferred to emphasize nonuse rather than "grow your own." Grapes became an important crop, and as many as 544 acres of grapes, yielding about 1,700 tons, were in production in 1875.[118] Santa Clara and Toquerville, both in Washington County, were the chief centers of production. One faithful churchman, John C. Naegle, was specifically called by Brigham Young to take charge of the wine industry in Dixie. He secured a wine press and distillery from California and made high quality wines and brandies — as much as 3,000 gallons per year. By exchanging these products in Salt Lake City, Naegle was able to obtain thousands of sacks of much-needed wheat and flour to distribute to the cotton missionaries.[119] Because of complaint against the poor quality of some of the homemade wine, and doubtless because of the quantity of grapes turned in as tithing which would otherwise spoil, the church tithing offices in Toquerville, St. George, and elsewhere entered largely into the production of wine.[120] There was constant temptation, however, to consume the product locally.[121] By the turn of the century, most of the vines had been pulled on the advice of church authorities, and that important source of cash income was closed.[122]

The one specialty which was a continuing success in southern Utah was the production of grain-sorghum molasses. "Dixie" molasses was a staple export, enjoying a ready market in Utah, Nevada, and even in Idaho and Montana. Through the years molasses was the chief means by which the farmers of southern Utah acquired breadstuffs and paid their tithing and taxes. A gallon of molasses for a bushel of wheat was the basis on which the cotton missionaries eventually attained equality with their more fortunate brethren to the north.[123]

The Cotton Mission was not the only phase of the calculated drive of the Mormons toward diversification and territorial self-sufficiency in 1859 and the 1860's. Other colonies were established, from southern Idaho in the north, to northern Arizona in the south, with the same purpose in mind. The town of Mantua, in Box Elder County, Utah, was founded as part of a church campaign to stimulate the production of flax. Twelve Danish families were appointed to settle in what was originally called Flaxville, to produce thread for use in making summer clothing, household linen, and sacks for grain.[124] Similarly, the town of Minersville, in Beaver County, Utah, was founded as a church mission in 1859 for the purpose of working a local lead, zinc, and silver deposit. With the encouragement and assistance of the church, many tons of lead bullion were produced for use in making bullets and paint for the public works.[125] The town of Coalville, in Summit County, Utah, was also founded as part of a church mission to mine coal. Soon after the discovery of this coal in 1859, it was being transported to Salt Lake City for church and commercial use. Several dozen persons were called to the region in the spring of 1860; improved roads to connect with Salt Lake City were built; new mines were discovered; and scores of church and private teams plied back and forth between Coalville and Salt Lake City throughout the 'sixties. These mines were of particular importance because of the increasing scarcity of timber in the Salt Lake Valley. Hundreds of men continued to find employment in Coalville, even after the Union Pacific Railroad introduced superior coal from Wyoming in the 1870's, particularly during depressions and in periods of alleged abuse by Union Pacific coal agents in Salt Lake City.[126]

THE AGRICULTURAL PROGRAM

The Mormon agricultural program of the 1860's was much broader than that indicated in the missions to raise cotton and other specialty crops. Perhaps as much as half of the recorded sermons of general authorities was devoted to agricultural problems — the proper use of water, the management of crop and livestock enterprises, and combatting the visitations of grasshoppers, crickets, and Indians. Agricultural diversification and self-sufficiency were not only desirable *per se,* they argued, but were indispensable to economic growth generally. Industrial development depended on the local production of fibers and on the importation of machinery. The latter could not be accomplished financially without eliminating the unfavorable balance of trade in food and clothing.[127]

Aside from the agricultural missions the Mormon agricultural program of the 1860's may be said to have included three phases or elements. First, church leaders discouraged the use of such imported "luxuries" or "vices" as tea, coffee, tobacco, and liquor. Beginning in 1859, and continuing with increased emphasis throughout the 1860's, a series of sermons was directed against the use of these commodities. "We can produce them or do without them," said Brigham Young. He estimated that in 1864 the territory expended in gold and silver approximately $100,000 on tobacco, and many thousands of dollars on tea, coffee, and liquor.[128] It was not so much a moral principle as a matter of sound economic policy:

> This community has not yet concluded to entirely dispense with the use of tobacco, and great quantities have been imported into our Territory. The silver and gold which we have paid out for this article alone, since we first came into

Utah, would have built several extensive cotton and woollen factories and filled them with machinery. . . . Instead of buying it in a foreign market and importing it over a thousand miles, why not raise it in our own country or do without it? True principles of domestic and political economy would suggest the production at home of every article of home consumption, for herein lies the basis of wealth and independence for any people. . . .

Tea is in great demand in Utah, and anything under that name sells readily at an extravagant price. This article opens a wide drain for the escape of much of our circulating medium. . . . Tea can be produced in this Territory in sufficient quantities for home consumption. . . . If we do not raise it, I would suggest that we do without it.[129]

On other occasions he suggested that all should do without tea and coffee, so that the money saved "might be applied to better purposes," as for example the Perpetual Emigrating Fund, the importation of machinery, and the improvement of agriculture.[130]

In addition to discouraging the importation of "useless" commodities, the church also adopted an internal improvement program which centered attention on the construction of canals and irrigation works intended to assure maximum use of available water resources. Communities building dams and ditches "did not have to rely on their own resources or depend on their unaided wisdom or experience." [131] Planning, direction, technical, and financial assistance were often provided by the church.[132] Most of the new land projects, as we have seen, were given the privilege, when necessary, of drawing on tithing offices for their seed, provisions, clothing, and implements. Such assistance was particularly important in the case of the new settlements opened up in the 1860's along the Sevier and Virgin rivers. Both rivers were subject to high quick floods alternated with prolonged dry periods, making the construction of costly irrigation works an annual affair.[133]

Such difficulties led to some attempts to plan the use of water on a river-valley basis. In its one major attempt to do this, however, the church was checkmated by a carpetbag governor, and this appears to have discouraged other efforts along the same line. This attempt called for the granting of a charter to the Deseret Irrigation and Navigation Canal Company. At a cost of perhaps half a million dollars, of which $50,000 was to be advanced by the trustee-in-trust, this company planned to undertake a comprehensive program to utilize the water flowing from Utah Lake into Salt Lake, via the Jordan River, for irrigation, power, and navigation purposes. Although a great deal of preliminary work was carried out under Brigham Young's personal supervision, and although the measure was passed by a huge majority in two successive territorial assemblies, the unfriendly Governor, Charles Durkee, vetoed it. While it "awakens my admiration by its magni-

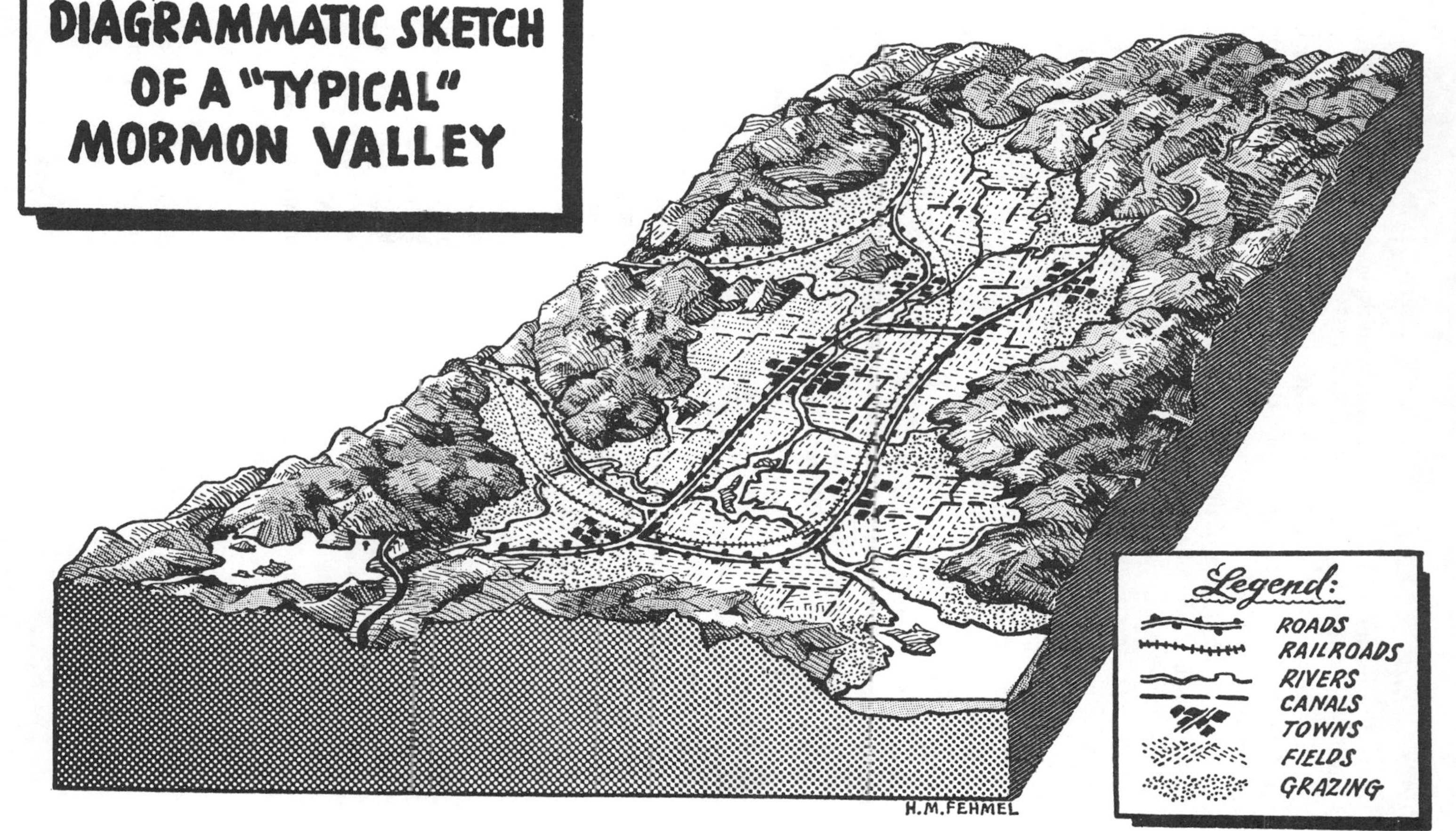
DIAGRAMMATIC SKETCH
OF A "TYPICAL"
MORMON VALLEY
Legend:
ROADS
RAILROADS
RIVERS
CANALS
TOWNS
FIELDS
GRAZING
H. M. FEHMEL

tude and boldness," he wrote, "it would exclude competition, and create a possible great and burdensome monopoly."[134]

The promotional and educational phase of the church's agricultural program in the 1860's was carried out under the aegis of its creation, the Deseret Agricultural and Manufacturing Society. The D.A.&M. Society had been incorporated by an act of the territorial legislature in 1856,[135] but due to the interruption of the Utah War its activities were not significant until the 1860's. In reality, the society represented both church and state. As an agent of the territory, the D.A.&M. received regular appropriations for the payment of premiums and subsidies; was accorded the responsibility of gathering the agricultural statistics of the territory; and was charged with receiving and disposing of the titles to the public lands apportioned to the territory by the Morrill Act for the purpose of establishing an agricultural college and experiment station.[136] The society was also designated recipient of the seeds and plants distributed by the U. S. Patent Office, and, later the Department of Agriculture. Finally, when the territorial assembly wished to promote a particular industry, as in the case of wool-growing, appropriations were made to the society to be expended by them in behalf of the particular industry singled out for assistance.

As an agent of the church the Deseret Agricultural and Manufacturing Society (largely officered by church authorities) held monthly meetings in church meetinghouses in Salt Lake City and in each county at which lectures were delivered on the culture of different tree and row crops and the breeding of livestock; published pamphlets containing treatises of "experts" on agricultural problems and detailing improved practices; and collected and maintained a library, consisting of standard works on agriculture and mechanics, and agricultural and scientific periodicals, for the use of members and the church generally.[137]

The society also held an annual exhibition or territorial fair in Salt Lake City, with local societies sponsoring fairs in each county. As with medieval fairs, the annual territorial fairs had religious significance. Most of them were held on the tithing grounds; they were held to coincide with the October general conference of the church; and the diplomas awarded for prize exhibits in each field of agriculture, manufacturing, and handicraft contained the All-seeing Eye, with the inscription, "Holiness to the Lord." Nearly all visitors to Utah commented on the excellence of these fairs, and upon the stimulus to improvement they provided. There is no doubt that church members were made to feel that agricultural improvement was an aspect of worship, indispensable to the building of the Kingdom.

Beginning in 1861, the D.A.&M. Society acquired a piece of ground in Salt Lake City to serve as an experimental garden. Seeds, roots, and cuttings received from the federal government and other sources were planted on this plot, and later were distributed to local societies and patrons.[138] Originally called Quarantine Farm, and later, Deseret Gardens, this may have been the first public experimental garden in the Mountain West. The society also attempted in various ways to improve the quality of livestock in the territory. This was particularly important — and comparatively easy — because of the fact that nearly all livestock were in cooperative village herds. At considerable expense, improved breeds of sheep, goats, and cattle were imported.[139] Some of this represented an investment by the society, and some was advanced by private interests. The society also invested in a fish farm. A number of specialized associations which had influence in their own areas grew out of the D.A.&M., including societies for the promotion of fruit culture, beekeeping, fish culture, and sericulture.

Perhaps the most important activity of the Deseret Agricultural and Manufacturing Society was the promotion of territorial production of commodities whose production was viewed by the church as essential to territorial self-sufficiency; that is, substitutes for articles whose importation represented a heavy drain on the floating currency. The society formed "companies" to produce and supply the Utah market with cane sugar, molasses, tobacco, flax, and hemp.[140] Machinery was imported to process sugar cane and to work up flax and hemp into cloth.[141] Similarly, sheep and wool production were encouraged by the distribution of information in relation to improved care, by the adoption of cooperative herding, and by the importation of machinery. Largely as the result of these efforts, the number of sheep in the territory rose from approximately 37,000 in 1860, to about 235,000 in 1880.[142]

As with many agricultural societies elsewhere in the nation a generation earlier, the society also devoted much effort to propagating the cause of sericulture. Mulberry seed (*morus multicaulis*) was obtained through the agency of Mormon missionaries in France and planted on a church farm in Salt Lake City. These trees were distributed widely through the territory in 1866, Brigham Young personally supervising the transplanting of about 100,000 trees.[143] At the same time, silkworm eggs were obtained, and the industry began to grow. Silk cooperatives were organized in all the leading settlements; the *Deseret News* carried many articles on the various phases of the industry; and one good brother, George D. Watt, was given a church mission to spread the gospel of silk. Utah, a French convert declared, was promptly becoming "the leading silk growing country on this [the American] continent."[144] Brigham Young, who thought the work "light and interesting" and especially suited to women, children, and the aged,[145] invested some $25,000 in the enterprise, including the construction of a model cocoonery to house 2,000,000 worms, the sending of a son to California to learn of experiences there, and the appointment of a wife to supervise this family industry.[146] A number of silk products resulted from his interest and similarly directed activities of others.

THE DESERET TELEGRAPH

An agency of the church which promoted the cultural and economic unity of the territory and assisted in its general development was the Deseret Telegraph line. The completion of the transcontinental telegraph line in 1861 had raised the question of the possibility of a regional line which would connect the hundred or more isolated Mormon settlements with Salt Lake and the "outside" world. The experience gained by the Saints in the construction of the transcontinental line would certainly facilitate the erection of a local line. In fact, on the very day communication was opened between Salt Lake City and the East, Brigham Young called in advisers to plan the construction of a North-South territorial line connecting all Mormon settlements.[147] Telegraphic instruments were sent for; a telegraphy school was established in Salt Lake City; and a short line was established to run from Brigham Young's Office to the Council House.[148] However, the Civil War prevented the Mormons from getting the necessary wire, batteries, insulators, sending and receiving sets, and other equipment until 1866.

With the end of the war, a campaign was launched to collect the necessary funds and commence construction. The *Deseret News* began a series of editorials; sermons were delivered on the subject in general conference and other church meetings; and the bishops were requested to present the matter before their wards for a determination of the contributions each would make. Circulars and instructions distributed to each settlement explained the plan of construction and the method of finance.[149] The line was to be built from Logan, in Cache Valley, to St. George, in Washington County, with a branch to connect the principal Sanpete settlements. Each valley would assume the burden of constructing, equipping, and staffing that part of the line running through the valley and half way to the next valley. The total cost was expected to be about $100,000 — an average of $200 per mile. The cash with which to buy wire and other equipment was to be collected during the winter of 1865–1866 and sent to Salt Lake City in time to be taken to the Missouri Valley with the Church Train of 1866. It was expected that sixty-five teams would be required to transport the wire and other equipment back to Utah, and each valley was required to send a proportionate share of such teams and teamsters. Each settlement desiring to have a station was to appoint one or two young men or women and send them to a church school of telegraphy to be held in Salt Lake City during the winter of 1865–1866. These young people were to regard their call as a church mission, for which they would be supported by their wards out of donations of food and clothing. The school was to be directed by John C. Clowes, operator in the Salt Lake office of the transcontinental line, and a newly won Mormon convert.

Under priesthood supervision, the line was surveyed, poles were cut, means were collected, and the line was well along toward completion when work was suspended to work on crops in the spring of 1866.[150] By the time Captain Horton D. Haight's train arrived in the territory in October with eighty-four tons of wire, insulators, batteries, and other equipment, volunteer teams were ready to put up the wire and connect the line. By the first of December, the line from Salt Lake to Ogden was connected. By the middle of February 1867, the entire line was in operation. The cost of the 500-mile line included $56,000 in cash for wire and equipment, and $24,000 in tithing credit for labor, making a total of $80,000, or $160 per mile.[151] Director John Clowes, who had been granted a leave from Western Union to supervise the work, and who had gained a testimony of Mormon organizational efficiency in the process, commented: "Not a man on this line ever worked a telegraph line before, the line was strung and put into operation in the middle of winter, it is about five hundred miles in length; taking all into consideration please permit me as an old operator to say that I think the working of the same almost a miracle." [152] The line was dedicated by Brigham Young with the following telegraphed message:

> In my heart I dedicate the line which is now completed . . . , to the Lord God of Israel, whom we serve, for the building up of His Kingdom, praying that this and all other improvements may contribute to our benefit, and the glory of our God; until we can waft ourselves by the power of the Almighty from world to world to our fullest satisfaction.[153]

In subsequent years the line was extended, also with tithing labor, to connect virtually all Mormon settlements from southern Idaho to northern Arizona, and most of the mining districts in Utah and southeastern Nevada. In 1867, during the Black Hawk Indian War, the church found it necessary to erect, at a cost of $25,000, Cove Creek Fort, 200 miles south of Salt Lake City, for use as a protection to the telegraph line. Situated in the middle of a sixty-mile stretch through the desert between Fillmore and Beaver, Cove Creek Fort served as a church-operated communications center, way place, supply station, and cattle ranch.[154] By 1880 there were approximately 1,000 miles of poles and 1200 miles of wire, and 68 offices or stations. The whole system was connected with the outside world at Salt Lake City.

Meanwhile, the territorial assembly incorporated the Deseret Telegraph Company and the company was organized on March 21, 1867, with Brigham Young as president.[155] Most of the other officers were general authorities of the church or local bishops. The company was capitalized for $500,000, with 5,000 shares of stock being issued with a par value of $100 each. Because of the cooperative nature of the construction, all of the stock, except qualifying shares, belonged to the trustee-in-trust of the church. The company was thus under church direction throughout its life.

The organization of the Deseret Telegraph Company gave business direction to the operation of the line, but did not change its essentially cooperative nature. Until the end of the century, the telegraph operators (except those in mining communities) were supported by voluntary donations collected by ward teachers; the charges for social correspondence via telegraph were nominal; news passed over the wire to all settlements almost as cheaply as it was received in Salt Lake City; and church business, including sermons, instructions, and queries, passed over the line without charge. It was not intended that the line pay expenses,[156] and most of the revenue came from connections with mining communities. Gross receipts from tolls were approximately $8,500 in 1868; $75,600 at the height of the mining boom in 1873; and $15,000 in 1885.[157] The company was subsidized by the tithing office until its sale to eastern interests in 1900.[158]

The Deseret Telegraph was a typical product of the 1860's. The community cooperation involved in the construction and operation demonstrates Mormon efficiency in organizing a barter society for the reception and use of a significant invention. To have their own line, "in the hands of, and under the direction of the Priesthood of God," as one of them expressed it,[159] was a symbol of Mormon determination to appropriate the technics of Babylon without becoming subject or beholden to Babylon. The line facilitated the effective administration of the expanding spiritual and temporal interests of the church; increased the security of the outlying settlements from attacks of Indians; and helped pioneers in scattered settlements to overcome the feeling of isolation, which must have overwhelmed them with loneliness before the line was built. It thus increased the permanency of many otherwise doubtful colonization projects. The line was also of some value to the United States Army. The first news of General Custer's defeat by the Sioux reached the world through the agency of the Deseret Telegraph.[160]

The telegraph, as with all improvements in communication and transportation, was generally thought to lead to a greater cosmopolitanism in thought and action, but it is doubtful that it had such an influence among the Mormons. By demonstrating the vitality of Mormon social and economic organization in providing a modern convenience at a comparatively early date, and with comparatively little sacrifice, the Deseret Telegraph actually may have contributed toward the perpetuation of Mormon social and economic institutions. The successful operation of this line at a time when grasshoppers were destroying their crops, Indians were stealing their livestock, and home industries were floundering by the dozen, unquestionably raised the *esprit de corps* of the community of Latter-day Saints. As with the Moscow subway, it made them proud of themselves, their religion, and their Zion. By placing them in closer touch with the world, however, it prepared Mormon leaders to appreciate more fully the problems which would be faced when the transcontinental railroad was completed in 1869.

THE KINGDOM THREATENED

[1869–1884]

* III *

The completion of the Pacific railroad in 1869 posed three threats to the Mormon Kingdom in the Great Basin: (1) Offering, as it did, opportunities for eastern and midwestern enterprisers to exploit new mines and markets, the railroad threatened the continuance of theocratic control of the region; (2) entailing increased commercial intercourse, it threatened the economic autonomy of the exclusively Mormon commonwealth; and (3) by involving the Mormons increasingly in "worldly" trade and exchange, the railroad threatened to break up the Kingdom of Saints into conflicting segments and to secularize economic relationships generally.

A well-directed program of "protection" combatted these tendencies with much success. With the adoption of a formalized system of "cooperation," branch railroads were built, trade was centralized, new enterprises were launched, and various devices were instituted for the preservation of group loyalties and the strengthening of community institutions. The joining of efforts through the United Orders, temple construction districts, and Zion's Central Board of Trade left the Mormons in 1884 nearer the realization of their ancient goals than when the ox-cart was outmoded in 1869.

CHAPTER VIII

Year of Decision: 1869

An improvement in transportation facilities produces many types of social change. More intricate division of labor, geographic specialization, extension of the market, greater mobility of capital and labor, replacement of local monopoly with regional and national monopoly — all are changes which result from the introduction and use of a major transportation facility. Religious, political, and economic ideologies are transformed, and local customs, beliefs, habits, and other forms of social differentiation are replaced by a new cosmopolitanism in thought and action. As the transcontinental railroad moved west in the 1860's the self-sufficient family and village economies widened into a national commercial organization. National commerce, in turn, involved regional and local specialization and a high degree of interdependence. Never was an economy of such magnitude knit together so quickly and so securely as the economy of the United States during the first few years after the end of the Civil War.

As with other sections of the country, the Mormon-occupied Great Basin was profoundly influenced by the junction of the Pacific railroads at Promontory, near Ogden, Utah, on May 10, 1869. That a social revolution did not occur, that the Mormon economy was not immediately or completely absorbed into the national free trade area, and that the economic and social changes in nineteenth-century Utah were never as great as those which transformed other Western states, can be attributed largely to the economic policies adopted by church leaders during the years immediately following the coming of the railroad. While the advance of "American civilization" must have descended like an avalanche upon their isolated theocratic commonwealth, Mormon officials attempted to make effective use of the limited defensive weapons at their disposal. Through agencies created by the church Mormon leaders carried out an economic action program which delayed and mollified the absorption of the Mormon economy into the broader social economy of the nation — an action program which constituted a unique response to the challenge of eastern competitive capitalism.

MORMON SUPPORT OF THE TRANSCONTINENTAL RAILROAD

There can be no doubt that the Mormons wanted the railroad completed. There is no evidence which supports the impression left by some contemporary writers that Mormon leaders opposed the Pacific railroad, fearing that it would "civilize" their followers and thus lead to an end of "superstition," "darkness," and "tyranny."[1] Not only did the church welcome the transcontinental road—though deploring some of its consequences—but facilitated its construction in many ways, and, after its completion, successfully promoted a number of interior branch railroads to connect Mormon settlements with it. As Brigham Young stated:

> Speaking of the completion of this railroad, I am anxious to see it, and I say to the Congress of the United States, through our Delegate, to the Company, and to others, hurry up, hasten the work! We want to hear the iron horse puffing through this valley. What for! To bring our brethren and sisters here.[2]

There is even some evidence that Brigham Young, while crossing the Plains in 1847 and 1848, gave consideration to a possible route for a Pacific railroad. It was said that Young predicted that if the nation would not build it, the Mormons would do so if granted statehood.[3] One of the first actions of the territorial legislature was the passage in 1852 of a memorial to Congress asking immediate consideration of a bill to secure construction of a railroad to the Pacific.[4] Two years later, after active surveying of the proposed rail route had been started, a mass assembly of Utahans called together by church and civic leaders met to petition once more for the construction of the railroad and to suggest that the line pass through Weber Canyon into Salt Lake City and then around the southern end of the Great Salt Lake to California.[5] At the same time, Brigham Young published a notice in the *Deseret News* instructing the Latter-day Saints to prepare to aid the project if it should be consummated:

> It is . . . advisable, to begin this season to build storehouses, in which to preserve all the surplus grain; that we may be able to supply the demand which will be made upon us for provisions to support the laborers on the Pacific Railroad.[6]

The Pacific Railroad Act, however, was not passed until July 1, 1862, when the cementing of the Union seemed to require it.[7] As a gesture of good will toward the Union Pacific Railroad Company, which was organized as a result of this act, Brigham Young, presumably on behalf of the church, subscribed for five shares of stock, with a par value of $1,000 each. At the time of the subscription he paid in the required ten per cent and later paid the remaining ninety per cent in full. Young was made a director of the company in 1865.[8]

In the preliminary exploration work which followed the passage of the Pacific Railroad Act the survey party was aided in many ways by the church.[9] Samuel B. Reed, who supervised the party reaching Salt Lake City in 1864, and who was later made General Superintendent and Engineer of Construction, wrote: "They all feel a great interest in the construction of the road and will extend to me every facility in their power to help forward the work."[10] The church agreed to provide Reed with men, means of transportation, and subsistence. At Reed's request, President Young placed his son, Joseph A. Young, in charge of the surveys over the Wasatch Mountains. When the men working with Joseph "struck for wages" in June 1864 Reed sent a messenger to Salt Lake City to report the matter to President Young. Reed reported that the church president wrote "a severe letter to the boys, bidding them complete all work I have for them to do before showing themselves in Salt Lake City, since which I have not heard a word about pay."[11] According to the contemporary historian, Edward Tullidge, the church "advanced all the money" for the preliminary surveys and explorations of the Union Pacific for the first two years, and "not a dollar of it" was paid back to Brigham Young until 1870, "and then the company reluctantly paid him his money, without any profit, and only 6 per cent. interest."[12]

The strongest indications of Mormon interest in the transcontinental railroad, however, are the letters, editorials, and sermons published in the years following the commencement of active construction in 1865. Few statements were made expressing downright displeasure with the project, and hundreds of messages express delight with the immense advantages which the railroad would offer upon completion. As Brigham Young said, Mormonism "must, indeed, be a —— poor religion, if it cannot stand one railroad."[13] As with the proverbial husband who wanted his wife to receive an inheritance but did not want it to destroy their marriage, the church president was concerned, not with the railroad itself as an evil, but with the influences accompanying it, which might tend to destroy the Mormon way of life.

Precisely, what was that way of life, and in what ways did the railroad threaten it? For convenience, one may characterize the Mormon economy before the coming of the railroad as one which was relatively self-sufficient, relatively equalitarian, and relatively homogeneous. It is true that church teams took to the Salt Lake Valley each year an average of up to fifty tons of merchandise, in addition to specialized equipment like the sugar beet factory and telegraph wire. For example, the church train of 1859 consisted of forty-three wagons loaded with more than fifty tons of freight, including seven tons of paper; two tons of cotton yarn; four tons of tea, coffee, and tobacco; three tons of sugar; ten tons of dry goods; two tons of axes, scythes, shovels, and spades; several carding machines, three cane sugar mills, two nail machines, a button machine, and several tons of such miscellaneous items as black pepper, raisins, files, candles, type, ink, anvils, steel, madder, and liquor.[14] It is also true that private and non-Mormon freighters imported even larger amounts of merchandise to the territory throughout the 1860's, although much of this was freighted from Salt Lake City to mining communities in Idaho and Montana. Nevertheless, the amount of church purchases in the East had been diminished substantially as the result of the self-sufficiency campaign of the 1860's. It seems clear that most of Utah's imports were in the form of capital goods, or were goods destined for non-Mormon consumers.

It is likewise true that a significant differentiation in income began to occur in the 1860's as the direct effect of the mining trade. A class of "merchant princes" was produced which bid fair to destroy Mormon social solidarity. Nevertheless, the Mormon economy was not marked by the wide divergence in income which marked contemporary American and European society. Acording to income tax lists, only thirty-seven persons in the territory had an income of more than $2,000 in 1867, and only two had an income of more than $10,000 in the same year.[15] Finally, the Mormons were importing large numbers of Scandinavians, Swiss, and Germans, as well as Englishmen, and while some national schisms did develop, the prevailing characteristic was still homogeneity.[16]

One unique element in Mormon society, of course, was the institution of polygamy. An estimated ten per cent of all Mormon families in the 1860's were polygamous, the great majority of the marriages having been solemnized in 1846 — the year of exodus, and in 1856 — the year of famine.[17] Most of these were two-wife families — not the harem played up by a sensational press. The effect of the institution was to create somewhat larger family units than was typical on the frontier. This permitted a high degree of specialization among family members, and, at the same time, a high degree of family self-sufficiency. Since land was usually allotted on the basis of families — that is, one lot and farming acreage for each wife and children — polygamy also created larger units of operation and greater play for managerial skill. This did not necessarily make for inequality in levels of living, however, since most of these plural households provided homes for the poor and unfortunate, either as wives or as helpers. Often, under strict church regulation, men who were spiritually, socially, and economically qualified, and whose first wives did not object, were "commanded" or requested to accept another spouse into the household to provide her a "righteous" home and the opportunity of a family. Frequently, the newcomer was a homeless immigrant, a spinster, or the wife of a deceased relative with a family to support.[18]

Other than this, however, polygamy lacked the force of economic logic and would probably have died out except for its function as a symbol of Mormon heterodoxy in religious and social affairs generally. As this symbol, it provided a focus for uniting the diverse groups opposed to the spread of Mormonism, and was thus the inevitable standard around which the Mormons themselves were forced to rally in defending their faith.

Most Mormon leaders and many national leaders would have preferred another issue as a basis for arguing the Mormon question, but Mormonism had long since been identified in the public mind with polygamy, and a coming-to-terms was no doubt inevitable. The dilemma of the more liberal-minded leaders of national thought was posed by Mrs. Frank Leslie, wife of the most famed publisher of the day, who visited Utah in the 1870's. Observing the remarkable industry which had converted barren plains into verdant fields, and finding that the Mormons were "better fed, better dressed, and better mannered" than other Westerners, and lived in neater cottages, amid flowers and garden produce in profusion, Mrs. Leslie confessed "a vague doubt and bewilderment" stealing over her womanly prejudices:

> Certainly, polygamy is very wrong, but roses are better than sage-brush, and potatoes and peas preferable as diet to buffalo grass. Also schoolhouses, with cleanly and comfortable troops of children about them, are a symptom of more advanced civilization than lonely shanties with only fever-and-ague and whisky therein.[19]

Mormon leaders recognized that the railroad would produce changes, and they attempted to prepare their followers for these changes. "The railroad," wrote the editor of the *Deseret News,* "is going to make a great change in affairs here, and our people should moderate their expectations and prepare themselves for the alteration which appears inevitable." [20] Some leaders spoke and acted as though they feared some sort of a coup on the part of their "enemies." In a session of the October 1868 general conference largely devoted to "the railroad problem," Apostle George Q. Cannon read an editorial from an anti-Mormon newspaper expressing this threat—a threat which the Mormons obviously thought had some substance:

> Hitherto this Territory [Utah] has only been of interest to the people of the United States because of the infamous establishment sought to be set up in the sacred name of religion. . . . But now, for the reason just mentioned, (viz.—the advent of the railroad) a commercial interest is added, and the two together will as surely as truth is right and right is right, crush out the vile thing and rid the country of the foul blot, peaceably if possible, but with the besom of destruction if that is inevitable.

Cannon then alluded to similar boasts of national leaders:

> We are told openly and without disguise that when the railroad is completed there will be such a flood of so called "civilization" brought in here that every vestige of us, our church and institutions, shall be completely obliterated.

The railroad, he concluded, would almost certainly add to the power of that group which "menaces us with utter destruction and overthrow."[21] Other sermons add up to essentially the same view; that is, that the Mormons wanted the railroad and the facilities it provided, but they recognized the threat it posed to their supremacy and were determined that it should not destroy the essential character of their society. Suspecting their local and national "enemies" of a design to utilize the new situation to crush out Mormonism entirely, they were prepared to recommend measures of defense — measures which are explicable only in terms of the struggle for power in which the Mormons thought themselves engaged.[22]

THE END OF ISOLATION

Three basic problems faced Mormon leaders, then, as the Pacific railroad approached the borders of their commonwealth. The first problem concerned the raising of cash to pay the railway fares of Latter-day Saint immigrants from Europe. No consideration was given to the idea of cutting down on immigration; missionary work and the gathering continued as prime articles of faith and as firm obligations upon the membership. Church members had been able to assist "the poor" in the 1860's with only a small amount of cash by forming the Church Trains. Acquiring the additional cash to pay the annual fare of an estimated 3,000 immigrants from Omaha to Ogden beginning in 1869 would be particularly difficult, Mormon leaders knew, because members already in the Great Basin would be strongly tempted to use their cash to buy previously unavailable commodities which would add to their personal comfort or sense of enjoyment. The way out of this dilemma — the way to obtain cash for the emigration fund — was to use moral sanction against the importation and use of such "wasteful" commodities as tea, coffee, tobacco, liquor, fashionable clothing, and elegant furniture.

The second problem was the manner in which to deal with the flood of cheap imports which was certain to follow in the wake of the railroad. There was great concern among Mormon leaders lest "dumping" from the East destroy local industries and put profits into the hands of non-Mormon merchants and traders who might use them against the interests of the church. Also, the arrival of cheaper manufactured goods would be certain to disemploy a considerable number of Mormons working in local industries. Orthodox economists had repeatedly asserted that such workers, if sufficiently mobile, would find work eventually in other fields or regions. For Mormon leaders, however, the telling point was that it would be difficult for them to find desirable employment in Zion. There would be little outlet for added employment in an expanded agriculture. Utah's high-cost (in the short run) irrigation agriculture could not compete with the extensive (and low-cost in the short run) agriculture of the prairies. Indeed, cheap wheat from Kansas and Nebraska might force Utah's agriculture to contract. Moreover, new local manufactures could hardly have been expected to be put on a paying basis unless special measures were adopted to stimulate and protect them. Mormon workers could have found employment in mining, of course, but the life of a western miner was hardly suitable for a Latter-day Saint. While, therefore, the local industries which were in danger of being destroyed would appear to have been uneconomic, and their destruction economically desirable, this may not have been true except (or even!) in the short run, and the preservation and development by church subsidy of local "infant" industries, from the long-run point of view of Mormon leaders, may have been economically justifiable.[23]

The third basic problem facing Mormon leaders as the Pacific railroad drew nearer was the probability of a tremendous expansion in Great Basin mining. The coming of the railroad would make the extensive mineral deposits in the Wasatch Range profitable to work. By concentrating on mining, Utahans could probably pay for imports from the States. The destruction of local industry and the probable contraction of Utah's agriculture might find ample compensation in the increase in mining. Comparative advantage, for the Mormon economy, clearly seemed to lie in the exploitation and exportation of the abundant mineral ores. What was the attitude of church leaders to mining development?

Church policy with respect to mining, as hammered out in the 1850's and 1860's, was based upon the proposition that the building of the kingdom required the orderly, balanced development of local resources by a unified people for the support of a permanent society. Mining and the "gold fever" were not allowed to dominate the thoughts and activities of the Latter-day Saints. The disintegrating moral influences and social losses of the "gold fever" were, as we have seen, important considerations. Of equal importance was the fact that a permanent society could not be built upon mining. Mines become exhausted; ghost towns develop; people move away; societies decay. Cultivating land, tending flocks, developing local industries using local resources — these were the activities which church leaders thought produced stable, contented societies. What people needed to be happy and prosperous, said Brigham Young, was "iron and coal, good hard work, plenty to eat, good schools, and good doctrine." [24] Finally, there was the purely economic consideration of whether mining would pay, with respect to which church leaders had taken the position during the Connor occupation of the 1860's that it would not. Sermons and editorials after 1868 continued to reflect the view that, as President George A. Smith expressed it, "the blanks in the lottery are numerous, while the prizes are few." [25] Brigham Young, who had had a great deal of experience with miners in the preceding twenty-five years, declared in a conference sermon that the most common poverty-pleaders in Zion were miners: "Whenever I see a man going along with an old mule that can hardly stand up, and a frying pan and an old quilt, I say, 'There goes a millionaire in prospect.' These millionaires are all over the county; they are in the mountains, on our highways and in the streets. And they haven't a sixpence." [26]

An important consideration in the 1868–1872 period was that almost all of the rich deposits in the Great Basin area were owned by non-Mormons. Most of them having been opened up by the California Volunteers, and those attracted to Utah by them, the profit involved in the expansion of mining would go, not to the church, but to the church's "enemies." The large-scale mining operations now made possible by the railroad connection were certain to attract non-Mormon miners, workers, and speculators from outside the territory in increasing numbers.[27] "If the mines must be worked, it is better for the saints to work them than for others to do it," said Apostle Erastus Snow.

> But we have all the time prayed that the Lord would shut up the mines. It is better for us to live in peace and good order, and to raise wheat, corn, potatoes and fruit, than to suffer the evils of a mining life, and do no more than make a living at last.[28]

Mormon leaders were determined that their Promised Valley would not be converted into a rip-roaring mining camp, despite the apparent short-run economic advantages associated with such a conversion.

Church leaders placed repeated emphasis on the fact that Utah mines must be used directly in the building of the Kingdom. This implied exploitation of mines and other resources under priesthood direction, and parallel development of manufacturing so that mineral resources would be processed primarily by local industry. The latter procedure would increase employment and income within the territory, and at the same time guard against early exhaustion of mineral reserves. These seem to have been the considerations in the minds of Mormon leaders when they voiced apprehension over the development of Utah mines by eastern capitalists.

When the railroad did come, when mining development was stimulated, when Mormon laborers were invited to work in the mines at favorable wages, church leaders demonstrated their acceptance of reality by encouraging such labor. The purpose of this encouragement was to render it unnecessary for mine owners to import help from outside the territory.[29] However, Mormon workers were requested not to go to the mines without getting the permission of their bishop, who would ascertain if their labor was needed in the village; they were told not to partake of the vices of the Gentiles with whom they associated; and they were advised to work for cash rather than for speculative mining claims. The cash, it was suggested, should be used in paying the government for their lands, importing breeding stock, and buying agricultural machinery.[30]

Utah's economic policy crisis in 1869 was pinpointed by the New Movement or Godbeite heresy. William Godbe, a prominent Mormon merchant and confidant of Brigham Young, felt that the time was ripe for the absorption of the self-sufficient Mormon economy into the larger capitalistic economy of the nation. Godbe and such talented Mormon intellectual "liberals" as E. L. T. Harrison, Edward W. Tullidge, W. H. Shearman, and Eli B. Kelsey, began a campaign for cooperation with the Gentiles, elimination of social and economic insularity, and development of mining. In a lengthy and brilliantly reasoned editorial on "The True Development of the Territory," the organ of this group, *The Utah Magazine,* contended that Utah's prosperity depended, not on the development of manufactures, but on the development of her mineral resources. The true policy for any nation or commonwealth, said Editor Harrison, must be to "devote its labors in developing those resources which will command the largest outside market, and thus establish a basis for obtaining the money that it needs." All countries or regions which fail to develop exportable specialties "must fall back to a greater or less extent upon the miserable and cumbrous system of 'trade,' as money will be out of the question." "The reason why we have had so little cash in Utah for so long a period, and have had to depend so much upon the hateful 'trade' system," he said, "is, simply, because we have, as yet, developed no specialty." He then examined areas in which potential exportable products might be found. It would be futile to look for a competing product in agriculture, he said; Utah's high-cost irrigation agriculture could not possibly compete with California, Missouri, and Iowa. Nor did the territory have preeminency in livestock grazing or the growing of sheep and wool. So far as manufacturing was concerned, the best the territory could hope to do would be to supply its own small and limited market. "Common sense would seem to say, develop that first which will bring money from other Territories and States, and then these factories and home industries which supply ourselves will have something to lean upon."

The question then arises — Have we a specialty of the kind in this Territory that will bring us the money we need? . . . the answer comes back from all parts of the Territory, that it is in MINERALS! We are one of Nature's vast mineral store-houses — a mineral Territory in fact. From one end to the other we walk over worlds of mineral wealth awaiting development. We have mountains of coal, iron, and lead, and enough copper and silver to supply the world — to say nothing of more precious metals. Here, then, is our specialty written on the face of the country — a department in which we can compete with almost any part of the world, and keep alive all our other industries as well. Here is the opening for our enterprise. Here nature needs no forcing to produce us what we need, she groans with profusion. To strain our souls out in fruitless endeavors to bend the climate and soil of the Territory in matching other countries in departments where we were evidently never intended to equal them, much more to excell, while our grand specialty lies almost untouched, is to turn our backs on the open hand of God. . . .

Summed up in a few words — we live in a country destitute of the rich advantages of other lands — a country with few natural facilities beyond the great mass of minerals in its bowels. These are its main financial hopes. To this our future factories must look for their life, our farmers, our stock, wool, and cotton raisers for their sale, and our mechanics for suitable wages. Let these resources be developed, and we have a future before us as bright as any country beneath the sun, because we shall be working in harmony with the indications of Nature around us.[31]

Intended to represent the "intelligent" and "progressive" Mormon's solution to "the railroad problem," the editorial also expressed the view of Utah's non-Mormons. It did not, however, convince church officials that the advocated policy was "the Mormon way." In the opinion of Brigham Young and associates, the "liberal" program would mean appeasement, one-sided adjustment, and assimilation — the end of the homogeneous, equalitarian, self-sufficient Kingdom. Far from persuading church officials that the development of mining, "foreign trade," and cooperation with Gentile and capitalistic enterprise were the way of the future, the open criticism of church policy found in this and related editorials caused Harrison, Godbe, and their fellow "liberals" to be placed on trial for their fellowship, and eventually to be excommunicated. It was apostasy, they were told, "to honestly differ with the Priesthood" on such important matters of temporal policy. One might as well expect "to differ honestly with the Almighty!"[32] Once more, the church's economic program was shown to be a matter of dogma, and not a purely secular concern.[33] Though the Godbeites undoubtedly had their influence, Mormon economic policy, in 1869 and immediately thereafter, was devoted almost fanatically to the preservation of the tightly-reined independent theocratic commonwealth.

THE MORMON RESPONSE: THE SCHOOL OF THE PROPHETS

As the Latter-day Saints faced the problems of 1868–1869, what steps did they take to mitigate the undesirable adjustments which the coming of the railroad was thought to entail? And what agencies were competent to translate church policy into an effective economic action program? In large measure the agencies which prevented the complete triumph of the eastern capitalist were the School of the Prophets and the Women's Relief Society. Together, these organizations countered an energetic and financially powerful laissez-faire capitalism with a vigorous, well-organized, socially minded, and theocratically directed program of economic action. Of the two, the School of the Prophets, as an organization of the priesthood, was the more important. The Relief Society, however, provided a valuable supplement.

The School of the Prophets was organized in December 1867 by Brigham Young and was named after a similar organization established by Joseph Smith in Kirtland, Ohio, in 1833. Its immediate predecessor, however, was the Council of Fifty, which had played an important role in shaping Mormon economic policy during the first decade in Utah. The central or Salt Lake "School" was composed of over nine hundred leading adult males, and was "parent" to branch "schools" established in all the principal settlements. Approximately 5,000 priesthood members belonged to various branch schools. Not a school in the usual sense, the School of the Prophets was a forum or town meeting of leading high priests in which theology, church government, and problems of church and community were discussed and appropriate action taken. The meetings were directed by the First Presidency and other general authorities, who frequently used the meetings to impart instructions to line officers of the church. So far as its secular phase was concerned, the School of the Prophets resembled an economic planning conference. In its meetings the economic problems posed by the coming of the railroad were amply discussed and measures were taken to accomplish the desired objectives. Admission was by card only, and the sessions were confidential. It was in the School of the Prophets that the Godbeite heresy was ventilated, and it was the school which voted to disfellowship Godbe and his group of "liberals" from the church.[34]

Both the rules of the school and the actions taken give strong evidence that the school was instituted, at least in part, expressly for the purpose of meeting the problems created for the Mormons by the approach and completion of the transcontinental railroad.[35] When the economic forces which compelled its attention were satisfactorily adjusted, partly by discrediting advocates of a "new order," and partly by the adoption of an "emergency" economic program, the school was disbanded. The central school in Salt

Lake City was dissolved in August 1872.[36] Some of the local schools continued to function until 1874, when they were absorbed into the United Order organizations.[37]

The economic policies of the School of the Prophets — and the programs initiated for the purpose of bringing those policies into effect — may be summarized as follows:

First, the school attempted to prevent, or minimize, an influx of those who might threaten the morality of the community or destroy its basic structure and function. The first problem in this connection was that created by the construction of the railroad itself. The school thought it important to prevent "the swarms of scalawags that the construction of the railroad would bring."[38] One member revealed the school's feeling when he wrote the following to a Mormon missionary in England:

> you can form some estimate of what the result would be to our cities and settlements of 5,000 or 6,000 Irish, German, and other laborers crowding through our peaceful vales. It is not the men actually working on the line that I should fear so much, though no doubt they would cause some trouble, and raise a muss occasionally, but it would be the bummers, gamblers, saloon and hurdy-gurdy keepers, border ruffians, and desperadoes generally, who prey upon the laborers, whom I should fear most.[39]

The school's solution to this problem was to sponsor a contract, taken in the name of Brigham Young, to construct the Union Pacific Railroad from the mouth of Echo Canyon to Ogden — a distance of some ninety miles.[40] That contract would, as one member stated, "free" Utah of all the "evidences of civilization" referred to above. It would have been "better," in his opinion, "for the Saints to do the work for nothing, if necessary, than to let outsiders do it, as it would cost us more to preserve our cattle and horses from thieves, and our families from insult, than to roll up our sleeves and go and do the work ourselves."[41]

Another advantage of the railroad contract, from the standpoint of the School of the Prophets, was that it would insure that the income earned under the contract would go to the church and its members. "Had the Gentiles had the contract," wrote George Reynolds, "they would have traded with Gentiles, and overflooded us with traders not of us, who would have crowded into the Territory and made all the money — if any — that is to be made."[42] With the contract in the hands of the School of the Prophets, however, "The *spending* of the means [wages and other income] after it is earned, will be as carefully looked to by our advisers as the *getting* of it."[43]

The School of the Prophets also sought to minimize an influx of undesirable "outsiders" by deflating the reports on Utah's mineral wealth, thus diminishing the prospect of a rush of miners to Utah. Where the expansion in mining provided additional employment, Mormon laborers were urged to do the work rather than make it necessary for the mining industry to import labor from outside the territory.[44]

Second, the school established locally owned "cooperative" enterprises designed to prevent unemployment and make the Mormon community less dependent on imports from the East. George Q. Cannon, apostle, called attention to the need for the establishment of these enterprises in a series of editorials in the *Deseret News*.

The railroad [wrote Cannon] will not be an unmixed benefit to us unless we prepare for it. It will not put an abundance of money in circulation unless we lay the foundation of branches of business that will bring it to us. It is a mistake to suppose that the Railroad, in and of itself, is going to make our country great and its people wealthy. While there is demand for labor upon its construction, and we have that labor to supply, money will flow into us; but when this demand ceases, and we have no products that can be transported at a profit for which money can be had in return, we will be in a worse position than if we had no railroad; for the ease with which the country can then be drained, at speculator's own prices, of breadstuffs and such articles as we now produce will be a detriment to us.

We must take the necessary steps to create new industries. . . . Our manufacturers, mechanics and merchants should endeavor to shape their various branches of business so as to be prepared for the coming change. Home manufacture must be extensively and persistently pursued.

The railroad, added Cannon, must be used to import raw materials rather than consumer goods, in order that intraterritorial employment might be maintained. "As for capital to carry out these plans, there is no people better situated than we to obtain it by co-operation — a principle that has been found to work well in carrying on many branches of business." [45]

As the result of the efforts of the School of the Prophets, a number of important cooperative Mormon enterprises were established at this time, including the Utah Manufacturing Company, which was organized in 1868 to manufacture wagons, carriages, and agricultural machinery; a furniture manufacturing enterprise; associations to further the development of a silk industry; the $300,000 Provo Woolen Mills; and a number of minor manufactures including a wooden-bucket factory, and ink and match factories.

The school was very critical of Mormon suppliers and buyers who refused to patronize these local enterprises. Consistent trading with competing eastern firms made the culprit *persona non grata* in the organization and endangered his fellowship in the church. Investment in these enterprises, though admittedly risky, was urged strongly on Mormon capitalists, and Brigham Young, as trustee-in-trust, also invested part of the common fund of the community in most of them.

Third, as the school discussed the possibilities and prospects of export manufactures, it was agreed that wage reductions were a necessary prerequisite to the placing of local industry on an export basis. Substantial agreement on this matter was reached in 1869 at the time when many of the enterprises referred to above were beginning their operations.[46] At an important meeting of the school in July 1869, at which the members of the First Presidency, several members of the Council of Twelve Apostles, and a full membership of the school were present, a decision was reached to elect a committeeman from each trade. The committeeman was expected to submit to his trade the proposition that wages be reduced "in order that Utah might be able to compete with the manufactures of the States."[47] The goal was to reduce wages by as much as one-third to one-half. The reactions of the tradespeople to this proposition are not chronicled, but it seems doubtful that the school was successful in reducing wages substantially or permanently. There seems, however, to have been a willingness on the part of many Mormon mechanics and artisans to make sacrifices for the cause of building up Zion. It is interesting to note that wage reduction was the first announced policy of the church which the Godbeites undertook to criticize in print.[48]

Fourth, another requisite to the success of larger-scale valley industry was the establishment of interior branch railroads. The prime need was the construction of a thirty-seven mile railroad from the Union Pacific terminal at Ogden to Salt Lake City. This road was commenced by the Utah Central Railroad Company — a "church" company — soon after the completion of the Union Pacific Railroad to Promontory. The financing of the Utah Central Railroad was handled largely by members of the School of the Prophets and was discussed several times in its meetings. Later Mormon efforts resulted in the construction of the Utah Southern, Utah Southern Extension, Utah Northern, and Utah Eastern Railroads.

Fifth, to the extent to which imports were necessary and desirable, the School of the Prophets attempted to canalize them through a church-established wholesale trading concern — Zion's Cooperative Mercantile Institution. One of the rules of the school was the following stipulation: "In all matters, their [the members'] dealings should be as much as possible with those in full fellowship in the Church of Jesus Christ of Latter-day Saints, but they must not deal with their enemies."[49] Before the organization of the School of the Prophets, church leaders had conducted, in 1865–1866, a "boycott" against merchants who were considered hostile to the interest of the Latter-day Saints. As the Pacific railroad entered Utah Territory, however, a general boycott on Gentile business and trading establishments was inaugurated.[50] This policy of not trading with "outsiders" was discussed in the School of the Prophets before its proclamation to the church-at-large, and plans for the establishment of a wholesale trading concern were expedited. President Brigham Young told the school that he had "tried to control the merchants, but could not do it. . . . They would go to hell, if they did not turn a short corner." The school voted "that those who dealt with outsiders should be cut off from the Church."[51] A few days later, in October 1868, the general boycott was presented to the semiannual conference of the church in Salt Lake City, and the "protective" course was sustained. Within two weeks the School of the Prophets had drawn up, discussed, and given final approval to the preamble, constitution, and by-laws of "Zion's Cooperative Mercantile Institution." Retail cooperative stores were then established in each of the one-hundred-odd settlements in Mormondom as outlets for the goods imported by Z.C.M.I. These retail cooperatives had a working monopoly on the local market, and all nonlocal goods were to be purchased through Z.C.M.I. Being, in their initial stage, community enterprises, they do not appear to have abused their monopolistic positions. Their establishment and operation were, in many cases, functions of the local branch of the School of the Prophets.

Sixth, another problem confronting the church when the transcontinental railroad was completed was that of preventing the railroad companies and other newcomers from acquiring title to land on which the Saints had settled. Until 1869 the Mormons had no "legal" property rights in Utah; that is, while Congress was confirming land titles in other Western states and territories, Mormon titles were not confirmed, nor the benefits of the Homestead Act applied to Utah, until after the completion of the railroad. This delay was undoubtedly purposeful, being based on the hope of forcing the Mormons to change their social institutions, but actually made it easier for the Mormons to establish and maintain their own somewhat unique property institutions. It is surprising, as one reads of the numerous and bloody contests between early rancheros and squatters in California, for example, that there was so little conflict over land in Utah, even after "the coming of the Gentile." With the completion of the railroad, however, it became necessary to establish a General Land Office in Utah, giving rise to a potential source of antagonism. Under the Pacific Railroad Act, the railroads were given alternate sections of land along their right of way, except where property rights were already vested in private citizens. As soon as this danger to the vested interests of Mormon squatters appeared (March 1869), the School of the Prophets appointed a committee to "post" themselves on the land question and "report to the people what steps were necessary to take to preserve their homesteads being claimed by the railroad companies."[52] This committee made periodic reports to the school, and sent individuals on missions to assist local settlers throughout the territory with their land title applications. There appears to have been a minimum of injustice done to the people of

Utah (viewing it from the Mormon position) as a result of the efforts of this committee and the School of the Prophets.[53]

Seventh, and finally, the School of the Prophets participated in the drive to raise cash for the Perpetual Emigrating Fund by pledging to cut down on personal consumption expenditures and donating the amount saved to that Fund. Most important was the pledge required of each member that he would observe the "Word of Wisdom."[54] The Word of Wisdom was a revelation announced by Joseph Smith at Kirtland, Ohio, in 1833, stating that strong drinks, tobacco, and such hot drinks as tea and coffee, were not good for man.[55] This revelation had not been a binding commandment in early Mormonism, nor in the 1860's when it was used in connection with the "grow your own or do without" program. With the establishment of the School of the Prophets in 1867, however, a campaign for complete abstinence was launched, with the object in view of stopping the cash drain from the territory and using the money saved to bring "the poor" home to Zion.

> It was our wish then, and, is still [said Brigham Young], that the money generally paid out for tea and coffee, liquor, tobacco, etc. be used to send for the poor Saints and bring them to a land where they can accumulate the common necessaries of life, instead of staying in their own land, and going down to an untimely grave for want of food.[56]

The minutes of the schools reflect the trials which countless Mormon men went through in living up to the rule.[57] But the misery of breaking the habit, particularly in regard to tobacco, was somewhat counterbalanced by the satisfaction that most of them felt in saving a soul from the fleshpots of Babylon. Mormon women took a similar pledge as they joined the Relief Society. Relief Society minutes also reflect the eventual triumph of pious resolves, particularly those to abstain from coffee and tea. Many a sister's coffee money went into the railroad fund of the P.E.F.

So effective was the Word of Wisdom campaign in 1867 and following years that in less than two decades abstinence from tea, coffee, tobacco, and intoxicating beverages was almost as strong a test of faith as carrying out a colonization or missionary assignment. Continued for reasons of "good health" in the twentieth century, it is one of the distinguishing traits of Latter-day Saints.

These were the principal activities of the territory-wide organization of the School of the Prophets. Just how the many problems were solved, especially those related to the railroad contracts, the construction of branch railroads, and the establishment of cooperative stores and industries, will be discussed in the chapters that follow. Each local school also discussed a variety of local problems, including such matters as the management of stock herds, support of cooperative stores, establishing the price of grain, elections, repair of fences, opening of roads, and the appointment of watermasters. On occasion, the schools also heard confessions of members who had been drunk, worked on Sunday, or allowed their livestock to run wild.

THE WOMEN'S RELIEF SOCIETY

Somewhat less important from the standpoint of policy, but equally effective in marshaling support behind the policies decided upon, was the Women's Relief Society. As early as April 1865, Brigham Young had suggested the establishment of an "organization of the sisters against purchasing goods at the stores," as part of the home industry and self-sufficiency campaign of the 1860's.[58] A number of "female home manufacturing societies" resulted. Late in 1867, at the time the School of the Prophets was being organized, a movement got under way to form, in each ward and settlement, a Women's Relief Society. Eliza R. Snow, poetess, feminist, and plural wife in turn of Joseph Smith and Brigham Young, was appointed by the First Presidency to take charge of the movement.[59] "Sister" Snow, as she was called, had been secretary of the "Female Relief Society of Nauvoo" organized by Joseph Smith in 1842, which was now being revived and expanded to meet the challenge posed by the coming of the railroad.

Ostensibly the Relief Societies were organized "to visit the sick and the helpless and the needy, and learn their wants, and, under their Bishops, collect the means necessary to relieve them."[60] Their actual task was far greater:

> Relieving the poor, in most instances, requires something beyond administering to present necessities. . . . To those who have strength to labor, it is far more charitable to give employment and so direct their energies that they can earn what they need, and thus realize the fruits of their own labors.[61]

The objects of the Relief Societies, in other words, were to teach the poor to provide for themselves and to establish institutions and programs which would assist the poor to live more comfortably and those not so poor to live more frugally. By requesting compliance with the traditional Mormon doctrine that they should clothe themselves in the workmanship of their own hands, church leaders hoped that the women would cut down their purchases from the stores, and at the same time find pleasant employment in their homes. Brigham Young, for example, said he did not mind seeing the "human form and the human face adorned," but he wanted the adorning to be the workmanship of Mormon hands.[62] It would seem that the underlying motive for the organization of the Relief Societies was the prevention or diminution of female extravagance, by the rich as well as by the poor, thus relieving hard-pressed husbands to devote a larger share of their production and time to the building of the Kingdom. The Relief Societies would relieve the territory of the burden of supporting both unnecessary importation and unnecessary poverty.

The approaching completion of the transcontinental railroad, then, appears to have been a major reason for the organization of Relief Societies in 1867–1868. It was not only that the railroad would tempt the sisters with such "vices" as tea and coffee; the railroad would also bring "outsiders" with new tastes and fashions. Any resulting increase in the demand for "needless" and "fashionable" imports would diminish the capital fund of the community and damage the cause of economic growth. Contemporary fashion, according to Brigham Young, "was most useless, unbecoming and ridiculous," and he illustrated his point with the Grecian Bend, mutton-legged sleeves, and the long, flowing skirts which were popular in his day. The Grecian Bend, he said, gave women a hump on their backs that made them look like camels; mutton-legged sleeves "took seven yards for the sleeves, and three for the dress"; and long trains would drag up the dirt, raise a dust, and represented a waste of many yards of cloth.[63] Rather than waste their money on "useless articles that do no good to the body of the persons who use them," Latter-day Saint women should make contributions to such worthy causes as the transportation of the "pure in heart" from abroad.

The effect of the railroad on the tastes of the young ladies was expected to be particularly strong. For that reason, when the Relief Societies had completed their own organization, they were requested to supervise and encourage the formation of "Retrenchment Societies" among the young ladies of the various settlements. The pattern was set in November 1869, when Brigham Young called his many wives and daughters together in the parlor of the Lion House in Salt Lake City and addressed them as follows:

> All Israel [the Mormon people] are looking for my family and watching the example set by my wives and children. For this reason I desire to organize my own family first into a society for the promotion of habits of order, thrift, industry, and charity; and, above all things, I desire them to retrench from their extravagance in dress, in eating, and even in speech. The time has come when the sisters must agree to give up their follies of dress and cultivate a modest apparel, a meek deportment, and to set an example before the people of the world worthy of imitation. . . .
>
> I want you to set your own fashions. Let your apparel be neat and comely, and the workmanship of your own hands. Wear the good cloth manufactured in our own mills, and cease to build up the merchant who sends your money out of the Territory for fine clothes made in the East.[64]

The Young Family voted its support, and under the leadership of Eliza R. Snow, the "Young Ladies' Department of the Co-operative Retrenchment

Association," with appropriate constitution, by-laws, regular meetings, and a carefully-worked-out program, was formed. One of those present wrote: "it was settled that night that a Spartan plainness of dress was to be one of the distinguishing marks of the new movement."[65] The signed articles of agreement included the following:

> Resolved, that inasmuch as the Saints have been commanded to gather out from Babylon and not partake of her sins, that they may receive not of her plagues, we feel that we should not condescend to imitate the pride, folly and fashions of the world. . . .
>
> Resolved . . . as fast as it shall be expedient, we shall adopt the wearing of home-made articles, and exercise our united influence in rendering them fashionable.[66]

The model of this association was carried by Sister Snow to the Relief Societies throughout the territory. Within a few months, several score Retrenchment Societies had blossomed throughout the Great Basin. The girls were taught to glean wheat, piece quilts, crochet, make hats, knit stockings, and to engage in many cultural activities. The fruits of their labor were commonly devoted to the P.E.F. and to other worthwhile church projects. The organization seemed to fulfill a useful purpose, even when the economic need which was responsible for its formation was passed, and in 1877 the emphasis on retrenchment was abandoned in favor of that of personal improvement. The organization has continued to the present under the name "The Young Ladies' Mutual Improvement Association," with church-appointed general officers, and with several hundred thousand members.

The emphasis on the formation of young ladies' retrenchment associations was so pronounced for a period that Brigham Young deemed it necessary to appoint Mrs. Mary Isabella Horne as an associate of Sister Snow to assure that the cause of retrenchment was not neglected by the older women. Mrs. Horne held meetings throughout the territory and organized Relief Society sisters into a Senior Department of the Retrenchment Association. Her addresses stressed the immediate possibility of community bankruptcy induced by excessive imports of things which the ladies could, if they would, make themselves or do without.[67] The response of the sisters to these addresses usually took the form of an adoption of a series of resolutions and the formation of a department of the Relief Society to carry them into effect. The resolution passed by the Retrenchment Department of the Salt Lake City Eighth Ward Relief Society was typical: "We will not follow the fashions of the wicked world, but will endeavor to attire ourselves as becometh Saints of God, and as much as possible in the workmanship of our own hands."[68] These organizations continued to function during the early 1870's. They began to disappear when the emergency created by the coming of the railroad had passed.

A second task assigned to the Relief Societies was that of assisting in the establishment and operation of cooperative general stores. The Relief Societies were advised to take stock in these stores, patronize them exclusively, and prepare to set up retail outlets for their own hand work.[69] In many cases, the Relief Societies actually took over the management of some of the cooperative stores originally established by the priesthood. The societies also operated a number of their own establishments.

In the third place, the Relief Societies were expected to give support to the home industry movement. "Every branch of the Relief Society," wrote the leaders, "is called upon to lay hold of this subject of home industry with a will, and to take active part in the great work of bringing about the perfect organization of a self-sustaining people."[70] Many industries were named as being at once practical and necessary, because of the large drain in purchasing power resulting from their importation; but getting the women to be "self-sustaining with respect to clothing" was given greatest stress. "Home industry," which once had typically meant "Mormon" industry, was now applied primarily to industries which would provide employment for women and children. No member of the Relief Society, declared its officers, "should be satisfied to acknowledge herself in all respects a non-producer. . . . Let the sisters think of what they can wear that is Zion made."[71]

Since wool and cotton clothing were successfully manufactured in the locally owned Provo Woolen Mills, Washington Cotton Factory, and similar enterprises, the assignment given to the Relief Society sisters to make their own clothing resolved itself into a mission to grow and manufacture silk, in order to make materials for their better dresses. Those women who wished fancy handkerchiefs, gloves, shawls, and dresses for formal wear would be expected to produce them of silk rather than waste territorial exchange in importing them. Under the aegis of the Relief Society, the "Deseret Silk Association" was organized to disseminate information on silk culture, distribute eggs, and import facilities for the reeling of silk. Bishops were urged to set aside a plot of ground for Relief Society mulberry trees and to facilitate the project in other ways. Nearly every one of the approximately 150 local Relief Society organizations had a silk project during the 1870's. By 1877, there were 5,000,000 silk worms in the territory.[72]

There were other activities of the Relief Societies, but those mentioned were the ones which had chief importance as the railroad approached the Mormons in 1869. Unlike the School of the Prophets, the women's organization has survived to the present day. Under the name "Relief Society of the Church of Jesus Christ of Latter-day Saints" it now has more than 200,000 members.

EFFECTIVENESS OF MORMON "PROTECTIONISM"

Leading politicians and preachers had confidently predicted that the railroad would mean the end of Mormonism—or at least the end of the distinctive elements in Mormonism. It was widely believed that Mormon society would succumb, much as other local societies and institutions had succumbed, to the "march of civilization" which followed in the wake of the railroad. The editor of *The Galaxy* expressed a typical view when he wrote:

For rolling back the tide of Anglo-American civilization, whenever that tide shall wash over the mountain bounds of Utah, Brother Brigham's bands will be just as efficient as old Mrs. Partington's mop in keeping the Atlantic Ocean out of her back kitchen. . . . When the United States goes to Utah, Mormonism will disappear like a puddle with Niagara Falls turned into it.[73]

So widely held was the view that the railroad would lead to the death of Mormonism that the strongly supported national antipolygamy legislation which had come to a head in the late 'sixties was momentarily abandoned in the hope that such measures would no longer be necessary when the transcontinental railroad was completed. Brigham Young and his associates, however, introduced a deliberate program whereby the machinery of civilization, usually designed for breaking up isolation, would make isolation more complete and better organized—or, at the least, make isolation sufficiently complete and well-organized to preserve the integrity of Mormon institutions. In full realization of the fact that they were fighting a rear-guard action, Mormon policymakers fought the immediate shift to a mining economy, the seemingly inevitable increase in imports and decrease in immigration, and the relinquishment of control over business institutions to eastern capitalists. Though these policies undoubtedly were carried out with less success than church leaders desired, they also were unquestionably more effective than most non-Mormons—and some Mormons—had anticipated. The church did not seem to grow appreciably weaker; and the religion of the Saints was not "mineralized." The Mormons remained, in some respects, a "peculiar people." Utah did not become, at least immediately, an economic province whose chief function was to supply raw materials to the industrial East. There was a noticeable tendency in that direction to be sure, but Utah managed to postpone, or at least slow down, the "colonial" status which characterized early Montana, Nevada, Colorado, and Wyoming. Utah, whose geography and resources were not greatly different from those of surrounding states, represented, during the succeeding three decades, a quite different type of social economy. There can be little doubt that church policies were influential in accomplishing this result.

From the standpoint of the Mormons, the School of the Prophets and Women's Relief Society were useful economic service agencies, for they established protective economic institutions and consolidated the weight of public opinion behind those institutions. They activated local producing and marketing enterprises, and implemented policies which aimed at preserving the unity and economic independence of the Mormon people. While they cannot be said to have been successful in achieving all of their objectives, they lessened and eased the inevitable adjustments in Utah's economy and prevented other adjustments which were regarded as undesirable. As essential institutions in the church's program of economic solidarity, the School of the Prophets and Relief Society managed to prevent, for good or for ill, the immediate and complete assimilation of Mormon institutions, in the years immediately after 1869, by the dominant laissez-faire institutions of post-bellum America. At least two decades were to pass before the Great Basin Kingdom was to make substantial accommodation to the more powerful institutions characteristic of America at the turn of the century.

CHAPTER IX

Mormon Railroads

A number of historians, both Mormon and non-Mormon, finding some evidence of discontinuity in Mormon policy, have treated 1869 as the great dividing peak in Mormon history — as the beginning of the decline of the Kingdom. It has been common, for example, to attribute to private enterprise most of the large endeavors of the Mormons after 1869. Such enterprises as Zion's Co-operative Mercantile Institution, Provo Woolen Mills, Washington Cotton Factory, Zion's Savings Bank & Trust Company, the Salt Lake City streetcar and gas companies, and the four Mormon railroads (Utah Central, Utah Southern, Utah Northern, and Utah Eastern) have been regarded as private; and this view seems to be confirmed by an examination of the incorporation papers of these companies. Yet, if the analysis in the preceding chapter be accepted, the collective response which typified Mormon activity in the era of the wagon train also characterized the Mormon response in the age of the railroad. As with the construction of roads and irrigation ditches in the 1850's, the railroads and factories of the 1870's were promoted by the church or by its agents, the trustee-in-trust and the School of the Prophets. The construction and initial ownership of these enterprises was semipublic, and the decision-making power in their subsequent operation rested to a considerable extent upon the shoulders of the church and its official family. Basic modification of the distinctive economic institutions of the Mormons, as will be seen, did not begin until two full decades after the "joining of the rails" in 1869.

To some extent, this misleading impression of church withdrawal from economic activity may have been deliberately fostered by the church to avoid punitive legislation. The important federal Anti-Bigamy Act of 1862, in addition to its penalties against plural marriage, contained provisions specifically designed to curb the economic power of the church. The near-passage of other proposals to tighten the enforcement of this law and to expand its scope seems to have led to a deliberate concealment of the church's participation in economic development.[1]

The particular clause of the 1862 act which created difficulty was one which disincorporated the Church of Jesus Christ of Latter-day Saints and limited the amount of real estate which it could hold to $50,000.[2] Any property acquired by the church in excess of that value was to be "forfeited and escheat to the United States." The object of this section, according to Senator Bayard of Delaware who sponsored it, was to prevent the accumulation, in Utah, of wealth and property in the hands of ecclesiastical corporations or "theocratic institutions inconsistent with our form of government."[3]

Although some thought this section of the act was unconstitutional,[4] and although no administrative apparatus was established to enforce it, the church thought it best to feign compliance by placing many of its properties in the hands of Brigham Young and other trustworthy individuals, to be administered by them on behalf of the church, but in a private capacity. Because of these arrangements, which were necessarily secret, most of the business of the church after 1862 was transacted in the name of Brigham Young. Contemporary travelers and writers contributed to the Great Man interpretation of Mormon history by attributing to Brigham Young activities and innovations which in reality were those of the church he represented. Only when one examines the papers connected with the settlement of the Brigham Young estate in the late 1870's does the scope and importance of church economic activity from 1869 to 1879 become clear. Brigham Young's primary economic role during this decade was that of trustee-in-trust of the church's financial affairs rather than that of a private enterpriser.[5] The construction and operation of early Utah railroads, usually considered to be a private affair involving Brigham Young and a few others, thus assumes an aspect or focus which was never understood by contemporaries and never corrected by modern writers. In many respects, Mormon railroads bore more resemblance to the community-built Deseret Telegraph, than to the hosts of privately built independent railroads in nineteenth-century America.

MORMON EXPERIENCE WITH THE TRANSCONTINENTAL RAILROAD

The Mormons who had looked forward with eagerness — and also with fear — to the completion of the transcontinental railroad found it disappointing in three respects: It did not follow the route preferred by the Mormons; the Mormon contract to grade part of the road was not paid on time or in full; and the independent roads built by the Mormons to connect it with their own settlements occupied such a precarious position with respect to earnings that they were eventually sold to interests connected with the transcontinental line. Mormon activity associated with railroad building was extensive and enthusiastic, but frustrating. In this respect, their experience was not unique.

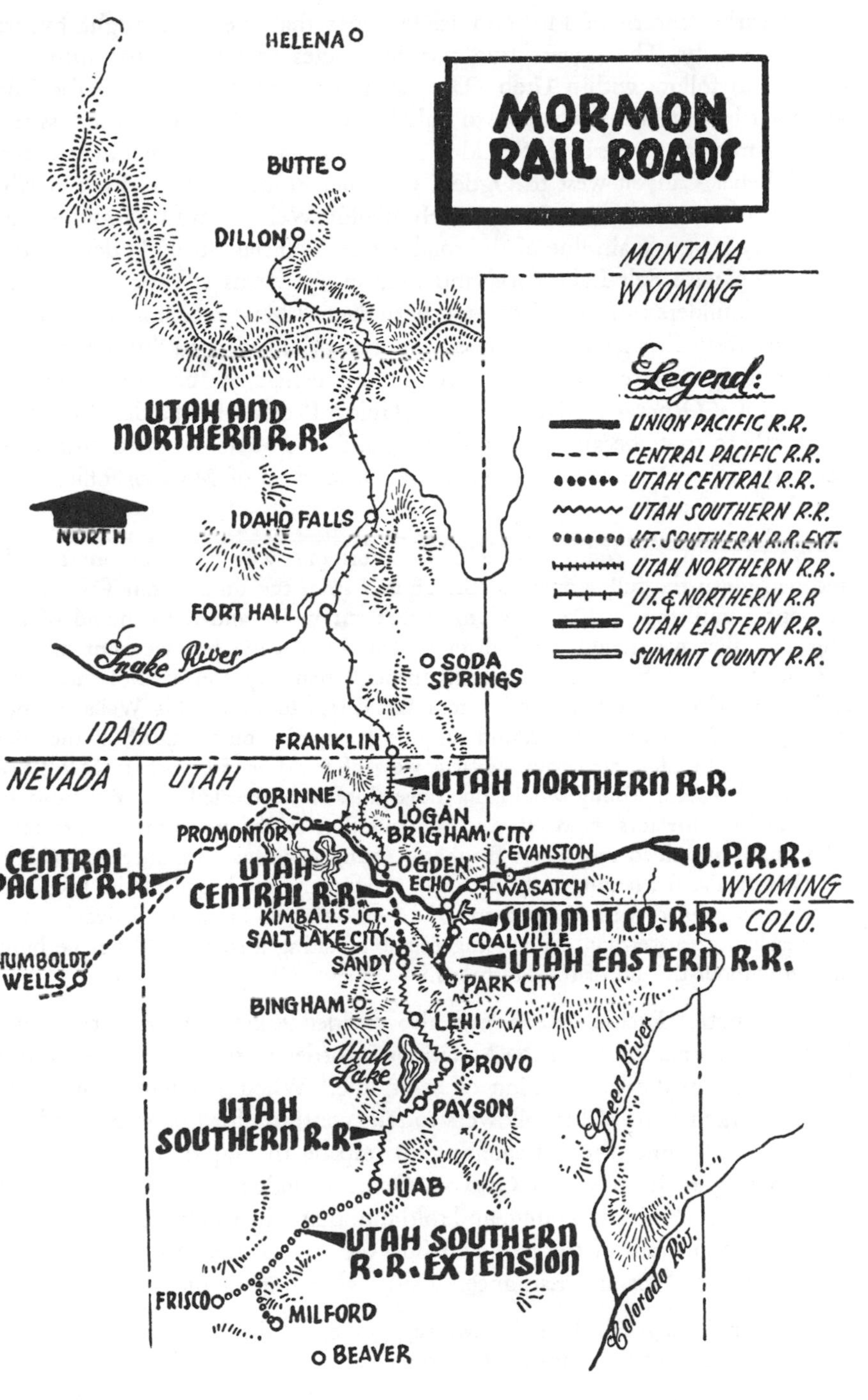
MORMON RAIL ROADS
HELENA
BUTTE
DILLON
MONTANA
WYOMING
Legend:
UNION PACIFIC R.R.
CENTRAL PACIFIC R.R.
UTAH CENTRAL R.R.
UTAH SOUTHERN R.R.
UT. SOUTHERN R.R. EXT.
UTAH NORTHERN R.R.
UT. & NORTHERN R.R
UTAH EASTERN R.R.
SUMMIT COUNTY R.R.
UTAH AND NORTHERN R.R.
NORTH
IDAHO FALLS
FORT HALL
Snake River
SODA SPRINGS
IDAHO
FRANKLIN
NEVADA
UTAH
UTAH NORTHERN R.R.
CORINNE
LOGAN
PROMONTORY
BRIGHAM CITY
EVANSTON
U.P.R.R.
CENTRAL PACIFIC R.R.
UTAH CENTRAL R.R.
OGDEN
ECHO
WASATCH
WYOMING
KIMBALLS JCT.
SUMMIT CO. R.R.
COLO.
SALT LAKE CITY
COALVILLE
SANDY
UTAH EASTERN R.R.
HUMBOLDT WELLS
PARK CITY
BINGHAM
LEHI
Utah Lake
PROVO
Green River
UTAH SOUTHERN R.R.
PAYSON
JUAB
UTAH SOUTHERN R.R. EXTENSION
Colorado Riv.
FRISCO
MILFORD
BEAVER

An early concern of Mormon leaders was that the road might bypass Salt Lake City. There were two possible routes that the transcontinental road could follow within Utah. The "southern route" would run the line southward from Weber Canyon to Salt Lake City, and then west across the Great American Desert of Nevada. The "northern route" would proceed from Weber Canyon west to Ogden, Corinne, Promontory, and the northern end of the Great Salt Lake to Humboldt Wells, Nevada, leaving Salt Lake City off the main line of the road. Church officials strongly desired the connection with Salt Lake City, and used every means at their disposal to influence builders in favor of the southern route.[6] Mass meetings were held; petitions were circulated; Congress was memorialized; and church writers and politicians were pressed into service on behalf of the cause. Despite these efforts, General Dodge and other Union Pacific officials decided upon the northern route because it was shorter, and was better supplied with timber and water. General Dodge wrote of the reaction of Mormon officials to this decision as follows:

> We had only one controversy with the Mormons, who had been our friends and had given the full support of the church from the time of our first reconnoissances until the final completion. It was our desire and the demand of the Mormons that we should build through Salt Lake City, but we bent all our energies to find a feasible line passing through that city and around the south end of the Great Salt Lake and across the desert to Humboldt Wells, a controlling point in the line. We found the line so superior on the north of the lake that we had to adopt that route with a view of building a branch to Salt Lake City, but Brigham Young would not have this, and appealed over my head to the board of directors, who referred the question to the government directors, who finally sustained me. Then Brigham Young gave his allegiance and aid to the Central Pacific, hoping to bring them around the south end of the lake and force us to connect with them there. He even went so far as to deliver in the tabernacle a great sermon denouncing me, and stating a road could not be built or run without the aid of the Mormons.[7]

The Central Pacific, which had also decided upon the northern route, kept this information from the Mormons in order to secure their assistance in speeding up the construction of their line.[8] When Brigham Young reportedly urged some of his followers to take contracts for the grading of the Central Pacific line, thus threatening to impede the rapid progress of the U. P. road west from Weber Canyon, General Dodge of the U. P. decided to "enlighten" President Young, and told him that "the Central Pacific wasn't going to build south of the lake and into the city, so the Mormons needn't look to that road for any assistance." Dodge's biographer then adds:

> Brigham Young called in the twelve apostles of the Mormon church and Dodge told them of the plans of the Union Pacific to build a first-class railroad

from Ogden down to Salt Lake; of the necessity of building the main line north of the lake; and of the impossibility of the Central Pacific's ever tapping the town owing to the fact that the Union Pacific would beat the California road to Ogden and shut out any attempt it might make to construct its own branch to the Mormon city.

Brigham Young was far too shrewd not to see the logic of Dodge's position, so he planned a great tabernacle service, explained the whole situation and "told his followers that the Lord, in another vision, had commanded the Mormons to help the Union Pacific." [9]

Thus, the prime desire of the church, that the road pass through their metropolis, was not to be consummated. Ironically, however, the old rail route around the northern shore of Great Salt Lake was finally abandoned early in the twentieth century in favor of the Lucin Cutoff whereby trains now run directly across the lake.

The second concern which disturbed church officials was the problem raised by the projected importation of several thousand "Gentile" laborers into the territory to do the construction work — a job which church leaders felt could profitably be performed by the Latter-day Saints. When asked by Samuel Reed if he would take a contract for some of the construction work near the Mormon settlements, Brigham Young was very much pleased and later reported to the School of the Prophets that "the hand of the Lord" had intervened in favor of the Latter-day Saints. The clerk of the school reported that:

> When the president expressed the hope that the job might be completed creditably with the saints, that in the halls of Congress it might be announced that no part of the national railway was completed more satisfactorily, the brethren in mass clapped their hands approving of the president's remarks.[10]

The construction contract was finally signed on May 21, 1868, in the Continental Hotel, Salt Lake City, between Brigham Young, representing the church, and Samuel B. Reed, representing the U. P. Under the terms of the contract the Mormons were to do all the grading, tunneling, and bridge masonry on the U. P. line for the 150-odd miles from the head of Echo Canyon through Weber Canyon to the shores of the Great Salt Lake.[11] The bulk of the work was to be completed by November 1, 1868, and was expected to require the employment of 5,000 men and several hundred teams. The consideration appears to have been $2,125,000. The U.P. Company entered into the contract before the location of the road was definitely determined to be north of Salt Lake City, and worded it to provide for grading of the route north or south of Great Salt Lake.

Immediately after the contract was signed, preparations were made to put the Latter-day Saints to work. The type of men and work required, together with the prices and conditions of subcontract arrangements, were published in the *Deseret News*. In general, the Mormon laborers were told that they could earn $2.00 per day for their work, of which eighty per cent was to be paid monthly as the work progressed and the remaining twenty per cent was to be paid when the entire job was finished and accepted. The Saints were urged to participate so that "those who owe may pay their debts and have the necessary funds to send for machinery and establish mercantile houses in the various settlements." However, bishops were cautioned to "see that a sufficient number of hands remain in the various Wards and settlements to take care of the crops . . . the fields should not be neglected." [12] Brigham Young also wrote to the church's Emigration Agent in Liverpool suggesting that emigrants during the 1868 season be prepared for work under the terms of the contract after reaching Utah. In this way they could repay immediately their indebtedness to the Perpetual Emigrating Fund, and, at the same time, earn cash for the purchase of farming equipment and land. Moreover, all men physically able to work were to be passed free, and their families at reduced rates, over the U. P. from Omaha to the terminus, thus saving travel expense.[13] The message concluded:

> For many reasons that will readily occur to you, this contract is viewed by the brethren of understanding as a God-send. There is much indebtedness among the people, and the territory is drained of money, but labor here and coming we have in large amount, and this contract affords opportunity for turning that labor into money, with which those here can pay each other, and import needed machinery, and such useful articles as we cannot yet produce, and those coming can pay their indebtedness, and have ready means with which to gather around them the comforts of life in their new homes.[14]

The reaction of the Mormon rank and file to the contract seems to have been one of unqualified approval. One of the more articulate, in a letter to the English Saints, listed three advantages of the contract to the Mormons:

> It will obviate the necessity of some few thousands of strangers being brought here, to mix and interfere with the settlers, of that class of men who take pleasure in making disturbance wherever they go. It will give the money expended in the work to citizens of this Territory, and work to employ them, which is very desirable at the present time. It will show that we are interested in forwarding the great national project, and ready to assist in consummating this great national good.[15]

Virtually all the subcontracts were let in May and June 1868. Most of the small ones were let to bishops of the various wards with members desiring work, while larger contracts involving such specialized work as the making of bridge abutments and the cutting of tunnels, were taken by John Sharp, assistant to the Superintendent of Public Works; Joseph A.

Young, a son of the church president; and Joseph F. Nounan, a non-Mormon businessman of Salt Lake City. The subcontracts were let at ten per cent less than the stipulation in the church contract with Union Pacific.[16] The church would thus make a tithe of all contract earnings.

While laborers and bosses were being recruited and put to work on the U. P. contract, Leland Stanford, representing the Central Pacific Railroad, also approached Brigham Young with the object of getting the church to assume responsibility for the construction of the C. P. road from Humboldt Wells, Nevada, to Ogden, Utah — a distance of about 200 miles. This contract was finally signed in the fall of 1868, and was taken in the names of Apostle Ezra T. Benson (grandfather of the Secretary of Agriculture in Dwight Eisenhower's cabinet), Lorin Farr, and Chauncey W. West. Benson was ecclesiastical leader in Cache Valley, while Farr and West were prominent churchmen in Weber County. The contract consideration was in the neighborhood of $4,000,000.[17]

President Young's letters during the summer and fall of 1868 reflect great satisfaction at the favorable turn of events. One excerpt also suggests the paternalistic view which the Mormon leader took of church and community projects:

> Work on my railroad contract is progressing rapidly; several jobs are already completed, and nearly all the light work would have been done ere this, had the work been staked out in time. The Western Company [that is, Central Pacific] are wishing me to contract to grade 200 miles for them, which I expect to begin as soon as the stakes are driven. These contracts give us many advantages, besides furnishing money for labor to those whom the grasshoppers have left but little to do, and who could not well otherwise supply themselves with food until another harvest.[18]

That the contracts with both the U. P. and C. P. companies were given careful supervision by the church president is abundantly indicated in the writings of both General Dodge and Leland Stanford. Stanford's letters to Mark Hopkins indicate a healthy respect for Brigham Young's hold over his followers:

> I cannot see Brigham, and until he is seen but little is seen here clearly. . . .
>
> The Mormons will not go west of their contract this winter but will work east unless Brigham Young should object. . . .
>
> Today I had a talk with Brigham Young. He will do our grading west from Ogden to the Promontory and will not make our work secondary to the U. P. That he will put plenty of men on both lines, I am satisfied he can do it. . . .
>
> Our work from Ogden to Monument goes very slowly. Our contractors have many excuses. But the real trouble is they are trying to do the work too close. But I have started Brigham after them and they give indications of doing better.[19]

Although a formally capitalistic arrangement, the completion of the Union Pacific and Central Pacific contracts was handled in much the same way that other church cooperative projects were undertaken. Workers were "called" or volunteered. Each was expected to consult his bishop before leaving. The usual arrangement was for a ward or group of wards to form a "company," resembling the colonizing companies of previous years, with a church-appointed president to look after their interests. These companies were almost invariably limited to church members and so-called "church standards" were usually adhered to; that is, there was to be no swearing, no work on Sunday, no drinking, and each man was to pay a faithful tithe. In some cases the profits on the contract were to go toward the building of a meeting house, or for some other religious purpose. Various ward companies vied with one another in the speed and excellence of their work.

One occurrence gave Mormon leaders much inner amusement. In December 1868 when the Union Pacific was rushing with all possible speed to beat the Central Pacific to Ogden, a swarm of "outsiders" was brought in to relieve the Mormons of some of their hardest and heaviest work on tunnels in the canyon. At the time Brigham Young wrote, "I could not have asked Dr. [Thomas C.] Durant to confer a greater favor." [20] A month later, according to Young's report, the U. P. was ready to give the contract back to the Mormons:

> The big tunnel which the company's men took off from our hands to complete in a hurry, has been proffered back again. They have not less than four men to our one constantly employed, and, withal, have not been doing over two-thirds as much work. Superintendent Reed has solicited us to resume it again. We were well pleased to have the job off from our hands when it was, as it enabled us to complete our other work on the line; but now that it is so nearly complete, probably we shall finish the tunnel. Bishop Sharp and Joseph A. Young are using the nitro-glycerine for blasting, and its superiority over powder, as well as the sobriety, steadiness and industry of our men, gives us a marked advantage.[21]

The U. P. road to Ogden was finally completed on March 8, 1869, and the junction of the Union Pacific and Central Pacific was accomplished in dramatic ceremonies on May 10, 1869, at Promontory Summit, fifty-three miles west of Ogden.[22]

For some time there was real controversy as to whether the junction would be located at Ogden or Corinne, twenty-five miles northwest of Ogden. Corinne was the last of the "Hell on Wheels" transcontinental railroad camps, and sported nineteen saloons. Gentile speculators had invested heavily in its real estate. Church officials, of course, preferred Ogden since it would provide direct connections to Salt Lake City and also labor for Mormon mechanics. While Ogden was superior as a source of labor and materials, Corinne had geographic advantages and sentimental attachments to many Gentiles. A further disadvantage of Ogden, on the surface, was the difficulty of acquiring sufficient property in proximity for terminals and shops.

In anticipation of this problem, Brigham Young, five months in advance of the completion of the transcontinental line, met with property owners in the western part of Ogden and "proposed conditionally to buy the same for the purpose of locating a railroad town and a depot upon it." Approximately 133 acres of urban property were involved. The church chronicles continue:

> Brigham Young and the brethren with him met with the proprietors of the 5 acre lots at Ogden, who all consented to let him have their land at $50 per acre, provided the property was for a railroad town.
>
> At Ogden those brethren who owned the land where the railroad station was to be built signed the agreement to sell. Brigham Young showed Dr. Durrant a fine place for railroad work shops a short distance above the site of Elder Taylor's mill, a few miles south of Ogden.[23]

A large share of this block of land was donated by the individual owners, or sold at less than its value, the owners realizing they could obtain, at a reasonable price in labor, a lot in some other location colonized by the church.[24] The land was offered to U. P. and C. P. officials free of charge on condition that they locate their depot and shops upon it, the church absorbing the cost of the land. The amazed railroad officials, who had not counted on this boon, and had not expected the church to swing it, agreed to recommend that the junction of the two roads be located at Ogden, rather than at Corinne.[25] Within ten years, the budding Gentile capital of Corinne was virtually a ghost town with nothing but its saloons and Opera House to remind it of its broken hopes and lost opportunity.[26]

SECURING PAYMENT ON THE CONTRACTS

By the time the Mormons had completed their contracts in the spring of 1869, they had been paid approximately a million dollars on each of their two contracts.[27] By August 1869, Central Pacific still owed a million dollars, and Union Pacific owed in excess of that amount.[28] While Central Pacific agreed to pay within the month all but $200,000 of its indebtedness, the failure of Union Pacific to make a similar concession, and the failure of both roads to meet all of their contract obligations produced a condition of near panic in Salt Lake City. Laborers were destitute and contractors were heavily in debt to merchants and other creditors. Worry over his own financial status was listed as a direct cause of the death of Apostle Ezra T. Benson.[29] Church officials were faced with the dual task of pressing both railroads to "keep faith with the Mormon people," and of quieting the followers with assurances that everything would be done to obtain satisfaction. A lengthy letter appeared in the *Deseret News* in September 1869, reciting the grievances of the Mormons against the roads, and explaining the conditions which had been produced by their failure to pay. Among other things, the statement charged that Mormon grading crews had been repeatedly delayed beyond reason by tardy U. P. surveying parties; that these delays had not only increased the cost of maintaining Mormon crews, but had forced graders to do much of their work in the winter; that the company had promised tools and equipment which were not forthcoming; and that, despite these difficulties, Mormon graders and construction crews, with the reputation of the church and territory at stake, had completed their work in good time and order, and that the work had been officially accepted and praised by U. P. officials. Nevertheless, the Union Pacific Railroad Company, after more than six months, still owed the people of the territory "upwards of a million of dollars." The Central Pacific had also, the statement continued, failed to fulfill its agreement and keep its faith with its contractors:

> A moment's reflection will convince every person that the withholding of a million and a quarter of dollars from a community no larger than ours must produce serious loss, embarrassment and distress . . . there is not a business man in the country who is not affected, and some very seriously . . . hundreds of poor men are literally destitute of the necessaries of life. . . . We know of sub-contractors who have stripped themselves and ran heavily into debt to pay their hands. . . .
>
> A whole community, embarrassed by the unparalleled and reprehensible failures of these companies to pay for the honest labor done at their bidding, loudly ask them why? [30]

Union Pacific's builders had found it necessary to devise a scheme for the attraction of large sums of capital, and this consisted of providing immediate and huge profits to investors through a financial association called "The Credit Mobilier of America." While drawing huge profits in stocks, bonds, and cash, however, the promoters failed to make adequate provision for the unpaid bills of contractors and subcontractors, much less for the working capital needed for the operation of the railroad. According to the report of a congressional investigating committee, the railroad paid $94,600,000 to the Credit Mobilier for construction, while the actual cost to the Credit Mobilier contractors was only $50,700,000, leaving a total profit of approximately $43,900,000.[31] The railroad company, squeezed into bankruptcy by its own promoter-contractors, was necessarily forced to reorganize.

In an attempt to obtain a satisfactory settlement with the U. P. Company, Brigham Young sent John Sharp to Boston to confer with U. P. officials. After an interview with Vice-president Thomas Durant and with other members of the board of directors, Sharp wrote: "they had no flattering news for me, so far as money is concerned, in the settlement."[32] They did offer him various construction materials, including iron, from the surpluses on hand at Echo and elsewhere. These could be used in building the Utah Central Railroad, which the church was planning to construct from Ogden to Salt Lake City. Sharp's reaction to this proposal was as follows:

> We need the iron, but we also need some money badly, for this great labour has made a very heavy draw on all business men in our city, as well as the farmer and labouring classes. The President and board of directors, however, have agreed to meet on Thursday next to investigate our claims, and try to come to a settlement, when I do hope the Lord will open up some way that we may get some money, although I do not believe we shall be able to get a final settlement for some time yet, and I shall have to stay here till we do.[33]

Sharp was forced to leave without a settlement. He returned to Boston later, and on September 3, 1869, he telegraphed the message "Amicable settlement" to Brigham Young, and indicated that the railroad was settling the indebtedness with $600,000 worth of iron and rolling stock to be forwarded from Omaha as soon as possible.[34] Another $200,000 was to be paid later, presumably in cash.[35] Although it is difficult to obtain details on this matter, it would appear that the amount of material and equipment actually delivered to Brigham Young may have amounted to less than $530,000.[36]

This settlement, whatever the amount, did not really liquidate the indebtedness involved in the contract. How were the workers to be paid? How were the merchants' credits to workers' families to be balanced? How were the Mormon subcontractors to meet their many obligations? The failure to obtain a cash settlement would cause, indeed had already caused, according to one report, a virtual return to barter in trading.[37]

The subcontractors and workers were paid, it appears, in tithing credit, stocks and bonds in the Utah Central Railroad Company, and in some cases with cash, credit, and/or produce obtained from the sale of the company's stocks and bonds. Most of this indebtedness was liquidated late in 1870, more than a year after the U. P. settlement had been effected. For the liquidation of Brigham Young's indebtedness to his subcontractors, and of their debt to their workmen, principal reliance was placed on an issue of $1,000,000 in first mortgage bonds using the Utah Central Railroad as security.[38] These bonds, which bore an interest of six per cent, were ready for sale in February 1870. It had been intended originally to offer these bonds on the New York market, but perhaps the market there was deemed insufficient, or perhaps it was thought best not to risk indebtedness to "outsiders."[39] At any rate, Brigham Young called a meeting of all his creditors at the tabernacle in Salt Lake City on February 5, at which time he explained his plan to sell the Utah Central bonds locally and use the proceeds to satisfy his debt. He asked the creditors to accept part payment in these bonds. Sales of the bonds went very slowly, however. In July 1870, the School of the Prophets took the matter in hand and appointed a committee of six, to which the Council of the Twelve was added, to visit the various wards in the territory and "get the people to buy bonds of the Utah Central Railroad, to enable the President to liquidate his indebtedness of the Union Pacific Railroad claims which were held against him."[40] Apostle George Q. Cannon is reported to have "argued the necessity of the Saints untying the hands of the President, that his mind might not be embarrassed but be free to minister to the Saints."[41] Among other things, the committee prepared the following circular to be sent to all bishops of wards and settlements:

Dear Brother: — A committee will shortly visit you to solicit your cooperation in the sale of the Bonds of the Utah Central Railroad in your settlement, this being the means adopted to enable that company to liquidate its indebtedness to myself, which will thus enable me to pay those of my Creditors, for work done on my Contract on the Union Pacific Railroad, whose accounts still remain unsettled.

It is deemed advisable, to give those who are not in circumstances to purchase a whole Bond, the opportunity to purchase a portion of a Bond, which is to be held in the settlement by the Bishop or some other responsible person who will pay to each one entitled thereto, his portion of the interest, as it becomes due. When a person purchases a whole Bond, he will of course, hold it himself.

To further facilitate this labor, stock, grain or whatever can readily be turned into cash, or that will be accepted as payment from me by any of my Creditors for work done on the Union Pacific Railroad may be taken on this account, and the idea should be brought prominently before the people, so that they may understand the advisability of turning out their surplus stock, grain etc., to make purchase in so good an investment as are the Utah Central Bonds.

You will also be requested by the Committee to pay any or all of that which you may receive on this account to persons to whom I am indebted; whom you will pay only on my written order. Should anything remain not paid out after honoring my orders, you will please write to my office for directions.

Further instructions with regard to the matter will be given you by the Committee, when they visit your settlement.

Your Brother in the Gospel,

Brigham Young[42]

There was very little response to this appeal and the campaign which followed its distribution.[43] The matter worried Brigham Young so much that he was moved to make the following statement at the general conference of the church held in Salt Lake City in October 1870:

It is the mind and will of God, that the Elders of Israel should take the Utah Central Railroad bonds, and own the road by paying for it; so that he [Brigham] could pay the debt of the Union Pacific, which we owe to the brethren.[44]

Nevertheless, few bonds were sold. Indeed, in order to meet some obligations with respect to extending the Utah Central, the president was forced to borrow $125,000 on his personal note from Oliver Ames, president of the Union Pacific Railroad Company (although why he should have had to borrow the money, at nine per cent interest, when according to his own statement Union Pacific owed him that much is not clear).[45] Several months later, on May 20, 1871, at a meeting of the School of the Prophets, Daniel H. Wells, a member of the First Presidency, was still giving "a good earnest exhortation against the stinginess of some at the canvass for the Utah Central Railroad."[46] It is probable that the church assumed most of the burden of the debt with tithing resources. At the time of Brigham Young's death in 1877 the church's burden was reported as $139,678 in Utah Central bonds and coupons.[47]

Before relating the story of the Utah Central Railroad whose construction was made possible by the iron received on the U. P. contract, however, comment should be made on two misinterpretations found in Utah histories dealing with the contract. Some writers, notably Stenhouse, have left the impression that the mismanagement or chicanery of Brigham Young was responsible for the failure of Mormon construction companies to get their pay. In a chapter pretending to illustrate the prophet's propensity for duplicity and financial jugglery, Stenhouse wrote:

Whether the work paid the men who toiled, or not, Brigham and his friends were certain of their percentage and made large sums of money, while a great many of the small contractors and labouring men were utterly ruined. It was many months after the completion of the Pacific Railroad before the needy men could get their pay, and then it was in Utah Central bonds that did not at the time command more than forty-five cents on the dollar in Salt Lake City. The merchants who had credited the brethren during the building of the road, and who had to wait an indefinite period for the return of their money, were seriously injured by this forced delay.[48]

It must be clear from what has been written that the financial calamities of 1869 were not the result of the designs of Brigham Young, but the failure of the two branches of the Pacific railroad to keep faith with their Mormon contractors.

Another misinterpretation has to do with the profits made by Brigham Young on the contract. Orson F. Whitney, a Mormon historian and later an apostle, uncritically repeated the assertion that Brigham Young realized a profit of about $800,000 on the Union Pacific contract alone.[49] This would have been almost forty per cent of the gross contract receipts, when the subcontracts were let at only ten per cent less! Actually, if any percentage was made at all, it would have been not more than ten per cent of the first $1,000,000 which was paid by the U.P., or $100,000, and out of this gross take would have to come the costs of the chief contractor. After Brigham Young's death in 1877, the clerks and administrators going over his accounts found that the "profits" on the railroad contract had been $88,000.[50] The administrators accepted the proof of the church that the contract was a church undertaking rather than a private arrangement, and placed the $88,000 in contract profits to the credit of the church rather than to the credit of the Young heirs in the settlement of the estate.[51] In contrast with that of the Credit Mobilier crowd, the fortune of Brigham Young was not made — if indeed one was made — on the Mormon Pacific railroad contract.

THE UTAH CENTRAL RAILROAD

The experience gained from the Union Pacific and Central Pacific contracts, together with the business contacts made in fulfilling them, gave Mormon leaders confidence that a network of interior branch lines could be constructed without extensive "outside" help, thus giving railroad connections to the principal settlements of the Latter-day Saints. The first goal of these plans was the construction of a line from Ogden to Salt Lake City — a distance of thirty-seven miles. On March 3, 1869, just two months before the completion of the transcontinental railroad, church officials met in Salt Lake City to discuss formation of a company to construct and operate such a road.[52] Five days later, on the very day on which the Union Pacific Railroad was celebrating its entrance into Ogden, the Utah Central Railroad Company was organized with a capital stock of $1,500,000, consisting of 15,000 shares valued at $100 each.[53] Brigham Young was chosen president and director; his son Joseph Young was to be general superintendent. Other officers and directors were prominent church and business leaders in Salt Lake City and vicinity. They included Daniel H. Wells, member of the church First Presidency and superintendent of church public works, who was elected treasurer and director; and Jesse W. Fox, the church surveyor, who was appointed chief engineer.[54] The principal subscribers were likewise Mormon businessmen and churchmen. Only 420 shares of stock, with a value of $42,000, were initially subscribed, but this was more than the required $1,000 per mile of road. Almost half of the stock, 200 shares, was taken by Brigham Young, as trustee-in-trust for the church.[55] Only ten per cent of the specified subscriptions were actually paid in to the treasurer.

Immediately after the organization of the company Treasurer Wells began to sell stock subscriptions to the general public, and the general superintendent and chief engineer proceeded to locate the road.[56] The hope was expressed by Brigham Young that the road would be completed early in the fall of 1869.[57] By the time Brigham Young returned from southern Utah in May 1869 the surveying had been completed, and in a meeting held May 12, 1869 the board of directors "decided to build the line . . . immediately."[58] Official ceremonies were held at Ogden, during which President George A. Smith dedicated the ground by prayer and Brigham Young broke the first ground with a shovel.[59]

These preparations appear to have met with general support. The editor of the *Deseret News* pointed out that it would help Salt Lake City to meet a pressing fuel problem which was threatening to "check . . . the growth, development and prosperity of the city." Food would also become cheaper:

> To have a large and prosperous community here, the first requisites are cheap food and cheap fuel. We cannot compete with other places in manufactures until these articles are cheap; for if the present high prices were to continue, the cost of living would be too high for operative labor and many kinds of manufacturing business would be driven from the city. . . . In our present circumstances the importance of this line cannot very well be overestimated.[60]

The real test of community support, however, was the response to the call of church officials to participate in the construction of the road. On June 10, 1869, Brigham Young and the other officers of the company followed the route of the Utah Central, met with local civic and ecclesiastical officials, discussed the exact location of the line, and arranged for each ward and settlement between Ogden and Salt Lake City to do its share of the grading. He explained that the enterprise was intended to be a cooperative venture; not only were local ward leaders and members asked to give their preference as to the location of the road, but they were also asked to specify the timber, supplies, and labor they would be prepared to furnish.[61] Property owners were asked to surrender rights of way as a part of their contribution.[62] This had been the procedure followed in other church ventures, but the *Deseret News* thought it a unique way to build a railroad:

> Probably their [the officers of the U. C. R. R.] course is unexampled in the history of railroad building. But the Utah Central Railroad is not being built by a company solely to make money or for its own benefit, but for the good of the people and country, and it is desirable that whatever is necessary to make the scheme a success should be done by the common consent of all concerned.[63]

The grading, building of bridges, and other work went on during the summer of 1869, with gangs of volunteer laborers doing most of the work. Labor was recruited and supervised by the bishops of the various wards along the line, to whom small contracts were let so as to distribute the work uniformly and add an element of friendly competition. For example, the officers of the various wards in the Ogden area met in June 1869 and agreed that each ward should contract to grade its "just share," according to the wealth and labor supply in the ward.[64] In some cases, the labor was performed in return for stock and/or bonds;[65] in other cases, railroad tickets were the only pay;[66] but most of the labor appears to have been done by immigrants who adopted this way of repaying the church for furnishing their transportation to Utah under the auspices of the Perpetual Emigrating Fund Company.[67] The church received shares of stock in return for this labor. "Most of the pay I got from the railroad, like others with whom I worked," declared one of the graders, "came in the form of merchandise. We didn't care, though, in what form it was given. We wanted a railroad and we didn't hesitate to work to that end." [68]

The settlement with Union Pacific, by which some $530,000 worth of iron, rolling stock, and construction equipment were secured, was not effected until September 1869. The last of this material, though promised immediately, was not delivered until December, thus delaying completion of the road before winter set in. The first rails were laid at Ogden on September 22, and seventy men laid a mile of track every other day during October and November. A corps of 150 men was hired to complete the track to Salt Lake City in December. The last spike was driven, as part of a public ceremony, on January 10, 1870. Freight houses, passenger and freight landings, and other facilities at the Utah Central depots in Salt Lake City and Ogden were completed soon afterward, and locomotives previously ordered were placed in operation. Two regular trains ran daily each way between Salt Lake and Ogden, and a third ran each way on Wednesdays, Saturdays, and Sundays.[69]

The dedication ceremonies reflect the role of the church in the promotion and construction of the road. An estimated 15,000 Saints were on hand to cheer the completion of what was called "the first road built and owned by the people of this Territory." [70] The last spike had been especially prepared for the occasion by the church blacksmith shop of native Utah iron. It was driven by Brigham Young with a steel mallet also made at the church public works. Both the spike and hammer bore the emblem of a beehive, the initials U. C. R. R., and the engraved inscription: "Holiness to the Lord." The road was dedicated in a formal prayer by Apostle Wilford Woodruff, after which Brigham Young made the following statement:

> Since the day that we first trod the soil of these valleys, have we received any assistance from our neighbors? No, we have not. We have built our homes, our cities, have made our farms, have dug our canals and water ditches, have subdued this barren country, have fed the stranger, have clothed the naked, have immigrated the poor from foreign lands, have placed them in a condition to make all comfortable and have made some rich. We have fed the Indians to the amount of thousands of dollars yearly, have clothed them in part, and have

sustained several Indian wars, and now we have built thirty-seven miles of railroad.

All this having been done, are not our cities, our counties and the Territory in debt? No, not the first dollar. But the question may be asked, is not the Utah Central Railroad in debt? Yes, but to none but our own people. . . .

We have felt somewhat to complain of the Union Pacific railroad company for not paying us for the work we did, in grading so many miles of their road. But let me say, if they had paid us according to agreement, this road would not have been graded, and this track would not have been laid today. It is all right. . . .

I also thank the brethren who have aided to build this, our first railroad. They have acted as Elders of Israel, and what higher praise can I accord to them, for they have worked on the road, they have graded the track, they have laid the rails, they have finished the line, and have done it cheerfully "without purse or scrip."

An official of the Union Pacific attending the celebration followed the same theme. He said:

The Utah Central Railroad, although thirty-seven or thirty-eight miles long, is perhaps the only railroad west of the Missouri River that has been built entirely without Government subsidies; it has been built slowly with money wrung from the soil which, a few years ago, we used to consider a desert, by the strong arms of men and women who stand before me.[71]

These and other speeches delivered on the occasion of the completion of the road manifested the pride felt by the Mormon people in building the road "without outside help." Knowing that the occasion would be widely publicized, and the national respect for self-reliance, church leaders wanted to underline Utah's qualifications for Statehood by accentuating Mormon industry and enterprise. It was also a source of satisfaction to church leaders, but not of dominating importance, that outside financial interests would not be controlling the railroad. Church Historian George A. Smith expressed the official sense of accomplishment in recording the following succinct summary of the dedicatory service:

Yesterday the last rail of the Utah Central Railroad was laid, and I think it would be difficult to find a railroad of its length and cost, that has been built without national or State aid or the assistance of some heavy capitalist, the iron was procured from the Union Pacific in part payment for labor done for them, by the people of Utah last year, which should have been paid in money one year ago, the ties, grading, tracking, and bridgeing had all been done by the people here who own the road, there being no debt against it outside the Territory.[72]

Exactly how was the Utah Central financed? According to Bishop John Sharp, who was one of the original promoters, and who was made general superintendent of the road in 1871, only ten per cent of the $1,500,000 authorized stock was paid in during the construction period.[73] This would have provided only $150,000 worth of cash, materials, and labor. There still remained a floating debt on the railroad amounting to approximately $100,000, however, and an additional six per cent was levied on the stock in June 1871 to pay this debt. By this time, $1,000,000 in bonds had been sold or exchanged for 80 per cent of par value, yielding $800,000. Virtually all of this was used to repay Brigham Young's indebtedness to his subcontractors on the Union Pacific contract, in return for which the Utah Central had the $530,000 worth of iron and rolling stock provided by U. P. in satisfaction of the contract. Thus, one may estimate the cost of the Utah Central at $850,000, of which $530,000 was for iron and rolling stock and approximately $320,000 for grading, bridge-building, and laying the track. The real burden, of course, rested with the men of the priesthood in northern Utah who labored on the U. P. contract and on the Utah Central for little more than "tithing pay."

Despite the church's pose of independence from Babylon at the time of the completion of the Utah Central, there were reasons why the First Presidency might wish to sell stock in the Utah Central. Such a sale would provide cash with which to construct additional railroad mileage in Utah, and it would relieve the church of the embarrassment of managing a railroad whose dependence on U. P. connections would prevent it from earning its keep. According to Bishop Sharp, Brigham Young asked him, in 1872, to negotiate with Union Pacific with the view to getting as much cash for the stock as possible. Sharp was instructed to offer all stock held in the name of Brigham Young, which amounted to 7,600 shares — slightly more than half of the 15,000 shares authorized. As the result of these transactions, Union Pacific officials bought 5,000 of these shares of stock at a price of $50.00 per share, or a total purchase price of $250,000.[74] The Mormon officials were retained in the management of the road, however, and their autonomy seems to have been almost complete until Jay Gould interested himself in the road in 1879.[75]

Not much is known about the operation of the Utah Central while it was under the management of the church. Various evidences point to policies which dovetailed with the needs of the Kingdom, as interpreted by church leaders. The road was used to speed up immigration and reduce immigration costs; special rates were offered during the weeks in which the annual and semi-annual general church conferences were held; summer excursions conducted under the supervision of the various wards were also accorded special low rates; and church officials and missionaries were given complimentary passes to facilitate their movement through northern Utah.[76] Moreover, one of the cars acquired from Union Pacific was made up into a special private car for Brigham Young and placed at his disposal for official visits. Decorated in keeping with Young's high position in the church, the ornamentation of the well-appointed interior included gilt and scrolls, "while angels and cherubim were painted on the ceiling."[77]

The effect of these policies on profits is difficult to determine. In 1872 the gross earnings of the road were said to be $420,000, while the expenses were approximately $210,000, leaving operating earnings of $210,000.[78] The chief traffic was coal bound for Salt Lake City, and ores bound for Ogden.

The most important economic influence of the road, of course, was in the field of mining. The railroad made scores of mines in the Salt Lake City area economical to work. Only a short time before the completion of the road the fabulous Emma Mine at Alta was opened. The rich ore from this mine was originally "rawhided" (that is, loaded into green skins and dragged by horse) to the mouth of Little Cottonwood Canyon and there transferred to ox-cart for hauling to the U. P. depot at Ogden. With the completion of the Utah Central these ores became its most lucrative traffic, with shipments averaging 100 tons a day for many months.[79]

THE SUMMIT COUNTY RAILROAD

Church officials had hoped that an important item of traffic from Ogden to Salt Lake City would be coal from the mines opened up near Coalville in the early 1860's. With the growing exhaustion of timber supplies and the increased need for coal in residences, and in industrial and commercial enterprises, Salt Lake consumers and businessmen naturally looked to the Coalville mines to supply the market with fuel. At the time of the construction of the Utah Central, church officials planned to construct a three-foot narrow-gauge railroad from Coalville north to the Union Pacific line at Echo, five miles distant. From Echo the coal would be carried on the U. P. lines some thirty-two miles northwest to Ogden for transmittal to the Utah Central and delivery in Salt Lake City. Later, it was proposed to build branch lines to the principal mines in the Coalville area. Following in the footsteps of the Utah Central, the Coalville and Echo Railroad Company was organized and plans were made to construct the road on the cooperative plan. Coalville residents would be expected to contribute labor, supplies, and equipment, in return for stock in the road; the rails and rolling stock would be furnished by the Utah Central, which expected to have enough left over from the rails and rolling stock given by the Union Pacific on the church contract to furnish the five miles of track. Although the grading was completed and the ties prepared, the Union Pacific failed to send more than enough iron to stock the Utah Central, and so the track was not laid. When the Union Pacific roads began to carry the superior coal from the Rock Springs, Wyoming, mines to Ogden, for transshipment to Salt Lake City, church authorities abandoned plans to purchase iron and lay the track of the Coalville and Echo. No compensation, unless in tithing credit, was given to the Coalville residents who had devoted months of labor to the task of grading the road and securing the ties. What coal was shipped out of Coalville during the next two seasons went by wagon north to the U. P. line at Echo, or, alternatively, southwest by team to Salt Lake City.[80]

The Union Pacific Railroad, however, seemed to play the part of the "grasping monopolist," at least in the eyes of the Utah citizenry.[81] Coal prices were high and supplies precarious. In 1871, the Coalville bishop was asked once more to superintend the construction of the Echo and Coalville road so that the Salt Lake area might be supplied with coal at competitive rates. The Summit County Railroad Company was formed, with a capital stock of $660,000. Plans were made to construct a narrow-gauge road from Echo Station to the Coalville mines, and on south through Summit County in the direction of Salt Lake City, for a total of twenty-six miles of road. Summit County persons would furnish the labor and ties, and bonds would be issued for the purchase of iron and rolling stock. Nine miles of the line were completed and stocked by the fall of 1873.[82]

The Summit County Railroad, however, did not "free the citizens from the clutches of the Union Pacific," as some of them put it. The coal had to be transferred at Echo Station to the Union Pacific track for transmittal to the Utah Central at Ogden. The U. P., which apparently was not eager to relinquish its hold on the lucrative Salt Lake coal market, did not regard the Summit County venture as a "feeder." Instead, for a brief period at least, U. P. officials retaliated by hiking coal rates from Echo to Ogden to prohibitive levels. One church official wrote of the "helpless condition of the entire city" and "the rapacity of the railroad monopolists."[83] "Our remedy," wrote George A. Smith, member of the First Presidency, "appears to be in building a railroad to the south [from Salt Lake City to southern Utah] until coal mines are struck, and by that means equalize the market."[84] Some private interests did build the Sevier Valley Railway and the Sanpete Railway to make connections with coal and other mines in central Utah, but these were also acquired by Union Pacific interests. The Summit County Railroad finally defaulted on its bonds in 1875, and Brigham Young arranged for the sale of the controlling interest to Union Pacific. Before the formal demise of the company in 1880, however, as we shall see, the Mormons were making one more effort to lay rails from Coalville to Salt Lake City. Their experience in that episode would prove equally futile.

THE UTAH SOUTHERN RAILROAD

The Utah Southern Railroad was a "natural" (that is, economic) extension of the Utah Central. Running south from Salt Lake City, the road was first completed to Sandy, then, in succession, to Lehi, Provo, Payson, York, Nephi, and Milford, Utah. Under Union Pacific auspices the road was eventually constructed to Los Angeles. The road was originally promoted by church authorities and Utah Central Railroad directors—largely the same persons—and the same procedure was used in its building (during the period it was a Mormon road) as was used in the building of Utah Central. No government subsidy except the right-of-way was involved.

A road stretching south from Salt Lake City was expected to have three advantages: it would provide closer rail connections with the quarry in Cottonwood Canyon from which the granite was extracted to build the Salt Lake Temple. This was an important consideration to Brigham Young, and serves to explain the use of tithing resources in the construction and financing of the first few miles of the Utah Southern.[85] Second, it would provide rail connections with important settlements south of Salt Lake City thus facilitating the marketing of their produce and the acquisition of supplies. Immigrants could be located with greater dispatch, and church authorities could keep in closer touch with local developments. In general, the road would connect the various Mormon settlements south of Salt Lake City with the spiritual and temporal capital of the region. Third, the road would tap the rich mining districts which had been located during the 1860's; this alone was expected to make the road profitable. By means of branch lines, the road could serve the mines in Little Cottonwood, Big Cottonwood and American Fork on the east side of the Jordan River; Bingham Canyon and Camp Floyd on the west end of Salt Lake City; and, by reaching south to Payson, the road would command the trade of the Tintic mines in Juab and Beaver Counties, as well as the rich mineral districts around Pioche, Nevada:

> The Utah Southern Railroad will do for mining in the central and southern portion of the Territory what the overland line has done for this region. It will give cheap and rapid transportation for ores and bullion, as well as for farm and garden produce; and what is now comparatively valueless in mining property in several parts of the Territory will become valuable with its progress.[86]

The Utah Southern Railroad Company was incorporated on January 17, 1871, just a year after the completion of the Utah Central.[87] Authorized capital stock consisted of 15,000 shares of $100 par-value stock, for a total capitalization of $1,500,000. Although the company hoped eventually to construct the road south as far as the Arizona border, the immediate plan was to build a narrow-gauge road from Salt Lake City to Payson — a distance of about 65 miles — with several branches for the shipment of granite and ore. William Jennings was listed as first president of the company, and the principal subscriber was Joseph A. Young, son of Brigham, who agreed to take 500 of the 801 shares ($80,100) initially subscribed.[88] Other shares were subscribed by prominent Mormon businessmen who also held stock in the Utah Central.

In February 1871, Brigham Young wrote that it had not been decided how far the road would be extended, but, he added, "with our limited resources prudence would dictate that we build only as far as present business will warrant."[89] The company first broke ground on May 1, 1871, in Salt Lake City, and contracts were let immediately thereafter for several miles of grading. Track-laying began a month later, with Brigham Young driving the first spike. The road was completed and open for traffic to Sandy, thirteen miles south of Salt Lake City, in September 1871. Shortly after the Sandy station was completed, large granite blocks, quarried in Little Cottonwood Canyon, and carried by ox-drawn wagons from that point to Sandy, were being transported via the Utah Southern to the depot in Salt Lake City, from which point a spur had been built to the site of the Salt Lake Temple.[90]

During the winter 1871–1872 contracts were let for the work of grading south from Sandy to Utah County, and this work continued until September 23, 1872, when the road was completed to Lehi, thirty-one miles south of Salt Lake City. This placed the Utah Southern in a position to handle the transportation of the Utah County harvest in 1872 and succeeding years.[91] It was during the fall of 1872 that the single-track Utah Southern found a typically Mormon solution to a problem which has often aggravated railroaders:

> The inevitable happened. Two trains, headed in opposite directions, came to a grinding stop at the Point of the Mountain, about twenty miles south of Salt Lake City. The engineers dropped from their diamond-shaped smokestack locomotives and were soon joined by their respective crews in heated argument. Someone would have to back down the hill to the passing track at the bottom. Finally, one conductor, a little more level-headed than the rest, said: "I've got Brigham Young in my hind car. Let's send for him." Brigham Young came and patiently listened, and then asked: "Which one of you engineers have paid your tithing?" One engineer hung his head, while the other fished in his coat pocket and came up with a greasy receipt. "That settles it," Brigham Young announced, "the engineer without the receipt backs down. Come on, let's be going. I've got a conference in the next town."[92]

Church officials and territorial businessmen also planned the construction of branches to run both east and west of the Utah Southern track. One narrow-gauge spur was built by Mormon and mining interests east of Sandy to complete railroad connections with the church's granite quarry and the Little Cottonwood district at Alta. Under the auspices of the Wasatch and Jordan Valley Railroad Company, this line was completed as far as Granite (now Wasatch), seven miles from Sandy, on April 4, 1873, and from that date the hauling of temple granite was handled entirely by railroad.[93] This freight made up a large proportion of the road's traffic. In 1875 the road was completed to Alta, ten miles farther up Little Cottonwood Canyon, and ores were freighted from that point to the sampling works at Sandy.

Another narrow-gauge spur ran about eighteen miles west from Sandy to Bingham, an important mining region in the Oquirrh Mountains. This road was built by the Bingham Canyon and Camp Floyd Railroad Company in 1873. The church was not involved in this company, as was also the case with the American Fork Railroad Company, organized in 1873, to build a twelve-mile narrow-gauge line from the Utah Southern connection at American Fork to the Sultana Smelter Works and other interests at Deer Creek. Both were financed entirely by outside capital.

The Utah Southern itself was financed partly with bond issues, and partly from sales of stock. On July 1, 1871, the directors approved the issuance of $1,500,000 worth of $1,000 first mortgage bonds, yielding seven per cent interest, and maturing in twenty years. These bonds were to be sold as the road progressed, and the issue was not to exceed $20,000 worth of bonds per mile actually completed.[94] Offered to the original purchasers at a discount of twenty per cent, or $800 for a $1,000 bond, the bonds were issued over the signature of Brigham Young, who was made president of the company for this very purpose.[95] A total of $15,000 in Utah Southern stock was issued to those buying Utah Southern bonds with the completion of each mile of road. This stock was assessed at five per cent. This made it possible for the Utah Central promoters who bought Utah Southern bonds to retain control of the Road. And Brigham Young, as trustee-in-trust of the church, thus became the principal bondholder and stockholder in the Utah Southern. Nevertheless, the bonds of the Utah Southern did not sell well. Other enterprises were absorbing Mormon capital; and outside capital was being frightened, or so church officials declared, by Gentile "crusaders" and "carpet-baggers" who sought to diminish the influence of the church. As a part of this campaign, strong contemporaneous efforts were allegedly made by certain non-Mormons to obtain capital to build a competing road from Salt Lake City to Pioche.[96] Mormon leaders had the feeling that Washington officials looked with approval on these efforts. The reaction of the church was expressed by George A. Smith, who had become a member of the First Presidency:

The effects of the corrupt course pursued by our Federal Administration were apparent in frightening away capital in the Territory, (which would otherwise be expended in the development of mines) and damaging railroad and other securities. The Utah Southern Railroad company are prosecuting their road, but the persecution against the people here has retarded its progress.[97]

Brigham Young worked out a plan whereby Union Pacific, which was acquiring control of Utah Central in 1872, was also permitted to acquire bonds and stock in the Utah Southern on the same basis as the original Utah Southern incorporators. Union Pacific interests agreed to provide iron and rolling stock in exchange for bonds (and stock); and President Young pledged that Latter-day Saints would provide the ties and labor, also for bonds (and stock).[98] While this arrangement was a "sell out" to Union Pacific, it was favored by the church because it gave the "Mormon roads" a powerful advocate in Washington. Thus, while the construction of the road from Salt Lake to Sandy had been financed entirely by sales of bonds to the trustee-in-trust and to Mormon capitalists, the iron for most of the distance from Sandy to Lehi was financed by U. P., and in this way U. P. was acquiring partial control of the road.

Union Pacific, however, failed to send iron to complete the road beyond Lehi.[99] According to John Sharp,

The government had enjoined that company [Union Pacific] from spending any money except for the running of their own road and the interest on their bonds. They, therefore, could not invest, not from lack of disposition, but from lack of ability.[100]

The church, of course, was particularly anxious to push the main line at least to the important Mormon settlement of Provo, which was seventeen miles from Lehi. At $20,000 per mile, such an undertaking would cost about $340,000. When commitments had been obtained in 1873 from certain eastern interests to furnish iron, the First Presidency and Quorum of the Twelve, along with officials of the Utah Southern, invited representatives of the various settlements in Utah County to a "railroad meeting," held in Lehi on July 21, 1873.[101] At the meeting President Young asked the residents of Utah County to volunteer to furnish cash, labor, and ties.[102] He asked that each ward and settlement take the responsibility of completing a proportionate share of the line. The financial arrangement would be that each ward and settlement buy a certain number of shares of stock, and the agreement was stated as follows:

As payment for the stock the people of the county agree to do the grading, supply the ties, lay the rails, and, in fact, to build the road, station houses, etc., from its present terminus to Provo, and also to continue the work beyond the latter point to Payson, subsequently. The shares will be distributed among the various settlements of the county, each taking as many or as few shares as it chooses.[103]

There were thirteen different settlements in Utah County, and each was given a quota of a certain number of shares. A committee of thirteen men, consisting of the bishop of each settlement, and A. O. Smoot, Presiding Bishop of Utah County, as chairman, was appointed to purchase on behalf of the county all of the 3600 shares ($360,000) required to be sold. At the same time, a contract was let for the necessary lumber, and the contractor (Orrawell Simons of Payson) was instructed to apportion the amount to be supplied among the different settlements according to the number of shares they agreed to take. The same was to be done with regard to the ties, Bishop William Bringhurst of Springville having been appointed to handle that phase of the construction.

Further progress was made in arranging for the construction at a series of meetings held at Alpine, Utah County, on July 26 and 27, 1873. Brigham Young attended these meetings and encouraged the people to invest. The people were praised for demonstrating "unity" and "the true spirit of co-operation. . . ."[104] Further assignments were made, subcontracts let, and the Utah County citizenry agreed to "commence and prepare for the iron" as soon as they had harvested their 1873 crops.[105] President George A. Smith wrote:

> The brethren in Utah County have undertaken to grade the road for the Utah Southern Railroad through their county, and also to furnish the ties for the road. They have taken shares of railroad stock to the amount of their labor and expense of construction, placing them on equality with the other stockholders of the company. How this cooperative operation will work in railroad building is now being tried.[106]

By these means the road was completed to American Fork by September 23, 1873, and to Provo by November 24, 1873. A special ceremony was held at Provo on November 28 to celebrate the completion of the road to that place.[107]

The following fall and winter, the Union Pacific was given freer rein in its activities, and completely financed the construction of the road to York, Juab County, twenty-seven miles from Provo.[108] Some of the construction contracts were taken by United Orders formed along the location of the line.[109] At this point the Utah Southern was in a position to tap the rich Tintic mines.

A month later a new corporation was formed, called the Utah Southern Railroad Extension Company, for the purpose of extending the road 200 miles further south to Washington County in southern Utah. The new corporation, capitalized at $4,000,000, was organized by Mormon businessmen who had been prominent in the formation of the Utah Central and the Utah Southern.[110] Although still in possession of many Utah Southern stocks and bonds, the trustee-in-trust appears to have taken no part in the formation or financing of the new company.[111] Actually, however, no construction was undertaken by this company until 1878–1879, when the road was extended another thirty miles to Chicken Creek (Juab), fourteen miles south of Nephi, Juab County. At this point the road was 105 miles from Salt Lake City.[112] This was the sum total of the construction efforts by the "Mormon" Utah Southern Extension.[113]

As this first "extension" was being completed, a new Utah Southern Railroad Extension Company was formed to run the road south from Chicken Creek to Milford, Beaver County, with a branch line running to Frisco — a distance of 130 miles. This company was formed by Jay Gould and S. H. H. Clark, of Union Pacific, in association with magnates of the Horn Silver Mine near Frisco and some representatives of the Utah Southern.[114] The obvious intention was to provide railroad connections for the newly opened mining claims in the San Francisco Mountains of Beaver County, which yielded over $50,000,000 in ore from 1875 to 1885. This extension was completed in 1880, and a year later, in June 1881, the Utah Central, the Utah Southern, the original Utah Southern Extension, and the Frisco Utah Southern Extension were all combined, under the auspices of Union Pacific, into a company called the Utah Central Railway System. The combined line ran from Ogden to Frisco, a distance of 280 miles. With this move, Mormon influence on the policy of roads originally built by the church became negligible. The Utah Central Railway was combined with the Utah and Northern Railroad to become part of the Oregon Short Line System in 1889, and of the San Pedro, Los Angeles, and Salt Lake, in 1903, after which it was completed to Los Angeles.

The year 1879 marks the end of the era of "Mormon railroads." In that year, Utah citizens were so thoroughly disillusioned with the financial manipulations of railroad magnates that a Provo newspaper remarked that people should go to general conference in Salt Lake City with their wagons before they rode on the Utah Southern and gave their money to Jay Gould.[115] Nevertheless, the road was a paying one, and a particular boon to the agricultural interests in central Utah who could enjoy the advantages of a railroad without having to underwrite its operation. (The mining interests did that.) Writing of the Utah Southern Railroad in 1890, Professor Marcus E. Jones gave perhaps the best appraisal:

> No railroad was ever built in Utah that was of so much value to the people as this one (except the Union Pacific, of course), because it gave an outlet for the produce of the richest valleys, enabled the mines to ship ore, and gave a great impetus to every branch of industry.[116]

THE UTAH NORTHERN RAILROAD

For reasons similar to those which induced church authorities to promote construction of the Utah Southern south of Salt Lake City, plans were made to construct a narrow gauge (three feet wide) railroad north of the Utah Central terminus at Ogden. Northern Utah was a rich agricultural area which could profit from railroad connections. Its most lucrative market had come to be the mining camps around Butte, Montana, which had been experiencing a boom since the middle 1860's. While Butte, Virginia City, and Helena, were fully 500 wagon miles north of Ogden, they had depended heavily on Mormon farmers for their food and freighting. Every mile that a railroad was pushed toward Butte, Montana, would increase the mutually profitable exchange between Butte and northern Utah.

Mention has been made previously that when the transcontinental railroad was completed in 1869, a strong effort was made to establish the Gentile town of Corinne as the Junction City. Indeed, the issue of Ogden *v.* Corinne as the junction of the Union Pacific and Central Pacific roads was not settled in favor of the former until June 1874. In the meantime, Corinne was proving to be the terminus for the Montana trade. Supplies and provisions destined for Butte and Helena went by rail to Corinne, by land around Great Salt Lake, or by boat across Great Salt Lake, and from there by ox-team north to Virginia City or the Northern Pacific terminal at Garrison. In order to be certain that the economic position of their own settlements was protected, church officials left no stone unturned in their effort to overthrow Corinne. They reasoned that a railroad connecting Ogden with Brigham City, Logan, and Franklin, Idaho, would consolidate the northern Mormon settlements, provide an outlet for their agricultural produce, and divert the Montana traffic from Corinne. This traffic, especially of ore from Montana destined for refining in Colorado, would make a northern railroad financially profitable.

Soon after the formation of the Utah Southern Railroad Company, therefore, John W. Young, son of Brigham, negotiated with Joseph and Benjamin Richardson, of New York City, in regard to financing the construction of a road from Ogden north to Soda Springs, Idaho, a distance of about 125 miles. The Richardsons agreed to furnish the rails and equipment provided Mormon interests would handle the rest of the financing. Conversations leading to the formation of a company were held in Logan, Utah, in August 1871. The Presiding Bishop of Cache Valley, William B. Preston, wrote Brigham Young asking his attitude about the arrangement:

> Will it be wisdom for us in Cache County to grade and tie a railroad from Ogden to Soda Springs, with a view to Eastern capitalists ironing and stocking

it, thereby giving them control of the road? The people feel considerably spirited in taking stock to grade and tie, expecting to have a prominent voice in the control of it; but to let foreign capitalists iron and stock it will, if my judgment is correct, give *them* control.[117]

Brigham Young replied immediately by Deseret Telegraph:

The foreign capitalists in this enterprise do not seek the control; this is all understood. What they want, and what we want, is to push this road with all possible speed, if you decide to have one, so that it shall run through and benefit your settlements and reach Soda Springs as soon as possible.[118]

Upon receipt of this telegram, seventeen leading church and businessmen of northern Utah agreed to "go to work and build the railroad, and take stock for grading and tying the road." [119] The Utah Northern Railroad Company was organized, on August 23, 1871, with John W. Young, president and superintendent; William B. Preston, vice president and assistant superintendent; and Moses Thatcher, secretary. The directors largely consisted of bishops of the settlements along the route of the projected line.[120]

The plan of construction called for the appointment of superintendents in each of the major areas of construction.[121] Labor was to be recruited directly by these men or through local bishops. Each priesthood-bearer was expected to do his share of the work. The men were to be paid principally in stock in the railroad, but in cases of necessity a certain amount would be given workers in "ready pay."

The company broke first ground at a religiously directed dedication ceremony held at Brigham City on August 26, 1871.[122] The first rail was laid the following March, and by July 1, 1872 freight and passenger trains were running regularly, twice daily, from Brigham City to Hampton's Station, on the edge of Cache Valley, a distance of twenty-three miles.[123] Goudy Hogan, who was to work on the project during the winter of 1871–1872, described what was doubtless a typical experience:

In the latter part of the summer [of 1871] there was a requirement made from headquarters to build a narrow gauge railroad from Ogden to Soda Springs and wished the people of Ogden, Boxelder and Cache Valleys to build road and own a good share interest in it, for the people to do a certain portion of labor to each man. I rigged up my teams and started out in company with William Fisher and we worked out our portion of work. We were the first that started work in Cache Valley on the divide between Cache Valley and Salt Lake Valley. I had fitted out three teams, took my wife Christiana, and Harriet, my daughter, to cook, Ira and Nels, my sons, and one hired man. Fisher had 4 teams. We bought 70 yards of tent cloth and made a new tent. . . . We did the work that was allotted to us in three weeks and were going to start south to work but John W. Young who had charge of the road wished us to stay and work on the Utah

> Northern. There were few could work on the road without some ready means having lost their crops for so many years but Bro. Young promised to pay us a portion of ready pay . . . and take stock in the road for the balance. I worked three months. . . . My estimate for 11 weeks amounted to $2600. Besides Fisher work I had 2 hired men besides my own folks to pay in wheat and part in vouchers. These were the railroad vouchers that circulated as money and paid off some of my debts.

Again, in the spring of 1872:

> This spring there was a loud call for help to work on the Utah Northern Railroad. The men were rather slow to turn out to work because of no ready funds. The Bishop called on me and Fisher publicly to go as missionaries and work on the R.R. I again took my whole force and began work. Bro. Fisher and I finished the large Casper Whittle Fill and worked on the Hamtons Y at the station. I went home to arrange for someone to do my farm work but couldn't hire anyone as they were all engaged on the railroad.[124]

Work was suspended during the summer of 1872 while Cache Valley farmers tended their crops, but the call began again after harvest, and nearly all wards in Cache Valley had crews at work. After another season's work under similar circumstances the road was completed to Logan on January 31, 1873.[125] Cache Valley citizens were so grateful for the completion of "their" road, and so strong in the feeling that it was, indeed, "their road," that when a severe snowstorm forced discontinuance of regular service soon after it was inaugurated, the people voluntarily turned out *en masse* to break the blockade:

> In breaking the Utah Northern Railroad snow blockade, the people here turned out to the tune of some three or four hundred, as far north as Franklin, and south to Paradise, each settlement contributing a portion of her young and old hardy pioneers. This labor was performed as an earnest of good feeling, for the property of the Utah Northern railroad. . . . The labor on the railroad was a voluntary donation. . . . This railroad is truly one of the greatest labors that has ever been performed by the people of Box Elder, Cache, and Oneida counties; a railroad built on faith, coupled with the labors of an obedient people.[126]

While the construction to Logan was being carried forward, plans were made to construct the line from Brigham City to the Central Pacific terminus at Corinne, and from Brigham City south to the U. P. and Utah Central terminals at Ogden. The four-mile road to Corinne, much the shorter of the two, was completed on June 9, 1873. The road from Brigham City to Ogden was completed February 5, 1874. As in Cache Valley, most of the construction of the Ogden branch was under the supervision of ecclesiastical officials, principally bishops and ward members in Brigham City, Willard, and Ogden.[127] Until this line was completed, all northward traffic from

Ogden, Salt Lake City, and points south, had to be sent to Corinne, then across on the branch line to Brigham, and thence on the direct route to Logan and points north. At the time of the connection with Ogden, Brigham Young and his counselor, George A. Smith, were in St. George. Learning that regular passenger service was about to begin between Ogden and Logan, they sent the following message over the Deseret Telegraph:

> We congratulate you on the successful joining of the track, and expect for the road a brilliant financial future, and that it will be great and lasting in its benefit to the people; and congratulate you on your zeal and perseverance in building your road, as all railroads should be built, by private enterprise, without the aid or patronage of the government.[128]

To be strictly correct, Cache County appropriated $4,000 in favor of the railroad, and extended other favors from time to time, including the abatement of taxes.[129] In addition, as indicated, the church assisted greatly in the financing.

While work was proceeding on the important Ogden and Corinne branches, plans were also being made for the extension of the line north from Logan. By an Act of Congress, on March 3, 1873, the road was granted a right-of-way to build north to Montana "by way of the Bear River Valley, Soda Springs, Snake River Valley and through Montana to a connection with the Northern Pacific Railroad" at Garrison, Montana. In a church conference held in Logan in June 1873, attended by the First Presidency and Council of the Twelve, definite plans were worked out for pushing the road further north. The congregation unitedly agreed to contribute labor and ties.[130] By September the grading was completed to Smithfield, and construction was completed to Franklin by May 2, 1874, making the Utah Northern the first railroad to be constructed on Idaho Territory.

Goudy Hogan relates the manner in which the Saints were organized to finish the road from Logan to Franklin during the winter and spring of 1873–1874:

> In the month of November [1873] the Bishop called upon me to take a half mile of grading to cross a wet piece of hay land. He gave me 22 names for me to call on to help me on this job as every body was required to labor on the railroad at that time. This was north from Richmond and south from Cherry Creek. It was a very disagreeable job but I obeyed the call and went at it with all my strength. I had a great deal of difficulty in obtaining help. I only got half the amount of hands the Bishop gave me. On account of so much cold water to work in and being late in the fall it was disagreeable. I worked some 6 weeks there with damp and many times wet feet so that I was taken down with rheumatism toward the latter part of this job and suffered with this complaint all that winter. . . .
>
> In the month of March [1874] all hands were called on to finish up their

job that had been left in the fall. There were some 2 feet of snow that I had to shovel off and I was not able to work but I rode a horse to see the brethren and get them to work. The railroad had to be crowded through to Franklin by a certain time.[131]

Some fourteen miles of grade were built northeast out of Franklin toward Soda Springs during the summer of 1874, but the track was not completed because of financial problems connected with the Panic of 1873, and because of the realization that the Soda Springs route to Montana was impractical.

The solution to the problems involved in the financing of the road from Ogden to Franklin, for a total of almost ninety miles of track, resembled that adopted in the cases of the Utah Central, Summit County, and Utah Southern. The road was initially described as "a people's road," and the men in northern Utah were told that it was their responsibility and privilege to assist the project by working on it and becoming part owners. And, indeed, the stock was principally held by the people of northern Utah and southern Idaho. Moses Thatcher, who was made president of the Utah Northern in 1873, said of it:

I suppose there is not a road in the United States of equal length the stock of which is distributed so extensively among the workingmen along its line. The iron and rolling stock have been furnished by Mr. Richardson, an eastern capitalist, the rest has been accomplished . . . by the best wealth the world possesses — union of interest and concert of action, backed by the bone and muscle of the independent farmer, the hardy lumberman, and the intelligent miner.[132]

Thatcher thought the "cooperative labor system" of construction was distinctly superior to the capitalistic contract system. Not the least advantage was that "working on the railroad" in a part-owner capacity had "changed the whole face of affairs, by making all more active and enterprising."

The road had cost about $1,400,000 for the whole line. About half of this went for iron and rolling stock, and the other half was an investment of the people along the line in labor, ties, and bridges. More than $1,000,000 in bonds bearing seven per cent interest had been issued on November 1, 1871, but the Richardsons were apparently permitted to buy these bonds at seventy per cent of face value, so that their investment was approximately $700,000, thus making the effective rate of interest ten per cent.[133] The Richardsons were also given, as a bonus, an unspecified quantity of assessable stock. The contribution of the men in northern Utah and southern Idaho was approximately equal to that of the Richardsons.[134] Some of this contribution represented purchases of stock, and some of it represented acceptance of company vouchers issued in lieu of better pay. Promises were made to those receiving vouchers that the vouchers would eventually be redeemed with double their face value in company stock. The company, however, was not able to redeem all these vouchers, and the church eventually agreed to redeem large numbers of them at the tithing offices. For assuming these obligations, the church appears to have been given equivalent value in the capital stock of the company. Thus, the church became an important stockholder in the Utah Northern and an important financial contributor-after-the-fact in its construction.

The failure of Joseph Richardson, as the principal eastern partner, to purchase additional bonds caused the terminus of the Utah Northern to remain at Franklin from 1874 to 1877. Richardson, according to the report, "was getting to the bottom of his purse . . . and he did not want to spend any more money."[135] Several unsuccessful attempts were made by church and business leaders in northern Utah and southern Idaho to secure funds to construct the road north to Fort Hall, near Pocatello, Idaho, eighty miles north of Franklin.[136] Their own financial resources being inadequate for the task, Mormon leaders solicited the cooperation of Sidney Dillon of the Union Pacific Railroad Company. But Dillon "scorned the idea of building railroads in the sage brush."[137] They did succeed in interesting Jay Gould in the venture, however. Gould gave Joseph Richardson approximately $400,000 for his interest in the road, and paid "the promoters" (presumably the Mormon investors) $80,000, or about ten cents on the dollar, for their stock.[138] The church apparently held on to its Utah Northern stock and bonds until 1877, and in the settlement of the Brigham Young estate they were traded to John W. Young for other properties. The latter, in turn, traded the securities to Union Pacific interests for railroad equipment to be used in another venture.[139] Considering that the railroad was not making enough money to maintain interest on the bonds, and that northern Utah would benefit enormously if the road were extended north to connect with Butte and other Montana cities, Mormon interests agreed to the transfer and cooperated with Gould in selecting the location of a route to Montana and in obtaining local labor and supplies.

Union Pacific later purchased Gould's interests in the Utah Northern. Under U. P. direction a new corporation, called the Utah and Northern Railroad Company, was formed on October 4, 1877. The new company represented a "coalition between the stockholders of the old company [Utah Northern] and some of the leading stockholders and directors of the Union Pacific."[140] With the formation of the new company, contracts were let to construct the road from Franklin to Fort Hall and beyond.[141] On December 2, 1877, the Utah Northern was permitted to default on the $1,453,765.32 due on bonds and interest, and on April 3, 1878, the assets of the Utah Northern were sold at auction to S. H. H. Clark, general superintendent of the Union Pacific Railroad Company, for the sum of $100,000.[142]

Contributing to the unprofitability of the Utah Northern as a local concern were the small volume of agricultural traffic due to annual grasshopper visitations, the continuation of much wagon-freight traffic to and from Corinne, and the failure of the Richardsons to furnish funds for the extension of the road sufficiently far to command the Montana traffic. In 1875, to take a typical year, gross earnings were only $137,000, while operating expenses were $77,000. Net earnings were not sufficient to meet the bonded debt, let alone pay dividends on stock.[143]

The subsequent history of the Utah and Northern is not unlike that of the Utah Southern after the church had sold its stock in that concern to Union Pacific. After the assets of the old Utah Northern had been conveyed to the new company, the Utah and Northern Railway Company was incorporated, on April 30, 1878. This third company was capitalized for $960,000.[144] Congress granted the new company the right of way through the public domain, and authorized it to extend its road to Helena, Montana, by way of Bear River, Marsh, and Snake River valleys in Idaho. Under U & N aegis construction was completed to Pocatello, Idaho, in August 1878; to Blackfoot, Idaho, in December 1878, to Camas, Idaho, in 1879; to Red Rock and Dillon, Montana, in 1880; to Silver Bow Junction and Butte, Montana, in 1881; and to the Northern Pacific connection at Garrison, Montana, in 1884. The distance from Ogden, Utah, to Garrison, Montana, was 466 miles. With its completion the line was one of the longest narrow-gauge railroads in the world, and one of the most profitable of all western railroads.[145] Battle Creek and Eagle Rock (now Idaho Falls) gradually replaced Logan as centers of maintenance and repair, and while this took away from Logan a lucrative payroll, Mormon colonization parties had followed the railroad north and established the Upper Snake River Valley as a Mormon stronghold. The whole road was broad-gauged beginning in 1887, and was incorporated in the Oregon Short Line system in 1889.[146] As with O.S.L., it is now a part of the Union Pacific Railroad system.

The principal item of interest in the construction of the Utah and Northern extension to Montana is the opportunity for work it provided to Mormons in northern Utah and southern Idaho, particularly those in Cache Valley. Marriner W. Merrill, bishop of Richmond, Utah, and later an apostle, became leading contractor and later general construction superintendent of the extension from Franklin to Idaho Falls. Other bishops and "practical men" took sub-contracts, and Cache Valley labor was used almost exclusively during the five years (1877–1881) this work went on.[147] This labor, which distributed almost $1,000,000 in cash in the valley, was arranged for by the church.[148]

THE SALT LAKE CITY STREETCAR AND GAS SYSTEMS

Two other enterprises in which the church played a prominent role in the 1870's and 1880's were the Salt Lake City Street Railroad and the Salt Lake City Gas Company. Upon the advice and encouragement of Brigham Young, some ambitious young Mormons formed the Salt Lake City Railroad Company, in January 1872, with a capitalization of $180,000, consisting of 3,600 shares of stock valued at $50 per share.[149] Only $9,500 was subscribed at the time of incorporation. Originally, the construction of nine miles of track was contemplated, at an estimated cost of $150,000. This was to be financed by selling treasury stock, at the rate of $20,000 for each mile of single track constructed. This proved to be impossible, and instead the company decided to sell bonds, at the rate of $15,000 per mile of track. Daniel H. Wells, now a member of the First Presidency and mayor of Salt Lake City, and H. B. Clawson, Brigham Young's son-in-law, agreed to furnish up to $135,000 for the nine-mile line, in return for the first mortgage bonds.[150]

When the Salt Lake City Council granted permission to the company to construct and operate the street railroad in April 1872, construction began at once, and on June 20, 1872, the first street car was put into service. This was a heavy secondhand horse car, pulled by four horses borrowed from Brigham Young's private stable. Later two additional cars were introduced, and the three were pulled by mules, twenty-four of which had been imported from Missouri in 1872 especially for the purpose.

On July 17, 1872, less than a month after the first car was put into service, the company had a mile and a half of single track (an expenditure of about $25,000), constructed in the center of the wide streets of Salt Lake City.

The line was not sufficiently profitable to pay interest on the bonded debt, and the Panic of 1873 made it impossible for Wells and Clawson to finance additional construction. In 1873, with church resources at his command, Brigham Young came to the rescue of the struggling, uncompleted line. As trustee-in-trust he acquired all of the bonds and 3,521 of the 3,600 shares of stock.[151] He assumed the presidency of the company and located its offices in the office of the president of the church. Under church sponsorship the lines were extended at first to a length of seven miles, and later to every important part of Salt Lake City. It is probable that more than $100,000 was expended by the church in the acquisition and expansion of the system. A popular line was run out to the Warm Springs Bath House (now the Wasatch Springs Plunge) on Second West and Eighth North, Salt Lake City. This line carried invalids and others in need of "health treatments."[152] From the church standpoint, however, the most valuable part of the line was that extending from the Utah Southern-Utah Central depot to Temple Block, which facilitated the transportation of granite blocks and other materials and equipment used in the construction of the Salt Lake Temple. This was perhaps the basic reason for the church purchase of the company in 1873. By 1883 the company had fourteen cars in operation, nine miles of track, eighty-four mules, and thirty regular employees.[153]

The church came into the control of the Salt Lake City gas system in much the same way. Incorporated in 1872 with an initial paid-up capital of $55,000, the Salt Lake City Gas Company erected and operated works for the manufacture of illuminating gas. A patented device to generate gas from wood was tried and given up in favor of a similarly patented scheme to make gas from Summit County coal. By the summer of 1873 pipe had been laid and the company was delivering gas to some 125 customers, principally business concerns, and furnishing lights for Salt Lake City streets. At the time of the organization of the company, Daniel H. Wells, who was chief promoter, had an understanding with Brigham Young and other leading church and civic officials that "the community would stand behind the project, endorse it and see it through."[154] When stockholders found themselves unable to furnish additional capital late in 1873, the City Council of Salt Lake City, over which Wells presided as mayor, furnished the company $50,000 in return for stock. Shortly thereafter, Wells made a settlement with the church in which the church acquired some 850 shares of Wells' stock, which constituted a controlling interest. This stock was valued at slightly less than $85,000. Whether Wells turned this stock over to the church as tithing, or gave it to the trustee-in-trust in satisfaction of his drawings on the church, is not clear.[155] At any rate, the church and other stockholders invested additional sums until a total of $250,000 had been expended before the company was turned over to the government receiver under the Edmunds-Tucker Act in 1888. The enterprise appears to have been a profitable one.[156]

CONCLUSION

The history of Mormon railroading exhibits the meaning of "cooperation" to Mormon leaders in the 1870's and 1880's. The church sought to cooperate with private enterprise and its members in developing the territory and securing the benefits which the civilization could afford. People in the localities were asked to contribute their labor and local supplies, while the church would make the necessary connections with eastern capitalists and furnish whatever additional help was required. Where private persons had undertaken projects with the encouragement of the church and had run into financial difficulties, as in the case of the Utah Northern Railroad and the Salt Lake streetcar and gas companies, the trustee-in-trust was prepared to recruit the labor and use the common fund to assure completion and continued operation. One might also infer from some of the transactions described in this chapter that the trustee-in-trust was willing to come to the rescue of those associated with him who, at his request, had sunk their private capital in schemes calculated to benefit the community.

The history of Mormon railroading also indicates that the principal purpose of the church in promoting these roads was to provide improved transportation facilities rather than to obtain profits or consolidate its own holdings of property. The most important roads constructed under church sponsorship were sold to the Union Pacific Railroad soon after they commenced to operate. Others were eventually sold to private interests. The church's interest, apparently, was purely promotional.

CHAPTER X

The Cooperative Movement

DEVELOPMENT OF COOPERATIVE MERCHANDISING

The cooperative movement which captured the imagination of farmers, laborers, and other ethically motivated individuals and groups in the nineteenth century spread into Utah from Europe and the East. Mormon missionaries in Europe had a particularly excellent opportunity to observe the operation of cooperatives in England, Scotland, and Scandinavia. Many of them vowed to assist in the establishment of similar institutions in Zion. Among the Mormons, however, more attention was paid to the purposes for which businesses were to be established, and their role in community life, than to the particular form which the organization took. Structurally, most Mormon "cooperatives" were nothing more than joint-stock corporations, organized under the sponsorship of the church, with a broad basis of public ownership and support. Functionally, however, most Mormon cooperatives appear to have been motivated principally by welfare rather than profit; patronage was an act of religious loyalty; the church participated in the organization, operation, and financing of most of the important establishments; and the whole cooperative movement was permeated with an unmistakable pietistic zeal and feeling of religious obligation.

While the Mormons had cooperated, in the broad sense of that term, in the founding of settlements, development of irrigation works, erection of public buildings and business enterprises, and, indeed, in the provision of most of the necessaries of life, "the cooperative movement" was a phase of Mormon economic organization which lasted from 1868 to 1884. It featured the establishment, in virtually every Mormon settlement in the West, of "cooperative" retail stores and factories. Probably as many as 200 separate enterprises bearing the name "cooperative" were founded in Mormon Country during this period.

Prior to 1868, despite self-sufficiency policies, the number and size of private trading companies, both Mormon and non-Mormon, had continued to rise. As has been noted, most merchandising was in the hands of non-

Mormons because of the stigma attached to "profiteering Saints," and because of the inability of Mormon traders to refuse credit to their "brethren" and force the payment of debts. Until 1857 there seemed to be little difference in the treatment and patronage accorded Mormon and Gentile stores. The primary concern of the church was the encouragement of home manufactures, the prevention of exorbitant profits, and cautions against what was called "speculation."[1] The outbreak of the Utah War, however, caused church leaders to lose faith in Gentile merchants, who were widely believed to have encouraged the invasion of federal troops for business reasons. Brigham Young, as we have seen, accused several merchants of courting the favor of the Mormons in Utah and, at the same time, plotting their "destruction" in Washington. While this feeling was doubtless exaggerated, and perhaps false, it nonetheless produced a coolness which had developed into a full-blown boycott against non-Mormon concerns by the end of 1868. During the 1860's the church not only frowned on the multiplication of trading centers in general, but was distinctly hostile to those which failed to use their profits in building up the Kingdom.[2] "There is a class of men," said Brigham Young, "who are here to pick the pockets of the Latter-day Saints and then use the means they get from us to bring about our destruction. . . . We should be of one heart and mind, and be determined not to put means in their power to create trouble for us, and bring us sorrow. . . . I am giving you my counsel upon this matter, that you have no deal or communication with men who would destroy you."[3]

In the summer of 1860 a number of prominent Mormon merchants and capitalists attempted to establish a concern in which the church, along with private investors, would have an interest. This plan for a cooperative and completely-Mormon wholesale buying, freighting, and selling association was outlined by W. H. Hooper, leading politician, merchant, and friend of Brigham Young. Shares were to sell at $100 each, draw 10 per cent interest, and be refundable in three years, together with dividends in cash and/or goods. A ledger account was to be kept on each article showing the purchase price, pro rata share of freight and handling, and selling price. One of the group (E. D. Woolley), according to the record, said,

> It was time something was done to stop bleeding the people. There was a prejudice existing against any "Mormon" who will embark in the business of merchandising, but none against non-Mormons, no matter how they imposed on us, and when trouble came on us, they pack up their goods and immense fortunes, and leave us to bear the burden.[4]

Evidently he thought a church-approved plan would cure the "prejudice." Upon the invitation of the group, Brigham Young met with them to determine church policy. Although there was almost unanimous support of the plan by the merchants present, it was vetoed by Brigham Young. His reasons are stated in the minutes, as follows:

> Brigham Young then remarked the plan was a good one, but from the experience he had had with this people [the Mormons] he believed that the people would not be willing to trust their means in the hands of the Association. He said, he did not think they would trust him, and he thought his credit was as good as any other persons. He said, that the brethren could do more good by putting the sheep's grey upon their backs and upon the backs of their families, than by bringing goods into this country; and if the people had not given [him] clothing, he would have worn sheep's grey for years. . . . He also said that he would have to repulse the operation as that kind of business was not for us, the Kingdom was for us, and if we went into it, [it] would not prosper, but it would be like the mail contract [the Y. X. Company], it would be a disastrous business.[5]

The approaching completion of the transcontinental railroad, however, forced the president to change his policy. Almost certainly, the volume of imports into Utah would increase. It was now necessary to make sure that there would be no exorbitant profits on these imports, and that what profits were made would be devoted to the purchase of machinery, the establishment of new enterprises, and other purposes which would clearly benefit the Mormon element in the territory. It was also in harmony with his self-sufficiency policy to want to insure preferential treatment to "home manufactures." Finally, church officials wished to guard against the development of a moneyed class among the Latter-day Saints themselves which would rend the social fabric and destroy cohesion and unity.[6]

The connection between cooperative merchandising and marketing and territorial development was brought to the attention of the Latter-day Saints many times during the late 1860's. Albert Carrington, apostle and editor of the *Deseret News,* described the merchants as a class "rapidly swelling"; "they come here on the wing, remain long enough to become comparatively rich, and depart with what they have acquired." They do not build houses, he added, nor make improvements ("except in their purses"), nor develop the country. They are the parasites "who have grown or are growing fat off the people." He stressed that all who derive benefits from residence in a community ought to pay back with equivalent improvements and investments. And yet these merchants had impudently advertised that they could sell cheaper than the "friendly" merchants because they did not have to pay tithing! "It is about time," concluded the apostle, "that this class should get the 'cut direct,' and be 'let severely alone.' We are, or ought to be, perfectly competent to do our own trading . . . and we can use the profits for building up ourselves, our Territory and the kingdom of God."[7] He suggested that the people become their own storeowners, in a cooperative way, and thus *"the money saved could be invested to bring more machinery and make us more self-sustaining."* [8]

This attitude was similar to that of the First Presidency of the Church, as given in an official message in 1867:

If the saints residing in the settlements over which you preside want dry goods and groceries, let them select brethren in whom they have confidence and place the means in their hands and send them to purchase goods in the Eastern states. . . .

We wish the Capitalists in your community to use their means for purchasing machinery — for manufacturing purposes — which will best meet the growing wants and necessities of the people of this territory . . . [thus] the great profits which will be realized on the manufacture of the raw material may be retained by those whose interest it is to build up the kingdom, whereas if the people do not improve the present opportunity and obey this counsel, aliens to the government of God will possess themselves of that which the Almighty intended his saints to enjoy.

Cease paying the exhorbitant prices demanded by disinterested persons and our enemies for all imported articles, and hundreds of thousands of dollars may be saved annually by the saints and the revenue, which has heretofore enriched those who have no interests with us, may be devoted to the building up of the Kingdom of God. . . .[9]

To implement this counsel the church had sponsored, in 1866, the Utah Produce Company — a semipublic joint-stock marketing agency which purchased produce from Mormon farmers, freighted it to mining camps and other markets in northern Utah, Idaho, and Montana, and sold it on terms favorable to the Utah cooperators.[10] But this had not prevented the accumulation of "all the money to a few hands." [11] As the railroad drew closer, attention shifted from cooperative marketing, as a means of retaining freighting costs and profits locally, to cooperative importing and merchandising, as a means of "constructing for the community a broader and more equitable system of commercial existence; so that all could participate, to the extent of their means, in the profits realized and the reduction in price of the cooperative system." [12]

The first step in the direction of church-sponsored cooperative merchandising was taken in September 1868 when Brigham Young suggested that the Mormon people should not "trade another cent" with a man "who does not pay his tithing and help gather the poor, and pray in his family." [13] This was accompanied by the adoption of the previously mentioned rule of the School of Prophets that members should deal "as much as possible with those in full fellowship in the Church." [14] The following month the school voted that "those who dealt with outsiders should be cut off from the Church," but this was a last resort.[15] Such "protective" measures, as they were sometimes called, were regarded not only as devices for countering the strength of the church's enemies, but they were also considered essential to the attainment of that spiritual and temporal unity for which Brigham Young and his associates had striven so long. "In the absence of the necessary faith to enter upon a more perfect order revealed by the Lord unto the Church," said a pronouncement of church authorities defending the action of 1868, cooperation "was felt to be the best means of drawing us together and making us one." [16]

Thus cooperative merchandising was proposed as a substitute for "trading with the enemy." Not only was this a way of assuring that mercantile earnings would be expended within the territory, they reasoned, but by the concentration of mercantile operations in a relatively few institutions, human resources would be more fully utilized, and earnings would be more surely channeled into fields which would promote self-sufficiency and home industry. Cessation of trading with "outside" speculators and freebooters, and the concentration of purchases in establishments which could be certain of expending earnings under the direction of the church, would facilitate, or so they thought, the building of the Kingdom.[17] With this thought in mind, church officials proposed to the general conference of the church, held in Salt Lake City in October 1868, that "we sustain [only] ourselves and those who sustain us." [18] Approved unanimously, this resolution laid the groundwork for the organization of cooperative merchandising.

While local cooperatives previously had been established at Brigham City and Lehi, therefore, generalized Mormon mercantile cooperation began with a series of sermons in the October 1868 general conference, accompanied by a series of editorials in the *Deseret News*. This softening-up process was followed by a series of meetings in the wards and settlements of the church, under the direction of a general church authority or other appointed representatives. Particularly invited to these meetings were local ecclesiastical officials and businessmen. The first such meeting was held in Salt Lake City on October 9, 1868, and meetings were held the following week in each of the twenty wards in Salt Lake City, and in each of the wards near by.[19] At the same time, the subject was being presented to Latter-day Saint congregations in each of the counties of the territory. Within two weeks after the close of the October general conference, the necessity of establishing cooperative merchandising concerns had been discussed in every Mormon community in the West.

The messages delivered in these meetings were essentially: (1) The Latter-day Saints should not trade with "outsiders"; (2) a cooperative wholesale house, or "Parent Institution," should be established in Salt Lake City which would purchase all goods imported into the territory for sale; (3) cooperative retailing establishments should be established in each ward and settlement, and these should patronize the parent wholesale house in Salt Lake City, and also control the trade within their respective communities; (4) the retail stores should use their profits in establishing local shops and factories which could supply the people's wants.

The reactions of the Latter-day Saints to these meetings, as reflected in their diaries and journals, are almost universally favorable. Particularly interesting was that of Charles Smith, as indicated in an entry dated October 11, 1868:

I went to Ward meeting Bro A M Musser and G Q Cannon occupied the time. They spoke upon this matter of our trading with those who were not of us. He shewed the advantages that would arise from our cooperating putting our means together to do away with this monopoly that . . . is in our midst that was continually draining our substance. This movement was intended to make us more united to bring us closer together, according to the pattern of the Gospel. Bro Cannon Said it was very evident that men were Seecking to get rich, and build themselves up, and to form that distinction of class in society, which thing was an abomination in the sight of God. He refered to the Nephites [a people described in the *Book of Mormon*] shewing that when they began to get rich they Drew off in Classes and despised the poor. This matter to which our attention was now being Called would bring about good results, and would prepare the minds of the people, to receive further those principles that pertained to the order of Enoch, as contained in the book of Covenants. At the close of the meeting subscriptions were handed in to carry forward the movement of a cooperative Wholesale Store.[20]

The contemporary comments of the Mormon people indicate a fear on their part that if they continued to trade freely with non-Mormon merchants after the completion of the transcontinental railroad, such merchants would gradually assimilate the means and property of the Mormons and eventually control the Mountain Kingdom. Charles Smith heard Brigham Young specifically tell one group that if they did not stop trading with outsiders they would soon be "driven from their homes." [21]

THE FOUNDING OF ZION'S CO-OPERATIVE MERCANTILE INSTITUTION

The success of the cooperative movement hinged on the formation and successful operation of a Parent Store, as it was called, or cooperative wholesale establishment. A number of meetings were held in Salt Lake City in regard to forming such an institution during October 1868, and a tentative organization was completed on the sixteenth. Brigham Young, of course, was elected president, and other positions were filled with church and business leaders in Salt Lake City.[22] The purpose of the new institution, said President Young, was "to bring goods here and sell them as low as they can possibly be sold and let the profits be divided with the people at large."[23] The constitution and bylaws of the association, which were finally approved on October 24, 1868, provided for an organization to be called "Zion's Co-operative Mercantile Institution," with an authorized capitalization of $3,000,000, consisting of 30,000 shares valued at $100 each. This association was later incorporated for twenty-five years on December 1, 1870, after the territorial general incorporation law had been passed.[24]

The original constitution of Z.C.M.I. is an interesting document. Beginning with the phrase "Holiness to the Lord!" the preamble declares:

> The inhabitants of Utah, convinced of the impolicy of leaving the trade and commerce of their Territory to be conducted by strangers, have resolved, in public meeting assembled, to unite in a system of co-operation for the transaction of their own business.

No limit was set on the amount of stock for which any person could subscribe, and stockholders were to have one vote per share, but no person was eligible to acquire or hold stock "except they be of good moral character and have paid their tithing according to the rules of the Church of Jesus Christ of Latter-day Saints."[25] The directors were instructed to tithe the net profits of the concern prior to any declaration of dividend "according to the rules of the Church." As in other church enterprises, all officers were required to serve without pay except the secretary and treasurer. The bylaws included a provision that "All houses wherein the business of this Institution may be transacted shall have placed over the main entrance the inscription: 'Holiness to the Lord: Zion's Co-operative Mercantile Institution.'" These signs were prepared under Brigham Young's direction and contained the legend "Holiness to the Lord" arched over the All-seeing Eye of Jehovah, below which were the words "Zion's Co-operative Mercantile Institution."[26] The erection of these signs in November 1868 really inaugurated "cooperation"; that is, trading exclusively with Mormon firms. The immediate effect of their erection was that of "emptying the stores of the brethren of nearly all their staple articles, the people having bought them."[27]

The business policies to be applied by the new enterprise, as worked out by the cooperating merchants,[28] were perhaps even more significant than the specifications in the constitution or charter. The most important of these policies was the agreement that in order to achieve unified action the board of directors of the wholesale institution be empowered to set standard retail prices, and these were to be charged by all cooperating concerns. Such prices were to be "reasonable," and "such as would tend to the satisfaction and benefit of both the merchants and the whole people."[29] The purpose of uniform retail prices was not to prevent price competition, it was declared, but to prevent the charging of exorbitant prices. According to the founders, it was not a question of uniformly high prices, but of uniformly low prices. The first such list of prices was adopted on February 25, 1869, "with the understanding that the superintendent of Z.C.M.I. be permitted to vary them according to circumstances."[30]

Another such policy called for the maintenance of a double price system: one for jobbers and one for consumers. Consumers were to be charged "the same price as their own [ward cooperative] store charges."[31] This was to permit any person to purchase goods on as favorable terms as in his own locality, but on no more favorable terms, thus eliminating the possibility of large firms driving the smaller ones out of business.

After the formation of the wholesale association, the adoption of the constitution and bylaws, and the working out of a common agreement on business practice, the next problem was the acquisition of a place of business and a stock of goods adequate to put the institution in business. It was the plan of Brigham Young that the association get its original stock of goods from participating Mormon retailers. Although more than $150,000 in money and goods had been subscribed by Salt Lakers by October 22, 1868, and although other subscriptions were expected from other communities with the distribution of a circular stating the purposes of the institution and inviting subscriptions, retailers were understandably reticent about transferring their stocks and inventories to the new concern.[32] The date of the transfer was postponed from November to December, and from December to January 1869. After all, the erection of the "Holiness" signs, and the enforcement of the boycott against noncooperators, turned trade in their favor. Why should they push the new venture?

Brigham Young became alarmed at the lagging interest in cooperation. He had originally said that if the merchants did not respond favorably to cooperation they would be left "out in the cold, the same as the Gentiles, and their goods shall rot upon their shelves."[33] Now he was prepared to force the issue by threatening to set up a church-backed wholesale establishment in Provo. This threat was not an idle one. Preliminary meetings were actually held in Provo on February 8, 1869, with the view to carrying it out. If Salt Lake merchants were left "out in the cold," President Young told the group, they had nobody to blame but themselves.[34] This action was enough to frighten cooperating merchants in Salt Lake City into making definite offers to the Board of Directors of Z.C.M.I. to exchange their inventories for capital stock in the new company. Each of the three largest firms of cooperating merchants — William Jennings, Eldredge and Clawson, and Saddler and Teasdale — made such offers in February.

Apparently, only one cooperating merchant voiced public opposition to the plan of "compulsory mercantile cooperation," in which merchants were asked to turn their entire stock over to the new concern. Henry W. Lawrence said that he could not understand how the people were going to benefit from the change. "It would merely concentrate the trade into a few stores and the rest would be empty and the men out of business." Lawrence thought that either the parent store (Z.C.M.I.) should go into retailing, as it eventually did, or the retailers should retain their inventories for the convenience of customers.[35] Brigham Young replied that there was need of a big department store to which people "from the country" could come and "get their goods cheaply"; and, anyway, there were too many people in the retailing business. Two-thirds of these merchants, he said, "ought to go into the field preaching and the others do the work."

Lawrence's opposition did not carry the day, and a committee was appointed to find a suitable building or buildings, and to acquire a stock of goods. When a preliminary report indicated that "the merchants without exception were exceedingly liberal in their offers," the committee was directed to "thoroughly examine the various stocks of goods . . . and purchase the same or any portion thereof that they may deem suitable; also rent suitable buildings for stores and forthwith start the wholesale business."[36] H. B. Clawson, of the firm of Eldredge and Clawson, a son-in-law of Brigham Young, was appointed general superintendent, and William Clayton, chief clerk. H. W. Naisbitt was chosen as eastern buying agent. Employees were to be paid "part in cash and part in orders on the retail stores in the various wards."[37]

The institution finally opened for business on March 1, 1869, in the Eagle Emporium, the site of William Jennings' store, a block south of church headquarters. In a solemn ceremony, the building and its contents were officially dedicated to Deity by Brigham Young, after which the president was permitted to make the first purchase. What was advertised as the first department store west of the Mississippi River was now ready for business.

The Eagle Emporium handled dry goods, clothing, hats and caps, boots and shoes, and similar goods. Another store was opened on March 10, 1869, in the Old Constitution Building, formerly occupied by Eldredge and Clawson, which carried groceries, hardware, stoves, queen's ware, and agricultural implements. Both were intended as wholesale establishments. A month later, on April 21, 1869, Z.C.M.I. opened its first retail department in a Main Street store formerly occupied by N. S. Ransohoff and Company. A drug store was opened in November 1869.[38]

The beginning stock of goods of Z.C.M.I. consisted of almost half a million dollars worth of goods acquired from leading Salt Lake merchants for stock or cash. Commodity acquisitions by March 1869 were as follows:[39]

William Jennings	$200,000
Eldredge and Clawson	75,000
N. S. Ransohoff & Co.	75,000
H. W. Lawrence	30,000
Bowman and Co.	15,000
David Day and Co.	10,000
Woodmansee Bros.	5,000
Sundry purchases	40,000
Total	$450,000

With the absorption of all important retail and wholesale firms in Salt Lake City, and with the formation of local cooperatives throughout the territory pledged to give it exclusive patronage, Z.C.M.I. was in a commanding position indeed.

At least half of the early purchases of Z.C.M.I. were made by the direct exchange of company stock. The paid-up capital in the institution on the day it commenced business amounted to $220,000, of which $60,000 had been paid in cash and the balance in merchandise.[40] By September 1869, paid-up capital was listed at $279,520, this amount having been contributed by a total of 347 shareholders, most of whom had subscribed for twenty-five shares ($2,500) or less.[41] There were more than 600 shareholders in March 1870.[42] Because of the unique financial arrangements, most of the capital stock of the company was owned by the cooperating merchants. This is demonstrated by the fact that the largest stockholders in 1869, representing two per cent of the total number of stockholders, owned over seventy per cent of the capital stock; while the smallest stockholders, representing seventy-eight per cent of all shareholders, owned less than four per cent of all the stock.[43]

The 1870 incorporation papers, which apparently include only the principal Salt Lake stockholders, show paid-up stock of $199,000, with an authorized capitalization of $1,000,000, consisting of 10,000 shares valued at $100 each. Twenty-two stockholders are listed, including the trustee-in-trust of the church, prominent Mormon merchants, and a few "ordinary" Mormon capitalists and workingmen. The list of stockholders with their respective shares exhibits the mixed ownership of this semipublic concern:[44]

Brigham Young, representing the church	772	$ 77,200
William Jennings, Utah's senior merchant	790	79,000
Other cooperating merchants	260	26,000
Other shareholders (a total of sixteen)	168	16,800
Total	1990	$199,000

THE ESTABLISHMENT OF LOCAL RETAIL COOPERATIVES

While final arrangements were being made for the establishment of Z.C.M.I., an intensive campaign was being waged by church officials and others to assure the establishment of a cooperative general store in each ward and settlement throughout the territory. That the campaign was effective is indicated by the fact that within six weeks after the opening of Z.C.M.I. there were seventy-eight Mormon cooperative stores in actual operation, and plans well advanced for many others.[45] By 1870 no known ward or settlement was without one, and Salt Lake City had seventeen. At least one hundred and fifty such cooperatives were founded during the decade after 1869.[46]

These stores were all established on the advice of Brigham Young and other ecclesiastical authorities. In general conference addresses on the subject in April 1869, the president declared:

> Taking up the system of our cooperative method of merchandising, it gives to the people ease and money. They are not obliged to run a mile or two through the mud to buy a yard of ribbon, they have it in their own Ward, and they can purchase it twenty or thirty per cent cheaper than they ever could before. . . .
>
> There are very few people who cannot get twenty-five dollars to put into one of these co-operative stores. There are hundreds and thousands of women who, by prudence and industry, can obtain this sum. And we say to you put your capital into one of these stores. What for? To bring you interest for your money. . . . These co-operative stores are instituted to give the poor a little advantage as well as the rich.[47]

Brigham Young suggested that everybody contribute toward the concerns, especially the poor:

> When you start your Co-operative Store in a ward, you will find the men of capital stepping forward, and one says, "I will put in ten thousand dollars;" another says, "I will put in five thousand," But I say to you, bishops, do not let these men take five thousand, or one thousand, but call on the brethren and sisters who are poor and tell them to put in their five dollars or their twenty-five, and let those who have capital stand back and give the poor the advantage of this quick trading.[48]

Local cooperative stores, in other words, were to be established by the pooling of the small investments of everyone. The rich, rather than use their capital in acquiring control of community stores, were asked to devote their surpluses to the importation of sheep, the building of woolen mills, the founding of tanneries, and the establishment of other home industries. "You are rich," they were told, "and I want to turn the stream [their money] so as to do good to the whole community."[49]

The organizations in these one hundred-odd local stores followed a common pattern. Nearly all of them used the name "Cooperative Mercantile Institution" in association with the name of the location; as, for example, the "Arizona Co-operative Mercantile Institution" at Snowflake, Arizona. Local organizers were instructed by church officials to model their cooperatives after the constitution and bylaws of the parent company in Salt Lake City. Membership was usually limited to Latter-day Saints, or to such Latter-day Saint organizations as the Relief Society. The institutions tithed their net profits; and the officers were usually the ecclesiastical officials in the ward. It was common for the ward bishop to serve as manager of the ward co-op. In all the houses in which these institutions did business throughout the territory, an inscription was placed over the main entrance reading "Holiness to the Lord." "Zion's Co-operative Mercantile Institution."

In practice, most of the cooperatives were formed, as was Z.C.M.I., by exchanging capital stock for the inventories of local retailers. Once set up in business, however, an attempt was made to get a broad basis of public support for the enterprise by valuing the shares at less than $50.00, usually at $5.00, so that it would be within the reach of the poorest ward members. Some of them added a stipulation that no person could hold more than one share of stock. In some cooperatives, members were limited to one vote each, while in others, those with more than one share were permitted to cast additional votes according to the number of shares owned. One cooperative solved the voting problem by agreeing that "all the shareholders present should have an equal choice in the matter [of management] irrespective of the number of their shares"; but in case there was any "division of sentiment" the votes were to be "regulated by the number of shares according to the Constitution." [50]

In respect to the distribution of profits there was also lack of uniformity. Some followed the Rochdale Pioneer plan of distributing profits to patrons according to the volume of purchases, while others followed the corporation practice of dividing profits among shareholders according to the number of shares held. Local cooperatives also differed in size. Some opened for business with a paid-in capital of only a few hundred dollars, while others were of considerable size. On the whole, most of them were highly profitable during the first few years.[51]

Originally, Z.C.M.I. owned none of the stock in these stores, but the relationship was the same as if it had.[52] Each of the stores gave virtually exclusive patronage to Z.C.M.I. and the latter, in turn, granted favorable prices, credit, and other arrangements to the advantage of local "co-ops." [53] The system was not dissimilar to that of modern chain stores, without the ownership tie-in.

Just as Z.C.M.I. was expected to have a monopoly in wholesaling, so each local cooperative was also expected to have a monopoly of retailing in its own area. The monopoly was a regulated monopoly, in theory at least, and the usual results of private monopoly were not expected to occur because of the broad basis of public ownership, and also because of the restraining hand of the priesthood. When the question of monopoly was raised, the usual answer was that cooperation was not an attempt to establish monopoly, but to destroy *private* monopoly and "disseminate means through the community."[54] Gentile retailers, of course, objected to the exclusive patronage requested by the church of these stores, and their economic loss in many instances was considerable. Mormon private enterprisers in some cases also protested. They did not want to sell out their own businesses for stock in the new cooperatives. Brigham Young, however, was adamant on the point that they should do so. He made use of the old mercantilist argument that production was more important than distribution and that much of the "waste" in distribution could be eliminated by excluding competition:

> As to these little traders, we are going to shut them off. We feel a little sorry for them. Some of them have but just commenced their trading operations, and they want to keep them up. They have made, perhaps, a few hundred dollars, and they would like to continue so as to make a few thousands; and then they would want scores of thousands and then hundreds of thousands. Instead of trading we want them to go into other branches of business. Do you say, what business? Why, some of them may go into raising broom corn to supply the Territory with brooms, instead of bringing them from the States. Others may go to raising sugar cane, and thus supply the Territory with a good sweet; we have to send to the States for our sugar now. We will get some more of them to gathering up hides and making them into leather, and manufacturing that leather into boots and shoes; this will be more profitable than letting hundreds and thousands of hides go to waste as they have done. Others may go and make baskets; we do not care what they go at, provided they produce that which will prove of general benefit. Those who are able can erect woolen factories, get a few spindles, raise sheep and manufacture the wool. Others may raise flax and manufacture that into linen cloth, that we may not be under the necessity of sending abroad for it. If we go on in this way, we shall turn these little traders into producers, which well help to enrich the entire people.[55]

As a part of his production-first program he suggested that women be hired to run the small ward cooperative stores so that the men could be released to become producers in agriculture and industry. His argument was as follows:

> Another thing I will say with regard to our trading. Our Female Relief Societies are doing immense good now, but they can take hold and do all the trading for these wards just as well as to keep a big loafer to do it. It is always disgusting to me to see a big, fat, lubberly fellow handing out calicoes and meas-

uring ribbon; I would rather see the ladies do it. The ladies can learn to keep books as well as the men; we have some few, already, who are just as good accountants as any of our brethren. Why not teach more to keep books and sell goods, and let them do this business, and let the men go to raising sheep, wheat, or cattle, or go and do something or other to beautify the earth and help to make it like the Garden of Eden, instead of spending their time in a lazy, loafing manner?[56]

The functions of the local cooperatives were, in short, to provide retail outlets for Z.C.M.I., to minimize the use of imported commodities, to provide an eventual basis for cooperative home industry, and to distribute the profits of mercantile operations among the people generally. These goals were realized to a limited degree only, and then for little more than a decade. Nevertheless, the church-sponsored concerns introduced a certain efficiency and economy in retailing. Without competition, they could operate "with less show"; they could handle goods of standard grade; there was little overhead to charge against the prices of commodities; and, of course, there was a uniformity of policy that ruled out destructive price competition.[57]

EXPANSION OF Z.C.M.I. AND LOCAL COOPERATIVES

Z.C.M.I., as the Parent Store, was an immediate and outstanding financial success. It quickly captured virtually all the wholesale trade of the territory and much of the retail trade in Salt Lake City. Considering the pledged support of all Mormon consumers and of all local cooperatives, this is not to be wondered at. Sales during the first full year of operation were $1,750,000, and by 1873 sales were running at the level of $4,400,000 annually. Dividends reflected the institution's profitability. A ten per cent cash dividend was declared in 1869, while a sixteen per cent cash dividend and 25 per cent stock dividend were declared in 1870. By the end of 1873, total dividends had amounted to more than half a million dollars, on an original investment of approximately $280,000.[58] Largely through stock dividends, the capital stock of the company had increased to $782,081 by September 30, 1873. In addition to these earnings, the superintendent of Z.C.M.I. claimed that during its first four years the institution had saved the Mormon people $3,000,000 in the form of lower prices.[59]

Most of the earnings of Z.C.M.I. reflect those which would have been earned by the cooperating merchants if the institution had not been established, but some of them may have been at the expense of non-Mormon and apostate-Mormon firms which left the territory or continued to operate in the face of the boycott. Some of these firms claimed to have sustained huge losses. The apostate Mormon firm of Walker Brothers, for example, alleged that their sales decreased in a brief space "from $60,000 to $5,000 per month," and that those of the Auerbach Brothers fell off in like ratio.[60] Both firms reported that they had offered to sell their property to Z.C.M.I. for fifty cents on the dollar and leave the territory, but that the offer had been refused.[61] These contentions are not borne out by the tax lists of the period. The monthly reports of dealers' sales, for example, give no perceptible decline in Walker Brothers' sales after Z.C.M.I. opened for business, and, indeed, their sales for March and April 1869 are almost double those reported for the same months in 1868.[62] Throughout the year 1869, the dealer sales of Z.C.M.I. averaged $106,000 per month, while those of Walker Brothers averaged only $29,000 per month. On the basis of the evidence available in tax memoranda, three things would appear to be true: (1) that Z.C.M.I. absorbed the business of its cooperating merchants, while Walker Brothers absorbed the business of the non-Mormon merchants who decided to leave the territory; (2) that Z.C.M.I. effectively prevented Walker Brothers from expanding as rapidly as they would have done upon the completion of the transcontinental railroad; and (3) that Walker Brothers' retail sales (as contrasted with their wholesale business) may have suffered temporarily from the church boycott.

Brigham Young, of course, made no apologies about the decline in overall business done by firms which were "opposed to the true interests of Utah,"[63] and in fact was delighted with it. Their profits, he asserted, had been too liberal and they had done "little or nothing to encourage or build up the Territory."[64] The destruction of such merchants, added Brigham, would make it possible for the church to extend its efforts "more vigorously and with greater effect than ever in the development of home resources, and to curtail the practice of importing articles that can be made here."[65] To those who were inclined to complain that Z.C.M.I. prices were not sufficiently low, or that they could in some cases get better bargains at Walker Brothers, the president simply reminded them of prices previously charged by Gentile stores and added:

> Among this people, called Latter-day Saints, when the devil has got the crowns, sovereigns, guineas and the twenty dollar pieces, it has been all right; but let the Lord get a sixpence and there is an eternal grunt about it.[66]

Victorious, temporarily at least, over both Jew and Gentile, Z.C.M.I. sought to extend its service and influence more widely throughout the territory by the establishment of branch houses, north and south of Salt Lake City. These were owned on a proprietary basis by the parent company. The first such branch was established at Ogden in May 1869, and was accompanied by absorbing the Ogden cooperative general store on the same terms that private merchants in Salt Lake City had been absorbed; that is, shareholders in the Ogden cooperative were given shares in Z.C.M.I. in exchange for the sale of the assets of the co-op to Z.C.M.I. By the same procedure branches were established at Soda Springs, Idaho, in March 1872, and at Logan, Utah, in August 1872. A branch to serve southern Utah was later established in 1883 in Provo; and another to serve eastern Idaho in 1889 at Idaho Falls. A final branch was opened at Pocatello, Idaho, in 1915.[67] As a part of the same expansionary process, Z.C.M.I. also completed new department store buildings in Salt Lake City.

In line with the announced objective of stimulating territorial development, Z.C.M.I. also established a number of manufacturing branches. This manner of utilizing earnings was intended not only to diminish territorial imports, but also to serve as an example for local cooperatives to imitate. The most important steps in this direction were taken in 1878–1879, under the leadership of Brigham Young's successor, John Taylor. At the time of the October 1878 general conference, President Taylor appointed a "committee on Cooperation, Home Manufactures, and Industries," with H. S. Eldredge, the superintendent of Z.C.M.I., as the chairman. The committee was charged with "introducing measures to promote the interests of that institution [Z.C.M.I.] as well as the general interests of the people throughout the Territory."[68] Noting that Z.C.M.I. had expended $125,000 on locally manufactured goods in 1878, this committee recommended, among other things, the furtherance of *industrial* cooperation, as contrasted with mercantile cooperation, and added that Z.C.M.I. would lead the way by appropriating its profits "for the development of home manufactures, the making of machinery, the introduction of self-sustaining principles and the building up of the Territory generally."[69] A tannery, boot and shoe factory, and clothing factory were established or enlarged as the result of this planning.

A branch for the manufacture of boots and shoes was first established by Z.C.M.I. on a small basis in 1870.[70] It expanded greatly in 1879 by absorbing the Deseret Tanning & Manufacturing Association, a Mormon-owned Salt Lake concern.[71] By exchanging $30,000, in company stock, and by the installation of additional equipment, Z.C.M.I. was able to boast of "the best appointed and most capable boot and shoe factory west of Chicago."[72] The output of the new factory during its first year was 83,000 pairs of boots and shoes, valued at $150,000, and requiring the employment of 160 persons. Within three years the factory was employing more than 200 people and producing up to 100,000 pairs of misses', women's, and men's shoes and boots per year.[73] "The Big Boot" as it was called, was immensely profitable, and its earnings were continuously reinvested in expanded facilities. A $110,000 factory was constructed in 1887–1888, permitting increase in output to 500 pairs of boots and shoes daily, or more than 160,000 pairs annually, with an average employment of 180 hands.[74] All of the sole leather and half of the uppers used in this manufacture were made at the Z.C.M.I. tannery. The tannery and boot and shoe factory were still being operated at capacity at the turn of the century.

A clothing manufacturing branch was also established by Z.C.M.I. during the same period. A "duck clothing" factory, opened in 1878, was soon expanded to include related cotton goods manufacturing, and by 1881 the factory turned out more than 50,000 overalls, "jumpers," lined coats and vests, overshirts, undershirts, and men's drawers, valued at more than $55,000. Most of the pieces were made from cloth manufactured by the Provo Woolen Mills. Approximately eighty hands were employed, producing clothing for both wholesale and retail sale.[75] By 1888, the daily output of overalls and men's underwear amounted to 4,300 items per week, and at the turn of the century, some 750,000 yards of denim and other material were being used in the production of an output valued at more than $100,000 per year.[76]

In addition to the maintenance of the tannery, boot and shoe factory, and clothing factory, Z.C.M.I. followed a regular purchase policy of giving preference to other products of Mormon manufacture. These purchases varied between $100,000 and $300,000 worth per year, and were strongly recommended by the church. George Q. Cannon, member of the First Presidency, boasted to the general conference in 1878:

> Our institution [Z.C.M.I.] . . . has carried many a struggling enterprise; it has been the beast of burden for almost every institution and every establishment and railroad, almost, in the country. It has accomplished an immense amount of good, far more than the mere paying of dividends, although it has done this to a surprising extent.[77]

Following the lead of Z.C.M.I., local cooperatives also limited dividends and devoted earnings to the promotion and expansion of cooperative butcher shops, blacksmith shops, dairies, carding machines, gristmills, sawmills, tanneries, boot and shoe shops, molasses mills, furniture shops, and enterprises of a similar character. Many village cooperatives used their first dividends to buy threshers and mowing machines for neighborhood farmers. The various cooperative stores also supported one another's cooperative mills and factories. Upon entering a cooperative store in Cache Valley, for example, one might find shoes and harnesses manufactured in Smithfield, brooms from Millville, woolen goods from Franklin, tinware from Richmond, shingles from Mendon, window casings from Logan Second Ward, hand tools from Logan First Ward, meat from Wellsville, and cheese from Hyrum — all from Cache Valley shops established and operated by cooperatives. Most co-ops had three or four such subsidiary industries.[78]

Perhaps the most consistently uniform connection was that between the cooperative store and the cooperative livestock herd. In the cooperative herds of the '50's and '60's each sheep and cattle owner marked his individual animals and combined his flocks and herds with those of others to be herded on nearby ranges by one or more persons, sometimes boys, appointed in the ward priesthood meetings. At shearing and lambing times, and when cows came fresh, each owner took out his own animals from the herd and kept them at home until they could be returned to the herd again. As the number of livestock in the territory increased, under the stimulus of the Deseret Agricultural and Manufacturing Society, sheep and cattle herds were separated and the owners and the herder came to an agreement under which each owner was entitled to a certain number of pounds of wool and head of lambs for each hundred head of mixed sheep. One disadvantage of this arrangement was the complicated bookkeeping required:

> When the number of sheep owned by one man was such that he was entitled to a specified number of lambs, plus a fraction of another, he was credited with that fraction, and each year and generation that fraction became more complicated. Many members had such imaginary animals as 7/12 or 19/48 of a sheep to their credit.[79]

Beginning in 1869, church leaders counseled the abolition of individual ownership of the sheep and the formation of a cooperative sheep association, in which each person, including the church, turned their sheep over to the co-op herd in return for an equivalent number of shares in the association. The herd was then managed by an elected set of directors and appointed managers, and profits were distributed according to the shares held.[80] Most of these associations were incorporated after the passage of a suitable incorporation law in 1870, and many of them are still in existence. Partly as the result of this cooperative arrangement, and partly due to the increase in the number of cooperative woolen mills, the number of sheep in the territory rose from approximately 60,000 in 1870, to more than 1,000,000 in 1890.[81] Through similar cooperative arrangements, the quantity and quality of cattle in the territory greatly increased.

CHURCH ASSISTANCE TO Z.C.M.I.

A number of interesting problems confronted Z.C.M.I. during its first quarter of a century. In the solution of each of these the church and its trustee-in-trust played a role consistent with the importance attached to the wholesale institution in the building of the Kingdom. The first of these problems grew out of a transportation tie-up during the winter of 1871–1872. Heavy snows delayed for four months the shipment of almost $120,000 worth of merchandise its buyers had ordered in the East. Payment for most of this merchandise fell due thirty days after date of the invoice, which was, of course, long before the shipment arrived in Salt Lake City for sale. Z.C.M.I. was hard pressed to obtain the cash with which to meet this heavy shipment. Determined to assure the financial soundness of the institution, Brigham Young, as trustee-in-trust of the church, loaned the company 200 Utah Central Railroad bonds (valued at $160,000), without interest, to be used as collateral in borrowing the money to meet its notes coming due. These bonds were sold to Union Pacific soon afterward, and the church apparently devoted $100,000 of this sum toward the purchase of Z.C.M.I. capital stock in 1872 in order to give the institution a more solid basis.[82]

An even more serious problem was presented as the effects of the Panic of 1873 spread to Utah. In the latter part of 1873, Z.C.M.I. owed more than half a million dollars, without a reserve sufficient to carry the debt. Mastery of this problem occupied the personal attention of Brigham Young for many months, he having assumed the presidency of Z.C.M.I. for the purpose. He called W. H. Hooper, territorial delegate to Congress and a man of wide mercantile experience and valuable eastern contacts, to superintend Z.C.M.I. during this period.[83] H. S. Eldredge, who had served the church as buying agent on many occasions, was called on a mission to negotiate with the eastern creditors of Z.C.M.I. Eldredge succeeded in getting extensions of credit amounting to $467,913.48 from firms in Boston, New York, Chicago, St. Louis, and Omaha. James Linforth, formerly a church agent in London, went to San Francisco for the same purpose and obtained credit extensions amounting to $99,110.04 in that city.[84] The interest rates on these extensions varied from 7 to 12 per cent. The ease with which Eldredge and Linforth obtained these extensions in a period of financial stringency was apparently due to their timely use of the credit standings of Brigham Young and of the church. R. G. Dun and Company recognized the importance of Z.C.M.I.'s backing by reporting: "At the back of the Institution is of course . . . the whole body of the Mormon people, and so long as they have a dollar, just so long will the support be given this concern."[85]

In the meantime, the institution retrenched by selling its retail dry goods and retail grocery departments, and by abolishing the clothing, trunk, and produce departments, thus paying off $497,000 in credit extensions by October 1874.[86] Credit renewals later made possible the reopening of several of its retail departments, and by April 1875, a year and a half after the difficulties started, Z.C.M.I. was in a sound enough position to consider the erection of its own facilities. The church agreed to subscribe for an additional 500 shares ($50,000), probably in tithing produce, materials, and labor, to make the construction possible. A building with a frontage of 50 feet and a depth of 318 feet was completed on the east side of Main Street, between South Temple and First South streets in Salt Lake City. Three stories high, with a full basement in addition, the building was completed in March 1876 at a cost of $136,544. All departments were transferred to the new store except the drug, wagon and machinery, and produce departments. Another addition was completed in 1880, at a cost of $50,000, which gave the institution an additional fifty foot frontage and increased the store space to 12,000 square feet. The building was expanded still further in 1891 by the erection of the North addition — a one-story building with a frontage of sixty feet, costing $20,000.[87] These expanded facilities resulted in substantially the same building as that occupied by the firm today. In terms of physical facilities Z.C.M.I., during the first fifty years, was on a par with similar establishments in major eastern cities.

Shortly after Z.C.M.I. had recovered from the effects of the Panic of 1873, another problem was posed with the attempts of the Collector of Internal Revenue to collect taxes on the institution's scrip. As with many western establishments, Z.C.M.I. had been operating in an economy almost completely devoid of United States money.[88] It had adopted the policy of paying its employees one-third in cash, and the remainder in "Z.C.M.I. scrip," or orders payable in company merchandise. This scrip was of unquestioned advantage to Z.C.M.I., as it was to the local cooperatives which accepted it at full value and used it in making purchases from Z.C.M.I. By the use of the due bill system, according to Professor Spahr who was considerably impressed with it, "the early Mormon settlers . . . got along with even less money than other primitive communities."[89] The orders also facilitated the granting of credit, for a customer could borrow from Z.C.M.I. by giving his note at the office and receiving scrip to the amount of the face value of the note. The scrip could then be used in making purchases at Z.C.M.I. or at any other establishment which would honor them. This widely circulated scrip bore considerable resemblance to money, and after 1873 was beautifully lithographed in denominations of 25 cents, 50 cents, and one, two, three, five and ten dollars. Approximately $20,000 of these bills, sometimes called "Co-op Shinplasters," enjoyed more or less continuous circulation between 1873 and 1878.[90]

On July 20, 1878, O. J. Hollister, U. S. Collector of Internal Revenue in Utah, and no friend to the Mormons, demanded a payment of $9,000 upon the orders of Z.C.M.I. issued from October 1876 to April 30, 1878.[91] Two additional $500 fines were assessed by the Commissioner of Internal Revenue in Washington on the orders issued during the month of May and June 1878.[92] These assessments, which were paid under protest, represented a tax of ten per cent on the scrip and were made on the ground that the scrip was being used as money. Hollister also gathered evidence in relation to the scrip issues of local Mormon cooperatives, and claimed that $50,000 (representing a tax on $500,000 in scrip) was due the government for scrip issued between

October 1876 and July 1878.[93] The most important of these were also required to pay ten per cent fines.

The church was greatly interested in these cases, and assigned its lawyers to work on them, because many church institutions, including the tithing offices, used similar scrip. While an appeal was being made the institution devised a new system of orders which would not be subject to taxation. On November 30, 1878, a total of $31,105.25 in old orders was destroyed.[94] The new orders were also assessed, however, and on August 22, 1879, an additional tax of $6,810.92 was paid the government under protest, making a total tax paid of $16,810.92. The institution's appeal was finally sustained on March 17, 1884, and the full sum was returned in January 1885, almost seven years after it was paid. Smaller cooperatives not involved in the court case were not refunded their protested assessments until 1898.[95]

DECLINE OF LOCAL COOPERATIVES

The retailing and industrial cooperatives which formed such an important part of the system established in 1869 did not flourish as did Z.C.M.I., although the latter seems to have maintained a liberal credit policy toward all member institutions. With some local cooperatives, the periodic depressions in trade brought about failure. With others, an excessively liberal credit policy with individual consumers was decisive. Poor and discontinuous management, particularly during periods of harassment by federal authorities, also caused difficulties. Few cooperatives survived the intense "persecutions" and prosecutions of the late 1880's.

The dominant tendency, however, was not the discontinuance of the cooperative as a business, but the gradual disappearance of its cooperative characteristics and its gradual replacement by private enterprise. Little by little, local business men acquired control of most local co-ops during the first few years of operation and ultimately bought out the minority stockholders. As the stock drifted into fewer and fewer hands, public interest diminished, and in time those holding the bulk of the stock began increasingly to regard the enterprise as a personal one. Of course, this was contrary to the original intent, but the church found no effective way of combatting the tendency. These closely controlled stores were really private enterprises, but continued for a time to enjoy the monopoly associated with church sponsorship and exclusive trading. Ultimately, however, the expansion in population coupled with the gradual abandonment of cooperative principles led to a considerable amount of criticism of the stores by consumers and by individuals who wished to establish competitive stores.

Fully cognizant of this trend toward free, private enterprise, President John Taylor and his colleagues in the First Presidency, on April 11, 1882, officially opened the field of retailing once more to individual Latter-day Saints. An epistle was printed for distribution to bishops, stake presidents, and other church and community officials declaring the end of the exclusive support of local cooperative stores by the church. The following excerpts are typical:

A feeling had been manifested by some of our brethren to branch out into mercantile business on their own account, and his [John Taylor's] idea, as to that, was, if people would be governed by correct principles, laying aside covetousness and eschewing chicanery and fraud, dealing honestly and conscientiously with others as they would like others to deal with them, that there would be no objection on our part for our brethren to do these things; that it was certainly much better for them to embark in such enterprises than our enemies. . . .

Under existing circumstances, it had been thought best to throw open the field of trading, under proper restrictions, but that we should do all we could to confine it as much as possible in the hands of our own people, who were honorable and upright, and good Latter-day Saints. All should be subject to the principle of co-operation, and not recede a particle from it; but we should put our own business people in the place of outsiders, and sustain them, inasmuch as they sustained the principle of co-operation themselves by acting honorably in their dealing, paid their tithing and donations, were willing to be counselled and advised, and had at heart the interest of the work of God.[96]

This decree created a minor boom in retail store construction in the early 1880's — a boom which inevitably overexpanded the retailing field, with a resultant heavy percentage of failures in the 1890's. Virtually all of these private enterprises, as well as the former cooperatives, patronized Z.C.M.I., so that the position of the Parent Institution was not affected by the decree.

OTHER MANIFESTATIONS OF COOPERATION

As we have seen, for many years after the beginning of the cooperative movement in 1868 the Mormons seem to have regarded cooperation as a distinctly Mormon way of doing business. Virtually every important enterprise organized by the Mormons after 1868 bore the name "cooperative." Mercantile cooperation was but the first step in a movement which saw the establishment of cooperative institutions in almost every realm of economic activity. Cooperative farming, cooperative herding, cooperative processing and manufacturing of grain, dairy products, leather, wool, cotton, and silk — cooperation in each activity and in each community was the dominant organizational pattern of Mormon economic life in the years immediately following 1869.

This spread of cooperation, it must be emphasized, was not a "natural" development. Cooperation was deliberately promoted by the church as a solution to its problems, both spiritual and material. Cooperation, it was believed, would increase production, cut down costs, and make possible a superior organization of resources. It was also calculated to heighten the spirit of unity and "temporal oneness" of the Saints and promote the kind of brotherhood without which the Kingdom could not be built. Cooperation was simply, or so they believed, the Mormon way of doing things,[97] the ultimate goal and inevitable tendency of which was the United Order of Enoch or "Order of Heaven."[98] "The time will come," said Brigham Young, "when this cooperative system which we have now partially adopted in merchandizing, will be carried out by the whole people, and it will be said: 'Here are the Saints.' The time will come when we can give all into the store house of the Lord and have our inheritances given out by those who will be appointed; and when we have had sufficient for the support of our families, the [surplus] supplies will be given into the storehouse of the Lord. Will there be any rich and poor then? No."[99] The president was trying to say that his goal was far more positive than that of driving Gentile businessmen out of the territory and protecting the church's temporal interests. The cooperative movement was just another stage in his incessant campaign to develop a completely self-contained Latter-day Saint community, with emphasis on local production of every needful thing, without financial or other aid from outside the realm of the church. If cooperation was practical in each separate field of economic activity, how much better a cooperative of cooperatives which would organize all fields of economic activity, under one directing head! This, as will be seen, is precisely what was attempted in 1874.

In the meantime, however, the church used the cooperative movement as a facility for organizing a number of large enterprises which had no immediate relationship to Z.C.M.I. and the local general stores and home industries. These included an iron enterprise, a commercial bank, a savings bank, and a number of textile factories.

Cooperative iron works. Under the general sponsorship of the church, the Union Iron Works was organized in 1870 to attempt the development of the resources of Iron Mountain. This association produced up to 2,500 pounds of "good" grey cast iron per day, and sold a variety of products to the silver and lead stamp mills at Bullion, Nevada.[100] The capital resources of this enterprise were strengthened in 1873 by the formation of The Great Western Iron Mining and Manufacturing Company, which imported engines, material, and machinery for moulding and casting iron, and constructed a substantial engine house, blast furnace, air furnace, pattern shop, and business office not far from Cedar City. Producing up to five tons of iron per day, the company turned out various pieces of cast iron, including stoves, flat iron, and mining machinery for sale in Nevada mining camps. Among other things, the company furnished the twelve life-sized iron oxen on which the baptismal font in the St. George Temple rests.[101]

Cooperative banks. A more important cooperative enterprise was the Bank of Deseret. At the time of the initiation of the cooperative boycott in the fall of 1868, William H. Hooper and Horace S. Eldredge, both prominent merchants, established a banking partnership. Other Mormon capitalists were invited to join the firm, and several did so. When Brigham Young, on private or church account (it is not clear which), became a leading stockholder in 1869, the bank was called "Zion's Co-operative Banking Institution," and its sign bore a representation of the All-Seeing Eye. In 1871, the bank increased its capital to $100,000 and incorporated as the Bank of Deseret, becoming the first "state" bank in Utah. Brigham Young was president of the institution. The "cooperative" bank further expanded in 1871 and, with a capital of $200,000, obtained a charter as the Deseret National Bank. It was the only Mormon commercial bank in Utah until 1881 and the leading bank in the territory until well into the twentieth century.

Because it cooperated in meeting the economic needs and social goals of the church, the historian, Edward W. Tullidge, regarded the Deseret National Bank as the "financial handmaiden" of the Mormon Church.[102] In 1873, as an immediate result of the financial panic of that year, Deseret stockholders and the church established Zion's Savings Bank & Trust Company to take over the savings department of the Deseret bank. The original officers and directors of the savings bank were largely church officials. The capital stock was originally listed at $200,000, of which one-fourth was paid up. Through its financial agent, James Jack, the church subscribed for one-half (2,000 shares) of the capital stock of the concern (par value, $50). Shortly after its organization, Brigham Young made the following statement in relation to Zion's Savings Bank & Trust Company, which will explain its purpose:

> This institution is a cooperative one, and we think it is likely to meet with favor. The interest allowed is at the rate of ten per cent., per annum, compounded semi-annually. It will be found of considerable advantage to those who wish to save money for the emigration of their friends, as the interest is large; and sums as low as $1 will be received, which, if continually added to, will soon reach a considerable amount, and the depositors will hardly miss the money. We expect in time to have branches of this Bank all over the Territory, and perhaps extend it into Europe, so that the Saints there may also have the advantage of a higher rate of interest. One important lesson is taught us by the late financial panic, and that is, to husband our own resources, and to avoid, as much as possible, all entangling alliances.[103]

Thus, the bank was intended to stimulate thrift, facilitate emigration to Utah, and mobilize savings for investment projects, particularly those in which the church itself was interested. Indeed, Zion's Savings claims to be "the first Western bank to make available long time loans."[104] During the first twenty-five years of its history, it made loans to Utah canal companies, railroads, real estate developments, salt companies, sugar companies, power companies, and, indeed, to the church itself, on such security as stocks, bonds, and mortgages. The "cooperative" nature of the bank was simply that it was a church or group enterprise rather than a purely private bank of the type that dotted the American countryside in the 1870's. The ten per cent interest, not at all unusual in the contemporary West, can be explained by the fact that returns on loans and investments could be very high, particularly just before and during the Panic which followed the organization of the bank. With the occasional assistance of the church, Zion's Savings Bank successfully weathered the crises of 1873, 1891, 1893, and 1932. Its resources grew from slightly more than $50,000 in 1873 to more than $50,000,000 in 1957.[105]

Cooperative textile factories. The greatest contribution of the cooperative movement to the industrial development of the territory, however, was in the field of textile manufacturing. Small "cooperative" mills were erected at Franklin, Idaho; Afton, Wyoming; Tuba City, Arizona; and in Hyrum, Ogden, Brigham City, Grantsville, Salt Lake City, Springville, Kingston, Beaver, Parowan, Washington, and Orderville, Utah. All of these were devoted to the production of woolen goods except the cotton factories at Parowan, Washington, and Springville, and the latter was converted into a woolen mill in 1875. Other woolen mills were projected and partially completed at Logan, Ephraim, and Cedar City, Utah, and in Paris, Idaho. The three cotton mills, of course, were established in the 1860's in connection with the Cotton Mission; the woolen factories were initiated during the cooperative movement of the 1870's, and most of them operated successfully, albeit on a minor scale, until the turn of the century. The census of 1880 shows twelve establishments manufacturing cotton and woolen goods, with a capital of $402,000, 306 wage-earners, and $136,763 value added by manufacture.

These factories were "cooperative" in the sense that the people in the locality participated by furnishing labor and local materials in return for stock in the enterprise, while the church and its leading capitalists furnished the necessary cash and/or the machinery which had to be imported from the East. Thus, there was cooperation between the community, the church, and private capitalists in financing the factory. This technique represented a conscious attempt to develop a manufacturing industry without the importation of capital from the East:

Some tell us that we want capital, and that we should send abroad and get men to come here with money to build factories. This is not what we need. If the cotton lord and the millionaire come here and hire you to build factories and pay you their money for their work, when the factory is erected they own it, and they set their price upon your labor and your wool or cotton — they have dominion over you. But if, by your own efforts and exertions, you co-operate together and build a factory, it is your own. You are the lords of the land, and if fortunes are made the means is yours and it is used to oppress no one. The profits are divided among those whose labor produced it, and will be used to build up the country. Hence it is not capital, that is, it is not so much money that is needed. It is unity of effort on the part of the bone, sinew, skill and ingenuity which we have in our midst, and which, in whatever enterprise has been attempted hitherto, under the direction of the servants of the Lord, with whole-souled unity on the part of the people, has proved successful.[106]

How much the Apostles were influenced in such views by their own and their followers' observations of English experience is difficult to say, but undoubtedly these had an influence.

"Cooperation" in textile and other manufacturing also implied an identity between the goals of the church and the objectives of management. The construction was superintended, and the concern managed and operated, primarily by persons appointed by general authorities of the church. These persons were expected to harmonize their decisions with the social and economic objectives of the church, even when this might necessitate sacrificing profits or increasing losses.

The two most important of these cooperative factories to be sponsored by the church were the Washington Cotton Factory, which for many years housed the largest asssortment of cotton machinery west of the Mississippi River, and the Provo Woolen Mills, which was the first large manufacturing establishment of any kind in Utah, and also for many years the largest woolen factory west of the Mississippi River.

The Washington Cotton Factory. As mentioned in Chapter VII, the Washington Cotton Factory was originally built in 1866–1867 in connection with the Cotton Mission. The original $25,000 structure was built largely with tithing labor and produce,[107] and additional wings and stories were added in 1868 and 1871, also with church assistance. The original $40,000 worth of machinery was provided by Brigham Young, as trustee-in-trust of the church.

As additional machinery was needed, Brigham Young suggested to the cotton missionaries in 1869 that they form a cooperative association, raise funds to buy additional machinery and supplies, and assume the responsibility for the financial success of the enterprise. The minutes of the conference summarized his message as follows:

> He [Brigham Young] asked the people to cooperate in raising cotton, wool and other raw materials, so, that when they choose, they may be separate from the wicked and be self sustaining. He said if the people would do this, they might have his woolen factory brought from the north and use it to work up the wool that can be raised here in such abundance. The people might enter into a cooperative association and have his [that is, the church's] cotton factory, allowing him an interest in it as a stockholder.[108]

Such an association was formed in April 1870 with the name "Zion's Co-operative Rio Virgen Manufacturing Association."[109] The leader of the cotton mission, Apostle Erastus Snow, was selected president, and the members of the board of directors were prominent ecclesiastical leaders in the southern settlements.[110] This association later incorporated and signed notes on $40,000 worth of cotton and woolen machinery which bore an annual rate of interest of ten per cent. Shortly after the association had been organized the woolen machinery was freighted to Washington.

At the same time, the new company authorized the superintendent to enlarge the factory further by purchasing additional cotton and woolen machinery in the East. Approximately $44,000 was expended in the purchase of looms, spinners, and carders, raising the capacity of the plant to 550 yards of cloth per day. All of the money for this machinery was "raised locally," and most of it consisted of contributions of grain, cotton, vegetables, and labor.[111] The end product of the factory was sold through cooperative stores in southern Utah, and to Z.C.M.I. in Salt Lake City. Sales to Z.C.M.I. were strategic because they provided the cash credits with which to buy dyestuffs, lubricating oil, and machinery replacements which had to be imported from California and the East.

Factory managers were often converts from the British Isles who had had experience in the textile factories of their homeland. Many of the operatives were also convert-immigrants. On one occasion the superintendent of the factory was called on a mission to England where his principal object seems to have been to convert and arrange for the immigration of suitable workers for the factory. He gathered several factory workers and their families in 1874 and brought them to America on the steamship *Nevada.* Their transportation, food, and clothing, were provided by the Perpetual Emigration Fund. Upon their arrival in the Salt Lake Valley, tithing teams and labor conveyed them to southern Utah. These operatives gave new impetus to the production of fabrics.[112]

The production of the factory suffered during the antipolygamy raids of the late 1880's, and in 1888 the capital stock of the company was transferred to the St. George Temple Association, an ecclesiastical association which also owned the St. George Temple, in trust for the church. The factory was finally closed in 1910 after almost a half century of operation.

Provo Woolen Mills. The discussions which led to the construction of the $300,000 cooperative woolen factory at Provo took place in the School of the Prophets at the time the cooperative movement was inaugurated in the fall of 1868. Provo was selected as the site for the woolen mills because of the excellent facilities for water power, because it was in the center of an excellent sheep-raising country, and because it was not far from the principal market in Salt Lake City. Eventually, it was also to be furnished with railroad facilities by the church-promoted Utah Southern Railroad Company. Under Brigham Young's leadership, the School of the Prophets effected an organization called the "Timpanogos Manufacturing Association," with the intention of raising money for the construction of the "Provo Co-operative Woolen Factory."[113] The factory buildings were completed in 1872, at a cost of about $155,000, with all of the labor and materials furnished by men from the surrounding area, who received stock in the enterprise for their contributions. Local governments in the county also assisted in the construction by furnishing tax wheat to feed the workmen. An estimated $100,000 in machinery was installed during the winter of 1872–1873. This included twenty-five small or narrow power looms and twenty broad looms, and more than a thousand spindles. By midsummer 1874, the factory operated 3,240 spindles, consumed some 300,000 pounds of wool per year, employed seventy mill hands, and was turning out more than five hundred yards of cloth per day. Most of the cash for the machinery was furnished by the church. By 1875, the company was handling half a million pounds of wool, costing some $125,000 per year; the number of employees had jumped to 125, earning an annual payroll of $60,000; and the factory was manufacturing 4,000 yards of cloth per week, valued at upwards of $125,000. The name of the company was changed in 1889 to the Provo Woolen Mills Company.[114] Total paid-up capital in 1873 was approximately $300,000.

The firm sold its blankets, shawls, yarns, overcoats, flannels, and underwear throughout the West. Indeed, almost half of the company's production during the period 1873 to 1900 found a cash market in eastern cities, San Francisco, and other areas outside Utah. The factory also served as a commission merchant in marketing the wool produced in the territory in excess of the factory's needs. In the year 1883, for example, the company's wool agency bought more than one million pounds of wool, which was about thirty-five per cent of the Utah wool crop in that year. Of this amount, roughly one-third was consumed by the factory, and the remainder was exported to the East. The factory continued to operate until 1932.

APPRAISAL OF THE COOPERATIVE MOVEMENT

In general, it can be said that Z.C.M.I. and its member cooperatives, and the Washington Cotton Factory, Provo Woolen Mills and other cooperating factories, were agents of the church in accomplishing desired social and economic objectives above and beyond those connected with the production, importing, and marketing of merchandise at reasonable prices. The executives of Z.C.M.I., to take the most important of the enterprises, did not neglect the pursuit of profits, as a perusal of its earnings history will demonstrate, but they did sacrifice the distribution of dividends when necessary to support and develop home industry. Moreover, under church influence, Z.C.M.I. stopped, or so it was claimed, "the old practise of dealing which prompted traders to increase the price of an article because of its scarcity." [115] Above all, Z.C.M.I. executives bore little resemblance to the sharp-practicing, profiteering speculators and freebooters who dominated much of the trade in the New West during the last half of the nineteenth century. The analogy of a resolute and responsible civil servant conveys more accurately the status and function of these and other Mormon business leaders. Among the Mormons the private capitalist was subordinated, but not by *dirigisme,* as in Europe today, as much as by the gratuitous submission of business to the priesthood with its broad, extra-economic conception of the welfare of Zion. The official Mormon view of the role of Z.C.M.I., expressed just prior to the official end of cooperation as an exclusive principle, was as follows:

> It has been the means as a distributor of imported goods, of furnishing merchandise at remarkably low prices, thus bringing them within the reach of the masses; it has been a regulator of trade; it has prevented "corners" in any article in general demand; it has kept large supplies at a convenient point for dealers in the various parts of the Territory, by which the people could obtain comforts at all seasons of the year without difficulty; it has also been a repository for many articles of home manufacture, by which they have been brought to the attention and patronage of the public.[116]

As reciprocation for the public functions exercised by Z.C.M.I., local cooperatives, and cooperating factories, the Mormon people were expected to patronize these establishments, and in some cases, violation of this principle brought excommunication from the church. Despite financial reverses, the church would not let the enterprises go under. Thus, "cooperation" meant not the practice of a certain form of business arrangement, but a partnership of church and business in building the Kingdom. Utah's cooperative concerns were unique, not because they were cooperatives, but because of the eccelesiastical participation and influence and the broad basis of public support.

The cooperative movement of the 1870's, in short, was simply another expression of the typical — by now, traditional — Mormon adherence to early ideals in seeking through collectivistic institutions to build and perpetuate the religio-economic Kingdom. It will not be surprising to learn, as in the next chapter, that the momentum of the movement did not stop until it had produced a comprehensive reorganization of Mormon society called the United Order of Enoch. Some of the contemporary opposition to these cooperative efforts, of course, was based on immediate economic self-interest. But the ridicule to which the Mormons were increasingly subjected in the national press for their solidarity in establishing and supporting cooperative stores and industries illustrates the degree to which the nation had come to embrace the apologetics for exaggerated private enterprise and uncontrolled laissez-faire in place of the traditional communitarian attitudes of antebellum democracy.

CHAPTER XI

The United Order of Enoch

The economic idealism which had been manifested in limited form in the Perpetual Emigration Fund, the consecration movement of the 1850's, and the cooperative movement of 1868–1869 contemplated an eventual comprehensive reorganization of society. What was needed, according to the early revelations still propounded by the church, was a system of relationships in which self-seeking individualism and personal aggrandizement would be completely replaced by common action, simplicity in consumption, relative equality, and group self-sufficiency. Much of the preaching in connection with the cooperative movement had alluded to the inevitability of instituting this more perfect society. "This co-operative movement," said Brigham Young in 1869, "is only a stepping stone to what is called the Order of Enoch, but which is in reality the order of Heaven." [1] In 1869 and succeeding years, sermon after sermon played upon the theme of unity and the necessity of extending the principle of cooperation to every phase of life.

The period of depression which followed the Panic of 1873 offered to Brigham Young and his associates precisely the opportunity they had desired to experiment more radically with the economic institutions of Mormon Country. That the Panic should have had any appreciable effect on the Mormon economy was due, of course, to the "entangling economic alliances" with the East which had been built up after the completion of the transcontinental railroad. Into the more or less self-enclosed system of the Mormons the railroad had catapulted an enclave of merchants, bankers, freighters, and prospectors. Although connected principally with the newly developed silver and lead mines in Utah, and with the older mines of Idaho, Montana, and Nevada, this enclave had punctured the official boycott which had attempted to isolate the Mormon economy from this newly developed commerce. By 1873, many hundreds — and perhaps thousands — of Mormon workmen were employed in these mines or otherwise dependent upon their operation. The pecuniary economy of the territory was almost entirely in Gentile hands. Of the seven banks in existence in Utah in 1873, six were initiated and owned by non-Mormons.[2]

The Panic of 1873 hit this enclave of "outsiders" with suddenness and severity.[3] The principal bank in the territory failed as the direct result of the Panic, and another failed when the mines closed down. During the twelve-month following the Panic, bank deposits in the territory dropped by approximately one-third.[4] Financial depression was converted into industrial depression as the mines closed down. The closing of the mines, in turn, affected the business of general stores, shops, and factories, and the market for agricultural produce. Thus, the depression penetrated in ever-deepening circles the heart of the Mormon economy. Tithing receipts in one valley dropped approximately thirty per cent in the first year after the market broke.[5]

A typical nineteenth-century response to panics and depressions was to attempt to insulate one's community from the spreading paralysis by greater attention to home industry and the inauguration of local self-help movements. If one adds a liberal mixture of religious idealism, and some "I-told-you-so's" in relation to the effect of the enclave, this was essentially the response of the Mormons. Under the stimulus of the church, each community was asked to extend the cooperative principle to every form of labor and investment, and to cut the ties which bound them to the outside world. The resources of ward members were pooled, and an attempt was made, under the aura of religious sanction, to root out individualistic profit-seeking and trade and achieve the blessed state of opulent self-sufficiency and equality.[6] This new order, recognized to be somewhat different from the law of consecration and stewardship, was called "The United Order of Enoch."[7]

THE BRIGHAM CITY COOPERATIVE

As first advocated during the winter of 1873–1874, the United Order, as it was usually called, appears to have been based upon the success of an experimental community which previously had been established by Apostle Lorenzo Snow in Brigham City, Utah. In 1864 Snow, who had been a student at Oberlin in the early 1830's, organized a mercantile cooperative in which a number of Brigham City people took shares.[8] As profits were made, members received dividends in kind, rather than in money. Cash resources were husbanded, ward members were encouraged to buy capital stock, and within four years the cooperative had accumulated sufficient funds to build a $10,000 tannery. The tannery soon produced all the boots, shoes, saddles, and harness needed in the community by using locally available hides. In 1870 the expanded Brigham City Cooperative Mercantile and Manufacturing Company founded a $35,000 water-powered woolen factory, which contained 200 spindles and seven looms and employed thirty-two hands. The policy of paying worker-capitalists with cooperatively produced goods was continued, and dividends were paid only in kind. By 1874 approximately forty branches or departments had been established covering almost every phase of industry and agriculture in the valley. The paid-up capital of $120,000 was owned by approximately 400 shareholders.

Almost every conceivable good and service, from brooms and hats to molasses and furniture was produced and sold in one of these departments. In addition to the general store, tannery, and woolen mill, the cooperative owned 5,000 sheep, 500 milk cows, and 100 hogs, and operated several farms devoted to specialized crops. A colony was established at nearby Mantua, Utah, to raise flax; and another near Washington, in southern Utah, to raise cotton and other semitropical products. Carpentry, brick, blacksmith, cabinet shop, and painting departments built homes and made furniture, while a public works department contracted with the county government to build roads, bridges, dams, canals, and public edifices. Nearly all the workmen in this village of two thousand people owned shares in "The Co-op" and were employed in one of the departments.

Brigham City came to be recognized as a "hive of industry" — one of the most prosperous and progressive settlements in the territory. Calculating that the cooperative was 85 per cent self-sufficient, the management paid 85 per cent of the wages and dividends in "Home D" scrip (scrip redeemable in products of the cooperative) and 15 per cent in "Merchandise" scrip (redeemable in imported merchandise). For the few items which had to be ordered from Salt Lake City, the cooperative traded locally produced leather, and some rather famous local cheese. In the single year 1875, the total production was valued at $260,000, of which $100,000 was said to have been reinvested in new cooperative enterprises.

When the Panic of 1873 struck Utah, Brigham City was left almost untouched, experiencing in that year its greatest expansion. The community, in fact, enjoyed a certain amount of notoriety. Newspaper reporters visited the area and reported such interesting features as the manner in which homes were built for the poor and widows; how a department was set up to provide labor for tramps and benefit from feeding them; how the cooperators planned to locate their shops and factories on a twelve-acre square around the center of town and run street cars from the square to various parts of the town; and how they maintained their own monetary and banking system. One reporter declared:

If the example of the inhabitants of this town was more generally followed, Utah would be far more prosperous and her people much better off. Our present suicidal policy of exporting raw materials and importing manufactured articles would be stopped, we would be far more independent of our sister states and territories; the financial panics of the east or west would not affect us; our people would all have good homes and enjoy more of the comforts of life than they can hope for under present regulations; and our children would stand a much better chance of receiving good educations and becoming useful members of society.[9]

Even social reformers in England heard of the cooperative community, and one of them, Bronterre O'Brien, wrote that the Brigham City Mormons had "created a soul under the rib of death."[10] Edward Bellamy paid them a week's visit, and may have received some of the inspiration for *Looking Backward* while observing their system.

Brigham Young seems to have been impressed with the manner in which Apostle Snow had succeeded in mobilizing labor and capital for the promotion of home industry and agriculture. The people were achieving unity and the whole system was based upon recognized corporate procedures and law. "Brother Snow," he said, "has led the people along, and got them into the United Order without their knowing it."[11]

When Brigham Young went to southern Utah in the winter of 1873–1874, therefore, the desirability of improving on the economic organization of Mormon communities, as in the case of the Brigham City example, seems to have been on his mind. In one of his talks given on the way south, he outlined his concept for a Utah Utopia. Instead of having every woman getting up in the morning and fussing around a cookstove or over the fire, cooking a few indigestible slapjacks for two or three or half a dozen persons, he said, he would have a village dining hall a hundred feet long with a cooking room and bakery attached. This would mean that most of the women could spend their time profitably making bonnets, hats, and clothing, or working in factories. Confusion in the dining hall could be avoided by installing a system by which each person could telegraph his order to the kitchen, and this order would be conveyed to him by a little railway under the table. "And when they have all eaten the dishes are piled together, slipped under the table, and run back to the ones who wash them. We could have a few Chinamen to do that if we did not want to do it ourselves." In order to remove the laborious burden of big family washings, he suggested they have cooperative laundries. These would not only relieve the women from drudgery, but would also "save the husbands from steaming walls, soap-suds, and ill-temper."

The community would eat together, pray together, and work together. City streets would be graveled and paths paved. Evening schools would furnish fruitful recreation and improvement. Each branch of industry would be organized according to a rational plan; and there would be no work on Sunday. "Half the labor necessary to make the people moderately comfortable" under their present arrangements, he said, would make them "independently rich" under this system. "A society like this," he concluded, "would never have to buy anything; they would always make and raise all they would eat, drink and wear, and always have something to sell and bring money, to help to increase their comfort and independence."[12] These thoughts — the possibility of setting up "families" of Saints in each settlement — were said to have been in the president's mind as he journeyed south in the fall of 1873.

THE UNITED ORDER MOVEMENT

When Brigham Young arrived in southern Utah for his winter visit in 1873–1874, he found the town of St. George to be in particular need of economic revitalization. The shutdown of mines in southern Nevada had closed off a lucrative market for southern Utah produce and labor, and periodic drouths and floods, and two successive annual visitations of grasshoppers, had depleted their stores and brought the community to the verge of destitution. Some way had to be devised to bring a livelihood for the hundreds of underemployed laborers and farmers. Moreover, in a previous visit, the president had initiated the construction of a temple in St. George. Economy in the use of labor was therefore essential, not only to increase the production of food and feed, but to liberate the labor force needed to complete in the shortest possible time this large religious structure.

After a series of talks and conferences in which local members indicated their enthusiasm for an economic reorganization, the president organized the United Order of the City of St. George. "Now is the accepted time," he said, "but if we are not disposed to enter into this Order, the curses of God will come upon the people . . . the time has come for this work to be commenced." About 300 persons (nearly all the adults in the city) subscribed their names on the United Order roll.[13]

While in retrospect the St. George order seems to have been particularly adapted to the needs of southern Utah communities, great care was taken in forming it because it was to be the model upon which about a hundred others would be constructed throughout the territory. The constitution, for example, is a document of great importance because of its subsequent adoption in substantially the original form by the church-at-large. It begins with a preamble which reflects both the self-sufficient goals of the church and the influence of the Granger Movement:

> Realizing the signs and spirit of the times and from the results of our past experience, the necessity of a closer union and combination of our labor for the promotion of our common welfare:
>
> *And whereas:* — we have learned of the struggle between capital and labor — resulting in strikes of the workmen, with their consequent distress; and also the oppression of monied monopolies.
> *And whereas:* — there is a growing distrust and faithlessness among men in the political and business relations of life, as well as a spirit for extravagant specula-

tion and over-reaching the legitimate bounds of the credit system; resulting in financial panic and bankruptcy, paralyzing industry, thereby making many of the necessities and conveniences of life precarious and uncertain.

And whereas: — our past experience has proven that, to be the friends of God we must become the friends and helpers of each other, in a common bond and brotherhood.

And whereas: — to accomplish such a desirable end and to become truly prosperous, we must be self-sustaining, encouraging home manufacturing, producing cotton, and other raw materials; and not only supply our own wants with manufactured goods, but also have some to spare for exportation, and by these means create a fund for a sure basis upon which to do all our business.

And whereas: — we believe that by a proper classification of our labors and energies, with a due regard to the laws of life and health, we will not only increase in earthly possessions, at a more rapid rate, but will also have more leisure time to devote to the cultivation and training of our minds and those of our children in the arts and sciences.

And whereas: — at the present time, we rely too much upon importation for a large share of our clothing and other necessities; and also bring from abroad many articles of luxury of but little value, for which we pay our money, most of which articles could be dispensed with.

And whereas: — we believe that the beauty of our garments should be the workmanship of our own hands, and that we should practice more diligently economy, temperance, frugality, and the simple grandeur of manners that belong to the pure in heart.

And whereas: — we are desirous of avoiding the difficulties above alluded to, and feeling the necessity of becoming a self-sustaining community, fully realizing that we live in perilous times, socially, morally, politically, and commercially.

Therefore, be it resolved: — That we, the undersigned, being residents of the places set opposite our respective names, do hereby, of our own free will and choice, and without mental reservation, or purpose of evasion, and also without any undue influence, constraining or coercion having been used by any party whatever, to direct and guide us in this action, — mutually agree, each with the others, and with our associates and successors, to enter into and form a co-partnership for the purposes and subject to the provisions as herein set forth.[14]

The provisions of the constitution include three significant features. First, each person in the community was asked to contribute his economic property to the Order in return for equivalent capital stock. The Order would thus be provided with the enterprises and the capital with which to commence its operations. Each member also pledged all of his "time, labor, energy, and ability." All of the property turned over to the Order, and all of the labor of those joining it, became subject to the direction of an elected Board of Management. Second, a number of articles included pledges to encourage home manufactures, cease importing, and deal only with members of the Order. All members were asked individually to signify their willingness to subsist on the products of the Order. Finally, there was to be spiritual as well as temporal "union." A long list of rules was drawn up according to which the community should live. There was to be no lying, backbiting, nor quarrelling. All were to live as good Christians ought to live; above all, they were to live frugally. They were to pray daily, not use liquors or tobacco, tea or coffee, and they must obey their leaders. As a part of the process of joining the United Order, each person was rebaptized in a ceremony in which he pledged to obey the rules of the United Order.

The newly instituted Order immediately began to process applicants, receive property, and organize for work. More grain was planted, the production of cotton was doubled, attention was given to the improvement of livestock, leather was tanned locally, hats were made of native materials, and agents were appointed to trade molasses and wine for such items as the community had to import from northern Utah and elsewhere. The whole community was managed as one vast enterprise. Small, inefficiently worked fields, which had suffered from fragmentation, were combined, as were labor and capital resources, and the marketing was handled on a unitary basis. Several new industries were started, and the Washington cotton factory and St. George cooperative were associated in the Order. The general impression one gets from a perusal of their records is that labor was applied more economically than under previous individualistic institutions, but that less attention was paid to the proper use and maintenance of tools and equipment. There was often dispute, even at the outset, over the pricing of labor and the products of labor, and, in general, over the use of the common product.

Immediately after the organization of the St. George United Order, corps of church authorities visited the twenty or more communities elsewhere in southern Utah and organized each into a United Order after the pattern of the St. George model. Then, in the spring of 1874, Brigham Young and other general authorities moved north from St. George organizing each of the thirty or more settlements they visited along the way into a United Order. When they reached Salt Lake City, in recognition of the practical impossibility of establishing a city-wide United Order in that place, they organized separate United Orders in each of the twenty wards. Teams of apostles then visited each of the thirty or more wards and settlements north of Salt Lake City and organized each into a separate United Order. Later, United Orders were established in each Mormon colony founded in northern Arizona and southern Nevada, and in new settlements opened up in Utah. All told, about 150 United Orders were organized. A central United Order was set up in Salt Lake City with Brigham Young as president to coordinate and direct the entire movement. All of the orders operated formally under a constitution and bylaws, and nearly all were legally incorporated. No count has been made of their combined net worth, but it would surely have amounted to several millions of dollars.

In the sermons, letters, and circulars which were delivered and circulated in connection with the organization of these orders, stress was given to three objectives: (1) The need for greater economic unity to fight depression, unfriendly merchants, and poverty; (2) the need to cut down imports, which had begun to rise, despite the boycott, in 1872–1873; and (3) the need to pool surplus capital to initiate new industries, develop new resources, and establish new colonies. It was clear to all that the United Order was an attempt to retard, and, if possible, to prevent, the development of a market-oriented economy dependent on extensive importation and exportation. The United Order, in fact, was a deliberate flight from the gradually developing exchange economy into the less advanced, but more autonomous, self-sufficing household and village economy of the frontier. To the anti-Mormon *Salt Lake Daily Tribune,* "the Prophet's idea of embarking in the many and varied industries necessary to supply the wants of the community and thus render them independent of the outside world" was "the most preposterous and crackbrained fantasy that ever deluded the judgment of a spiritual or temporal leader."[15] This opinion, of course, was no deterrent, and served, if anything, to solidify Mormon support behind the plan's objectives. There was no opposition movement within the church comparable to the Godbeite movement which fought the measures of 1868–1869. Many Mormons saw it as a longed-for attempt to eliminate the profit motive and institute a more perfect Christian society. Others were still sufficiently reminiscent of early trials and persecutions to welcome any scheme which had any chance of lessening the "tribute" which they thought the territory was paying to its "enemies."

TYPES OF UNITED ORDERS

Four kinds of United Orders can be distinguished. First, there were the St. George-type orders in which persons in the community contributed all of their economic property to the Order and received differential wages and dividends depending upon their labor and the property contributed. Gains were achieved through the increased specialization of labor and the rationalization of agriculture by cooperative farming. However, in most of these communities a few residents failed to join, and this caused some practical problems which were not always satisfactorily resolved. Equally important were the frequent disagreements over the use of property and the rewards of labor. Each family was given "credits" for work performed and for dividends earned on capital stock. Each family was also permitted to make regular withdrawals in the form of consumer goods and services. The most persistent questions were: Should persons who were ill, or who had large families, or who were lazy, be permitted to overdraw their credits? To put it more precisely, should the Order be conducted as a "well-regulated family" with each member contributing according to his ability and drawing from the storehouse according to his need? Church officials usually left it up to the locality to decide this basic question, but advised that if there was serious division over this question, this was a sign that the people were not quite ready to live "the Gospel plan." Church officials, however, advised all that "the grand feature of the Order is retrenchment," for only in that way could the desired investment in the future be made.

Approximately half of these orders lasted no more than one year, the most common cause of difficulty being disagreement over the practical workings of the plan. One critic called it "Priestcraft instead of Priesthood."[16] The response of Apostle Erastus Snow, the "Apostle of Southern Utah": "I beseech all the Saints to refrain from attributing our failures to the Lord."[17] In some cases, individuals with property lacked faith in the ecclesiastical officials who bore the major responsibility in making decisions. In others, the industrious hated to share with the indolent. In still others, leading figures revolted at the evident waste and improvidence. In all cases where the operation of an order created division in the community which threatened the health and growth of the local church organization, no effort was made to perpetuate the order. At the time the St. George Order was dissolved in 1878, only a handful of St. George-type orders remained.

A second type of United Order did not involve the consecration of all one's property or labor, but contemplated an increase in the community ownership and operation of cooperative enterprises. This is the Brigham City plan, and was introduced in communities where the cooperative system was already widespread. Thus, the United Order was simply used as a device to reinforce and extend the cooperative network already in existence. The rebaptisms and the adoption of a set of United Order rules, however, were insisted upon. So far as organization was concerned, an elected United Order Board of Management replaced the Board of Directors of the cooperative, and the community structure remained virtually as before except for the progressive spread of cooperative labor and enterprises. Among the towns organized in this fashion which have been studied were Brigham City and Hyrum, Utah, and Paris, Idaho. As with the Brigham City Cooperative, the Hyrum and Paris co-ops began with a general store which plowed back its earnings into cooperative sawmills, lath and shingle mills, blacksmith shops, tanneries, boot and shoe shops, millineries, sheep and dairy herds, and creameries. The Hyrum co-op was based upon an exploitation of the grazing and timber resources in Blacksmith Fork Canyon, in northern Utah, and when those resources were about exhausted in the 1880's, the

Hyrum cooperatives began to fail. The Paris co-op was based primarily upon the rich grazing lands in Bear Lake Valley and adjoining canyons and the knowledge of cheese-making of Swiss immigrants. Branches of this cooperative functioned until late in the 1880's.

The fortunes — or misfortunes — of the Brigham City Cooperative are perhaps symbolic of the difficulties experienced by many cooperative communities. During the years 1877–1879 its woolen mill was destroyed by fire; an "unfriendly" federal official placed an embargo on the withdrawal of timber from the area in which its steam sawmill was operating; an "unfriendly" tax collector assessed a tax of $10,200 on its issues of scrip; and the grasshoppers destroyed much of the grain crop. The enterprise began to retrench in 1879 and most of the cooperative enterprises were liquidated in 1885 when Superintendent Lorenzo Snow was sentenced to the penitentiary for the practice of polygamy. Even before these disasters, however, Apostle Snow was experiencing difficulty in superintending the forty or more separate enterprises operated by the Brigham City Order. In a little-known letter to Brigham Young in 1877, Snow described his problems as follows:

> Over one thousand persons, little and big are depending entirely upon the Institution for all their supplies, for their food, their clothing, and all their comforts and conveniences. Over one thousand more living in our City are more or less dependent upon this Institution because in its progress it has gradually monopolized and gathered to itself all the main arteries and channels of business. . . .
>
> When Israel left their leeks and onions by the direction of Moses they looked to him for their supplies, and became very quarrelsome and troublesome whenever they failed. This is a feature in the United Order which I contemplate with no small degree of anxiety, viz., concentrating a multitude of individual responsibilities upon one man or a few men. One man may assume the responsibility of looking after the general interest of a community but to be required to provide for their daily wants, their food and clothing, one might do very well in prosperous times, but not very desirable in a financial crisis unless abounding in resources.[18]

Feeling that, as he expressed it, he had an "elephant" on his hands, with accumulating responsibilities that were "difficult or even impossible to discharge," Snow may have been not unwilling to disband the Order in the early 1880's after misfortune had struck.

A third type of United Order was essentially a modification of the Brigham City arrangement. Designed for wards in the larger cities of the territory — Salt Lake City, Ogden, Provo, and Logan — a single cooperative or corporation was organized in each ward to promote some needed enterprise. All ward members were asked to participate in financing it. The theory seems to have been that, if economic reorganization was impossible because of a considerable number of Gentile residents, the wards could still contribute toward territorial self-sufficiency by initiating an industry whose products had been imported previously. Thus, while there would be little or no opportunity for cooperative labor, surplus capital would be mobilized to create employment and develop the territory. In Salt Lake City, for example, the Eighth Ward operated a hat factory; the Eleventh Ward, a tailor's shop; the Nineteenth Ward, a soap manufactory; and the Twentieth Ward, a boot and shoe shop, all of which were referred to as United Order enterprises. In Logan, the First Ward initiated a large foundry and machine shop in which were produced sawmills, planing machines, and various kinds of agricultural implements and tools; the Second Ward, in turn, operated a planing mill and woodworking shop in connection with seven sawmills, and a United Order store; and the Third Ward owned a dairy. Most of these specialized U. O. enterprises lasted until the middle 1880's, when the antipolygamy "Raid" and other factors compelled the abandonment of such group projects. Most of them continued operation under private auspices.

Perhaps the most interesting of the orders were those established on a communal plan. In some quarters this plan was called the Gospel Plan. Settlers contributed all their property to the community United Order, had no private property, shared more or less equally in the common product, and lived and ate as a well-regulated family. The best known of these communal orders was established at Orderville, Utah, but others functioned in Price City, Springdale, and Kingston, Utah; Bunkerville, Nevada; and in a number of newly founded Arizona settlements. These communities, with populations varying from fifty to seven hundred and fifty, achieved a remarkable degree of self-sufficiency. They ate at a common table and wore clothes from the same bolt of cloth. The labor of all was directed by a Board of Management, and their life was regulated by a United Order bugler who signaled the community to rise, to eat, to attend to prayers, to go to work, to return from work, and so on. Put to the test of living like the ancient Christian Apostles, the members appear to have lived and worked together in remarkable harmony. Most of these orders continued in operation until the antipolygamy prosecutions of the 1880's.

The experience of the Orderville United Order is instructive. Orderville, situated on the Virgin River in Long Valley, in southern Utah, was founded for the express purpose of establishing a United Order. And, indeed, the twenty-four families (150 souls) who founded Orderville were uniquely trained in precisely the type of disciplined cooperation required for a successful communal order. They were part of the group which had been called in the 1860's to form colonies on the Muddy River to raise cotton and to maintain a stopping place for emigrants and freighters on the way to and from California. These colonies were not a success, however. The valley of the Muddy was hot and dry, and subject to insect infestation, flash floods, and disease. The settlers eked out a living in a condition approaching outright destitution. Only the practice of mutual helpfulness and the patriarchal organization of the community made survival possible. When these colonists were recalled to Utah in 1870–1871, many of them went to Long Valley where, once more, cooperation and unselfish division of product facilitated survival.

The Orderville United Order was instituted in 1875, when all the property of the colonists, both real and personal, was deeded to the community corporation. This property included several hundred acres of land, houses, cattle, horses and mules, sheep, hogs, chickens, agricultural machinery and equipment, sawmills, and a large variety of provisions and supplies. Although each donor was given book credit for capital stock in the corporation according to the value of his contribution, it was formally agreed that such stock did not entitle the "owner" to dividends or to any share of the corporation assets. In a deeply moving religious ceremony, all participants agreed that all property would belong "to the Lord," and that each would be a good steward over his time and the property left in his charge.

By cooperative labor they built apartment house units or "shanties" in a semi-fort arrangement around the town square and constructed a large common dining hall in the center. At appropriate locations, they also built a United Order office and store room, shoe shop, bakery, blacksmith shop, carpenter shop, cooper shop, tannery, schoolhouse, telegraph office, woolen factory, garden house, and dairy barns and sheep sheds. Newcomers were invited to participate in this experiment in Christian living, and within five years, there were 700 persons in Orderville. Food was served by relays in the dining room, and women took turns doing kitchen duty.

The Order operated a number of farms, gardens, and orchards, including a cotton farm, a poultry project, three dairies, a sheep enterprise, a steam sawmill and water-powered gristmill, and several molasses mills — each in the charge of an appointed overseer or foreman. Almost complete self-sufficiency was attained. Out of local materials and productions they made their own soap, brooms, hats, containers, silk thread, leather products, furniture, grey goods, and linsey. United Order carpenters made the looms for their own woolen factory, while United Order midwives delivered their babies. The Order had its quota of blacksmiths, clerks, artists, musicians, and teachers, and even an herb doctor.

Order members produced an excess of furniture, leather goods, and other products which were sold in southern Utah communities to build up a capital fund with which to buy additional land and equipment. The Order also furnished lumber, tar, and labor for the construction of the St. George

Temple, and supported two members who helped to erect the temple at Manti, Utah. A number of gospel missionaries were also supported in England and Europe. Ten per cent of the "net increase" of the Order was paid to the church each year for tithing.

During the first two years the members worked without wages or wage credits. Each family was permitted to withdraw food and supplies from the storehouse according to need. Early in 1877, however, on the advice of Brigham Young, the Order inaugurated a system of bookkeeping which awarded compensation in the form of book credit for all work done. The scale of credits was uniform according to age, without differentiation as to the type of labor or occupation. Each assignment was considered the equal of every other assignment. No dividends were declared, so there were no property incomes. Each withdrawal was entered into a debit column. Even under this arrangement, however, it was agreed that those who had more credits than debits at the end of the year should consecrate to the Order "of their own free will and consent" all their surplus credit. All overdrawals or net debits were cancelled. The financial statements indicate that there was always a balance of credits over debits, showing remarkable discipline and self-restraint.

The principal problems of the Order were the lack of restrictions on new members, the growing discontent of the young people, the management of property, and the lack of wage differentials. Church officials advised them not to "overload the boat" by accepting too many new members, but the Order members were so charitable in this respect that population began to press upon their limited resources. The rules governing admission were, in general, moral and religious rather than economic. In a number of instances, the Order provided transportation for the families of prospective members too poor to pay their own way to Orderville. According to an officer, they believed that "it would be as wrong to deny them" the privilege of joining "as it would be for a Repentant believer to be denied of baptism."[19] Similarly, the Order was probably unduly generous in giving property to those who withdrew from the Order and went elsewhere.

Orderville had been founded in an atmosphere of dire poverty, and the common action which took place in the Order made it possible for members to eat and dress better than they had for years — better, in fact, than many residents in surrounding settlements where United Orders had not functioned successfully. When the Utah Southern Railroad was completed to Milford, Utah, however, the rich mines at Silver Reef, not far from Orderville, were exploited to the full. Within five years, more than $10,000,000 worth of silver was extracted. Orderville's neighbors, profiting from this boom, suddenly found themselves able to buy imported clothing and other store commodities. The Saints in Orderville became "old fashioned." Their floppy straw hats, "gray jeans," "valley tan" shoes, and one-room shanties suddenly became objects of ridicule and derision. Orderville adolescents began to envy the young people in other communities, and their discontent spread to the older members of the Order. Mark Pendleton relates the story of a certain young man who felt the need of a new pair of trousers:

As he gained in stature, the pants he wore seemed to shrink, but as there were no holes in them, and no patches, his application for a new pair was denied. But where "there is a will there is a way." There was a big crop of lambs that spring. When the lambs' tails were docked, the young brother surreptitiously gathered them and sheared off the wool which he stored in sacks. When he was assigned to take a load of wool to Nephi, he secretly took the lambs' tail wool with his load and exchanged it for a pair of store pants. On his return, he wore his new pants to the next dance. His entrance caused a sensation. The story is that one young lady rushed to him, embraced and kissed him. The president of the Order demanded an explanation, and when it was truthfully given, he said: "According to your own story these pants belong to the Order. You are requested to appear before the Board of Management tomorrow evening at half past eight, and to bring the store pants with you."

At the meeting, the young brother was commended for his enterprise, but was reminded that all pants must be made of cloth from the same bolt. However, to prove its good will, the Board of Management agreed to have the store pants unseamed and used as a pattern for all pants made in the future, and further, the young man in question would get the first pair. Mark Pendleton continues:

The tailoring department was soon swamped with orders for pants. The elders of the Order protested. The boys went to work, as usual, but loafed on the job. It was noticed that the everlasting pants worn by the boys were getting thin in spots, and even some holes had developed. These boys were often on their knees when at prayers, or when weeding in the garden, but not much time was spent sitting down. Why was this unusual wear on the seat of the pants? When the elders saw the boys going in groups to the shed where the grindstone was housed, they became suspicious and investigated. Yes, the boys were wearing out their pants on the grindstone. The elders protested and then capitulated. A load of wool was dispatched to Washington Mills to trade for cloth. The tailor shop was a busy place. The boys were hard at work. The pants rebellion was over! [20]

Church officials recognized that the future of Orderville children was not exactly propitious, though they might never know unemployment. While some of the older members of the Order compared their position with the days of poverty on the Muddy, Orderville youth compared its opportunities with those of young people in other communities who were acquiring property of their own. The solution to this problem recommended by the church was that a certain proportion of each year's income be set aside to buy capital stock for maturing young people. "In this way you will show to the rising generation that you have their interest at heart; and it will be the means of binding them more closely to your organization."[21] This remedy was applied too late to be effective.

Other problems related to the management of property and the payment of wage differentials. In the early 1880's, these were partially solved by contractual stewardships, in which individuals were given limited rights in the property they managed; and by allowing certain enterprising individuals, and those with heavy responsibilities, to earn higher wages than those with ordinary assignments. When a flood filled the bakery with sediment and caved in the brick ovens, they also abandoned the common table and distributed supplies to individual families for preparation and serving in their own individual apartments.

The community continued to experiment with improved institutions, with the encouragement and support of church officials, until the enforcement of the Edmunds Act drove most of their leaders into hiding, and caused some to be committed to the penitentiary. Church authorities counseled dissolution in 1885. In an auction in which each man was allowed to use his credits to buy the property of the Order, the common possessions of all were distributed among the one hundred or more families who had remained in the Order. There was little or no complaint over the procedure followed. With the disintegration of their collective institutions, after ten years of "cooperative living," the older members began to reflect on the advantages of their previously enjoyed communal existence over the encroaching spirit of competitive individualism. The chafing under restrictive regulations, the disagreements, the yearning for privacy were all forgotten, and their memories were sweet. Almost every published reminiscence of life under the Order mentions it as the closest approximation to a well-ordered, supremely happy Christian life that was possible of achievement in human society. When a number of Orderville families moved to Cave Valley, Chihuahua, Mexico, during the 1890's, they formed themselves into a United Order organization which closely resembled that under which they had lived in Orderville.

ACHIEVEMENTS OF THE UNITED ORDER

As previously indicated, the generalized United Order movement was over by 1877. By that time, the economy was not so depressed, the necessity of group action not so immediate, and the death of Brigham Young in that year removed its chief advocate. Only here and there, in isolated communities like Orderville and the Little Colorado settlements in Arizona, or in places like the Virgin River Valley in southern Utah, Cache Valley in northern Utah, and Bear Lake Valley in southern Idaho, where cooperative financing was the only method of progress, did United Order enterprises continue to function. Even in those areas private enterprise became almost universal in the late 1880's.

While it was (and is) common to say that the United Order was a failure because so many orders were disbanded so soon after their organization, there is much evidence in favor of the idea that they were originally designed as temporary organizations, and that no hope was held out that they would last longer than the depressed conditions which followed the Panic of 1873. Whatever the soundness of this hypothesis, Mormon leaders, as in other instances, were more interested in achieving goals than in making systems work.[22] If the goals were to diminish importation, increase production, increase investment, and diminish inequality among the Latter-day Saints, there can be no doubt (though it is difficult to cite concrete evidence) that much progress was made toward each of these goals. The entanglements produced by the coming of the railroad, which had been minimized but not eliminated by the cooperative movement and other activities of the School of the Prophets and the Women's Relief Society, were almost erased in many communities, and greatly reduced in many others. It is a testimony to the effectiveness of the cooperative and United Order movements that Mormon cooperative ventures and collective institutions had to be destroyed, as most of them were during the "Raid" of the 1880's, before the "peculiar" theocratic economy of Zion could be accommodated and absorbed into the general economy of the nation. Regardless of the fate of individual organizations, therefore, the United Order movement may be said to have promoted thrift and made possible a more rapid accumulation of funds with which to buy machinery and equipment; created additional employment for the Mormon people; and assured a more rapid development of resources, particularly in areas where Utah had a comparative disadvantage. The United Order, in other words, helped to keep Utah economically independent of the East longer and more completely than would otherwise have been the case.

The First Presidency, in appraising the influence of the United Order in 1877, expressed their belief that it had tempered the growing spirit of acquisitiveness and individualism with a more saintly selflessness and devotion to the building of the Kingdom. When "the good and prosperity of Zion" had been proposed in counteracting such adverses as the Panic of 1873, they wrote, the question too frequently asked had been "Will it pay?" Workmen required the highest wages they could extract, regardless of the difficulties the employer had in carrying on his business. With both labor and capital, the First Presidency continued, the welfare of Zion often had been secondary, and the elements around them went to waste, manufacturing failed to pay, trade languished, enterprise was checked, and many of the people were unemployed. The principles of the United Order had been urged upon the people to combat these forms of selfishness, and after three years of United Order preaching, they were able to see the possibility of "great improvement" in the devotion to building the Kingdom.[23] "It was not a part of this Order," concluded Brigham Young, "to take away the property of one man and give it to another, neither to equally divide what we possessed." Its primary purpose, he said, was "to afford to all the opportunity of enriching themselves through their diligence" and to devote the surplus property thus made available to the task of "carrying on the work of God generally." [24]

One phase of the Order, and of the "carrying on of the work of God generally," which is seldom recognized was the construction of temples at Salt Lake City, St. George, Logan, and Manti. On each of these four temples from two to three hundred persons were employed almost continually during part or all of the United Order period, and very often the activities of United Order enterprises were geared toward temple construction rather than toward purely economic ends. Each temple project involved hundreds of thousands of hours of labor, and massive quantities of rock and lumber. Some idea of their size and importance can be gleaned from the following tabulation:[25]

Temples Constructed in Utah, 1847–1900

Location	Years of Construction	Approximate Cost
Salt Lake City	1853–1893	$4,000,000
St. George	1871–1877	450,000
Logan	1877–1884	650,000
Manti	1877–1888	1,000,000

The Mormon temple, as is well known, was a structure in which marriages, baptisms, and other sacred ordinances were performed. Its construction was therefore the kind of other-worldly project which the preachments of the spiritual phase of the United Order tended to activate. Similarly, the voluntary cooperative activity involved in the construction and financing of these edifices was precisely the form of economic organization contemplated in the United Order. In dedicating the site for one of the temples, Brigham Young expressed official church policy with respect to the building of temples, as follows:

> We now call upon the people, through the several Bishops who preside in this and the neighboring settlements for men to come here with teams and wagons, plows and scrapers, picks and shovels, to prepare this ground for the mason-work. Let this work be commenced forthwith; and as soon as possible we

shall expect from fifty to one hundred men every working day throughout the season to labor here.

We intend building this Temple for ourselves, and we are abundantly able to do it; therefore no man need come here to work expecting wages for his services. The neighboring settlements will send their men, and they can be changed whenever, and as often as, desirable; and they can get credit on Labor Tithing or on Donation Account for their services, and we expect them to work until this Temple is completed without asking for wages. It is not in keeping with the character of Saints to make the building of Temples a matter of merchandise. . . .

We call upon the sisters also to render what assistance they can in this matter. They can do a great deal by way of encouraging their husbands and sons, and also by making clothing of various kinds for them, and in otherwise providing for them while they are working here.

Now, Bishops, if any person should enquire what wages are to be paid for work done on this Temple, let the answer be "Not one dime." And when the Temple is completed, we will work in God's holy house without inquiring what we are going to get, or who is going to pay us, but we will trust in the Lord for our reward, and he will not forget us.[26]

In order to carry out this policy, church authorities organized the Salt Lake, St. George, Logan, and Manti temple districts, comprising the stakes in the vicinity of each temple. Officers of the temple districts were charged with organizing the labor, produce, and cash resources within the district for the building of the temple. In most instances the trustee-in-trust placed at the disposal of each district the tithing paid by members living in the district during the period the temple was being constructed. Within each district, the presidents of stakes and bishops of wards were assigned the responsibility of supplying the construction needs of the temple from their ward or settlement. Each ward, then, under the chairmanship of the bishop, selected a temple committee, and these committees were responsible for organizing their areas and providing the needed assistance upon proper notice.

Within each district a number of industries were established to supply needed materials. Thus, each temple had its sawmills, lime kilns, rock quarries, and carpentry shops. Most of these industries contributed revenue to the temple fund by selling a part of their production on the market. For the utilization of donations in supplying its workers, each temple also had a dining hall, meat market, laundry, and general store. Nearly all of the hundreds of men engaged in obtaining materials, and in working on the temples were individual volunteers or were supported by local church groups through cooperative fund-raising ventures. All such men were called "temple missionaries." The contributions which went into the building of the Logan Temple illustrates the extent of the barter economy involved:[27]

Labor	$380,082
Wagons and teams	2,637
Farm produce	71,157
Livestock	29,472
Merchandise	30,231
Cash	93,484
Total	$607,063

Three-fifths of these contributions ($371,543) came from the 25,000 church members residing in the temple district, while approximately two-fifths ($214,653) was furnished by the trustee-in-trust of the church.[28] The trustee-in-trust contributions represented appropriations of tithing labor, tithing merchandise, tithing livestock, tithing produce, and approximately $35,000 in cash. Temple records indicate an enormous variety of objects donated toward the cause. As the superintendent wrote to one would-be contributor: "We shall be pleased to accept some fat sheep or anything else we can use, if it is the hide of a yellow dog, we can use that for many purposes." [29] Many of the materials used were produced in specialized cooperative and United Order enterprises.

ZION'S CENTRAL BOARD OF TRADE

The abandonment of the church-wide campaign to organize United Orders coincided roughly with the death of Brigham Young in 1877. John Taylor, who replaced Young as president of the church, viewed the United Order as "a step in the right direction," and as a desirable expedient in fighting the problems facing the church in 1874; but he and his associates seem to have recognized that some new type of economic planning must supplant the failing United Orders. While they were entranced with the beauty of the Gospel Plan so earnestly advocated by Brigham Young, they did not identify the ideal economic system of Mormon thought with the particular orders which Young had established. "We shall have a United Order by and by," said President Taylor. "But we have not yet had the order that we shall have." [30] With their petty restrictions on man's agency, the United Orders were neither popular nor practical, and they often produced precisely that disunity and division which they were intended to correct. The particular form of Brigham's United Order, they confessed, had been influenced to a considerable degree by the imperfect nature of the laws under which they were forced to live. The Lord would have no objection, they reasoned, if other organizational devices were tried which pointed to the same goals as the United Order, and, at the same time, effectively reconciled individual freedom and the welfare of the group. The independent Kingdom of God was still the object in view—there was still no thought of easing the adjustment to the institutions of private capitalism—but the Lord would not be displeased with them if they tried cooperation on a somewhat less intensive scale.[31]

The new organization developed to replace or supplement the village United Orders was called Zion's Central Board of Trade. As established in 1878, Zion's Central Board of Trade was an organization of religious and secular leaders, with John Taylor as president, William Jennings and Edward Hunter, vice presidents, and a board of directors of fifty men which included the "leading men" of each valley or stake. The organization was modeled after one which had functioned since 1872 in Cache Valley. Under the leadership of the manager of the Logan Branch of Z.C.M.I., Moses Thatcher, the twelve cooperatives in Cache Valley had agreed to offer uniform prices for the farm products brought to them for marketing, use their influence in improving the quality of products brought to them, and find markets for the exportable products of the valley.[32] Their aim in doing this was to eliminate the "peddlers and middlemen" who, allegedly, had "bought up everything for which a market could be found," at low prices, and "hauled it off" to sell in mining camps at enormous profits to themselves. The Cache Valley Board of Trade, as the organization established in 1872 called itself, could perform the marketing function itself and thus save "to the people" the profits which were going to outside middlemen. While a few independents and outsiders viewed the Board of Trade as a means of tightening the monopoly powers of the church-sponsored cooperatives, Thatcher saw it as the means of "regulating the commerce of producers and consumers and introducing a more healthy and stable condition of supply and demand."[33]

Faced with a general breakdown of cooperative institutions because of the failure of the United Orders, John Taylor saw the Cache Valley Board of Trade as the type of organization which, under church direction, would encourage and strengthen cooperative marketing, cooperative buying, the development of new industries, and the regulation of trade in the interests of the group as a whole; and, at the same time, prepare the way for a more completely cooperative society such as that contemplated in Mormon theology. Each valley, county, or stake, it was decided, should have a board of trade, and representatives of these could meet as a central board of trade at the time of the general conferences of Saints in April and October of each year. President Taylor could preside over these meetings, just as he presided over the religious conferences, and thus maintain an identity of means and ends between the church and the board of trade. Finally, the decisions would be made by consulting with "practical men"; that is, "the best" Mormon businessmen and farmers. By providing businesslike direction to the initiation and operation of programs aimed at developing the region, the board of trade could avoid the pitfalls of the ecclesiastically dominated United Order. Territorial or regional self-sufficiency would replace village self-sufficiency as the goal of the new plan, but the other goals of equality, resource development, and unity of action would remain.[34] "And should there at any time be anything wrong in our systems of doing business, tending in the least to prevent perfect union," a member of the First Presidency declared, the central board of trade could devise the necessary measures "and bring about a concert of action upon all hands."[35]

All of these ideas and proposals relating to what were called "the temporal interests of Zion" were presented to the general conference in October 1878 and approved "unanimously."[36] "If mistakes and blunders had been made in trying to establish the United Order," said President Taylor, "that should not prevent us from carrying out the revelations of God, to be united together in our temporal and spiritual affairs; for unless 'we were one,' we were not the Lord's. . . . All who felt to endorse and carry out the principles of union, as dictated by the Presidency and Twelve would say amen." A "hearty and universal response" was reported to have been given.[37] It was at the conclusion of this conference that Zion's Central Board of Trade was organized.[38] Later, Moses Thatcher, who was afterwards made an apostle, and several members of the Council of Twelve were sent out to organize a local board of trade in each of the stakes. Organizations were established in Bear Lake, Cache, Weber, Salt Lake, Davis, Utah, Sanpete, Juab, Millard, Sevier, and Washington valleys and counties in Utah, and also one in Snowflake, Arizona to serve Mormon settlements on the Little Colorado River.[39] It was intended that the board of trade organization be church-wide in coverage.

The declared objects of Zion's Central Board of Trade were as follows:[40]

1. To maintain a commercial exchange.
2. To seek remunerative markets for the produce of the brethren and help to bring to them as cheaply as possible what they have to buy.
3. To aid in organizing and sustaining such home industries as will tend to the independence and self-sustenance of the people.
4. To attempt to prevent the Saints from overstocking the market and introducing and sustaining among themselves hurtful competition.
5. To promote uniformity in the customs and usages of producers, manufacturers, and merchants.
6. To acquire and disseminate valuable agricultural, manufacturing, commercial, and economic information.
7. To bring home producer and manufacturer into close business relations with the consumer, preventing intermediate parties from exacting margins for

transacting business which, with a little forethought and care, the people, through the Board of Trade can do as well for themselves.

8. To help the producer fix living prices on the fruits of his own toil.

9. To foster capital and protect labor, uniting them as friends rather than dividing them as enemies.

10. To facilitate the speedy adjustment of business disputes.

11. To arrange for transportation.

12. Generally, to secure to its members the benefits of cooperation in the furtherance of their legitimate pursuits, and to unite and harmonize the business relations of the stake Boards of Trade.

Stated more succinctly, the Board of Trade movement was an attempt on the part of the church to get together a group of her best business and professional people to help work out solutions to the various economic problems which would arise from time to time. The organization would work down from the central board to the stake boards, and up from the stake boards to the central board during the conventions. The boards would represent a sort of "citizens' advisory committee" with an organization capable of bringing the various suggestions to a successful issue. The boards would "look after the manufacturing, mercantile, and other interests of Zion," as President Taylor stated, "and should there at any time be anything wrong . . . tending in the least to prevent perfect union, the necessary measures would be devised to remedy these things and bring about a concert of action upon all hands."[41] President Taylor added,

Our true policy is to make, as far as possible, at least what we need for home consumption, with an eye to future exports of those articles which we can sell abroad at a profit. To determine what can be produced and manufactured to the best advantage, on sound business principles, in this Territory, and to devise measures by which those articles can be produced for the benefit of the community and the advantage of all engaged in these enterprises, . . . are the purposes which will be served by the organization of Zion's Board of Trade.[42]

And when we get things into a proper fix we will pull with a long pull and a strong pull and a pull all together. We will strive to be one; . . . we will begin with this, and then cooperate in all the different Stakes, not only in our merchandising, but in our manufacturing affairs and in our producing affairs; and in everything it will be the duty of this general Board of Trade to regulate the interests of the whole community, honestly and faithfully, at least we will do it according to the best ability we have; and if there should be any mistakes arise, we will try to correct them; if they are on the part of the people, we will talk to them about it, if on the part of the institution, we will talk to its management about it. And we will keep working and operating until we succeed in introducing and establishing these things that God has desired, and until Zion shall be a united people and the glory of all the earth.[43]

It should be noted that a major instrumentality in carrying out many of these policies was intended to be Zion's Co-operative Mercantile Institution. To effectuate that purpose the directors of Z.C.M.I. were liberally represented on the central board of trade. Z.C.M.I. was specifically charged by the church with introducing more "justice" into the business relations of the territory. After its close call with bankruptcy in 1873, Brigham Young had tended to emphasize financial soundness in operating that institution, and this had caused some criticism. President Taylor took the attitude that since Z.C.M.I. was called "Zion's Mercantile Institution," it ought to operate, as the name indicated, in the interests of Zion. "While it is being sustained and helped by all," he declared, it ought in turn to "shield, protect and help all, that a mutual reciprocity of feeling and action may exist."[44]

The contemporary historian, Edward Tullidge, called the organization of the Central Board of Trade "the greatest industrial event that has occurred in the settling and growth of our Territory."[45] Of the many types of activities in which Zion's Central Board of Trade engaged during its six-year existence, the most fruitful was the sponsorship of a four-day convention in Salt Lake City from May 17 to May 20, 1881. Present at this conference were all the members of the Central Board of Trade and almost complete representation from the stake boards of trade. This group attempted a comprehensive review of the resources of Mormon Country, and discussed the possibilities of initiating home industries which would develop these resources in the following specified fields: iron, lead, glass, wool, clothing, silk, wagons and agricultural machinery, paper, leather, dairy products, flour, soap, sugar, matches, salt, glue, hats, horticulture, and animal husbandry. "Here is the grandest opportunity," wrote the editor of the *Deseret News,* "for the building up of a self-sustaining, industrial and powerful system of co-operative effort ever offered in the history of the world. . . . What is needed? Practical cooperation. Union of capital and labor, mutual interest between consumer and producer."[46]

In the case of each of the nineteen industry groups and fields of interest the conference appointed a permanent committee of leading men to study ways and means of developing the industry in question. The committee was also to take such action as might seem desirable, such as organizing a company, calling a special convention to further the industry, or publishing information with regard to proper practices. Active steps were taken to develop new manufacturing in nearly all fields, although the efforts were not always successful. Typical of the attempts to promote development were those in the fields of iron, sugar, and wagon and agricultural implement manufacture.

Iron. The Board of Trade convention appointed a committee to organize a company for the manufacture of iron and coke. The Utah Iron Manufacturing Company, with a paid-up capital of $50,000, was organized in August 1881. With financial and other assistance from the church, this company acquired coal and iron lands on Iron Mountain previously worked by the Deseret Iron Company, Union Iron Works, and Great Western Iron Company, and was prepared to experiment with iron manufacture when some of its claims were allegedly "jumped" by a wealthy non-Mormon, and the case remained in the courts until 1884. When the litigation was nearing completion the First Presidency of the Church, with the assistance of the Board of Trade committee, organized a new company called the Iron Manufacturing Company of Utah, with $250,000 capital stock. The church subscribed about one-fourth of the stock, including about $25,000 in tithing credit, for the patenting of iron and coal land claims, and for the support of laborers engaged in developmental activities. The Iron Manufacturing Company hired an experienced ironmonger and built a furnace, factory, and storehouse. Some twenty men were employed during the winter of 1883–1884. A small railroad, twenty miles in length — the Pioche and Bullionville Railroad — was purchased and rails, cars, and equipment were transported to southern Utah for use in carrying coal to the iron furnace. Another railroad was laid out, running from Iron City to the Utah Southern line at Milford.

In spite of the enthusiasm of all this preparatory work, however, there were some who doubted the wisdom of spending half a million dollars to develop an industry of such questionable profitability. A special Board of Trade committee was selected to make an exhaustive study and recommendation. The report of Apostle Moses Thatcher, as the chief investigator, was under consideration at the time of the commencement of the anti-polygamy crusade, which effectively forestalled these efforts to develop southern Utah's iron and coal resources.[47]

Sugar. A Board of Trade committee was appointed to study the relative advantages of sugar cane, grain sorghums, and sugar beets. At the instigation of this committee, the territorial legislature offered a bounty for the development of locally produced marketable sugar. After a considerable amount of experimentation, a small company was organized in 1886 to manufacture cane sugar. The principal product of these activities, however, was the formation, in 1889, of the Utah Sugar Company, which, as will be shown in a later chapter, figured prominently in the development of Utah's important beet sugar industry.

Wagons and agricultural implements. Of special interest to a predominantly agrarian society was the provision of cheap farm wagons and machinery. An outstanding Board of Trade committee gave serious attention to this industry. After the failure of at least two attempts to manufacture these items in Utah, the committee decided to organize a cooperative company to import wagons, carriages, implements, and tools. In 1883 the Co-operative Wagon and Machine Company was organized with a capital of $100,000. This company later merged with the Consolidated Implement Company to form the Consolidated Wagon and Machine Company, with a capital of $2,500,000. The latter company sometimes regarded as a "church" company, occupied a strategic position in this field in the intermountain area for almost four decades.

The three industries mentioned do not, of course, exhaust the efforts of the Central Board of Trade to stimulate home industry. In wool, silk, paper, leather, dairy products, soap, and salt manufacture Board of Trade committees took active steps to establish "cooperative" enterprises. Success crowned Board of Trade efforts in stimulating manufacturing in all of these industries mentioned with the exception of silk and soap manufacture, in which the local firms soon succumbed to "outside" competition.

The Central Board of Trade also sponsored an outstanding territorial fair in 1881, succeeded in reducing freight rates on agricultural exports from Utah, and found markets for surplus grain during the hard-hitting depression of 1884. Perhaps the least-known of its activities had to do with the resurrection of a plan to transport cheap coal from Coalville to Salt Lake City. The increasingly adverse fuel situation in Salt Lake City, and the opening of silver and lead mines in Park City in the late 1870's, led Board of Trade officials, the Presiding Bishopric of the church, and officers of the Ontario Mining Company of Park City to form, in December 1879, the Utah Eastern Railroad Company. With a projected capital of $700,000, they planned to build a railroad from Coalville to Park City, and from Park City to Salt Lake City, a distance of about fifty miles. In order to insure that Union Pacific — still regarded as "the great monopoly" — would not buy up a controlling interest in the road, three trustees were elected in whose hands was placed a majority, or $400,000, of the stock. This stock was to be inalienable for fifteen years. That is, the stock could be sold but would still be subject to the control of the trustees for voting purposes. Two of these trustees were members of the Presiding Bishop's Office; the other was a non-Mormon Salt Lake businessman.[48]

Large numbers of Latter-day Saints subscribed labor and cash to buy stock, the road was bonded, and construction from Coalville to Park City was completed in December 1880. The public subscription had been insufficient to pay even half of the cost of the iron and rolling stock, however, and the money for this purpose was advanced by the Ontario Mining Company in return for mortgage bonds and a bonus of treasury stock. This stock appears to have been given to the mining company by a Utah Eastern officer without the knowledge or approval of the trustees. Eventually, Union Pacific obtained the bonus stock, used it in electing its own officers and directors, and closed the railroad down in November 1883.[49]

Nevertheless, Union Pacific's "monopoly" was short-lived. With the active encouragement of Board of Trade members, the impudent little Denver & Rio Grande Western pushed into Salt Lake City in the early 1880's with competitive coal from the rich new mines in Carbon and Emery counties, in eastern Utah. An "outside" competitor had accomplished what the Mormons had sought in vain to do.

The activities of stake boards of trade were even more extensive, but can only be summarized here. These boards, being arms of the church as well as local representatives of the Central Board of Trade, were, in a sense, business agents of the stake presidencies of their respective stakes. The following activities are known to have been carried out by one or more of the stake organizations.

1. Stake boards of trade served as media through which contracts were acquired for the construction of the Utah Northern, Southern Pacific, and Denver & Rio Grande Western railroads. These contracts provided lucrative employment to hundreds of men, especially during winter months, and at the same time insured cooperative division of contracting profits. These group contracts also made it possible for Mormon laborers to practice, in their camps, the observances of their religion.[50]

2. Several of the stake boards of trade established a centralized marketing agency for the disposal of farm produce. For years the Cache Valley Board of Trade marketed almost all the butter, eggs, and grain which were shipped out of Cache Valley to San Francisco, Montana, and other large buying centers. The Salt Lake Board of Trade established a central wool-marketing agency which is reported to have increased wool prices to farmers and stockmen by a considerable margin.

3. Before the organization of the church-approved Cooperative Wagon and Machine Company in the late 1880's, several stake boards established agencies for the importation and retailing under cooperative principles of agricultural implements, wagons, and buggies.

4. In some instances a local board of trade actually set up agencies for the regulation of the prices of local farm and other products. The Snowflake, Arizona, board, for example, set prices on hay and grain.

5. There were cases in which local trade competition was effectively "regulated" by the industry-group concerned, under the direction of a board of trade, to prevent "excessive" price and product competition. An example of these activities was the regulation of the Cache Valley lumber industry by the Cache Board of Trade.

6. Several boards of trade made strenuous, and at times successful, efforts to reduce freight rates for local produce for export from the producing area,

and also on products imported into the local area. In the minds of several board of trade leaders, their outstanding accomplishment was countering the "monopoly" and "discriminatory tactics" of the Union Pacific Railroad Company during its heyday in Utah.

Although a creature of the First Presidency and general conference of the church, Zion's Central Board of Trade did not strive to build up the church and its business interests at the expense of the people. Its planning was devoted to increasing private production and employment in the region by a comprehensive plan of resource development, and by a calculated policy of "regulated" competition. It was primarily interested in whole-group rather than business-group welfare. As a temporal organization with a quasi-spiritual purpose, it hoped to speed the process of building up Zion. With greater recognition of the advantages of commercialized agriculture and specialized industry, the movement might well have played as important a role in the expansion of market activities in the 1880's and 1890's as the Perpetual Emigrating Company played in the expansion of immigration in the 1850's and 1860's. However, in 1884, the very year in which the board of trade movement seemed to be making greatest headway in the accomplishment of its aims, it died as the result of "The Raid." Despite its obvious partisanship, there was some justification to the confiding Mormon in the following explanation of the demise of Zion's Central Board of Trade, given by the editor of the *Deseret News* ten years later:

> It seems inseparable from history, that whenever any beneficial project was afoot for the benefit of the people of Zion, all the malignity of the opposition has been evoked to frustrate and prevent success, and instances in great number could be given as evidences of this fact. In this special instance [that is from 1879 to 1884 under the Boards of Trade] when unanimity was growing, when prices of produce was being held up, and the masses were prospering exceedingly, and promise was beyond all past experience, that infamous raid was commenced which compelled almost every leading citizen into exile or into privacy, the organization meanwhile struggling along in a decapitated condition, until finally, they succumbed to compulsory inaction.[51]

KINGDOM IN RETREAT

[1885–1900]

* IV *

That the Mormon Kingdom should continue as a permanent enclave in the American commonwealth was unthinkable to a large segment of American opinion. The system of plural marriage, though admittedly practiced by a small minority of Mormons, was an unspeakable vice; the theocratic economy interfered with the spread of capitalistic institutions; and the supposed church control of political life was thought to be inconsistent with democracy. As Congress sought to end Mormon "peculiarities" with increasingly restrictive legislation, the church fought back with every available weapon. With the formal disincorporation of the church and the confiscation of its properties under the Edmunds-Tucker Act, however, the days of the independent, exclusive Kingdom were numbered. When the Supreme Court approved the Edmunds-Tucker Act in 1890, a program of accommodation was inaugurated. The "People's Party" was dissolved, the church sold most of its business interests, and President Woodruff's Manifesto declared the end of polygamy. By the end of the century, the most objectionable — and some of the most praiseworthy — aspects of Mormon life were eliminated. Nevertheless, Mormon life, even today, emphasizes community and cooperative activity, and the ideals and methods of the Great Basin Kingdom still inspire a million and a half members.

CHAPTER XII

The Raid

Under the influence of the programs of the School of the Prophets, the Women's Relief Society, and the United Order of Enoch, the Mormon economy of the 1870's was highly diversified, relatively self-sufficient, and much more equalitarian than contemporary American society. The church was still more or less in control of the economy, and the devotion of the citizenry to church and the Kingdom appears to have been as great as during the 1850's and 1860's. While the flow of shepherded immigration was not quite so great as during the 1860's, it still amounted to several thousand persons per year. The number of Gentiles in the territory had increased, but they were still no numerical threat to Mormon supremacy, either in politics or in business. There were an estimated 150,000 Mormons in Utah and surrounding states in 1880. Annual church revenues amounted to a little over $1,000,000, of which about $540,000 was in tithing, and the remainder in the form of donations to temples, contributions to the Perpetual Emigration Fund, and "profits" on church investments in land and livestock, Z.C.M.I., railroads, and other enterprises. The principal expenditures were for the construction of temples ($235,000), general church administration ($91,000), poor relief and the Indians ($28,000), and economic promotion. The annual migration of converts to Utah in 1880 consisted of 812 British, 515 Scandinavians, 90 Swiss, 34 Germans, 5 Dutch, 2 Irish, and 1 French, for a total of 1,459.[1]

When the great colonizer-financier, Brigham Young, died in 1877, many predicted the church would fall apart. But his successor, John Taylor, took over the reins with hardly a ripple. A different kind of personality from Brigham Young, this gifted Englishman soon demonstrated equal performance as an organizer and builder. He had had wide experiences in church economic enterprises from the early 1840's, and as a writer and sermonizer he had had large influence on the church during Brigham Young's administration. Taylor chose for his counselors in the First Presidency George Q. Cannon and Joseph F. Smith. Both were young enough to have reached their majority in Utah, and both were energetic, intelligent, talented, and devoted to the ideals of "ancient Mormonism." No one would have dreamed, when this triumvirate assumed the reins of church government, that within a decade the church would be passing through a trial even greater than that of Jackson County, Far West, and Nauvoo. Under federal pressure, the goal of the Kingdom would have to be tragically revised, or largely abandoned.

The prime economic problem of Mormon Country in the late 1870's and early 1880's was overpopulation. In every valley there were signs that the continued flow of immigration, and the natural increase in population, had filled up the land. Young married couples were not able to find farms; older people found themselves underemployed. "I find," wrote one observer, "the settlements crowded up to their utmost capacity, land and water all appropriated, and our young people as they marry off have no place to settle near home . . . the resources of the people are about exhausted, unless they go into manufacturing."[2] The church's program in these years reflects official recognition of the deterioration in the ratio of people to the land. Projects to increase the supply of irrigable land were sponsored by ward, stake, and general church organizations. Here and there, from Blackfoot, Idaho, in the north, to Mesa, Arizona, in the south; from Manassa, Colorado, in the east, to southern Nevada in the west, available patches of land were reclaimed from the desert and put in the way of raising grains, hay, and vegetables. Many of these were subsidized with church resources. Not only new projects in the older valleys, but scores of church colonizing missions opened up new valleys for settlement. New settlements were founded in the Little Colorado and Salt River valleys in Arizona and New Mexico, in the San Luis Valley of southern Colorado, in the Upper Salt River Valley of western Wyoming, Upper Snake River Valley in eastern Idaho, and Goose Creek Valley in western Idaho. All told, at least a hundred new Mormon settlements were founded outside of Utah during the four-year period 1876 to 1879. In addition, at least a score or more of important new colonies were founded within Utah, in such unlikely spots as the San Juan country of southeastern Utah, Rabbit Valley (Wayne County) in central Utah, and remote areas in the mountains of northern Utah and southern Idaho. With the exception of the initial colonization of Utah in 1847–1851, it was the greatest single colonization movement in Mormon history. Eventually, as we shall see, it spread to Alberta, Canada, and Sonora and Chihuahua, Mexico. Each of the new settlements was designated as a gathering place, and nearly all were founded in the same spirit, and with the same type of organization and institutions, as those founded in the 1850's and '60's. Colonizing companies moved as a group, with church approval; the village form of settlement prevailed; canals were built by cooperative labor;

and the small holdings of farm land and village lots were parceled out in community drawings. Many of the colonies were given tithing and other assistance from the church.[3]

For those who remained in the settled valleys, the problems of poverty and underemployment remained. These problems were attacked partly by the continued establishment of local industries, and partly by the redistribution of wealth and income. Zion's Central Board of Trade, and the church itself, promoted and subsidized scores of "home industries," including enterprises designed to manufacture wool, cotton, silk, clothing, and iron; tan leather and make boots, shoes, and other leather products; and manufacture sugar, salt, soap, and paper. All were intended to provide gainful employment and, at the same time, build the Kingdom.

In addition to the continuous sharing of common resources through the fast offering and tithing funds, and through church employment on temples and other projects, the church undertook to secure a general cancellation of debts in 1880. In that year the church was celebrating the fiftieth anniversary of its founding. President Taylor and his associates decided to sponsor an Israelitish Jubilee, which was a traditional fifty-year cancellation of debts. The Jubilee began in April 1880 with a three-phase program designed to "free the worthy debt-bound brother."[4] To begin with, one-half of the debts owed to the Perpetual Emigrating Company were canceled. By 1880, approximately $704,000 on principal and $900,000 on interest were owed by some 19,000 persons who had been assisted by the Fund. Under the instructions of the church, bishops were permitted to cancel part or all of the indebtedness of all families in their wards who, in their judgment, deserved it. This, said President Taylor, was for the benefit of the poor, not of those who were able to pay. "The rich can always take care of themselves — that is, so far as this world is concerned. I do not know how it will be in the next."[5] By vote of the conference, approximately $802,000 was scratched from the books of the Fund. Similarly, one-half of all the delinquent tithing was canceled. The members of the church had charged themselves with a total of $152,000 on the tithing books which through poverty, misfortune, or neglect they had been unable or unwilling to pay. By conference action half of this amount was remitted, thus salving the consciences of those poorer members to whom the full payment of tithes was a matter of honor and religious obligation. At the same time, those who were better off were reminded that "they should pay up and keep their record right before the Lord."

The second phase was a general redistribution of wealth in favor of the poor. This was accomplished by turning over to the poor 1,000 head of cattle ("good cows — not one-teated animals") and 5,000 sheep, and by lending to the poor without interest 35,000 bushels of seed wheat which had been accumulated and stored by the Women's Relief Society. The cattle and sheep were obtained partly from church herds and partly from private donations.

The final phase was a general cancellation of debts by Mormon capitalists, banks, and business houses — after a strong recommendation to do so had been made by church officials. Z.C.M.I., whose role in the religious and economic life of the Mormons can hardly be overemphasized, set the pattern by relieving all who were distressed of their obligations, "so far as prudence would permit." The cancellations applied not only to individuals, but also to the more hard-pressed cooperative and United Order enterprises.[6] How universally this pattern was followed is not known.

THE GROWTH OF "ANTI-MORMON" LEGISLATION

The dominant theme of Mormon economic policy in the 1880's, however, is not the positive one of counteracting unemployment and building the Kingdom, but the negative one of attempting to preserve it from federal harassment and spoliation. While the Mormons were struggling to surmount the problems of town and countryside, powerful groups elsewhere in the nation were seeking to strengthen federal controls over their society. These groups included Western businessmen, hampered by church interferences with the free market; Protestant ministers and lady's aid societies, indignant over the continued practice of plural marriage; and northern politicians, fresh from triumphs over the South, and eager to apply the doctrine of federal supremacy to another impudent territory. That the issue of polygamy played a major role in this campaign can hardly be denied, but it seems to have been neglected that Mormon collectivism, in economics and politics, was also under attack. The crusade which stamped out polygamy also succeeded largely in putting an end to most of the unique and noncapitalistic economic institutions for which the Mormons had been noted.

It will be recalled that Congress had passed an act in 1862 which prohibited polygamy, disincorporated the church, and prohibited it from owning more than $50,000 worth of property other than that used directly and exclusively for devotional purposes. Although this law was generally considered to be unconstitutional, the church did attempt a kind of surface compliance with it by permitting only one civil marriage, calling the others "sealings," and by placing properties acquired by the church in the hands of Brigham Young. The latter arrangement created special problems when Brigham Young died, particularly in federal courts disposed to favor private interests over church interests, but the giant share of the church properties in his name was eventually turned over to his successor, John Taylor.[7] Taylor continued the policy of secretly holding certain church business properties in the names of individual trustees.

Unsuccessful in the 1862 law, Congress continued to debate ways and means of handling "The Mormon Question." Among the bills considered were the following:

1. The Wade Bill. Proposed by Senator Benjamin F. Wade of Ohio in 1866, this bill would have placed the Nauvoo Legion under full control of the federally appointed governor; prohibited officers of the church from solemnizing marriages; given authority to the United States Marshal to select all jurors; given authority to the governor to appoint county judges; taxed all real and personal property of the church in excess of $20,000; and required the trustee-in-trust to make a full report, under oath, each year, to the governor of all financial operations, including property acquired and disposed of, bank deposits, and investments. This bill failed to pass. Most of its features were incorporated in a bill presented by Senator Aaron H. Cragin of New Hampshire in 1867 and 1869. The latter also proposed to abolish trial by jury in cases arising under the 1862 law. The Cragin Bill was withdrawn in favor of the Cullom Bill.

2. The Cullom Bill. Proposed by Representative Shelby M. Cullom of Illinois in 1869–1870, this would have placed in the hands of the United States Marshal and the United States Attorney all responsibility for selecting jurors; polygamy cases would have been confined to the exclusive jurisdiction of the federal judges; plural wives would have been deprived of immunity as witnesses in cases involving their husbands; and "cohabitation," as distinct from polygamy, would be declared a misdemeanor. This bill also authorized the president, in order to enforce the law, to send a portion of the United States Army to Utah, and to raise 25,000 militia in the territory. The property of all Mormons leaving the territory on account of the law, or imprisoned, was to be confiscated and used, under Gentile jurisdiction, for the benefit of Mormon families. This bill passed the House but failed in the Senate.

3. The Ashley Bill. Proposed by Congressman James M. Ashley of Ohio in 1869, this bill provided for "the dismemberment" of Utah by transferring large slices of it to Nevada, Wyoming, and Colorado. Failed of passage.

4. The Poland Act. Authored by Representative Potter Poland of Vermont, this bill passed in 1874. It strengthened the 1862 law by transferring to federal judges the jurisdiction over criminal, civil, and chancery cases in Utah; transferred to federal officials the duties of the territorial attorney general and marshal; and gave federal judges considerable leeway in the selection of jurors. This law was upheld by the United States Supreme Court in the Reynolds case in 1879.[8]

In addition to these laws, ostensibly aimed at the practice of polygamy, but having the effect of separating church and state and church and the economy, there was a parade of "crusading" judges and governors, who sought in various ways to accomplish the same result. Upon several occasions

Brigham Young, members of the First Presidency, and other prominent churchmen were held in custody for indefinite periods on various charges. One of Grant's appointees, Chief Justice James B. McKean, reflected perhaps the view of these Gentile "crusaders," when he declared:

The mission which God has called upon me to perform in Utah, is as much above the duties of other courts and judges as the heavens are above the earth, and whenever or wherever I may find the Local or Federal laws obstructing or interfering therewith, by God's blessing I shall trample them under my feet.[9]

In general, the techniques applied by McKean and others resembled those which had been used with indisputable effectiveness in the political reconstruction of the South.[10]

In 1881 the Supreme Court pointed out certain crucial weaknesses in the antipolygamy legislation.[11] This led the national administration to recommend, and Congress to approve, the drastic provisions of the Edmunds Act.[12] Passed in March 1882, the Edmunds Act, named for Senator George F. Edmunds of Vermont, "put teeth" in the 1862 law and attempted to eliminate the Mormon Church as a power in Utah by vesting the political machinery of the territory in federal non-Mormon appointive officers. Specifically, the Edmunds Act provided heavy penalties for the practice of polygamy; defined cohabitation with a polygamous wife as a misdemeanor, punishable by a fine of not to exceed $300, by imprisonment not to exceed six months, or both; declared all persons guilty of polygamy or cohabitation incompetent for jury service; and disfranchised and declared ineligible for public office all persons guilty of polygamy or unlawful cohabitation. To carry out the purposes of the law all elective and registration offices in Utah were declared vacant. A five-man "Utah Commission" was appointed by the President, with the advice and consent of the Senate, to supervise registration of voters, conduct of elections, eligibility of voters, counting of votes, and issuance of certificates to elected candidates. As a matter of practical administration, the Utah Commission and the territorial courts and other federal appointive officials in Utah, Idaho, and Arizona, tended to interpret the Edmunds Act to mean that persons professing belief in polygamy or cohabitation as a religious principle, whether or not proved guilty of their practice, were ineligible to vote and to hold public office. This meant all believing Mormons. The effectiveness of this decision is borne out by the fact that the Utah Commission was able to report that in the first year of its existence it had excluded some 12,000 men and women from registration and voting.[13]

Although the Utah Commission began to function within a few months after the passage of the 1882 law, and although federal officials began immediately to gather evidence against the Latter-day Saints, particularly their leaders, there was widespread belief that the Edmunds Act was unconstitutional.[14] "Congress shall make no law respecting the establishment of religion, or interfering with the free exercise thereof" read the Constitution, and plural marriage was a holy, religious principle to the Mormons. In taking over the governmental machinery of Utah Territory after the effective date of the Edmunds Act, therefore, federal officials moved slowly in bringing indictments under the law until a test case was tried. When Rudger Clawson, a leader in the community of Brigham City, and later to become one of the Twelve Apostles of the church, was convicted of polygamy in October 1884, deputies began to move through the territory gathering evidence against polygamists. And when, on March 3, 1885, the Supreme Court denied Clawson's appeal and upheld the constitutionality of the law, territorial officials commenced the systematic and intensive prosecution of Mormon leaders in Utah and elsewhere known as "The Raid."[15]

Polygamous marrige being difficult to establish in the courts, the most common charge against the Mormons was that of unlawful cohabitation, punishable by a $300 fine or six months in jail, or both. This offense went through a process of gradual redefinition by the courts, as they found it increasingly difficult to establish evidence of sexual association or other "living together" among alleged polygamists and their wives. Eventually, simple refusal to deny the existence of a charged plural marriage tie was held to constitute unlawful cohabitation.[16] These various interpretations were all sustained by the Supreme Court, which balked, however, when one Utah judge held that polygamous association over three six-month intervals constituted three separate offenses and sentenced the accused to three times the imprisonment called for under the Edmunds Act.[17]

There were 1,004 convictions for unlawful cohabitation under the Edmunds Act between 1884 and 1893, and another 31 for polygamy,[18] but these hardly measure the magnitude of the effect of the Act upon Mormon society. The period from 1885 to 1890 was marked by intensive "polyg hunts" for "cohabs." Officials of the church made a grave decision to fight each and every charge under the law. Having taken sacred covenants to remain true to their wives "for time and all eternity," they regarded it as unthinkable that they should desert these women in order to avoid the punishment provided in this law of Babylon.[19] Accordingly, when it became clear early in 1885 that the rigorous enforcement and interpretation of the law were to be held constitutional, church leaders — nearly all of whom had one or more plural wives — went "underground." Leading out in this action was the church president, John Taylor, whose last public appearance was in the Salt Lake City Tabernacle, February 1, 1885. President Taylor died while in hiding on July 25, 1887 — a martyr, so the Mormons thought, to the principles of his faith. Both of President Taylor's counselors likewise went into hiding. President Joseph F. Smith went to Hawaii and did not return until 1889. President Cannon, more sought after than any other person because of his influence, seldom spent two nights in the same place and was pursued all over the West by the United States marshal and his deputies. On February 13, 1886, Cannon was captured while en route to Mexico; during his return to Salt Lake City, he escaped, but was later recaptured. Released on $45,000 bail, pending trial, he forfeited the bail and went to Arizona. Later, after Cannon and others had aided President Taylor's successor, Wilford Woodruff, in putting church affairs in order, he surrendered himself to federal officials and served nine months in the Utah penitentiary.[20]

With almost all leaders of Latter-day Saint communities in prison or in hiding, business establishments were abandoned, or were kept in operation by inexperienced wives and children. The ownership of most of the cooperatives drifted into the hands of a few individuals and eventually were converted into private enterprises. Those United Orders which had survived until this period were discontinued. There were no further meetings of Zion's Central Board of Trade. Almost every business history, in short, shows stagnation; almost every family history records widespread suffering and misery. Above all, the church, as the prime stimulater, financier, and regulator of the Mormon economy, was forced to withdraw from participation in most phases of activity. The Raid, in other words, was a period of crippled group activity of every type, of decline in cooperative trade and industry — a period when, above all, church economic support was essential but not forthcoming — a period when planning would have saved much, but when the planners dared not plan.

> A more despairing situation than theirs, at that hour, has never been faced by an American community. Practically every Mormon man of any distinction was in prison, or had just served his term, or had escaped into exile. Hundreds of Mormon women had left their homes and their children to flee from the officers of the law; many had been behind prison bars for refusing to answer the questions put to them in court; more were concealed, like outlaws, in the houses of friends. . . . Old men were coming out of prison, broken in health.[21]

THE EDMUNDS-TUCKER ACT

Nevertheless, the Edmunds law was unable to force a change in the attitude of Latter-day Saint authorities. It was an unwilling cross, but one which the great majority of members seemed prepared to bear rather than yield on what they regarded a religious principle. Congress therefore moved almost immediately to increase the pressure, and after considering several proposals during a number of sessions, adopted, on February 19, 1887, an amendment to the 1862 law known as the Edmunds-Tucker Act.[22] Enacted into law without the signature of President Grover Cleveland, this "Anti-Polygamy Act," as it was entitled, amended the 1862 law to provide as follows:

1. That the Corporation of the Church of Jesus Christ of Latter-day Saints, insofar as it had, or pretended to have, any legal existence, was dissolved. The United States Attorney General was directed to institute proceedings to accomplish the dissolution.

2. That the Attorney General institute proceedings to forfeit and escheat all property, both real and personal, of the dissolved church corporation held in violation of the 1862 limitation of $50,000, which was reaffirmed. The property was to be disposed of by the Secretary of the Interior and the proceeds applied to the use and benefit of the district schools in Utah.

3. That the Perpetual Emigrating Company be dissolved, its charter annulled, and its resources escheated and expended by the Secretary of the Interior for the use of the district public schools of Utah. The territorial assembly was forbidden to approve the charter of any similar corporation designed "to accomplish the bringing of persons into the said Territory for any purpose whatsoever."

4. That the court be empowered to compel the production of books, records, papers, and documents relating to properties held by the president of the church, as trustee-in-trust over its properties, in which, as trustee-in-trust, he held an interest.

5. The act also abolished woman suffrage in Utah; disinherited children of plural marriages; prescribed a comprehensive "test oath" to eliminate polygamists from voting, holding office, and serving on juries; vested all judicial, law enforcement, and militia powers in the Utah Commission and other federal appointees; suspended the territorial school laws; and placed the territorial schools under the control of the territorial supreme court and a court-appointed commissioner. The act required all marriages to be certified by certificate in the probate courts, wiped out all existing election districts, and dissolved the Nauvoo Legion.

The Edmunds-Tucker Act was a direct bid to destroy the temporal power of the Mormon Church. Congressional leaders reasoned that the church would have to yield on the principle of plural marriage or suffer destruction as an organization of power and influence. Church leaders did not see the matter in this light, however. They believed (and were supported in this belief by several constitutional lawyers of national reputation) that several features of the Edmunds-Tucker Act were unconstitutional. They further declared that they could not revoke the principle of polygamy: Only God could do that; and, if He so decided, He would do so by direct revelation to the president of the church — not by prohibitory national legislation. Just as they had refused to surrender on the issue of plural marriage after the passage of the Edmunds Act, they now refused to surrender the role of the trustee-in-trust in the world of business. "We cannot violate," said President Taylor, "the compact we have made with our God." Because of the "plotting" of "Christian nations . . . against the welfare of Zion," he said, it was necessary for the Latter-day Saints to take such measures as would be most conducive to protect them from "the aggression of the ungodly and lawless and those who are trampling under foot the constitution of the United States."

In anticipation of the passage of the Edmunds-Tucker Act, therefore, President Taylor and other general church authorities secretly decided to place church properties in the hands of individuals and local congregations and thus help, Taylor said, "to protect us in our personal and proprietary rights so far as our legal status will entitle us to protection." Thus, he concluded, "any plans instituted against us," would be "against the people in their individual capacity . . . and in direct interference with their proprietary rights which this nation and all other civilized nations professed always to respect."[23] The program was threefold.[24]

First, continue for the time being Brigham Young's policy of asking certain members of the church to hold property on a secret trust in order to avoid possible forfeiture to the government. These properties, by 1887, included the tithing office and grounds in central Salt Lake City; three lots adjoining the tithing grounds; the Church Historian's Office and lot; the office and residence of President Taylor; the lots on which Zion's Savings Bank, Z.C.M.I., and other church enterprises were erected; the granite quarry in Little Cottonwood Canyon containing the stone used in building the Salt Lake Temple; some coal mines near Coalville; all of the capital stock of the Deseret News Company; half of the capital stock of the Zion's Savings Bank & Trust Company; and two-thirds of the stock of the Bullion, Beck, and Champion Mining Company. Other properties whose exact ownership status was not established by subsequent judicial investigation may have been similarly held. These included some lots fronting Temple Block in Salt Lake City; the Salt Lake City Social Hall; the iron and coal claims of the church near Cedar City; Lee's Ferry, Arizona; the sugar plantation and works in Laie, Hawaii; shares of stock in the First National Bank of Ogden and the First National Bank of Provo; and real estate along the Mormon Trail in Iowa and Nebraska.

Second, church officials proceeded to organize separate nonprofit associations to hold certain real and personal property which belonged to the church. The St. George, Logan, and Manti temple associations were organized in 1886 for the purpose of placing legal custody of the three temples in the hands of local ecclesiastical authorities.[25] Similarly, the Salt Lake Literary and Scientific Association was given title in 1885 to some church properties facing the Salt Lake Temple Block, including the Council House and the Deseret Museum.[26] Finally, the numerous ward and stake ecclesiastical associations were given title between 1884 and 1887 to local meetinghouses, tithing houses, granaries, and to capital stock in community stock herds, general stores, irrigation projects, and other local enterprises in which the local or general church had a financial interest.[27] These properties had been held variously in the name of general and local church leaders. Not transferred to the stake and ward ecclesiastical associations at this time were the tithing receipts, the value of which on hand throughout the territory at any moment of time probably varied between $200,000 and $300,000, which was approximately one-half the value of a year's tithing receipts.[28] Although physically located in the wards and stakes, tithing properties remained in the name and at the disposition of the trustee-in-trust.

Third, in the event of passage of enforceable confiscatory legislation such as the anticipated Edmunds-Tucker law, church authorities determined to transfer by outright sale or by trust assignments to individuals, real and personal property which was held in the name of the church trustee-in-trust and would otherwise be forfeited to the government.[29] This included tithing receipts, some church office buildings, church farms and livestock herds, church-operated Indian farms, the Salt Lake Temple Block, and controlling shares of stock in Z.C.M.I., the Deseret Telegraph Company, the Salt Lake City Railroad Company, the Salt Lake Gas Company, the Provo Woolen Mills, and the Salt Lake Dramatic Association (an association which owned and operated the Salt Lake Theatre). In order to insure their placement in friendly hands, and, if possible, to preserve them from spoliation, all of these properties were secretly "sold" or transferred to private individuals shortly before the effective date of the Edmunds-Tucker Act, with the exception of some church office buildings, the Temple Block, and the church Indian farms. Shares of stock in the Deseret Telegraph were distributed to various stake ecclesiastical associations.

The most important of these transactions was that affecting the tithing. On or about February 28, 1887, after the law had passed Congress but before it became effective, John Taylor, as trustee-in-trust, ordered the personal property in the church tithing offices transferred to the ecclesiastical associations of the stakes in which it was physically located. Approximately $270,000 worth of tithing property was thus transferred out of the hands of the trustee-in-trust.[30] The amounts transferred varied from the $2,717 transferred to Morgan Stake Association to the $45,036 transferred to the Cache Stake Association. The transferral included approximately $66,000 worth of cattle, $20,000 in horses, $15,000 worth of sheep, $61,000 worth of grain, office furniture and equipment valued at $13,000, $10,500 worth of hay, $10,000 worth of flour, $8,100 worth of building material, and such other items as vegetables, dairy products, farming implements, meats, and molasses.[31] Each stake, in a special conference, formally accepted the properties and conferred power on the directors of the respective stake associations to manage and dispose of the properties.[32] Tithing properties and receipts were henceforth disbursed by the presidents of the various stakes, and devoted to the construction and maintenance of temples, meetinghouses, and local academies (high schools). More than a score of stake academies were initiated in 1887–1888 with the tithing returned to the stakes.[33]

Coincident with the transferral of the tithing to the stake associations, most of the livestock on the church ranches at Star Valley, Wyoming; Oxford, Idaho; and Pipe Springs, Arizona, was sold to Mormon capitalists and semipublic livestock associations. Approximately 3,000 horses and cattle were sold in this way, some of them in such a way as to suggest that the "sale" was merely the assignment of a trust.[34]

At the time of the passage of the Edmunds-Tucker Act, and before its effective date, the trustee-in-trust also "sold" or transferred certain properties to Z.C.M.I., Zion's Savings Bank, church officers, and syndicates of Mormon capitalists, as summarized in the table on the opposite page.[35]

Most of the trust assignments were "sales" in which the prospective trustee or trustees gave his (their) personal note. They were not the result of arms-length bargaining, nor does the evidence indicate that the notes were presented for payment when they matured.

These transactions, if recognized as legitimate, left the trustee-in-trust, on March 3, 1887, in possession of the Salt Lake Temple Block, the Office of the President of the Church in Salt Lake City, the Church Farm in Salt Lake City, Indian farms located at four points in the territory; and cash and negotiable instruments to the amount of approximately $240,000.[36] These were the properties which, it was hoped, the government receiver would find belonging to the church. It was expected that the Temple Block would be exempt from escheat as being devoted to religious worship; and that the office of the church president would be exempt as a parsonage. The Indian farms were liabilities rather than assets; and national sentiment would probably discountenance their seizure. Finally, the cash was being expended for charitable purposes and for the construction and maintenance of church temples. In short, church legal advisers dared to hope that only the Church Farm in Salt Lake City would be seized by the government under the Edmunds-Tucker Act. Since that Act also disincorporated the church and abolished the position of trustee-in-trust, the Presiding Bishopric of the Church was appointed by the April 1887 general conference to hold in trust, for the unincorporated body of worshipers known as the Church of Jesus Christ of Latter-day Saints, the meetinghouses, parsonages, burial grounds, and other properties belonging to that body.[37] The church was prepared, as well as it could hope, for the sword of Damocles.

Property	Market Value	Disposition
Real estate near Temple Block	$ 80,000	Sold to church business institutions
1,000 shares of stock in the Deseret News Company (face value, $100,000)	5,000	Held in trust by a syndicate of Mormon writers and publishers
Tithing Office equipment and tools	13,000	Held in trust by the Presiding Bishop
30,000 head of sheep	60,000	Sold to Mormon stockmen
3,500 shares of stock in Z.C.M.I. (face value, $350,000)	350,000	Held in trust by a syndicate of Mormon businessmen
4,732 shares of stock in Deseret Telegraph Company (face value $473,200)	22,500	Assigned to stake ecclesiastical associations
2,800 shares of stock in the Salt Lake Street Railroad Company (face value, $160,000)	45,000	Held in trust by a Mormon capitalist
1,000 shares of stock in the Provo Woolen Mills (face value, $100,000)	23,500	Held in trust by church business interests
800 shares of stock in the Salt Lake City Gas Company (face value, $80,000)	45,000	Held in trust by the church treasurer
1,450 shares of stock in the Salt Lake Dramatic Company	25,000	Held in trust by a syndicate of Mormon actors
Total	$639,000	

SURRENDER OF CHURCH PROPERTY

The sword fell on the day following the burial of President John Taylor. On July 30, 1887, pursuant to the provisions of the Edmunds-Tucker Act, the United States Attorney for Utah, George S. Peters, commenced suit in the Supreme Court of the Territory to recover all property held by the trustee-in-trust in excess of $50,000, acquired after 1862, and to formally dissolve the Corporation of the Church of Jesus Christ of Latter-day Saints and the Perpetual Emigrating Company.[38] The government contended that the church had real estate subject to escheat valued at over $2,000,000, and personal property subject to escheat amounting to over $1,000,000. The appointment of a receiver to hold church properties pending final adjudication of the suit was formally requested.[39]

The church's answer to the government suit was filed in the court some two months later, on October 1, 1887.[40] Church attorneys denied that the church was a corporation at any time after July 1, 1862, having been dissolved by the Morrill Anti-Bigamy Act; denied that the church, as a corporation, had bought, acquired or held any real estate after July 1, 1862; denied that the corporation held $2,000,000 of real estate or $1,000,000 of personal property on February 19, 1887; and asserted as follows:

That since July 1, 1862, the Church of Jesus Christ of Latter-day Saints has been "a voluntary religious and charitable association, composed of numerous members and congregations, and that the objects of said association are the dissemination of the principles of the gospel as taught by our Saviour Jesus Christ, and in aiding the poor and incompetent, and in providing for their sustenance and wants.

That its purposes and objects are purely religious and charitable, and as such it has at all times and does now, receive donations from its members in limited amounts, which are used for the sole purposes aforesaid.

That as such society or association it has held through its trustee, from time to time, its real and personal property, and has from time to time used and disposed of portions of the same.

That John Taylor is the sole trustee of the sole association; that on or before February 28, 1887, the trustee-in-trust disposed of all the personal property of said association except sufficient to pay its debts.

That on April 8, 1887, the church appointed three trustees, W. B. Preston, Robert T. Burton, and J. R. Winder, to hold the real property of the church; that since their appointment, all real property of the church has been deeded to them, and that all this real property was held by the church before July 1, 1862 except the parsonage and offices.

That the church has acquired no other real property or personal property save that donated to the church (and held by the above-mentioned three trustees) for use in building and caring for its houses of worship, and in maintaining and supporting the poor.

With regard to the Perpetual Emigrating Company, church attorneys asserted further that:

it has never held or owned at any time since its incorporation any real estate whatsoever;

That the contributions to its funds have been by it expended, as they have been contributed, and that at no time has any fund remained on hand for any length of time;

That it did not, on the 19th day of February, 1887, nor on the 3rd of March, 1887, hold, own or possess any real or personal property whatsoever, save and except certain promissory notes, which had been heretofore given to it by emigrants in payment of advances by the said corporation to them to assist them in their emigration, and which said notes are for the most part barred by the statute of limitations, uncollectable, of no value and wholly worthless.[41]

On October 17, the date set for hearing arguments in the suit, the church filed a demurrer charging that the territorial supreme court was not competent to hear the suit and execute the provisions of the statute. The purpose of the demurrer seems to have been to force the matter into the United States Supreme Court for a technical ruling, and thus delay the appointment of a receiver to take over the properties of the church to be escheated under the law. This effort did not succeed, and the court ruled that the question of the receiver should be brought up first.[42] There followed several days of argument and testimony on the question of appointing a receiver.[43] The case of the government was admittedly weak, and the technique used by government lawyers to break down the case of the church resembled poker more closely than jurisprudence. Henry W. Hobson, United States Attorney for Colorado, who was called to Utah as special pleader for the government, explained this technique in a letter to Solicitor General George A. Jenks in Washington, D. C., on the day after the government had closed its case.

When I got out to Salt Lake, I found that Mr. Peters had been able to get little or no testimony at all to support the motion for a receiver, and his failure to do so, was not any fault of his, I think, but his misfortune. The Mormons had run off all the witnesses he had counted upon getting, except a few who could only make statements of the most general character. I was quite solicitous lest we should be left without any evidence at all which would have amounted to anything, and after consultation with Mr. Peters, he and I adopted the policy of making a great noise about the testimony we were going to put in, and we got the other side a little scared for fear we would open up things a good deal more than they wished. Really we could not have done so, but they did not know how much testimony we had. In consequence of this, we got them to agree to the statement of facts . . . ,[44] and which substantially shows that ever since this Act of Congress was passed, the church has been making away with its property. I do not think the defendants rely upon any failure of proof upon our side with regard to the necessity of a receiver. In the argument, they relied almost entirely upon the unconstitutionality of the Act of Congress.[45]

The bluffing strategy of government attorneys paid off. On November 5 the court made the unanimous decision to appoint a receiver.[46] The court accepted the belief of the United States Attorney and his staff that the church had a large amount of real and personal property subject to escheat; it also took cognizance of the transferral of the $268,982 of church livestock and tithing produce and other properties from the trustee-in-trust to the stake ecclesiastical corporations. Finally, the court noted that the property admittedly in the hands of the Presiding Bishopric, representing the church, included the Temple and Tithing Blocks, and the Gardo House (President Taylor's office and residence), all together worth far in excess of $50,000. This satisfied the court that the church had property subject to escheat and that the appointment of a receiver was necessary.

The Court appointed Frank H. Dyer, United States Marshal in Utah since 1886, as receiver for both properties of the Corporation of the Church of Jesus Christ of Latter-day Saints (for which he was required to post a bond of $250,000), and the Perpetual Emigrating Company (for which bond was fixed at $50,000).[47] Both Mormon and non-Mormon businessmen signed Dyer's bonds, and he took the oath of receivership November 10, 1887. The court then overruled the demurrers of the church in regard to its own incompetency, and the church attorneys immediately filed their intention to appeal the decision to the United States Supreme Court.[48] The receiver began immediately to take possession of properties which were known to belong to the church.

The extenuating circumstances which led to the appointment of the United States Marshal as receiver for the property of the late church corporation were afterwards related by Dyer in a letter to President Benjamin Harrison:

> The hostility of the Mormon people to this law [the Edmunds-Tucker Act] and the proceedings to enforce it are well known. It was believed that in anticipation of its passage large amounts of property really owned by the Church, but held in the names of private parties in trust in its favor, had been conveyed to evade the enforcement of the law. It seemed to the Supreme Court, that the means and powers which as Marshal I had at command, would greatly facilitate my acquisition of this property as Receiver. . . . I accepted this post with hesitation, though had I then known of its magnitude I would have declined it altogether. . . . Although there was voluntarily delivered to me by the Church authorities property to the amount of One Hundred and Forty-Five thousand dollars in value, in less than eight months I had with the aid of persons . . . in my employment unearthed of property held in secret trusts and reduced into my possession . . . a further amount . . . aggregating nearly Six Hundred thousand dollars.[49]

In succeeding weeks, upon the request of the receiver and with the reservation that an appeal would be made, church authorities voluntarily surrendered the structures built on Temple Block, the General Tithing Office, the Church Historian's Office, the Gardo House, the Church Farm in Salt Lake City, the Office of the President of the Church (including all financial records), and the assets of the Perpetual Emigrating Company. Temple Block was leased back to the church for the nominal sum of $1.00 per month, but work on the temple was stopped; the General Tithing Office and Church Historian's Office were rented back to the church for $300 (later reduced to $200) per month until March 1890, when the rent was raised to $500 per month; the Gardo House was rented to the church for $75 per month until April 1890, when the rent was raised to $450 per month; and the Church Farm was leased to the church for $50 a month until June 1889, when the rent was raised to $401 per month. Clerks in the Office of the President of the Church were discharged and two deputy marshals were placed in charge. The seized assets of the Perpetual Emigrating Company included an office safe, a desk, records, account books, $2.25 in defaced silver coins, 131¾ shares of stock in the Parowan Cooperative Stock Raising Company, and promissory notes amounting to $417,958.50. Virtually all of the latter were long since barred by the statute of limitations. An attempt was made to collect some of the notes, but this was unsuccessful. The receiver also demanded the tithing, religious structures, and other properties in the hands of the Weber and Cache stake ecclesiastical associations, in Ogden and Logan, but little progress was made toward obtaining possession of them.[50]

In the meantime, in the suit U.S. *v.* Church of Jesus Christ of Latter-day Saints, testimony was taken from various church officials and employees in an attempt to demonstrate that the church had tried to defeat the purposes of the Act by transferring personalty to the stakes and to private individuals under secret trusteeships, and also by transferrals under deeds fraudulently antedated.[51] After a considerable amount of prodding, the church treasurer was induced to surrender the 800 shares of stock in the Salt Lake Gas Company which he held in trust for the church.[52] This "victory" led government attorneys to press a test case for the surrender of the building equipment, furniture, and other properties in the hands of the Presiding Bishop, W. B. Preston.[53] Upon being successful in winning this property also, Dyer and his attorneys then instituted separate suits in the territorial district courts for the surrender of each and every piece of real and personal property which they had any reason to believe had belonged to the church prior to the passage of the Edmunds-Tucker Act. The undisguised purpose of these suits was to vex church officials into surrendering all such property in order to avoid a mass of petty suits which would hold up the appeal and final decree.[54] Considering the importance of obtaining a ruling from the Supreme Court on the constitutionality of the entire legislation, and considering that nearly all directing heads of the church were "in exile for their religion," as they expressed it, and could not manage the proceedings as they would have desired, the church determined, in June 1888, to compromise these suits to secure their dismissal. The compromise offered by the church, accepted by the receiver, and approved by the court, was that upon the payment of $157,666.15 by the church, all of these suits would be dismissed and the receiver would present no further claim for the properties involved. The properties involved included the following:[55]

Three important lots on which church businesses were erected	$ 84,666.15
Stock in the Salt Lake Street Railroad Company	51,000.00
Stock in the Provo Woolen Mills	22,000.00
Total	$157,666.15

All of these properties, although their ostensible value was surrendered, would remain in the hands of the church. Soon after this transaction, the church sold two of the lots to Z.C.M.I. and Zion's Savings Bank, and transferred its stock in the street railroad to Francis Armstrong, a prominent Mormon capitalist.

A second compromise, made at the same time, had to do with the $268,982.39½ in tithing property which was admittedly transferred by the trustee-in-trust to the stake associations on February 28, 1887.[56] This transferral was now generally regarded as indefensible from the legal point of view, and Dyer had demanded all of the properties involved in the transfers. In seeking to take possession of the church's herds of cattle and horses, however, he discovered that most of the hay, grain, and other feed had been consumed by the time he was appointed. Furthermore, the herds were widely scattered and it would have been costly for him to recover them completely. After negotiation with church leaders, therefore, Dyer agreed to a compromise whereby the church promised to turn over to him $75,000 worth of cattle, payable at the price at which the cattle were inventoried on the February 28 lists; or, if sufficient cattle could not be rounded up, the church agreed to pay $75,000 in cash.[57] The cattle (or cash) were to be turned over to Dyer, along with the $157,666.15 in cash, on September 1, 1888, and church officials were required to give Dyer promissory notes to signify their acceptance of the responsibility of making these deliveries on the date indicated.

The receiver and his attorneys, sensing from these compromises that the church would yield on minor points to concentrate efforts on winning the major case before the Supreme Court, immediately demanded and received the following properties whose status had previously been in question: Coal mines near Coalville, Utah; the $5,000 received by the church from the "sale" of Deseret News Company stock; 30,000 head of sheep; 4,732 shares of stock in the Deseret Telegraph Company; and promissory notes with a value of $27,000 covering stock in the Salt Lake Dramatic Association. Thus by July 11, 1888, the receiver had taken possession of over $800,000 worth of property alleged to belong to the trustee-in-trust. A complete list of this property then in the hands of the receiver is presented below:[58]

	Description of Property	*Stipulated Value*
1.	The Temple Block	No value stipulated
2.	The Tithing Yard and Offices	$ 50,000
3.	The Historian's Office	20,000
4.	The Gardo House	50,000
5.	The Office of the President of the Church	Value not stipulated
6.	The Office of the Presiding Bishop	12,000
7.	The Church Farm in the Salt Lake Valley	150,000
8.	Note for aggregate amount of values settled by order of Supreme Court on July 9, 1888.	157,666
9.	Coal interests at Grass Creek, near Coalville	100,000
10.	Note promising delivery of cattle (or cash) in lieu of church livestock herds and tithing produce transferred to stake ecclesiastical associations on February 28, 1887.	75,000
11.	30,000 head of sheep @ $2.00 per head	60,000
12.	Stock (4,732 shares) in Deseret Telegraph Company	22,000
13.	Stock (800 shares) in Salt Lake Gas Company	75,000
14.	Dividends received on Gas Company stock	4,000
15.	Notes for Salt Lake Dramatic Company stock	27,000
16.	Payment in satisfaction of receiver's claim to capital stock in Deseret News Company	5,000
	Total Stipulated Value	$807,666

When one considers the value of the items not stipulated, and the gross undervaluation of some of the properties, it is probable that the actual value of the properties surrendered was well in excess of $1,000,000. Nevertheless, a comparison of the properties confiscated with the list of properties which belonged to the church shows that the stratagems of the trustee-in-trust paid off in part. The receiver probably did not get a third of the value of the properties belonging to the church at the time of the passage of the Edmunds-Tucker Act. Of greatest importance to the Mormon economy, the receiver did not take possession of the church's bank stocks, nor of its holdings in that key institution, Zion's Co-operative Mercantile Institution.

Involved in this surrender was cash amounting to $239,266.15. This included the cash settlement negotiated and approved July 9, 1888; the payment in lieu of cattle; the payment for Deseret News stock; and a portion of the dividends on the gas stock. The church's cash assets having been spent on temples and other disbursements, officials at first met this obligation with short-term notes to the receiver and 2,000 head of cattle. But Dyer refused the cattle, insisting that they were "scrubs" and "culls," and demanded that the church's notes be endorsed by competent (that is, Gentile) banks.[59] On October 4, 1888, the church borrowed $240,700 from Salt Lake City banks to meet these obligations.[60] Since the cash expenses of the church for charity, education, and legal fees were greater than usual during this period, and since tithing receipts and business earnings were much less than usual for the same reason, the church found it impossible to pay these notes as they came due out of a budget surplus. Old notes were met by new notes, and the church's debt continued to increase as the interest pyramided. The problem of finding cash to carry on normal and extraordinary church activities was not the least of the worries produced by the Raid.

Church authorities placed their hopes for "financial salvation" on an appeal of the principal suit. Through the agency of its three trustees, the Presiding Bishopric, the church prayed for confirmation of its title to the Temple Block, the Tithing Office, the Historian's Office, and the Gardo House. The Temple Block, they declared, was set apart for the use of the church as a place of worship; the Tithing Office property had been acquired and used by the church prior to July 1, 1862; and the Gardo House and Historian's Office were set apart as parsonages. The trustees also prayed that if the court find the church corporation dissolved, then the personal property of that church, to the amount of about $800,000, ought to be turned over to its duly appointed trustees for the use and benefit of the members of the church.[61]

Upon the urging of the court, opposing counsel, on October 8, 1888, finally made an agreement upon facts, reached a decision on the property to be held by the receiver, and arrived at a basis upon which the case would be taken through the courts. The Utah Supreme Court then issued its decree and findings.[62] All prayers of the Mormon defendants were denied, except with regard to the Temple Block which the court ordered the receiver to release to trustees Preston, Burton, and Winder on the condition that it be used exclusively for religious worship.

Some other problems were to arise in the territorial court before the decision of the U. S. Supreme Court was finally handed down in May 1890. The first was concerned with fixing the compensation of the receiver and his attorneys.[63] The receiver asked $25,000 for himself and $10,000 for each of his attorneys. The principal objector to these high fees was one of the territorial judges, Charles S. Zane, who had served as Chief Justice on the previous term of the court. Zane, a non-Mormon, claimed to represent the 1,000 trustees of the 300 school districts in the territory who were interested in the disposal of the church property escheated to the government, lest the whole amount be taken for receiver's and attorneys' fees and incidental expenses.[64] Zane filed a petition in court representing that the claims for compensation were "grossly exorbitant, excessive and unconscionable." He severely arraigned the receiver and his attorneys, Peters and Williams.[65]

One of Zane's charges was that there was an indiscreet connection between the receiver and the government. Theoretically, he said, a receiver should be free of prejudicial connection with either side in such a suit. Yet the following illustrated the injudicious arrangements in the case.[66]

1. The United States Marshal was appointed receiver in a case in which the United States was a party to the suit. He retained the position of marshal while serving as receiver.

2. The federally appointed Territorial Superintendent of District Schools (P. L. Williams) was chosen attorney for the receiver, while it should have been his duty to look after the interests of the District Schools which, if the suit was successful, were to receive the benefits of the confiscation. Out of the property so seized he wanted $10,000 which meant that much less for the schools of which he was superintendent.

3. The United States District Attorney (Peters), who represented the government in the suit, was also an attorney for the receiver, and wanted $10,000 more for his services in that capacity, while the rule in law was that an attorney for a receiver must not be engaged in the litigation by either party to the suit. Thus, in the hearings on the compensation of the receiver and his attorneys, no one appeared for the government.

One is tempted to add to this compilation the action of Judge Zane, himself, for he was now vigorously representing one interested group in the case, and during the next term of the court, as he may have supposed, he would be sitting on the bench as Chief Justice directing the activities of the receiver.[67]

In the course of these hearings, the Court examined the receiver in regard to his administration of the forfeited property and his deals with the church.[68] Charges were made that Dyer had been too lenient in making compromises with the church for properties which had been spirited away; that he had rented forfeited properties back to the church at unduly low figures; that he had rented the 30,000 sheep to one of the sureties on his bond (a non-Mormon) at half the customary figure; and that the sheep herds had suffered heavy losses through mismanagement. Although Dyer and his staff were exonerated of the charge of mismanagement, his compensation was fixed at $10,000 per year; and that of his attorneys, at $5,500 and $4,000 respectively.[69]

THE CHURCH SUIT

Argument in the case of The Late Corporation of the Church of Jesus Christ of Latter-day Saints *v.* United States, testing the legality of the government seizure, took place in January 1889. Attorneys for the church were James O. Broadhead and Joseph E. McDonald, of national prominence, and Franklin S. Richards and John M. Butler, of Utah. The government case was argued by Solicitor General G. A. Jenks. Both sides prepared their briefs with great care on the assumption that there was real doubt as to how the court would hold. The principal questions raised in the arguments were two: First, whether Congress had the power to repeal the territorial charter by which the church was incorporated; and second, whether Congress and the courts had the power to seize the property of the corporation and hold it for the purposes specified in the Edmunds-Tucker Act.[70] Church attorneys, relying on the Dartmouth College and other cases, contended that the charter which created the church corporation was a vested right or contract which could not be altered or repealed by any subsequent act of the territorial legislature or Congress. They also contended that there was no rule of law by which personal property could escheat to the United States; that personal property was not subject to escheat on account of any failure or illegality of the trusts to which it was dedicated at its acquisition and for which it had been used by the corporation; that real estate in which the church had vested rights could not be disturbed; and that under the averments of the bill there was no authority to appoint a receiver.

Government attorneys, on the other hand, argued that the legislative power of Congress over the territories was general; that Congress had the power to repeal the charter under the Organic Law; that the alleged charter was void because the power exercised in the passage of the act of incorporation was among the powers forbidden by the constitution; that if the charter was a valid one, it was a public corporation, and therefore not within the principle announced by the court in the Dartmouth College case; that even if the corporation was a legal private one, its charter was rightfully dissolved, for misuse and abuse of its corporate powers; that whether the alleged corporation was legal or *de facto,* public or private, or had or had not abused its powers, it was rightfully dissolved under the police powers of the government; and that if the corporation was a public one, as they contended it was, on its dissolution its property became vested in the sovereign.

The decision of the court was read May 19, 1890 — approximately seventeen months after the case was argued. In finding for the government, a majority of the court held that the power of Congress over the territories was general and plenary; that is,

> Congress may not only abrogate laws of the Territorial Legislatures, but it may itself legislate directly for the local government. It may make a void Act of the Territorial Legislature valid, and a valid Act void. . . . Congress, for good and sufficient reasons of its own . . . had a full and perfect right to repeal its charter and abrogate its corporate existence.

With regard to the second general issue, whether Congress and the courts had the power to seize the property of the corporation and hold it for the charitable purposes specified in the 1887 law, the court declared that the government, "necessarily" had the disposition of the funds of the dissolved corporation and that the only limitations on the use of such funds was that they must be used "with due regard to the objects and purposes . . . to which the property was originally devoted, so far as they are lawful and not repugnant to public policy." The court then stated that the church had taken property dedicated to religious and charitable uses and had devoted it to spread and promote the doctrines of the church, "one of the distinguishing features" of which was polygamy—"a crime against the laws, and abhorrent to the sentiments and feelings of the civilized world." The state had "a perfect right to prohibit polygamy" and to apply the misdirected church properties to "other charitable objects." After ruling that the attempt, after the passage of the Act on February 19, 1887, to transfer the property from the trustee-in-trust to other persons, was an evasion of the law and void, the court concluded with a quotable paragraph which was to be spread on almost every newspaper in the land which reported the case:

> Then looking at the case as the finding of the facts presents it, we have before us—Congress had before it—a contumacious organization, wielding by its resources an immense power in the Territory of Utah, and employing those resources and that power in constantly attempting to oppose, thwart and subvert the legislation of Congress and the will of the government of the United States. Under these circumstances we have no doubt of the power of Congress to do as it did.

The court opinion stated that it would have more to say on the disposition of the forfeited personal property in a subsequent decision, and that the case was being held open for that purpose. Until then, the properties in the hands of the receiver would be undisturbed.

The opinion, final and definite as it was, was not unanimous. The Chief Justice (Fuller), two associate justices (Field and Lamar) concurring, wrote a short but vigorous dissent based on the States' Rights doctrine which had reached its farthest in the Dred Scott decision.[71] Wrote the Chief Justice:

> In my opinion, Congress is restrained, not merely by the limitations expressed in the Constitution, but also by the absence of any grant of power, express or implied, in that instrument. . . . If this property was accumulated for purposes declared illegal, that does not justify its arbitrary disposition by judicial legislation. In my judgment, its diversion under this Act of Congress is in contravention of specific limitations in the Constitution; unauthorized, expressly or by implication, by any of its provisions; and in disregard of the fundamental principle that the legislative power of the United States, as exercised by the agents of the people of this Republic, is delegated and not inherent.

EFFECTS OF THE SUPREME COURT DECISION

The Supreme Court decision produced two immediate effects. The first effect was a rather considerable national interest in the conduct of the receivership. Now that the escheat had been approved and the receivership confirmed, administration officials, and Senator Edmunds and the Committee on Territories began to express a not unnatural interest in the handling of the properties confiscated. In general, they were alarmed at the manner in which the costs of the receivership were eating into the fund. "I am very much afraid," wrote Senator Edmunds to the Attorney General, "that the conduct of the affairs thus far in respect of the receivership and the operations conducted under it, has been scandalous and unjust to the fund, to whomsoever it may belong or to whatever use it may be applied." [72] Edmunds suggested that the Attorney General inquire into the "astonishing" amount being paid for receiver's allowances and for counsel,[73] whereupon the Attorney General wrote to the United States Attorney in Utah, Charles S. Varian for confirmation or denial of the Senator's fears. Varian replied as follows:

> It is true that very heavy drafts have been made upon this fund, . . . somewhere near $53,000.00, I think, but it is not to be wondered at, for upon the examination before the Examiner directed to take testimony upon the question of the compensation of the Receiver, and of his counsel, the Government was not represented; the District Attorney appearing and examining for the Receiver and in his own behalf, and but two or three of the so called expert witnesses were cross-examined at all. . . .
>
> I may also say, that the last report of the Receiver shows that he has used for his personal ends, without authority some $11,000 of this fund, which he has since returned with interest.
>
> As at present advised I agree with Senator Edmunds, that this entire proceeding has been and is a scandal upon the administration of justice, and I shall use my best endeavors to arrest further raids upon this Trust Fund, and to put its administration into more competent hands.[74]

Varian might have added two other evidences of maladministration. Learning, in his capacity as a receiver, that the Salt Lake Gas Company was an extremely good investment, Dyer (and his attorneys) personally purchased 913 shares of stock, thus giving him control of the company in a private capacity. Thus, it would appear that Dyer, the receiver, sold the controlling interest to Dyer, the businessman, and deposited the proceeds of the sale into the receivership. The other questionable aspect was the investment of the cash resources. At a time when money was in great demand in Utah, the receiver placed $250,000 of the church's cash in non-Mormon banks and required no interest, thus losing for the fund up to $15,000 per year.[75]

Four days after the above letter was written, Dyer resigned from the position of receiver,[76] probably at the request of the United States Attorney, and filed a complete report on his activities.[77] An examination of the report and the body of testimony given at the time it was presented leads one to conclude that the receivership system, rather than Dyer personally, was responsible for the heavy drain on the fund. The salaries of the receiver and his attorneys were largely an unnecessary expense, while the judicial direction of the receiver's activities was not conducive to good business management.[78] By February 1891, over seventeen per cent (or some $58,000) of the personal property (including rent paid by the church for the use of its own property) in the hands of the receiver had been "frittered away" in expenses. As Attorney Varian stated "It would seem desirable to close this business and as soon as possible, as it seems to me that a receiver is too expensive a luxury for the fund." [79] This recommendation was not followed, however, and Dyer was replaced as receiver by Henry W. Lawrence, who had been active in the Godbeite movement of 1869–1870, and was an apostate Mormon. Lawrence, whose appointment was regarded as "obnoxious" by the Mormons,[80] was allowed $250 a month for his services, and his attorney received $150 per month. He continued as receiver until August 31, 1894, when John R. Winder, a member of the Presiding Bishopric, replaced him.

The second effect of the Supreme Court decision upholding the constitutionality of the Edmunds-Tucker Act was the church "Manifesto" proclaiming an end to the performance of plural marriages. The church, which at its inception had had to ask a poor farmer to mortgage his farm to print the first edition of its sacred book, and which by 1887 had reached the point where it was able to carry out missionary, educational, charitable, and economic activity on a wide scale, now found the financial wherewithal with which to continue this activity imperiled by processes which were declared by a majority of the court to be perfectly legal and proper. The aged president of the church, Wilford Woodruff (successor to John Taylor), had been a member of the church almost from its birth and had participated in nearly all of the experiences which had seen the Mormons driven in ever-larger groups from Missouri, Ohio, and Illinois to the Great Basin. For several weeks and months he "wrestled mightily with the Lord." Finally, on September 25, 1890, he wrote in his journal: "I have arrived at a point in the history of my life as the president of the Church . . . where I am under the necessity of acting for the temporal salvation of the church." [81] On that date, just four months after the fateful decision of the Supreme Court, President Woodruff issued the "Official Declaration" which proclaimed the end of polygamy among the Mormons:

> Inasmuch as laws have been enacted by Congress forbidding plural marriages, which laws have been pronounced constitutional by the court of last resort, I hereby declare my intention to submit to those laws, and to use my influence with the members of the Church over which I preside to have them do likewise.[82]

In the October 6 session of the general conference of the church, the congregation "unanimously sustained" this declaration as "authoritative and binding." Polygamy no longer had official sanction.

As he had no doubt anticipated, President Woodruff's "Manifesto," and its acceptance by most Mormons, removed some of the pressure built up during the Raid. Northern purity leagues lost interest in trying to reform Utah and "Christianize" the Mormons. "Polyg hunts" by deputy marshals became less and less frequent; judges showed more and more leniency in dealing with "cohabs" brought before the law. Government attorneys, with the acquiescence of the Attorney General in Washington, adopted the policy of being "light" and "humane" in their prosecutions.[83] There was a noticeable decline in the vigor with which government attorneys pressed the church case, the receivership, and the escheat of church property. Territorial judges reflected the same policy of leniency by slowing down the judicial processes by which the church would be finally deprived of its wealth. As the church demonstrated its good faith by strengthening its enforcement of the Manifesto, there was a growing opinion among political circles that to complete the escheat of church property would be both unfair and dangerous — dangerous from the political point of view because of the possible reaction of sympathy toward a group which was believed to have suffered much persecution in the past.

After a long and tortuous process, involving judicial hearings and decisions not particularly germane to the present discussion,[84] the church's personal property — or what was left of it — was returned to the First Presidency on January 10, 1894. The property returned was as follows: Furniture in the Office of the President of the Church, in the Church Historian's Office, and in the Office of the Receiver; 4,732 shares of stock in the Deseret Telegraph Company; and $438,174.39 in cash. The church real estate was returned on June 8, 1896, and consisted of Tithing Office property, Historian's Office, Gardo House, Church Farm, and Summit County coal lands.

This is a far different list from that originally possessed by the receiver and would lead one to suspect, in the absence of other evidence, that there was a studied attempt on the part of the receivers and courts to dispose of church interests for cash and "get the church out of business." However, there is no hint that the receivers disposed of such properties for less than their market value.

The Manifesto declaring an end to officially sanctioned plural marriages also enabled the Mormons to achieve the goal of statehood, which had been denied them for over forty years. Statehood gave them the prospect of getting rid, once and for all, of the unwanted and unfriendly federally appointed governors, judges, marshals, attorneys, and commissioners who had fought against them since 1852. As a part of the "deal" by which this was arranged, church officials are said to have given congressional and administration leaders to understand that they would support a proposition to prohibit forever the practice of polygamy in Utah; that the church would dissolve its Peoples' Party and divide itself into Republican and Democratic supporters; and that the church would discontinue its alleged fight against Gentile business and relax its own economic efforts. Some or all of these pledges may not have been made, but certain people later alleged that they were made and that the granting of statehood to Utah in 1896, the restoration of church property in 1894 and 1896, and the amnesties granted to Mormon polygamists in 1893 and 1894, were all conditioned upon this understanding. The Raid had finally culminated in the long-sought goal of statehood, but had produced capitulation in many areas of Mormon uniqueness, not the least of which was the decline in the economic power and influence of the church. The temporal Kingdom, for all practical purposes, was dead — slain by the dragon of Edmunds-Tucker.

CHAPTER XIII

Aftermath

The "surrender" of the church on the issues of polygamy, political control, and economic intervention which followed the Supreme Court decision approving the Edmunds-Tucker Act meant a change of direction and diminished acceleration, but not a complete halt in church activity in these fields. President Woodruff's Manifesto did not announce that polygamous living would be discontinued; it simply said that no more plural marriages would be sanctioned. The church did not promise to stay out of politics; it merely agreed that the old church party would be dropped. And the church did not give anyone to understand that it would discontinue its efforts to promote economic development, although there seems to have been a definite understanding that the old Mormon-Gentile dividing lines would be obliterated. Everyone understood that these elements in the "surrender" would take time — that the cessation of polygamous living and the separation of church and state and of church and the economy would not occur overnight. That it must occur, sooner or later (sooner rather than later), was the basic insistence of national political leaders.

Another factor was producing the same result — the "end of the frontier" in the Great Basin and Rocky Mountain regions. Mormons found it more and more difficult to find new areas to settle. By 1900 virtually all habitable locations had been occupied. Most of the new Mormon colonies founded at the end of the century were near non-Mormon communities. Mormon settlers usually found it necessary to accommodate their ways to those of the Gentiles around them. With "outsiders" attracted in ever greater numbers to Utah, and with Mormons settling in increasing numbers in non-Mormon communities and neighborhoods, the days of the proud, isolated, self-sufficient Kingdom were at an end.

The decade of the 1890's reflects this transition from Utah, the Mormon Commonwealth, to Utah, a State in the national commonwealth. The transition can be seen in the changes in immigration, colonization, enterprise, and in the measures taken by the church at the end of the century to promote economic development and compensate for the end of the frontier.

CHANGES IN CONCEPTS AND PRACTICES

Immigration. Mormon immigration was already beginning to slow down when the Raid commenced. Despite the speed, comfort, and convenience of the steamship and the railroad, there were approximately 7,000 fewer immigrants in the eight years following 1869, than in the eight years preceding it.[1] Whereas almost 4,000 immigrants had journeyed by sailing packet and ox-wagon to Utah in each year in the 1860's, approximately half that number went by steamship and railroad each year in the 1870's and 1880's. This decline, of course, was partly the result of the improvement of economic opportunities in England and Scandinavia in relation to those in Utah; and partly the effect of the decline in the extent and type of immigration aid rendered by the church. The church was not able to assume the financial burden of emigrating proselytes from Europe to Utah during the era of railroads and steamships primarily because payments to these "outside" agencies had to be made in cash, and there was no compensating build-up of cash in Utah. If the immigrants, upon their arrival in Utah, could have earned, in a reasonable length of time, sufficient in liquid funds to repay the loan, no obstacle would have been presented. But immigrants could do little more than assist, as immigrants had done since 1850, with the church public works. Thus, while the P.E. Company remained intact, continuing its many services at the ports of embarkation and debarkation and at the various railroad terminals along the way, the immigration of the 1870's and 1880's was financed primarily with private funds. The term "P.E. emigrants," to denote those whose entire journey was financed and provided by the P.E.F., does not occur in the records of the company after 1869. The P.E.F. did, however, accept deposits of cattle and grain from Utahans for the immigration of specific individuals and families.

The railroad and steamship era, of course, coincided with the build-up of antipolygamy legislation. A particular object of attack was the P.E.F. on the ground that it was feeding the church and polygamy. It had also become, in the eyes of many, "a repository or holding company for church wealth."[2] This "rich corporation," wrote Governor Eli H. Murray in 1883, "continues as a part of the Church and State machinery to gather converts from all parts of the world."[3] Agreeing with the governor's recommendations, President Grover Cleveland, in 1884, declared: "Since the people upholding polygamy in our Territories are reenforced by immigration from other lands, I recommend that a law be passed to prevent the importation of Mormons into the country."[4]

At first, an attempt was made to control or eliminate Mormon immigration through administrative regulation. American diplomatic and consular agents were instructed to discourage Mormon immigration in every possible way. Secretary of State William Evarts, in 1879, even went so far as to call the matter to the attention of several European powers, implying that it would be an unfriendly act for them not to take measures to stop the export of Mormon converts from their country to Utah.[5] Finally, in 1887, as we have seen, the Edmunds-Tucker Act dissolved the P.E. Company and enjoined the territorial legislature from chartering or recognizing "any corporation or association having for its purpose the bringing of persons into Utah for any purpose whatsoever." [6] While the charges of exorbitant wealth in the treasury of the P.E.F. were preposterous and quickly discovered to have no foundation in fact, the Edmunds-Tucker Act administered the *coup de grace* to the Mormon system of assisted immigration.

> Zion, once preached with so much intensity and conviction and expressed in a great program of immigration, was no longer a closed society. . . . With the establishment of a state Bureau of Immigration in 1911, what had been almost exclusively a Mormon enterprise turned secular, and Commissioner H. T. Haines in a letter to T. V. Powderley could advertise Utah as "a splendid state for the best classes of immigrants." [7]

Throughout its thirty-eight-year existence the Perpetual Emigrating Company helped directly or indirectly to immigrate over 100,000 persons, of which some 87,000 were from England and northern Europe.[8] From forty to fifty thousand of these were directly assisted in a financial way by the Fund.[9] The cost of all of this immigration, as measured by the cost to the immigrants if they had used commercial channels instead of the P.E.F., was approximately $25,000,000, of which it is estimated that the church through the P.E.F. expended (or would have expended if commercial channels had been used) approximately $12,500,000.

As the most important single enterprise undertaken by the Mormons in the nineteenth century, the Perpetual Emigrating Company implemented the gathering, imported enough people to qualify Utah for statehood, and furnished people to settle the territory and pre-empt its valuable lands before the Gentiles could come in. It also provided the conditions essential to profitable business by providing manpower in quantity and quality, by importing without special charge machinery and equipment for industry, and by furnishing labor for the construction of public buildings, the telegraph line, railroads, home industries, and other projects. In forcing the abolition of the Emigration Fund, however, Congress was merely "hastening what social and economic conditions were already accomplishing." [10] Where immigrants formerly had come by shiploads, they now came in handfuls. The lifeline of the Kingdom was broken.

Colonization. Despite the progressive decline in immigration as the end of the century approached, the need to establish new colonies continued. The high birthrate in Utah, the unfavorable economic situation produced by the Raid, and the long agricultural and mining depression of the period 1873–1896 combined to produce a continuing need for population outlets. The large colonization movement which had commenced in the late 1870's, therefore, continued throughout the 1880's and 1890's. The Mormons found a few waste places in Utah which could be irrigated — the Pahvant Valley in central Utah, the Uintah Basin of northeastern Utah, and the Grand Valley in southeastern Utah — but essentially the "last pioneers" had to look elsewhere for a home. Some of them settled in White Pine County, Nevada; the Big Horn Basin, in northern Wyoming or Star Valley in southern Wyoming; the Grande Ronde Valley in eastern Oregon; and scattered locations in Idaho, Arizona, and New Mexico. A number of Mormon settlements were planted in southern Alberta, Canada, and in northern Chihuahua and Sonora, Mexico. Some of these colonies were directly related to the Raid in the sense that polygamous husbands sought to find locations for their families in out-of-the-way places unlikely to be visited by federal deputies. Obviously, in such areas the opportunities for an economic livelihood were not particularly good.

Welcome as these outlets for population were, however, they were insufficient for the rapidly growing membership of the church. Large tracts of land — the last of the Western frontier — were offered for sale to the church in Bitter Root Valley, Montana; Grande Ronde Valley, Oregon; British Columbia; and in Argentina; but the church's financial condition was such that it could not purchase.[11] By 1899 church officials were forced to conclude that it was no longer advisable for converts to gather in Zion, even at their own expense.[12]

The change in colonizing techniques from pioneer style to the atomistic family movement which has characterized Mormon migration in the twentieth century reveals the process of accommodation. The essential ingredient in Mormon colonization in the period 1847–1884 was the submergence of individualism and the mobilization by ecclesiastical authorities of human, capital, and natural resources for building new communities. While property rights were not usually communal, they were in every case incidental to the common purpose. Until 1884, in other words, a Mormon colonizing "company" was a group of individuals, specially called and directed, working as a unit to found a settlement and develop its resources. All cast their lot with the common enterprise, and each benefited from the joint efforts of all.

During the 1880's, when ecclesiastical corporations were formed to hold church property and when mercantile and industrial cooperatives became incorporated as joint-stock concerns, new colonizing ventures followed the same practice. Companies were incorporated, shares of stock were subscribed, dividends were distributed, and property rights were precisely described and apportioned. Thus were organized The Mexican Colonization and Agricultural Company, which promoted colonization projects in Colorado and Mexico beginning in 1888; the Iosepa Agricultural & Stock Company, which founded a Hawaiian colony in Skull Valley, Utah, in 1889; the Deseret and Salt Lake Agricultural and Manufacturing Canal Company, established in 1889 to promote settlement in Millard County, Utah; the Alberta Land and Colonization Company, organized in 1896 to promote the development of projects in southern Alberta, Canada; the Nevada Land & Livestock Company, formed in 1897 to develop Mormon settlements in White Pine County, Nevada; and the Big Horn Basin Colonization Company, incorporated in 1900 to handle the colonization of Latter-day Saints in northern Wyoming. The capitalizations of these companies ranged from $50,000 to more than $1,000,000. The church assisted each of these companies financially, and held an important block of stock in each, and this influence submerged the tendency to convert them into ordinary commercial enterprises. Nevertheless, this was the "way of Babylon," not the "way of the Lord."

In 1899 officials became so concerned over the scattering of church members through the movement of unorganized bodies that they appointed a member of the Council of the Twelve, Apostle Abraham O. Woodruff, to supervise all Mormon colonization efforts.[13] The exhaustion of new lands for settlement, however, made the mission short-lived. With the death of Apostle Woodruff in 1904, official supervision of Mormon colonization largely terminated.

Enterprise. The position of the firm in Mormon social organization also went through two phases as it accommodated to the national pattern. The first phase began in 1882 when the First Presidency announced the end of the Gentile boycott and opened the fields of retailing and manufacturing to private enterprise. There followed a proliferation of independent private enterprises, quite outside the realm of church influence and control. These were financed partly by the private savings of merchants and mill owners and partly by banks which were established at the same time. These private corporations, a new phenomenon in the territory, were not organized in public meetings, as had been done earlier, and stock was not given in exchange for labor; but they were almost all Mormon enterprises. Among businesses organized during this period were banks, mercantile houses, utilities, mining enterprises, lumber concerns, foundries and machine companies, publishing companies, and various kinds of manufacturing concerns. Because of the conditions of the Raid, a number of important enterprises were successfully initiated by Gentiles.

In harmony with this multiplication of private concerns, most of the so-called church concerns were sold out to private interests or secularized in their policies. These included most local cooperative retailing and industrial enterprises which originally had public sponsorship at the local level; and also such general church concerns as the Salt Lake Street Railroad Company, Salt Lake City Gas Company, Zion's Savings Bank & Trust Company, Provo Woolen Mills, Z.C.M.I., and several land and irrigation projects. The trend toward secularization even transformed the Deseret Agricultural and Manufacturing Society, which in 1896 came directly under the control of the new state government. As an appointed state agency, the name of the D.A.&M. Society was changed in 1907 to the Utah State Fair Association, and its sole function since then seems to have been the sponsorship of the annual Utah State Fair.

Perhaps even more significant, Mormon businessmen were encouraged to unite with others in support of local chambers of commerce. In a formal discussion of this matter in 1898, the First Presidency and Quorum of the Twelve admitted that "the Saints never expected to be so mixed up with Gentiles as circumstances had led them into." It was still a principle of Mormon belief, in other words, "that the United Order would be established" eventually, and that ideal financial relationships would not exist "until that system should prevail among the Saints." Nevertheless, "under the present laws of the land, it would not be possible to establish that order," and thus it was proper for Mormon businessmen to cooperate with those not of their faith in improving the business systems of their communities.[14]

The most important symbol of the change in the function of church enterprises in the 1890's, however, was Z.C.M.I., which, it will be recalled, had been "sold" to a syndicate of young Mormon businessmen and financiers during the days of the Raid. Their assumption of management — and perhaps their policies — caused many church members to conclude that Z.C.M.I. had become "just another company" — had become, to use the phrase of President George Q. Cannon, who deprecated it, a "private corporation" with "no obligations to sustain it over and above another private corporation."[15] Z.C.M.I., for example, had regularly paid over to the church a tithe on all cash dividends declared since its formation. Approximately $161,000 had thus been paid between 1869 and 1891. Only once had a stockholder objected, and on that occasion the directors simply gave him his particular dividend without the tithe subtracted. In 1891, however, in accordance with a legal opinion rendered by the church attorney, and no doubt as the effect of the gradual disconnection between the trustee-in-trust and the institution, the Board of Directors dropped the practice. During the same year the Board removed the prohibition against the ownership of stock by non-Mormons, "provided, of course, that the control of the stock be kept here, and that no change take place in the management and defined policy of the Institution."[16] The subsequent history of Z.C.M.I. was not unlike that of similar large mercantile houses in the West. It continued to be profitable, and had more than 700 employees at the turn of the century. No longer, however, did the church and its officials urge their followers, as an act of religious loyalty, to patronize Z.C.M.I. or its branches.

The second phase in the accommodation of Mormon enterprise to the national pattern is evident in the arrangements made to finance new companies initiated in the 1890's. The church, in this phase, did not abandon its role as entrepreneur or innovator, as some Gentile enthusiasts hoped, nor did it relax the interest it had always shown in the development of local resources and the stimulation of home industry, as some Mormons feared. Moreover, as with the Provo Woolen Mills, the Washington Cotton Factory, and Z.C.M.I., the church used its own credit to supplement that of private enterprise, for the economic benefit of its members. But, as will be seen in the discussion of three typical cases, church policy broke with the past by actively soliciting financial assistance from outsiders. And the concessions made to these outside financial interests paved the way for absentee ownership and control. Eventually, the leviathan of American finance capitalism finally ruled Utah as it had long ruled Montana and other Western states and territories.

CASE STUDIES OF CHURCH PROMOTION IN THE 1890'S

A discussion, in some detail, of the transactions which led to outside control in three strategic industries reveals the process by which Mormon enterprise was accommodated to the national pattern. In each instance, the church played the predominant role in getting the industry established. In each case, the church used its financial resources to "rescue" the industry during the depression of the 1890's. Finally, in each industry, the church found it necessary to apply the "profit calculus" rather than the "welfare calculus" in order to preserve its own faltering credit.

The manufacture of sugar. Despite the failure of the Deseret Manufacturing Company in the 1850's, the church continued its interest in developing a local sugar industry. This was a matter of considerable economic import, for an estimated $1,000,000 was "lost" to the territory each year because of the necessity of having to import sugar.[17] With church encouragement and approval, Arthur Stayner, a Mormon horticulturist, experimented with sugar cane and sugar beets throughout the 1880's, and in 1887 received a $5,000 bounty from the territorial legislature for the first 7,000 pounds of marketable sugar produced in Utah.[18] Stayner twice solicited the financial support of the church to erect a factory to manufacture sugar from beets and/or cane during the period of the Edmunds-Tucker Act. Both times, President Woodruff declined such assistance because of "the unsettled condition of the church" and the confiscation of church property.[19] Nevertheless, Stayner visited the experimental plant of the government near Fort Scott, Kansas, and the new beet sugar plant of the Standard Refining Company at Alvarado, California.[20] He called a number of meetings to which church officials and Mormon businessmen were invited, and the First Presidency ultimately became convinced of the practicability of the industry. When a prospectus for the Utah Sugar Company was drawn up in the spring of 1889,[21] the First Presidency and Quorum of the Twelve supported a fund-raising drive with the following circular:

> Your attention is invited to the feasibility and practicability of establishing the industry of making sugar in this Territory.
>
> Amongst the many articles of importation for which we have been paying large sums of money annually, the article of sugar stands forth prominently as one of the most costly.
>
> For many years there existed a grave doubt whether or not the soil and climate of this Territory were suitable to the profitable production of sugar from any known sugar-bearing plant, but experiments made here during the past few years with sorghum cane and the introduction of the principle of diffusion in the extraction of the juice, have placed beyond doubt the practical and profitable production of sugar from that plant; and this success being assured, it is confidently believed that beets raised here in carefully selected localities can also be worked for sugar as readily and profitably as those raised in California, where the beet sugar production is a pronounced success. . . .
>
> As this industry when fully established will provide labor for hundreds, save the outgo of a very large amount annually, and yield a good profit to investors, we recommend it to the careful consideration and palpable support of all who desire to aid in the development of our Territory.[22]

President Woodruff had come to believe, he said, that it was "the mind and will of the Lord" that the sugar beet industry be established.[23]

As the result of this campaign sufficient capital stock was subscribed and paid by August 1889 to incorporate the Utah Sugar Company. Company and church officials then investigated the type of plant that should be erected, imported seed and initiated experimental plots for raising grain sorghum and sugar beets, and examined potential locations for the factory. It was determined to build a sugar beet factory, rather than a sugar cane factory, and to build it in Lehi, Utah County. The committee recommended a plant capable of working 350 tons of beets per day, at an estimated cost of $400,000, which would make it the largest sugar beet plant in the United States.[24] After meetings between the First Presidency of the Church, the Council of Twelve Apostles, the board of Zion's Savings Bank & Trust

Company, church lawyers, the board of the Utah Sugar Company, and other Mormon businessmen, the contract to build the factory was let in November 1890 to E. H. Dyer, who had built the plants for Claus Spreckels and associates at Alvarado and Watsonville, California.[25] The contract provided for immediate construction of the plant.

Most of the money which had been subscribed to the Utah Sugar Company seems to have consisted of promises, and after the first assessment, amounting to ten per cent of the stock subscribed, made in October 1890, the officers of the company found that there was a tendency, in the words of Wilford Woodruff, "to harden the work."[26] Many of the subscribers, "hard up for cash" in the fall of 1890, were unable or unwilling to fulfill their commitments. By the time the first $50,000 down payment on the construction contract was due on December 9, 1890, only $15,000 in cash seems to have been available for that purpose.[27] The remaining $35,000 was raised by borrowing, on the note of the company, endorsed by the First Presidency, from Zion's Savings Bank & Trust Company.[28] Having become convinced that the church should assure the establishment of the sugar beet industry, President Woodruff (with the support of his colleagues) was determined to use whatever church funds were available to assist the enterprise to get on its feet.[29] The considerations in the minds of the First Presidency were described four years later by President Joseph F. Smith as follows:

> We saw that we had reached a point in our history where there was not a single enterprise of a public character that was calculated to give employment to our people. The railroads had gone into the hands of the outsiders, . . . and instead of their pursuing a wise policy, they abandoned the course that had been pursued by their predecessors, and discharged the Mormon people from their service, brought strangers from the east and west, and gave them employment. . . . We began to feel that there was a responsibility resting upon us which required something to be done, in a small way at least, in the direction of giving employment to our people.[30]

After the cornerstone for the factory had been laid, the First Presidency issued a formal call to the leading financial men in the various wards and stakes to subscribe for stock in the concern and thus raise money to meet the company's notes and the construction costs as they came due.[31] In support of the circular, members of the Council of Twelve Apostles visited conferences and priesthood meetings in the various wards and stakes and urged the faithful to support the enterprise—at first by subscribing for stock, and later by buying its sugar.[32] In these speeches, church authorities stressed the employment it would provide, the scriptural admonitions to become self-sufficient, and the unfavorable treatment which Mormons were receiving from eastern corporations being established in the territory.[33]

The response to these appeals was niggardly. Remembering the failure of the Deseret Manufacturing Company, many thought that the alkali in the soil would prevent the crystallization of sugar from locally grown sugar beets. With others, fortunes had been depleted by the Raid or had been committed to such new industries as wool manufacturing, merchandising, banking, or real estate. Mormon capitalists were becoming more and more independent of the operations and suggestions of the church. Apostle Heber J. Grant, who was appointed to call on various Mormon bankers and capitalists in relation to the sugar company, related his experience as follows:

I was called upon a mission, and a letter was given to me in connection with other members of the Council of apostles. We were sent out to ask men to subscribe for stock in the Utah Sugar Company.

I took individual letters to different men asking them to subscribe. I delivered a letter to the late David Eccles [father of Marriner S. Eccles of Federal Reserve Bank fame], than whom I never met a clearer-headed business man in my life, and I have met men who draw their hundred thousand dollars and more every year in salary. He had a comprehensive grasp of business affairs which to me was superior to that of any man I ever met. David smiled when the letter was presented to him, signed by President Woodruff and his counselors, asking him to invest five thousand dollars, or seven thousand five hundred dollars.

He said, "Well, I would like to get off at the lowest figure. You can put me down for five thousand dollars." Then he added: "I hope they will buy lumber from me, so I may make a profit on a part of the five thousand dollars; and after I get my stock, if you can find someone who would like to buy it for twenty-five hundred dollars, I will be much obliged to you if you will come and get the stock." [34]

Men who would invest ten, twenty, thirty, fifty thousand dollars in sheep, and then go in debt in addition, would not put more than fifty or sixty dollars in this industry intended to create employment for the Latter-day Saints, and to benefit the farmers. . . . Many wealthy men whom I went to, with a letter from the Presidency of the Church, asking them to help that industry — and they were abundantly able to do it — declined to do so, and said they did not believe the Church had any business to put money in a sugar factory, that it was not within the province of the Church to do such things.[35]

Grant compared his efforts in raising money for the sugar company, in which he was armed with a circular letter from the Presidency of the Church "asking the Saints to subscribe of their means for the advancement of the kingdom of God," with another canvassing job in which "there was no circular from the Presidency of the Church, but the prospects of a good dividend were good." In the case of the sugar campaign, he said, he raised only half the amount required, whereas in the other, although $200,000 was wanted, $500,000 was obtained "without going out of Salt Lake City." [36]

With the Panic of 1891, many of those who had pledged support were unable to fulfill their commitments. The church itself was in debt by more than $300,000 as the result of the Edmunds-Tucker seizures, and found its credit position none too good. Apostle Grant was called on a mission to visit leading financial houses in the East and attempt to dispose of stocks, bonds, or notes of the company, but this mission was completely unsuccessful. Finally, in January 1891, the First Presidency decided to "shoulder the load and responsibility of the question of the manufacture of sugar" and appropriated $50,000 in tithing funds to make the first payment on the factory.[37] The First Presidency also signed notes for $150,000 borrowed from Salt Lake City banks; signed a note (along with twenty-four leading Mormon capitalists) to borrow $100,000 from the Wells-Fargo Bank, of San Francisco; and succeeded in obtaining $200,000 in subscriptions from some 700 Mormon stockholders.[38] Appeals were also made to Mormon farmers to plant sugar beets for eventual sale to the factory.[39] The factory was finally completed in October 1891, and the 10,000 tons of beets which had been dug and transported to the site were successfully refined into sugar.

While the enterprise had been proven to be a technical success, it was not yet a financial success. It took several years for farmers to learn to grow the crop successfully, with good yields and high sugar content. Apparently, some time was also required to convince prospective buyers that the sugar was as desirable as cane sugar. Thus, the company was not able to finance its early growth out of earnings. By 1893 the liabilities and net worth of the company totaled $679,000, of which only $277,000 was represented by capital stock. The church held approximately $70,000 of this capital stock, and also held or endorsed approximately $325,000 of the company's notes.[40] When the deepening national depression made it more and more costly to renew these notes, even with church endorsement, the company decided in 1895 to fund its indebtedness by issuing $400,000 worth of first mortgage bonds, with the factory and other real estate as security. When eastern investors failed to buy these bonds, the trustee-in-trust purchased them and then resold them, with a church guarantee, to Joseph Banigan, of Providence, Rhode Island, for $360,000.[41] Banigan, an Irish Catholic who had made a fortune in the production of rubber goods, was reported to have been induced to invest with the Mormons because of their "integrity, industry, and thrift."[42] George Q. Cannon, who represented the church in these negotiations, stated that he emphasized to Banigan and other eastern investors the conservative nature of the Latter-day Saints and the consequent risklessness of investment in their enterprises:

> I have endeavored to create the impression that in the mountains there was a conservative element that could be relied upon in the days of trouble. They would not organize into mobs, they would not raise riots, they would not be carried away by the ridiculous ideas which find circulation from time to time

throughout the country; but in days when other people would be quaking and trembling, and perhaps breaking forth in riot, they could be relied upon as conservative and stable. . . . I have also called attention to the fact that we were a people who were true to our engagements; that when we created an obligation that obligation would be maintained, and that our country was not plastered with mortgages, as many parts of the land were.[43]

The successful sale of the bond issue in 1895 marked the turning point in the financial standing of the company. Thereafter, it was able to meet all its outstanding accounts. In January 1896, near the end of the 1895–1896 season, the company paid its first cash dividend,[44] and from that time until the end of the century, the company operated in the black. The sale of the bonds also removed the burden of financial help from the shoulders of church officials. By July 1, 1898, the only church investment in the enterprise consisted of 8,520 shares of stock, with a face value of $85,200.[45] Indeed, by that date, the company was in a position to assist the church in its own financial difficulties. At that time, the company held three notes of the trustee-in-trust, signed in August, October, and November, 1897, respectively, amounting to a total of $75,993.25.[46] The shoe was now on the other foot!

By 1899 the factory was processing 36,000 tons of beets per season, with comparatively high content of sugar and purity. The factory employed more than 100 hands and provided additional income to more than 600 farmers. Considering the favorable rates of the Dingley Tariff, the company's prospects were so good that the directors planned to spend from half a million to a million dollars in doubling the capacity of the Lehi plant. The company also erected a million dollar factory in Garland, Utah, in 1903. At the same time a rash of Mormon companies, largely private in conception and financial backing, erected plants at Ogden, Logan, and Lewiston, Utah, and at Idaho Falls, Sugar City, Blackfoot, and Nampa, Idaho. The industry was well on its way toward permanent and profitable establishment. In 1907 most of these plants were united under the Utah-Idaho Sugar Company, a $13,000,000 combination which was essentially promoted by the church.[47]

The manufacture of salt. While the attempts were being made to establish a local sugar industry, a similar effort was being made to manufacture salt and develop other industries along the shore of the Great Salt Lake. Since 1847 the Mormons had mined and refined salt along the shores of Salt Lake for use within the territory and for export to mines in Montana, Idaho, and Nevada. The first sustained efforts to manufacture salt on a large scale came in the 1880's when at least three important companies were organized for this purpose. The most important of these was a group of young Mormons, under the leadership of the church treasurer, James Jack, who acquired 1,000 acres of land along the shore, formed the Inland Salt Company, and installed a system of pumps to pump salt water into specially constructed beds for evaporation.[48] The concern was incorporated for $100,000, of which $25,000 in stock was held by Jack, possibly in trust for the church. Whether or not any of the charter stock was held by the church, the First Presidency had associated itself with the enterprise by 1889.[49] At that time, during an official inspection tour of the plant, the First Presidency was pleased to note that the company employed fifty men and was prepared to produce fifty tons of "pure fine salt," most of it destined for the livestock yards and packing houses in Omaha.[50] In addition, the company made up a carload (about 100 tons) of loose salt for shipment to Montana mines.[51] This company was sold for a reported $200,000 to a Midwest syndicate in April 1891, and was reincorporated as the Inland Crystal Salt Company.[52] The latter company speeded up the expansion program and soon had 200 men at work on the grounds. Its production in 1892 was estimated at 250,000 tons, of which 50,000 tons consisted of refined "Royal Crystal" salt.

Apparently using the money obtained from the sale of the Inland Salt Company, church officials and those associated with them in the Inland enterprise, entered upon other projects to develop the resources of the Great Salt Lake shoreline. In June 1891, they formed the Saltair Beach Company for the purpose of establishing a bathing resort and place of recreation "for the benefit of the Latter-day Saints."[53] It was the design to build a sixteen-mile railroad from Salt Lake City to the resort and later, if feasible, extend the line toward Los Angeles. To this end the Saltair Railway Company was organized in September 1891. A few months later, as the planning became more ambitious, the name of the company was changed to Salt Lake & Los Angeles Railway Company.[54]

The initial sixteen-mile road was completed in 1893 at an estimated cost of $200,000, of which the church apparently advanced $110,000. In addition, beach properties worth $125,000 were acquired from Matthew White, who had ambitious plans of his own, and preparations were under way in 1891–1892 to engage in what was called "a grand enterprise"—an enterprise which, including beach resort, railway, and salt interests, cost $600,000.[55] About 200 new bath houses were constructed, and an immense oriental-like pavilion, called "Saltair," was constructed on the lake in 1893 at a cost of approximately $350,000.[56] The church furnished at least $185,000 and possibly more. Providing employment for church members was one purpose of this large expenditure; another was the desire to provide a wholesome place of recreation under the control of the church.[57] The plush pavilion became a popular resort, but was never financially profitable. It was partially burned in 1925.

In the meantime, essentially the same group incorporated the Intermountain Salt Company, erected a large salt refinery a few miles west of Salt

Lake City in 1893, and produced up to thirty tons of table and dairy salt each day. In 1895, the annual production was 50,000 tons of refined salt.[58] The company also acquired the Mormon-controlled Nebo Salt Company, incorporated 1893, which manufactured up to 500 pounds of dairy salt daily from beds near Nephi, Utah.[59]

In 1897 the refining works of the Intermountain Salt Company were "totally destroyed" by fire, and the loss was only partially covered by insurance.[60] This led to a "deal" in 1898 by which the church acquired a controlling interest in the lucrative Inland Crystal Salt Company, and through the latter bought out the Intermountain Salt Company. This gave the trustee-in-trust and the prominent Mormons associated with him a virtual monopoly on the salt and other interests at Great Salt Lake.[61] The church apparently invested $300,000 in these enterprises, of which approximately $110,000 was expended on the building of the railroad, $75,000 on the Saltair Pavilion, and $110,000 on the projects of the Inland Crystal Salt Company.[62] The salt company was the only one of the three enterprises which paid regular dividends. The companies operating all three properties were heavily overcapitalized.

It should be noted that these enterprises differed from those promoted in the 1870's in at least three respects. (1) Whereas the 1870 ventures were constructed with battalions of volunteer workers recruited from the various settlements, laboring primarily for tithing pay or stock in the enterprise, the salt plant, railroad, and pavilion were all constructed on a contract basis by private enterprise motivated by profit. It would even appear that no preference was given to Mormon workers. (2) Whereas in the 1870 ventures "the building of the Kingdom" and "the welfare of Zion" were paramount, more attention was paid to profit in the operation of the Great Salt Lake enterprises of the 1890's. It was originally intended, for example, that the Saltair pavilion would be closed on Sunday, and no barroom would be permitted. But when it became clear that neither the railroad nor the pavilion would be paying propositions on that basis, the First Presidency, mindful of the church's financial difficulties, allowed a private group to take over the management of the resort, open up saloons, operate on Sunday, and in return guarantee a certain return to the church.[63] There were also charges that the Pavilion permitted gambling machines. This placed the church in the embarrassing position of owning a resort which served liquor and having in the interests of profit to work up patronage for it. (3) The salt company, which was the only really profitable concern of the three, achieved some of this profit by its monopolistic position. It did not hesitate to eliminate competition by purchase and moral suasion, and thus to some extent achieved profits from scarcity rather than abundance.[64] This was a policy which had never been applied before by a "church" company.

Hydroelectric power plants. Among the newcomers to Utah near the end of the century was a remarkable young engineer, Charles K. Bannister. Bannister and a group of younger men in Weber Valley, some of whom were Latter-day Saints, were among the first to sense the enormous potential for hydroelectric power in the waterfalls of the Wasatch Mountains. These young men sought the assistance of the church in a project, and on November 27, 1893, just twenty days after the construction of the first hydroelectric plant in the West at Redlands, California, the Pioneer Electric Power Company was organized at Ogden, Utah.[65] The company's object was to build a dam across Ogden River, in Ogden Canyon, about ten miles east of Ogden, create a huge reservoir of water for power, culinary, and irrigation purposes, and provide power for the city of Ogden, for the use of electric railways in Ogden and Salt Lake City, and for factories of every description in northern Utah. It was expected that up to 20,000 acres of arid land in the northwestern part of Weber Valley could be irrigated with the surplus water stored in the eastern end of Ogden Canyon. This land was thought to be peculiarly adapted to the culture of sugar beets, and the company expected to establish a power-operated factory near Ogden to transform the beets into sugar. Consideration was also given to the trade potential resulting from the attraction of tourists to the reservoir. Water would be conveyed from the dam to the powerhouse nearer Ogden by means of a wooden pipeline, six miles long, reinforced by bands of steel.[66]

In order to lend their names and influence to the effort to interest eastern and European capital in the venture, the First Presidency of the church subscribed for $520,000 (out of $1,000,000) in stock and participated in the planning. Although this stock was listed as fully paid, it would appear that most of it was issued as a gift or in lieu of land and water rights turned over to the company by the church.[67] President Woodruff's first counselor, George Q. Cannon, was made president of the company.

In the spring of 1894, several months after the company was formed, the promoters succeeded in interesting a New York broker by the name of George A. Purbeck in the scheme. Purbeck, whose firm reputedly had branch offices in London, Paris, and Amsterdam, went to Utah in May 1894, in company with Thomas S. King, consulting engineer of the New York elevated railroads, and Warren H. Loss, construction engineer of international reputation, and entered into a series of conferences with church officials that lasted two weeks.[68] "I have felt," wrote President Woodruff in his diary, "that the Lord has raised up that man [Purbeck] to assist us in our temporal deliverance." [69] On May 22, 1894, Wilford Woodruff, as church president, entered into a contract with Purbeck whereby the latter agreed to act as the church financial agent to raise $1,250,000 to finance the Ogden project.[70] Although Purbeck and Frank J. Cannon, the company manager, developed eastern and European contacts, and even went to New York, Liverpool, and Paris for discussions, the necessary capital was not obtained. The national depression undoubtedly had something to do with their failure, as did uncertainties in regard to the technical possibility of transporting power over long distances — a thing which had never before been attempted. Some engineer-consultants may have advised delay until this was demonstrated to be feasible.

In the meantime, during 1894 and 1895, the engineer carried on a program of exploration and development. Over the signatures of church officials, an estimated $100,000 was borrowed for this purpose from local banks.[71] The site for a dam was located, a contract was let to manufacture and lay the water pipe, and sections of land to be irrigated were acquired and placed on the market.

In August 1895, when Joseph Banigan bought $400,000 of church-guaranteed bonds of the Utah Sugar Company, he indicated an interest in other Mormon projects.[72] Negotiations were entered into which resulted in his agreement, in November 1895, to invest $1,500,000 in the Ogden project. A new company, The Pioneer Electric Power Company, was organized, with a capitalization of $2,000,000, and the deal was closed in February 1896.[73] George Q. Cannon, of the First Presidency, was made president and treasurer of the new concern, and chairman of its finance committee. In the new corporation the church held approximately $350,000 of the $400,000 in common stock issued at the time of the reorganization, and most of the stock issued thereafter on a pro rata basis. The precise arrangements, as worked out in February and March 1896, stipulated that the Pioneer Electric Power Company would issue 1,500 gold bonds, each with a face value of $1,000 and bearing six per cent interest. The bonds would mature in intervals of four years, the last being payable on July 1, 1916. Banigan agreed to purchase the whole issue of these bonds in return for which the bonds would be "unconditionally and absolutely guaranteed" by Wilford Woodruff, George Q. Cannon, and Joseph F. Smith, of the First Presidency, and by Wilford Woodruff as trustee-in-trust for the church. Because of this guarantee, and the general importance of the project, the First Presidency took a principal role in the management of the concern.[74] Most of the church's large stockholdings were predicated or awarded on the basis of this guarantee. As Banigan said, perhaps not quite accurately, "You people who will not actually have invested a dollar of money will have $1,700,000 of stock in a paying enterprise. It is only my absolute confidence in the . . . honest character of your people which prompt me to make an offer." [75]

With financial help assured, several hundred men were employed and the actual construction proceeded apace. A long canal was dug from the damsite to west Ogden—"one of the finest canals in the Western world," wrote President Woodruff.[76] The company's arrangement with farmers was that they give up an acre of land in return for sufficient water to water an acre. A temporary dam strong enough to allow the generation of a supply of electricity was completed by the end of 1896, and the permanent dam was completed in the spring of 1898 at a cost of $250,000. A power plant with a capacity of 10,000 horsepower was completed in 1897.

The construction was a major engineering achievement.[77] Machine shops were built for the fashioning of the steel pipe (which had a diameter of six feet). Special planing mills were erected to produce staves for the pipe from the 2,000,000 cubic feet of special Oregon pine, completely free from knots, which was shipped from Portland and Seattle for the company's use. The laying of the pipeline required cutting through towering cliffs, and one tunnel 600 feet long was cut through solid rock. The construction of the electric line to Salt Lake City, a distance of about thirty-seven miles, was also unprecedented in American engineering. Until its completion, the farthest distance which power had been transmitted was the General Electric line from Niagara to Buffalo, completed in 1895, which was twenty-six miles in length. The Pioneer line, designed to work at 15,000 volts, was the first long-distance transmission from a man-made dam especially constructed to generate electricity. The 2,500 poles required for the line were made from Idaho cedar, shipped from Lake Pend Oreille in northern Idaho, some 1,100 miles north of Ogden. The dam extended from canyon wall to canyon wall, and was 340 feet long, 93 feet thick, and 60 feet high.

After construction of its facilities was completed, the company immediately obtained a franchise to provide electricity in Salt Lake City, and made plans to buy out or consolidate with the Salt Lake and Ogden Gas and Electric Light Company, the Citizens' Electric Light Company, and the Big Cottonwood Power Company, all of which had been providing gas and electrical service in Salt Lake City previous to the completion of the Pioneer plant.[78] The fruit of these negotiations was a giant combine called the Union Light & Power Company, incorporated August 9, 1897.

The companies which were consolidated in this maneuver were partly Mormon and partly Gentile. The largest of the group was the Mormon-promoted Big Cottonwood Power Company, which was organized shortly after the Pioneer Power Company for the purpose of developing the electric power generating potentialities of Big Cottonwood Canyon, fourteen miles southeast of Salt Lake City. What the Pioneer Power Company was doing for Weber Valley and north Salt Lake City, the Big Cottonwood Power Company would do for Salt Lake City and the southern part of the Salt Lake Valley. As with the Pioneer company, the Big Cottonwood company was also held up by the depression of 1893–1894 and the technical difficulty of long-distance power transmission. When the technical problem was solved, the company borrowed from Zion's Savings Bank & Trust Company and from other sources and completed its installations in 1896–1897, during the time the Pioneer company was doing the same. The Big Cottonwood plant had a capacity of 2,000 kilowatts, and its line to Salt Lake City was designed to work at 10,000 volts. Municipal and private contracts were obtained in Salt Lake City and Murray, and by the time of its transfer to Union Light & Power the company was worth about $500,000.[79]

The other two companies had no connection with the church, but had constructed steam plants and operated natural and artificial gas works. The smaller of the two, the Citizens' Electric Light Company, later incorporated as the Cottonwood Water, Power and Electric Company, was organized in 1896 with a capital of $100,000 to develop power facilities on Little Cottonwood Creek, southeast of Salt Lake City.[80] The larger, the Salt Lake and Ogden Gas and Electric Company, was a successor of the Salt Lake City Gas Company. Shortly after the latter company was purchased by the church receiver, Frank H. Dyer, and his attorneys in 1890, all of the stock of the Salt Lake Power Light & Heating Company (in operation since 1880) was acquired. The combined assets were then sold in 1893 to J. Elliott Condict of San Francisco for the sum of $400,000. The latter then absorbed its assets in the newly organized Salt Lake and Ogden Gas and Electric Company. This company, with $1,500,000 in bonds held by English capitalists, owned most of the public utilities in Ogden, and had gas and electric production and distribution systems in Salt Lake City.[81]

The combine which united all of these, the Union Light & Power Company, was capitalized at $4,550,000, with 18,295 of the 45,500 shares of capital stock held by members of the First Presidency of the church.[82] Eastern interests held 15,977 shares, and the remainder was held by Zion's Savings Bank and by Mormon and other Utah capitalists. George Q. Cannon was president of the new company, as he had been of its predecessor. On the basis of the properties acquired from the companies which were consolidated in its formation, the Union company was able to issue $2,250,000 in consolidated mortgage bonds to sponsoring English capitalists and others, and an additional $1,500,000 in first mortgage bonds to exchange for the Pioneer Electric bonds held by Banigan. This made a total bonded indebtedness of $3,750,000. The church was happy to sponsor the consolidation because it removed some of the immediacy from the church guarantee of the $1,500,000 bonds of the Pioneer Electric Power Company. Before the church could be pressed for payment of the guarantee, in other words, the Union Light & Power Company would have to fail.[83] As it turned out, however, the church was forced to pay nearly all the interest on the Banigan bonds during the years 1897–1898 because neither the Pioneer nor the Union companies earned sufficient revenue to do so.[84] For performing this financial service, the church was rewarded with an equivalent value of consolidated mortgage bonds of the Union company.[85]

The Union Light & Power Company was thought by Utah people to be the most extensive and complete system for the distribution of electrical energy and power over a wide area in the United States, and this may have been true. Its system embraced the Salt Lake and Weber valleys, and the total capacity of the machinery already installed was over 8,000 horsepower. The company owned 200 miles of overhead line construction, and about 10,000 poles. It obtained power from the Ogden River, Big Cottonwood River, and two steam plants in Salt Lake and one in Ogden. The company also owned plants for manufacturing and distributing coal gas in Salt Lake and Ogden, and controlled the entire production of the natural gas wells near Salt Lake City.[86]

Nevertheless, the revenue was far from sufficient to meet the interest on the heavy bonded indebtedness. Technical difficulties were experienced regularly, reflecting the unsettled state of electrical technology at the time. Despite economies achieved through physical consolidation, and the improvement of service through joint hookups and better machinery, there was dissatisfaction with interruptions and delays. There were frequent clashes with the company's chief competitor, the newly organized Utah Power Company, and the company's contracts were none too sure, particularly when confronted with the newly elected anti-Mormon city government of Salt Lake City. The church newspaper also claimed, in a lengthy editorial, that the company had gone beyond the call of duty in extending its service to the general public, charging low rates, and installing technological improvements. "The uniform policy of the directors," wrote the editor, "has been broad and liberal towards the public." [87] Illustrative of its financial difficulties, the company's minutes state, on November 19, 1897: "Our present revenue falls short some $120,000 per year of meeting our fixed expenses." During a subsequent twelve-month period the earnings were only $35,000, forcing the company to sell $750,000 in prior lien bonds in order to meet interest payments on the previously issued consolidated bonds. This increased the total bonded debt to $4,500,000, which was undoubtedly well in excess of the value of the company's physical properties.[88] One year later, the church was forced to pay $180,000 on interest on bonds which the company was unable to pay and which the church had guaranteed.[89]

This situation continued until it was universally recognized that a reorganization was inevitable. A reorganization plan was approved in June 1899, and instituted in December of the same year. Under this agreement, the value of outstanding bonds was scaled down from $4,500,000 to $3,000,000, thus reducing annual interest charges by $130,000. The church agreed to guarantee one per cent interest on the preferred stock, and, in return for the surrender of the guarantee on the $1,500,000 first mortgage bonds held by the Banigans, the church agreed to pay the Banigans $225,000, for which it would receive additional preferred stock in its own name.[90] Upon the completion of the signing of papers, exchange of securities, and deliveries of cash in December 1899, a successor company, the Utah Light and Power Company, came into existence.

As already stated, the outstanding bonded debt of the Utah Light and Power Company was $3,000,000, with an additional $500,000 to be issued for construction and improvement.[91] The par value of stock in the new concern equaled this figure, with a total of 80,000 shares of preferred and 42,500 shares of common stock. The largest block of preferred, 43,660 shares, went to eastern trusts representing English capitalists; 26,340 shares to the trustee-in-trust of the church; and 10,000 shares to the Banigan heirs. The largest block of common stock, 20,492 shares, went to the trustee-in-trust of the church, another 15,980 shares to the New York trusts, and the remainder consisted of small holdings owned principally by Utah Mormons. Once more, George Q. Cannon was elected president of the concern, and all other officers were prominent Mormon businessmen.

Caught up in the tide of McKinley prosperity, the Utah Light and Power Company was increasingly profitable. The church guarantee was lifted in 1903,[92] and in 1904 the company merged with its only competitor, the Consolidated Railway and Power Company of Salt Lake City (which in the meantime had acquired control of the Utah Power Company), to form the Utah Light and Railway Company.[93] In this company the church, through its trustee-in-trust, President Joseph F. Smith, shared a controlling interest with A. W. McCune, a wealthy Mormon mining magnate and architect of the Consolidated Railway and Power Company. The Utah Light & Railway Company had a working monopoly on all the street railways in Salt Lake and Ogden (including the Salt Lake Street Railroad Company promoted by the church in 1872), and all the electrical generating facilities in Weber, Davis, and Salt Lake counties. With a capitalization of $10,000,000, it was the largest corporation formed in Utah until the incorporation of the Utah-Idaho Sugar Company in 1907.

Other enterprises. In mitigating the effects of the depression of the 1890's the church, through the agency of the First Presidency, attempted to promote other enterprises calculated to provide employment and develop the resources of the region. Among these was an attempt to develop the coal resources near Coalville and Cedar City. Another looked toward the working of the iron mines at Iron Mountain. Still another plan was to construct a railroad from Salt Lake to Los Angeles. Finally, there were plans to improve transportation facilities in Utah by constructing several hundred miles of new railroad track. In each case, companies were formed, capital was solicited in the East, and developmental and surveying work was financed by the church. At one point, a giant scheme was planned requiring $75,000,000 to finance.[94] "Had the Latter-day Saints observed the instructions of God," stated Apostle Abraham H. Cannon, who represented the church in many of these negotiations, "there would not now be poor and unemployed in our midst. . . . It was not only the duty of those in authority in Zion to attend meetings and look after the spiritual welfare of the people, but also to see that their temporal wants were complied with; men and women who were cold and hungry could not worship God as they should do." [95] He continued:

If our Utah people do not awaken to the situation, one of these days, after their Rip Van Winkle sleep, they will peep out and see all these valuable resources taken up and operated by outsiders. Eastern capitalists and foreign capital will do for us what we ought to unite and do for ourselves. We may be sure we will have to pay dearly for our privileges.[96]

Fortunately or unfortunately, the prolonged depression of the 1890's, making it difficult to secure outside capital, and the increasing church debt, made it impossible to carry out any of these gigantic plans.[97] However, the church spent at least $100,000 on the exploratory phases of these projects.

THE CHURCH DEBT

It will be recalled that the church went into debt to the extent of about $300,000 as the direct effect of the Edmunds-Tucker Act and the creation of the government receivership of church property. The church also undertook to care for the families of those in prison, to aid poorer members in the payment of lawyers' fees and court costs, and maintained a sizeable "Defense Fund" of its own to pay legal fees and finance a campaign in the East to fight the law and its action.[98] At the same time, however, tithing receipts dropped from an average of more than $500,000 per year, during the 1880's, to a little more than $300,000 in 1890.[99] This was due, of course, to the unsettled nature of church finance. Why turn tithing over to the church if the government was going to get it? Moreover, the idea of tithing as a compulsory payment had been played upon so effectively by hostile writers and speechmakers that the trustee-in-trust was forced, in order to prevent confiscation of current tithing receipts, to substitute the word "voluntary offerings" for "tithing" on certificates issued during the late 1880's and early 1890's.[100] While the personal and real properties forfeited under the Edmunds-Tucker Act were returned to the church during the 1890's, their value was considerably reduced because of mismanagement and waste and the sale of several revenue-producing properties. Moreover, the church did not have the benefit of the use of a large share of the confiscated properties during the eight-year period of the receivership. Consequently, the long-run effect of the Edmunds-Tucker law was to throw the church, which had previously enjoyed a creditor status, into a debt of at least half a million dollars.

There were certain obligations and commitments which served to swell this debt during the 1890's. The first was the completion of the Salt Lake Temple. President Wilford Woodruff, in his eighty-third year by 1890, was anxious to finish this sacred structure in his lifetime. The stepped-up efforts of the church during Woodruff's administration, involving an expenditure of about $1,000,000, made possible the completion and dedication of this $4,000,000 structure in 1893.[101] A second obligation of the church was education. The First Presidency distributed a circular to stake presidents and bishops in 1890 bemoaning the fact that the desire for learning had "in too many instances . . . been lost sight of in the toil for daily existence," and requesting an expansion in local educational programs. A General Board of Education for the church was established for the purpose of assisting and coordinating the educational efforts of local communities. A considerable share of the annual church budget was allotted for this purpose each year.[102] The academies which were built with tithing properties in 1888–1890 received appropriations from this source as did the Brigham Young Academy in Provo, the Brigham Young College in Logan, and the Latter-day Saint College of Salt Lake City, all of which embarked on expansion programs in the field of higher education.[103] Welfare expenditures also increased during the depression of the 1890's. Finally, as has been noted, large sums were expended on the development of the sugar, salt, and hydroelectric power industries. By 1898, the church's debt amounted to over $1,250,000.[104]

The wherewithal to meet church expenditures came from tithing and donations, and from credit extended by banks, business houses, and private individuals. Tithing receipts in 1890 were about $350,000, and rose through the years to a total of about $600,000 in 1898.[105] This, of course, was quite insufficient to carry on the enlarged construction, educational, and economic program of the church. In 1893, as tithing receipts dropped off sharply and the need of funds to protect the church business interests rose equally, the financial predicament of the church was presented in a special meeting to all stake presidents, and a total of $105,000 was borrowed from these men and their constituents at that time.[106] Later in the same year, the church obtained $200,000 from J. B. Claflin of Chicago, for a period of three years, at six per cent interest and a bonus of $50,000.[107] This loan was renegotiated when due and was not finally repaid until March 1899. Additional credit, amounting to perhaps as much as $100,000, was obtained from Salt Lake City banks before the end of the year.[108] Indeed, the church's financial problem by 1894 had become so acute that the trustee-in-trust found himself borrowing from one bank to pay another. "We are passing through a great financial difficulty," wrote President Woodruff in his journal, "the Lord alone can help us out. . . . Our debts are very heavy . . . money matters are crowding hard upon us." [109]

The fiscal position of the church was so desperate that at one point the church was almost prepared to rely on a gold mine to rescue it from the abyss. During the winter of 1893–1894, when the general authorities had under consideration a proposal to build a railroad from Salt Lake City to Los Angeles, three men who had been hired to make a survey of the road discovered a gold mine in southwestern Nevada. When this matter was properly reported, a Utah corporation called the Sterling Mining and Milling Company was organized to work the claim. The church put approximately $180,000 into this mining venture in 1894–1896, with very little return. That the church was willing to go to this extreme to ease its financial burden demonstrates the seriousness with which its officials viewed its predicament.[110]

The increased expenditures of the church in the face of inadequate receipts caused the deficit to continue to mount. In January 1895, a committee of men appointed to ease the church's burden obtained $500,000 from New York sources, on the security of the note of the church president. One of those participating in the negotiations wrote: "Our credit rested on the belief that the Mormon people were ready to consecrate all their possessions at any time to the service of the Church at the command of the president." [111] Some of this credit was used in meeting other debts coming due, but most of it represented an addition to the total church debt. Additional credit was solicited in succeeding years from banks, business houses, and members of the church, so that by July 1898 the church owed $935,000 to banks (about half was owed to banks outside Utah), more than $100,000 to business houses in Salt Lake City, and more than $200,000 to individual Latter-day Saints.[112] Almost $200,000, or one-third of the church's budget in 1898, was required to meet interest on indebtedness and sinking fund. At least half of the debt bore an interest of ten per cent or more.

The enormity of the church's expenditure on interest, and the constant harassment of creditors pressing for the payment of this note and that, led the church, in 1898, to fund the debt by issuing bonds. When extended negotiations between the church and eastern financial interests for the sale of $1,500,000 in church bonds fell through, Lorenzo Snow, who had assumed the presidency of the church upon the death of Wilford Woodruff in September 1898, decided to borrow the money "among ourselves," rather than, as he expressed it, "go into the world for the means." [113] After determining that the trustee-in-trust had the power to issue bonds, three bond issues of

$500,000 each were planned. The bonds would mature in eleven years (redeemable in five), bear an interest rate of six per cent, and have maturity values of $100, $500, and $1,000.[114] Although the church's assets were far in excess of the contemplated issue, it was decided not to issue the bonds with specific security. Each issue of $500,000 was to be redeemed by setting aside $30,000 of the tithing for interest, and $50,000 for a sinking fund.[115] The first issue of $500,000 was offered for sale on January 1, 1899, and was sold within a few weeks. A second issue of equal size was placed on the market on January 4, and was disposed of within the year. Nearly all of the bonds were purchased by Mormons and Mormon financial institutions.[116] The improving financial fortunes of the church made it unnecessary to issue a third series. Half of the total issue was redeemed by 1903, and the remainder of the debt was extinguished by 1907. Total interest payments during the years the issues were outstanding amounted to $200,000.[117] One reason for the ability of the church to pay the interest and retire the debt so quickly, in the face of heavy expenditures for missionary work, education, welfare, and construction, was the strong emphasis on the payment of tithes during the years the debt existed.[118]

SALE OF CHURCH BUSINESS ASSETS

The combination of events which followed the Edmunds-Tucker Act, the Woodruff Manifesto, and the granting of Statehood, as has been intimated, worked inexorably to change official Mormon economic policy. But though the mills of the gods grind finely, to switch a famous line, they also grind exceeding slow. At least this is the way it seemed to many of the "reformers" bent on bringing the Mormons back into the dominant cultural pattern of the nation. The stubbornness with which some Mormons held to the principle of polygamy was one object of attack; but a far more important charge was directed against the church's economic policies. All could see that major changes had occurred: Tie-ups had been made with eastern capital; the corporate form had replaced the theocratic and cooperative forms of a generation earlier; Mormons were joining Chambers of Commerce, civic clubs, and working closely with Gentiles in Utah in many business ventures; and the church no longer insisted that members "ask counsel" and "take counsel" in regard to economic affairs. Most of the goals of the pioneer church — the gathering, the Mormon village, unique property institutions, economic independence, the theocratic Kingdom — were abandoned, or well on their way toward abandonment, at the end of the century. But in the eyes of many this was not enough. The church was still an active force in the economic life of the community, as a promoter and proprietor, and this was deemed inconsistent with the laissez-faire and free enterprising concepts of national policy. In a period when it was popular to attack the "trusts," it seemed the essence of consistency to attack the Mormon Church as a gigantic holding company controlling the strategic industries of the region. This appeared to be demonstrated by the activities of the church in stimulating the development of the sugar, salt, and hydroelectric power industries and in promoting grandiose railroad and mining projects. The church, asserted its detractors, was attempting to prolong and strengthen its control over the industries of the region, to the detriment of its competitors and followers.

An indication of the generality of dissatisfaction with the speed of the church's adjustment to prevailing national sentiment was furnished in the Roberts case of 1898–1900. Brigham H. Roberts, a gifted writer and orator and member of the First Council of Seventy of the church, was elected as Utah's Congressman in the election of 1898. He had been convicted of unlawful cohabitation in 1889, which some considered sufficient disqualification for the office. When he was elected by a considerable majority, however, the charge was made that in sending Roberts as congressman-elect the people of Utah had violated a "compact" with the United States. The "compact" was variously interpreted, but had reference to the unwritten agreement or understanding that the church would adopt the dominant cultural pattern of the nation in return for statehood and presidential amnesty. After a brief investigation, it seemed clear to the majority of Congressmen that Roberts' election, considering his Mormon fealty, was indeed a violation of the compact and that this was a sufficient basis for excluding him from membership. This position was reinforced by petitions, said to bear the signatures of 7,000,000 persons, protesting his admission. By a vote of 268 to 50 Roberts was refused his seat, and Utah was forced to choose another to represent her interests in the 56th Congress.[119]

The case which touched off a much more important investigation involved the seating of Utah's senator-elect Reed Smoot. Reed Smoot was not a polygamist, as Roberts had been, but he was a member of the Quorum of Twelve Apostles, a higher position in the church than Roberts had held. Following Smoot's election in 1903, a group of Salt Lake citizens lodged a formal protest with the Senate praying that Smoot "be not permitted to . . . sit as a member of the United States Senate, for reasons affecting the honor and dignity of the United States and their Senators in Congress." The prayer was denied, and Senator Smoot was seated, but petitions began to pour in from all parts of the country — petitions containing in excess of 1,000,000 signatures. The Senate Committee on Privileges and Elections then commenced an investigation of the church and its "hierarchy" in what is known as the "Smoot trial." The investigation lasted three years, and the testimony of witnesses and arguments of counsel comprise five volumes of about 4,000 pages. It was, wrote Professor Garner, "the most thorough and exhaustive investigation of Mormon affairs ever made."[120] "The charge here, in its widest scope," said one of the investigating senators, "is that the Mormon Church controls the politics and industries of Utah."[121]

Coincident with the Smoot investigation a "crusade" was launched in a number of national magazines designed to "expose" and destroy the "tyranny" of the church, particularly in the field of business. In such magazines as *McClure's, Everybody's, Pearsons,* and *Cosmopolitan* — and even in such august journals as the *North American Review* and the *Atlantic* — the church was referred to as a viper and a lawbreaker, and its business activities were linked up with the current bugaboo, "the trusts."[122] Two British observers, accepting this literature and its insinuations at face value, came to the conclusion, in a serious work, that the Mormon Church was virtually the mother of all trusts:

> The Church . . . is said to draw a hundred per cent. dividend from money invested in the Rubber Trust, formed by Senator Aldrich; to have an interest in the great National City Bank at 52 Wall Street, New York, and in many other banks; and to be in greater or less degree a partner with the trusts that control in the United States the wool, beef, tin, oil, tobacco, iron, and farming-implement industries.[123]

The reasoning was simple: Reed Smoot's first loyalty was to the church. Reed Smoot supported tariff legislation which protected all of these trusts. Therefore, the Mormon Church must be linked up with the trusts in a financial way. For a small, relatively isolated community, lodged in the inhospitable wastes of the Great Basin, the allegation of partnership with these giant combines was almost a compliment!

The main charge under consideration in the Smoot trials was that Reed Smoot allegedly was one of a "self-perpetuating body of fifteen men," who controlled the temporal and spiritual, civil and religious affairs, of Mormon Country, and was therefore not entitled to a seat in the Senate. The general authorities of the Mormon Church, witnesses declared, interfered in politics, conducted business affairs on a large scale, and made use of the public schools to inculcate the doctrines of the Mormon religion. The church owned and operated street railways, electric light and power plants, coal mines, salt works, sugar factories, mercantile establishments, publishing houses, and theaters, and, according to the charge, refused to permit competition on the part of non-church and non-Mormon enterprises. That the church was accused of proprietary monopoly rather than of radical progressivism, as had been true through much of its earlier history, was a sign of the transformation which had occurred in Mormon policy and practice between 1890 and 1904. The transformation was not lessened by the fact that it was largely involuntary.

The church responded to these charges by stating the obvious truth that many non-Mormon churches also owned and managed income-producing property, that its interests in many of these properties was not controlling, and that its economic policies were permissive, not compulsive. The counsel for Smoot also argued that, whether or not these policies of the church were reprehensible, this had no relation to the qualification of Reed Smoot to retain his seat in the United States Senate. Finally, the church argued that many of the enterprises in which it had an interest were established to provide employment and income for the poor, and that this concern for man's physical and economic welfare was a legitimate object of religion. "Food for the stomach, clothes for the back, and shelter for the body are all part of our religion," said President Joseph F. Smith. By the church's "wise counsels, persuasively given and willingly followed," the First Presidency added, "the resources of various localities have been developed, community industries diversified, and the people, especially the poor, given increased opportunity for employment and a better chance to become self-sustaining."[124] The basic reply to all this was condensed in the statement of one senator that the Senate must "serve notice . . . that the nation is supreme; that the institutions of this country must prevail throughout the land."[125]

At the conclusion of the investigation, Smoot was permitted, by a close vote, to retain his seat in the Senate. He served a long and distinguished career in that body. Nevertheless, the widely believed charges against "the hierarchy" struck a responsive blow in church headquarters. So strong was the pressure for conformity with "national institutions"—whatever they were—so uncomfortable was the "anti-American" label which had been attached to the church, so overwhelming the national opposition to church participation in business, that Joseph F. Smith, president of the church after 1901, undertook to get the church out of business. By the end of the Smoot trial, late in 1906, Smith was able to testify that the church did not hold a controlling stock interest in any corporation but the Salt Lake Theatre. By that time, most of its important business properties had been sold to national corporations.

Actually, the desire to sell church assets had been spawned in 1899 when the campaign commenced to get the church out of debt. Lorenzo Snow, who had succeeded Wilford Woodruff in 1898 as church president, was aghast at the heavy burden of debt which had accumulated during the 1890's, and equally disturbed by the financial involvement of the church in business and speculative ventures.

He believed [wrote his secretary] that if half the means used for business enterprises in which the Church was interested, had been used in circulating our printed word, a mighty work might have been accomplished. But we were in debt and without money. . . . He believed that the Lord was displeased with us for borrowing or going into debt to the extent of nearly two millions of dollars for business enterprises.[126]

President Snow initiated a definite policy of retreat and retrenchment, vis-à-vis participation in business ventures. "The church was not investing any means," he declared, "but on the contrary was getting out of debt as fast as possible."[127] This policy was continued by Joseph F. Smith after Snow's death in 1901, with particular emphasis during the period of the Smoot trial. The following important properties were disposed of during this period of retraction and retrenchment:

1. The Deseret Telegraph system. This property, which had greatly depreciated during the Raid and the subsequent government seizure, was sold in February 1900 for $10,000 cash to the Western Union Company.[128]

2. The Utah Sugar Company. When Henry O. Havemeyer, president of the monopolistic American Sugar Refining Company, offered in November 1901 to purchase one-half of the capital stock of the Utah Sugar Company, church authorities agreed to negotiate with his representatives. In March 1902, some 75,000 shares of stock (one-half of the capitalization) were sold to him at approximately $17.80 per share (par value $10.00), or a total of $1,334,934.[129] The church insisted that all smaller stockholders who wished to dispose of their stock must be given the opportunity at the same price, and about 90 per cent of the 800 stockholders are said to have sold at that time. In the announcement which made the conditions of sale public, the following statement is pertinent:

> The question as to who should control has cut no figure, as it is stipulated, and was in fact one of the requirements made by the eastern parties that President Joseph F. Smith should remain at the head of the company; that Mr. [Thomas R.] Cutler should remain its manager; that a majority of the board of directors should reside in Utah, and that the new board to be elected at the annual meeting, April 7, should hold office for a term of five years.[130]

The church subsequently participated with Mr. Havemeyer in the formation of the Idaho Sugar Company, capitalized for $1,000,000, which built an extensive plant at Idaho Falls, Idaho, where a large Mormon colony was located. Of the 75,000 shares of stock (par value $10.00) subscribed at the time of the incorporation of that concern, some 3,720 shares were subscribed by the church or its representatives.[131] The Idaho Sugar Company built a large plant at Sugar City, Idaho, and by 1905 had a capitalization of $3,000,000. With Havemeyer's funds, the Utah Sugar Company also built a large new factory at Garland, Box Elder County, Utah. The arrangement with Mr. Havemeyer was made "on the basis of the New York man's supplying 50 per cent of the capital for new plants, in consideration for which he got one-half of the stock of the company."[132]

On July 18, 1907, the Idaho Sugar Company and the Western Idaho Sugar Company (which owned a factory at Nampa, Idaho) merged with the Utah Sugar Company to form the Utah-Idaho Sugar Company. The capitalization of the consolidated firm was $13,000,000, with 1,000,000 shares of preferred, and 300,000 shares of common stock, each valued at $10.00 per share. At the time of the merger the investment of the trustee-in-trust in these enterprises approached $500,000.[133] The controlling interest in this combination, of course, belonged to Havemeyer, although neither he nor his representatives seem to have taken a prominent part in the negotiations which preceded the merger. All of the officers and directors of the Utah-Idaho Company were Utah men, and the trustee-in-trust was chosen as its president and board chairman. In 1957 the Utah-Idaho Sugar Company had a net worth approximating $20,000,000. At that time the church owned 80 per cent of the preferred stock and about 50 per cent of the common.

3. Utah Light and Railway Company. In 1906, two years after the formation of the Utah Light and Railway Company, the church and other stock was sold to Edward H. Harriman, who at that time also controlled the Union Pacific Railroad. Harriman was reported to have paid $10,000,000 for the concern, which would have given the church a "profit" on its promotional activities of almost $3,000,000.[134] The Utah Light and Railway Company later became a part of the Utah Power and Light Company, a Maine corporation which until 1946 was a subsidiary of Electric Bond and Share.

4. Saltair properties. In 1906 the church also sold its interests in the Saltair Beach Company and in the Salt Lake and Los Angeles Railroad Company to a Salt Lake syndicate for a price reported to be in excess of $500,000. The syndicate was composed of Nephi W. Clayton, Charles W. Nibley, J. E. Langford, and other Salt Lake residents. "Through this deal," the church newspaper reported, "the 'Mormon' Church goes out of the pleasure resort business in every shape and form. . . . By parting with these properties, the Church unloads something that has been a source of great anxiety and care for a long time." [135] The name of the Salt Lake & Los Angeles Railroad was changed to Salt Lake, Garfield & Western R. R. The church's interests in the Inland Crystal Salt Company were not part of this sale, and it would appear that the church held on to these interests until their sale to the Morton Salt Company about 1923.

5. Mining land and other property. In connection with the promotion of a railroad from Utah to California in the 1890's the church had "taken up" and made payments on a large quantity of arid land, including land adjacent to the Cedar City coal mines. This land was "let go" to private parties in Utah in order to save the church the money required to keep up the annual payments on it.[136] Also, in the years 1903 and 1905, the church sold its interests in its iron and coal claims near Cedar City. Capitalists associated

with the Colorado Fuel & Iron Company, of Pueblo, Colorado, purchased some the these properties,[137] but they were not developed until the 1920's by the Columbia Iron Mining Company, a subsidiary of U. S. Steel. Church coal mine claims near Coalville were also sold during this period.

With these sales, and with the abolition of tithing in kind in 1908, the self-sufficient Kingdom may be said to have been brought to an end. A more acceptable adjustment between spiritual and secular interests was attained. And with this adjustment, the church no longer offered a geographic and institutional alternative to Babylon. Faith became increasingly separated from community policy, and religion from society. Individualism, speculation, and inequality — once thought to be characteristics of Babylon — were woven into the fabric of Mormon life.

MORMON POLICIES AT THE END OF THE CENTURY

The great capitulation — and it can be called that, although induced by coercive federal legislation — did not completely or permanently remove the church from the world of business. The church re-acquired about twenty-five per cent of the stock of Z.C.M.I. and a controlling interest in the Provo Woolen Mills, held on to its control of the savings bank, and resumed control of the Utah-Idaho Sugar Company after the Federal Trade Commission forced Henry Havemeyer to break up the American Sugar Refining Company in 1914. In addition, in the half-century after 1900, the church assisted in promoting and financing hotels, apartment houses, insurance companies, publishing houses, banks, textile mills, food processing enterprises, an airline, a radio and television station, an agricultural implement concern, a number of ranches and hospitals, and several score of irrigation companies. By 1958 the church owned or held a controlling interest in business corporations worth an estimated $200,000,000, and, in addition, owned an estimated $30,000,000 worth of fixed assets in hundreds of smaller, nonprofit, "welfare" enterprises, including farms, ranches, coal mines, factories, canneries, grain elevators, and pineapple and sugar plantations. Its annual expenditures, for "religious" and educational purposes alone, approached $60,000,000.[138]

In many of these concerns, the church president has been invariably elected president of the corporation, but the management has been left free to pursue normal business policies. The means and ends, in other words, were closely related, if not identical, with those of the world of capitalism about them. Church investments, which were mostly promotional and developmental in the nineteenth century, often became, in the twentieth century, such income-producing investments as rural and urban real estate and stocks and bonds in established industrial and commercial enterprises. By and large, the church's role became that of the *rentier* capitalist, with a social, educational, and ecclesiastical mission. The number, the significance, and the progressiveness of church social and economic programs seemed to decline. The success of this search for acceptance by "the world" is measured by the fact that a high church official now (1958) serves as Secretary of Agriculture in the president's cabinet, and that former missionaries and adherents have served variously as director of the United Nations Food and Agricultural Organization, as chairman of the Board of Governors of the Federal Reserve System, and as executives of such large corporations as Standard Oil of California, American Motors Corporation, and American Broadcasting Company.

The pattern of economic development in Mormon Country, in other words, came to resemble, in this century, the pattern of economic development in the remainder of the Mountain West. Agricultural development has been largely the product of the efforts of the Department of Agriculture and the Bureau of Reclamation. Industrial development has stemmed primarily from the investments of outside corporations. Recognizing the futility of attempting to perpetuate a cooperative and self-sufficient commonwealth in the highly integrated, market-oriented industrial economy of the modern world, Mormon leaders have eased the accommodation of the Mormon economy to that of the national economy. Secular government and secular industry have come to exert greater influence than the church on the development and regulation of the local Mormon economy. In a world of big cities, big business, and big labor, the church has made an adjustment which was theologically difficult, but socially necessary, and has therefore continued to grow. Only since the depression of the Thirties has the cooperative approach reasserted itself in the promotion by the church of community hospitals, "Welfare farms," and "Welfare industries."

The remarkable thing about Mormon economic policy over the century is not that it varied to meet changing circumstances and conditions, which it did, but that it held fast as long as it did to the original program. Mormon institutions and policies, although admittedly efficacious in making the desert blossom, evoked opposition from many quarters. Many on the national scene sought to exploit "the Mormon question" for political advantage. Others saw opportunities for profit in gaining access to Mormon-controlled resources and markets. Still others believed that forceful measures were essential to crush polygamy. Finally, there were those who saw in the theocratic institutions of Mormonism a barrier to the spread of private capitalism and the competitive market economy. The combined influence of these pressures, as we have seen, produced a stream of laws, administrative directives, judicial decisions, and occupation armies which progressively reduced the scope of church and group economic activity. Nevertheless, despite interferences both natural and human, the church and its members adhered stubbornly to "revealed" policy, until to continue to do so would have brought consequences worse than losing the Kingdom. And even today, having no doubt of its attainability and inevitability, Mormons still discuss the type of society that will exist when the Kingdom is finally realized. God's great design, they believe, will eventually prevail.

Even without attaining their goal, however, the Mormons could show two solid accomplishments. By the end of the century they had provided the basis of support for half a million people in an area long and widely regarded as uninhabitable. And Mormon agriculture and industry, stimulated by an activist church, supplied the burgeoning economies of Colorado, Montana, Idaho, and Nevada — not to mention the construction gangs of the transcontinental railroads and telegraph lines — with a veritable lifeline of flour, beef, fruits, and other goods and services. The spectacular development of the Mountain West was attributable in significant measure to the early and substantial achievements of the Mormons.

If, as some have believed, Mormon economic policies and practices were superior, for the time and place, it was due to the happy conjuncture of geography, economics, and ideology. Considering the nature of the Great Basin, and the difficulties encountered in developing it, it is doubtful that a substantial degree of progress could have been achieved except with the aid and direction of the dominant church. The heavy expense of constructing irrigation works, the tremendous cost of importing machinery and other capital goods, and the inability to produce a sizeable agricultural surplus, all conspired to keep the Mormon economy in a state of perpetual deficit. A group tightening-of-the-belt, facilitated by strong organization and cohesive solidarity, and attended by timely windfalls, made possible most of the investment which converted the barren wastes of the Great Basin into an oasis of beauty and strength.

The policies and practices applied by the Mormons in developing their desert habitat, it should be recalled, although different from those generally applied on other Western frontiers, had their origin in the cultural milieu of ante-bellum America. Thus, they had much in common with traditional American experience. If there was anything distinctive in the Mormon venture, it was the scale on which the experiment was carried out, the degree of success achieved in the face of overwhelming obstacles, and the intensity of application and continuity of policy over an extended period. Above all, in an era increasingly hostile to all forms of collectivism, the Mormons demonstrated the effectiveness of central planning and voluntary cooperation in developing a large semi-arid region. As the waste involved in the short-sighted, unplanned, and ruthless exploitation of other Western frontiers became more apparent, the Mormon pattern became increasingly appreciated — became recognized as prophetic of the pattern which the entire

West would ultimately have to adopt. By government decree and otherwise, this pattern is being followed in many parts of the world, at times with conscious knowledge of the Mormon antecedent. The design of the Kingdom, once despised as backward, is now part of the heritage which Americans are passing on to governments and peoples in many parts of the world.

1. Brigham Young, Mormon President for thirty years and Utah's first governor.

2. *Joseph Smith.*

3. *Daniel H. Wells.*

4. *John Taylor.*

5. *George Q. Cannon.*

PROMINENT MEN IN THE FORMULATION AND EXECUTION OF ECONOMIC POLICY, 1830–1900.

6. The Mormon city of Nauvoo, Illinois, in 1845.

7. Mormon camp in Iowa, along the route to Winter Quarters, after the expulsion from Nauvoo in 1846.

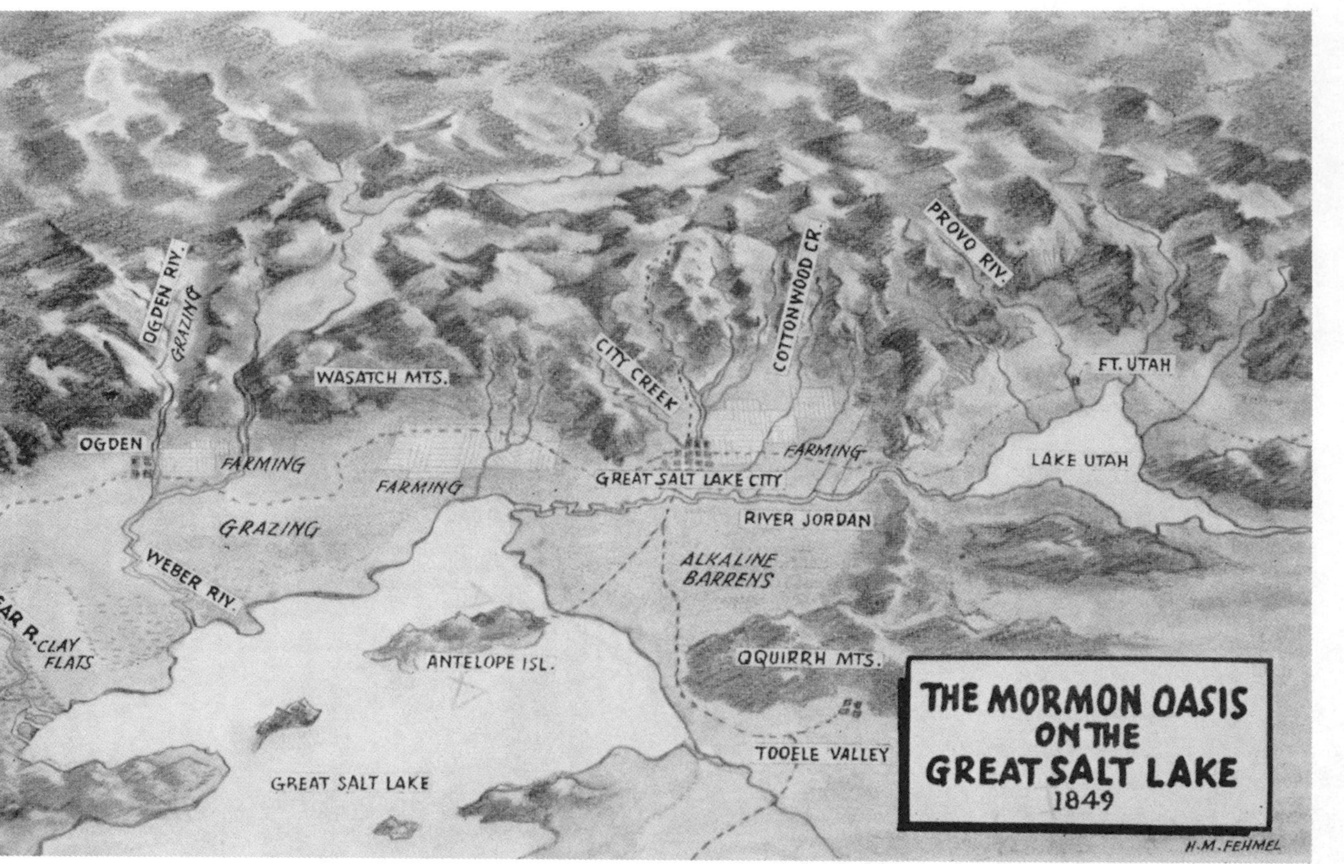

8. *The Mormon oasis on the Great Salt Lake, 1849.*

Edward Stevenson Block 67 Lot 6
City
paid 50
1848 J Bullock

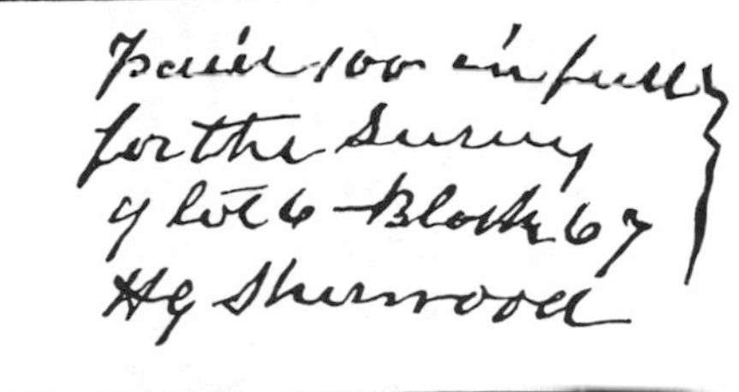

paid 100 in full
for the Survey
of lot 6 Block 67
H G Sherwood

9. *One of the first titles or deeds to city lots in Salt Lake City, 1848.*

G. S. L. City. Jan. 20. 1849.
No 2.00
GOOD to N K Whitney or bearer
two DOLLARS on demand. B Young
2.00
Tho Bullock Clerk. H. C. Kimball

10. *First printed currency issued in Salt Lake Valley.*

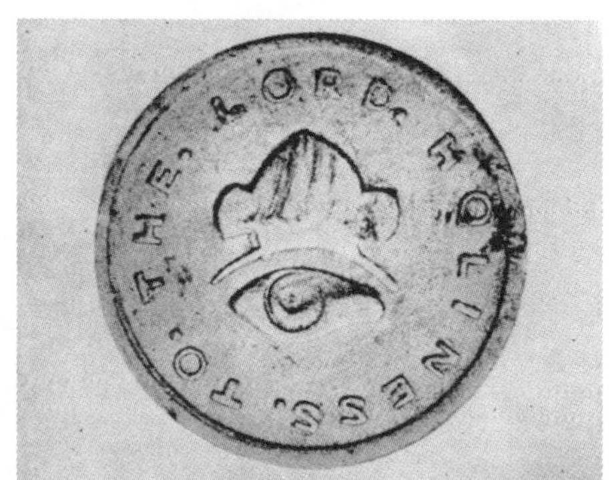

11. *Gold coin minted in Salt Lake City in 1849.*

— Brigham Young's daily transactions — in gold dust —

1848			Received $	Cents		Paid out $	Cents
Dec.	10	Received from William J. Follett 14½ Dust	232	00	x	–	–
"	12	Paid William J. Follett — — Coin	–	–	x	52	50
"	"	Received from John Y. Green — — Dust	11	00	x	–	–
"	"	— " — Brigham Young — — Dust	47	66		–	–
"	"	— " — Ebenezer Brown (Tithing) B.Y. Dust	98	00		–	–
"	"	— " — James Craig — — — Dust	15	87	x	–	–
"	"	Paid James Craig — — — Coin	–	–	x	10	50
"	"	Paid William Beers — — — Coin	–	–	x	21	00
"	"	Received from William Beers — — Dust	161	13	x	–	–
"	"	— " — Asahel A. Lathrop (settled) Dust	92	19	x	–	–
"	"	Paid Asahel A. Lathrop — — Coin	–	–	x	31	50
"	"	Received from Shadrack Holdaway (tithing) B.Y. Dust	270	80		–	–
"	"	— " — Ephraim Green by J. J. Willis (settled) Dust	30	80	x	–	–
"	"	Paid Ephraim Green by J. J. Willis — Coin	–	–	x	10	50
"	"	Received from Daniel Z. Dennett — (settled) Dust	34	30	x	..	–
"	"	Paid to Daniel Z. Dennett .. .. .. Coin	–	–	x	10	50
"	15	Paid Shadrack Holdaway — — — Coin	–	–	x	31	50
"	"	Received from Shadrack Holdaway (settled) Dust	187	82½	x		
"	"	— " — Edmund Ellsworth (settled) Dust	37	13			
"	"	— " — John Y. Green — (settled) Dust	16	76½	x		
"	"	— " — Joseph C. Kingsbury (settled) Dust	4	00	x		
"	"	— " — Willard G. McMullen (settled) Dust	7	65	x		
"	"	— " — David H. Jones (settled) Dust	56	73	x		
"	"	— " — Ira N. Spalding (settled) Dust	18	30			

12. Record of gold dust turned in for coinage and tithing, illustrating the care with which the Latter-day Saints kept accounts.

BE IT KNOWN BY THESE PRESENTS,

That I Alexander Beckstead

of West Jordan, in the county of Great Salt Lake, and

Territory of Utah, for and in consideration of the good will which I have to the CHURCH OF JESUS CHRIST OF LATTER DAY SAINTS, give and convey unto BRIGHAM YOUNG, Trustee in Trust for said Church, his successors in office, and assigns, all my claim to, and ownership of the following described property, to wit:—

	$	C.
Two Parcels of Land Viz Acre Qr Rod — 37 2 10. — Beginning at the S.E. Corner of Sm Egberts Survey of 22 3 10 on Jordan running thence W 97 Rods to said Egberts S W Corner, thence S 51 Rods to said Egberts N W Corner of 45 3 2 Survey thence East 160 Rods to the N E Corner of said Egberts last named Survey thence down the W bank of Jordan to the place of beginning	925	00
Acre Qr Rod — 44 2 14 — Begin at the S E Corner of Sm Egberts Survey of 45.3.2 on Jordan running thence W 151 Rod to said Egberts S W Corner, thence S 43 Rods to the N W Corner of Marcus Ensigns Survey of 41 1 15 — Thence E 178 Rods to said Ensigns N E Corner, thence Down the W bank of Jordan to the place of beginning.	1100	00
— Dwelling House 1000 — Out Houses Stabling etc 400.	1400	00
— Household Furniture and farming Implements etc	500	00
— 14 Horses $1190. — Sheep $1200.	2390	00
— Horned Cattle 48 Head	1200	00
— 3 Wagons $350. — Hides and Leather $160	510	00
— Vegetables $75. — Wheat $750. Corn $100.	925	00
— Wool & Cloth.	150	00
	$9030	00

Together with all the rights, privileges, and appurtenances, thereunto belonging or appertaining. I also covenant and agree, that I being the lawful claimant and owner of said property, and will warrant and forever defend the same, unto the said Trustee in Trust, his successors in office, and assigns, against the claims of my heirs, assigns, or any person whomsoever.

WITNESSES:

Thomas Allsop

Edwin D Woolley

Alexander Beckstead

Territory of Utah:

County of Great Salt Lake } I, Edwin D Woolley Recorder in and for said County ~~Great Salt Lake City~~ certify

that the signer of the above transfer, personally known to me, appeared this 23rd day of January A.D. 1855, and acknowledged that he of his own choice, executed the foregoing transfer.

Edwin D Woolley

13. One of the "deeds of consecration" in which church members signed over their property to the church, expecting to receive most of it back in the form of a stewardship. For various reasons the church never took possession of any of these properties.

14. Artist's conception of Fort Supply, Wyoming, erected by the Mormons in 1854, burned and abandoned in 1857 during the Utah War.

15. Main Street in Salt Lake City about 1861. Note water flowing through irrigation ditches on each side of the street.

16. General Tithing Office and Storehouse in Salt Lake City about 1856.

17. Note issued by the church-sponsored Deseret Currency Association to liquidate debts occasioned by the Utah War and the Move South.

18. Church cotton and woolen factories, in Parley's Canyon near Salt Lake City, 1869.

19. *A Mormon village before the coming of the railroad: Coalville, Utah, in 1869.*

20. Mormons assembling rocks at Temple Block in Salt Lake City for smooth cutting. The huge Mormon Tabernacle, completed in 1867, is in the rear.

21. Mormon "cooperative" cotton mill built in 1867 at Washington, Utah.

22. *Isolation ends: a Mormon wagon train meets the newly completed Union Pacific near the shores of the Great Salt Lake.*

23. *The Emporium, Salt Lake City, original home of Zion's Co-operative Mercantile Institution, 1869.*

24. Brigham Young addressing general conference in the Tabernacle, Salt Lake City, in 1869.

25. Mormon laborers grading for the Utah Central Railroad, 1869.

26. A local Mormon cooperative organized in 1869.

27. Salt Lake City about 1890. In the foreground are the General Tithing Office and its facilities: barns, stables, corrals, sheds, and stores for the receipt and disbursement of tithes.

28. Harvesting salt on the edge of Great Salt Lake, about 1900. On the right is the Salt Lake and Los Angeles Railway.

BIBLIOGRAPHY
NOTES AND REFERENCES

BIBLIOGRAPHY

MANUSCRIPT COLLECTIONS

The most extensive collection of manuscript and printed sources for the history of Utah, the Mormons, and the West is the Historian's Office and Library of the Church of Jesus Christ of Latter-day Saints, Salt Lake City, Utah. The manuscript materials uniquely found there can be divided into six categories, as follows:

1. The "History of Brigham Young," a multi-volume work kept by historians and clerks under the direction of Brigham Young, for the years 1847–1877, contains an account of affairs in the church and territory coming to the attention of church headquarters. This history is not available to scholars except for checking.
2. The "Journal History of the Church," compiled under the supervision of the late Andrew Jenson, comprises approximately 750 large volumes of chronologically arranged documents. It includes typescripts from diaries, letters, reports, office journals, and newspaper clippings, and extends from 1830 to the present. The bulk of it, for the period 1847–1877, consists of typescripts from the "History of Brigham Young." Essentially, it is a massive scrapbook with a day-by-day account of happenings in the Mormon Church from 1830 to the present. A useful boiled-down version was published in Andrew Jenson, *Church Chronology* (2nd ed., Salt Lake City, 1899).
3. The journal histories of the stakes and missions of the church, one or more volumes for each stake and mission. These are chronologically arranged documentary histories of the various settlements and ecclesiastical units of the Latter-day Saints, made up to resemble the "Journal History of the Church." They include relevant typescripts of diaries, letters, reports, minutes of meetings, sermons, and newspaper clippings pertaining to the locality concerned. They have been published in abbreviated form in Andrew Jenson, *Encyclopedic History of the Church of Jesus Christ of Latter-day Saints* (Salt Lake City, 1941).
4. Original journals, account books, minute books, and other records of immigration and colonizing parties, of ecclesiastical organizations, and of associations, corporations, and other business enterprises with which the church and its officers have been associated.
5. Several hundred original diaries of Mormon pioneers and church officials, not all of which are available for study. The most complete and informative diaries are those of Wilford Woodruff and George Q. Cannon.
6. Miscellaneous collections of letters, several steel cases of material filed under assorted headings, and near-complete collections of all Mormon (and anti-Mormon) books, periodicals, and newspapers.

The Utah State Historical Society, Salt Lake City, in its library and archives divisions, has much primary source material not available in the Church Historian's Office, including territorial and state documents, and the great mass of materials accumulated and typed by the Utah Works Progress Administration. The Salt Lake Public Library is a particularly valuable source for early Utah newspapers and periodicals, both Mormon and non-Mormon. The libraries of the University of Utah, Utah State University, and Brigham Young University each have extensive holdings of printed and manuscript materials dealing with Utah, the Mormons, and the West. Each has prepared, or is preparing, a bibliography of such holdings. The Utah Humanities Research Foundation, of the University of Utah, is particularly strong in folk history, as is the large collection of Professor Austin E. Fife, at Occidental College, in Los Angeles. The Daughters of Utah Pioneers, in their Pioneer Memorial Building, Salt Lake City, have collected a large number of manuscripts and ephemera, which are not generally available, but which have been and are being reproduced, under the editorship of Kate B. Carter, in *Heart Throbs of the West* (12 vols.; Salt Lake City, 1936–1951); and *Treasures of Pioneer History* (6 vols.; Salt Lake City, 1952–1957). With the recent establishment of their Pioneer Village, in Salt Lake City, the Sons of Utah Pioneers have also commenced the accumulation of materials of interest to the historian.

Outside of Utah, important collections are found in the Henry E. Huntington Library & Art Gallery, San Marino, California; Bancroft Library, University of California, Berkeley, California; and in the Coe Collection, Yale University, New Haven, Connecticut. The Bancroft collection is described in S. George Ellsworth, "A Guide to the Manuscripts in the Bancroft Library Relating to the History of Utah," *Utah Historical Quarterly,* XXII (1954), 197–247. The Yale holdings are described in Mary C. Withington, comp., *A Catalogue of Manuscripts in the Collection of Western Americana Founded by William Robertson Coe, Yale University Library* (New Haven. 1952). The Huntington collection, which has never been described, features a large number of diaries and journals. A valuable part of the Bancroft holdings is a 550-page manuscript excerpt from the "History of Brigham Young" which was copied by clerks in the Church Historian's Office and sent to H. H. Bancroft at the time he was writing his *History of Utah* in the 1880's. This material is bound into three volumes entitled "Early Records of Utah [1847–1851]," "Incidents in Utah History [1852–1854]," and "Utah Historical Incidents [1855–1867]."

The National Archives, Washington, D. C., contains a wealth of documents pertaining to territorial history; and the Library of Congress and New York Public Library have extensive printed holdings. The Library of Congress also has the large collection of typescripts of Mormon diaries and journals prepared by the Works Progress Administration. The Houghton Library, Harvard University, has a large Mormon pamphlet collection, while the New York Public Library is particularly rich in early Mormoniana. The list of items in the Berrian Collection of the latter is an excellent beginning bibliography, and is available in the *New York Public Library Bulletin* for March 1909. A list of museums, which frequently contain manuscripts, is published in the *Utah Historical Quarterly,* XXI (1953), 43–56.

GENERAL WORKS ON UTAH AND THE WEST

General histories of the West invariably include one or more chapters on Utah and surrounding states. Outstanding among these are Ray Allen Billington, *Westward Expansion: A History of the American Frontier* (New York, 1949), and *The Far Western Frontier, 1830–1860* (New York, 1956); Dan Elbert Clark, *The West in American History* (New York, 1937); Katherine Coman, *Economic Beginnings of the Far West* (2 vols.; New York, 1912); LeRoy R. Hafen and Carl Coke Rister, *Western America: The Exploration, Settlement, and Development of the Region Beyond the Mississippi* (New York, 1941); Rupert N. Richardson, *The Greater Southwest* (Glendale, Calif., 1934); Frederick L. Paxson, *History of the American Frontier, 1763–1893* (Boston, 1924); Robert E. Riegel, *America Moves West* (New York, 1947); and Cardinal Goodwin, *The Trans-Mississippi West (1803–1853): A History of Its Acquisition and Settlement* (New York, 1922). The best interpretive selection is Avery Craven, "Utah and the West," *Western Humanities Review,* III (1949), 276–284. The economic setting of the area settled by the Mormons and their neighbors is treated in Morris E. Garnsey, *America's New Frontier: The Mountain West* (New York, 1950).

General histories of Utah include: H. H. Bancroft, *History of Utah, 1540–1886* (San Francisco, 1889); Edward W. Tullidge, *History of Salt Lake City and Its Founders* (Salt Lake City, c. 1886); and Orson F. Whitney, *History of Utah* (4 vols.; Salt Lake City, 1892–1904). The latter is available in condensed form as *Popular History of Utah* (Salt Lake City, 1916). Nels Anderson's penetrating and instructive *Desert Saints: The Mormon Frontier in Utah* (Chicago, 1942), is as much a history of Utah to 1900 as it is a study of the Mormons and their social system. The outstanding social and economic history covering a limited period of time is Andrew Love Neff, *History of Utah, 1847 to 1869,* Leland Hargrave Creer, ed. (Salt Lake City, 1940). The earliest industrial history is Marcus E. Jones, "Commercial, Industrial, Transportational and other Interests of Utah," *House Exec. Doc. No. 6,* Pt. 2, 52nd Cong., 2nd sess. (Washington, 1890), pp. 841–954; the most recent is ElRoy Nelson, *Utah's Economic Patterns* (Salt Lake City, 1956). Wain Sutton, ed., *Utah: A Centennial History* (3 vols.; New York, 1949), contains many chapters of value. The years just before and after statehood are given coverage in S. A. Kenner, *Utah As It Is Today* (Salt Lake City, 1904); and Noble Warrum, *History of Utah Since Statehood* (4 vols.; Chicago, 1919). Levi Edgar Young's *The Founding of Utah* (New York, 1923); John Henry Evans, *The Story of Utah: The Beehive State* (New York, 1933); Milton R. Hunter, *Utah in Her Western Setting* (Salt Lake City, 1943), and *Utah: The Story of Her People, 1540–1947* (Salt Lake City, 1947) have all been used as texts, as has *Utah — Resources and Activities* (Salt Lake City, 1933), prepared under the direction of the State Department of Education. An authorized text is currently (1958) being prepared by Professor S. George Ellsworth, Utah State University.

Reference works include: J. Cecil Alter, ed., *Utah: The Storied Domain, A Documentary History of Utah's Eventful Career* (3 vols.; Chicago, 1932), the first volume of which contains chronologically arranged selections from contemporary books, newspapers, and magazines; and *Utah: A Guide to the State* (New York, 1945), prepared by the Utah Works Progress Administration under the editorship of Dale Morgan and others. The latter has an excellent classified bibliography. The Works Progress Administration also conducted an extensive Historical Records Survey which included the writing of county histories in connection with the compilation of inventories to materials in each of the counties. Useful gazetteers and directories were published in 1869, 1874, and 1884 by Edward L. Sloan, of Salt Lake City. There is also much useful economic information in O. J. Hollister, *The Resources and Attractions of Utah* (Salt Lake City, 1882). The best compilation of statistics is *Measures of Economic Changes in Utah, 1847–1947,* published in 1947 by the Bureau of Economic and Business Research of the University of Utah as Vol. VII, No. 1, of *Utah Economic and Business Review.* A number of historical maps have been published by Nicholas G. Morgan, Sr., Salt Lake City, on behalf of the Sons of Utah Pioneers.

The Daughters of Utah Pioneers, historical societies, and other groups and individuals have published histories of most of the counties and important cities in the state. The most valuable interpretative studies are: Edward W. Tullidge, *History of Northern Utah and Southern Idaho* (Salt Lake City, 1889); Joel E. Ricks, ed., Everett L. Cooley, assoc. ed., *The History of a Valley: Cache Valley, Utah-Idaho* (Logan, Utah, 1956); Joseph Earle Spencer, "The Middle Virgin River Valley, Utah: A Study in Culture Growth and Change" (unpublished Ph.D. dissertation, University of California, 1937); Andrew Karl Larson, *The Red Hills of November: A Pioneer Biography of Utah's Cotton Town* (Salt Lake City, 1957); and Odell E. Scott, "Economic History of Provo, Utah: 1849–1900" (unpublished Master's Thesis, Brigham Young University, 1951).

Biographical sources include: Andrew Jenson, *Latter-day Saint Biographical Encyclopedia* (4 vols.; Salt Lake City, 1901–1936), which gives biographies of prominent Mormons; Frank W. Esshom, *Pioneers and Prominent Men of Utah* (Salt Lake City, 1913); and biographical sections in the Tullidge, Whitney, Sutton, Warrum, and Alter volumes mentioned above. Particularly valuable are the biographies of Brigham Young. These include the skeptical and entertaining M. R. Werner, *Brigham Young* (New York, 1926); the useful Preston Nibley, *Brigham Young: The Man and His Work* (Independence, Missouri, 1936); Edward W. Tullidge, *Life of Brigham Young; or, Utah and Her Founders* (New York, 1876); and Susa Young Gates, *The Life Story of Brigham Young,* in collaboration with Leah D. Widstoe (New York, 1931).

The most important contemporary newspaper in pioneer Utah was the *Deseret News* (Salt Lake City), published by the Latter-day Saints' church. Founded in 1850, it had a weekly edition until 1922, and a daily edition from 1867 to date. Microfilm copies have been made available to libraries by the Church Historian's Office. It is a veritable mine of information on all aspects of Utah history. Good introductions to it are provided in Wendell J. Ashton, *Voice in the West: Biography of a Pioneer Newspaper* (New York, 1950), and A. R. Mortensen, "The *Deseret News* and Utah, 1850–1867" (unpublished Ph. D. dissertation, University of California, Los Angeles, 1949). Also valuable are *The Herald* (Salt Lake City), published daily from 1870 to 1909, during most of its life a Mormon, but not church-owned, paper; and the *Salt Lake Tribune,* a non-Mormon paper published daily from 1871 to date. The best guide to pioneer newspapers is J. Cecil Alter, *Early Utah Journalism* (Salt Lake City, 1938).

The *Utah Historical Quarterly,* published by the Utah State Historical Society since 1932, has published hundreds of useful documents and annotated articles on phases of Utah history. Also useful is *The Utah Genealogical and Historical Magazine,* published quarterly by the Genealogical Society of Utah (31 vols.; Salt Lake City, 1910–1940).

Most of the published contemporary travel accounts deal chiefly with the geography, conditions of travel, and the peculiarities of the Mormon religion. The best bibliography of such accounts is in Henry R. Wagner, *The Plains and the Rockies: A Bibliography of Original Narratives of Travel and Adventure, 1800–1865* (3d ed., revised by Charles L. Camp; Columbus, Ohio, 1953). The most useful will be mentioned in connection with specific chapters. An exciting volume of Utah and Mormon commentaries, *Among the Mormons: Historic Accounts by Contemporary Observers,* edited by William Mulder and A. Russell Mortensen, was published in 1958 by Alfred A. Knopf.

GENERAL WORKS ON THE MORMONS

An authoritative official history of the church is B. H. Roberts, *A Comprehensive History of the Church of Jesus Christ of Latter-day Saints: Century I* (6 vols.; Salt Lake City, 1930). This is a capable work, beautifully printed, with emphasis on relations between the church and the government. A frequently used one-volume ecclesiastical history is Joseph Fielding Smith, *Essentials in Church History* (13th ed.; Salt Lake City, 1953). A contemporary document of value is George A. Smith, *The Rise, Progress and Travels of the Church* (Salt Lake City, 1869, 1872, 1873). Somewhat resembling it is Charles H. Ellis, *Utah, 1847 to 1870* (Salt Lake City, 1891). There are, of course, introductions to Mormon history, government, and thought in such histories of Utah as the Bancroft, Neff, Sutton, and W.P.A. volumes. A useful introduction to sources is William E. Berrett and Alma P. Burton, *Readings in L. D. S. Church History, from Original Manuscripts* (3 vols.; Salt Lake City, 1953–1958).

Of the large number of histories by non-Mormons the earliest is [Charles Mackay], *The Mormons, or Latter Day Saints* (London, 1851). This evenly tempered volume is often attributed to Henry Mayhew. A work often cited, but often unreliable, is William A. Linn, *The Story of the Mormons* (New York, 1902). Happily it has been superseded by the readable and informative *Kingdom of the Saints: The Story of Brigham Young and the Mormons,* by Ray B. West, Jr. (New York, 1957). T. B. H. Stenhouse, *The Rocky Mountain Saints* (New York, 1873), was written in the heat of apostate repudiation but contains valuable firsthand information and commentary when properly sifted.

Mormon doctrine, the knowledge of which is basic to an understanding of Mormon social philosophy and economic practice, is expounded in the so-called "standard works"—*The Bible,* the *Book of Mormon, The Pearl of Great Price,* and especially *The Doctrine and Covenants of the Church of Jesus Christ of Latter-day Saints,* containing revelations given to Joseph Smith and his successors (Salt Lake City, many editions) — and in the compiled sermons and writings of the eight prophets of the Church: Joseph Smith, Brigham Young, John Taylor, Wilford Woodruff, Lorenzo Snow, Joseph F. Smith, Heber J. Grant, George Albert Smith, and David O. McKay, published separately by Salt Lake City publishers. Complete texts of the sermons of nineteenth-century prophets and other general church authorities were published periodically in the *Journal of Discourses* (26 vols.; Liverpool, 1854–1886). The variety of subjects covered in these addresses reflect official interest and church participation in all phases of pioneer life. Since 1898, transcripts of the sermons and proceedings of each annual and semiannual conference have been published separately by the church. Official textbooks on church doctrine include James E. Talmage, *A Study of the Articles of Faith* (19th ed., Salt Lake City, 1940); and Lowell L. Bennion, *The Religion of the Latter-day Saints* (Salt Lake City, 1940). An appraisal which has been particularly valuable in the present study is Carl J. Furr, "The Religious Philosophy of Brigham Young" (unpublished Ph. D. dissertation, University of Chicago, 1937).

The earliest general interpretation of Mormon social history is E. E. Ericksen, *The Psychological and Ethical Aspects of Mormon Group Life* (Chicago, 1923), in which particular attention is paid to "the genetic development of Mormon group consciousness." Hamilton Gardner followed with "Economic Activities of the Mormons," a book-length typescript, written in 1925, which unfortunately was never published. Copies were made available recently to the University of Utah and Utah State University. More recent works include: William John McNiff, *Heaven On Earth: A*

Planned Mormon Society (Oxford, Ohio, 1940); Gustive O. Larson, *Prelude to the Kingdom: Mormon Desert Conquest — A Chapter in American Cooperative Experience* (Francestown, N. H., 1947); and Leonard J. Arrington, "Mormon Economic Policies and Their Implementation on the Western Frontier, 1847–1900" (unpublished Ph. D. dissertation, University of North Carolina, 1952). Only a small portion of the latter study is included in the present work. A work by a sociologist with a deep understanding of Mormon social philosophy is Thomas F. O'Dea, "Mormon Values: The Significance of a Religious Outlook for Social Action" (unpublished Ph. D. dissertation, Harvard University, 1953). Part of this brilliant work is now available as *The Mormons* (Chicago, 1957).

Other interpretative studies are Therald N. Jensen, "Mormon Theory of Church and State" (unpublished Ph. D. dissertation, University of Chicago, 1938); S. George Ellsworth, "A History of Mormon Missions in the United States and Canada, 1830–1860" (unpublished Ph. D. dissertation, University of California, Berkeley, 1951); G. Homer Durham, "Political Interpretation of Mormon History," *Pacific Historical Review,* XIII (1944), 136–150; and Gaylon L. Caldwell, "Mormon Conceptions of Individual Rights and Political Obligation" (unpublished Ph. D. dissertation, Stanford University, 1952). A skillful short interpretation, with emphasis on the gathering, is William Mulder, *The Mormons in American History* (Salt Lake City, 1957), which was the 1957 Reynolds Lecture at the University of Utah. Professor Mulder carries out the same theme at greater length in his highly readable *Homeward to Zion: The Mormon Migration from Scandinavia* (Minneapolis, 1957). A brief study of Mormon economic organization is P. A. M. Taylor and Leonard J. Arrington, "Religion and Planning in the Far West: The First Generation of Mormons in Utah," forthcoming in *Economic History Review.*

For many persons the best introduction to "the Mormon way" will be found in the disarmingly accurate and charming essays of Wallace Stegner in *Mormon Country* (New York, 1942). Also of interest is Austin and Alta Fife, *Saints of Sage & Saddle: Folklore Among the Mormons* (Bloomington, Indiana, 1956).

The Latter-day Saints' Millennial Star, published monthly in Manchester, England, from 1840 to 1842; monthly in Liverpool, 1842 to 1845; semimonthly from 1845 to 1851; and weekly, from Liverpool, January 1, 1852, to date, is of tremendous value because of its reports of general conferences in Salt Lake City, its letters from church authorities to agents in England describing events in the Great Basin, and because of its extensive coverage of the church picture in the West. Also of value are *The Contributor* (Salt Lake City), published monthly by the church from 1879 to 1896; and its successor, *The Improvement Era* (Salt Lake City), published monthly from 1897 to date. Occasionally there have been articles of historical value in the *Juvenile Instructor* (Salt Lake City), published semimonthly by the church 1866–1888, monthly 1889–1929, and monthly as *The Instructor* from 1930 to date.

NOTES AND REFERENCES

In referring to the manuscripts, publications, and archives described above, the following abbreviations or symbols are used:

BYU Brigham Young University Library, Provo, Utah
CHO Latter-day Saints Church Historian's Office and Library, Salt Lake City, Utah
HBY Extracts from the "History of Brigham Young" in the Bancroft Library, Berkeley, California
JD *Journal of Discourses* (26 vols.; Liverpool, 1854–1886)
JH Journal History of the Church of Jesus Christ of Latter-day Saints, located in the Church Historian's Office, Salt Lake City
UHS Library and Archives of the Utah State Historical Society, Salt Lake City
USU Utah State University Library, Logan, Utah
UU University of Utah Library, Salt Lake City

CHAPTER I: EARLY ECONOMIC EXPERIENCES OF THE MORMONS

General works which describe and interpret the social and intellectual atmosphere of early Mormonism include: Whitney R. Cross, *The Burned-over District: The Social and Intellectual History of Enthusiastic Religion in Western New York, 1800–1850* (Ithaca, New York, 1950); Alice Felt Tyler, *Freedom's Ferment: Phases of American Social History to 1860* (Minneapolis, 1944); David M. Ludlum, *Social Ferment in Vermont, 1791–1850* (Montpelier, Vermont, 1948); Meade Minnigerode, *The Fabulous Forties, 1840–1850: A Presentation of Private Life* (New York, 1924); Arthur Eugene Bestor, Jr., *Backwoods Utopias: The Sectarian and Owenite Phases of Communitarian Socialism in America, 1663–1829* (Philadelphia, 1950); Delavan L. Leonard, *The Story of Oberlin: The Institution, the Community, the Idea, the Movement* (Boston, 1898); and Carl Russell Fish, *The Rise of the Common Man, 1830–1850,* Volume VI of *A History of American Life,* edited by Arthur M. Schlesinger and Dixon Ryan Fox (New York, 1929). General intellectual histories which treat Mormonism only incidentally but which contain valuable background commentary are Vernon L. Parrington, *Main Currents in American Thought: An Interpretation of American Literature from the Beginning to 1920* (3 vols.; New York, 1930); Merle Curti, *The Growth of American Thought* (2nd ed., New York, 1951); Arthur E. Ekirch, *The Idea of Progress in America, 1815–1860* (New York, 1944); Ralph Barton Perry, *Puritanism and Democracy* (New York, 1944); and Van Wyck Brooks, *The Flowering of New England, 1815–1865* (New York, 1936).

Explanations of Mormon theologic origins are found in Thomas F. O'Dea, *The Mormons* (Chicago, 1957); George B. Arbaugh, *Revelation in Mormonism* (Chicago,

1932); and David Brion Davis, "The New England Origins of Mormonism," *New England Quarterly,* XXVI (1953), 147–168. The latter advances the thesis that the Mormon religion represented, in essence, an attempt to restore or reproduce seventeenth-century New England Puritanism.

The basic official sources for the early history of the Mormons are: Joseph Smith, *History of the Church of Jesus Christ of Latter-day Saints: Period I,* B. H. Roberts, ed. (2nd ed.; 6 vols.; Salt Lake City, 1946ff.); a seventh volume, under the same title, published in 1932 for the "Apostolic Interregnum (1844–1847)" period, with notes and introduction by B. H. Roberts; and the following church periodicals published during the period: *The Evening and The Morning Star* (14 monthly numbers; Independence, Missouri, 1832–1833); *The Evening and Morning Star* (10 monthly numbers; Kirtland, Ohio, 1833–1834); *The Latter Day Saints' Messenger and Advocate* (3 vols.; Kirtland, Ohio, 1834–1837); *The Elders' Journal* (4 monthly numbers; Kirtland, Ohio, and Far West, Missouri, 1837–1838); and *The Times and Seasons* (6 vols.; Nauvoo, Illinois, 1839–1846). A national periodical with occasional mention of early Mormon affairs is *Niles' National Register* (Baltimore), XL-LXX (1831–1846).

Useful histories of the pre-Utah phase include: Fawn M. Brodie, *No Man Knows My History: The Life of Joseph Smith, the Mormon Prophet* (New York, 1946), which interprets Mormonism as largely the product of the personal magnetism and experiences of Joseph Smith; John Henry Evans, *Joseph Smith, An American Prophet* (New York, 1933); Inez Smith Davis, *The Story of the Church* (4th ed.; Independence, Missouri, 1948); and James H. Kennedy, *Early Days of Mormonism* (New York, 1888). The Turner "frontier" thesis, as applied to early Mormonism, finds expression in Dean D. McBrien, "The Influence of the Frontier on Joseph Smith" (unpublished Ph. D. dissertation, George Washington University, 1929).

Specialized treatments of the Jackson County period include B. H. Roberts, *The Missouri Persecutions* (Salt Lake City, 1900); Joseph A. Geddes, *The United Order Among the Mormons (Missouri Phase): An Unfinished Experiment in Economic Organization* (Salt Lake City, 1924); Hamilton Gardner, "Communism Among the Mormons," *Quarterly Journal of Economics,* XXXVII (1922), 134–174; Leonard J. Arrington, "Early Mormon Communitarianism: The Law of Consecration and Stewardship," *Western Humanities Review,* VII (1953), 341–369; and Eleanor M. Johnson, "The Gathering of the Mormons in Jackson County, Missouri" (unpublished Master's Thesis, University of Nebraska, 1927). An illuminating personal and social history of a participant is Emily M. Austin, *Mormonism; or, Life Among the Mormons* (Madison, Wisconsin, 1882), esp., pp. 63–92.

The best comprehensive history of the Kirtland phase of Mormonism is R. Kent Fielding, "Growth of the Mormon Church in Kirtland, Ohio" (unpublished Ph. D. dissertation, Indiana University, 1957). Other treatments are: Eva L. Pancoast, "The Mormons at Kirtland" (unpublished Master's Thesis, Western Reserve University, 1929); Harlan Hatcher, *The Western Reserve: The Story of New Connecticut in Ohio* (Indianapolis, 1949), Chap. X; and Willis Thornton, "Gentile and Saint at Kirtland," *Ohio State Archaeological and Historical Quarterly,* LXIII (1954), 8–33.

The Far West phase of Mormonism is usually treated as a postlude to the Jackson County and Kirtland phases, or as prelude to the Nauvoo phase. A recent but inadequate study of Mormon Nauvoo is George R. Gayler, "A Social, Economic, and Political Study of the Mormons in Western Illinois, 1839–1846: A Re-evaluation" (unpublished Ph. D. dissertation, Indiana University, 1955). Other studies include Thomas Ford, *A History of Illinois . . .* (Chicago, 1854), esp. pp. 251–278, 313–369, 403–436; B. H. Roberts, *The Rise and Fall of Nauvoo* (Salt Lake City, 1900); William V. Pooley, *The*

Settlement of Illinois from 1830 to 1850, Bulletin No. 220 of the University of Wisconsin (Madison, 1908), esp. pp. 508–525; Clyde E. Buckingham, "Mormonism in Illinois," *Journal of the Illinois State Historical Society,* XXXII (1939), 173–192; J. Earl Arrington, "The Building of the Nauvoo Temple," a scholarly book-length typescript in the CHO; E. Cecil McGavin, *Nauvoo the Beautiful* (Salt Lake City, 1946); and Reta L. Halford, "Nauvoo — The City Beautiful" (unpublished Master's Thesis, University of Utah, 1945).

The exodus from Nauvoo to the Missouri River, and from the Missouri River to the Salt Lake Valley, is described in James A. Little, *From Kirtland to Salt Lake City* (Salt Lake City, 1890); E. Cecil McGavin, *The Mormon Pioneers* (Salt Lake City, 1947); Preston L. Nibley, *Exodus to Greatness: The Story of the Mormon Migration* (Salt Lake City, 1947); William J. Peterson, "Mormons on the March," *Palimpsest,* XXVII (1946), 142–157; Bernard De Voto, *The Year of Decision: 1846* (Boston, 1943), pp. 75–101, *et passim;* Andrew L. Neff, "The Mormon Migration to Utah" (unpublished Ph. D. dissertation, University of California, 1918); and Jay Monaghan, *The Overland Trail* (Indianapolis, 1947), pp. 318–340. The settlements in the Missouri River Valley are described in Clyde B. Aitchison, "The Mormon Settlements in the Missouri Valley," *Nebraska State Historical Society Proceedings,* XV (1907), 7–25; also his similar article in *Oregon Historical Society Quarterly,* VIII (1907), 276–289; E. Widtsoe Shumway, "History of Winter Quarters, Nebraska" (unpublished Master's Thesis, Brigham Young University, 1953), and "Winter Quarters, Nebraska, 1846–1848," *Nebraska History,* XXXV (1954), 115–125; and Belle Palmer, "The Sojourn of the Mormons at Kanesville, Pottawattamie County, Iowa, 1846–1852" (unpublished Master's Thesis, Colorado State College of Education, 1936). The best contemporary treatments of the exodus are the address of Colonel Thomas L. Kane before the Historical Society of Pennsylvania, published as *The Mormons* (Philadelphia, 1850); and the Diary of Hosea Stout, typescript at BYU, original at UHS.

Studies of the Mormon Battalion include: Daniel Tyler, *A Concise History of the Mormon Battalion in the Mexican War, 1846–1847* (n. p., 1881); B. H. Roberts, *The Mormon Battalion: Its History and Achievements* (Salt Lake City, 1919); Frank A. Golder, *The March of the Mormon Battalion from Council Bluffs to California; Taken from the Journal of Henry Standage* (New York, 1928); *House Exec. Doc. No. 41,* 30th Cong., 1st sess., 551–563; and Hamilton Gardner, "The Command and Staff of the Mormon Battalion in the Mexican War," *Utah Historical Quarterly,* XX (1952), 331–351. Firsthand sketches of life in the Battalion are found in Joseph M. Tanner, *A Biographical Sketch of John Riggs Murdock* (Salt Lake City, 1909); John Q. Cannon, ed., *Autobiography of Christopher Layton* (Salt Lake City, 1911); and "Historical Sketch of J. E. Forsgren," *Box Elder News* (Brigham City, Utah), August 1, 1916. The Huntington Library has unpublished diaries of several members of the Battalion.

Early Mormon social and economic ideals are given excellent analysis in O'Dea, *The Mormons;* and in Gustive O. Larson, *Prelude to the Kingdom* (Francestown, N. H., 1947). The evolution of the organizational pattern of the Mormon Church is suggested in S. George Ellsworth, "A History of Mormon Missions in the United States and Canada, 1830–1860" (unpublished Ph. D. dissertation, University of California, 1950); and J. Keith Melville, "The Political Ideas of Brigham Young" (unpublished Ph. D. dissertation, University of Utah, 1956), pp. 30–50. A contemporary study is John Taylor, *Items on Priesthood* (Salt Lake City, *ca.* 1880). The twentieth century pattern is described in John A. Widstoe, *Priesthood and Church Government* (Salt Lake City, 1939); and in G. Homer Durham, "Administrative Organization of the Mormon Church," *Political Science Quarterly,* LVII (1942), 51–71.

1. From April 1830 to May 1834, the title of the church was "The Church of Christ," when it was changed to "The Church of the Latter-day Saints." In April 1838, the name became "The Church of Jesus Christ of Latter-day Saints." Joseph Smith, *History of the Church,* II, 62–63; III, 23–24. The popular name, Mormon Church, comes from the church use and acceptance of the *Book of Mormon.*

2. While Mormonism originated in western New York State, and while it is common to regard it as a "frontier" religion, two recent scholars, one Mormon, one non-Mormon, working quite independently, and using different approaches and data, came to the somewhat startling conclusion that Mormonism was not a "frontier" religion. See S. George Ellsworth, "A History of Mormon Missions," esp. Chap. XIII; and Whitney R. Cross, *The Burned-over District,* Chap. VIII. The more common "frontier" interpretation is found in McBrien, "The Influence of the Frontier on Joseph Smith"; Ray Allen Billington, *Westward Expansion: A History of the American Frontier* (New York, 1949), pp. 532ff.; and Tyler, *Freedom's Ferment,* pp. 86ff.

3. *Book of Mormon,* 2 Nephi, 1:5.

4. Bill Hickman said that he once heard Joseph Smith say "in a public audience that the Constitution of the United States was a part of his religion, and a good part too." William A. Hickman, *Brigham's Destroying Angel . . .* (New York, 1872), p. 37. Joseph Smith also said, "I am the greatest advocate of the Constitution of the United States there is on earth. . . . We say that God is true, that the Constitution of the United States is true." JH, October 15, 1843, March 25, 1839. See also Therald N. Jensen, "Mormon Theory of Church and State" (unpublished Ph. D. dissertation, University of Chicago, 1938), p. 24.

5. Thomas J. Yates, "Count Tolstoi and the 'American Religion,'" *Improvement Era* (Salt Lake City), XLII (1939), 94. Tolstoi found a certain agrarianism in "the Mormon myth" which attracted him. For example, he told White that "on the whole he preferred a religion which professed to have dug its sacred books out of the earth to one which pretended that they were let down from heaven." *Autobiography of Andrew Dickson White* (2 vols.; New York, 1907), II, 87.

6. A. S. P. Woodhouse, *Puritanism and Liberty . . .* (London, 1938), p. 38.

7. *The Evening and The Morning Star,* I (September 1832), [2]. Some scholars have assumed that this revelation was given to quiet those who objected to Joseph Smith's interferences in their "private" affairs. The principal evidence in support of this view is a sermon by Brigham Young in the Salt Lake Tabernacle on September 11, 1853, in which he made the following significant observations: "What were the feelings of the people, almost universally, in the infancy of this Church? Men of science and talent in this Church believed — or they said they believed . . . that Joseph Smith did not understand anything about temporal matters. They believed he understood *spiritual* things — that he understood the Spirit of the Lord, and how to build up the spiritual kingdom among men; but when temporal matters were talked of, men were ready to decide at once, that *they* knew more than the Prophet about such matters; and they did so decide. . . . For men of principle, and seemingly of good sense, to believe [that] the Prophet Joseph, who was inspired to build up the kingdom of God temporally as well as spiritually, did not know as much about a picayune as about God's spiritual kingdom, about a farm as about the New Jerusalem, is folly in the extreme, it is nonsense in the superlative degree. Those who entertain such ideas ought to have their heads well combed, and subjected to a lively course of friction, that peradventure a little common sense might dawn upon their confused ideas. . . . Do you think that God would set a man to lead his people who does not know as much about a picayune or a farm, as about God's spiritual kingdom, or the New Jerusalem? Shame

on those who would entertain such ideas, for they debase and corrupt the hearts of the community who imbibe them." JD, I, 74–76.

8. Sermon of June 22, 1864, JD, X, 329. Another early apostle, Orson Hyde, put the matter a little more bluntly: "When we descend to the matter of dollars and cents, it is also spiritual." Sermon of September 24, 1853, JD, II, 118.

9. The word "temporal" in Mormon literature can mean either that which pertains to time, and therefore to the world, as contrasted with that which is outside the world of time and space; or it can mean that which pertains to the material or economic aspects of life and living. See Thomas F. O'Dea, "Mormonism and the American Experience of Time," *Western Humanities Review,* VIII (1954), 181–190. In this chapter, the term is used in the former sense, but in certain quotations elsewhere in the book the word is clearly synonymous with economics.

10. There is support for this conclusion in the statements of Brigham Young. For example: "The first revelations given to Joseph were of a temporal character, pertaining to a literal kingdom on the earth. And most of the revelations he received in the early part of his ministry pertained to what the few around him should do in this or in that case—when and how they should perform their duties; at the same time calling upon them to preach the Gospel and diffuse the Spirit and principles of the kingdom of God, that their eyes might be open to see and gather the people together—that they might begin and organize a literal, temporal organization on the earth." Sermon of January 17, 1858, JD, VI, 171.

11. Dean D. McBrien, "The Economic Content of Early Mormon Doctrine," *Southwestern Political and Social Science Quarterly,* VI (1925), 180. McBrien used the Lamoni, Iowa, 1911 edition of the *Doctrine and Covenants* published by the Reorganized Church of Jesus Christ of Latter-day Saints, Independence, Missouri. This is not identical with Salt Lake City editions.

12. S. A. Davis in *The Glad Tidings, and Ohio Christian Telescope,* as reprinted in the *Latter Day Saints' Messenger and Advocate,* III (April 1837), 489–491.

13. *Time,* October 18, 1948, p. 75.

14. A prominent early theologian of the church, Orson Pratt, published a pamphlet in Liverpool in 1849 entitled *Absurdities of Immaterialism.*

15. Tawney, who was perhaps unduly critical of the growing separation of religion and economics in the eighteenth century, describes that trend in the following words: "In the eighteenth century both the State and the Church had abdicated that part of the sphere which had consisted in the maintenance of a common body of social ethics; what was left of it was repression of a class, not the discipline of a nation. . . . And the Church was even more remote from the daily life of mankind than the State. Philanthropy abounded; but religion, once the greatest social force, had become a thing as private and individual as the estate of the squire or the working clothes of the laborer. . . . God had been thrust into the frigid altitudes of infinite space." R. H. Tawney, *The Acquisitive Society* (New York, 1920), pp. 11–12.

16. "It has always been a cardinal teaching with the Latter-day Saints, that a religion which has not the power to save people temporally and make them prosperous and happy here, cannot be depended upon to save them spiritually, to exalt them in the life to come." Joseph F. Smith, "The Truth About Mormonism," *Out West,* XXIII (1905), 242. See also the editorial, "Religion and Business," *Deseret News* (Salt Lake City), October 29, 1877.

17. "A Prophecy Given to the Church of Christ, March 7, 1831," *The Evening and The Morning Star,* I (June 1832), [2].

18. The "heart" of the law of consecration and stewardship was first published

in *The Evening and The Morning Star,* I (July 1832), [1], under the title, "Extract From the Laws for the Government of the Church of Christ." It was later reproduced more completely in *A Book of Commandments, for the Government of the Church of Christ . . .* (Zion [Independence, Missouri], 1833), Chap. XLIV. Somewhat expanded, and slightly altered, the law was again reproduced in a reprint of *The Evening and The Morning Star* (called *Evening and Morning Star*) issued at Kirtland, Ohio, beginning in January 1835. In this form, the law was incorporated, with other revelations, in the 1835 edition of the *Doctrine and Covenants of the Church of the Latter Day Saints,* Section 13. Subsequent editions of the *Doctrine and Covenants* have carried the law in the 1835 version, but the law is now found in Section 42 of that work. Other revelations, published in *The Evening and The Morning Star,* the *Book of Commandments,* and the *Doctrine and Covenants,* explain and elaborate upon the system as first announced in February 1831.

19. *The Evening and The Morning Star,* I (July 1832), [1].

20. Revelation of March 1831, *Book of Commandments,* Chap. LII, verse 20, p. 97.

21. John Corrill, *A Brief History of the Church of Christ of Latter-day Saints . . .* (St. Louis, 1839), p. 45.

22. The original Plat of the City of Zion and the written instructions of Joseph Smith are in the Church Historian's Office, Salt Lake City. It has been given careful study in: Feramorz Y. Fox, "The Mormon Land System: A Study of the Settlement and Utilization of Land Under the Direction of the Mormon Church" (unpublished Ph. D. dissertation, Northwestern University, 1932), pp. 13–15; and Lowry Nelson, *The Mormon Village: A Pattern and Technique of Land Settlement* (Salt Lake City, 1952), p. 39, *et passim.*

23. "The Elders Stationed in Zion to the Churches Abroad . . . ," *The Evening and The Morning Star,* II (July 1833), 110–111.

24. These phrases are from a communication from the elders in Zion to the church, published in *The Evening and The Morning Star,* I (July 1832), [5].

25. *Autobiography of Parley Parker Pratt,* edited by his son, Parley P. Pratt (3rd ed.; Salt Lake City, 1938), 72, 93. Another participant, Newel Knight, mentioned the "cheerful hearts" of the people and said that they were "united, and peace and happiness abounded." "Newel Knight's Journal," in *Scraps of Biography* (Salt Lake City, 1883), 72, 73, 75. See also Davis, *The Story of Our Church,* p. 124.

26. See a specimen of a lease-loan in Joseph Smith, *History of the Church,* I, 365–367.

27. Joseph Smith, Jr., to Edward Partridge, May 2, 1833, as printed in O. F. Whitney, "The Aaronic Priesthood," *The Contributor* (Salt Lake City), VI (1884), 7.

28. *History of the Church,* I, 364–365.

29. See particularly C. W. Wandell, *History of the Persecutions!! Endured by the Church of Jesus Christ of Latter Day Saints, in America* (Sydney, Australia, 1852), p. 12. A copy of this rare pamphlet is in the Huntington Library.

30. See JH, May 1, 1834ff.

31. Williams Brothers, pub., *History of Geauga and Lake Counties* (Philadelphia, 1878), 248, cited in Willis Thornton, "Gentile and Saint at Kirtland," p. 16. See also [Warren A. Cowdery], "Our Village," *Messenger and Advocate,* III (1837), 444.

32. Remarks of Daniel H. Wells, April 7, 1869, JD, XIII, 22. See also sermon of Brigham Young, October 9, 1852, JD, I, 214–216.

33. Brodie, *No Man Knows My History,* p. 202.

34. This would have made it the largest bank in Ohio. Indeed, the entire paid-in

capital of all the banks in Ohio at the time was less than $10,000,000. Thornton, pp. 21–22.

35. The largest single stockholder was Joseph Smith, whose pledged stockholdings (probably church property) were said to have been valued at the highly speculative figure of $300,000. See Brodie, p. 195.

36. Davis, *The Story of the Church,* p. 240.

37. Articles of agreement are given in the *Messenger and Advocate,* III (January 1837), 441–442. There was apparently no president or cashier of this "industrial stock company." Management was in the hands of twenty-three managers. A list of some 200 subscribers to the institution, including such later notables as Brigham Young, is given in the *Messenger and Advocate,* III (March 1837), 475–477.

38. A large collection of the bank notes in various denominations may be seen at the Western Reserve Historical Society in Cleveland.

39. Orson F. Whitney, *Life of Heber C. Kimball . . .* (Salt Lake City, 1888), p. 111.

40. *The Mormons, or, Knavery Exposed,* published by E. G. Lee (Philadelphia, 1841), p. 14.

41. *The Mormons,* p. 14; John A. Clark, *Gleanings by the Way* (Philadelphia, 1842), p. 352. On the other hand, Reed Peck said that Joseph Smith and others, prior to the establishment of the bank had procured "enormous sums of specie," principally from loyal Latter-day Saints. See "The Original Reed Peck Manuscript," dated Quincy, Illinois, September 18, 1839, p. 16., MS., Mormon File, Box 10, Huntington Library.

42. The *Messenger and Advocate* commented editorially in June 1837: "a sullen, we can almost say, a desponding gloom hangs over us, sufficient at least to show a striking contrast between this and last year. One year since and our village was all activity, all animation — the noise and bustle of teams with lumber, brick, stone, lime or merchandise, were heard from the early dawn of morning till the grey twilight of evening. . . . The starting up, as if by magic, of buildings in every direction around us, were evincive to us of buoyant hope, lively anticipation, and a firm confidence . . . ; but we too feel the pressure, occasioned by the derangement of the currency, the loss of credit, the want of confidence or by overtrading. . . ." (II, 520–521).

43. The first explanation by the church of the failure of the bank was contained in an editorial in the *Messenger and Advocate,* III (July 1837), 535–539. Factors mentioned include the failure to obtain a charter and the unpopularity of Mormonism. The bank did well, according to the editorial, until the money panic hit Kirtland in May and June of 1837. When money became scarce and real estate values declined, there was a clamor in the church to have the bank issue more new bills to stimulate trade. "These causes . . . operated to induce the officers of the bank to let out larger sums than their better judgements [sic] dictated. . . . Hundreds who were enemies, either came or sent their agents and demanded specie till the officers thought best to refuse payment." (p. 536). Shortly after this failure, Joseph Smith and Sidney Rigdon severed their connections with the bank and Frederick G. Williams and Warren Parrish became president and cashier of the institution. The editorial suggests that it had been a mistake to depend too heavily upon civil or church leaders for leadership and direction: "Whenever a people have unlimited confidence in a civil or ecclesiastical [sic] ruler or rulers, who are but men like themselves, and begin to think they can do no wrong, they increase their tyrany [sic], and oppression. . . ." (p. 538). Later on, in 1837 and 1838, the church began to spread the view that the bank's failure was attributable to the defalcation of Warren Parrish with $25,000 in bank funds. The *Elder's Journal* (Far West, Missouri), I (August 1839), 57–58. This sum could

hardly have been specie, as that amount would have been sufficient to have saved the bank long before he allegedly absconded with it. Benjamin Winchester's charge seems more likely; that is, that Parish printed up $25,000 or more in additional notes at a time when the bank should have been curtailing its issue, and circulated them without the prefix "Anti" in front to denote the lack of a charter. The circulated notes then "came pouring in upon the firm like a flood. . . . Of course they suspended." Letter of B. Winchester, February 19, 1841, published in [E. G. Lee], *The Mormons,* p. 20. Brigham Young's explanation of the Kirtland Bank failure, which has some interest, was given in a sermon reprinted in JD, XI, 11.

44. Thornton, "Gentile and Saint at Kirtland," p. 32. The train of some 70 wagons that left Kirtland for Far West in the summer of 1838 is known in Mormon history as "The Kirtland Camp."

45. *The Book of Doctrine & Covenants . . .* (Liverpool [1845]), sec. CVII.

46. "The Original Reed Peck Manuscript," p. 13.

47. See Joseph Smith, *History of the Church,* III, 63–64.

48. Letters of "Brother Winchester," September 6 to November 19, 1838, cited in Brodie, *No Man Knows My History,* p. 221–222.

49. Corrill, *History of the Church,* p. 46.

50. Sermon of George A. Smith, May 7, 1874, JD, XVII, 60.

51. Joseph Smith, *History of the Church,* III, 250–254.

52. While there are no exact figures of the peak population of Mormon Nauvoo, most sources estimate it at 20,000. In addition, several thousand Mormons were across the river in Iowa and elsewhere in the agricultural countryside around Nauvoo.

53. Brodie, *No Man Knows My History,* p. 262.

54. "The building of the Temple has sustained the poor who were driven from Missouri, and kept them from starving; and it has been the best means for this object which could be devised." Joseph Smith, sermon of October 15, 1843, *History of the Church,* VI, 58.

55. *Ibid.,* pp. 58–59.

56. Dean D. McBrien, "Influence of the Frontier on Joseph Smith," pp. 263–264; Pooley, *The Settlement of Illinois,* p. 513; *History of the Church,* IV, 303–305; *ibid.,* V, 436–438.

57. See "An Epistle of the Twelve Apostles to the Saints of the Last Days," Nauvoo, Illinois, December 13, 1841, *History of the Church,* IV, 472–475.

58. Brigham Young, "An Epistle of the Twelve to the Church . . . , August 15, 1844, *History of the Church,* VII, 251.

59. John Taylor, "Address to the Saints in Great Britain," *Latter-day Saints' Millennial Star* (Liverpool), VIII (1846), 114; Oscar O. Winther, ed., *The Private Papers and Diary of Thomas Leiper Kane: A Friend of the Mormons* (San Francisco, 1937), pp. 31–32.

60. *Millennial Star,* VIII (1846), 115; also *Niles' National Register,* LXX (May 30, 1846), 208.

61. Benjamin Brown, *Testimonies for the Truth . . .* (Liverpool, 1853), p. 24–25. Benjamin Johnson in *My Life's Review* (Independence, Mo., 1947), wrote that he sold his Nauvoo property "at prices one-tenth, perhaps, their true cost." p. 108.

62. *History of the Church,* VII, 465.

63. "It was in the intimate camp life of that protracted expedition from Ohio to Missouri [Zion's Camp] that Brigham Young became so well acquainted with Joseph Smith; and it was to that experience that he later attributed his knowledge as to how

to lead Israel in its great exodus and settlement. Concerning that trip with 'Zion's Camp' Brigham Young spoke as follows: 'I have travelled with Joseph a thousand miles, as he has led the camp of Israel. I have watched him and observed everything he said or did. . . . I watched every word and summed it up, and I knew just as well how to lead this kingdom as I know the way to my own house.'" Jensen, "Mormon Theory of Church and State," p. 43.

64. George A. Smith, *The Rise, Progress and Travels of the Church . . .* (Salt Lake City, 1869), p. 16.

65. See Jensen, "Mormon Theory of Church and State," p. 44; P.A.M. Taylor, "Emigrants' Problems in Crossing the West, 1830–70," *University of Birmingham Historical Journal,* V (1955), 99–102.

66. See particularly, F. Y. Fox, "The Mormon Land System," pp. 29–35; B. H. Roberts, *A Comprehensive History of the Church . . .* (6 vols.; Salt Lake City, 1930), III, 54–55.

67. President Polk's version of the conferences is given in *The Diary of James K. Polk,* Milo Milton Quaife, ed. (4 vols.; Chicago, 1910), I, 444–450.

68. Roberts, *Comprehensive History,* III, 83, 95.

69. Golder publishes a letter from officers of Company A of the Mormon Battalion to Newel K. Whitney, bishop of the church, and others, authorizing the payment of their paychecks to representatives of the church. Brigham Young's reply: "by the wisdom of heaven we will make every dollar sent us count as good as two or three at ordinary traffic. . . ." Golder, *The March of the Mormon Battalion,* pp. 133–134, 145; also Tyler, *History of the Mormon Battalion,* pp. 131, 136. In the Church Historian's Office, Salt Lake City, is a journal kept by John D. Lee while on a mission with Howard Egan to go to Santa Fe to pick up Mormon Battalion pay. They apparently obtained $5,860.

70. JH, August 16, 1846. Also *Journals of John D. Lee, 1846–1847 and 1859,* edited by Charles Kelly (Salt Lake City, 1938), entries for February 27, March 17 and 24, 1847.

71. JH, August 14, 1846.

72. Golder, *March of the Mormon Battalion,* pp. 34–36.

73. JH, December 31, 1846.

74. This document is reproduced in JH, January 14, 1847, and in *Doctrine and Covenants* (Salt Lake City, 1935), sec. 136.

75. When the Mormons called Joseph Smith and his successors prophets, they meant much more than that they predicted events yet to come. Mormon prophecies and revelations were proclamations of the intention to progress — "expectation impenetrated with aspiration. . . ." Smith's prophetic revelations, in other words, were a blueprint of economic action. See O'Dea, "Mormonism and the American Experience of Time," p. 182.

76. This section represents a distillation of the revelations, because the principles given here do not appear in systematic form in any Mormon scripture or treatise. An official summation of early Mormon policy and its continuity throughout the century was given by the (then) president of the church, Joseph F. Smith, in "The Truth About Mormonism," *Out West,* XXIII (1905), 239–255. President Smith's statement expresses the spirit, if not the detail, of the treatment given here.

77. *The Evening and The Morning Star,* I (September 1832), [2]. Nearly all of the published revelations to Joseph Smith were couched in biblical (King James version) language. See also the revelation of November 3, 1831, *The Evening and The*

Morning Star, I (May 1833), [1]; Andrew Jenson, "The Principle of Gathering," *The Contributor,* XII (1891), 261–266; William Mulder, "Mormonism's 'Gathering': An American Doctrine with a Difference," *Church History,* XXIII (1954), 3–19.

78. The original source of the thirteen Articles of Faith of the Mormon Church is "The Wentworth Letter," written by Joseph Smith in 1842, and published in *History of the Church,* IV, 541.

79. Nelson, *The Mormon Village,* p. 53.

80. In an address before the School of the Prophets, JH, November 21, 1868.

81. *History of the Church,* IV, 541.

82. James E. Talmage, *A Study of the Articles of Faith* (19th ed.; Salt Lake City, 1940), p. 377. Also see *The Evening and The Morning Star,* I (September 1832), [2]. There is an obvious similarity between this concept and the biblical injunction to "Be Fruitful, multiply, and replenish the earth and subdue it. . . ." *Genesis,* 1:28.

83. It is true that certain Latter-day Saint scriptures speak of a miraculous purification process which is to precede "the great and dreadful day of the Lord." Among Mormon educators, however, there is an increasing tendency to interpret this in a figurative rather than a literal sense, on the supposition that it refers to the purification of the souls of men and their acceptance of Christianity.

84. Many early revelations contain injunctions against idleness. For example, "Thou shalt not be idle; for he that is idle shall not eat the bread, nor wear the garments of the laborer." *The Evening and The Morning Star,* I (July 1832), p. [1]. According to world traveler Richard Burton, it was common for early statements of church belief to contain the statement, "an idle or lazy person cannot be a Christian, neither have salvation. He is a drone, and destined to be stung to death, and tumbled out of the hive." Richard F. Burton, *The City of the Saints* (London, 1861), p. 480.

85. "A Practical Religion," *Deseret Weekly* (Salt Lake City), October 16, 1897, p. 553.

86. Sermon of February 23, 1862, JD, IX, 283–284. Similar remarks may be found in many of Brigham Young's sermons.

87. "In the new church work is honorable, the recovery of barren places noble, the production of corn and oil, of fruit and flowers, of gum and spices, of herbs and trees, a saving act; the whole earth being regarded by the Saints as a waste to be redeemed by labor into the future heaven. . . . With them, to do any piece of work is a righteous act; to be a toiling and producing man is to be in a state of grace." W. H. Dixon, *New America* (Philadelphia, 1867), pp. 195, 200. See also Carl J. Furr, "The Religious Philosophy of Brigham Young" (unpublished Ph. D. dissertation, University of Chicago, 1937), pp. 53–60.

88. "Extract From the Laws . . . of the Church of Christ," *The Morning and The Evening Star,* I (July 1832), [1].

89. "Revelation given January 1831," *ibid.,* I (January 1833), [5].

90. Sermon of October 7, 1859, JD, VII, 280.

91. Sermon of January 12, 1868, JD, XII, 153.

92. Revelation of March 1832, *Doctrine and Covenants* (Kirtland, Ohio, 1835), sec. 75, verse 1, p. 204.

93. *Ibid.,* sec. 23, verse 1, p. 150. Revelation of May 1831.

94. *Ibid.,* sec. 26, verse 3, p. 153. Revelation of November 1831.

95. *Ibid.,* sec. 86, verse 4, p. 220.

96. *The Evening and The Morning Star,* I (June 1832), [2]; Orson Pratt, *The Kingdom of God* (Liverpool, 1848–1849), and *New Jerusalem; or, The Fulfillment of*

Prophecy (Liverpool, 1849); Parley P. Pratt, *A Voice of Warning and Instruction to All People, Or an Introduction to the Faith and Doctrine of the Church of Jesus Christ of Latter Day Saints* (Manchester, England, 1841).

97. At the outset, there were only elders; later seventy elders who were appointed to preach; still later High Priests who were empowered to officiate in a superior capacity. The priests acted in a supervisory capacity under the direction of the bishops; the teachers were the bishops' representatives in teaching and instructing the Saints and in mediating quarrels; the deacons were the bishops' assistants in caring for the poor.

98. Joseph Smith said, "I go for a theo-democracy." JH, April 15, 1844. This was explained as an arrangement where God was the king, His people were His subjects, His revealed will was the law of the Kingdom; the priesthood was the administrator of those laws, yet individual persons still had free agency, and the organized community of Saints had the right to accept or reject their officers and the general doctrines said to be God's revelation. See *Times and Seasons,* IV (December 1, 1842), 24–25.

99. Cf. Max Haenle, "Some Inter-relations Between Religion and Economics," *Improvement Era,* XXXII (1928), 108.

100. Levi Edgar Young, "The New England Town Government in Early Day Utah," *Proceedings of the Pacific Coast Branch of the American Historical Association,* 1927, pp. 41–58.

101. "Moroni Historical Record," November 15, 1867, MS., CHO.

102. A careful reading of the Mormon diaries in the Library of Congress, Huntington Library, and in the libraries of Brigham Young University and Utah State University provides convincing evidence of the near-universality of obedience to church command. Because of the shame attached to refusing a call, however, it is probable that some instances of disobedience are prudently left unmentioned.

103. The term "trustee-in-trust," which seems to have currency only among the Latter-day Saints, may have been a corruption of the common legal phrase, "trustee, in trust for. . . ." This phrase, in Mormon literature, would become "trustee-in-trust, in trust for. . . ." The position of trustee-in-trust was created at a general conference of the church held at Nauvoo, Illinois, on January 30, 1841. Joseph Smith, then president of the church, was the first trustee-in-trust. He was to hold office during life, his successors to be the First Presidency of the church. He was "vested with plenary powers . . . to receive, acquire, manage or convey property, real, personal, or mixed, for the sole use and benefit of said Church. . . ." *History of the Church,* IV, 286–287. He was subject only to God and the "sustaining vote" of the general conference of Saints.

104. The First Presidency and Council of the Twelve Apostles had general oversight of the church's missionary system which, in many aspects, was under the immediate direction of the "Presidents of the First Council of Seventy." This council consisted of a continuous group of seven men. Their authority in economic matters was relatively unimportant. The same can be said of a chief "patriarch," who gave special blessings to church members.

105. For a discussion of this belief, see particularly B. H. Roberts, *The Rise and Fall of Nauvoo,* pp. 178–182; James R. Clark, "The Kingdom of God, the Council of Fifty, and the State of Deseret," *Utah Historical Quarterly,* XXVI (1958), 131–148; and Hyrum L. Andrus, *Joseph Smith and World Government* (Salt Lake City, 1958).

106. Joseph Smith, *History of the Church,* VI, 260–261; Brigham Young and Willard Richards to Reuben Hedlock, May 3, 1844, *Millennial Star,* XXIII (1861), 422;

"History of Brigham Young," *ibid.*, XXVI (1864), 328; Brigham Young's Sermon, August 9, 1874, JD, XVII, 156; and Brodie, *No Man Knows My History*, pp. 356–366. Benjamin Johnson, who claimed to be the youngest member of the group, referred to it in his recollections as the "Colonial Council." Benjamin F. Johnson to George S. Gibbs, 1903, pp. 22–23, typescript, Huntington Library.

107. John D. Lee, *Mormonism Unveiled . . .* (St. Louis, 1878), p. 173; Diary of Hosea Stout, February 18, 1845, UHS.

108. Correspondence of Bishop George Miller, pp. 21, 24, 37, typescript, O'Neil Collection, Mormon File, Huntington Library; Benjamin F. Johnson, *My Life's Review* (Independence, Mo., 1947), pp. 104, 105, *et passim; History of the Church*, VII, 379–380; "Statement of Elder Samuel W. Richards," MSS., Mormon File, Huntington Library, Film No. 166; Dale Morgan, ed., "The Reminiscences of James Holt: A Narrative of the Emmett Company," *Utah Historical Quarterly*, XXIII (1955), 7; *Journals of John D. Lee*, entry for January 18, 1847, p. 53.

109. *Harper's Weekly*, II (December 4, 1858), 781.

110. Ellsworth, "A History of Mormon Missions," pp. 308–309.

111. Joseph F. Smith, "The Truth About Mormonism," pp. 246–248.

112. Frank Knight once pointed out that a theocracy had more power than a political despotism "because it is in a better position to make its own public opinion." There may be "coercion," and yet, in a theocracy, "the victims may not feel coerced at all." F. H. Knight, "Professor Heimann on Religion and Economics," *Journal of Political Economy*, LVI (1948), 485.

113. Professor Ely concluded that "in Mormonism we find precisely the cohesive strength of religion needed . . . to secure economic success" under the physiographic conditions of the Great Basin. Professor Ely also supports the thesis of this chapter that the peculiar features in the economic and social life of the Latter-day Saints is an outgrowth of religion and of church discipline. "Faith comes first of all, and the discipline which proceeds from religious organization rests upon faith." Richard T. Ely, "Economic Aspects of Mormonism," *Harper's Monthly Magazine*, CVI (1903), 667–669.

114. Many writers, Mormon and non-Mormon, have characterized Joseph Smith as being imaginative, unstable, and sometimes spiritual, but always thoroughly impractical; and have reserved their admiration for Brigham Young, with respect to whom such words as "good organizer," "sound administrator," and "brilliant leader" are used. There can be no doubt that many of the "practical" measures adopted by Brigham Young were suggested and first applied by Joseph Smith. While many of Joseph Smith's enterprises failed, this may have been due to the turbulent history of early Mormonism and to Smith's greater concern for "the cause" than for the "soundness" and financial "success" of individual enterprises.

115. See the review of recent research on the role of government in ante-bellum America in Robert A. Lively, "The American System: A Review Article," *Business History Review*, XXIX (1955), 81–96.

CHAPTER II: A NEW WORLD

The first systematic work on the geography of the Great Basin, and still one of the best, is John C. Fremont, *Geographical Memoir upon Upper California, Senate Exec. Doc. No. 148*, 30th Cong., 1st sess., 1847–1848 (serial No. 511). Some insights into the work are also found in Fremont's autobiography: *Memoirs of My Life, Including Five Journeys of Western Exploration . . .* (Chicago, 1887); and in John Charles Fremont,

Narratives of Exploration and Adventure, Allan Nevins, ed. (New York, 1956). Fremont's work was followed by Howard Stansbury's *Expedition to the Valley of the Great Salt Lake of Utah . . .* (Philadelphia, 1852). Later studies include: J. H. Simpson, *Report of Explorations Across the Great Basin of the Territory of Utah . . . in 1859* (Washington, 1876); J. W. Powell, *Report on the Arid Regions of the United States* (Washington, 1879); and Grove Karl Gilbert, *Lake Bonneville,* monographs of the United States Geological Survey, Vol. I (Washington, 1890).

General and historical geographies of particular value to the economic historian are: E. W. Gilbert, *The Exploration of Western America, 1800–1850: An Historical Geography* (Cambridge, England, 1933); Ralph H. Brown, *Historical Geography of the United States* (New York, 1948); N. M. Fenneman, *Physiography of Western United States* (New York, 1931); and J. Russell Smith and M. Ogden Phillips, *North America* (New York, 1940). C. O. Paullin's *Atlas of the Historical Geography of the United States* (Washington, 1932) is an indispensable map reference. Excellent chapters of descriptive geography are also found in the W.P.A., *Utah: Guide to the State* (New York, 1945); and Wallace Stegner, *Mormon Country* (New York, 1942). The geographic and economic importance of Salt Lake City is carefully detailed in Chauncy D. Harris, *Salt Lake City: A Regional Capital* (Chicago, 1940); and also to some extent in Dale L. Morgan, *The Great Salt Lake* (New York, 1947). A recent study published by the Department of Geography of the University of Utah is *Mormon Country: A Survey of Utah's Geography* (Salt Lake City, 1955).

The early explorations of the Mormons in the Great Basin are told in the "History of Brigham Young" in the Bancroft Library, and in the diaries of the participants: *William Clayton's Journal . . .* (Salt Lake City, 1921), 306–347; Orson Pratt, "Interesting Items Concerning the Journeying of the Latter-day Saints . . . (Extracted from the Private Journal of Orson Pratt)," *Millennial Star,* XII (1850), 178–180; *Pioneering the West, 1846 to 1878: Major Howard Egan's Diary,* Wm. M. Egan, ed. (Richmond, Utah, 1917), pp. 103–131; "From Nauvoo to Salt Lake in the Van of the Pioneers: The Original Diary of Erastus Snow," Moroni Snow, ed., *Improvement Era,* XIV–XV (1911–1912), later republished, with improved editorship, as "Journey to Zion: From the Journal of Erastus Snow," *Utah Humanities Review,* II (1948), esp. 276–284; and "Norton Jacob's Record," typescript, BYU. Much of the information in these diaries and of some unpublished ones, has been copied in the "Journal History of the Church" for the dates mentioned. Good general treatments are L. H. Creer, *The Founding of an Empire: The Exploration and Colonization of Utah, 1776–1856* (Salt Lake City, 1947); Milton R. Hunter, *Brigham Young the Colonizer* (Salt Lake City, 1940); and Joel E. Ricks, "Forms and Methods of Early Settlements in Utah and the Surrounding Region, 1847–77" (unpublished Ph. D. dissertation, University of Chicago, 1930).

The early activities of governing authorities and the colony in the first two years are noted in daily entries in the "Journal History of the Church," in monthly entries in the "History of Brigham Young," in A. L. Neff, *History of Utah, 1847 to 1869* (Salt Lake City, 1940), and in the diaries and reminiscences of participants. In addition to those mentioned above, the latter include: George Q. Cannon, "History of the Church," appearing serially in *The Juvenile Instructor,* VIII–IX (1873–1874); "A Short Sketch of the Life of Levi Jackman, 1797–1876," mimeographed, BYU; Robert Glass Cleland and Juanita Brooks, eds., *A Mormon Chronicle: Journals of John D. Lee* (2 vols.; San Marino, California, 1955); James S. Brown, *Life of a Pioneer* (Salt Lake City, 1900); *Journal of Jesse Nathaniel Smith . . .* (Salt Lake City, 1953); Diary of Hosea Stout, typescript, BYU; "Journal of Priddy Meeks," *Utah Historical Quarterly,* X (1942), 145–223; Joseph M. Tanner, *A Biographical Sketch of John Riggs Murdock*

(Salt Lake City, 1909); Flora Bean Horne, ed., *Autobiography of George Washington Bean . . .* (Salt Lake City, 1945); and the diaries of Lorenzo Dow Young and his wife Harriett in *Utah Historical Quarterly,* XIV (1946), esp. pp. 163–176. The best contemporary general accounts are in Stansbury's *Expedition,* pp. 122–150; J. W. Gunnison, *The Mormons, or Latter-day Saints . . .* (Philadelphia, 1856); and Jules Remy and Julius Brenchley, *A Journey to Great-Salt-Lake City* (2 vols.; London, 1861).

The origins of government are discussed in Thomas C. Romney, *The Story of Deseret* (Independence, Missouri, 1948); Dale L. Morgan, "The State of Deseret," *Utah Historical Quarterly,* VIII (1940), 65–251; L. H. Creer, "The Evolution of Government in Early Utah," *Utah Historical Quarterly,* XXVI (1958), 23–42; and Eugene E. Campbell, "A History of the Government of Utah, 1847–1851" (unpublished Master's Thesis, University of Utah, 1940). The land problem is analyzed and discussed in Feramorz Young Fox, "The Mormon Land System: A Study of the Settlement and Utilization of Land Under the Direction of the Mormon Church" (unpublished Ph. D. dissertation, Northwestern University, 1932). The irrigation problem is treated in George Thomas, *The Development of Institutions Under Irrigation, With Special Reference to Early Utah Conditions* (New York, 1920); and Charles H. Brough, *Irrigation in Utah* (Baltimore, 1898). Special studies of the monetary arrangements include: F. Y. Fox, "Hard Money and Currency in Utah," *Deseret News,* August 17, 1940; Sheridan L. McGarry, "Mormon Money," *The Numismatist,* LXIII (1940), 491–604, 698–706, 732–744, 830–840; and Leonard J. Arrington, "Coin and Currency in Early Utah," *Utah Historical Quarterly,* XX (1952), 56–76.

The quotations from John D. Lee's diary, *A Mormon Chronicle,* appear through the kind courtesy of the Henry E. Huntington Library & Art Gallery, San Marino, California.

1. Joseph Smith, *History of the Church . . .* (2nd ed.; 6 vols.; Salt Lake City, 1946ff.), V, 85, entry for August 6, 1842; also B. H. Roberts, *A Comprehensive History of the Church . . .* (6 vols.; Salt Lake City, 1930), II, 181–182.

2. *History of the Church,* VI, 222–227; Roberts, *Comprehensive History,* II, 210–212.

3. *History of the Church,* VI, 275–277; Roberts, *Comprehensive History,* II, 212–216.

4. Fawn Brodie, *No Man Knows My History . . .* (New York, 1946), pp. 360–361.

5. See "Memorial to the Queen for the Relief, by Emigration, of a Portion of Her Poor Subjects," *Latter-day Saints' Millennial Star* (Liverpool), VIII (1846), 142; J. B. Munro, "Mormon Colonization Scheme for Vancouver Island," *Washington Historical Quarterly,* XXV (1934), 278–285.

6. *History of the Church,* VI, 370–372.

7. *History of the Church,* VI, 548.

8. B. H. Roberts, *The Rise and Fall of Nauvoo* (Salt Lake City, 1900), p. 268; *Millennial Star,* VII (1846), 65; John C. Fremont, *Report of the Exploring Expedition to the Rocky Mountains, 1842* (Washington, 1844). Fremont's 1842 report was later reprinted and incorporated with his explorations of 1843–1844 and published in 1845.

9. Neff, *History of Utah,* p. 42; Roberts, *Comprehensive History,* II, 521.

10. Journal of John Taylor, cited in Roberts, *Comprehensive History,* II, 521; *History of the Church,* VII, 439; Diary of Hosea Stout, entries for October-December, 1845.

11. "History of Brigham Young," Book 2, p. 107, entry for August 9, 1846, CHO.

12. Roberts, *Comprehensive History,* III, 84–86. Jim Bridger apparently advocated Bear River Valley. Father De Smet saw the Mormons at Winter Quarters in November 1846, and wrote of this experience: "They [the Mormons] asked me a thousand questions about the regions I had explored and the spot which I have just described to you [the basin of Great Salt Lake] pleased them greatly from the account I gave them of it. Was that what determined them? I would not dare to assert it. They are there." H. M. Chittenden and A. T. Richardson, eds., *Life, Letters and Travels of Father Pierre-Jean De Smet, S. J., 1801–1873* (4 vols.; New York, 1905), I, 56.

13. Diary of Hosea Stout, September 9, 1846, March 22, 1847; JH, July 3, 1847.

14. *William Clayton's Journal,* pp. 76–77, entry for April 16, 1847.

15. It is not difficult to find strong statements, made by Brigham Young and other leaders at the time of the expulsion from Nauvoo and later, which indicate, to put it mildly, displeasure with the United States. For example, the statements attributed to Brigham Young by John D. Lee in *A Mormon Chronicle,* I, 27, dated May 14, 1848. On the basis of such statements, and the newspaper statements of apostates and others that the Mormons were going to set up an opposing government, Paxson and others seem to have drawn the not unreasonable conclusion that the Treaty of Guadalupe Hidalgo was unwanted by the Mormons and that after it was concluded there was nothing for the Saints to do "but make the best of these facts and to seek from the United States the same sort of autonomy they had received from Illinois." Frederic L. Paxson, *History of the American Frontier, 1763–1893* (New York, 1924), p. 349. This overlooks the continuous Mormon pleas for civil aid and federal recognition before their departure. It also overlooks the repeated Mormon assertions, if they are worth anything, that all the troubles they had been through had not alienated them from "the institutions of our country." See the "Circular" of the High Council of Nauvoo, dated January 20, 1846, published in Frank Golder, *The March of the Mormon Battalion . . .* (New York, 1928), pp. 70–73. Bancroft's conclusion seems nearer the truth: "The Mormons did not, however, hope to remain an independent republic, nor did they probably wish to do so." H. H. Bancroft, *History of Utah . . .* (San Francisco, 1889), p. 444. For a fuller discussion of the evidence, see Therald Jensen, "Mormon Theory of Church and State" (unpublished Ph. D. dissertation, University of Chicago, 1938), pp. 49–53.

16. Roberts, *Comprehensive History,* III, 90; JH, August 9, 1846; Diary of Hosea Stout, August 9, 1846.

17. JH, October 10, 1848.

18. JH, July 4, 1847; Jensen, p. 126.

19. JH, July 28, 1847; Journal of Wilford Woodruff, as cited in Hunter, *Brigham Young the Colonizer,* p. 32.

20. "Should the brethren at any time discover any specimens or beds of chalk, lime, coal, iron, lead, copper, or any other minerals, we wish they would report the same to the Council, who will keep a record of the same with the specimens, the place where found, and by whom, which record may be of great worth hereafter." JH, September 8, 1847.

21. See the discussion on settlement in JH, July 28, 1847.

22. Samuel Bowles, *Across the Continent . . .* (Springfield, Mass., 1865), p. 131.

23. John C. Fremont, *Report of the Exploring Expedition to the Rocky Mountains in the Year 1842, and to Oregon and North California in the Years 1843–'44* (Washington, 1845), p. 160. This was presumably among the parts read orally before the Quorum of the Twelve in December 1845.

24. Heber C. Kimball, on August 22, 1847, as recorded in Egan, *Pioneering the West,* p. 127.

25. JH, August 8, 1847.

26. HBY, 1847, pp. 11–13.

27. Erastus Snow, "From Nauvoo to Salt Lake . . . ," *Improvement Era,* XV (1912), 551, entry for August 8, 1847.

28. *William Clayton's Journal,* p. 326, entry for July 28, 1847; Journal of Wilford Woodruff, July 25, 1847, cited in Roberts, *Comprehensive History,* III, 269; "Norton Jacob's Record," July 25, 1847. These words were similar to Brigham Young's instructions of September 9, 1847: "We have no land to sell to the Saints in the Great Basin, but you are entitled to as much as you can till, or as you need for your support, providing you pay the surveyor for his services, while he is laboring for you; . . . none of you have any land to buy or sell more than ourselves; for the inheritance is of the Lord, and we are his servants, to see that everyone has his portion in due season." JH, September 9, 1847.

29. Remarks of July 28, 1847, as reported in "Norton Jacob's Record," p. 74.

30. Fox, "The Mormon Land System," pp. 159–161; JH, March 6, 1848.

31. HBY, 1847, p. 17; JH, November 16, 1847. Actually, the committee left before Captain Brown arrived with the money, but they seem to have spent Mormon Battalion money.

32. JH, November 9, 20, 1847, March 6, 1848.

33. JH, November 28, 1847. On October 17, 1847, Albert Carrington was appointed "to foot up papers of public work." JH, that date.

34. JH, October 13, 1847.

35. JH, November 28, December 1, 2, 1847. In September 1848 Crismon's toll was legally raised from one-sixteenth to one-tenth of the grain. JH, September 30, 1848.

36. JH, March 6, May 15, 1848.

37. Roberts, *Comprehensive History,* III, 269.

38. HBY, 1848, p. 22; JH, March 27, 1848.

39. The genesis of price control in 1847–1848 is described by Levi Jackman, a member of the High Council, in his journal at BYU, as follows: "January 1848. . . . It having cost the people so much to fetch provisions so far, some appeared to be disposed to make the necessities of the destitute their opportunity, and sold things I thot, rather high. I feared that such a principle if not checked might prove our destruction. I went to Father John Smith who was then the President of the place and recommended that prices should be set by the council for labor, provisions, etc. The proposition was opposed but it was finally carried into effect and the results were good. Some few were not pleased with the arrangement but it changed the drift of things much for the better. The most of the people were desirous to do right and were kind and did all they could to help the poor and needy and to build up the Kingdom of God on the earth. I had expected that we had left the thieves behind, but in this I was disappointed for we found they were in this place. But as fast as they were detected they were dealt with according to law."

40. "There was a little corn cracker mill on City Creek, built by Charles Crismon; there was no smutter and no bolt to this mill; we took some of our wheat, there was some smut in it, and some of the leaves and seeds of sunflowers; the result was a little of the worst flour I ever saw." *Journal of Jesse N. Smith,* p. 14.

41. George Q. Cannon, "History of the Church," *Juvenile Instructor,* VIII (1873), 203.

42. "Journal of Priddy Meeks," p. 164.

43. Thomas L. Kane, *The Mormons* (Philadelphia, 1850), p. 66.

44. "Journal of Priddy Meeks," p. 164; HBY, 1848, p. 30. As a result of this "miracle" the seagull came to be held in sacred remembrance in Utah. Laws were enacted prohibiting anyone from killing them. Later a statue was erected on Temple Block in their honor. Finally, in this century, the state legislature officially named the seagull to be the state bird of Utah.

45. HBY, 1848, p. 30.

46. Because of its secret nature, the written references to the Council of Fifty are often veiled and vague. John D. Lee often refers to it as "The Council of YTFIF"—fifty spelled backwards. Other diaries and journals refer to it as "a council," or "the legislative council," or "a meeting of leading citizens." The diaries of John D. Lee and Hosea Stout, HBY, and JH provide information of its activities from early December 1848 to late January 1850. Recent research suggests that the council continued in a behind-the-scenes capacity until the organization of the School of the Prophets in 1867.

47. *A Mormon Chronicle,* I, 80.

48. The Brigham Young manuscript gives the following explanation for the organization of the State of Deseret: "In consequence of Indian depredations on our horses, cattle, and other property, and the wicked conduct of a few base fellows who came among the Saints, the inhabitants of this Valley, as is common in new countries, generally, have organized a temporary government, to exist during its necessity, or until we can obtain a charter, for a Territorial Government, a petition for which is already in progress." HBY, 1849, p. 74.

49. Actually, the State of Deseret was disorganized in 1851, when the territorial government took over, but was reorganized in 1862 when the Mormons thought that, due to the Civil War, there was some chance of reaching their goal of becoming a state. In the high tide of reconstructionism after the war, Mormon pretensions toward state government seemed both futile and a provocation, and the ghost legislature ceased to meet after 1870.

50. JH, September 24, 1848.

51. JH, September 30, 1848, *et. seq.*

52. JH, October 2, 1848. In a letter written a few days later to Apostle Ezra T. Benson, Brigham Young wrote: "I have been all the day crowded by an anxious inquiring people to allot them their inheritances, to set out their farming-land . . . ." JH, October 7, 1848.

53. "Epistle to Orson Hyde . . . ." JH, October 9, 1848.

54. Roberts, *Comprehensive History,* III, 269.

55. Elwood Mead, *Irrigation Institutions: A Discussion of the Economic and Legal Questions Created by the Growth of Irrigated Agriculture in the West* (New York, 1907), p. 62; also pp. 319ff.

56. Wells A. Hutchins, *Mutual Irrigation Companies in Utah,* Utah Agricultural Experiment Station Bulletin 199 (Logan, Utah, 1927), pp. 1–15.

57. JH, August 22, 1847.

58. Thomas, *Development of Institutions Under Irrigation,* p. 27.

59. Approved February 4, 1852. *Acts, Resolutions, Memorials* (Salt Lake City, 1852).

60. Neff, *History of Utah,* p. 255.

61. Cited in F. Y. Fox, "Cooperation Among the Mormons," Chapter III, p. 20, typescript, CHO.

62. Neff, *History of Utah,* p. 162.

63. The daily journal in which labor and produce contributions toward the public works were entered is in CHO, listed as "Great Salt Lake Labor Account Book, 1848–1850."

64. HBY, 1849, p. 92; Mary Reynolds, "Boweries on the Temple Block," typescript, CHO.

65. JH, April 9, June 10, July 8, 1849.

66. HBY, 1849, p. 42.

67. *Ibid.,* p. 97.

68. *Ibid.,* p. 82–83.

69. According to Bancroft, "about $50" brought by Brigham Young in 1847 was at that time virtually "the only money in Utah" to care for the needs of almost 1700 persons. When the 1848 companies swelled the population to some 4200 the monetary stock was replenished with $84.00 in small change brought by Brigham Young from Winter Quarters. *History of Utah,* p. 762; JH, January 1, 1849.

70. *Deseret News Weekly* (Salt Lake City), May 1, 1897, p. 627.

71. For example: "Ebeneezer Brown paid in tithing six ounces of gold dust and six dollars; total $100." JH, November 23, 1848.

72. JH, November 25, 1848.

73. "Brigham Young's Daily Transactions in Gold Dust," MS., CHO; JH, December 13, 15, 1848.

74. *Ibid.;* Fox, "Hard Money and Currency in Utah."

75. JH, December 27, 1848; also "Norton Jacob's Record," January 6, 1849.

76. JH, January 1, 1849. Hosea Stout's diary notation is also of interest:

"*Thursday Dec 28th 1848.* Meeting called this morning for the purpose of consulting the practicability of issuing Bills of credit or notes to answer for currency for the time being as the gold dust cannot be coined for the want of crusibles at present. The gold dust to be deposited with the President & no more than the amount to be issued in bills. which plan was agreed upon.

"*Tuesday Jany 2nd 1849.* Today the National Bank commenced its operations & those who had gold dust were depositing it in the Bank at a rapid rate. It seems to take well among the people. I was there awhile & today received 25–00 of it for a rifle."

77. "Brigham Young's Transactions in Gold Dust."

78. JH, December 29–31, 1848, January 1–2, 1849.

79. JH, January 3, 4, 5, 1849.

80. JH, January 6, 1849.

81. JH, January 6, 8, 9, 10, 1849; "Transactions in Gold Dust."

82. JH, January 22, 1849.

83. Diary of Hosea Stout, February 4, 6, 1849; also JH, February 3, 1849; *A Mormon Chronicle,* I, 88.

84. Fox, "Hard Money and Currency in Utah."

85. JH, March 9, 1849.

86. HBY, 1848, p. 39. Fort Hall, near present-day Pocatello, Idaho, was originally built in 1834 by Nathaniel Wyeth, a fur trapper, and was sold by him to Hudson's Bay Company in 1837. The Hudson's Bay Company operated the fort until 1855.

87. "First General Epistle of the First Presidency . . . ," *Millennial Star,* XI (1849), 228.

88. *A Mormon Chronicle,* I, 81–82.

89. HBY, 1849, pp. 51–52.

90. *A Mormon Chronicle,* I, 100.

91. HBY, 1849, p. 86.

92. JH, February 3, 1849.

93. *Millennial Star,* XI (1849), 230.

94. *A Mormon Chronicle,* I, 89. In this and other quotations from Lee in this chapter, Lee's original spelling and capitalization have been slightly altered for purposes of clarity.

95. *Ibid.,* I, 86.

96. *Ibid.,* I, 88. Also see Diary of Hosea Stout, February 4, 1849.

97. *Ibid.,* I, 89–90.

98. Diary of Hosea Stout, June 23, 1849.

99. *Millennial Star,* XI (1849), 245; HBY, 1849, pp. 67, 72.

100. James S. Brown, *Life of a Pioneer,* p. 120.

101. HBY, 1849, p. 69.

102. From epistles published in *Millennial Star,* XI (1849), 230, 247.

103. Sermon of February 4, 1849, as reported in Brown, *Life of a Pioneer,* pp. 121–122. Another report of the same meeting makes Brigham's language even stronger: "He said that none should leave here & carry off the gold & silver &c without he pleases to let them; that they can not get away unless he sees fit & those who go away contrary to council he will confiscate their property, for he is Boss. . . ." Diary of Hosea Stout, February 4, 1849. Apparently, according to this report, Brigham Young was particularly concerned that "deserters" did not carry away with them any of the floating capital of the community.

104. Brown, *Life of a Pioneer,* p. 123.

105. See Oscar and Mary Flug Handlin, *Commonwealth — A Study of the Role of Government in the American Economy: Massachusetts, 1774–1861* (New York, 1947); Louis Hartz, *Economic Policy and Democratic Thought: Pennsylvania, 1776–1860* (Cambridge, Mass., 1948); James Neal Primm, *Economic Policy in the Development of a Western State: Missouri, 1820–1860* (Cambridge, Mass., 1954).

106. See, for example, the challenging interpretation in Avery Craven, "Utah and the West," *Western Humanities Review,* III (1949), 276–284.

CHAPTER III: THE HARVEST OF '49

The only systematic study of the Gold Rush, the Mormon Battalion, and the Gold Mission, and their relationship to church policy, is Eugene Edward Campbell, "A History of the Church of Jesus Christ of Latter-day Saints in California, 1846–1946" (unpublished Ph. D. dissertation, University of Southern California, 1952). That work has been particularly useful in preparing the present chapter.

General treatments of the Gold Rush have done very little with the Salt Lake experience, but among the best are: John Walton Caughey, *Gold is the Cornerstone* (Berkeley, California, 1948); Rodman W. Paul, *California Gold: The Beginning of Mining in the Far West* (Cambridge, Mass., 1947); Owen C. Coy, *Gold Days* (San Francisco, 1929), and *The Great Trek* (San Francisco, 1931); David M. Potter's introduction to *Trail to California: The Overland Journal of Vincent Geiger and Wakeman Bryarly* (New Haven, 1945); and the delightful Arthur B. Hulbert, *Forty-Niners: The Chronicle of the California Trail* (Boston, 1931). One of the most sensitive narratives of the forty-niners is that of Sarah Royce, mother of Josiah Royce, published under the editorship of Ralph Henry Gabriel as *A Frontier Lady: Recollections of the Gold Rush and Early California* (New Haven, 1932). Another contemporary journal, with much information about Salt Lake Valley, but reflecting a distinctly hostile feeling, is Franklin Langworthy, *Scenery of the Plains, Mountains and Mines . . .* (Ogdensburgh [N. Y.], 1855), esp. 72–106.

The trail from Salt Lake southwest to California is described in John Walton Caughey, "Southwest from Salt Lake in 1849," *Pacific Historical Review,* VI (1937), 143–164; and in LeRoy R. Hafen and Ann W. Hafen, *Journals of Forty-niners: Salt Lake to Los Angeles . . .* (Volume II of The Far West and the Rockies Historical Series, 1820–1875, Glendale, California, 1954). The history of the Humboldt trail and the story of Mormon Station, Nevada, are told in Dale L. Morgan, *The Humboldt: Highroad of the West* (New York, 1943). John Walton Caughey's *California* (New York, 1940) also has a chapter on the Gold Rush, as does Hubert Howe Bancroft, *History of California* (7 vols.; San Francisco, 1884–1890).

The basic facts with respect to the Gold Mission are related in the journals and reminiscences of several participants. The best of these is Henry Bigler's Journal, Book B, MS., Huntington Library, which is a daily account of the first company. After his return, Bigler copied this diary, with some amplification, into Henry W. Bigler's Journal, Book A, MS., also in the Huntington Library. The latter was typed by the Works Progress Administration and is in the WPA Collection of Mormon diaries in the Library of Congress. Extracts from Bigler's journals were also published in the *Utah Historical Quarterly,* V (1932), 35–64, 87–112, 134–160. Other treatments of the first company include: George Q. Cannon, "Twenty Years Ago: A Trip to California," *The Juvenile Instructor,* IV (1869), 13ff., which is a beautifully written series of recollections based upon journals which Cannon kept during the mission; "Autobiography of James Henry Rollins," dictated in 1898, typescript, UHS; Diary of William Farrer, typescript, BYU; and Benjamin F. Johnson, *My Life's Review* (Independence, Mo., 1947), esp. p. 129. Extracts from the Bigler and Farrer diaries, the recollections of Rollins, and the diaries and reminiscences of Charles C. Rich and Sheldon Stoddard, all members of the first company, were also published in the Hafen, *Journals of Forty-niners,* pp. 141–272. Our knowledge of the second company comes primarily from "Journal and Diary of Albert King Thurber," in Kate B. Carter, ed., *Treasures of Pioneer History,* III, 273–290, which is a recollection (1862) based on original journals.

Perhaps the best contemporary Mormon source for the events of 1849–1851 is *The Frontier Guardian,* published weekly in Kanesville, Iowa, 1849–1852. The paper is full of letters and reports from Utah. Beginning on June 15, 1850 the church also published the newsworthy Salt Lake weekly, *The Deseret News.*

The standard reference on early Mormon colonization is Milton R. Hunter, *Brigham Young the Colonizer* (Salt Lake City, 1940). A short interpretative account is William R. Palmer, "The Pioneering Mormon," *Improvement Era,* XLV (1942), 538ff. The San Bernardino colony has been studied in: George William Beattie and Helen Pruitt Beattie, *Heritage of the Valley: San Bernardino's First Century* (Pasadena, Calif., 1939), pp. 170–318; John Henry Evans, *Charles Coulson Rich: Pioneer Builder of the West* (New York, 1936), pp. 171–225; H. F. Raup, "San Bernardino, California: Settlement and Growth of a Pass-Site City," *University of California Publications in Geography,* Vol. 8, no. 1 (Berkeley, 1940); and a chapter in Robert V. Hine, *California's Utopian Colonies* (San Marino, Calif., 1953).

Early village institutions in Utah are described in Lowry Nelson, *The Mormon Village: A Pattern and Technique of Land Settlement* (Salt Lake City, 1952); George W. Rollins, "Land Policies of the United States as Applied to Utah to 1910," *Utah Historical Quarterly,* XX (1952), 219–251; and Leonard J. Arrington, "Property Among the Mormons," *Rural Sociology,* XVI (1951), 339–352. The early town government of the Mormon communities, as reflected in priesthood and other meetings is described in Levi Edgar Young, "The New England Town Government in Early Day Utah," *Proceedings of the Pacific Coast Branch of the American Historical Association,* 1927, pp. 41–58. Thematic treatments of coöperative irrigation projects include: Juanita Brooks, "The Water's In!" *Harper's Monthly Magazine,* CLXXXII (1941), 608–613; and Leonard J. Arrington, "Taming the Turbulent Sevier: A Story of Mormon Desert Conquest," *Western Humanities Review,* V (1951), 393–406.

1. On Brannan, see Paul A. Bailey, *Sam Brannan and the California Mormons* (Los Angeles, 1953); Reva L. Scott, *Samuel Brannan and the Golden Fleece: A Biography* (New York, 1944); William Glover, *The Mormons in California,* ed., Paul Bailey (Los Angeles, 1954); Douglas S. Watson, "Herald of the Gold Rush — Sam Brannan," *California Historical Society Quarterly,* X (1931), 298–301.

2. *Memoirs of General William T. Sherman, By Himself* (2 vols., New York, 1875), I, 52; William T. Sherman, *Recollections of California, 1846–1861* (Oakland, Calif., 1945), p. 40.

3. "Eleventh General Epistle of the Presidency," April 10, 1854, *Deseret News,* April 13, 1854.

4. Cited in Preston Nibley, *Brigham Young the Man and His Work* (Salt Lake City, 1936), p. 254.

5. JH, July 8, 1849.

6. JH, May 26, 1850.

7. JH, September 6, 1850. Father Thomas Rhodes, according to an early observer, is said to have brought "several sacks of gold" from California in 1848 including one sack weighing sixty pounds. This sack, valued at perhaps $15,000, is said to have been turned over to the church for equivalent tithing office pay; that is, the church built him a home, gave him a herd of cattle, and furnished food supplies. From the notes of Colonel Joseph M. Lock, in the possession of Sheridan L. McGarry, Salt Lake City, Utah.

8. HBY, 1849, p. 84.

9. This estimate is based upon "Brigham Young's Daily Transactions in Gold Dust," MS., CHO; "Joint Tithing and Collection Record of Lyman and Rich," MS., CHO; and notations by Brigham Young's secretary copied into JH.

10. HBY, 1849, p. 99.

11. George A. Smith, *The Rise, Progress and Travels of the Church* (Salt Lake City, 1869), p. 17.

12. "Fourth General Epistle of the First Presidency," September 27, 1850, *Millennial Star,* XIII (1851), 49.

13. JH, April 8, May 13, September 27, 1850; Brigham Young, sermon, October 6, 1854, *Deseret News,* November 2, 1854.

14. According to a letter written by John Taylor, there were "many small merchants who brought from two to ten thousand dollars worth of goods with them, who found it indispensably necessary to sell out in the Valley." The largest was "the Messrs. Pomeroy of Missouri, with about fifty thousand dollars worth [which] consisted mostly of men's ready made clothing." Apparently all of this was sold on the Salt Lake market. *Frontier Guardian,* January 9, 1850.

15. Benjamin Brown, *Testimonies for the Truth: A Record of Manifestations of the Power of God, Miraculous and Providential . . .* (Liverpool, 1853), pp. 27–29. A copy of this rare pamphlet is in the Huntington Library.

16. Dale L. Morgan, *The Great Salt Lake* (Indianapolis, 1947), p. 222, estimates

10,000. Contemporary Mormon estimates of the overland migration through the Salt Lake Valley vary from 12,000 to 20,000 per year. See correspondence in the *Millennial Star,* XI (1849), 340–343. On the other hand, John Walton Caughey places the number at a tenth or more of the total overland migration in *Gold is the Cornerstone,* p. 112. In his *History of California,* VI, 159, Bancroft estimates 25,000 went by way of the South Pass in 1849. All scholars agree that less than half of these went by way of Salt Lake City. An estimate that more than 40,000 passed Fort Laramie in 1850 is given in P. A. M. Taylor, "Emigrants' Problems in Crossing the West," *University of Birmingham Historical Journal,* V (1955), 83n.

17. Robert Glass Cleland and Juanita Brooks, eds., *A Mormon Chronicle: The Diaries of John D. Lee, 1848–1876* (2 vols., San Marino, Calif., 1955), I, 110–111, 114, entries for July-August 1849. William Adams puts the price of flour near the end of July 1849 at $25.00 per hundred, "and scarce at that price." "Autobiography of William Adams," typescript, BYU, p. 18. See also "Diary of Hosea Stout," entries for June, July, and August 1849, typescript, BYU; *Millennial Star,* XII (1850), 350.

18. *Frontier Guardian,* September 15, 1849. Babbitt, who had been elected Delegate to Congress from the State of Deseret, was on his way from Salt Lake to Washington when he made this statement. He suggested to Missouri Valley merchants that "as a grand speculation" they ought to go to Salt Lake and "lay in their fall stock of goods!" "They can buy plenty of wagons there for less than one half what the iron costs in St. Louis and any number of cattle to haul them back."

19. "Journal of Priddy Meeks," *Utah Historical Quarterly,* X (1942), 183–185.

20. HBY, 1850, pp. 112–113; also "Record of Andrew Jackson Allen," May 1850, typescript, USU.

21. Sermon published in the *Deseret News,* July 20, 1850.

22. Matt Lagerberg, "The Bishop Hill Colonists in the Gold Rush," *Journal of the Illinois State Historical Society,* XLVIII (1955), 467; see also Charles Kelly, "Gold Seekers on the Hastings Cutoff," *Utah Historical Quarterly,* XX (1952), 27.

23. Andrew Macfarlane to Margaret L. McFarlane, November 19, 1850, *Utah Historical Quarterly,* XXII (1954), 60.

24. Parley P. Pratt to Orson Pratt, JH, July 8, 1849; Diary of Hosea Stout, April 10, 1850.

25. *A Mormon Chronicle,* I, 112, August 5, 1849.

26. See Dale Morgan's introduction to "The Mormon Ferry on the North Platte: The Journal of William A. Empey, May 7–August 4, 1847," *Annals of Wyoming,* XXI (1949), esp. 111–117.

27. The church historian noted in October 1849 that several hundred California-bound emigrants arrived too late in the season to continue the journey by the northern route. Many contemplated wintering at Salt Lake until they learned of the unavailability of food. So, "on the 8th Jefferson Hunt started with a company of about 100 wagons [some 500 persons], by the southern route." There was much suffering among those who left in this company and some of them perished in the desert in the experience which gave Death Valley its name. HBY, 1849, p. 98; Hafen and Hafen, *Journals of Forty-niners;* William Lewis Manly, *Death Valley in '49 . . .* (San Jose, Calif., 1894); *Pioneer Notes: From the Diaries of Judge Benjamin Hayes, 1849–1875* (Los Angeles, 1929), pp. 67, 72–73.

28. This estimate is given in the contemporary pamphlet: N. Slater, *Fruits of Mormonism, or a Fair and Candid Statement of Facts Illustrative of Mormon Principles, Mormon Policy, and Mormon Character, by More than Forty Eye-witnesses* (Coloma, Calif., 1851), pp. 4, 8, 11, a copy in the Huntington Library.

29. Addison Crane, "Journal of a trip from Lafayette, Indiana, to Volcano, Calif., via Fort Laramie, Salt Lake City, and the Humboldt River, March 26, 1852 to August 28, 1852," p. 56, MS., Huntington Library; Jules Remy and Julius Brenchley, *A Journey to Great-Salt-Lake City* (2 vols., London, 1861), II, 269.

30. Slater, pp. 6–9, 11.

31. Howard Stansbury, *An Expedition to the Valley of the Great Salt Lake of Utah . . .* (Philadelphia, 1852), p. 63.

32. *A Mormon Chronicle,* I, 112.

33. HBY, 1850, p. 107.

34. Diary of Joseph Holbrook, I, 71, typescript in possession of the writer.

35. JH, April 12, 1849.

36. Embossed reproductions of the coins are found in Jacob R. Eckfeldt and William E. Du Bois, *New Varieties of Gold and Silver Coins, Counterfeit Coins, and Bullion; with Mint Values* (Philadelphia, 1850), p. 24. Eckfeldt and Du Bois were assayers of the United States Mint, and received some of the Mormon coins on January 10, 1850.

37. JH, October 27, 1849; also JH, October 31, November 28, 1849.

38. *Deseret News,* October 5, 1850.

39. JH, May 28, 1850; *Frontier Guardian,* May 16, 1851.

40. Eckfeldt and Du Bois, p. [61]. The fineness was found to be 899. In the 1851 edition of the same work (p. 9), the writers give the fineness as 886.

41. Ira B. Cross, *Financing an Empire: History of Banking in California* (4 vols.; Chicago, 1927), I, 128–129, 137.

42. The *Deseret News* of January 10, 1852, concluded an editorial on the subject of "Valley coin," by asserting: "if valley coin in exchange, is not as valuable as goods, at the current prices offered in our market, we recommend our friends to keep their coin, and not insult their neighbors with such miserable trash as virgin gold."

43. JH, August 31, 1851.

44. Professor E. E. Campbell of Brigham Young University, and the writer, have collaborated in an unpublished paper "The L. D. S. Gold Mining Missions of 1849–1850," from which some of the material in this section has been borrowed.

45. "Henry W. Bigler's Journal, Book A," pp. 162–163 [96–97]. "Father" John Smith held the position of "Presiding Patriarch" of the church. He was 68 years of age and had participated in all of the Mormon "wars" and migrations.

46. *Ibid.*

47. Cannon, "Twenty Years Ago: A Trip to California," *The Juvenile Instructor,* IV (1869), 13.

48. Cannon, p. 13.

49. Bigler, January 6, 1850, p. 196 [128].

50. Bigler, September 23, 1850, pp. 204 [136]. Elders Gibson, Flake, Burnham, Kinion, Gould, and Bills died of causes incident to the mission.

51. Bigler, October 6, 1850, p. 207 [139].

52. It will be remembered that Bigler indicated he had previously earned $836. If all twelve earned equally — a reasonable assumption — their combined previous earnings had been $10,032.

53. *Ibid.,* p. 207 [139].

54. "Journal and Diary of Albert King Thurber," p. 280.

55. *Ibid.,* p. 284.

56. "Autobiography of James Henry Rollins." See also "Tales of the Old Santa Fe

and Salt Lake Trail to California [Life of Sheldon Stoddard]," *Sante Fe Magazine,* VIII (1914), 28.

57. Thurber, p. 289.

58. The committee consisted of Willard Snow, John S. Fullmer, Lorenzo Snow, John D. Lee, and Franklin D. Richards. HBY, 1849, p. 95; JH, September 9, 1849.

59. "The brethren who come from the mines bring the gold with them, and many are glad to have an opportunity, now they are able, of fulfilling their covenant made in relation to gathering the Saints to a resting place." Brigham Young *et al* to Orson Hyde, JH, November 19, 1849.

60. JH, October 6, 1849.

61. The act of incorporation is reprinted in [Dale L. Morgan], "The State of Deseret," *Utah Historical Quarterly,* VIII (1940), 187–190. When the Territory of Utah was established it was necessary for the territorial legislature to recharter the company, which it did on October 4, 1851. That charter was slightly reworded by amendment and confirmed by the legislature on January 12, 1856.

62. The First Presidency to Orson Hyde, October 16, 1849, *Millennial Star,* XII (1850), 124.

63. JH, January 31, 1852; also *Frontier Guardian,* November 14, 1851.

64. "Seventh General Epistle of the Presidency . . . ," *Millennial Star,* XIV (1852), 325.

65. See HBY, 1852, p. 17.

66. HBY, 1849, p. 97.

67. Associated in the venture were Shadrach Roundy, Jedediah M. Grant, John S. Fullmer, George D. Grant, and Russell Homer. JH, December 11, 26, 1849. Abraham O. Smoot was also associated in the venture, although it is doubtful that he was an original partner. See William R. Palmer, "Abraham O. Smoot, Pioneer," *The Instructor,* November 1944, pp. 518–519.

68. Letter of Shadrach Roundy *et al,* December 24, 1849, *Frontier Guardian,* January 9, 1850; John Taylor, *ibid.*

69. Brigham Young, *Deseret News,* November 21, 1855; George L. Strebel, "Freighting Between the Missouri River and Utah — 1847–1869" (unpublished Master's Thesis, Brigham Young University, 1954), p. 209.

70. *Frontier Guardian,* January 9, 1850.

71. "Church Store Day Book A," October 26, 1850 to June 28, 1852, MS., CHO.

72. "Record of Business Meetings of the Bishops and Lesser Priesthood of Provo City [1868–1875]," December 22, 1868, p. 35, microfilm, BYU.

73. *Ibid.* The church attempted in October 1850 to establish a second carrying and trading company without success. JH, October 16, 1850. Apparently, many persons felt that the Gold Rush trade would make commercial importation into Utah unprofitable.

74. JH, November 21, 1849.

75. J. F. Frederick, *Ben Holladay, The Stagecoach King: A Chapter in the Development of Transcontinental Transportation* (Glendale, Calif., 1940), pp. 28–33; *Deseret News,* December 13, 1851.

76. Kinkead's name is variously spelled Kinkade, Kincaid, Kinkaid, and Kinkhead.

77. Remarks of George A. Smith, October 8–9, 1868, JD, XIII, 122; *Tullidge's Quarterly Magazine,* I (1881), 354.

78. As told in Sarah Hollister Harris, *An Unwritten Chapter of Salt Lake: 1851–1901* (New York, 1901), pp. 32–33.

79. Slater, *Fruits of Mormonism,* p. 10, says "four or five thousand dollars per day."

80. John Taylor in *Frontier Guardian,* January 9, 1850.

81. Harris, pp. 32–33.

82. Crane, "Journal," p. 58.

83. Santiago [James H. Martineau], "Pioneer Sketches: A Journey in 1854," *The Contributor,* XI (1890), 183.

84. Sermon published in the *Deseret News,* May 26, 1869.

85. Sermon, April 9, 1852, JD, I, 52; also sermon in JH, October 9, 1852.

86. JH, October 22, 1850.

87. Statement of Brigham Young, *Deseret News,* November 21, 1855.

88. The church exchanged cattle for 1,300 bushels of wheat and 60,000 pounds of flour, and approximately $20,000 worth of boots and shoes, hats, groceries, supplies, dry goods, and other commodities from a Mr. I. L. Mason of the firm of Mason and Perry in May 1855, which were disposed of in the church store. Heber C. Kimball to William Kimball, JH, May 29, 1855; *Deseret News,* May 30, 1855; "Invoice Book A, Church Store, 1855, MS., CHO.

89. Sermons in JH, May 25, 1851, October 6, 1852.

90. Sermon of October 9, 1852, JD, I, 214–216; also his sermon of October 8, 1855, in Neff, *History of Utah,* p. 347.

91. *Ibid.*

92. Neff, *History of Utah,* p. 209.

93. Hampton Sidney Beatie, "The First in Nevada," p. 6, MS., Bancroft Library, cited in Hunter, *Brigham Young the Colonizer,* p. 257.

94. Milton R. Hunter, "The Mormon Corridor," *Pacific Historical Review,* VIII (1939), 179–200.

95. "Early History and Records of Provo, Utah, 1849–1872," entry for November 26, 1849, p. 25, microfilm, BYU; HBY, 1849, p. 100; Epistle of the Twelve to Orson Pratt, JH, March 9, 1849; also Brigham Young in JH, October 27, 1850.

96. Parley P. Pratt, "A Report of the Southern Exploring Company," JH, November 23, 1849 to February 2, 1850, particularly, JH, January 31, 1850. Also Isaac C. Haight's diary, pp. 63–72, typescript, BYU.

97. Milton Hunter, p. 192.

98. JH, December 29, 1849.

99. Manuscript History of Brigham Young, March 23, 1851, as cited in B. H. Roberts, *A Comprehensive History of the Church . . .* (6 vols.; Salt Lake City, 1930), III, 349.

100. JH, November 18, 1847.

101. Evans, *Charles Coulson Rich,* p. 201.

102. JH, September 22, 1851; *Millennial Star,* XIV (1852), 75. Rich and Lyman thought they were buying an 80,000 to 100,000 acre ranch, but a subsequent government survey cut it down to 35,500.

103. Evans, p. 210; Campbell, pp. 169–170; JH, February 1, 1852.

104. Remy and Brenchley, *A Journey to Great-Salt-Lake City,* II, 456–457; Neff, *History of Utah,* p. 221.

105. Campbell, pp. 180–181; Evans, pp. 201–202.

106. Cp. Hunter, *Brigham Young the Colonizer,* pp. 361–366.

107. "History of Goudy E. Hogan," p. 51, typescript, BYU.

108. "Journal of the Iron County Mission," Gustive O. Larson, ed., *Utah Historical Quarterly,* XX (1952), 370–373.

109. "Journal History of Snowflake Stake," 1879, CHO.

110. Lowry Nelson, "Early Land Holding Practices in Utah, and Problems Arising from Them," *Journal of Farm Economics,* IX (1947), 354.

111. *Utah Pioneer and Apostle, Marriner Wood Merrill and His Family,* ed. Melvin Clarence Merrill (Salt Lake City, 1937), p. 36. Goudy Hogan makes no mention of the affair in his own journal, which is at BYU.

112. From a dispatch by "J. W. R." in *The Semi-weekly Inter Ocean* (Chicago), June 2, 1881, Ritch Collection, Huntington Library.

113. Nelson, p. 353.

114. This problem is discussed at some length in Leonard J. Arrington, "Mormon Economic Policies and Their Implementation on the Western Frontier, 1847–1900" (unpublished Ph. D. dissertation, University of North Carolina, 1952), pp. 164–198.

115. From the address of George Q. Cannon on accepting the chairmanship of the Third National Irrigation Congress, Denver, Colorado, September 1894. Published by the Utah Irrigation Commission in *Irrigation in Utah* (Salt Lake City, 1895), p. 35. See also the address of Wilford Woodruff, "My Twenty Acre Farm," *ibid.,* pp. 65–68.

116. Neff, *History of Utah,* pp. 678–690.

117. The absence of such banks, in turn, explains the lack of a sensational history of currency, inflation, credit, etc. in pioneer Utah. The early monetary and banking history of the territory deals principally with the church's attempts to provide cash and credit for transaction and import purposes.

118. JH, March 26, May 13, 17, 20, 1850.

119. The words of Sir Francis Bacon, as cited in R. H. Tawney, *The Acquisitive Society* (New York, 1920), p. 181.

CHAPTER IV: ORGANIZATION FOR GROWTH AND DEVELOPMENT

Travelers' and other accounts which depict the Mormon economy of the 1850's include: J. W. Gunnison, *The Mormons, or Latter-day Saints . . .* (Philadelphia, 1856); William Chandless, *A Visit to Salt Lake . . .* (London, 1857); S. N. Carvalho, *Incidents of Travel and Adventure in the Far West* (New York, 1858); Jules Remy and Julius Brenchley, *A Journey to Great-Salt-Lake City* (2 vols.; London, 1861); Richard F. Burton, *The City of the Saints . . .* (New York, 1862); John Hyde, Jr., *Mormonism: Its Leaders and Designs* (New York, 1857); Benjamin G. Ferris, *Utah and the Mormons* (New York, 1854); and Nelson Winch Green, *Fifteen Years Among the Mormons, Being the Narrative of Mrs. Mary Ettie V. Smith . . .* (New York, 1858).

The first study of Mormon immigration was *Route from Liverpool to Great Salt Lake Valley, Illustrated with Steel Engravings and Wood Cuts from Sketches Made by Frederick Piercy,* edited by James Linforth (Liverpool, 1855). This quarto volume is a masterpiece of artistic excellence, with a firsthand travel commentary by Mr. Piercy, who accompanied one of the Mormon companies from Liverpool to Salt Lake City; detailed geographical and historical notes by Mr. Linforth; and a compilation of immigration statistics. In the course of a study of London labor and poor in 1850, Charles Mackay became interested enough in the activities of the Mormons preparing to emigrate from Liverpool to write *The Mormons, or Latter Day Saints* (London, 1851), which devotes much space to emigration. Charles Dickens also applied his graphic powers to a description of a Mormon emigration company in *The Uncommercial Traveller.* More recent studies include a series of articles by Andrew Jenson in *The Contributor,* XII and XIII (1891–1892); Gustive O. Larson, *Prelude to the Kingdom*

. . . (Francestown, N. H., 1947); William Mulder, *Homeward to Zion: The Mormon Migration from Scandinavia* (Minneapolis, 1957); and Philip A. M. Taylor, "Mormon Emigration from Great Britain to the United States 1840–70" (unpublished Ph. D. dissertation, University of Cambridge, 1950), from which have appeared: "Why Did British Mormons Emigrate?", *Utah Historical Quarterly*, XXII (1954), 249–270, "Mormons and Gentiles on the Atlantic," XXIV (1956), 195–214, and "The Mormon Crossing of the United States, 1840–1870," XXV (1957), 319–337. Other studies include Wilbur S. Shepperson, "The Place of the Mormons in the Religious Emigration of Britain, 1840–1860," *Utah Historical Quarterly*, XX (1952), 207–218; and M. Hamlin Cannon, "The 'Gathering' of British Mormons to Western America: A Study in Religious Migration" (unpublished Ph. D. dissertation, American University, 1950), from which have been published "Migration of English Mormons to America," *American Historical Review*, LII (1947), 436–455; and "The English Mormons in America," *American Historical Review*, LVII (1952), 893–908.

An early treatise on industrial development in the 1850's is John G. Crook, "The Development of Early Industry and Trade in Utah" (unpublished Master's Thesis, University of Utah, 1926). The best account of the sugar enterprise is Fred G. Taylor, *A Saga of Sugar* (Salt Lake City, 1944). Mining history is reviewed in Robert G. Raymer, "Early Mining in Utah," *Pacific Historical Review*, VII (1939), 81–88. Particularized accounts of the iron industry include William R. Palmer, "The Pioneer Iron Company," distributed in mimeographed form in the "Christmas Bulletin" of the Minnequa Historical Society, December 1938; and Leonard J. Arrington, "Planning an Iron Industry for Utah, 1851–1858," *The Huntington Library Quarterly*, XXI (May, 1958), 237–260. A day-by-day chronicle of the Las Vegas lead and Indian mission is found in Andrew Jenson, ed., "History of Las Vegas Mission," *Nevada State Historical Papers*, V (Reno, 1926), 117–284. An autobiographical account is in Flora Bean Horne, ed., *Autobiography of George Washington Bean* (Salt Lake City, 1945), pp. 114–126.

1. "Economic Aspects of Mormonism," *Harper's Monthly Magazine*, CVI (1903), 668. Professor Ely thought the German Army in its heyday was superior.

2. See B. H. Roberts, *A Comprehensive History of the Church . . .* (6 vols.; Salt Lake City, 1930), III, 487–488 for a discussion of population statistics.

3. There were 32,894 Mormon members in England in 1851 and 29,441 in 1854. Taylor, "Mormon Emigration from Great Britain to the United States," pp. 69–70.

4. *Utah Historical Quarterly*, VIII (1940), 187.

5. *Route from Liverpool*, p. 9. Up to 1855, priority in emigration was apparently given to mechanics, even over veteran church members. In fact, the veteran members were not all removed to Utah until 1868. Taylor, p. 90.

6. For example, the epistle of December 23, 1847, published as Douglas C. McMurtrie, ed., *The General Epistle of the Latter-Day Saints* (Chicago, 1935).

7. JH, April 8, 1849.

8. *Millennial Star*, XI (1849), 246–249, XII (1850), 141.

9. *Route from Liverpool*, pp. 16–17.

10. *Economic Beginnings of the Far West* (2 vols.; New York, 1912), II, 184. A recent study goes farther: "Considering the well-ordered operation of the program and the loyalty to original purpose shown by the emigrants after their arrival in America, the Mormons produced the only successful, privately conducted emigration system of the period." Shepperson, "The Place of the Mormons in the Religious Emigration of Britain, 1840–1860," *Utah Historical Quarterly*, XX (1952), 218.

11. A discussion of the ten and thirteen pound companies by their organizer is found in "Discourse by S. W. Richards delivered in the Tabernacle, on Sunday, Oct. 29, 1854, J. V. Long, Reporter," photostat in the Huntington Library, Mormon File, Box 11.

12. A table of Mormon emigration from the British Isles and the Continent, 1840–1870, is given in Taylor, "Mormon Emigration from Great Britain to the United States, 1840–1870," pp. 193–194.

13. Larson, *Prelude to the Kingdom* . . . pp. 167, 235. Two Europeans who visited Utah in 1855 made the following observations in relation to the work of the P.E.F.: "By means of the good management of its agents, the Church has often reduced the cost of the journey to a tenth of what it might otherwise have been, and moreover has, by compelling the converts to go in large bands, been able to protect them from being way-laid and plundered by the Indians. It is owing to this paternal care, which shows as much ability as integrity in the administrators, that the expense of a journey from Liverpool to Great Salt Lake City has been reduced to the astonishing minimum of £20 for each adult, and even sometimes so low as £10. To comprehend this extraordinary cheapness, we must first take into account the incalculable advantages of association, and then be aware that wherever the emigrants stop to victual, they find missionaries who, aware of their coming, have arranged everything as to avoid all delay, and make any overcharge or extortion impossible." Remy and Brenchley, *A Journey to Great-Salt-Lake City,* II, 220.

14. *Millennial Star,* XIX (1857), 570.

15. Franklin L. West, *Life of Franklin D. Richards* (Salt Lake City, 1924), p. 133.

16. T. B. H. Stenhouse, *The Rocky Mountain Saints* . . . (New York, 1873), p. 340.

17. As given in William E. Smythe, *The Conquest of Arid America* (Rev. ed.; New York, 1905), p. 68.

18. From Ward Teachers' Report Slips of the Logan First Ward, found in the Cache Stakehouse Vault, Logan, Utah.

19. Logan Tithing Office Account Book, 1863–1868, MS., Cache Stakehouse Vault.

20. Receipt Book of the Perpetual Emigrating Fund Company, MS., UU.

21. *Utah Historical Quarterly,* VIII (1940), 238, also 226–227.

22. Receipt Book, the Perpetual Emigrating Fund Company; also *Deseret News,* May 15, 1852.

23. JH, September 27, 1850; *St. Louis Luminary,* September 1, 1855.

24. JH, September 16, 1855, October 6, 1860.

25. Brigham Young sermon, JH, September 13, 1860.

26. A specimen of the full contract is found in Roberts, *Comprehensive History,* III, 409–410. According to Roberts, interest was not required "whenever there was anything like promptness in the payment of the principal, or where misfortune had been encountered. . . ."

27. JD, III, 5.

28. "Circular To Presidents and Bishops of the Church . . ." (Salt Lake City, 1856); *Names of Persons and Sureties Indebted to the Perpetual Emigrating Fund Company from 1850 to 1877 Inclusive* (Salt Lake City, 1877).

29. *Route from Liverpool,* p. 20; Mackay, *The Mormons, or Latter Day Saints,* pp. 270–272.

30. However, when 300 Welsh and German Mormons offered to take the *Great Eastern,* the large, jinx-haunted, iron ship, in 1861, the management, despite the fact that the ship sailed with one-fortieth of passenger capacity, turned the Mormons down

on the ground that they had "peculiar habits." James Dugan, *The Great Iron Ship* (New York, 1953), pp. 92–93.

31. Mackay, pp. 270–273.

32. Charles Dickens, *The Uncommercial Traveller,* Vol. VI of *The Works of Charles Dickens* (New York, n.d.), pp. 635–638.

33. See also *Parliamentary Papers, House of Commons,* Report from the Select Committee on Emigration Ships, 1854, XIII, 163, 349.

34. Cited in *Route from Liverpool,* p. 18. The story of the "Mormonite elder" who testified at these hearings is given in Samuel W. Richards, "Missionary Experience," *The Contributor,* XI (1890), 155–159. See the analysis in Cannon, "Gathering of British Saints," pp. 107–108.

35. The outfitting point moved West as facilities for transportation improved and supplies became available. In 1853 Keokuk, Iowa, was the western outfitting point, and in succession the following cities: Kansas City (1854); Iowa City (1856); Florence, Nebraska (1857); Wyoming, Nebraska (1864); Benton, Nebraska (1868); and, later in 1868, Laramie, Wyoming. After the transcontinental railroad was completed in March 1869, emigration companies traveled all the way to Utah by rail.

36. An outfit for a party of six persons in 1860 cost $491. Burton, *The City of the Saints,* pp. 138–139.

37. *Route from Liverpool,* p. 19.

38. E. W. Tullidge, *The History of Salt Lake City* (Salt Lake City, c. 1886), pp. 666–667.

39. Andrew M. Israelsen, *Utah Pioneering: An Autobiography,* Orson W. Israelsen, ed. (Salt Lake City, 1938), p. 21.

40. H. H. Bancroft, *History of Utah,* p. 483n.

41. Nels Anderson, *Desert Saints: The Mormon Frontier in Utah* (Chicago, 1942), p. 96.

42. *Deseret News,* October 16, 1852.

43. Sermon of October 3, 1852, *ibid.,* May 11, 1854.

44. See Robert S. Ellison, *Fort Bridger, Wyoming: A Brief History* (Casper, Wyoming, 1931); Victor H. Cohen, "James Bridger's Claims," *Annals of Wyoming,* XII (1940), 228–240; Jerome Thomases, "Fort Bridger: A Western Community," *Military Affairs,* V (1941), 177–188, esp. p. 178; Roberts, *Comprehensive History,* IV, 2–3; JH, October 16, 1858, December 9, 1868.

45. Published in full in *Route from Liverpool,* pp. 11–12.

46. *Millennial Star,* XXVI (1864), 813.

47. *Deseret News,* July 6, 1854.

48. W. H. Dixon, *New America* (Philadelphia, 1867), p. 177. Interesting in this connection is the plea made by Heber C. Kimball from the pulpit in 1856: "I hope the bishops will step forth and get places for those who have just come in, and I hope the people will employ them and not let them lay in their tents, for if they stay idle they will become sick, but if you set them to work they will stay well. . . ." Cited in *Heart Throbs of the West* (12 vols.; Salt Lake City, 1936–1951), I, 220.

49. *Deseret News,* April 13, 1854.

50. *Ibid.,* December 13, 1851.

51. JH, January 26, April 10, May 6, 1850.

52. When Hosea Stout was called on a mission in 1852, he paid the public works $440 for which they agreed to build "a comfortable house," 18 feet square, "with a good cellar under it," for his family to live in while he was gone. Diary of Hosea Stout, September 30, 1852, typescript, BYU.

53. JH, December 13, 1851, May 14, 1855.

54. JH, August 29, 1858; *Millennial Star,* XXI (1859), 719–720.

55. JH, April 7, 1861; "Diary of George Laub," typescript, BYU.

56. HBY, 1851, pp. 125–126; *Millennial Star,* XIV (1852), 18.

57. Wilford Woodruff to George A. Smith, JH, April 1, 1857; also JH, February 1, April 27, August 31, 1855, June 14, 1856. Parts of the canal were used for irrigation and the propelling of machinery.

58. JH, February 26, 1854; also JH, August 23, 27, 1853; *Deseret Weekly,* June 19, 1897, pp. 23–28; sermon of George A. Smith, June 20, 1869, JD, XIII, 85.

59. Most of the literature pertaining to the "home industry" movement of 1852 can be read in issues of the *Deseret News,* beginning January 24, 1852, and continuing through succeeding issues.

60. JH, January 5, 1852.

61. *Deseret News,* December 25, 1852; also Remy and Brenchley, I, 460.

62. JH, January 26, 1852.

63. Brigham Young sermon, April 7, 1861, *Deseret News,* May 22, 1861.

64. *Ibid.,* February 3, 1861; *Salt Lake Tribune,* August 14, 1898.

65. *Salt Lake Tribune,* August 14, 1898; *Deseret News,* October 3, 1860, April 7, 1861, April 28, 1876.

66. *Deseret News,* May 14, 1862.

67. *Deseret Weekly,* April 4, 1896, p. 485.

68. George Goddard, "Ten Months Among Paper Rags," *Deseret News,* August 20, 1862.

69. "Fourth Epistle of the Presidency . . . ," September 27, 1850, *Millennial Star,* XIII (1851), 49.

70. Addison Crane states that sugar sold at 40 cents a pound in 1852, "Journal," p. 56, MS., Huntington Library. Carvalho bought four pounds at $1.00 a pound in 1854, which "was a favor." *Incidents of Travel,* p. 247. Chandless found the price to be 40 cents a pound in 1855. *A Visit to Salt Lake City,* p. 345. Also *Deseret News,* May 30, 1855.

71. J. M. Bernhisel to Brigham Young, JH, March 27, 1850.

72. Governor's Message, December 2, 1850, *Utah Historical Quarterly,* VIII (1940), 193.

73. See "Addenda to the Fifth General Epistle . . . ," *Deseret News,* April 19, 1851; *ibid.,* November 15, 1851; Neff, *History of Utah,* pp. 294–295.

74. Phillip De LaMare, "History of the Deseret Manufacturing Company," MS., CHO.

75. Phillip De LaMare came from a family of builders and contractors. His father built the Victoria and Albert Piers on the coast of Jersey. Phillip was converted to Mormonism by Apostle Taylor and agreed to fill a six-months' mission with Taylor working on the sugar and other enterprises.

76. The dollar equivalent is given in the original records as averaging $4.84. Subscribers were Phillip De LaMare, £1,000; a Mr. Collinson, Liverpool boot manufacturer, £1,000; John W. Coward, Liverpool salt dealer, £1,000; a Capt. Russell, Scotch shipbuilder, £9,000. Apostle Taylor was awarded £2,000 worth of stock for his promotional efforts. All subscribers were converts to the Mormon faith. B. H. Roberts, *Comprehensive History,* III, 396–397.

77. According to the "Summary Exhibit of the Stock invested by Shareholders," found in Cash Book of the Deseret Manufacturing Company, 1851–53, MS., CHO. £3,420.8.0 ($16,587) of this amount was spent in England and France, £1700

($8,220.08) was taken to the United States in the form of letters of credit, and £1,525.1.1 ($7,366) was used to buy specie to take to the States.

78. JH, March 13, 1851, March 6, 1852; Roberts, III, 397. The company cash book seems to refer to the company as "Fawette & Co."

79. Taylor, *A Saga of Sugar,* p. 30; *Deseret News,* April 19, 1851; JH, June 30, 1851; Franklin D. Richards to Brigham Young, JH, February 24, 1852.

80. Cash Book of the Deseret Manufacturing Company, p. 5. JH for July 2, 1852 notes simply that "Elder John Taylor paid about $4,000 duty at New Orleans Custom House on his sugar machinery." The duty was forty per cent ad valorem. Apostle Taylor visited Washington hoping to get Congress to refund the duty, but his efforts were unavailing.

81. JH, June 27, 1852.

82. Roberts, III, 397–398; also Taylor, pp. 34–38.

83. The reminiscences of Elias Morris, a subcaptain, are given in the *Deseret Weekly* (Salt Lake City), March 26, 1898, p. 454. Captain of the train was De LaMare.

84. See statement of John Taylor, *Deseret News,* November 6, 1852.

85. The company cash book shows that at the time the shipment reached Salt Lake City in November 1852, total expenditures had been $37,335.31, while total receipts from shareholders had been only $32,173.08. By the time the books of the company were officially closed, on June 14, 1853, an additional $9,786.92 had been expended by the church on behalf of the company, raising total expenditures to $47,122.23, of which $32,173.08 was raised from private sources in Europe, $631.07 came from private sources in the United States, and the remaining $14,318.08 was advanced by the church out of tithing resources. "Summary Exhibit" (cited note 77 above). Among other things, the church paid the tariff assessed at New Orleans, paid for the second group of wagons actually used in crossing the Plains, paid for the flour and other supplies purchased by the company at Fort Bridger, and assumed the burden of hauling the equipment from Salt Lake City to Provo and return.

86. JH, December 20, 1852.

87. *Autobiography of George Washington Bean,* pp. 87–88.

88. JH, February 10, 12, 14, 1853; Taylor, p. 43.

89. Brigham Young to H. S. Eldredge, JH, February 26, 1853; Orson Hyde, *Deseret News,* March 5, 1853.

90. Sermon, April 10, 1853, *Deseret News,* July 27, 1854; also May 28, 1853.

91. Virtually the sole source for the story of the construction is the diary of church architect Truman O. Angell. Copious extracts from it are published in Taylor, pp. 45–51.

92. "Journal A. Sugar Works' Book [1853–1857]," MS., CHO.

93. JH, April 10, 1853.

94. HBY, 1855, p. 70; also JH, March 17, 1855. The molasses, several hundred gallons of it, was distributed to public works hands. George A. Smith to F. D. Richards, February 7, 1855, *Millennial Star,* XVII (1855), 270.

95. *Deseret News,* December 10, 1856.

96. The total value of all tithing resources devoted to the sugar enterprise after the church assumed control, by actual count, amounted to $49,593.87. Prior to church proprietorship, the company had expended $47,122.23. Total listed expenditures: $96,716.10, of which $59,380.79 was disbursed by the church. "Journal A. Sugar Works Book"; "Summary Exhibit."

97. Roberts, III, 399–401; De LaMare, MS., CHO; Taylor, p. 50.

98. JH, April 14, May 17, 1858, January 28, 29, 1859.

99. JH, October 14, 1849.

100. JH, February 24, 1851.

101. *Laws, Resolutions, Memorials,* 1852, pp. 205–206.

102. JH, March 13, September 22, 1851.

103. Brigham Young to Horace S. Eldredge, JH, February 26, 1853.

104. *Millennial Star,* XXIV (1862), 235; JH, February 10, 22, September 14, 1862; remarks of Brigham Young, JH, January 19, 1863. A portion of the machinery was hauled to Utah in 1859. Brigham Young to Horace S. Eldredge, March 4, 18, May 5, 1859, typescripts, UHS.

105. JH, June 1, 1864. The factory was clearly church property, and was undoubtedly listed in Young's name because of the prohibitions against church ownership in the Anti-Bigamy Act of 1862.

106. Neff, *History of Utah,* pp. 273–275, 284–292.

107. Malicent C. Wells, "History of John Murray Murdoch," typescript in possession of Mrs. Cleone Baird Arrington, Twin Falls, Idaho.

108. According to the record book of the company in possession of William R. Palmer, Cedar City, Utah.

109. *Deseret News,* December 13, 19, 1851.

110. "Sixth General Epistle . . . ," September 22, 1851, *Millennial Star,* XIV (1852), 20. Also JH, June 30, 1851, February 24, 1852.

111. A synopsis of the conference is in JH, April 6, 1852.

112. A report on their activities is found under the title "Manufacture of Iron in Utah," *Millennial Star,* XVII (1855), 2.

113. "Minute Book of the Deseret Iron Company," MS., in the possession of William R. Palmer, Cedar City, Utah. Extracts from the minutes are found in John G. Crook, "The Development of Early Industry and Trade in Utah," pp. 39ff.

114. *Millennial Star,* XVII (1855), 2.

115. The records of the Pioneer Iron Company state: "On the 29th of November [1852] a meeting was held in the schoolhouse by the brethren of the Iron Company, when it was resolved that the company sell out to Snow and Richards. Also resolved that the company agree to take whatever Snow and Richards say they will give, and that it be left entirely with them." At a meeting held that evening Snow and Richards offered the company $2,865.64, which was unanimously accepted, and the next day, November 30, 1852, a bill of sale was drawn up and executed, and the property duly passed to the Deseret Iron Company.

116. *Deseret News,* December 25, 1852.

117. Henry Lunt, *Deseret News,* December 25, 1852, February 26, 1853.

118. Copies of the acts approved December 27, 1852, and January 5, 17, 1853, are in *Deseret News,* January 22, 1853, and *Acts, Resolutions and Memorials* (Great Salt Lake City, 1855), pp. 235–237.

119. *Millennial Star,* XVII (1855), 5; *Deseret News,* December 25, 1852, April 2, 1853.

120. *Ibid.,* February 26, 1853. A portion of the daily journal of the company indicates that sixty-eight men worked 2,106 days for the company from January 1 to April 1, 1853. Crook, pp. 50–51.

121. William R. Palmer, "Pioneer Fortifications," *Improvement Era,* LIV (1951), 149ff.; JH, October 6, 1853; Carvalho, *Incidents of Travel,* p. 276.

122. *Millennial Star,* XVII (1855), 3.

123. A curious financial statement is found in *Millennial Star,* XVII (1855), 3.

124. "Journal of Isaac C. Haight," Part II, typescript, Library of Congress (Utah,

W.P.A. Collection), p. 13. Under date of October 8, 1853, Haight wrote: "I had much rather have stayed here [Salt Lake City], but am willing to obey the counsel of my Brethren."

125. Matthias F. Cowley, ed., *Wilford Woodruff, . . . : History of His Life and Labors as Recorded in His Daily Journals* (Salt Lake City, 1909), p. 346.

126. Isaac C. Haight to Franklin D. Richards, September 24, 1854, *Millennial Star,* XVII (1855), 5–6; *Deseret News,* January 4, 1855.

127. See Brigham Young, Governor's Message, *Deseret News,* December 14, 1854.

128. *Acts, Resolutions and Memorials* (Great Salt Lake City, 1855), pp. 399–400.

129. The shares of Utah Territory were purchased by a transferal to the Perpetual Emigrating Fund Company in Salt Lake which, in turn, issued a warrant in favor of the iron company. The church paid for its two shares by transferring to the iron company accounts from the local tithing offices, as follows: from the Cedar City Tithing Office, $2897.20; from Harmony Tithing Office, $105.57; from Parowan Tithing Office, $1837.25. The company then drew a general assortment of goods from these offices. "Records of the Deseret Iron Company," Crook, pp. 49, 58.

130. *Deseret News,* May 2, 1855; "Journal of Isaac C. Haight," p. 16; *Millennial Star,* XVIII (1856), 60.

131. *Deseret News,* May 27, 1855; Address of Brigham Young, May 27, 1855, JD, II, 281–283.

132. *Millennial Star,* XVIII (1856), 14, 251.

133. *Deseret News,* March 5, December 10, 1856; *Heart Throbs of the West,* II, 216; "Journal of Isaac C. Haight," p. 21.

134. Robert S. Lewis and Thomas Varley, *The Mineral Industry of Utah,* Bulletin No. 12, Utah Engineering Experiment Station (Salt Lake City), p. 67.

135. Sermon of May 27, 1855, JD, II, 282.

136. Christopher J. Arthur, clerk of the company store, who had just been married, wrote in his journal: "1856 — have been a hard year — grasshoppers — scarcity of breadstuff — Weeds and bran bread. It has been kisses without the bread and cheese, but we had happiness & contentment." "Autobiography, Part II," typescript, Library of Congress (W.P.A. Collection), p. 16, also "C. J. Arthur's Diary," p. 111, film from the original in the Mormon File, Huntington Library.

137. "Journal of Isaac C. Haight," p. 21, entry for September 1857.

138. *Ibid.,* p. 25.

139. JH, October 7, 1858.

140. Heber C. Kimball to William H. Kimball, February 29, 1856, *Millennial Star,* XVIII (1856), 397; Jenson, "History of Las Vegas Mission," p. 270.

141. Jenson, p. 270.

142. Jenson, p. 271. In anticipation of immediate results from the mission, the church public works cast five lead molds. JH, July 3, 1856. Soon afterward, a number of teams were requested to go to Vegas to pick up lead and lead ore.

143. Jenson, p. 232.

144. Horne, *Autobiography of George Washington Bean,* pp. 125, 273.

145. Jenson, pp. 265–266. Wilford Woodruff gives only 1,000 or 1,200 pounds (letter to George A. Smith, JH, April 1, 1857). On February 12, 1857, the General Tithing Office in Salt Lake City received 1,562 pounds of lead, presumably that produced at Las Vegas. See JH, February 12, 1857. In addition, some of the lead may have been left with some of the southern settlements. Certainly none of it went into commercial channels.

146. Jenson, p. 275; Horne, p. 120. Apparently, no attention was given to property rights — not an unusual thing in a Mormon mission enterprise.

147. *Deseret News,* April 3, 1861.

148. Sermon of May 27, 1855, JD, II, 282.

149. "Again, all that has been said, and all the praying that has been done, and all the faith that has been exercised, and all the combination and union of effort among the Saints have not brought to pass one say of the President's in regard to iron; he said, let there be iron, but there is no iron yet. Br. Wells has told you the reason, this morning. A man says, 'I am going to make iron, and I will have the credit of making the first iron in the Territory. I will have the credit of knowing how to flux the ore that is found in these regions, and bringing out the metal in abundance, or no other man shall.'" Sermon of March 16, 1862, *Deseret News,* May 28, 1862. Wells' sermon is in *Deseret News,* June 4, 1862. Similar remarks were made by Young on April 7, 1861, recorded in *Deseret News,* May 22, 1861.

150. Oscar and Mary Flug Handlin, *Commonwealth — A Study of the Role of Government in the American Economy: Massachusetts, 1774–1861* (New York, 1947), p. 53.

151. Brigham Young sermons, December 5, 1853, October 6, 1863, JD, I, 341, X, 210, 270.

CHAPTER V: WAYS AND MEANS

Mormon newspapers and magazines which contain many informative reports on activities in the Great Basin in the 1850's, particularly with respect to matters discussed in this chapter, include: *The Mormon* (New York, 1855–1857), *Saint Louis Luminary* (St. Louis, 1854–1855), *The Seer* (Washington, D. C., 1853–1854), and *The Western Standard* (San Francisco, 1856–1857).

Records of the General Tithing Office and of the trustee-in-trust, which provide a detailed understanding of the functioning of Mormon financial practices and improvisations, are in CHO but are not generally available. A detailed treatment of the system of tithing, based largely on the records of the Cache Valley Tithing Office, is given in Leonard J. Arrington, "The Mormon Tithing House: A Frontier Business Institution," *Business History Review,* XXVIII (1954), 24–58. The function of Brigham Young as trustee-in-trust is discussed in Leonard J. Arrington, "The Settlement of the Brigham Young Estate, 1877–1879," *Pacific Historical Review,* XXI (1952), 1–20.

The consecration movement of the 1850's is described in Feramorz Y. Fox, "The Consecration Movement of the Middle Fifties," *Improvement Era,* XLVII (1944), 80ff., 146ff. A. L. Neff, *History of Utah* (Salt Lake City, 1940), also has a good treatment. An excellent contemporary discussion is found in Orson Pratt, "The Equality and Oneness of Saints," *The Seer* (2 vols.; Washington, D. C., 1853–1854), II.

Any study of the handcart companies must begin with the moving, and at times pathetic, accounts left by participants. The following have been published: "Journal of Archer Walters," *Improvement Era,* XXXIX (1936), 612, 635, 764; XL (1937), 43, 112, 154, 253; Mary Ann Hafen, *Recollections of a Handcart Pioneer of 1860* (Denver, 1938); The Narrative of John Chislett, in T. B. H. Stenhouse, *The Rocky Mountain Saints* (New York, 1873), pp. 312–338; and "Brief Record of the First Handcart Company," *Utah Genealogical and Historical Magazine,* XVII (1926), 247; XVIII (1927), 17, 49. The best systematic treatment is a book manuscript by LeRoy and Ann Hafen scheduled for early publication. Shorter treatments by Dr. Hafen include, "Handcarts to Utah, 1856–1860," *Utah Historical Quarterly,* XXIV (1956), 309–317; and

"Hand Cart Migration Across the Plains," in James F. Willard and Colin B. Goodykoontz, eds., *The Trans-Mississippi West . . .* (Boulder, Colo., 1930), pp. 103–121. Other studies include: Jay Monaghan, "Handcarts on the Overland Trail," *Nebraska History,* XXX (1949), 3–18; Edgar R. Harlan, ed., "First Mormon Handcart Trip Across Iowa," *Annals of Iowa,* 3d series, XX (1936), 444–449; and Ruth A. Gallaher, "The Handcart Expeditions," *Palimpsest,* III (1922), 214–226. Gustive Larson's *Prelude to the Kingdom* (Francestown, N. H., 1947) also has done much with the handcart episode, as has Wallace Stegner in "Ordeal by Handcart," *Colliers,* CXXXVIII (July 6, 1956), 78–85.

1. The Church of Jesus Christ of Latter-day Saints was first incorporated by the Provisional State of Deseret on February 8, 1851. When the territorial government was organized later that year, the newly elected assembly brought over and approved this act on October 4, 1851. In a subsequent revision the charter grant was confirmed on January 19, 1855. A copy of the act of incorporation is reproduced in [Dale Morgan], "The State of Deseret," *Utah Historical Quarterly,* VIII (1940), 223–225.

2. During the period 1873–75 the trustee-in-trust was George A. Smith, counselor to Brigham Young in the First Presidency. In 1887 the position of trustee-in-trust was eliminated by action of Congress and the responsibilities of the position for the next ten years were lodged by action of the general conference in the three members of the Presiding Bishopric.

3. Under the Anti-Bigamy Act of 1862 the church was prohibited from owning more than $50,000 worth of property (houses of worship, parsonages, and burial grounds excepted). In order to prevent the complete breakdown of the church's economic program, the trustee-in-trust simply transferred much of the church's business property to private individuals (particularly Brigham Young) to hold in trust for the church. See Arrington, "The Settlement of the Brigham Young Estate."

4. Parley P. Pratt, sermon, October 7, 1849, *Millennial Star,* XII (1850), 134; Brigham Young, sermon, JH, September 8, 1850; *Deseret News,* November 29, 1851.

5. *Millennial Star,* XIV (1852), 25; Diary of Joseph Holbrook, Book II, p. 72, typescript in possession of the writer.

6. Sermon of June 7, 1857, in Carter, ed., *Heart Throbs of the West* (12 vols.; Salt Lake City, 1936–1951), VII, 278–279. On another occasion, he said that those who were not willing to labor on the public works, "for the pay we get as Tithing, are at liberty to leave when you please, and never strike another blow. We want 200 workmen, who will work there, for such pay as we get, and who will not push my soul out of me for Money, *Money,* MONEY, M O N E Y !!!!" Sermon of October 7, 1852, *Deseret News,* October 16, 1852.

7. According to his own statement, sermon of June 7, 1863, JD, X, 205.

8. Daniel H. Wells, April 6, 1863, JD, X, 140.

9. Editorial in the *Deseret News,* January 10, 1852.

10. JH, February 12, 1857.

11. Brigham Young to Horace S. Eldredge, June 30, 1857, typescript, UHS.

12. *Deseret News,* April 17, 1852; Brigham Young sermons of April 9, 1852, May 8, 1853, JD, I, 52–53, 110; C. Langdon White, "The Agricultural Geography of the Salt Lake Oasis," *Denison University Bulletin,* Vol. XXV, No. 6 (1925), pp. 240–241.

13. "Journal Extracts of Henry W. Bigler," *Utah Historical Quarterly,* V (1932), 141, entry for May 14, 1857. These cattle were collected primarily to satisfy the church debt in connection with supplying the Brigham Young Express & Carrying Company, as explained in the following chapter.

14. *Deseret News,* January 10, 1852.

15. *The China Mail,* March 18, 1852, citation furnished by S. George Ellsworth.

16. *Deseret News,* August 7, 1852.

17. *Ibid.*, August 9, 1854.

18. Heber C. Kimball, address of June 7, 1857, JD, IV, 337.

19. Sermon of October 8, 1860, JD, VIII, 201.

20. JH, September 13, 1860; also sermon of April 9, 1852, JD, I, 51–52.

21. The evidence points two ways. The general conference vote to assess a ten per cent levy on all property stipulated that all who would not thus tithe themselves be cut off from the church. (*Millennial Star,* XIV [1852], 25; Diary of Hosea Stout, September 9, 1851, BYU.) This was apparently used as a threat, but not carried out in practice. In 1853, however, five persons who "openly and with deadly Weapons" resisted officers of the Nauvoo Legion who were seeking to carry into effect an order of Brigham Young with respect to requisitioning "surplus stock" to drive to Salt Lake City were charged by a military court of inquiry with "mutinous conduct." ("Records of the Southern Military Department, Nauvoo Legion, 1853," MS., UHS.) During a period of scarcity in 1863, the First Presidency of the Church distributed a circular to the bishops urging them to gather grain tithing and forward it immediately to the Salt Lake tithing office "so that we can feed those depending upon us for bread." And they added, "If any one refused to pay his proper Tithing in its kind, it should, we think, be made a matter of fellowship." (JH, October 26, 1863.)

The weight of the evidence, however, suggests that, while some bishops exercised more zeal in this matter than others, it was not common for tithing delinquents to be disfellowshipped or excommunicated. John D. Lee wrote, when such an order was issued in southern Utah by Erastus Snow, "To carry out the Letter & spirit of the Epistle would cause ¾ of this community to be cut off from this church. He certainly is ahead of the Times." (Cleland and Brooks, eds., *A Mormon Chronicle* . . . [San Marino, 1955], II, 96.) For evidence that Brigham Young did not consider it appropriate to excommunicate a person for not paying tithing, see JD, XII, 36; VIII, 202; XIV, 89; *Millennial Star,* XXVII (1865), 415, 781–782; Franklin D. Richards, "Narrative," pp. 60–61, MS., Bancroft Library.

22. Arrington, "The Mormon Tithing House," p. 29; Sermon of Bishop L. W. Hardy, April 7, 1880, in *The Year of Jubilee: Fiftieth Annual Conference of the Church* . . . (Salt Lake City, 1880), p. 65.

23. Compiled from Cache Valley Ward Tithing Ledger, 1860–86 and Cache Valley Stake Tithing Ledger, 1887–1900, MSS., Cache Stakehouse Vault, Logan, Utah.

24. *Ira Allen: Founder of Hyrum,* compiled by his grandson, Alvin Allen [Logan, Utah, *ca.* 1941], p. 33.

25. William Clayton Letterpress Copybook (1869–85), p. 161, MS., UHS. This was a notarized statement signed by William Clayton, Auditor of Public Accounts for Utah Territory, and also Church Auditor. The amounts in parenthesis are given to the nearest unit.

26. *Millennial Star,* XIV (1852), 323–324.

27. *Ibid.,* XIV (1852), 18, 321; *Deseret News,* January 16, 1856, and many other places.

28. Sermon of April 9, 1852, JD, I, 52.

29. Sermon of June 3, 1855, JD, II, 306–307.

30. Sermon of October 6, 1860, JD, VIII, 317.

31. F. H. Ludlow, *The Heart of the Continent* (London, 1870), pp. 540–541.

32. Brigham Young and Heber C. Kimball to the Presidency of Parowan, JH, October 28, 1851.

33. Brigham Young to Isaac Morley, JH, December 23, 1850.

34. Sermon of September 16, 1860, JD, VIII, 170. One prominent visitor to Utah in 1853 asked Apostle John Taylor why no public account was made of the use of tithing, as would be normal in a democratic society. Taylor is said to have replied that "in the end it would be better for the more intelligent and educated men to take care of the people's affairs than to have them fight and quarrel about everything." James Schiel, "Journey through the Rocky Mountains . . . ," Maria Williams, transl., in Nolie Mumey, *John Williams Gunnison (1812–1853)* . . . (Denver, 1955), p. 96.

35. Sermon of June 27, 1873, JD, XVI, 111.

36. *Deseret News,* February 21, 1852; records of Utah Territory, MSS., UHS; records of Salt Lake City and County, MSS., City and County Building, Salt Lake City.

37. Compiled from the account of Thomas Edwin Ricks in "Logan General Tithing Office Book B, 1864–65" MS., Cache Stakehouse Vault.

38. A. N. Sorensen, *Biography of Hezekiah Eastman Hatch* (Logan, Utah, 1952), p. 42.

39. "Diary of John Clark Dowdle, 1836–1894," typescript, BYU, entries for 1864, pp. 11–12.

40. From a note in "Account Book of Erastus Bingham," microfilm, BYU.

41. As told in *Reminiscences of Alexander Toponce* (Ogden, 1923), pp. 186 187.

42. John Codman, *The Round Trip* (New York, 1879), p. 174.

43. For example, sermon of February 14, 1853, JD, I, 279.

44. A systematic study of Utah territorial finance is sorely needed. A comparison of federal contributions to Utah with those contributed to neighboring territories would prove particularly illuminating. From a study of Mormon sources one gets the distinct impression that the federal government failed to carry its share of administrative expenses. This is said to have been due to the fear that the Mormons would divert federal grants toward their own purposes.

45. Brigham Young to Amasa Lyman and Charles C. Rich, JH, October 17, 1852.

46. Sermon of April 9, 1852, JD, I, 52.

47. *Millennial Star,* XVI (1854), 427–428; Diary of Hosea Stout, April 7–8, 1854.

48. Eleventh General Epistle of the Presidency, April 10, 1854, *Deseret News,* April 13, 1854.

49. Twelfth General Epistle of the Presidency, *Deseret News,* April 25, 1855.

50. Several dozen completed forms are in CHO.

51. Fox in "The Consecration Movement of the Middle Fifties," p. 120.

52. Young's deed, dated April 11, 1855, is recorded in Book A, p. 249, Pioneer Records, MS., Salt Lake County Recorder's Office. It was published in full in Fox, pp. 83, 124.

53. John Zimmerman Brown, ed., *Autobiography of Pioneer John Brown, 1820–1896* (Salt Lake City, 1941), p. 144.

54. Fox, pp. 146–147.

55. See S. N. Carvalho, *Incidents of Travel and Adventure in the Far West* (New York, 1857), pp. 208–209; John Hyde, *Mormonism: Its Leaders and Designs* (New York, 1857), pp. 37–38; and William Chandless, *A Visit to Salt Lake* . . . (London, 1857), pp. 274–276.

56. *Messages and Documents, 1856–1857,* Part I, serial 893, cited in Neff, *History of Utah,* p. 540.

57. See the year-by-year commentary in Jules Remy and Julius Brenchley, *A Journey to Great-Salt-Lake City* (2 vols.; London, 1861), I, 455–464.

58. Neff, *History of Utah,* p. 180; W. Turrentine Jackson, *Wagon Roads West: A Study of Federal Road Surveys and Construction in the Trans-Mississippi West, 1846–1869* (Berkeley, California, 1952), pp. 140–146.

59. *Ibid.,* p. 146.

60. Carvalho, pp. 221–222, 247.

61. Autobiography of Samuel Roskelley as published in Emma R. Hansen, ed., *The Roskelley Organ* (Smithfield, Utah), June 1, 1951, p. 14.

62. The 1856 population of Utah was estimated at 38,000. *Hunt's Merchant's Magazine and Commercial Review,* XLI (1859), 259. The 1860 census listed 39,229 persons in Utah.

63. William Jennings, "Material Progress of Utah," 1884, MS., Bancroft Library, p. 6.

64. Ralph H. Brown, *Historical Geography of the United States* (New York, 1948), pp. 384–386; "The Rocky Mountain Locust, or Grasshopper of the West," *Report of the Commissioner of Agriculture, 1877* (Washington, 1878).

65. Jennings, pp. 4–7.

66. George A. Smith, in HBY, 1855, pp. 78–81.

67. Diary of Joseph Holbrook, Vol. I, 74.

68. HBY, 1855, pp. 78–80.

69. Richard F. Burton, *The City of the Saints* (New York, 1862), p. 557, estimated a one-third reduction. The church historian, in HBY, 1855, pp. 78–81, leaves the very definite impression that nearly all was destroyed.

70. Diary of Joseph Holbrook, I, 73–74.

71. Heber C. Kimball to William Kimball, February 29, 1856, *Millennial Star,* XVIII (1856), 395.

72. HBY, 1855, p. 81; Brigham Young to Franklin D. Richards, July 30, 1855, *Millennial Star,* XVII (1855), 666.

73. Approved December 18, 1855. *Resolutions, Acts and Memorials* (Great Salt Lake City, 1855), p. 22; Albert Carrington to Elias Smith, December 23, 1855, *Deseret News,* January 2, 1856.

74. Joel E. Ricks, ed., *The History of a Valley: Cache Valley, Utah-Idaho* (Logan, 1956), p. 29; JH, August 31, 1855.

75. Ricks, p. 30.

76. Wilford Woodruff to John Taylor, JH, May 29, 1856; Burton, p. 557, more conservatively estimated that half the stock in the territory had perished during the winter of 1855–56.

77. *Millennial Star,* XVIII (1856), 396–397, 476.

78. Chandless, *A Visit to Salt Lake,* p. 143.

79. Diary of Joseph Holbrook, I, 75.

80. *Millennial Star,* XVIII (1856), 395.

81. Heber C. Kimball to William Kimball, April 13, 1856, *Millennial Star,* XVIII (1856), 476.

82. Autobiography of Samuel Roskelley, *The Roskelley Organ,* p. 16.

83. Remy and Brenchley, I, 216; Chandless, *A Visit to Salt Lake,* p. 345; *Deseret News,* May 30, 1855.

84. Bearing out the scarcity are the Autobiography of Samuel Roskelley, p. 16; James S. Brown, *Life of a Pioneer* (Salt Lake City, 1900), p. 372; Dale Morgan, ed., "Reminiscences of James Holt," *Utah Historical Quarterly,* XXIII (1955), 170.

85. The circular is published in *Deseret News,* February 13, 1856.

86. *Deseret News,* July 9, 1856; JH, June 25, 1856.

87. John E. Booth, "History of the Provo Fourth Ward," p. 52, typescript, BYU.

88. The number of plural marriages in relation to population was sixty-five per cent higher in 1856–1857 than in any other two-year period in Utah history. Stanley S. Ivins, "Notes on Mormon Polygamy," *Western Humanities Review,* X (1956), 231. Most writers, including Ivins, attribute the burst of plural marriages to the Mormon religious "Reformation" of 1856. The present writer believes that there is a good case for the hypothesis that the Reformation itself was an outgrowth of the famine of 1855–1856. See also Gustive O. Larson, "The Mormon Reformation," *Utah Historical Quarterly,* XXVI (1958), 45–63.

89. JH, February 29, May 6, 8, 1856; *Millennial Star,* XVIII (1856), 396.

90. George A. Smith, *The Rise, Progress and Travels of the Church . . .* (Salt Lake City, 1869), p. 17.

91. Sermon of October 8, 1855, JD, III, 122.

92. Heber C. Kimball to William Kimball, February 29, 1856, *Millennial Star,* XVIII (1856), 395–396.

93. JH, June 8, 1856.

94. Wilford Woodruff to John Taylor, JH, August 30, 1856.

95. JH, March 4, 1860.

96. JH, June 8, 1856.

97. Heber C. Kimball to William Kimball, p. 397.

98. Circular of the First Presidency, *Deseret News,* February 13, 1856; *Millennial Star,* XVIII (1856), 477.

99. George W. Brimhall, *The Workers of Utah* (Provo, Utah, 1889), p. 33; Chandless, *A Visit to Salt Lake,* p. 141; Smith, p. 17. Several contemporary sources indicate no deaths from starvation.

100. "Circular" of the P.E. Company (Salt Lake City, 1856), microfilm, BYU.

101. Brigham Young to Franklin D. Richards, July 30, 1855, *Millennial Star,* XVII (1855), 666.

102. Thirteenth General Epistle, October 29, 1855, *Millennial Star,* XVIII (1856), 51–52.

103. Brigham Young to Franklin D. Richards, September 30, 1855, *Millennial Star,* XVII (1855), 813.

104. Dated October 29, 1855, and published in *Millennial Star,* XVIII (1856), 52, 54.

105. *Millennial Star,* p. 122.

106. A cut of a handcart is found in T. B. H. Stenhouse, *Rocky Mountain Saints* (New York, 1873), p. 315.

107. Hafen, "Handcarts to Utah, 1856–1860," p. 311.

108. Wilford Woodruff to Orson Pratt, September 30, 1856, *Millennial Star,* XVIII (1856), 794–795.

109. Stenhouse, *Rocky Mountain Saints,* pp. 339–342; Brigham Young sermon, November 2, 1856, *Deseret News,* November 12, 1856.

110. A list is given in JH, October 7, 1856. See also sermons and instructions published in *Deseret News,* October 15, 1856.

111. Hafen, p. 314; also Bancroft, *History of Utah,* pp. 423–430.

112. Sermon of November 30, 1856, *Deseret News,* December 10, 1856.

113. See Caroline Addy, "James Godson Bleak, Pioneer Historian of Southern

Utah" (unpublished Master's Thesis, Brigham Young University, 1953), p. 9. Bleak was with the ill-fated Martin company.

114. See his sermon of November 16, 1856, *Deseret News,* November 26, 1856.

115. Brigham Young to Franklin D. Richards, April 11, 1856, *Millennial Star,* XVIII (1856), 466.

116. Brigham Young to Orson Pratt, JH, August 30, 1856; also JH, January 31, 1857.

117. Larson, *Prelude to the Kingdom,* pp. 215, 235–236; Hafen, p. 316.

CHAPTER VI: MOBILIZATION, 1856–1858

The most complete treatment of Utah history during the years 1856–1858 is B. H. Roberts, *A Comprehensive History of the Church . . .* (6 vols.; Salt Lake City, 1930), IV, 181–471. Based primarily on the documentation in the "History of Brigham Young," the narrative and analysis is replete with citations and annotations from other sources. With some exceptions, the approach is detached and scholarly. A documentary account is LeRoy R. Hafen and Ann W. Hafen, *The Utah Expedition, 1857–1858* (Glendale, Calif., 1958). Two excellent monographs on the period are Leland Hargrave Creer, *Utah and the Nation* (Seattle, 1929); and Richard D. Poll, "The Mormon Question, 1850–1865: A Study in Politics and Public Opinion" (unpublished Ph. D. dissertation, University of California, 1948). The latter presents the Mormon question in relation to the national political scene. The events of the period, as reflected in the pages of the *Deseret News,* are also treated in A. R. Mortensen, "The *Deseret News* and Utah, 1850–1867" (unpublished Ph. D. dissertation, University of California, Los Angeles, 1950). Two chapters from this work have been published in the *Utah Historical Quarterly* as: "A Pioneer Paper Mirrors the Breakup of Isolation in the Great Basin," XX (1952), 77–92; and "A Local Paper Reports on the Utah War," XXV (1957), 297–318.

A contemporary running commentary on the Mormon War and on Utah affairs in general is found, among other places, in successive issues of *Harper's Weekly* (New York, I–II (1857–1858); and *Daily National Intelligencer* (Washington, D. C.), 1857–58. The best Mormon commentary, which includes many documents not elsewhere available, is in successive issues of the *Millennial Star,* XX (1858). The crosscurrents of emotion are also captured in Juanita Brooks, *The Mountain Meadows Massacre* (Stanford, 1950). In the present work heavy reliance is placed on the little-used extracts from the History of Brigham Young in the Bancroft Library.

Although the activities of the Brigham Young Express and Carrying Company have never been the subject of an essay, the background is discussed in LeRoy R. Hafen, *The Overland Mail, 1849–1869: Promoter of Settlement; Precursor of Railroads* (Cleveland, 1926); and Curtis Nettels, "The Overland Mail Issue During the Fifties," *Missouri Historical Review,* XVIII (1924), 521–534. Good personal accounts are in Daniel W. Jones, *Forty Years Among the Indians . . .* (Salt Lake City, 1890); and Joseph M. Tanner, *A Biographical Sketch of John Riggs Murdock* (Salt Lake City, 1909).

The best available monograph on the Utah War is Everett L. Cooley, "The Utah War" (unpublished Master's Thesis, University of Utah, 1947). M. Hamlin Cannon's study, "The Mormon War: A Study in Territorial Rebellion" (unpublished Master's Thesis, George Washington University, 1938), is brief and relies almost entirely on federal sources. The most disappointing attempt is E. Cecil McGavin, *U. S. Soldiers Invade Utah* (Boston, 1937), which uses much primary material but lacks documentation, perspective, and depth. A fast-moving brief account is Paul Bailey, "Holy Smoke:

A Dissertation on the Utah War," in *The Westerners Brand Book* (Los Angeles, 1948), pp. 101–120.

The Utah Expedition has been the subject of a number of monographs, the earliest being [Albert G. Browne, Jr.], "The Utah Expedition," *Atlantic Monthly,* III (1859), 361–375, 474–495, 570–584, which was written by a correspondent with Johnston's Army. These articles also contain useful descriptions of contemporary Mormon social and economic institutions. A military account is W. R. Hamilton, "History of the Mormon Rebellion of 1856–57," *The United Service* (Philadelphia), new series, IV and V (1890–1891), serialized. The lieutenant, who pours out his vitriol on Mormons and scheming politicians alike, relies heavily on William Prescott Johnston's *The Life of Gen. Albert Sidney Johnston . . .* (New York, 1878), who in turn relies heavily on T. B. H. Stenhouse, *Rocky Mountain Saints* (New York, 1873). A later study is Nils Henderson Lago, "The Utah Expedition, 1857–1858" (unpublished Master's Thesis, University of Oklahoma, 1939). The supply operations of Russell, Majors and Waddell are described in Raymond W. Settle and Mary Lund Settle, *Empire on Wheels* (Stanford, 1949), esp. pp. 17–32.

Contemporary personal accounts include Jesse A. Gove, *The Utah Expedition, 1857–1858,* Otis G. Hammond, ed. (Cleveland, 1928); "The Utah War: Journal of Albert Tracy, 1858–1860," *Utah Historical Quarterly,* XIII (1945), 1–128; Cornelius Conway, *The Utah Expedition . . .* (Cincinnati, 1858), which is an account by "a Wagonmaster of the Expedition"; "The Echo Canyon War," *The Contributor,* III and IV (1881–1883), serialized, which gives Mormon accounts; and Hamilton Gardner, ed., "A Territorial Militiaman in the Utah War: Journal of Newton Tuttle," *Utah Historical Quarterly,* XXII (1954), 297–320. The activities of one division of the Nauvoo Legion are recorded in "Record of Orders, Returns and Courts Martial &c of 2nd Brigade, 1st Division, Nauvoo Legion, Headquarters 14th Ward, Great Salt Lake City [1857–1868]," typescript, BYU. One phase of the call back to Zion in 1857 is told in Dale Morgan, *The Humboldt, Highroad of the West* (New York, 1943), pp. 234–247. Much of the political history of the times can be reconstructed from letter books in the Utah Territorial Papers, National Archives.

Much interesting social history in connection with the Move South is published in Kate B. Carter, ed., *Heart Throbs of the West* (12 vols.; Salt Lake City, 1936–1951), X, 233–268. The financial aspects, particularly those associated with the Deseret Currency Association, are described in Leonard J. Arrington, "Mormon Finance and the Utah War," *Utah Historical Quarterly,* XX (1952), 219–237.

1. Brigham Young sermons of April 6, July 5, 1857, *Deseret News,* April 15, July 15, 1857; "The Express and Carrying Company," *ibid.,* April 1, 1857; Brigham Young to Orson Pratt, March 1, 1857, *Millennial Star,* XIX (1857), 363

2. *Ibid.,* p. 410.

3. Henry Lunt to Albert Carrington, October 7, 1856, *Deseret News,* April 8, 1857.

4. Hafen, *The Overland Mail,* pp. 60–61; Neff, *History of Utah,* pp. 325–326.

5. The proposal is outlined in a lengthy letter from Brigham Young "To Those Who Are Engaged in Freighting on the Western Waters," *Deseret News,* November 21, 1855.

6. William Chandless, *A Visit to Salt Lake . . .* (London, 1857), p. 277.

7. "Acts, Resolutions and Memorials . . . 1852–1861," pp. 177–178, MS., UHS. The following prominent Mormon merchants, freighters, and explorers were listed as incorporators: Jesse C. Little, Leonard W. Hardy, Orrin Porter Rockwell, Franklin

Neff, Almon W. Babbitt, William H. Hooper, Thomas S. Williams, Joseph L. Heywood, Albert P. Rockwood, Orson Hyde, Enoch Reese, Judson Stoddard, George D. Grant, William H. Kimball, John S. Fullmer, Parley P. Pratt, and William A. Hickman.

8. *Deseret News,* February 6, 1856; JH, February 14, 1856.

9. The Postmaster General's advertisement for bids, dated May 31, 1856, appeared in the *Deseret News* for August 6, 1856. Brigham Young wrote that "the best course to secure the contract" was to do so in Kimball's name. Brigham Young to H. S. Eldredge, correspondence, April 1, 1857, typescript, UHS.

10. *House Exec. Doc, No. 96,* 35th Cong., 1st sess., p. 353.

11. Brigham Young to Feramorz Little, February 5, 1857, cited in Neff, *History of Utah,* p. 329; also Brigham Young to Orson Pratt, March 1, 1857, *Millennial Star,* XIX (1857), 362–363. The contract was not received in Salt Lake City until March 24, 1857. On the books of the company, Kimball was given $1,000 credit as "compensation for contract." "Express and Carrying Co.'s Ledger," MS., CHO.

12. *Deseret News,* May 20, June 3, 1857.

13. "Journal of John Pulsipher," *Utah Humanities Review,* II (1948), 376; Brigham Young to Feramorz Little, February 5, 1857, cited in Neff, *History of Utah,* p. 329.

14. Brigham Young to Orson Pratt, March 1, 1857, *Millennial Star,* XIX (1857), 362–363.

15. *Ibid.,* p. 363.

16. Brigham Young to H. S. Eldredge, February 25, 1857.

17. *Deseret News,* April 1, 1857.

18. Brigham Young to Feramorz Little, February 5, 1857, cited in Neff, *History of Utah,* p. 329; Brigham Young to Lewis Robison, February 6, 1857, *ibid.;* Brigham Young to H. S. Eldredge, April 1, 1857.

19. *Deseret News,* April 1, 1857. Hooper and Stewart were repaid by the church in 1858 with Deseret scrip which was later redeemed with horses.

20. The company's ledger contains 454 separate accounts, of which a few are duplications. "Express and Carrying Co.'s Ledger."

21. JH, June 11, 1857; Brigham Young sermons, June 7, 14, 1857, *Deseret News,* June 17, 24, 1857; also JH, June 16, 1857; *Millennial Star,* XIX (1857), 557.

22. *Deseret News,* April 1, 1857.

23. "Ira Nathaniel Hinckley: Some Events of His Life," p. 5, mimeographed, Huntington Library.

24. "I put in one yoke of oxen a saddle and bridle and some hundred weight of flour with meat, etc." Diary of Joseph Holbrook, I, 81, typescript, possession of the writer.

25. Brigham Young sermon, April 6, 1857, *Deseret News,* April 15, 1857; *Millennial Star,* XIX (1857), 525. Most of the sermons in the general conference sessions of April 6 and 7, 1857 were devoted to explaining the Y. X. enterprise, and urging participation in it and contributions to it upon the basis of religious sentiment. A list of some of the men called on special missions to assist the company in locating stations and establishing settlements is found in JH, April 21, 1857. See also JH, July 24, 1857.

26. Brigham Young to Orson Pratt and Ezra T. Benson, June 30, 1857, *Millennial Star,* XIX (1857), 556.

27. *Deseret News,* April 29, 1857.

28. Henry J. Hudson to John Taylor, July 1, 1857, *Millennial Star,* XIX (1857), 607.

29. JH, July 24, 1857; John Taylor to W. I. Appleby, *The Mormon* (New York City), August 29, 1857.

30. JH, July 24, 1857.

31. Brigham Young to George Q. Cannon, July 4, 1857, cited in Neff, *History of Utah,* p. 331.

32. Brigham Young to H. S. Eldredge, May 29, 1857.

33. Brigham Young called the cancellation "arbitrary, unjust and illegal . . . a great national loss, in a financial point of view, and a great legal and moral outrage." Brigham Young to Thomas L. Kane, October 22, 1858, *Utah Humanities Review,* II (1948), 57–58.

34. Smoot's recollections of these events are published in E. W. Tullidge, *History of Salt Lake City* (Salt Lake City, c. 1886), pp. 156–157.

35. Mormon and Utah historians have left the impression that Brigham Young was completely surprised about the Utah Expedition. However, in a sermon delivered the preceding June 7, he revealed that "some poor, miserable people" had been telling him that the Mormon people would soon be forced to leave their Great Basin retreat. *Deseret News,* June 17, 1857.

36. JH, July 24, August 12, 1857; also sermons of Brigham Young and others in the general conference of July 26, 1857, *Deseret News,* August 5, 1857.

37. *Deseret News,* September 23, 1857.

38. *Deseret News,* December 9, 1859; Brigham Young to Thomas L. Kane, October 22, 1858, *Utah Humanities Review,* II (1948), 57. In speaking to the Utah legislature, Young said the enterprise had involved an immediate expenditure of "upwards of $125,000," *Deseret News,* December 23, 1857. The company's ledger showed total debits of $106,810. This did not include all the "volunteer" labor.

39. Stenhouse, *Rocky Mountain Saints,* p. 346.

40. According to Sir Richard Burton, Harney had boasted that he would "hang Brigham first and try him afterward." *The City of the Saints* (New York, 1862), p. 558.

41. *House Exec. Doc. No. 2,* 35th Cong., 1st sess., p. 21.

42. John Bassett Moore, ed., *The Works of James Buchanan* (Philadelphia, 1910), X, 152; also Moore, XII, 212–218.

43. The documents are published in *House Exec. Doc. No. 71,* 35th Cong., 1st sess., X, pp. 1–215; and in Tullidge, pp. 129–152.

44. Scott's letter with a discussion of its significance is published in M. Hamlin Cannon, "Winfield Scott and the Utah Expedition," *Military Affairs,* V (1941), 208–211.

45. Scott said: "The expedition set on foot by Mr. Secretary Floyd, in 1857, against the Mormons and Indians about Salt Lake was, beyond a doubt, to give occasion for large contracts and expenditures, that is, to open a wide field for frauds and peculation . . . observing the desperate characters who frequented the Secretary, some of whom had desks near him, suspicion [of this result] was at length excited." *Memoirs of Lieut.-General Scott, LL. D., Written by Himself* (2 vols.; New York, 1864), II, 604.

46. This argument is advanced in John C. Robinson, "The Utah Expedition," *Magazine of American History,* XI (1884), 335–341.

47. Evidence in support of this view is offered in M. H. Cannon, "The Abstracted Indian Trust Bonds," *Improvement Era,* XLV (1942), 430ff., 502ff.

48. This possibility is discussed in Poll, p. 92.

49. *Ibid.,* p. 94. The letter of instructions on July 11, 1857, to the new governor

stated: "With any peculiar opinions of the inhabitants, however deplorable in themselves or revolting to the public sentiment of the country, the Executive Government has no legitimate concern, and no design to interfere. . . . The great object is to assert the supremacy of the law." Utah Territorial Papers: Letter Books, I, National Archives, courtesy of Howard R. Lamar.

50. Creer, *Utah and the Nation,* p. 159.

51. *Ibid.,* pp. 123, 232; Cannon, "The Abstracted Indian Trust Bonds," p. 431.

52. Letter of November 11, 1857, *Messages and Documents, 1857–1858,* Part I, serial 942, cited in Neff, *History of Utah,* p. 441. See also Alban W. Hoopes, *Indian Affairs and Their Administration with Special Reference to the Far West, 1849–1860* (Philadelphia, 1932), pp. 131–159.

53. Sermon of Daniel Carn, July 5, 1857, cited in Neff, *History of Utah,* p. 349.

54. According to a dispatch in the St. Louis *Republican,* August 7, 1857, copied into HBY, 1857, pp. 6–7.

55. Church chronicles mention that on November 26, 1857, Ben Simons, an Indian trader, reported on the condition of the federal troops near Fort Bridger. He declared that the merchants (that is, Gentiles who had previously done business in Utah) "were suffering for want of food." The church reaction, as reported by the historian, was "they ought to suffer, for they had been the means of bringing on this war in a great measure." HBY, 1857, p. 57.

56. JH, October 26, 1857. According to the Mormon chronicle, the merchants simply "stood and took it." See JH, July 6, 1858, March 30, 1859.

57. Tullidge, p. 130.

58. HBY, 1857, p. 50. That Buchanan expected the Mormons to oppose the troops is indicated by the secrecy in which the whole movement was couched — the failure to seek Congressional approval, the discontinuance of mail service, and the failure to communicate directly with Governor Brigham Young. The first intimation the Mormons had of the overall design of the government came from the army freighter, William H. Russell. Tullidge, p. 156.

59. Diary of Hosea Stout, September 19, 1857, typescript, BYU. Several reports of Mormon spies are copied into HBY, 1857. For example, Charles Decker and Jesse Earl reported that they had disguised themselves as California emigrants, and "went in among the soldiers" and inquired what they were going to do. "Scalp old Brigham," they replied. "Have you seen him?" "Yes." "How does he feel?" "Rather scary," the Mormons answered (p. 13). Another report stated that the officers of the Tenth Regiment were "young and full of fire, and they swore they would come into our settlements any how, for they could whip out Utah." The Second Regiment, however, was officered by older men who "thought it an imposition to be sent out here as a political movement, to kill innocent people or to get killed (p. 14). Officers' journals reflect similar attitudes. "If the Mormons will only fight," wrote Captain Gove, "their days are numbered. We shall sweep them from the face of the earth and Mormonism in Utah shall cease. Our campaign will then be at an end. I sincerely hope that they will, at least, go far enough to compel us to take quarters instead of hiring." Jesse A. Gove, *The Utah Expedition, 1857–1858,* Otis G. Hammond, ed. (Cleveland, 1928), entry for September 18, 1857, p. 58.

60. The proclamation, dated September 15, 1857, is reproduced in *House Exec. Doc. No. 71,* 35th Cong., 1st sess., X, pp. 34–35.

61. [Edward W. Tullidge], "The Reformation in Utah," *Harper's New Monthly Magazine,* XLIII (1871), 603.

62. The document in which these instructions appear is published in Juanita

Brooks, *The Mountain Meadows Massacre,* p. 13. See also Roberts, *Comprehensive History,* IV, 240.

63. James K. P. Miller, from whose diary the above was taken, added: "The horses resembled the guns, the cavalry arms resembled the horses, and the men matched the kit to perfection." This quotation furnished by Professor Andrew F. Rolle, of Occidental College, who has been authorized to edit and publish this important Western diary.

64. These orders, signed by Daniel H. Wells, and dated October 4, 1857, were found on Major Joseph Taylor when captured by government troops. They are published in R. B. Marcy, *Thirty Years of Army Life on the Border* (New York, 1866), pp. 270–271; and in *House Exec. Doc. No. 71,* 35th Cong., 1st sess., X, pp. 56–57.

65. Roberts, IV, 279.

66. In the back of the company's ledger is a section, dated September 1857, entitled "Outfit for Eastern Expedition." This lists properties assigned to Captain H. B. Clawson's company of lancers, Lot Smith's "express" expedition, General Wells' expedition, and several companies comprising, perhaps, 300 individuals.

67. "Journal and Diary of William Marsden," *Heart Throbs of the West,* XII, 155.

68. "Manti Historical Record, Book C," entry for October 25, 1857, cited in Therald Jensen, "Mormon Theory of Church and State" (unpublished Ph. D. dissertation, University of Chicago, 1938), p. 111.

69. Ralph Hansen, "Administrative History of the Nauvoo Legion in Utah" (unpublished Master's Thesis, Brigham Young University, 1954), p. 55.

70. HBY, 1857, pp. 19, 40, 51, 55.

71. JH, March 21, May 19, August 7, December 31, 1857, February 23, 1858, March 22, 1860. Samuel Colt had great admiration for Brigham Young, regarding him as "the one really great leader living" and a "true statesman who knows how to rule and does so." Such a man, he said, who had "wrested an empire from wilderness and savage," could hardly be expected to "tolerate interference from pettifogging politicians who begged the appointment because they could not make a living in any other way." Young was just the sort of man who could appreciate "the advantages of possessing arms of my invention," in order to protect himself and his people "from the raids of savages" and from the "white marauders who are always ready to rob honest persons who have not the power to protect themselves." Colt presented a pair of his finest gift revolvers to the Mormon leader who then "purchased the consignment of several hundred revolvers, paying cash." Colt's agents may have given the church permission to duplicate some of the patented revolvers. See Jack Rohan, *Yankee Arms Maker: The Incredible Career of Samuel Colt* (New York, 1935), pp. 232–233. See also Hansen, "The Nauvoo Legion," p. 62.

72. The letter to the Carson Valley Saints, as found in the church letter-books, is published in Brooks, *The Mountain Meadows Massacre,* p. 20. See also Roberts, *Comprehensive History,* IV, 240–242. Professor Eugene Campbell, in his history of the Mormons in California cited in Chapter III, offers evidence that the San Bernardino colony was written off before the Utah War, and that the latter offered a convenient excuse for abandonment.

73. Stenhouse, *Rocky Mountain Saints,* p. 353.

74. A particularly good account of the losses of one family during the "Big Move" from California to Utah is in the "Journal of Louisa Barnes Pratt," *Heart Throbs of the West,* VIII, 325–330.

75. HBY, 1858, p. 11.

76. *Millennial Star,* XIX (1857), 766.

77. The commander of one of the trains, a Mr. Dawson, pled "For God's sake, don't burn the trains!" To which Major Smith replied, "It is for His sake that I am going to burn them." Lot Smith's Narrative in "The Echo Cañon War," *The Contributor,* III (1882), 273. The list of supplies destroyed is given in *House Exec. Doc. No. 71,* X, p. 63.

78. Mormon guerilla activity is described by participants in: "Santiago [James H. Martineau]," "A Scouting Party," *The Contributor,* XI (1890), 395–398; and William A. Hickman, *Brigham's Destroying Angel* (New York, 1872), pp. 118–123.

79. Henry S. Hamilton, *Reminiscences of a Veteran* (Concord, 1897), pp. 80–81. The soldiers eventually managed to get some fast mules and captured three of the "Mormon marauders." They were tried for "treasonous behavior" but exonerated by President Buchanan's amnesty.

80. Some of the difficulties were described by a teamster for Russell, Majors and Waddell in "Diary of William Wallace Hammond, 1837–1869," pp. 10–15, typescript, Huntington Library.

81. Eugene Bandel, *Frontier Life in the Army, 1854–1861,* Olga Bandel and Richard Jente, transl.; Ralph P. Bieber, ed. (Glendale, Calif., 1932), p. 218.

82. Circular from Army Headquarters to Chiefs of Staff in *House Exec. Doc. No. 2,* II, pp. 31–32.

83. H. M. Chittenden and A. T. Richardson, eds., *Life, Letters and Travels of Father Pierre-Jean De Smet . . .* (4 vols.; New York, 1905), II, 728. De Smet was chaplain of the expedition.

84. *Congressional Globe,* 35th Cong., 1st sess., 1084, 1177, 1516–1519; Browne, "The Utah Expedition," p. 478.

85. Browne, "The Utah Expedition," p. 478. Browne was a correspondent with the expedition. In their account of the activities of Russell, Majors and Waddell in *Empire on Wheels,* the Settles do not substantiate all of Browne's obviously biased but widely believed allegations. Copies of the transportation contracts of this firm are in the Waddell Collection, Huntington Library.

86. Chittenden, *Father De Smet,* I, 70; II, 725. Also see Alexander Majors, *Seventy Years on the Frontier,* pp. 142–144.

87. See Cleland and Brooks, eds., *A Mormon Chronicle . . .* (2 vols., San Marino, Calif., 1955), I, 144–145, entries for January 13, 19, 1858.

88. Diary of Joseph Holbrook, Vol. II, p. 2.

89. "A List of Donations Towards Fitting Out Soldiers for the Army of Israel," MS., BYU, cited in Hansen, "The Nauvoo Legion," pp. 53–54.

90. HBY, 1858, pp. 1, 4; Roberts, *Comprehensive History,* IV, 333.

91. JH, February 21, 22, 23, 1858.

92. "You may query will the soldiers be really permitted to enter Salt Lake Valley? No! They will not!! . . . we are determined to enjoy it [peace] if we have to fight for it." Brigham Young to Horace S. Eldredge, August 7, 1857, UHS. Also the following passage in a letter to his nephews in the Hawaiian Islands: "We had determined years ago, if a mob again attacked us, whether led by their own passions, or unconstitutionally legalized by the general government, or by the government of any of the states, or territories, that we'll resist their aggressions by making an appeal to God and our own right arms, for that protection which has been denied us by christianized and civilized nations. Our former determination remains unshaken." *Memoirs of John R. Young* (Salt Lake City, 1920), p. 97. The sermons of church officials delivered in the fall of 1857 and published in the *Deseret News* and *Journal of Discourses* seem strong enough, but Brigham Young admitted that "considerable of

the pepper" had been "extracted" from the published versions. Brigham Young to Horace S. Eldredge, August 7, 1857.

93. This report from a California-bound party which passed through Salt Lake City in December 1857 was published in *National Intelligencer,* January 28, 1858, and cited in Poll, "The Mormon Question," p. 117.

94. Oscar O. Winther, ed., *The Private Papers and Diary of Thomas Leiper Kane: A Friend of the Mormons* (San Francisco, 1937). Colonel Kane was directly apprised of the Mormon difficulties by dispatches from Brigham Young forwarded by Utah's congressional delegate, John M. Bernhisel. Obviously, neither Kane nor Young intimated that Kane's intervention was the result of collaboration between the two. See Roberts, *Comprehensive History,* IV, 242.

95. In essence, the army personnel believed that they had been betrayed by political schemers and that the entire campaign had been all for nought. Few seem to have questioned that the march on Utah was justified. A teamster with the Utah Expedition wrote that a story circulated among the soldiers of the expedition that when word came from Washington that there was to be no fighting, Johnston and his chief of staff were furious. "Johnston took off his hat with the insignia of a general on it, threw it on the ground, stamped on it, and said: 'Damn such a government. Here we have starved and froze all winter and, now that we have these fellows right where we want them, they are going to get off without shedding so much as one drop of blood. Damn such a government.'" *Reminiscences of Alexander Toponce* (Ogden, Utah, 1923), pp. 37–38. Whether or not this story is true, it reflects either the attitude of the soldiers or the general or both.

96. *Campaigns in the West, 1856–1861: The Journal and Letters of Colonel John Van Deusen Du Bois . . . ,* George P. Hammond, ed. (Tuscon, Arizona, 1949), p. 69, entry for June 21, 1858.

97. "Journal of Captain Albert Tracy," p. 23, entry for June 21, 1858.

98. HBY, 1858, p. 4. This had previously been considered, but only as a last resort in case resistance to the army failed. Roberts, *Comprehensive History,* IV, 361. On January 6, 1858, Brigham Young had written: "We have an abundant supply of grain and cattle, and if necessity compels us to flee to the mountains, bread and beef will appease our hunger. . . . Rather than see my wives and daughters ravished and polluted, and the seeds of corruption sown in the hearts of my sons by a brutal soldiery, I would leave my home in ashes, my gardens and orchards a waste, and subsist upon roots and herbs, a wanderer through these mountains for the remainder of my natural life." Letter cited in Ray B. West, Jr., *Kingdom of the Saints* (New York, 1957), p. 263.

99. During the Crimean War, the Russian general who evacuated Sebastopol stated: "It is not Sebastopol which we have left to them, but the burning ruins of the town, which we ourselves set fire to, having maintained the honour of defence in such a manner that our grandchildren may recall with pride the remembrance of it and send it on to all posterity." Justin McCarthy, *A History of Our Own Times . . .* (11th ed.; 4 vols.; London, 1879), II, 339–340. That the Mormons were stimulated, as were most Americans, by the news reports from Sebastopol, is indicated by diary entries of many pioneer Utahans. For example, see Diary of Hosea Stout, July 4, 9, 1855.

100. "History of Brigham Young," March 21, 1858, as cited in Roberts, *Comprehensive History,* IV, 360.

101. *A Series of Instructions and Remarks by President Brigham Young, at a Special Council, Tabernacle, March 21, 1858 . . .* (Salt Lake City, [1858]), p. 5, copy in the Yale Library. The reference to Sebastopol is on page 11.

102. Young to Thomas L. Kane, March 22, 1858, cited in Poll, "The Mormon Question," p. 127.

103. "Manti Historical Record, Book C," entry of March 28, 1858, cited in Jensen, "Mormon Theory of Church and State," p. 111. Notice of objections is found in Roberts, *Comprehensive History,* IV, 361; Stenhouse, p. 394.

104. "Instructions" of Brigham Young, March 28, 1858, *Deseret News,* April 14, 1858.

105. George A. Smith to T. B. H. Stenhouse, April 5, 1858, HBY, 1858, p. 8.

106. *Ibid.,* pp. 5–6.

107. *A Series of Instructions and Remarks . . . ,* p. 7; also Stenhouse, pp. 385–386.

108. [James H Martineau?], "Seeking a Refuge in the Desert," *The Contributor,* XI (1890), 249.

109. Roberts, *Comprehensive History,* IV, 362. In addition to these two parties, John D. Lee wrote that he was appointed to locate an isolated place in southern Utah where members of the First Presidency and their families could find a "resting place." *A Mormon Chronicle,* I, 149, entries for February 8, 9, 1858.

110. HBY, 1858, pp. 19, 30; also Roberts, *Comprehensive History,* IV, 362–363; Flora Bean Horne, ed., *Autobiography of George Washington Bean* (Salt Lake City, 1945), pp. 132–134.

111. The interesting story of the Dame party is told in [James H. Martineau?], "Seeking a Refuge in the Desert," *The Contributor,* XI (1890), 249–251, 296–300. See also *A Mormon Chronicle,* I, 158–159, entry for April 13, 1858; *Journal of Jesse Nathaniel Smith . . .* (Salt Lake City, 1953), pp. 29–30.

112. HBY, 1858, pp. 27–29; *Memoirs of John R. Young,* pp. 105, 110, 114–115. After listening to the earnest advocacy of Walker's agents, Brigham Young is said to have replied: "Gentlemen, God Almighty made these everlasting hills to be bulwarks of liberty for the oppressed and down-trodden of the earth. We shall never leave here and go to a country where we should have six hundred miles of sea coast to defend, and where any nation at their pleasure could send war ships to bombard our cities. Furthermore, gentlemen, should the desire ever come, we have hundreds of boys, just as capable of going to Nicaragua, and of taking possession and holding it, too, as General Walker of New York." *Ibid.,* pp. 114–115.

113. Diary of Hosea Stout, March 21, 24, 28, 30, 1858.

114. One hundred men were appointed to remain in Box Elder County, 300 in Weber County, 75 in Davis County, 30 in Tooele County, and 300 in Salt Lake County. Somewhat more than the appointed number remained in Salt Lake. HBY, 1858, p. 20.

115. HBY, 1858, pp. 8–9; Diary of Hosea Stout, April 6, 1858.

116. The manner in which the wards were organized is illustrated in the minutes of the Big Cottonwood Ward, published in *Heart Throbs,* X, 239–240.

117. Neff, *History of Utah,* p. 502; *A Mormon Chronicle,* I, 156–158; *Journal of Jesse N. Smith,* p. 28.

118. HBY, 1858, p. 5; JH, March 25, 30, April 13, 27, May 28, 1858, June 28, 1864.

119. See Roberts, *Comprehensive History,* IV, 386.

120. HBY, 1858, p. 23.

121. HBY, 1858, p. 20; Roberts, *Comprehensive History,* IV, 397–398. Governor Cumming's reflections on the Move South are contained in his letter to the Secretary of State, Lewis Cass, May 2, 1858, in Utah Territorial Papers: Letter Books, I, N. A.

122. JH, June 12, 1858.

123. HBY, 1858, p. 27.

124. *Memoirs of John R. Young,* pp. 113–114.

125. G. W. Brimhall, *The Workers of Utah* (Provo, Utah, 1889), pp. 28–29.

126. Cited in McGavin, *U. S. Soldiers Invade Utah,* pp. 216–217.

127. *A Mormon Chronicle,* I, 145; Sermon of Brigham Young, March 28, 1858, *Deseret News,* April 14, 1858.

128. Journals of the Territorial Assembly, 7th Annual Session, 1857–1858, MS., UHS.

129. Diary of Hosea Stout, January 19, 1858; *A Mormon Chronicle,* I, 145.

130. Diary of Hosea Stout, January 19, 1858. I have been unable to find a copy of the charter of the bank although the "Diary of Charles L. Walker," typescript, BYU, entry for January 19, 1858, distinctly states that the charter was read, alterations made, and approved.

131. "Diary of Charles L. Walker," p. 19, entry for January 21, 1858.

132. JH, June 26, 1856, August 5, 1858.

133. *A Mormon Chronicle,* I, 164–165, entry for May 23, 1858.

134. "Deseret Currency Association Account Book," MS., CHO.

135. JH, June 18, 1859.

136. Remarks of Daniel H. Wells, *Deseret News,* April 14, 1858. The Daughters of Utah Pioneers have on display in their Pioneer Memorial Building in Salt Lake City a specimen of the promissory notes.

137. G. W. Mills to T. B. H. Stenhouse, April 5, 1858, *Millennial Star,* XX (1858), 461–462.

138. See J. H. Simpson, *Report of Explorations Across the Great Basin . . .* (Washington, 1876), p. 137.

139. JH, June 6, 7, 1858, June 14, 20, 1859; Brigham Young to H. S. Eldredge, November 20, 1858; *Autobiography of George Washington Bean,* p. 135. Brigham Young, presumably as trustee-in-trust, owned 200 shares in the Provo Canyon Company.

140. JH, May 10, 1858.

141. *Ibid.;* Diary of John McEwan, pp. 163–164, entry for May 16, 1858, MS. in possession of Mark K. Allen, Provo, Utah.

142. *A Mormon Chronicle,* I, 178, entry for August 3, 1858.

143. This is clearly indicated in General Tithing Office of the Trustee-in-trust and Perpetual Emigration Fund Receipt Book, MS., UU. This book also contains a record of the various amounts of currency turned in and for what purpose. For example, the people of Parowan, in Iron County, turned in $492.00 of Deseret Currency on August 30, 1858, of which $227.00 was donated to the P.E.F., $102.00 to the tithing office, $138.00 to be placed "on deposit," and the remaining $25.00 to be used as subscriptions for the *Deseret News.*

144. The marshal was eventually forced to pay to Brigham Young, as president of the association, damages of $1,668, plus $648.66 costs of court, for trespass in the case of the plates. See Minute Book of the Salt Lake County Probate Court, MS., Office of the County Clerk, Salt Lake City. Also JH, July 11, August 22, September 3, 1859, September 6, 8, 1860.

145. JH, June 14, 18, 20, 1859. All of the currency was burned in 1867. See JH, December 1, 1867.

146. *House Exec. Doc. No. 2,* 35th Cong., 2nd sess., II, 113.

147. Oliver Lyman Spaulding, *The United States Army in War and Peace* (New York, 1937), p. 239.

148. Browne, "The Utah Expedition," p. 490.

149. "Journal of Captain Albert Tracy," p. 27, entry for June 26, 1858.
150. *Memoirs of John R. Young,* p. 115.
151. *Campaigns in the West,* pp. 69–70, entry for June 24 [26], 1858.
152. "Journal of Albert Tracy," p. 28.
153. Roberts, *Comprehensive History,* IV, 447.
154. *Campaigns in the West,* p. 71.
155. Hamilton, *Reminiscences of a Veteran,* p. 108.
156. Brimhall, *The Workers of Utah,* p. 31; William Jennings, "Material Progress of Utah," 1884, MS., Bancroft Library, p. 2. Jennings, who was later mayor of Salt Lake City, wrote that "women were so scantily dressed [due to lack of clothing] as scarcely to cover their nakedness, barefooted and bleeding too, with no means for supplying their needs. They dressed sometimes in sacking or with remnants of rag carpets thrown about them."

CHAPTER VII: A DECADE OF PLANNING FOR SELF-SUFFICIENCY AND GROWTH

The most complete general account of the 1860's is in Neff, *History of Utah,* pp. 617–908, but a number of monographs have greatly enlarged our understanding of this significant decade. Outstanding among these for its scholarly study of the documents of the period is Robert Joseph Dwyer, *The Gentile Comes to Utah: A Study in Religious and Social Conflict (1862–1890)* (Washington, D. C., 1941). A fine bibliographical essay is included. A good analysis of the impact of the events of the 1860's on Mormon society is A. R. Mortensen, "The *Deseret News* and Utah, 1850–1867" (unpublished Ph. D. dissertation, University of California, Los Angeles, 1949). Valuable for their treatments of subjects included in this chapter are Gustive O. Larson, *Prelude to the Kingdom* . . . (Francestown, N. H., 1947); and William J. McNiff, *Heaven On Earth: A Planned Mormon Society* (Oxford, Ohio, 1940).

Contemporary studies include E. M. Tullidge [Edward W. Tullidge], "Views of Mormondom," and "The Mormon Commonwealth," in *The Galaxy* (New York), II (1866), 209–214, 351–364; and the following studies and commentaries by visitors to Mormonland: Richard F. Burton, *The City of the Saints* . . . (New York, 1862); Horace Greeley, *An Overland Journey from New York to San Francisco in the Summer of 1859* (New York, 1863); Samuel Bowles, *Across the Continent* . . . (Springfield, Mass., 1865); Albert D. Richardson, *Beyond the Mississippi* . . . (Hartford, Conn., 1867); Charles Wentworth Dilke, *Greater Britain: A Record of Travel in English-Speaking Countries during 1866 and 1867* (2 vols.; 2nd ed.; London, 1869); [William Elkanah Waters], *Life Among the Mormons, and a March to their Zion* (1868); Fitz Hugh Ludlow, *The Heart of the Continent* . . . (London, 1870); James F. Rusling, *Across America: Or, the Great West and the Pacific Coast* (New York, 1874), esp. pp. 157–222; Augustus L. Chetlain, *Recollections of Seventy Years* (Galena, Illinois, 1899), esp. pp. 117–139; Julius C. Birge, *The Awakening of the Desert* (Boston, 1912), esp. pp. 303–438; and William Henry Jackson, *Time Exposure: The Autobiography of William Henry Jackson* (New York, 1940). A useful contemporary Mormon narrative is George W. Brimhall, *The Workers of Utah* (Provo, 1889).

The activities of Colonel Connor and his California and Nevada Volunteers and their influence on the development of mining in Utah, are described in their newspaper, the *Daily Union Vedette* (Salt Lake City, 1863–1867), and in: Fred B. Rogers, *Soldiers of the Overland* . . . (San Francisco, 1938); Richard H. Orton, comp., *Records of California Men in the War of the Rebellion, 1861–1867* (Sacramento, 1890), pp. 505–519; "The Mines of Utah," *Tullidge's Quarterly Magazine,* I (1880), 179–190; Robert G. Raymer, "Early Mining in Utah," *Pacific Historical Review,* VIII (1939), 81–88; T. A. Rickard, *A History of American Mining* (New York, 1932), pp. 179–201; and Muriel Sibelle Wolle, "Utah: The Army Turns Prospector," in *The Bonanza Trail: Ghost Towns and Mining Camps of the West* (Bloomington, Ind., 1953), pp. 363–393.

The role of Gentile freighters, merchants, and bankers is told in *Reminiscences of Alexander Toponce* (Ogden, 1923); J. F. Frederick, *Ben Holladay, The Stagecoach King: A Chapter in the Development of Transcontinental Transportation* (Glendale, Calif., 1940); Archer B. Hulbert, ed., "Letters of an Overland Mail Agent in Utah [Hiram S. Rumfield]," *Proceedings of the American Antiquarian Society* (Worcester, Mass., 1929); and Leonard J. Arrington, "Banking Enterprises in Utah, 1847–1880," *Business History Review,* XXIX (1955), 312–334, and "Taxable Income in Utah, 1862–1872," *Utah Historical Quarterly,* XXIV (1956), 21–47. The Mormon response to the activities of these "outsiders" is detailed in Leonard J. Arrington, "Agricultural Price Control in Pioneer Utah," *Agricultural History,* XXX (1956), 104–113.

Other monographs dealing with phases of the 1860's are: Margaret M. Fisher, ed., *Utah and the Civil War* (Salt Lake City, 1929); George D. Pyper, *The Romance of an Old Playhouse* (Salt Lake City, 1928); Stewart Grow, "A Historical Study of the Construction of the Salt Lake Tabernacle" (unpublished Master's Thesis, Brigham Young University, 1947), and *A Tabernacle in the Desert* (Salt Lake City, 1958); James E. Talmage, *The House of the Lord* (Salt Lake City, 1912); Ivan J. Barrett, "History of the Cotton Mission and Cotton Culture in Utah" (unpublished Master's Thesis, Brigham Young University, 1947); Andrew Karl Larson, *The Red Hills of November: A Pioneer Biography of Utah's Cotton Town* (Salt Lake City, 1957); Milton R. Hunter, "The Mormons and the Colorado River," *American Historical Review,* XLIV (1939), 549-555; and the following by Leonard J. Arrington: "The Mormon Cotton Mission in Southern Utah," *Pacific Historical Review,* XXV (1956), 221–238; "The Deseret Agricultural and Manufacturing Society in Pioneer Utah," *Utah Historical Quarterly, XXIV* (1956), 165–170; "Taming the Turbulent Sevier: A Story of Mormon Desert Conquest," *Western Humanities Review,* V (1951), 393–406; and "The Deseret Telegraph — A Church-owned Public Utility," *Journal of Economic History,* XI (1951), 117–139.

1. Remarks of October 24, 1857, HBY, 1857, p. 50.

2. JH, March 28, 1858; Brigham Young to H. S. Eldredge, November 20, 1858, typescript, UHS.

3. So said A. O. Smoot to the Provo Bishops, "Early Records of Provo, Utah, 1868–1875," p. 320, microfilm, BYU. This belief is implicit in many of the sermons of Brigham Young. He is reported to have used the expression, "Tie the calf at home, and the cow is sure to return. Where a man's treasure is, there will his heart be also." T. B. H. Stenhouse, *The Rocky Mountain Saints* (New York, 1873), p. 502n.

4. *An Overland Journey,* p. 247. Johnston's command, including employees, was estimated at 7,000 to 8,000 men, in *Harper's Weekly,* II (October 30, 1858), 694.

5. A. B. Miller, who was associated with Russell, Majors and Waddell, told Mormon officials in July 1859 that 1,100 three-ton merchant wagons were on the way to Utah and that 1,500 additional wagons were at that time ready to leave Fort Leavenworth for Camp Floyd. HBY, 1859, pp. 33–34.

6. JH, June 22, July 9, 1858; Cleland and Brooks, eds., *A Mormon Chronicle . . .* (2 vols.; San Marino, Calif., 1955), 1, 182, entry for August 20, 1858; Diary of

A. J. Allen, *Heart Throbs of the West* (12 vols.; Salt Lake City, 1936–1951), X, 254.

7. Daniel H. Wells, JH, October 6, 1858.

8. Diary of Joseph Holbrook, II, 3, typescript in possession of the writer.

9. Brimhall, *The Workers of Utah,* p. 31; T. S. Kenderdine, *A California Tramp and Later Footprints . . .* (Newton, Pa., 1888), pp. 94ff.; "The Utah War: Journal of Albert Tracy, 1858–1860," *Utah Historical Quarterly,* XIII (1945), 21, 24, 28, 29, 41, and 42; Eugene Bandel, *Frontier Life in the Army 1854–1861,* transl. Olga Bandel and Richard Jente; ed. Ralph P. Bieber (Glendale, Calif., 1932), pp. 228–230.

10. Bandel, p. 230.

11. *Deseret News,* July 21, October 6, 1858; JH, July 10, October 7, 1858.

12. "Journal of Albert Tracy," p. 35; HBY, 1858, p. 54.

13. Brigham Young to H. S. Eldredge, December 30, 1858; HBY, 1858, pp. 73–74.

14. Greeley, *An Overland Journey,* p. 246; Kenderdine, *A California Tramp,* p. 101; Burton, *City of the Saints,* p. 242; Brigham Young sermon, October 8, 1860, *Millennial Star,* XXIII (1861), 49; account books of the Big Cottonwood Lumber Company, 1855–1863, CHO.

15. Kenderdine, *A California Tramp,* p. 94; also Brigham Young to H. S. Eldredge, November 20, 1858.

16. "Autobiography of James McBride," p. 39, typescript, BYU.

17. Alexander Majors, *Seventy Years on the Frontier* (Chicago, 1893), p. 145; *Deseret News,* May 16, 1860.

18. *Millennial Star,* XXIII (1861), 613; H. H. Bancroft, *History of Utah* (San Francisco, 1889), p. 575; E. W. Tullidge, *History of Salt Lake City* (Salt Lake City, c. 1886), p. 248; B. H. Roberts, *A Comprehensive History of the Church . . .* (6 vols.; Salt Lake City, 1930), IV, 541. A search of the National Archives for the army records detailing the sales in July 1861 proved to be unsuccessful.

19. Roberts, *Comprehensive History,* IV, 541; Schuyler Colfax, "Journal from the Missouri River to California," *Western Galaxy,* I (1888), 349; Toponce, *Reminiscences,* p. 39.

20. Hamilton Gardner, *History of Lehi* (Salt Lake City, 1913), p. 137.

21. William Clayton to George Q. Cannon, July 16, 1861, *Millennial Star,* XXIII (1861), 566.

22. Frederick, *Ben Holladay;* Majors, *Seventy Years on the Frontier.*

23. JH, December 20, 27, 1860, September 2, 1861; James Gamble, "Wiring a Continent," *The Californian,* III (1881), 556–563; Ben Hur Wilson, "From Coast to Coast," *The Palimpsest,* VII (1926), 233–242; Leonard J. Arrington, "Brigham Young and the Transcontinental Telegraph Line," *Improvement Era,* LIV (1951), 510ff.; Ann Eliza Young, *Wife No. 19 . . .* (Hartford, Conn., 1876), pp. 446–453.

24. JH, December 15, 1861.

25. JH, August 16, 1861.

26. *Letters of an Overland Mail Agent,* p. 44.

27. JH, June 30, 1862. See also Brigham Young sermon, April 7, 1862, JD, X, 97–98.

28. This will be discussed further in Chapter VIII.

29. *Deseret News,* October 29, 1862; JH, October 30, 1862. The Mormons probably did not realize that loyalty oaths had been introduced rather generally elsewhere in the nation as a phase of the consolidation of pro-Unionist sentiment during the Civil War. See Harold Melvin Hyman, *Era of the Oath: Northern Loyalty Tests During the Civil War and Reconstruction* (Philadelphia, 1954).

30. Rogers, *Soldiers of the Overland,* p. 112.

31. *Ibid.*, pp. 111–117; Orton, *Records of California Men,* pp. 505–510.

32. Connor to R. C. Drum, Assistant Adjutant General, U. S. Army, July 21, 1864, cited in *Tullidge's Quarterly Magazine,* I, 185.

33. H. H. Bancroft, *History of Washington, Idaho, and Montana, 1845–1889* (San Francisco, 1890), pp. 405–406, 621, and *History of Nevada, Colorado, and Wyoming, 1540–1888* (San Francisco, 1890), 92ff., 376ff.

34. Rogers, *Soldiers of the Overland,* p. 117; *Tullidge's Quarterly Magazine,* I, 179, 187; Stenhouse, *The Rocky Mountain Saints,* pp. 714–719; "Mineral Resources of the States and Territories, 1868" in *House Exec. Doc. No. 54,* 50th Cong., 3d sess., p. 168; George A. Smith in JH, February 19, 1868, November 11, 1869.

35. JH, November 30, 1863, January 17, August 31, December 5, 1864, March 13, April 20, 1865. An added consideration was that the government had not yet passed laws under which land could be owned in Utah. Several Mormons expressed the view that if any rich finds were made by Mormons, their claims would be jumped by Gentiles, and the latter would get preferential treatment in the courts because of prevailing anti-Mormon prejudices. See a discussion of this in a reminiscence by George Q. Cannon in *Deseret Evening News,* February 11, 1893.

36. *The Wealth of Nations* (Modern Library edition, New York, 1939), pp. 529–530.

37. Diary of Wilford Woodruff, July 1865, as reported in Matthias F. Cowley, ed., *Wilford Woodruff: History of His Life and Labors as Recorded in His Daily Journals* (Salt Lake City, 1909), p. 442. Also *Deseret News,* October 8, 1881.

38. For example, *Deseret News,* June 22, 29, August 8, November 30, 1864, January 4, June 14, 1865, May 3, September 6, 1866, March 6, December 17, 1867, March 21, 1868, August 18, 1880, October 8, 1881.

39. Sermon of October 6, 1863, JD, X, 271.

40. Remarks recorded in JH, April 9, 1868.

41. Sermon of October 25, 1863, *Deseret News,* November 18, 1863. Some of the statements of Brigham Young and other church officials at this time have been used as evidence that the church was opposed to mining. This widely held interpretation, found in nearly every history of the state, Mormon and non-Mormon, is based on a misreading of the events of the 1860's. The many mining missions sponsored by the church in the 1850's, '60's, and '70's, and the church promotion of railroads to the mines after 1869, should be proof that the church was never opposed to mining as such, even to the mining of gold and silver. (See, among others, JH, October 27, 1861, June 11, 1864, January 23, February 11, 1873; James S. Brown, *Life of a Pioneer* [Salt Lake City, 1900], pp. 440–445.) But the church was opposed to Connor's premature efforts, and particularly to his objective of accomplishing the development by means of a stampede of "outsiders" which would infiltrate and subvert the Mormon commonwealth. It is simply not true, as Samuel Bowles wrote in 1865, that "The policy of the Mormon leaders has been to confine their people to agriculture." (*Across the Continent,* p. 93). Mormon policy was, rather, the achievement of a workable self-sufficiency, and this required attention (by the Mormons themselves) to all aspects of development: agriculture, mining, manufacturing, transportation, and marketing. Church criticism of Connor's activities was not unlike that of political and religious leaders of so-called backward countries in objecting to opportunistic exploitative foreign investment. (See Brigham Young sermon, October 6, 1863, JD, X, 254–255.) No one seems to have advanced the possibility that Colonel Connor himself may have had a part in spreading the popular theory of Mormon retardation of mining in Utah. Eager to make the strongest case against the Mormons, and not willing to admit his

own miscalculation of economic factors, the Colonel, in his conversations with visiting writers and businessmen, may have pinned the blame for unproductive ventures on Mormon opposition rather than on the unsuitability of fuel and high cost of transportation. Particularly objectionable to Connor and others was an "outrageous" bill to levy a tax of 20 per cent on the "proceeds" of all mines in Utah. The bill was passed by the Mormon legislature but vetoed by the non-Mormon governor. See Schuyler Colfax, "The Mormon Defiance for a Quarter-Century," *The Advance* (Chicago), August 24, 1882, Ritch Collection, Huntington Library.

42. Apostle Erastus Snow, leader of the Mormons in southern Utah, said in 1865 that "he wished any man that would go to the western mines as a miner to be cut off the Church." JH, August 31, 1865. There are no discoverable instances of such excommunications, but it was doubtless used as a threat when reason failed. See also "The Mormons and Mining," Salt Lake *Herald,* September 18, 1887.

43. See esp., "Reminiscences" of William Jennings, *Heart Throbs,* VII, 441–442.

44. Such a telegram to the residents of Providence, Utah, dated July 8, 1867, is recorded in *Providence and Her People* (Logan, 1949), p. 239.

45. JH, December 21, 1863, January 14, 1864. The Mormons viewed this as something of a concession, since the current tithing office price was $6.00 per bushel.

46. Connor to General Halleck, February 15, 1865, *Records of California Men,* p. 516.

47. LeRoy R. Hafen, "Utah Food Supplies Sold to the Pioneer Settlers of Colorado," *Utah Historical Quarterly,* IV (1931), 62–64; *Deseret News,* September 5, 1860, May 8, 1861; A. B. Miller to W. B. Waddell, September 6, 1860, MS., Waddell Collection, Huntington Library.

48. JH, October 10, 1865.

49. *Deseret News,* August 17, 1864; *Millennial Star,* XXVI (1864), 717.

50. *Millennial Star,* XXVII (1865), 62; *Deseret News,* December 28, 1864, February 1, 1865.

51. *Across the Continent,* p. 94.

52. Toponce, *Reminiscences,* pp. 87–88, *et passim.*

53. For a detailed discussion of the Farm Price Convention and Utah Produce Company, see Arrington, "Agricultural Price Control in Pioneer Utah."

54. *Millennial Star,* XXI (1859), 8–9.

55. Hafen, "Handcarts to Utah, 1856–1860," *Utah Historical Quarterly,* XXIV (1956), 315.

56. This is clear from notations in the "General Tithing Office of the Trustee-in-trust and Perpetual Emigration Fund Receipt Book," MS., UU.

57. *Deseret News,* May 11, September 14, 1859.

58. *Ibid.,* October 10, 1860.

59. JH, February 28, 1861.

60. Joel E. Ricks, ed., *The History of a Valley: Cache Valley, Utah-Idaho* (Logan, 1956), pp. 166–167. A good personal experience narrative of a participant in the Church Trains of 1861, 1862, 1863, and 1864 is in J. M. Tanner, *A Biographical Sketch of John Riggs Murdock* (Salt Lake City, 1909), pp. 136–153.

61. Larson, *Prelude to the Kingdom,* pp. 227, 236. My calculations show more men and animals to have been involved in the Church Trains than Larson reports.

62. The estimates on cost are based on Brigham Young, sermon of August 21, 1864, JH, August 22, 1864; report of the trustee-in-trust read by George Q. Cannon before the general conference, JH, April 9, 1865; George A. Smith estimate in JH,

August 13, 1868; also see Joseph W. Young to George Q. Cannon, January 17, 1863, *Millennial Star,* XXV (1863), 157–159.

63. William Clayton to George Q. Cannon, JH, February 22, 1862; *Deseret News,* May 7, 21, 1862; JH, January 30, 1862.

64. *Deseret News,* April 29, 1863; H. S. Eldredge to George Q. Cannon, May 19, 1863, *Millennial Star,* XXV (1863), 413.

65. This information, from the records of the Harmony Ward, is found in greater detail in William R. Palmer, "The Pioneering Mormon," *Improvement Era,* XLV (1942), 540.

66. "Cache Valley High Priests Minute Book, 1859–1883," MS., USU.

67. Although built on the order of Brigham Young, and generally regarded as Brigham Young's personal project, the theater was awarded to the church in the settlement of the Young estate, and may be considered as having been a church project rather than a purely private one.

68. *Across the Continent,* p. 103.

69. Pyper, *Romance of an Old Playhouse,* p. 80; also pp. 74–81.

70. JH, August 21, 1861.

71. JH, January 7, 1862.

72. Pyper, pp. 277, 279.

73. The Jarvis story is told by Nels Anderson in *Desert Saints* (Chicago, 1942), pp. 232–233, and in his "Utah's Unemployment Problem," a speech delivered before the Utah State Conference of Social Work, held at Salt Lake City, November 15, 1940, a mimeographed copy of which is in the library of USU.

74. Ludlow, *The Heart of the Continent,* pp. 370–371.

75. *Utah: A Guide to the State* (New York, 1945), p. 178.

76. At the time of its dedication, March 6, 1862, Brigham Young delivered an address on "The Capacity of the Human Body and Mind for Development," in which he expressed the Mormon view that the theater was a desirable form of recreation and amusement so long as the atmosphere was wholesome. No liquor was to be served, nor drunkenness permitted; performances were to be opened and closed with prayer; and actors and actresses were expected to set a wholesome example to the community. JD, IX, 243–245. Brigham Young further expressed his views on theaters and theatrical performances in an open letter to the *Deseret News,* January 11, 1865, and reprinted in McNiff, *Heaven on Earth: A Planned Mormon Society* (Oxford, Ohio, 1940), pp. 231–235. See also John S. Lindsay, *The Mormons and the Theatre* (Salt Lake City, 1905).

77. The active architect of the exterior, Henry Grow, had been a bridge builder in Pennsylvania. He procured the right to the use of the Remington Patent of arch construction of bridges, and applied it on many bridges in the Territory of Utah. At each point on the arches where timbers intersected, four holes were drilled and wooden pegs were driven through. The ends of the pegs were then split with wooden wedges, which were permanently driven into the pegs to secure them solidly. "Wherever the timbers were cracked they were wrapped with green rawhide which contracted when dry and made a tight binding. This rawhide is still steel tight." Grow, "A Historical Study of the Construction of the Salt Lake Tabernacle," pp. 74–76.

78. Grow, p. 78. Some handmade nails were used in the construction of the stand inside the tabernacle.

79. Even today, the guides on Temple Square seat visitors in the rear of the building and drop a pin on the raised platform in the front with audible results.

80. Christoffer Jensen Kempe to C. Widerborg, *Skandinaviens Stjerne* (Copenhagen), January 15, 1866, p. 122. This letter was brought to my attention and translated by Professor William Mulder of the University of Utah.

81. Grow, pp. 161–162.

82. JH, March 16, 1856.

83. "Every Salt Laker of the age of thirty-five years and downward recalls, as a boy, the curious spectacle of six or eight toiling oxen drawing a cart, underneath which was suspended by chains a monster rock from the mountains. It frequently took four days to bring a single rock from the quarry to the Temple Block, and the road was strewn with the wreckage of wagons and carts unable to bear the strain put on them." "The Salt Lake Temple," *Deseret News,* January 1, 1893.

84. Daniel H. Wells, April 6, 1863, JD, X, 139–140.

85. JH, February 26, March 2, 1862.

86. Priesthood groups as far south as Millard County (130 miles south of Salt Lake City), and as far north as the Bear Lake region (130 miles north of Salt Lake City) hired some of their members to go to Salt Lake to work for six months or a year at a time on the temple.

87. Milton R. Hunter, *Brigham Young the Colonizer* (Salt Lake City, 1940), pp. 362–364.

88. Sermon, April 20, 1863, JD, X, 225.

89. *Senate Document No. 986,* 53 Cong., 3 sess., 1895, II, 364.

90. JH, October 8, 1861.

91. Brigham Young to Orson Hyde, JH, October 13, 1861.

92. *Deseret News,* October 1, 1862.

93. George A. Smith sermon, October 8, 1862, *Deseret News,* March 25, 1863; JH, October 19, 1862.

94. *Deseret News,* October 1, 1862.

95. One of the missionaries recalled the experiences of the first few months as follows: ". . . we had a good time for we was united in everything we went at in these days we had no rich nor poor our tents and wagons and what was in them was about all we had, and we had all things common in those days and very common too especially in the eating line for we did not even have sargom [sorghum molasses] in those days[.]" "Biography and Journal of Robert Gardner, Jr.," p. 53, typescript, BYU.

96. George A. Smith to John Fidoe, November 15, 1862, *Millennial Star,* XXV (1863), 61–62.

97. JH, April 16, 1862; *Deseret News,* September 24, 1862.

98. *Ibid.,* May 13, 1863.

99. *Memoirs of John R. Young* (Salt Lake City, 1920), pp. 118–123.

100. *Deseret News,* July 15, 1863.

101. Barrett, "History of the Cotton Mission," p. 226; JH, March 20, 1864.

102. Journal History of St. George Stake, p. [165], CHO.

103. Barrett, p. 152.

104. Brigham Young and H. S. Eldredge, with church help, were setting up a small factory in Salt Lake City; Houtz and Bringhurst were erecting one in Springville, Utah; A. O. Smoot had one under construction in Provo; Ebenezer Hanks was enlarging and improving his factory at Parowan; and a number of individuals had acquired some paraphernalia for working cotton on a family basis. *Deseret News,* November 11, 1863.

105. JH, October 8, 1864; *Millennial Star,* XXVI (1864), 769. Many diaries of pio-

neer settlers in southern Utah describe their abject circumstances, particularly during the "famine" of 1864. One missionary recorded the events prior to the October, 1864, conference resolution as follows: "Now During the year of 1864 there was a scarse time for bread in this Suthern Settlements we had to haul our bread stuff from the Northren Settlements in which the Northren Brethren took the Advantage of our needcesity while we ware oblidgd to sell our wagons and cattle at a Sacrifice to obtain bread to Sustain and uphold and upbuild these places in Dixey South in order that we might Raise our own cotten to Sustain our selvs in cotten clothing and open the pass for the forin emegration and our merchendise to come through this portion of the country from the California gulf and thence up the Colerado . . . ." "Diary of George Laub, 1814–1880, Vol. II," p. 101, typescript, BYU.

106. *Millennial Star,* XXVI (1864), 761.

107. The donations included 16,677 pounds of flour, including 1,500 pounds furnished by the General Tithing Office, and 160 bushels of wheat furnished by Brigham Young in return for cotton. JH, May 31, 1865. The flour in tithing offices in Parowan and Cedar City was also mobilized to meet the emergency.

108. Barrett, p. 153.

109. It was called Brigham Young's Cotton and Woolen Factory, but the evidence clearly indicates that it belonged to Brigham Young as trustee-in-trust of the church, and that it was not his private property.

110. Bleak's notes, JH, October 5, 1866.

111. Barrett, pp. 155–156.

112. George A. Smith to John E. Smith, JH, November 9, 1866.

113. Harrisberg correspondent to Smith, JH, January 4, 1867.

114. Brigham Young to F. D. Richards, October 18, 1867, *Millennial Star,* XXIX (1867), 763.

115. JH, October 7, 1868.

116. Milton R. Hunter, "The Mormons and the Colorado River"; Neff, *History of Utah,* pp. 805–812.

117. Leonard J. Arrington, *Orderville, Utah: A Pioneer Mormon Experiment in Economic Organization* (Logan, Utah [Utah State Agricultural College Monograph Series], 1954).

118. Bancroft, *History of Utah,* p. 726.

119. George C. Naegle, "Sketch of the Life of John Conrad Naegle," typescript, W.P.A. MSS., Library of Congress, p. 6.

120. In March 1887, the St. George Tithing Office reported a supply of 6,610 gallons of wine, valued at 50 cents per gallon. Anderson, *Desert Saints,* p. 320.

121. A Toquerville school teacher wrote in his diary under the date April 10, 1876: "A great deal of wine is manufactured here, and I am grieved to see some elders abuse this blessing, by becoming dissipated with the beverage. Some of the youth in Zion are following diligently the example of thoughtless and foolish fathers. . . ." "Diary of Levi Mathers Savage," typescript, W.P.A. MSS., Library of Congress, p. 17.

122. Anderson, *Desert Saints,* p. 374.

123. Joseph Earle Spencer, "The Middle Virgin River Valley, Utah . . ." (unpublished Ph. D. dissertation, University of California, 1937), p. 138.

124. Daughters of Utah Pioneers of Box Elder County, *History of Box Elder County* (Brigham City, Utah, 1937), pp. 286, *et passim.*

125. "Daughters of Utah Pioneers of Beaver County," *Monuments to Courage: A History of Beaver County* (Beaver, 1947), pp. 209–216; S. A. Kenner, *Utah As It Is*

(Salt Lake City, 1904), pp. 322–323; *Journal of Jesse Nathaniel Smith: The Life Story of a Mormon Pioneer 1834–1906* (Salt Lake City, 1953), pp. 35–36; JH, November 12, 1858, April 13, August 5, 11, 1859, March 26, April 4, July 18, 1860, March 28, June 13, 1861.

126. "Daughters of Utah Pioneers of Summit County," *Echoes of Yesterday: Summit County Centennial History* (Salt Lake City, 1947); JH, July 12, December 23, 30, 1859, April 23, August 24, September 17, 27, October 27, 1860. See also Account Books of Arza E. Hinckley, MSS., in possession of Mrs. A. E. Smith, Tooele, Utah.

127. Perhaps the clearest statement of his policy of autarchy by Brigham Young is in his sermon of June 7, 1863, JD, X, 200ff.

128. "Instructions" of June and July 1865, JD, XI, 113; sermon of June 7, 1863, JD, X, 202.

129. Sermon of April 20, 1863, JD, X, 226. See also sermon of October 9, 1865, JD, XI, 140.

130. JH, April 1, 1867.

131. Elwood Mead, *Irrigation Institutions: A Discussion of the Economic and Legal Questions Created by the Growth of Irrigated Agriculture in the West* (New York, 1907), p. 55.

132. George Thomas, *The Development of Institutions Under Irrigation* (New York, 1920), pp. 61–78; Wells A. Hutchins, *Mutual Irrigation Companies in Utah,* Utah Agricultural Experiment Station Bulletin 199 (Logan, 1927), pp. 28–29.

133. See Arrington, "Taming the Turbulent Sevier," pp. 393–406.

134. Neff, *History of Utah,* p. 759. Durkee also mentioned the fact that titles to real estate in Utah were not perfected. See also JH, November 26, 1864, February 15, 1865, January 18, 1867; *Millennial Star,* XXVII (1865) 62, 207; "Record of the Deseret Irrigation and Navigation Canal Company's Proceedings," MS., CHO.

135. *Resolutions, Acts, and Memorials,* . . . (Great Salt Lake City, 1855 [1856]). Also "Minutes of the General Conference," *Deseret News,* April 9, 1856.

136. *Acts, Resolutions and Memorials* . . . (Great Salt Lake City, 1865), pp. 54–55.

137. Minutes of the Deseret Agricultural and Manufacturing Society, MS., UHS; also HBY, 1861, p. 6.

138. *Deseret News,* March 20, April 3, 1861; JH, April 4, 1861.

139. *Deseret News,* March 4, 6, 1869; February 16, 1872; Minute Book, *passim.*

140. JH, January 28, 29, 1859.

141. JH, February 18, April 9, September 1, 1859, December 15, 1868; *Deseret News,* March 7, 1860.

142. *Measures of Economic Changes in Utah 1847–1947* (Salt Lake City, 1947), p. 51.

143. JH, July 29, 1866, March 30, 1868.

144. *Deseret News,* December 7, 1868.

145. Sermon of April 8, 1868, *ibid.,* May 13, 1868.

146. JH, November 4, 18, 1868; *Deseret News,* December 7, 1868, July 22, 1870; Salt Lake *Herald,* June 25, 1870, June 25, 1872.

147. JH, October 17, 1861.

148. JH, September 22, 1862, January 2, 1863.

149. *Deseret News,* November 9, December 7, 1865.

150. *Ibid.,* December 7, 1865.

151. The wire estimate is based on E. W. Tullidge, *Life of Brigham Young; or, Utah and Her Founders* (New York, 1876), supplement, p. 67. The labor estimate is based upon an incomplete list of community contributions of labor compiled by the

secretary of the Deseret Telegraph, William Clayton. Clayton listed contributions totaling $14,797 by forty-one wards and communities, of which $2,988 was contributed to apply on the Perpetual Emigrating Fund. See the report of February 1, 1868, given in William Clayton Letterpress Copybook, I [1860–1865], [40–47], MS., Bancroft Library.

152. JH, February 18, 1867.

153. *Deseret News Extra,* December 1, 1866.

154. George A. Smith, in JH, May 2, 1870; "Ira N. Hinckley," pp. 8–10.

155. *Deseret News,* April 3, 1867.

156. Statement of the treasurer, George Q. Cannon, *Deseret News,* October 20, 1891.

157. Orson F. Whitney, *History of Utah* (4 vols.; Salt Lake City, 1892–1904), IV, 275; *Deseret News,* June 15, 1889.

158. JH, March 28, 1900.

159. Chauncey W. West in JH, November 21, 1865.

160. Marie Danielsen, *The Trail Blazer: History of the Development of Southeastern Idaho* (Preston, Idaho, 1930), p. 35.

CHAPTER VIII: YEAR OF DECISION: 1869

The most discerning discussions of Mormon economic policies in 1868–69 and thereafter are found in *The Utah Magazine* (3 vols., weekly, Salt Lake City, 1868–1869); the *Mormon Tribune* and *Salt Lake Tribune* (2 vols., weekly, Salt Lake City, 1870–1871); and the *Salt Lake Daily Tribune* until it became a Gentile paper in April 1871. These papers were edited by E. L. T. Harrison, and included contributions by W. S. Godbe, Edward W. Tullidge, W. H. Shearman, and Eli B. Kelsey. The significance of the magazine and of the ideas it espoused was summarized in Edward W. Tullidge, "The Reformation in Utah," *Harper's New Monthly Magazine,* XLIII (1871), 602–610; and in *Tullidge's Quarterly Magazine* (Salt Lake City), I (1880), 14–86. Another participant also reviewed the Godbeite or New Movement in T. B. H. Stenhouse, *The Rocky Mountain Saints . . .* (London, 1873), pp. 622–645.

Other contemporary discussions of the policy crisis of 1869 and its aftermath include: Samuel Bowles, *Our New West* (Hartford, Conn., 1869); John W. Clampitt, *Echoes from the Rocky Mountains* [in Utah 1866–1869] (Chicago, 1889), esp. pp. 253–428; James Bonwick, *The Mormons and the Silver Mines* (London, 1872), particularly, pp. 164–175; John Codman, *The Mormon Country . . .* (New York, 1874); John Todd, *The Sunset Land . . .* (Boston, 1870), esp. 161–212; and two significant articles: Charles Marshall, "Salt Lake City and The Valley Settlements," *Fraser's Magazine* (London), n. s., IV (1871), 97–108; and R. H. Seeley, "The Mormons and their Religion," *Scribner's Monthly* (later, *The Century,* III (1872), 396–408. Travelers' and other accounts of the 1870's include: R. Guy McClellan, *The Golden State: A History of the Region West of the Rocky Mountains . . .* (Philadelphia, 1872), pp. 549–599; Miriam F. Leslie, *California: A Pleasure Trip from Gotham to the Golden State* (New York, 1877), esp. pp. 70–103; George R. Bird, *Tenderfoot Days in Territorial Utah* (Boston, 1918); and the charming and sympathetic account of the wife of Thomas L. Kane, published as Mrs. Eliza D. Kane, *Twelve Mormon Homes Visited in Succession on a Journey through Utah and Arizona* (Philadelphia, 1874).

An attempt to interpret and appraise church policy, in the light of the suggestions of Harrison, Godbe, Tullidge, and others is presented in Leonard J. Arrington, "The Transcontinental Railroad and Mormon Economic Policy," *Pacific Historical Review,*

XX (1951), 143–157, a few paragraphs from which have been incorporated in the present chapter. Other studies of the period include Dwyer, "The Golden Spike is Driven Home," in *The Gentile Comes to Utah; A Study in Religious and Social Conflict (1862–1890)* (Washington, D. C., 1941), pp. 29–58; and the following by Leonard J. Arrington: "Taxable Income in Utah, 1862–1872," *Utah Historical Quarterly,* XXIV (1956), 21–47; "Banking Enterprises in Utah, 1847–1880," *Business History Review,* XXIX (1955), 312–334; and "The Economic Role of Pioneer Mormon Women," *The Western Humanities Review,* IX (1955), 145–164.

1. Certainly there was a sizeable body of Latter-day Saints that feared the end of isolation and the encroachment of "civilization," but most of the Mormon leaders had traveled widely throughout the world and had successfully expounded and defended Mormonism in such centers of culture and commerce as Boston, New York, and London. Their confident view prevailed. See Edward W. Tullidge, "Brigham and His Problem," "The Era of Isolation," "Our Social Redemption," and "Do We Fear Civilization?" in *The Utah Magazine,* II (1868), 66, 102; III (1869), 394, 454.

2. JD, XII, 54.

3. JH, June 1, 1868, November 28, 1873.

4. Approved March 3, 1852. *Laws, Resolutions, Memorials* (Salt Lake City, 1852).

5. The complete minutes of the meeting are given in the *Deseret News,* February 2, 1854.

6. *Ibid.,* March 30, 1854.

7. 12 Stat. L. 489.

8. Photostat No. 1419 furnished the writer by the Union Pacific Railroad Company, Omaha, Nebr. Young subscribed in his own name, but this was after the passage of the Anti-Bigamy Act of 1862 when he was handling virtually all church business in his own name. See Leonard J. Arrington, "The Settlement of the Brigham Young Estate, 1877–1879," *Pacific Historical Review,* XXI (1952), 1–20. The stock was disposed of sometime before Young's death in 1877, possibly in 1872.

9. Dr. T. C. Durant, vice president of Union Pacific, selected Engineer Peter A. Dey to supervise the reconnaissance from the Missouri River to the Salt Lake Valley. Dey organized surveying parties in the fall of 1863 to determine the line. Grenville M. Dodge, "How We Built The Union Pacific Railway," *Senate Document No. 447,* 61st Cong., 2nd sess., pp. 9–11.

10. See reports to Dey and Durant in *Report of Organization and Proceedings of the Union Pacific Railroad Company* (New York, 1864); Union Pacific Railroad, *Report of Thomas C. Durant . . .* (New York, 1866), pp. 1, 12; also letters from Reed to his wife in David H. Mann, "When the Rails Came West," *Improvement Era,* XLII (1939), 77. Reed's letters are in the Union Pacific Museum at Omaha, Nebr., No. 179-B-4.

11. Mann, p. 77.

12. E. W. Tullidge, *History of Northern Utah and Southern Idaho* (Salt Lake City, 1889), p. 533.

13. Bowles, *Our New West,* p. 260.

14. *Millennial Star,* XXI (1859), 719–720; "Inventory of Goods Loaded into Church Wagons, Florence, N. T., May 1859," MS., CHO.

15. Arrington, "Taxable Income in Utah," p. 42. This study gives statistical evidence in support of the view that the distribution of income in Utah in the 1860's was much more equal than in the United States during the same period.

16. The most searching study of this problem is William Mulder, *Homeward to*

Zion: The Mormon Migration from Scandinavia (Minneapolis, 1957). Mulder concludes that the degree of integration of Scandinavians was uncommonly high.

17. Studies of polygamy and its incidence among the Mormons include: Kimball Young, *Isn't One Wife Enough?* (New York, 1954); Stanley S. Ivins, "Notes on Mormon Polygamy," *Western Humanities Review,* X (1956), 229–239; Nels Anderson, *Desert Saints* (Chicago, 1942), pp. 390–419; Thomas F. O'Dea, *The Mormons* (Chicago, 1957), pp. 60–63, 138–140, 245–249; S. George Ellsworth in Joel E. Ricks, ed., *History of a Valley* (Logan, 1956), p. 111; William Mulder, pp. 239–241; Juanita Brooks, "A Close-up of Polygamy," *Harper's Monthly Magazine,* CLXVIII (1934), 299–307; John A. Widstoe, *Evidences and Reconciliations* (Salt Lake City, 1943), pp. 306–319; John Henry Evans, *Joseph Smith, An American Prophet* (New York, 1933), pp. 266–275; and Benjamin F. Johnson to George S. Gibbs, 1903, typescript, Mormon File, Huntington Library.

18. "So far is polygamy from being opposed in spirit to democracy, that it is impossible here, in Salt Lake City, not to see that it is the most levelling of all social institutions — Mormonism the most democratic of religions. A rich man in New York leaves his two or three sons large property, and founds a family; a rich Mormon leaves his twenty or thirty sons each a miserable fraction of his money, and each son must trudge out into the world, and toil for himself. Brigham's sons — those of them who are not gratuitously employed in hard service for the Church in foreign parts — are cattle-drivers, small farmers, ranchmen. One of them was the only poorly clad boy I saw in Salt Lake City. A system of polygamy, in which all the wives, and consequently all the children, are equal before the law, is a powerful engine of democracy." Sir Charles Dilke, M. P., *Greater Britain: A Record of Travel in English-Speaking Countries . . .* (2 vols.; 2nd ed.; London, 1869), I, 179.

19. Leslie, *California: A Pleasure Trip from Gotham to the Golden State,* p. 71.

20. *Deseret News,* May 21, 1868.

21. Sermon of October 7, 1868, JD, XII, 290. See also remarks of Orson Pratt, October 6, 1868, JD, XII, 305–307; and of Brigham Young, JD, XII, 301, 310, 312.

22. See also Hamilton Gardner, "Economic Activities of the Mormons," p. 209, typescript, UU.

23. See arguments in Edward W. Tullidge, "Capital and Labor," and "To Our Home Manufacturers," *Utah Magazine,* II (1868), 78, 90.

24. JH, May 29, 1870.

25. George A. Smith, *The Rise, Progress and Travels of the Church . . .* (2nd ed., Salt Lake City, 1872), p. 60.

26. JH, April 7, 1873.

27. "If Mormons have seemed to oppose the development of mines by Gentiles, it is because they have realized the probability of the influx of a great population, which, through the influence of lying priests and politicians, might seek to re-enact the scenes of Missouri and Kansas. If there were some competent power to make a treaty for the Gentile population, which would be honored, and if it were stipulated that the Mormons would receive fair and honest treatment forever at their hands, the latter would not raise a voice in opposition to their coming." "The Mormons and Mining," in the Salt Lake *Herald,* September 18, 1887.

28. JH, June 5, 1870.

29. See sermons of George A. Smith, *Deseret News,* October 8, 9, 1870; JH, November 8, 1870.

30. Brigham Young to Horace S. Eldredge, JH, February 16, 1871; Brigham Young sermon, April 9, 1871, JD, XIV, 82, 85, 86.

31. *Utah Magazine,* III (October 16, 1869), 376–378.

32. *The Utah Magazine,* III (October 30, 1869), pp. 406ff. contains a review of the debates and trials which led to the excommunications. Tullidge, who was one of the dissenters, wrote that the basic question involved in the Godbeite heresy was whether or not Brigham Young, as president of the church, had the right to dictate to them in all things temporal and spiritual. "The Reformation in Utah," p. 606.

33. The emphasis on conformity to church policy with regard to economic policy provoked Editor Harrison to remark that for a number of years "temporalities" had been "the all-absorbing theme" of Mormonism: "It is temporalities upon the street, in the garden, in the meeting and in the council — temporalities from the rising of the sun to the going down of the same, and from one year's end to another. We have but one kind of subject — houses, fences, dry-goods and money, worlds without end." Among other things, the Godbeites wanted less emphasis on the temporal, and more emphasis on the spiritual aspects of Mormonism. That the two were inseparably bound, they did not deny. "We Are Nothing, If Not Spiritual," *Utah Magazine,* III (October 23, 1869), 390–391.

34. Only the Salt Lake High Council was competent to excommunicate the Godbeites, which it did on October 26, 1869.

35. The rules are given in JH, September 19, 1868. Brigham Young stated that the School of the Prophets was "the place where correction may be given and explanations made upon all matters which pertain to the temporal and spiritual lives of the Saints." JD, XII, 159.

36. JH, August 3, 1872.

37. George Goddard to Joseph F. Smith, JH, September 10, 1874. The School of the Prophets was reconstituted by President John Taylor in 1883, and it functioned for about two years. The group of members was small, however, and the meetings were devoted to such sacred ordinances as the washing of feet, partaking of the Lord's Supper, the relating of visions, and other spiritual experiences. JH, September 28, October 10, 11, 1883.

38. JH, May 22, 28, 29, 1868.

39. George Reynolds to George F. Gibbs, June 4, 1868, *Millennial Star,* XXX (1868), 443.

40. "Last Friday [May 22, 1868], and also yesterday [May 28, 1868] the first class of the School of the Prophets had under consideration the best measures to adopt to get the work of grading the railroad before the people, and *they* engaged upon it. The plan of operation, the letting of contracts, and many of the *minutiae,* were critically discussed. Its advantages to us just now as a people were presented in a very favorable and satisfactory light." Samuel W. Richards to Franklin D. Richards, *Millennial Star,* XXX, 410.

41. Reynolds to Gibbs, *Millennial Star,* XXX (1868), 443.

42. *Ibid.*

43. Richards to Richards, *Millennial Star,* XXX (1868), 410.

44. *Deseret News,* October 8, 9, 1870.

45. "The Railroad — Changes It Will Produce," *ibid.,* August 12, 1868.

46. JH, March 27, June 5, 12, 1869.

47. JH, July 3, 1869.

48. "Our Workmen's Wages," *Utah Magazine,* III (August 28, 1869), 262–264.

49. JH, September 19, 1868.

50. Roberts, *A Comprehensive History of the Church . . .* (6 vols.; Salt Lake City, 1930), V, 209–211, 223. The boycott did not prevent leading Mormons from remaining

on friendly terms with a few "Gentiles," such as, for example, F. H. and S. H. Auerbach. This fact somewhat qualifies the absoluteness of the general boycott against "outsiders."

51. JH, October 3, 1868.

52. JH, March 20, 1869; Diary of Hosea Stout, March 20, 1869, typescript, BYU.

53. JH, March 20, April 24, May 8, 1869, December 9, 1871.

54. JH, September 19, 1868.

55. *Doctrine and Covenants of the Church of the Latter Day Saints* (Kirtland, Ohio, 1835), sec. LXXX, p. 207. In modern editions of the *Doctrine and Covenants* the "Word of Wisdom" comprises Section 89.

56. JH, October 30, 1870.

57. See minutes of the Grantsville School of the Prophets in "Diaries and Records of Joshua R. Clark and Mary Louisa Woolley Clark," James R. Clark, ed., pp. 138–182, typescript, BYU; "Minutes of the School of the Prophets Held in Parowan, 1868–1872," typescript, USU.

58. JH, April 10, 1865.

59. See Emmeline B. Wells, "History of the Relief Society," *Woman's Exponent* (Salt Lake City), XXXII (1903), serialized.

60. *Deseret News,* December 6, 1867.

61. *Ibid.,* April 22, 1868.

62. This is the theme of several sermons. See e. g., sermon of April 6, 1868, *ibid.,* April 29, 1868; also Halbert S. Greaves, "Doctrine on Dress," *Utah Humanities Review* (Salt Lake City), II (1948), 46–47.

63. "If I were a lady . . . I would not have eighteen or twenty yards to drag behind me, so that if I had to turn around I would have to pick up my dress and throw it after me, or, just as a cow does when she kicks over the milk pail, throw out one foot to kick the dress out of the way. That is not becoming, beautiful or convenient . . . you would . . . think there was a six horse team travelling there, with a dozen dogs under the wagon. . . . This is not modesty, gentility or good taste; it does not belong to a lady at all, but to an ignorant, extravagant or vain-minded person, who knows not true principles." See sermons of May 26, August 18, October 9, 1872, *Deseret News,* June 5, August 28, October 23, 1872.

64. Susa Young Gates, *History of the Young Ladies' Mutual Improvement Association of the Church . . .* (Salt Lake City, 1911), pp. 8–9.

65. *Ibid.,* pp. 10–12.

66. *Ibid.*

67. *Woman's Exponent,* IV (1875), 18.

68. Gates, p. 64.

69. "Woman and Her Mission," *Deseret News,* May 19, 1869.

70. *Woman's Exponent,* III (1875), 157.

71. *Ibid.;* also *ibid.,* IV (1875), 52.

72. JH, July 18, 1877.

73. *The Galaxy,* II (1866), 381. Compare Dilke, *Greater Britain,* pp. 178, 181.

CHAPTER IX: MORMON RAILROADS

The earliest history of Utah railroads is in Marcus E. Jones, "Commercial, Industrial, Transportational and other Interests of Utah," *House Exec. Doc. No. 6,* Pt. 2, 52nd Cong., 2nd sess. (Washington 1890), pp. 854ff. A recent attempt at a comprehensive study is David F. Johnson, "The History and Economics of Utah Railroads" (unpublished Master's Thesis, University of Utah, 1947). This is substantially reproduced in Wain Sutton, ed., *Utah: A Centennial History* (3 vols.; New York, 1949), II, 813–873. While it is a capable thesis, Johnson was not able to make use of documents in the National Archives, Library of Congress, New York Public Library, or the Bureau of Railway Economics Library, Washington, D. C. Much information can be found in Howard Fleming, *Narrow Gauge Railways in America* (New York, 1875); testimony before the Pacific Railway Commission, *Senate Exec. Doc. No. 51,* 50th Cong., 1st sess. (9 vols.; Washington, 1887), III, 2154ff.; and also in "The Utah Central and Other Railroads," Kate B. Carter, ed., *Treasures of Pioneer History* (6 vols.; Salt Lake City, 1952–1957), I, 1–36.

Studies of individual roads include: Gustive O. Larson, "Building of the Utah Central: A Unique Cooperative Enterprise," *Improvement Era,* XXVIII (1925), 217–227; Albert L. Zobell, Jr., "Utah Saddles the Iron Horse," *Western Humanities Review,* III (1949), 23–32; David H. Mann, "When the Rails Came West," *Improvement Era,* XLII (1939), 77ff.; Robert L. Wrigley, Jr., "Utah and Northern Railway Co.: A Brief History," *Oregon Historical Quarterly,* XLVIII (1947), 245–253; Merrill D. Beal, "The Story of the Utah Northern Railroad," serialized in Volume I (1957) of *Idaho Yesterdays;* and Leonard J. Arrington, "Railroad Building and Cooperatives, 1869–1879," in Joel E. Ricks, ed., *The History of a Valley: Cache Valley, Utah-Idaho* (Logan, 1956), pp. 172–186. Some paragraphs of the latter have been incorporated in the section on the Utah Northern Railroad. General background sources are: Nelson Trottman, *History of the Union Pacific* (Chicago, 1923); and Robert E. Riegel, *The Story of the Western Railroads* (New York, 1926).

1. Brief reviews of congressional proposals for restricting the powers of the Mormon Church are found in Nels Anderson, *Desert Saints . . .* (Chicago, 1942), pp. 263–265; and Richard D. Poll, "The Political Reconstruction of Utah Territory, 1866–1890," *Pacific Historical Review,* XXVII (1958), 111–126.

2. 12 Stat. L. 501 (1862).

3. E. W. Tullidge, *History of Salt Lake City* (Salt Lake City, 1888), p. 263. Bayard said there was "great danger" that the church would become the owner "in perpetuity of all the valuable land in that Territory, and so afford a nucleus for the permanence of their general institutions. . . ."

4. The act was eventually declared constitutional by the federal supreme court in the case of Reynolds *v.* U. S. (1878), 98 U. S. 145, but the property restrictions were not ruled upon until 1890, when they were also held to be constitutional in 136 U. S. 1–68 (1890).

5. Documentation in support of this view is presented and discussed in Leonard J. Arrington, "The Settlement of the Brigham Young Estate, 1877–1879," *Pacific Historical Review,* XXI (1952), 1–20.

6. See minutes of the mass meeting held on June 10, 1868, *Deseret News,* June 11, 1868.

7. Grenville M. Dodge, "How We Built the Union Pacific Railway," *Senate Doc. No. 447,* 61st Cong., 2nd sess., pp. 27–28.

8. Leland Stanford relates this strategy in a letter to Mark Hopkins, dated Salt Lake City, June 9, 1868: "Brigham . . . and everybody here was dead set for the southern rout. How to meet this bothered me a good deal. . . . There does not seem any of them to be aware of the location from Humboldt Wells to the north end of the Lake. I have not thought it advisable to enlighten them." Cited in George T. Clark, *Leland Stanford . . .* (Stanford, California, 1931), p. 245. It is quite apparent that the

Mormons had no faith in the premature report in the Gentile newspaper, *The Daily Union Vedette,* of October 2, 1867, that it was "a settled fact" that the Pacific Railroad would by-pass Salt Lake City.

9. Jacob R. Perkins, *Trails, Rails and War: The Life of General G. M. Dodge* (Indianapolis, 1929), pp. 229–230. Dodge gave a great deal of credit to the Mormons for their assistance in completing the road in "miraculously" rapid time: ". . . we had the sympathy of the whole Mormon Church with us. President Young giving the matter personal attention, and seeing that the line over the Wasatch Mountains down the canyon and westward was covered by Mormons, to whom we let contracts. . . ." Dodge, p. 27.

10. JH, May 22, 1868.

11. The original contract covered the ninety miles from the head of Echo Canyon to the mouth of Weber Canyon. The contract was later extended to include construction from Ogden to the shores of the Great Salt Lake. *Deseret News,* May 21, 1868; *Millennial Star,* XXX (1868), 410; testimony of John Sharp before the U. S. Pacific Railway Commission, *Senate Exec. Doc. No. 51,* 50th Cong., 1st sess., (1887–1888), pp. 2172–2173. The unit prices specified in the contract appear to have been no greater, and in some cases were materially less, than those allowed other contractors on the line. Union Pacific Railroad File, "Mormons," photostat no. 1420 in possession of the writer. See also account books of Samuel B. Reed, Union Pacific Museum, Nos. 178-B-4 and 179-B-4.

12. *Deseret News,* May 21, 1868.

13. Brigham Young to Franklin D. Richards, JH, May 23, 1868. In June 1868, Vice President Durant instructed the Omaha superintendent as follows: "In consideration of the large grading contract made with Brigham Young, this company will transport passengers on his orders or those of his agents, at the same rate charged contractors, allowing 100 pounds of baggage to each. Children between 5 and 13 at half price. Extra baggage at one-half first freight class rates." U. P. R. R. file, "Mormons," photostat no. 1425 in possession of the writer.

14. Young to Richards, JH, May 23, 1868.

15. Samuel W. Richards to Franklin D. Richards, May 24, 1868, *Millennial Star,* XXX (1868), 410.

16. T. B. H. Stenhouse, *The Rocky Mountain Saints* (New York, 1873), p. 635.

17. Young to Richards, JH, August 4, 1868; Clark, pp. 245–263; John Henry Evans and Minnie Egan Anderson, *Ezra T. Benson: Pioneer — Statesman — Saint* (Salt Lake City, 1947), pp. 311ff.; Neff, *History of Utah,* p. 749.

18. Young to F. D. Richards, JH, August 4, 1868.

19. Clark, *Leland Stanford,* pp. 248, 250, 263.

20. Young to Albert Carrington, JH, January 5, 1869.

21. Young to Carrington, JH, February 4, 1869, *Millennial Star,* XXXI (1869), 164.

22. The ceremonies are given in *Deseret News* for March 9, May 12, 19, 1869. Important and epoch-making as these ceremonies were, Brigham Young attended neither. Piqued at the roads' decision to bypass Salt Lake City, the Mormon leader, on the very day the U. P. was celebrating its entrance into Ogden, was organizing the Utah Central Railroad Company to construct a branch line from Ogden to Salt Lake. At the time of the Promontory celebration, he was on a tour of Mormon settlements south of Salt Lake City.

23. JH, December 31, 1868, January 1, 4, 1869.

24. Testimony of David H. Peery, mayor of Ogden, *Senate Exec. Doc. 51,* pp. 2208–2210.

25. Under date of February 2, 1869, Charles Smith wrote to a friend: "A few weeks ago he [Brigham Young] went to Ogden to make some purchases of the brethren, of land, for So as to accomodate the directors of the railway with space enough for their purpose[.] after talking with the brethren, they came freely forward, and gave up their claims. Dr. Durant was present . . . he said their was not another Man on earth could have done the same . . ." "Diary of Charles Smith 1819–1905," February 2, 1869, typescript, BYU.

26. The fascinating rise and fall of Corinne is told in Jesse Jameson, "Corinne: A Study of a Freight Transfer Point" (unpublished Master's Thesis, University of Utah, 1952); and Bernice Gibbs Anderson, "The Gentile City of Corinne," *Utah Historical Quarterly,* IX (1941), 141–154.

27. Among the papers of William West Durant in the Manuscripts Division of the Library of Congress is a memorandum, dated August 6, 1869, that a total of $550,000 had been paid to Brigham Young by the U. P. R. R. Co. in a series of five installments, dated October 10, 1868, and January 12, 20, February 5, and 19, 1869. Sometime later a short-term note, "with a stiff rate of interest," was given to Young by the railroad in the amount of $346,017.23. U. P. R. R. file, "Mormons," photostat no. 1423 in possession of the writer.

28. Mormon sources (for example, *Deseret News,* August 24, 1869) leave the impression that U. P. owed as much as $1,125,000 on the church contract. On the other hand, in the "Boston records" in the Museum vault of the Union Pacific Railroad Company in Omaha, Brigham Young himself asserted, in a letter to Oliver Ames dated May 19, 1869, that the unpaid balance amounted to "some three-fourths of a million dollars." It is possible that the $750,000 figure was based on the original contract, and that the delay in payment led the Mormons to add interest and other charges, so that by the fall of 1869 the Mormons could regard the railroad's debt to them as upwards of $1,000,000.

29. Evans and Anderson, p. 318.

30. *Deseret News,* September 6, 1869.

31. Levi O. Leonard and Jack T. Johnson, *A Railroad to the Sea* (Iowa City, 1939), p. 237. U. P. records definitely indicate that Brigham Young, although a stockholder of U. P., "did not participate in the stockholders' agreement with the Trustees under the Ames and Davis construction contracts, and therefore did not share in the distribution of profits under these contracts, nor under the Credit Mobilier of America." U. P. R. R. file, "Mormons," photostat no. 1425 in possession of the writer.

32. Sharp to Carrington, JH, August 3, 1869.

33. Sharp to Carrington, JH, August 3, 1869.

34. Young to Carrington, JH, September 4, 1869.

35. Young to Oliver Ames, April 24, 1870, "Boston Records," U. P. R. R. Museum.

36. U. P. R. R. file, "Mormons," photostat no. 1424 in possession of the writer. This source, however, indicates a balance due Young of only $70,000, and professes to know nothing of the $200,000 claimed by Young.

37. Joseph Hall, *Millennial Star,* XXXI (1869), 648.

38. *Utah Central Railroad Company to Horace S. Eldredge and Abram O. Smoot, Trustees, First Mortgage, dated January 1, 1870* (New York, 1870).

39. JH, January 15, 1870.

40. JH, July 30, 1870.

41. JH, August 6, 1870.

42. JH, August 18, 1870.

43. At least one of these $1,000 bonds was purchased by the Sunday School of

Richmond, Utah. This bond was finally sold in February 1890 for the full face value. *Marriner Wood Merrill and His Family,* edited by M. C. Merrill (Salt Lake City, 1937), p. 107.

44. JH, October 7, 1870.

45. See G. M. Dodge and Sidney Dillon to Oliver Ames, December 7, 1870, and related statements, U. P. R. R. file, "Mormons," photostats nos. 1426 and 1427 in possession of the writer. Learning of the Mormon financial predicaments, and of their overtures to C. P. Huntington of Central Pacific, U. P. loaned the money to prevent C. P. from gaining a dominant position in the Salt Lake Valley.

46. JH, May 20, 1871.

47. "Diary of L. John Nuttall," entries for January 4, April 10, 1878, typescript, BYU.

48. Stenhouse, *Rocky Mountain Saints,* pp. 635–636.

49. Orson F. Whitney, *History of Utah* (4 vols.; Salt Lake City, 1892–1904), II, 244. Stenhouse, who is totally unreliable on Young's connection with the Utah Central, wrote that Young's profits were said to be $250,000. *Rocky Mountain Saints,* p. 666.

50. "Diary of L. John Nuttall," December 21, 31, 1877, January 4, April 10, 1878. Nuttall was a key figure in the examination of Brigham Young's accounts.

51. See also Arrington, "The Settlement of the Brigham Young Estate," p. 14.

52. *Deseret News,* March 4, 1869.

53. "Articles of Association of the Utah Central Railway Company," Bureau of Railway Economics Library, Transportation Building, Washington, D. C. The territorial legislature had passed a railroad incorporation law in February 1869.

54. Other officers were William Jennings, vice president and director; John W. Young, secretary; Feramorz Little and Christopher Layton, directors.

55. It was supposed at the time that this was a private investment of Brigham Young. I have explained that this and subsequent stock purchases by him were church investments in "The Settlement of the Brigham Young Estate," p. 14. It is true that the testimony of John Sharp, one of the promoters of the Utah Central, as given before the Pacific Railway Commission in 1887, places Brigham Young's interest in the Utah Central as a personal one. In view of the conclusiveness of the evidence on the other side, I am convinced that Sharp did not know about Brigham Young's financial arrangements with the church. See *Senate Exec. Doc. No. 51,* 50th Cong., 1st sess., III, 2154ff.

56. *Deseret News,* March 10, 1869.

57. Young to Carrington, JH, April 13, 1869.

58. JH, May 12, 1869.

59. Young to Carrington, JH, May 22, 1869.

60. *Deseret News,* May 17, 1869.

61. A newspaper account of the visits of Brigham Young and others to the settlements along the line, and their response, is found in the *Deseret News,* June 16, 18, 1869. As there was no timber between Ogden and Salt Lake City, most of the ties seem to have been taken from Pine and Dry Canyons, east of Tooele, and were drawn from there by team 12 miles to the Great Salt Lake, whence they were rafted to Farmington, Davis County, for distribution north and south. John A. Bevan, Salt Lake *Herald,* January 3, 1920.

62. The enterprise was inaugurated in the summer of 1869 after Congress had adjourned and for that reason the firm had not been able to apply for a right of way through the public domain. (The officers had assumed it would be given without

question.) When the road was completed, the application was made, and a year later, on January 10, 1871, church officials received word that the bill granting the right of way had been passed by Congress on December 15, 1870, and approved by the president. *The Grants, Rights, and Privileges of the Utah Central Railroad Company of the Territory of Utah, under National and Territorial Legislation: The Articles of Association, and by-laws thereof, and the Mortgage executed by the Company to Secure their First Mortgage Bonds* (Salt Lake City, 1871). This document is in the Library of Congress, but the Articles of Association have unfortunately been removed. The act granting right of way is also found in *House Exec. Doc. No. 26,* 46th Cong., 3rd sess., p. 974.

63. *Deseret News,* June 10, 1869.

64. Joseph Belnap, Salt Lake *Herald,* January 1, 1920.

65. John Martin, in *Treasures of Pioneer History,* I, 6; *Autobiography of Christopher Layton,* John Q. Cannon, ed. (Salt Lake City, 1911), p. 160.

66. A. I. and A. P. Stone received $100 of the amount due them in "railway tickets good for passage between Ogden and Salt Lake." *Deseret News,* January 3, 1920. John Farrington, a lad of seventeen who assisted in the grading, received compensation in "socks, overalls and car tickets." Salt Lake *Herald,* January 1, 1920. Thomas Roberts of Woods Cross, who drove an ox-team and hauled dirt for the roadbed, made a dollar a day "in transportation from Woods Cross to Salt Lake." He added that the fare was 70 cents round trip, so that: "I would work nearly all day for my railroad fare." *Treasures of Pioneer History,* I, 26.

67. William Jennings, who was vice president of the Utah Central, stated that the grading was largely financed with tithing and P. E. F. funds. Kate B. Carter, ed., *Heart Throbs of the West* (12 vols.; Salt Lake City, 1936–1951), VII, 441. Elias Morris substantiates this view in a letter to Albert Carrington, October 11, 1869, *Millennial Star,* XXXI (1869), 741. Since tithing resources consisted of contributions of livestock, produce, merchandise, and labor, the widespread reports that laborers were paid in foodstuffs and clothing appear to be true. See also Morris to Carrington, February 23, 1870, *ibid.,* XXXII (1870), 187; and Zobell, "Utah Saddles the Iron Horse."

68. *Treasures of Pioneer History,* I, 26.

69. *Deseret News,* September 14, 22, 1869; *Millennial Star,* XXXI (1869), 744, 792; XXXII (1870), 157, 173, 185–186.

70. A complete account of the ceremonies is found in the *Deseret News,* January 11, 1870.

71. *Ibid.*

72. George A. Smith to William H. Hooper, JH, January 11, 1870. See also *Autobiography of Christopher Layton,* p. 162. Smith had written previously: "Our golden-browed neighbors of Nevada and Colorado have been memorializing the general government for years for subsidies of land and money to enable them to connect their principal cities with the great national railroad. Utah, containing an agricultural and not a mining population, builds her road and memorializes Congress afterwards." Smith to N. S. Elderkin, JH, November 11, 1869.

73. Testimony of John Sharp, *Senate Exec. Doc. No. 51,* III, 2156–2157.

74. *Ibid.,* pp. 2154–2155.

75. Gould had bought into the U. P. in 1877, but did not "interfere" with Utah Central until 1879. Evidence of autonomy after 1872 and before 1879 is seen in the following incident. In June 1874 the U. P., according to the *Deseret News,* "suddenly raised the freight on coal from Echo to Ogden from $1.50 to $3.76 per ton." The purpose of this action, according to the editor of the *News* was "to make a monopoly of

the coal trade in favor of the Union Pacific Company, who own the Rock Springs [Wyoming] mine, and extends not only to this City [Salt Lake City], but also westward to Sacramento and eastward to Omaha, the tariff having been raised eastward as well as west to Ogden." The Utah Central Railroad, although a U. P. branch, "refused to receive their coal under the increased rates." This action, of course, greatly injured the Utah Central, which carried upwards of 45,000 tons of coal per year, but the management, still Mormon, refused to carry coal under such a "hold-up." See "The Coal Question," *ibid.*, July 1, 1874.

76. Zobell, p. 29–30; Young to Carrington, JH, July 23, 1872. Brigham Young's complimentary pass was salvaged from a mass of Utah Central papers destroyed by Union Pacific, and was reproduced in *Railway Age, LXXXVIII* (June 14, 1930), 1438.

77. David H. Mann, "Brigham Young's Road," *Railroad Magazine,* XXXVII (1945), 29; also C. Frank Steele, "What Ever Happened to Brigham Young's Private Car?" *Salt Lake Tribune,* February 24, 1952.

78. Brigham Young to editor, New York *Herald,* JH, April 10, 1873.

79. Edward L. Sloan, *Gazeteer of Utah and Salt Lake City Directory* (Salt Lake City, 1874), p. 30.

80. Edward W. Tullidge, *History of Northern Utah and Southern Idaho* (Salt Lake City, 1889), 131; *Deseret News,* June 4, November 1, 17, 1869; *Millennial Star,* XXXII (1870), 121.

81. Contemporary reactions to U. P. policies are discussed in Leonard J. Arrington, "Utah's Coal Road in the Age of Unregulated Competition," *Utah Historical Quarterly,* XXIII (1955), 35–63.

82. *Deseret News,* October 29, 1873; Salt Lake *Herald,* October 23, 1873; Fleming, *Narrow Gauge Railways,* pp. 89–90.

83. John Morgan, in Salt Lake *Herald,* July 22, 1874.

84. JH, July 2, 1874.

85. Brigham Young to H. S. Eldredge, JH, April 11, 1871.

86. "The Railroad and the Mines," Salt Lake *Herald,* August 22, 1871; also John Sharp's interview for the *New York Sun,* as found in JH, July 19, 1871.

87. At the same time a petition was prepared requesting Congress to grant right of way through the public domain. The Utah Southern Railroad Act, which granted the request, was passed in February 1871.

88. The articles of incorporation are filed in the General Records of the Department of Interior, National Archives. The officers at the time of incorporation were William Jennings, president; John Sharp, vice president; S. J. Jonasson, secretary; James T. Little, treasurer; Feramorz Little, superintendent of construction; and Jesse W. Fox, chief engineer.

89. Young to Eldredge, JH, February 16, 1871.

90. JH, June 20, 1872. The spur was built by the Salt Lake City Railroad Company, also a church-assisted line.

91. *Deseret News,* August 10, September 27, October 28, 1872.

92. A. L. Zobell, Sr., "I've Been Working on the Railroad," cited in "Utah Saddles the Iron Horse," pp. 31–32.

93. Young to Carrington, JH, April 19, 1873. The Wasatch and Jordan Valley Railway was constructed in 1873 by Mormon businessmen and eastern mining interests.

94. *Utah Southern Railroad Company to William H. Hooper and Henry B. Hammond, Trustees, First Mortgage, dated July 1, 1871* (New York City, 1871).

95. Immediately before and after July 1, 1871, William Jennings was listed as the president of the road. The promotion of the Utah Southern, as already mentioned, was

handled by the leading stockholders of the Utah Central. As the latter road was still controlled by the trustee-in-trust in 1871, the attachment of Brigham Young's name was perfectly proper.

96. JH, April 18, May 4, 29, 1872.

97. George A. Smith to J. S. Harris, JH, May 14, 1872.

98. Testimony of John Sharp, *Senate Exec. Doc. No. 51,* III, 2155–2157.

99. Young to Carrington, JH, December 11, 1872, April 19, 1873.

100. Salt Lake *Herald,* July 23, 1873.

101. JH, July 21, 1873.

102. Salt Lake *Herald,* July 23, 1873.

103. *Deseret News,* July 28, 1873.

104. *Ibid.*

105. Salt Lake *Herald,* July 31, 1873.

106. Smith to Carrington, September 12, 1873, *Millennial Star,* XXXV (1873), 634.

107. See Brigham Young's interesting address in JH, November 28, 1873.

108. Salt Lake *Herald,* November 1, 1873.

109. *Deseret News,* November 30, 1874.

110. The original officers of the Utah Southern Extension were all prominent Mormon businessmen: William Jennings, president; John Sharp, vice president; William H. Hooper, H. S. Eldredge, Feramorz Little, James Sharp, and John Sharp, Jr.; directors; and James T. Little, secretary and treasurer. *Deseret News,* December 31, 1874; incorporation papers, the Salt Lake County Clerk's Office, Salt Lake City.

111. At the time of Brigham Young's death in 1877, his estate owned 894 shares of Utah Southern Railroad stock and 29 first mortgage Utah Southern bonds. Some of these were awarded to the church and some to the Young heirs.

112. The extension was financed, and the bond issue of 1871 redeemed, by the issuance of $1,950,000 in bonds on July 1, 1879. See *Utah Southern Railroad Company to William H. Hooper and James M. Ham, Trustees, General Mortgage, dated July 1, 1879* (New York, 1879).

113. Salt Lake *Herald,* March 3, 29, June 13, 1879.

114. *Ibid.,* January 16, 1879.

115. *Territorial Enquirer* (Provo), March 8, 1879.

116. Marcus E. Jones, "Commercial, Industrial, Transportational and other Interests of Utah," *House Exec. Doc. No. 6,* Pt. 2, 52nd Cong., 2nd sess. (Washington, 1890), p. 855.

117. Preston to Young, August 15, 1871, published in *Biographies,* p. 51, supplement to Edward W. Tullidge, *History of Northern Utah and Southern Idaho.*

118. Young to Preston, *Biographies,* p. 51.

119. Tullidge, p. 52. Cf. the statement of Moses Thatcher to a conference in Pocatello, Idaho, as published in *The Deseret Weekly* (Salt Lake City), July 26, 1890, p. 143.

120. The directors were: Joseph Richardson and Le Grand Lockwood (New York City), William B. Preston and Hezekiah Thatcher (Logan), Franklin D. Richards (Ogden), Lorenzo Snow and Samuel Smith (Brigham City), William Maughan (Wellsville), O. N. Liljenquist (Hyrum), William Hyde (Hyde Park), Samuel Roskelley (Smithfield), Marriner W. Merrill (Richmond), and Lorenzo H. Hatch (Franklin).

121. These were Lorin Farr, from Ogden to Willard; Samuel Smith, from Willard to the border of Cache Valley; Joseph West, from Brigham City to Corinne; William B.

Preston, in the south end of Cache Valley; and Marriner W. Merrill, in the north end of Cache Valley and beyond.

122. *Deseret News,* August 27, 1871.

123. *Ibid.,* July 1, 1872.

124. "History of Goudy E. Hogan, 1829–1898," typescript, BYU, pp. 38–40. Similar accounts of other work-parties are given in the diaries of Ralph Smith, entries for August 23, 1871, *et. seq.;* and of Henry Ballard, entry of October 30, 1871, typescripts, USU.

125. *Deseret News,* February 4, 1873.

126. L. H. Hatch, Salt Lake *Herald,* March 15, 1873.

127. *Deseret News,* February 6, 1874.

128. JH, February 7, 1874.

129. Cache County appropriated $4,000 to the company on January 6, 1873. Other counties probably gave similar assistance. *Utah Pioneer and Apostle Marriner Wood Merrill and His Family,* p. 67.

130. JH, June 28, 1873; *Deseret News,* June 30, 1873.

131. "History of Goudy E. Hogan," pp. 41–42.

132. JH, December 11, 1874.

133. The General Records of the Department of Interior, National Archives, contain documents indicating that on November 1, 1871, the Utah Northern issued 1,012 bonds of a series of 1,500 bonds of $1,000 denomination, payable in 20 years, and bearing 7 per cent interest. John Sharp testified that the Richardsons spent about $700,000 on the road. *Senate Exec. Doc. No. 51,* III, 2173. Moses Thatcher stated that the bonded indebtedness of the Utah Northern was "within a fraction of only a third" of that of the Utah Central. JH, December 11, 1874. The Utah Central and Utah Southern bonded indebtedness at the time was about $2,000,000.

134. The Utah Northern distributed $780,000 to residents of Cache Valley for construction, and this was largely in the form of capital stock in the enterprise. *Utah Pioneer and Apostle Marriner Wood Merrill and His Family,* pp. 64–65.

135. Testimony of Sharp, p. 2173.

136. JH, December 11, 1874.

137. As reported by Moses Thatcher, *Deseret Weekly,* July 26, 1890, p. 143.

138. Sharp, p. 2173; *Deseret Weekly,* July 26, 1890, p. 143. Gould testified before the Pacific Railway Commission, *op. cit.,* p. 572, that he paid about 40 cents on the dollar for Utah Northern bonds and received a controlling interest in Utah Northern stock "as a bonus." Later in 1875, according to his statement, he turned the bonds and stock over to Union Pacific at the same price they had cost him. Gould may have turned the stock over to U. P. in 1877 rather than in 1875.

139. JH, April 17, 1878; Logan Temple Letter Book, No. 1 [1877–1878], MS., CHO.

140. Utah Northern vouchers were to be settled for in stock certificates at the face figures of the vouchers. Union Pacific also promised that the new company would have the privilege of selling coal — a privilege previously denied Utah Northern by U. P., which exercised a monopoly on the coal trade in Utah. The directors of the new company included Royal M. Bassett, Sidney Dillon, Jay Gould, Joseph Richardson, John Sharp, Monroe Salisbury, and Benjamin Richardson of Union Pacific, and Moses Thatcher, W. B. Preston, George W. Thatcher, M. W. Merrill, Lorin Farr, Samuel Smith, and Milton D. Hammond of the Utah Northern. *Deseret News,* October 6, 1877.

141. Salt Lake *Herald,* October 5, 1877.

142. *Deseret News,* April 3, 1878.

143. Fleming, *Narrow Gauge Railways,* pp. 91–92.

144. Of the outstanding shares at the time of incorporation, 395 were held by Sidney Dillon, 395 shares by Benjamin Richardson, 1 share by S. H. H. Clark, and 1 share each by all Mormons who were to be connected with the road as officers and managers. Directors of the new company were Dillon, Clark, Richardson, John Sharp, William Jennings, and Royal M. Bassett, of the U. P., and Moses Thatcher from Cache Valley, who was the only holdover from the Utah Northern. Incorporation papers, Salt Lake County Clerk's Office, Salt Lake City.

145. *Deseret News,* July 9, 1879; Salt Lake *Herald,* March 17, 1881. The 1880 report of the controller of the Territory of Idaho called the line "the most important narrow gauge in the world." In 1880 a net profit of $247,000 was realized. 17,000 passengers were carried, 35,600 tons of freight were handled, and 293 employees were at work for the line. *Biennial Report of the Territorial Controller, 1879–1880* (Boise, 1880).

146. The Oregon Short Line was built during the years 1878–1884, from Granger, Wyoming, across southern Idaho, to Huntington, Oregon. It connected with the U & N at Pocatello in 1882. The line was built to give Union Pacific access to the Pacific Northwest.

147. A diary account of one workman is that of Ralph Smith, typescript, USU.

148. Merrill reported that when the road had been completed to Eagle Rock he wanted to stop, but President John Taylor "advised him to continue." Merrill reported that he "could have made money for himself out of the contract, if he had acted as a Gentile would have done, but the people got the benefit of every cent of the profit." JH, December 17, 1896. Merrill's salary was $150 per month.

149. The original stockholders were John W. Young, Brigham Young, Jr., Seymour B. Young, Le Grand Young, John N. Pike, Moses Thatcher, W. B. Preston, P. L. Williams, Hamilton G. Park and William W. Riter. Each of these men subscribed for a few shares of stock with the exception of John W. Young, who subscribed for 170 shares. Incorporation papers, Salt Lake City Railroad Company, Office of the Secretary of State, Salt Lake City.

150. Minute Book of the Salt Lake City Railroad Company, April 29, 1872, MS., archives of the Utah Power and Light Company, Salt Lake City.

151. In 1878, the capital stock was reduced and in the settlement of the Brigham Young estate the following year the church received 2,165 shares out of the 2,800 outstanding. Their market value at the time was estimated at $55,050. *Deseret News,* June 30, 1879; also Stock Certificate Account Book, MS., CHO.

152. It will be recalled that the Warm Springs Bath House was originally developed by the church as a resort for invalids and others. It was later given to the City of Salt Lake, which owned it during the last quarter of the nineteenth century.

153. Minute Book of the Salt Lake City Railroad Company; *Deseret News,* October 3, 1873, April 17, May 8, 1875, May 5, 1877; JH, June 20, 1872, May 8, 1875; also articles by Harold Snow, *Deseret News,* August 14, 1926; Jack Thomas, Salt Lake *Telegram,* June 4, 1934; and C. W. McCullough, "The Passing of the Streetcar," *Utah Historical Quarterly,* XXIV (1956), 123–129.

154. Clara Hedges Anderson, *Heart Throbs,* V, 456–457.

155. In testimony before a House committee on territories considering Statehood for Utah, Franklin S. Richards, the church attorney, admitted that the church held one-third of the stock of the company and said that the stock had come into the pos-

session of the church "partly by donation and partly otherwise." Salt Lake *Herald,* January 20, 1889.

156. W. N. Peterson in *Heart Throbs,* V, 457–460; incorporation papers, Office of the Secretary of State; Minute Book in possession of the Utah Power and Light Company, Salt Lake City; *Deseret News,* December 20, 1872, August 23, 1873, June 30, 1879; Salt Lake *Herald,* September 3, 1872, August 26, 1873; JH, December 22, 1872, April 19, October 3, 1873.

CHAPTER X: THE COOPERATIVE MOVEMENT

The first published treatise on Mormon mercantile cooperation was by the Utah historian Edward W. Tullidge, in *Tullidge's Quarterly Magazine,* I, 353–432. This was followed by [Dyer D. Lum], *Social Problems of Today; or, the Mormon Question in its Economic Aspects* (Port Jervis, N. Y., 1886). In the same year, Professor Amos G. Warner made a similar study of "Cooperation Among the Mormons," which was published by the American Economic Association in 1887 as part of a larger monograph entitled *Three Phases of Cooperation in the West* (Publications of the American Economic Association, Vol. II, no. 1), 106–119. Hamilton Gardner contributed brilliant insight in "Cooperation Among the Mormons," *Quarterly Journal of Economics,* XXXI (1917), 461–499.

These studies culminated in an outstanding dissertation by Professor Arden Beal Olsen which made liberal use of hitherto unavailable minute books, ledgers, and manuscript materials in the possession of Z.C.M.I. and other primary and secondary sources: "The History of Mormon Mercantile Cooperation in Utah" (unpublished Ph. D. dissertation, University of California, Berkeley, 1935), which has been summarized in "Mormon Mercantile Cooperation in Utah," *Journal of Marketing,* VI (1941), 136–142; and "Merchandising Struggle in Early Utah; the Success of Z.C.M.I.," in Harold H. Dunham, ed., *1950 Brand Book,* Volume VI (Denver, 1951), 283–306. Specific treatments of cooperative enterprises include Ivan J. Barrett, "History of the Cotton Mission and Cotton Culture in Utah" (unpublished Master's Thesis, Brigham Young University, 1947); Leonard J. Arrington, "The Provo Woolen Mills: Utah's First Large Manufacturing Establishment," *Utah Historical Quarterly,* XXI (1953), 97–116, and "Railroad Building and Cooperatives, 1869–1879," in Joel E. Ricks, ed., *The History of a Valley: Cache Valley, Utah-Idaho* (Logan, Utah, 1956), pp. 170–204.

1. See Brigham Young sermons in JH, October 6, 1850, October 8, 1855.

2. Summary of Instructions given by President Brigham Young to the people on his visit to Utah, Juab and Sanpete Counties in June and July 1865, as reported in *Deseret News,* August 9, 1865.

3. JH, December 23, 1866; also his letter to a group of sixteen non-Mormon merchants who volunteered to sell out to the church and leave the territory in JH, December 21, 1866.

4. JH, July 4, 1860.

5. JH, July 11, 1860.

6. Regarding the events preceding the cooperative movement church officials wrote: "A condition of affairs existed among us which was favorable to the growth of riches in the hands of a few at the expense of the many. A wealthy class was being rapidly formed in our midst whose interests, in the course of time, were likely to be diverse from those of the rest of the community. The growth of such a class was dangerous to our union; and, of all people, we stand most in need of union and to

have our interests identical. Then it was that the Saints were counseled to enter into co-operation. In the absence of the necessary faith to enter upon a more perfect order revealed by the Lord unto the Church, this was felt to be the best means of drawing us together and making us one." Circular to the Latter-day Saints of the General Authorities of the Church, JH, July 10, 1875.

7. *Deseret News,* November 2, 23, 1865.

8. *Deseret News,* November 30, 1865. Italics in original.

9. Circular from the First Presidency "To the Presidents, Bishops and Saints Generally," JH, January 9, 1867. Paragraphing supplied. The circular was signed by Brigham Young, Heber C. Kimball, and Daniel H. Wells.

10. The Utah Produce Company has been discussed in Leonard J. Arrington, "Agricultural Price Control in Pioneer Utah," *Agricultural History,* XXX (1956), 111–113.

11. *Tullidge's Quarterly Magazine,* I (1881), 358.

12. *Ibid.*

13. JH, September 16, 1868.

14. JH, September 19, 1868.

15. JH, October 3, November 28, 1868, May 22, 29, 1869, and others. The minutes of the School of the Prophets indicate several instances in which members, including a brother of Brigham Young, were brought before the school and rebuked for violating the principle of cooperation and patronizing non-Mormon establishments. On one occasion, a certain brother "was charged with having bought goods from a Jew. He confessed, asked forgiveness and promised not to do so any more." JH, November 28, 1868.

16. JH, July 10, 1875.

17. Another motivating factor in the institution of "cooperation" may have been Mormon envy of Gentile mercantile success. Brigham Young often recited the many advantages to the church if the sums paid over to Gentiles could be "saved" to the church and devoted to such causes as missionary work, immigration, temple-building, and home manufactures.

18. JH, October 6, 1868.

19. See *Deseret News,* October 10, 1868.

20. "Diary of Charles Smith, 1819–1905," typescript, BYU. Some punctuation and capitalization supplied to add clarity.

21. *Ibid.,* October 29, 1868.

22. Besides Brigham Young, the officers were John M. Bernhisel, vice president; William Clayton, secretary; David O. Calder, treasurer; Brigham Young, John M. Bernhisel, George A. Smith, George Q. Cannon, Horace S. Eldredge, Henry W. Lawrence, and William Jennings, directors. *Deseret News,* October 16, 1868. W. H. Hooper later replaced Bernhisel as vice president; T. G. Webber replaced Clayton as secretary; and Thomas Williams succeeded Calder as treasurer. Lawrence resigned his directorate in 1869.

23. Olsen, "History of Mormon Mercantile Cooperation," p. 80.

24. The authorized capitalization of the 1870 charter was $1,000,000. Z.C.M.I. was reincorporated in 1895 and in 1945.

25. This provision was not in the charter by which the institution was incorporated on December 1, 1870, although there were no non-Mormon stockholders at the time.

26. JH, October 29, 1868; *Deseret News,* November 14, 1868. A contemporary traveler wrote that the Gentiles ridiculed the iconography on Mormon stores. "The eye they irreverently call the 'bull's eye,' and say it is put there because many of the

Mormons cannot read, but can follow the eye, and hit upon the proper stores." W. L. Humason, *From the Atlantic Surf to the Golden Gate . . .* (Hartford, Conn., 1869), p. 32.

27. Brigham Young to Albert Carrington, JH, November 18, 1868.

28. Brigham Young apparently left the planning of Z.C.M.I. up to coöperating Mormon merchants. Edward W. Tullidge, who had personal knowledge of some of the events connected with the founding of Z.C.M.I., wrote that the committee appointed in 1868–69 to commence operations waited upon the president for advice. He replied "Go to work and do it." When they pressed him further, Young again replied, "Go to work and do it." These replies reveal the confidence the church president reposed in such men as William Jennings, William H. Hooper, and Horace S. Eldredge, who, as Tullidge wrote, "*could* go to work and do it" better than Young could advise them. *Tullidge's Quarterly Magazine,* I, 367.

29. Olsen, p. 81.

30. *Ibid.,* p. 93. The pricing committee, consisting of H. B. Clawson, W. S. Godbe, and H. W. Naisbitt, had made its first report on December 12, 1868.

31. *Ibid.,* p. 103.

32. George A. Smith to Jesse N. Smith, JH, October 22, 1868; *Tullidge's Quarterly Magazine,* I, 386–388.

33. As reported in *ibid.,* I, 366.

34. *Ibid.,* III (1884), 253–254.

35. Olsen, p. 99.

36. *Ibid.,* p. 100.

37. *Ibid.,* p. 103.

38. *Ibid.,* pp. 105–107, 169.

39. *Ibid.,* p. 160.

40. *Ibid.,* p. 104.

41. *Ibid.,* p. 162.

42. *Deseret News,* March 3, 1870.

43. Olsen, pp. 161–162.

44. Incorporation papers, County Clerk, Salt Lake City, Utah. Also see *Zion's Cooperative Mercantile Institution: Agreement, Order, Certificate of Incorporation and By-Laws* (Salt Lake City, 1870), among the Mormon pamphlets, Harvard University Library. It is not usually recognized that Brigham Young's investment was church-financed. The best evidence is the treatment of church shares in the settlement of the Brigham Young estate. A total of 1,180 shares, valued at $118,000, out of 1,216 shares held by Young, were awarded to the church at that time. "Diary of L. John Nuttall," April 10, 1878, typescript, BYU. The original subscription of 772 shares in 1870 and prior years was increased by stock dividends in 1870, 1871, 1872, and 1873. The result was about equivalent to 1,180 shares. In addition, Brigham Young purchased in the name of the church 1,000 shares in 1872, and 500 shares in 1876. The church's holdings by 1878 were 2,730 shares, which, with an additional stock dividend in 1880, and other small investments and gifts, brought the church's holdings to 3,664 shares by 1885. This represented about 36 per cent of the $1,000,000 worth of Z.C.M.I. stock outstanding in 1885. The dividends are listed in an appendix to Olsen. Also see Olsen, p. 196.

45. JH, April 10, 1869.

46. Olsen, pp. 130–133, found at least 150 co-op stores organized in Utah from 1868–1880. The writer knows of a few overlooked by Dr. Olsen.

47. Sermon of April 6, 1869, JD, XII, 374–375.

48. Sermon of April 8, 1869, JD, XIII, 35.

49. JD, XIII, 36.

50. "Minute Book of the Logan Co-operative Mercantile Institution," p. 8, typescript, USU.

51. See Olsen's discussion of various local cooperatives, pp. 126–129.

52. During the depressions of the 1890's and 1930's, Z.C.M.I., as the principal creditor, took over the management of many of these stores in order to secure payment of debts. As many as thirty of these stores was under Z.C.M.I. management in the 1930's.

53. Brigham Young saw to it that the stores gave exclusive patronage to Z.C.M.I. On March 19, 1869, for example, he met with the retail storekeepers in Salt Lake Valley and "made enquiries relative to the course they meant to pursue in regard to making their purchases. All agreed to buy their goods from the parent store." JH, March 19, 1869.

54. To use the words of Peter Maughan, bishop of the Cache Valley Ward, and vice president of the Logan Co-operative Mercantile Institution. "Minute Book," p. 16.

55. Remarks of April 6, 1869, JD, XII, 374. A similar statement was made in general conference the following day: "This co-operative movement . . . will stop the operations of many little traders, but it will make them producers as well as consumers. You will find that if the people unitedly hearken to the counsel that is given them, it will not be long before the hats, caps, bonnets, boots and shoes, pants, coats, vests and underclothing of this entire community will all be made in our midst." Sermon of April 7, 1869, JD, XIII, 3.

56. Remarks of April 6, 1869, JD, XII, 374–375.

57. Cf. the response of President John Taylor to a correspondent of the Denver *Tribune,* dated July 25, 1883, and reprinted in the Ogden *Daily Herald.*

58. Cash dividends from 1869–1873 amounted to $350,189.24, while stock dividends totaled $197,309.27 during the same period. These represented 78 per cent and 49 per cent respectively of capital stock. Olsen, appendix.

59. As reported in E. E. Ericksen, *The Psychological and Ethical Aspects of Mormon Group Life* (Chicago, 1923), pp. 53–54.

60. "Merchants and Miners of Utah: Biographies of the Walker Brothers," p. 3, MS., Bancroft Library; H. H. Bancroft, *History of Utah* (San Francisco, 1889), p. 654.

61. Walker Brothers and Auerbachs both expanded with the development of mining and the resulting influx of Gentiles. Frederick Auerbach wrote the following to H. H. Bancroft, in relation to his business: "Our business gradually increased until 1868, when the institution known as Zion's Co-operative Mercantile Institution was started, which for a time seemed to threaten our existence here as merchants, and had it not been for the discovery of minerals here, and the steady development of the mining industry it would certainly have proved unprofitable for us to stay here in this Territory." (Interview between H. H. Bancroft and Frederick H. Auerbach, in Salt Lake City, *ca.* 1883, p. 9, Bancroft MSS., Bancroft Library.) Another Gentile businessman, Fred T. Kiesel of Ogden, wrote Bancroft that the commencement of mining saved the Gentiles from "the despotism of Brigham Young" and was, in fact, "the salvation of us [Gentiles] out here." (Interview between H. H. Bancroft and Fred T. Kiesel, in Ogden, p. 52, Bancroft MSS.)

62. U. S. Bureau of Internal Revenue, Utah District, Tax Lists, 1864–1873, MSS., Bancroft Library.

63. Brigham Young to Albert Carrington, JH, April 13, 1869.

64. Cf. "Autobiography of Horace S. Eldredge," *Tullidge's Quarterly Magazine,* I, 412.

65. Young to Carrington, JH, April 13, 1869.

66. Sermon of April 6, 1869, JD, XII, 373.

67. The Soda Springs branch was discontinued in 1885, the one at Logan in 1897, and the branch at Ogden in 1906.

68. JH, October 8, 1878.

69. To appropriate the words of President Taylor as reproduced in *Tullidge's Quarterly Magazine,* I, 396.

70. *Deseret News,* August 4, 1870; Salt Lake *Herald,* December 23, 1870.

71. During the United Order movement of 1874, a group of about twenty-five Salt Lake shoemakers organized the Workingmen's Co-operative Association for the purpose of operating a boot and shoe shop. The association was not conspicuously successful and was purchased in 1877 by William H. Rowe, an English convert to Mormonism and employee of Z.C.M.I., who had had experience in shoe factories in England. In 1878 the Deseret Tanning and Manufacturing Association, which was initiated by members of the Salt Lake 19th Ward in 1877, and which operated the only important tannery in the City, merged with Rowe to form Salt Lake's largest leather manufacturing firm. Rowe was appointed superintendent of the combined concern. Z.C.M.I. purchased the company's assets in 1879. *Tullidge's Quarterly Magazine,* I, 205–208; Salt Lake *Herald,* April 6, 1879; Olsen, p. 190.

72. *Deseret News,* December 20, 1881.

73. *Ibid.,* March 19, 1883; Salt Lake *Herald,* June 3, 1883; Olsen, p. 190.

74. *Deseret News,* March 21, 1889.

75. Salt Lake *Herald,* January 7, 1882.

76. Union Pacific Railroad, *Utah* (11th ed., Omaha, 1904), p. 64.

77. JH, October 6, 1878.

78. Joseph C. Felix, "The Development of Cooperative Enterprises in Cache Valley, 1865–1900" (unpublished Master's Thesis, Brigham Young University, 1956).

79. Edward Norris Wentworth, *America's Sheep Trails* (Ames, Iowa, 1948), p. 228.

80. Articles of Association and minute books of such coöperative herds are in USU, BYU, and CHO. Also see *Deseret News,* November 9, December 7, 1870.

81. *Measures of Economic Changes in Utah, 1847–1947* (Salt Lake City, 1947), p. 51.

82. Olsen, pp. 172, 196.

83. H. B. Clawson, who had served as superintendent of the institution from its founding, was replaced by Hooper in the latter part of 1873.

84. Olsen, p. 176.

85. Olsen, "Mormon Mercantile Cooperation in Utah," *Journal of Marketing,* VI (1941), 140.

86. JH, August 29, September 10, 13, October 3, 1874; Olsen, "History of Mormon Mercantile Cooperation in Utah," p. 177.

87. Olsen, pp. 178, 198.

88. The shortage of money, of course, was partly due to the self-sufficiency of the Utah economy, and partly to the speed with which cash was spent in the East for emigration, purchase of machinery, and purchase of consumer goods.

89. This is tantamount to saying that Z.C.M.I. and other scrip was the practical currency of the Mormons. Charles B. Spahr, "America's Working People: X — The Mormons," *The Outlook,* LXIV (1900), 310.

90. Salt Lake *Herald,* April 26, 1873; Marcus E. Jones, *Utah* (Washington, 1890), p. 862.

91. The assessment was made pursuant to the National Banking Act of 1863, as amended February 8, 1875, which imposed a tax of ten per cent on certain types of notes used as money and redeemable in money. Congress had in mind removing the state bank notes from circulation in competition with greenbacks and national bank notes.

92. *Deseret News,* August 12, 1879; Olsen, pp. 170–171.

93. *Deseret News,* September 26, 1878.

94. Olsen, pp. 188–189.

95. *Deseret News,* March 18, 1884, January 12, 1885; JH, January 10, February 2, 1898.

96. John Taylor, *An Epistle to the Presidents of Stakes, High Councils, Bishops and other Authorities of the Church* (Salt Lake City, 1882), pp. 1–4. The circular was also signed by George Q. Cannon and Joseph F. Smith, counselors to President Taylor.

97. In the Rochdale Pioneer sense, however, Mormon coöperation was neither new nor unique; and, in fact, was not coöperation! Nevertheless, what the Mormons did practice was unique, and that was community organization under church auspices for the accomplishment of the goals of self-trading and self-production.

98. Sermon of Brigham Young, April 7, 1869, JD, XIII, 2.

99. JH, January 2, 1870.

100. *Deseret News,* May 10, 1870, June 18, 1870, August 30, 1871; Salt Lake *Herald,* December 16, 1871; "Record of Incorporations," Iron County Courthouse, Book A. This company was also known as the Pinto Iron Company because Iron City was located on the Little Pinto Creek. Principals in the company were Ebenezer Hanks, Seth M. Blair, Chapman Duncan, Homer Duncan, and Peter Shirts.

101. *Deseret News,* October 1, 1873, June 24, 1874, October 1, 1875; George A. Smith to Joseph F. Smith, JH, November 26, 1874.

102. *Tullidge's Quarterly Magazine,* I (1881), 522–523.

103. Brigham Young to Albert Carrington, October 3, 1873, *Millennial Star,* XXXV (1873), 681.

104. *A Half-Century of Service,* published by Zion's Savings Bank & Trust Company (Salt Lake City [1923]), p. [7].

105. Incorporation papers, Office of the County Clerk, Salt Lake City; *Deseret News,* August 22, September 18, October 1, 1873, January 2, 1884; Stockholders' Minute Book, MS., bank archives, Salt Lake City.

106. Remarks of George A. Smith, May 1870, JD, XIV, 14.

107. See documents in the envelope "Cotton Factory," filed in the steel case, CHO.

108. JH, May 2, 1869.

109. George A. Smith to Albert Carrington, JH, April 5, 1870; JH, June 5, 1870.

110. Zion's Coöperative Rio Virgen Manufacturing Association was incorporated in January 1871, with an authorized capital of $100,000. The incorporation made it necessary to renegotiate the $40,000 note made in favor of Brigham Young in 1870. On March 28, 1871, the company signed eight notes for $5,000 each, bearing ten per cent interest, to be paid over a period of eight years. The $4,000 interest due for the year 1870–71 was added to the first note. In order to secure the loan, a mortgage on the factory and other property of the company was executed in favor of Brigham Young. President Young liked to do business in a business-like manner, even though he must have known full well that he would never collect the notes nor foreclose the

mortgage. See Barrett, "History of the Cotton Mission and Cotton Culture in Utah," pp. 250–251.

111. Barrett, pp. 247–249.

112. Barrett, pp. 268, 270.

113. See minutes of the secretary, L. John Nuttall, in *Tullidge's Quarterly Magazine,* III, 255. Also JH, June 1, 1869.

114. Articles of incorporation, Office of the Secretary of State, Salt Lake City.

115. This point is stressed in a circular of the general authorities of the church found in JH, July 10, 1875.

116. *Deseret News,* April 20, 1881.

CHAPTER XI: THE UNITED ORDER OF ENOCH

The most detailed account of the United Order is Feramorz Y. Fox, "Experiments in Cooperation and Social Security Among the Mormons," 1938, typescript, CHO. Marked by painstaking research, comprehensive coverage, and intelligent analysis, this useful and informative book-length treatise has never been published. The best published work is Edward J. Allen, *The Second United Order Among the Mormons* (New York, 1936). Shorter treatments include: Angus M. Woodbury, "The United Order," typescript, USU; William R. Palmer, "United Order in Utah," *Improvement Era,* XLV (1942), 788ff.; XLVI (1943), 24ff., 86ff.; "United Order," published by the Daughters of Utah Pioneers in *Heart Throbs of the West* (12 vols.; Salt Lake City, 1936–1951), I, 50–71; and some vivid and informative chapters in Nels Anderson, *Desert Saints* . . . (Chicago, 1942). The historical background is traced in Hamilton Gardner, "Communism Among the Mormons," *Quarterly Journal of Economics,* XXXVII (1922), 134–174. One of the most successful and enduring of the orders has been described with some detail in Leonard J. Arrington, *Orderville, Utah: A Pioneer Mormon Experiment in Economic Organization* (Utah State Agricultural College Monograph Series, Vol. II, No. 2, 1954). A bibliographical essay is included. The only treatment of the movement which followed the United Order is Leonard J. Arrington, "Zion's Board of Trade: A Third United Order," *Western Humanities Review,* V (1951), 1–20.

Contemporary discussions of Mormon economic policies and organization in the 1870's and 1880's are found in: *Tullidge's Quarterly Magazine* (Salt Lake City, 1880–1885); *Salt Lake Daily Tribune;* John Codman, *The Round Trip* (New York, 1879); Phil Robinson, *Sinners and Saints* (Boston, 1883); and in most county histories. The best accounts of temple construction during the period are Juanita Brooks, "The St. George Temple," *Improvement Era,* XLIX (1946), 370ff.; and Melvin Larkin, "History of the L. D. S. Temple in Logan, Utah" (unpublished Master's Thesis, Utah State University, 1954). Mr. Larkin had access to all of the ledgers, time books, minute books, correspondence, and other contemporary documents related to the building and operations of the Logan Temple during its first twenty years, and pieced together an authentic and fascinating picture of voluntary community cooperation in a major construction project.

1. Sermon of April 7, 1869, *Deseret News,* June 2, 1869.

2. Leonard J. Arrington, "Banking Enterprises in Utah, 1847–1880," *Business History Review,* XXIX (1955), 312–334.

3. See editorials in the Salt Lake *Herald* and *Deseret News,* beginning in July 1873 and running through 1874.

4. Arrington, pp. 331–332.

5. Leonard J. Arrington, "The Mormon Tithing House: A Frontier Business Institution," *Business History Review,* XXVIII (1954), 30.

6. In a Salt Lake sermon delivered in April 1874 Brigham Young listed the objects of the United Order as (1) to cut down imports and be self-sustaining; (2) to "classify" labor, so that every man could work at his own specialized trade; (3) to eliminate poverty and make the poor comfortable and happy. JH, April 12, 1874.

7. The Order of Enoch was the socio-economic system supposed to have been established by an Old Testament Prophet named Enoch, whose people had achieved such remarkable harmony and righteousness that they were taken up into Heaven. The following early Mormon scripture had impressed itself deeply into Mormon thought: "And the Lord called his [Enoch's] people Zion, because they were of one heart and one mind, and dwelt in righteousness; and there were no poor among them." Joseph Smith, *The Pearl of Great Price,* Book of Moses, 7:18 (Salt Lake City, 1923).

8. In addition to general sources, the Brigham City Coöperative is briefly described in Eliza R. Snow Smith, *Biography and Family Record of Lorenzo Snow* (Salt Lake City, 1884); Journal History of Box Elder Stake, CHO; and *History of Box Elder County,* compiled and published by the Daughters of Utah Pioneers of Box Elder County (Brigham City, 1937).

9. "Successful Co-operation," in the Salt Lake *Herald,* October 25, 1876.

10. *Tullidge's Quarterly Magazine,* II, 400.

11. As repeated by Apostle Snow, sermon of April 21, 1878, JD, XIV, 347.

12. Sermon of October 9, 1872, as cited in extenso in M. R. Werner, *Brigham Young* (New York, 1925), pp. 438–441. See also the editorial, "United Order of Enoch," *Salt Lake Daily Tribune,* April 28, 1874.

13. Journal History of St. George Stake, February 15, 1874, CHO.

14. Allen, *The Second United Order Among the Mormons,* pp. 136–137. This preamble was copied by Allen from the original on file in the St. George Temple.

15. "United Order of Enoch," *Salt Lake Daily Tribune,* April 28, 1874. Among the papers of Jacob Smith Boreman in the Huntington Library are a number of critical commentaries on the United Order. Boreman was a non-Mormon appointed judge in Utah Territory in the 1870's.

16. JH, October 7, 1877.

17. JH, December 15, 1878.

18. From an undated letter in "Scribbling Book," MS., in the possession of Le Roi C. Snow, Salt Lake City, Utah.

19. Samuel Claridge Autobiography, pp. 35–36, MS., in possession of S. George Ellsworth, Logan, Utah.

20. Mark A. Pendleton, "The Orderville United Order of Zion," *Utah Historical Quarterly,* VII (1939), 153–154.

21. George Q. Cannon to Thomas Chamberlain, June 2, 1884, cited in *ibid.,* pp. 157–158.

22. In a circular distributed to local church leaders in 1877, the First Presidency asserted that they had urged the great importance of the principles of the United Order upon the people in order to build up Zion, and this was to be accomplished by "the proper combination of labor, so as to furnish employment to all," by developing "home industries and all the resources of our country," and by "obviating the necessity of importing from abroad." The circular, which is bound in Volume VII of the L. D. S. Pamphlets in the E. H. Peirce Collection, Harvard University, then goes on to point

out specific ways in which the economic cause of Zion can be advanced, through proper organization and policies.

23. These views are expressed in the 1877 circular of the First Presidency, previously cited.

24. JH, April 6, 1877.

25. Based on "Temple Construction," in Leonard J. Arrington, "Mormon Economic Policies and Their Implementation on the Western Frontier, 1847–1900" (unpublished Ph. D. dissertation, University of North Carolina, 1952), pp. 310–329. The cost estimates, of course, are in terms of contemporary prices and wages.

26. JH, April 25, 1877.

27. "Current Record, Logan Temple," MS., Logan Temple Archives, Logan, Utah. The final completed cost of the temple was $660,749. See Larkin, "History of the Logan Temple."

28. Another $20,867 came from private sources outside the temple district.

29. Card to Fisher, 1880, as cited in Larkin, "History of the L. D. S. Temple in Logan, Utah," p. 89.

30. JH, April 5, 1884.

31. For representations on official views on the United Order in 1877 and thereafter, see Epistle of the First Presidency (Salt Lake City, 1882); JH, November 25, 1877, June 9, August 4, September 5, 21, October 5, 6, 7, 8, 1878; Erastus Snow in *Deseret News,* May 9, 1877 and JH, June 10, 1883; *Memoirs of John R. Young* (Salt Lake City, 1923), pp. 226–227, 251–252; and Thomas Robertson to Reddick Allred, August 18, 1883, Journal History of Kanab Stake, CHO.

32. *Deseret News,* April 10, 1872.

33. "Cache Valley Historical Record, Book A," February 1, 1879, MS., CHO.

34. See remarks of President Taylor and George Q. Cannon, his counselor in the First Presidency, JH, September 5, October 6, 8, 1878.

35. George Q. Cannon, JH, October 6, 1878.

36. JH, October 8, 1878.

37. JH, October 8, 1878.

38. Salt Lake *Herald,* October 19, 1878.

39. The diaries of Moses Thatcher, in possession of Mrs. George H. Ryan, Logan, Utah, contain many entries in 1878 and 1879 in relation to Thatcher's call by the First Presidency, and his activity in organizing stake boards of trade.

40. From a printed circular distributed by the society in May 1880, specimen in possession of the writer; and from the objectives read by Moses Thatcher at stake conferences, as published in the *Deseret News,* February 11, 1879.

41. JH, October 6, 1878.

42. *Deseret News,* April 20, 1881.

43. JH, October 8, 1878.

44. JH, October 8, 1878.

45. *Tullidge's Quarterly Magazine,* I (1881), 420.

46. *Deseret News,* April 20, 1881.

47. See Leonard J. Arrington, "Iron Manufacturing in Southern Utah in the Early 1880's: The Iron Manufacturing Company of Utah," *Bulletin of the Business Historical Society,* XXV (1951), 149–168.

48. The trustees were John R. Winder, Leonard W. Hardy, and Fred H. Auerbach.

49. The story of the Utah Eastern is told in Leonard J. Arrington, "Utah's Coal Road in the Age of Unregulated Competition," *Utah Historical Quarterly,* XXIII (1955), 35–63.

50. See official statement of the First Presidency in *Deseret News,* October 23, 1880.

51. *Ibid.,* July 14, 1894.

CHAPTER XII: THE RAID

The era of the Raid has been given surprisingly little treatment by historians of Utah and the West, but the raw material is there in abundance in the newspapers, diaries, and letters of the time. The *Deseret News* and *Salt Lake Tribune,* with completely opposite points of view, pled their diverse causes without mercy. Several dozen diaries bearing on the period are in typescript at BYU. The long "lost" documents of the Utah Commission have been "found" and are now in UHS. Finally, there are the government documents of the period in the National Archives, hardly any of which have been touched. Especially useful in preparing this chapter have been the General Records of the Department of Justice: Year File, 1887; also useful are the N. A. file for Utah, 1887–1888, and Instruction Books Y and Z. The most rewarding diaries are those of Wilford Woodruff, in CHO, and L. John Nuttall, typescript, BYU. The atmosphere of the period is captured in Kimball Young, *Isn't One Wife Enough?* (New York, 1954), pp. 349–409; William Mulder, *Homeward to Zion . . .* (Minneapolis, 1957), pp. 240–243, 274–302; and in Samuel W. Taylor, *The Family Kingdom* (New York, 1951), which is a novelized history of the fortunes of the families of Apostle John W. Taylor, son of President John Taylor.

The only studies of the period relate to the political aspect. They include: Stewart L. Grow, "A Study of the Utah Commission, 1882–1896" (unpublished Ph. D. dissertation, University of Utah, 1954); and Merle W. Wells, "The Idaho Anti-Mormon Movement, 1872–1908" (unpublished Ph. D. dissertation, University of California, Berkeley, 1951). From the latter have been published "Origins of Anti-Mormonism in Idaho, 1872–1880," *Pacific Northwest Quarterly,* XLVII (1956), 107–116; and "The Idaho Anti-Mormon Test Oath, 1884–1892," *Pacific Historical Review,* XXIV (1955), 235–252. The story is also treated in Grenville H. Gibbs, "Mormonism in Idaho Politics, 1880–1890," *Utah Historical Quarterly,* XXI (1953), 285–305; and S. George Ellsworth, "Political Developments," in Joel E. Ricks, ed., *The History of a Valley: Cache Valley, Utah-Idaho* (Logan, 1956), pp. 109–139. The general political framework of the period is described in Earl S. Pomeroy, *The Territories and the United States, 1861–1890: Studies in Colonial Administration* (Philadelphia, 1947).

The role of the Mormon Question in national politics is explored in Richard D. Poll, "The Political Reconstruction of Utah Territory, 1866–1890," *Pacific Historical Review,* XXVII (1958), 111–126. Discussions of the allegedly "anti-Mormon" activities of the appointed governors and judges, and of the anti-Mormon legislation which culminated in the Raid are found in: B. H. Roberts, *Comprehensive History of the Church . . .* (6 vols.; Salt Lake City, 1930), V and VI; Neff, *History of Utah,* pp. 864–885; Nels Anderson, *Desert Saints . . .* (Chicago, 1942), Chapters X–XII; E. W. Tullidge, *History of Salt Lake City* (Salt Lake City, c. 1886), pp. 373–620, 818–860; R. J. Dwyer, *The Gentile Comes to Utah . . .* (Washington, D. C., 1941), pp. 215–249; W. A. Linn, *The Story of the Mormons* (New York, 1902), pp. 590–608; and Everett L. Cooley, "Carpetbag Rule: Territorial Government in Utah," *Utah Historical Quarterly,* XXVI (1958), 107–129. Background of the alleged church-government compact is examined in the above works and in R. Davis Bitton, "The B. H. Roberts Case of 1898–1900," *Utah Historical Quarterly,* XXV (1957), 27–46.

Books and articles which reflect national attitudes on the Mormon question include: W. G. Marshall, *Through America; or, Nine Months in the United States* (London, 1882), pp. 147–236; C. P. Lyford, *The Mormon Problem . . .* (New York, 1886); C. C. Goodwin, "The Mormon Situation," *Harper's New Monthly Magazine,* LXIII (1881), 756–763; James W. Barclay, "A New View of Mormonism," *Nineteenth Century,* XV (1884), 167–184; Ernest Ingersoll, "Salt Lake City," *Harper's New Monthly Magazine,* LXIX (1884), 388–404; Eli H. Murray, "The Crisis in Utah," *North American Review,* CXXXIV (1882), 327–346; and John Taylor and Eli H. Murray, "Ecclesiastical Control in Utah," *ibid.,* CXXXVIII (1884), 1–23.

1. *Salt Lake Tribune,* April 7, 1880, April 6, 1881, summarizing the financial reports to the April general conferences in 1880 and 1881.

2. F. A. Hammond, *Deseret News,* April 29, 1885.

3. A sample Mormon colonizing episode of the late 1870's is treated in Charles E. Redd, "Short Cut to the San Juan," in *1949 Brand Book* of The Westerners (Denver, 1950), pp. 3–24.

4. The proceedings of the conference are published in *The Year of Jubilee: A Full Report of the Proceedings of the Fiftieth Annual Conference of the Church . . .* (Salt Lake City, 1880). Action taken was summarized in the report of George Q. Cannon, JH, October 8, 1880, April 6, 7, 1881.

5. Sermon of April 7, 1880, *Year of Jubilee,* p. 62.

6. For example, Z.C.M.I. cancelled $3,584 of the indebtedness of the Brigham City Co-operative, and $2,539 of the debt of the Coalville Co-operative Institution. Arden B. Olsen, "The History of Mormon Mercantile Cooperation in Utah" (unpublished Ph. D. dissertation, University of California, 1935), p. 203.

7. See Leonard J. Arrington, "The Settlement of the Brigham Young Estate, 1877–1879," *Pacific Historical Review,* XXI (1952), 1–20. The papers of Jacob S. Boreman, who tried the Brigham Young estate case, are in the Huntington Library.

8. Reynolds *v.* U.S., 98 U.S. 145 (1879). See also George Q. Cannon, *Review of the Reynolds Decision* (Salt Lake City, 1879); Bruce R. Trimble, *Chief Justice Waite: Defender of the Public Interest* (Princeton, 1938), pp. 242–245.

9. Cited in Edward W. Tullidge, *Life of Brigham Young; Or, Utah and Her Founders* (New York, 1876), pp. 420–421.

10. McKean resorted to extraordinary measures in using his office to combat the Mormons, but his rulings were overturned by a unanimous decision of the Supreme Court in the Englebrecht case, 80 U.S. 434 (1872). On one occasion, in speaking to Mormon jurors, McKean stated: "the day is not far in the future, when the disloyal high priesthood of the so-called Church of Jesus Christ of Latter-day Saints, shall bow to and obey the laws that are elsewhere respected, or else those laws will grind them to powder." (*Deseret News,* March 22, 1871). On another occasion, when trying Brigham Young for assorted crimes, including "murder," the judge said that "while the case at bar is called *The People versus Brigham Young,* its other and real title is *Federal Authority versus Polygamic Theocracy. . . .* A system is on trial in the person of Brigham Young. Let all concerned keep this fact steadily in view; and let that government rule without a rival which shall prove to be in the right." (*Ibid.,* October 18, 1871). Judge McKean was regarded by many non-Mormons as a judicial extremist, but his recommendations were largely realized in the Poland Act.

11. Miles *v.* U.S., 103 U.S. 304 (1881).

12. 22 Stat. L. 30 (1882).

13. The published reports of the Utah Commission are included in the annual reports of the Secretary of the Interior. It is true that there were some differences

between the Idaho and Utah interpretations, and that some monogamous Mormons (e.g., John T. Caine) were elected to office, but the generalizations given in the text seem to this writer to be descriptive and fully warranted.

14. The Reynolds case, cited in note 8, settled that Congress could legislate on plural marriage. While I have specifically mentioned the First Amendment in the text, the ruling on the Edmunds Act did involve other issues. See, for example, Grow, "A Study of the Utah Commission."

15. See Clawson *v.* U.S., 114 U.S. 55 (1885); Snow *v.* U.S., 120 U.S. 274 (1886); and Cannon *v.* U.S., 116 U.S. 55 (1885).

16. The president of the Twelve Apostles, Wilford Woodruff, stated that it was the Mormon understanding that the federal courts would regard each instance in which a man was under the same roof with a suspected plural wife for part of a day as a separate offense of cohabitation. Thus, the courts could pyramid the sentences of individuals where it could be established that they had visited their alleged plural wives several times after 1882. Diary of Wilford Woodruff, October 3, 1885.

17. Richard D. Poll, "The Twin Relic: A Study of Mormon Polygamy and the Campaign of the United States Government for its Abolition, 1852–1890" (unpublished Master's Thesis, Texas Christian University, 1938), pp. 206–224.

18. Grow, "A Study of the Utah Commission," p. 268. Professor Poll estimates there were 1,300 convictions in "The Twin Relic," p. 258.

19. Wilford Woodruff, one of the Twelve Apostles, wrote: "As an apostle of the Lord Jesus Christ, I will not desert my wives and children and disobey the commandments of God for the sake of accommodating the public clamor of a nation steeped in sin and ripened for the damnation of hell!" *Deseret News,* April 1, 1879.

20. See M. H. Cannon, ed., "The Prison Diary of a Mormon Apostle [George Q. Cannon]," *Pacific Historical Review,* XVI (1947), 393–409. After the abolition of polygamy in 1890, and the granting of statehood to Utah (1896), Congress, by special act, returned President Cannon's bail.

21. Frank J. Cannon and Harvey J. O'Higgins, *Under the Prophet in Utah* (Boston, 1911), p. 25.

22. 22 Stat. L. 635–641 (1887).

23. The full letter of President Taylor to Latter-day Saints in the Logan Temple District, July 2, 1884, and accompanying remarks recorded in "Logan Temple Association Minute Book," pp. 3–4, from which these phrases are taken, are in the Logan Temple Archives, Logan, Utah.

24. Most of the following is revealed in testimony published in the *Deseret News,* July 9, October 9, November 15, 1888, February 7, 1889; in notations found in the diary of L. John Nuttall; and in other sources, as indicated.

25. See "Minute Book of Logan Temple Association," MS., Logan Temple Archives, Logan, Utah; minutes of the St. George Temple and Manti Temple Associations in the History of St. George and Sanpete stakes, respectively, CHO.

26. "Minute Book of the Salt Lake Literary and Scientific Association," MS., CHO.

27. The records of a number of these associations are preserved in CHO. See also the diary of L. John Nuttall, who was instrumental in organizing these associations.

28. In 1891, President George Q. Cannon testified that the average annual receipts of the church during the preceding seven or eight years had varied between $500,000 and $750,000. *Deseret News,* October 20, 1891.

29. According to George Q. Cannon, President John Taylor was personally averse to putting the church property out of his hands with a view to saving it from seizure. He had wanted to meet the issue squarely and openly. He was dissuaded from this

view by some of his advisers, however, and every effort was made to save the property of the church from spoliation. Roberts, *Comprehensive History,* VI, 195–196; *Millennial Star,* L (1888), 235.

30. *Deseret News,* November 7, 1887; 5 Utah 361, 380; testimony of James Jack, *Deseret News,* May 2, 5, 1888.

31. "Statement of Personal Property alleged to be on hand at the various Tithing Offices Throughout the Territory of Utah and Adjoining Territories" (N.A., D.J. Year File, 1887); also United States *v.* Church of Jesus Christ of Latter-day Saints, 6 Utah 9, 61.

32. For examples, see Ogden *Herald,* April 18, 1887; *Deseret News,* April 30, May 7, 1887; *Territorial Enquirer* (Provo), April 26, 1887; also stake association minute books, MSS., CHO.

33. The relationship between the Edmunds-Tucker Act and the founding of the Mormon academies in 1888 has never before been pointed out. See JH, October 10, 1887, June 8, 1888; also John Clifton Moffitt, *The History of Public Education in Utah* (n. p., 1946); M. Lynn Bennion, *Mormonism and Education* (Salt Lake City, 1939).

34. Testimony published in the *Deseret News,* May 1, 1888, February 6, 7, 1889.

35. This list is based largely upon testimony recorded in *ibid.,* February 29, April 28, May 1, 2, 5, 14, July 11, November 15, 1888, February 11, 1889, October 20, 1891; *Millennial Star,* L (1888), 235, 406; Minute Book and Treasurer's Book of the Church Association of Salt Lake Stake, MSS., CHO; "Minute Book of the Salt Lake Literary and Scientific Association"; and Leonard J. Arrington, "The Deseret Telegraph," *Journal of Economic History,* XI (1951), 134–136. Arden Olsen, in his "Mormon Mercantile Cooperation," pp. 196–197, states that the transfer of Z.C.M.I. stock occurred on March 11, 1886, which would have been well before the passage of the Edmunds-Tucker Act.

36. See *Deseret News,* October 9, 1888.

37. Statement on file in the Salt Lake County Clerk's Office; also Roberts, *Comprehensive History,* VI, 196. The Presiding Bishop's Office served as the office of the trustee-in-trust of the church until April 1897, when the function was restored to the First Presidency. JH, April 12, 1896, April 12, 1897.

38. Details of the suit are given in the *Deseret News,* July 30, 1887; also United States *v.* Church of Jesus Christ of Latter-day Saints and others, 5 Utah 361 (June 1887 term of court).

39. A collection of letters from the district attorneys to the Attorney General's office, reporting the progress of the case and requesting further instructions, is in the National Archives files, mentioned above.

40. See *Deseret News,* October 4, 1887; and Peters to Jenks, October 2, 1887 (N. A., D.J. Year File, 1887).

41. *Ibid.*

42. See *Deseret News,* October 17, 1887.

43. The arguments of the church attorneys against the appointment of a receiver can be found in the *Deseret News* for October 20, 21, 22, 1887.

44. This statement of facts is found in the *Salt Lake Tribune,* October 20, 1887. In essence, the statement of facts to which the church agreed consisted of a tacit admission that the church, after February 19, 1887, had disposed of real and personal property worth $237,666.15.

45. Hobson to Jenks, October 31, 1887 (N.A., D.J. Year File, 1887).

46. The court opinion is given in the *Deseret News,* November 7, 1887. President Wilford Woodruff wrote in his diary under November 5, "The Court finally decided

to appoint a receiver and the government sues me and the Twelve for about $3,000,000. I doubt if they will get that much."

47. See Salt Lake *Herald,* November 7, 1887. This action was tantamount to selecting the plaintiff as receiver. The Chief Justice of the Utah Supreme Court, Charles S. Zane, objected to the appointment of Dyer as receiver. Peters' reaction to this objection was that a change should be made in the Chief Justiceship and he wrote the Solicitor General requesting it. The change was made (probably not as the result of this request) in July 1888 when Elliott Sandford replaced Zane. Peters to Jenks, November 10, 1887 (N.A., D.J. Year File, 1887). Zane was restored to the Chief Justiceship in May 1889. This change was quite probably a matter of party patronage—Cleveland ousting Zane and Harrison restoring him.

48. *Deseret News,* November 10, 1887.

49. Dyer to Harrison, March 9, 1889 (N.A., D.J. Appointment File, Utah).

50. For reports of the activities of the receiver, see *Deseret News,* November 11, 18, 22, 25, December 7, 1887, April 2, 14, July 11, November 17, 1888, July 7, October 1, 1890; Salt Lake *Herald,* May 18, 1888; *Millennial Star,* L (1890), 223; Varian to the Attorney General, October 27, 1890 (N.A., D.J. Year File, 1887).

51. Most of the testimony is given in *Deseret News,* February 10, 1888, *et. seq.*

52. Hobson to Jenks, February 14 and March 19, 1888 (N.A., D.J. Year File, 1887).

53. *Deseret News,* January 24, April 7, May 2, 1888; "Church Association of Salt Lake Stake Minute Book," report of W. B. Preston, on September 1, 1888, MS., CHO.

54. Hobson to Jenks, March 19, 1888 (N.A., D.J. Year File, 1887); Dyer's report as published in the *Deseret News,* July 9, 1888.

55. *Ibid.;* Salt Lake *Herald,* February 21, 1889.

56. United States *v.* Church . . . , 6 Utah 9, 62–3.

57. Testimony of Dyer, *Deseret News,* November 15, 1888.

58. *Deseret News,* July 11, 13, 1888. For some reason or other the Offices of the President and Presiding Bishop and the $5,000 on *Deseret News* stock were not listed in the published statement, although Dyer had certainly possessed them before that date and there is no evidence that he had relinquished control over them by July 11, 1888. However, church officials were permitted to use the Offices of the President and the Presiding Bishop throughout the period of the receivership, and they were not listed as possessed by Dyer in the findings of the Utah Supreme Court of October 9, 1888.

59. United States *v.* Church, 6 Utah 9, 62–3.

60. The notes involved in these loans are on file in the CHO. See also statement of Wilford Woodruff, JH, October 5, 1891.

61. See *Deseret News,* October 6, 1888.

62. The court findings and judgment are given in the *Deseret News,* October 9, 1888. They are also summarized in The Late Corporation of the Church of Jesus Christ of Latter-day Saints *v.* United States 136 (1890), 1–68. This decree of the Utah Supreme Court was actually drafted by the government attorneys, Hobson and Peters, and transmitted to the United States Attorney General on August 25, 1888, a month and a half before the court issued the decree as its own, and before it had heard all the prayers of the defendants. The decree, as returned from the Attorney General's office, was almost exactly like the decree finally handed down by the court on October 9. Varian to Attorney General, October 27, 1890 (N.A., D.J. Year File, 1887). This admission by the United States Attorney tends to support the charge of the Mormon press that the case was prejudicial.

63. The hearings and decision are reported in United States *v.* Church . . . , 6 Utah 9 (January 1889 term); *Deseret News,* October 6, November 15, 16, 17, 1888.

64. *Ibid.;* 6 Utah 9, 13.

65. *Deseret News,* November 28, 1888.

66. Mormon writers seized on Judge Zane's charges to show lack of justice throughout. See, for example, the editorial in the *Deseret News,* November 19, 1888, entitled, "The Scramble for Spoils."

67. For example, *Deseret News,* June 29, 1889. The reaction of the government attorneys to Zane's statements is given in the letters of Hobson and Peters to the Attorney General, both dated November 30, 1888 (N.A., D.J. Year File, 1887). A copy of the answers of Dyer, Peters, and Williams are found in Peters to the Attorney General, December 10, 1888 (N.A., D.J. Year File, 1887).

68. The *Deseret News* covered the examination fully. See February 5, 6, 7, 11, 12, 1889. See also the *Salt Lake Tribune* for February 13, 1889. Also United States *v.* Church, 6 Utah 9, 13, *et passim;* Senator Edmunds to Attorney General, May 1, 1889 (N.A., D.J. Appointment File, Utah), with enclosures.

69. *Deseret News,* March 2, 1889.

70. The summaries and excerpts are taken from 136 U.S. 1–68. The complete text of the court's opinion is also given in the *Deseret News,* June 10, 1890.

71. The dissent is discussed briefly in Willard L. King, *Melvin Weston Fuller, Chief Justice of the United States, 1888–1910* (New York, 1950), pp. 147–148.

72. Edmunds to the Attorney General, June 26, 1890 (N.A., D.J. Year File, 1887).

73. Edmunds to the Attorney General, July 7, 1890 (N.A., D.J. Year File, 1887).

74. Varian to the Attorney General, July 10, 1890 (N.A., D.J. Year File, 1887).

75. *Deseret News,* June 22, 1889, March 13, 1890; also Dyer's report mentioned below.

76. *Deseret News,* July 15, 1890.

77. One copy of the report was filed with the Utah Supreme Court and another was mailed by Varian directly to Senator Edmunds. Varian to the Attorney General, July 26, 1890 (N.A., D.J. Year File, 1887). The report is now filed in N.A., D.J. Year File, 1887, with a letter from Varian to the Attorney General, dated July 3, 1891, entitled, "Requests an answer to his last letter about his compensation." Dyer's report is approximately 70 pages long. A microfilm copy is in the possession of the writer.

78. The 30,000 sheep, for example, had been leased out to private stockmen. When the first contract was up, the court ordered Dyer to divide the herd into flocks, hire men, and herd them himself. The losses were heavy, for reasons both legitimate and illegitimate, and during the third season the receiver was ordered to sell all the sheep, which he did at a considerable loss to the fund. In testifying in regard to his accounts while receiver, Dyer stated that the sheep enterprise, far from adding to the fund, had diminished the fund by almost $30,000. See *Deseret News,* October 5, 1889, July 29, Septemper 1, 10, 20, 1890.

79. Varian to Attorney General, October 27, 1890 (N.A., D.J. Year File, 1887). Also *Deseret News,* February 13, 1891.

80. *Deseret News,* July 17, 1890. The *Salt Lake Tribune,* on the same day, declared: "There is poetic justice in the appointment. . . . On principle Mr. Lawrence found it necessary to oppose some of the pretensions of Brigham Young. His manhood made that necessary. As a result he was excommunicated under circumstances that tried his courage to the utmost. It would have required but a word to have caused the fierce fanatics around him to rend him limb from limb. . . . Now he, as an American, is

given the place of Receiver to manage and dispose of the property which, under the law, has been seized from the church and is to be turned over to the school fund. No better appointment could have been made."

81. Cited in Roberts, VI, 220.

82. The complete text of the declaration is found at the end of every modern edition of the church's *Doctrine and Covenants.*

83. Varian to Attorney General, November 13, 1890 (N.A., D.J. Year File, 1887).

84. See 140 U.S. 665 (1891); 150 U.S. 145 (1893); United States *v.* Church, 8 Utah 310 (1892); U.S. *v.* Tithing Yard and Offices, 9 Utah 273 (1893); U.S. *v.* Gardo House and Historian's Office, 9 Utah 285 (1893); U.S. *v.* Church Coal Lands, 9 Utah 288 (1893); U.S. *v.* Church Farm, 9 Utah 289 (1893). Also *Deseret News,* November 5, December 24, 1890; February 13, 14, May 26, July 2, October 20, 27, November 11, 1891; January 15, April 1, June 7, July 6, 7, September 2, November 12, December 17, 1892; March 20, April 22, July 15, September 19, October 6, 21, 23, 27, 1893; January 10, 11, 1894; and JH, January 15, 17, 23, February 4, March 13, 18, 24, April 2, 20, June 8, 1896.

CHAPTER XIII: AFTERMATH

There are five excellent general appraisals of the Mormon social economy at the end of the century. They are: Richard T. Ely, "Economic Aspects of Mormonism," *Harper's Monthly Magazine,* CVI (1903), 667–678; Ray Stannard Baker, "The Vitality of Mormonism: A Study of an Irrigated Valley in Utah and Idaho," *The Century Magazine,* LXVIII (1904), 165–177; William E. Smythe, "Utah As An Industrial Object-Lesson," *Atlantic Monthly,* LXXVIII (1896), 610–618; Charles B. Spahr, "America's Working People: The Mormons," *The Outlook,* LXIV (1900), 305–317; and Albert Edgar Wilson, "Gemeinwirtschaft und Unternehmungsformen im Mormonenstaat," in Gustav Schmoller's *Jahrbuch für Gesetzgebung, Verwaltung und Volkswirthschaft im Deutschen Reich* (39 vols.; Leipzig, 1877–1915), XXXI (1901), 1003–1056. An English translation of the latter, by Philip Flammer, is in USU. A similar work by a French economist, though a generation later, is G. H. Bousquet, "Une Théocratie Économique: L'Église Mormone," *Revue d'économie politique,* L (Part 1, 1936), 106–145. An English translation by Lincoln Bell is also available in USU. An indispensable but not completely reliable contemporary history is Frank J. Cannon and Harvey J. O'Higgins, *Under the Prophet in Utah* (Boston, 1911). Cannon was an important participant who later apostatized. The work is bitter in tone but has revealing glimpses into church procedures and policies. A companion work, by Cannon and George L. Knapp, *Brigham Young and His Mormon Empire* (New York, 1913), is so distorted that it reflects only the extreme to which a self-styled "calm, impartial" history of the Mormons could go early in the present century.

Other published essays which deal with phases of Mormon immigration, colonization, and industrial development near the end of the century are: Glen Miller, "The Mormons: A Successful Cooperative Society," *The World's Work,* V (1902), 2881–2894; William Mulder, "Immigration and the 'Mormon Question': An International Episode," *Western Political Quarterly,* IX (1956), 416–433; J. H. McClintock, *Mormon Settlement in Arizona: A Record of Peaceful Conquest of the Desert* (Phoenix, 1921); Thomas C. Romney, *The Mormon Colonies in Mexico* (Salt Lake City, 1940); M. D. Beal, *A History of Southeastern Idaho* (Caldwell, Idaho, 1942); Lowry Nelson, "The Mormons in Alberta," in *Group Settlement: Ethnic Communities in Western Canada,* by C. A. Dawson (Volume VII of *Canadian Frontiers of Settlement,* W. A. Mackintosh and W. L. G. Joerg, eds.) (Toronto, 1936); Leonard J. Arrington, "The L. D. S. Hawaiian Colony at Skull Valley," *Improvement Era,* LVII (1954), 314ff.; and Fred G. Taylor, *A Saga of Sugar: Being a Story of the Romance and Development of Beet Sugar in the Rocky Mountain West* (Salt Lake City, 1944). The archives of Utah Power & Light Company, Salt Lake City, contain corporate histories, minute books, and other records of predecessor companies engaged in the production, distribution, and consumption of electricity. Especially vauable is "Historical Sketch of Financial and Physical Data of Predecessor Companies to the Utah Light & Traction Company," mimeographed. Cynical commentaries on Mormon "trust-building" after 1900 are two pamphlets by C. G. Patterson: *Business, Politics and Religion in Utah: The Utah-Idaho Sugar Company versus The People of Utah and Idaho* [Salt Lake City, 1916]; and *Business, Politics and Religion in Utah: Utah and Her Railroads* [Salt Lake City, 1916].

The church struggle with economic problems is revealed in the following diaries and biographies of leading participants: Diary of Wilford Woodruff, MS., CHO; Matthias F. Cowley, ed., *Wilford Woodruff: History of His Life and Labors as Recorded in His Daily Journals* (Salt Lake City, 1909); Thomas C. Romney, *The Life of Lorenzo Snow* (Salt Lake City, 1955); Joseph Fielding Smith, *Life of Joseph F. Smith* (Salt Lake City, 1938); Bryant S. Hinckley, *Heber J. Grant: Highlights in the Life of a Great Leader* (Salt Lake City, 1951); Melvin C. Merrill, ed., *Marriner Wood Merrill and His Family* (Salt Lake City, 1937); and Diary of L. John Nuttall, typescript, BYU. The Journal History of the Church for the period 1896–1906 contains typescripts of the minutes of meetings of the First Presidency and Quorum of the Twelve. The mass of testimony of high Mormon officials and others in the *Proceedings Before the Committee on Privileges and Elections of the United States Senate in the Matter of the Protests Against the Right of Hon. Reed Smoot . . . to Hold His Seat* (4 vols.; Washington, 1904–1906) is also an indispensable reference on Mormon policy and practice. Official statements of Mormon beliefs, including beliefs with respect to temporal affairs, are: Lorenzo Snow, " 'Mormonism,' by its Head," *Land of Sunshine* (Los Angeles), XV (1901), 252–259; and Joseph F. Smith, "The Truth About Mormonism," *Out West,* XXIII (1905), 239–255.

The pattern of change in economic philosophy, as Mormons worked with non-Mormons to hammer out a new constitution for Utah in 1895, is alluded to in Stanley S. Ivins, "A Constitution for Utah," *Utah Historical Quarterly,* XXV (1957), 95–116. The significance of the change in economic policy is discussed in Leonard J. Arrington, "Objectives of Mormon Economic Policy," *Western Humanities Review,* X (1956), 180–185. A bitter picture of Mormon political activity is sketched in Josiah F. Gibbs, *Lights and Shadows of Mormonism* (Salt Lake City, 1909). An intelligent and revealing discussion of "the Mormon encounter with modern secular thought," including the "sources of strain and conflict" in modern Mormonism, is presented in Thomas F. O'Dea, *The Mormons* (Chicago, 1957), pp. 222–263.

1. Gustive O. Larson, *Prelude to the Kingdom . . .* (Francestown, N. H., 1947), pp. 227, 236.
2. Nels Anderson, *Desert Saints . . .* (Chicago, 1942), p. 319.
3. "Annual Report of the Governor of Utah," in Secretary of the Interior, *Annual Report, 1883, House Exec. Doc. No. 1,* Part V, XI, 627–637, 48th Cong., 1st sess.
4. James D. Richardson, ed., *A Compilation of the Messages and Papers of the Presidents, 1789–1908* (Washington, 1908), VIII, 362.
5. Mulder, "Immigration and the 'Mormon Question,' " pp. 416–433.

6. 24 Stat. L. 635.

7. Mulder, *op. cit.,* p. 433.

8. Larson, "The Story of the Perpetual Emigration Fund," *Mississippi Valley Historical Review,* XVIII (1931), 185.

9. Neff estimates the number at 50,000 in his *History of Utah,* p. 579. Romney estimates 40,000 in *The Story of Deseret* (Independence, Missouri, 1948), p. 193.

10. Mulder, p. 433. See also Baker, "The Vitality of Mormonism," p. 166.

11. JH, April 16, July 1, 1897, July 21, 1899, August 10, 1905.

12. JH, January 19, 1899. As late as 1898, however, a member of the First Presidency was still arguing for the gathering: [George Q. Cannon], "The Gathering—Its Advantages," *Juvenile Instructor,* XXXIII (May 1, 1898).

13. JH, July 28, October 8, 1898, January 19, March 30, July 9, 1899, January 23, 1900.

14. JH, January 27, 1898.

15. Remarks cited in Arden B. Olsen, "History of Mormon Mercantile Cooperation in Utah" (unpublished Ph. D. dissertation, University of California, 1936), p. 212.

16. *Ibid.,* pp. 198–200.

17. Arthur Stayner in the Salt Lake *Herald,* December 25, 1887; *Deseret Evening News,* February 4, 1889.

18. *Deseret Evening News,* December 27, 1890.

19. Diary of L. John Nuttall, August 9, 1887; Taylor, *A Saga of Sugar,* pp. 65–66.

20. Salt Lake *Herald,* December 25, 1887; *Deseret Evening News,* February 1, 1888.

21. The prospectus is reproduced in Salt Lake *Herald,* February 10, 1889; see also circular in *Deseret Evening News,* March 15, 1889.

22. *Ibid.,* March 27, 1889.

23. Remarks of Heber J. Grant, *Ninetieth Annual Conference of the Church* . . . (Salt Lake City, 1919), pp. 8–9.

24. The Alvarado and Watsonville, California plants had capacities of 200 and 300 tons respectively; and the new plant at Grand Island, Nebraska, had a capacity of 300 tons.

25. *Deseret Evening News,* October 9, November 8, 1890; Taylor, *Saga of Sugar,* p. 77.

26. Diary of Wilford Woodruff, December 8, 1890.

27. Apostle Heber J. Grant stated in 1903 that only $10,000 was available at the time. "All Israel," he stated, meaning the Mormon people, "in the greatest industry that has yet been established here, invested the enormous amount of ten thousand dollars at the time of the first payment had to be made on that factory." Remarks, *Seventy-Fourth Semi-Annual Conference of the Church* . . . (Salt Lake City, 1903), pp. 9–10.

28. *Deseret Evening News,* December 9, 1890; Diary of Wilford Woodruff, December 8, 9, 1890.

29. Remarks of Heber J. Grant, *Ninetieth Annual Conference of the Church* . . . (Salt Lake City, 1919), pp. 8–9.

30. Sermon of October 8, 1893, *Deseret Evening News,* December 16, 1893.

31. Letter published in Taylor, *Saga of Sugar,* pp. 78–79.

32. See, e.g., *Deseret Evening News,* December 8, 1890, January 22, 1891; *Mariner Wood Merrill and His Family,* pp. 135–137; Diary of L. John Nuttall, December 3, 11, 15, 16, 18, 21, 1891.

33. See esp. remarks of President George Q. Cannon, *Deseret Evening News,* March 3, April 6, 1891.

34. Remarks of Heber J. Grant, *Ninetieth Annual Conference of the Church . . .* (Salt Lake City, 1919), pp. 8–9.

35. Remarks of Heber J. Grant, *Seventy-Fourth Semi-Annual Conference of the Church . . .* (Salt Lake City, 1903), pp. 9–10.

36. *Deseret Evening News,* July 16, 1894.

37. Diary of Wilford Woodruff, January 30, 1891.

38. JH, April 8, 1896; Hinckley, *Heber J. Grant,* pp. 62–64.

39. *Deseret Evening News,* April 6, 1891.

40. See Taylor, *Saga of Sugar,* p. 179.

41. Diary of Wilford Woodruff, March 20, 21, August 23, 1893, February 16, 1894, August 19, 20, October 9, 29, 1895; Cannon and O'Higgins, *Under the Prophet in Utah,* p. 141; *Deseret Evening News,* July 16, 1895.

42. *The Deseret Weekly,* December 28, 1895, pp. 33–34. For an account of Mr. Banigan's participation see also his biography in William R. Cutter, *New England Families: Genealogical and Memorial,* Third Series, Volume II (New York, 1915), pp. 994–997. Most Utah sources spell his name "Bannigan."

43. Sermon of August 6, 1893, *Deseret Evening News,* August 26, 1893.

44. JH, January 15, 1896. The company had previously declared a 15 per cent stock dividend. *Deseret Evening News,* April 16, 1894.

45. "Statement of Assets and Liabilities of the Trustee-in-trust, July 1, 1898," typescript obtained by the writer from an authentic private source.

46. *Ibid.*

47. Incorporation papers, Office of the County Clerk, Salt Lake City.

48. Incorporation papers, Inland Salt Company, Office of County Clerk, Salt Lake City; Salt Lake *Herald,* November 23, 1887.

49. Diary of L. John Nuttall, August 27, 30, 1889.

50. *Ibid.,* February 28, 1889; *Deseret News,* February 28, March 28, 1889; Salt Lake *Herald,* November 14, 1888; JH, January 1, 1889.

51. Salt Lake *Herald,* September 6, 1890.

52. Incorporation papers, Office of the Secretary of State, Salt Lake City; Diary of L. John Nuttall, April 7, 1891; *Deseret News,* September 24, 1892.

53. Diary of L. John Nuttall, June 2, 1891, August 17, 22, 1892.

54. Incorporation papers, Office of Secretary of State. In 1916 the name was changed to the Salt Lake, Garfield, and Western.

55. Salt Lake *Herald,* March 6, April 20, 1890; *Deseret News,* January 12, 1892, May 1, 1893; Diary of L. John Nuttall, August 22, 24, 29, September 17, 1892.

56. *Deseret News,* January 14, 1893.

57. JH, June 19, 1898, January 5, April 21, 1899.

58. *Deseret News,* September 21, 1892, October 26, 1893, October 31, 1895; Incorporation papers, Office of the County Clerk, Salt Lake City.

59. *Deseret News,* August 27, 1897.

60. *Ibid.,* March 2, 1898; *Deseret Weekly,* March 12, 1897, p. 399.

61. O. F. Whitney, *Popular History of Utah* (Salt Lake City, 1916), p. 560; *Deseret Weekly,* March 19, 1898; JH, November 2, 1898, April 1, 1899.

62. "Statement of Assets and Liabilities of the Trustee-in-trust, July 1, 1898"; also, JH, April 21, 1899.

63. JH, June 19, 1898, January 5, April 21, December 26, 1899, August 17, 1900;

Salt Lake *Herald,* August 5, 1901. In 1901, 1902, and 1903, when the church was in a better financial condition, the Quorum of the Twelve recommended, and the First Presidency approved, a proposal to discontinue the sale of liquor. JH, January 10, 1901, April 17, 1902; *Deseret News,* June 12, 1902, May 13, 1903.

64. JH, November 2, 1898, April 1, 21, September 7, 1899; *Deseret News,* April 20, 1905; Cannon and O'Higgins, *Under the Prophet in Utah,* pp. 323–324.

65. Incorporation papers, Secretary of State, Salt Lake City. The significance of the Utah plants in the development of hydroelectric power in America is discussed in John Winthrop Hammond, *Men and Bolts: The Story of General Electric* (New York, 1941), pp. 232–233, 250–251.

66. Ogden *Standard,* October 19, 1896.

67. Diary of Wilford Woodruff, entries for November 14, 22, 24, 27, 1893.

68. Ogden *Standard,* May 15, 1894.

69. Diary of Wilford Woodruff, May 17, 1894.

70. Minutes, Pioneer Electric Power Company, May 22, 1894, Utah Power & Light Co. archives; Diary of Wilford Woodruff, May 22, 1894.

71. Diary of Wilford Woodruff, August 29, November 12, 1895, March 27, 1896; Ogden *Standard,* October 19, 1896.

72. Diary of Wilford Woodruff, August 19, 1895.

73. Incorporation papers, Office of Secretary of State; JH, February 26, 27, 29, 1896; Diary of Wilford Woodruff, March 3, 1896.

74. JH, March 14, 31, April 1, 9, July 10, November 17, 1896, July 28, 1897. The original church guarantee, dated March 2, 1896, is in a file of papers relating to the Pioneer Electric Power Company in the steel case, CHO.

75. Minutes, Pioneer Electric Power Company, November 26, 1895.

76. Diary of Wilford Woodruff, May 26, 1896.

77. A lengthy description, with much historical material, is given in a special edition of the Ogden *Standard,* October 19, 1896. See also *The Journal of Electricity* (San Francisco), III (August 1896), 35–36.

78. *Deseret News,* June 22, 23, 1897; JH, June 18, 1897; Minutes, The Pioneer Electric Power Company, July 25, 1897, Utah Power & Light Co. archives.

79. *Deseret Weekly,* February 8 and September 26, 1896; *Deseret News,* October 5, 1896; JH, April 24 and June 15, 1896; *The Journal of Electricity,* III (August 1896), 21–24.

80. Incorporation papers, Office of the Secretary of State; *Deseret Weekly,* November 2, 1895, February 8, 29, 1896; *Deseret News,* November 25, 1896.

81. Incorporation papers, Office of the Secretary of State; *Deseret News,* February 15, 1893.

82. JH, August 5, 1897; *Deseret Weekly,* August 14, 1897, June 18, 1898; *Salt Lake Tribune,* January 1, 1898.

83. JH, November 29, 1898.

84. JH, January 2, 4, 1899.

85. The church guarantee was modified upon the death of Joseph Banigan, shortly after the Union Light & Power Company was formed. Banigan's heirs sought new arrangements and eventually obtained a large block of preferred stock, valued at $250,000, and bearing 2 per cent interest, in exchange for surrender of the guarantee on the old bonds, and they also obtained 1,500 thousand-dollar bonds of the consolidated company to replace those of the Pioneer company surrendered. In this exchange, the church agreed to guarantee 1 per cent interest on the preferred stock of the company and paid $225,000 in cash to the Banigans. The church's gain consisted of large

quantities of preferred stock. The agreement, dated June 30, 1899, is filed with documents of the Pioneer Electric Power Company, CHO.

86. *Salt Lake Tribune,* January 1, 1898.

87. *Deseret News,* June 11, 1898.

88. *Salt Lake Tribune,* March 1, 1898; JH, March 1, 1898.

89. JH, July 5, 1899.

90. The arrangements are detailed in JH, June 29, 30, July 5, 1899; *Deseret News,* July 6, December 30, 1899.

91. Incorporation papers, Office of Secretary of State.

92. JH, October 7, 22, 1903.

93. Incorporation papers, Office of Secretary of State; *Deseret News,* June 21, August 9, 1901, various articles in April 1905.

94. *Marriner Wood Merrill and His Family,* p. 167, entry for June 1, 1893.

95. Journal History of Utah Stake, April 15, 1894.

96. *Deseret Weekly,* April 4, 1896. The word "they" has been changed to "we" in one instance.

97. The plans are discussed in the Diary of Wilford Woodruff, 1893–1897; Minutes of the Utah Company, MS., CHO; file of documents of the Utah Company, MSS., CHO; articles of incorporation, Utah Company, Salt Lake County Clerk; *Deseret News,* September 13, 1894; incorporation papers, Utah and Pacific Improvement Company, Utah and California Railway Company, and Salt Lake and Pacific Railroad, Office of the Secretary of State; Minutes copied into the JH, 1894 1897.

98. See, esp. Diary of Wilford Woodruff, October 24, 1888.

99. Statement of George Q. Cannon, *Deseret News,* October 20, 1891. "The seizure of the Church property," testified Cannon, "had a very marked effect upon the income [of the church], very many members of the Church fearing to give what they otherwise would lest further seizures might take place." See also the editorial, "A Groundless Apprehension," *Deseret News,* July 14, 1888.

100. JH, July 10, 1899.

101. The completion of the Salt Lake Temple provided an occasion for the reaffirmation of Mormon belief in the theocratic Kingdom. At a special prayer meeting, to which 115 leading church officials were invited, the group unanimously acknowledged "that the Presidency of the Church are set to govern and control the affairs of the Church and Kingdom of God . . . that upon their shoulders rest the responsibility of teaching, governing, controlling and counselling the Church and Kingdom of God in *all* things on the earth." Diary of L. John Nuttall, April 19, 1893.

102. Circular of October 25, 1890, CHO; also documents in the office of the Church Board of Education, Salt Lake City. It would be fair to say that the primary reason for the slow development of a public school system in Utah — beside the obvious one that people engaged in conquering an inhospitable wilderness could not afford the luxury of much education — was the conflict between Mormons and Gentiles. Gentiles objected to public schools because Mormon teachers would expose their children to Mormonism; Mormons, to protect the standing of their own faith, refused to alienate control to non-Mormon elements.

103. John Clifton Moffitt, *The History of Public Education in Utah* (n. p., 1946); M. Lynn Bennion, *Mormonism and Education* (Salt Lake City, 1939).

104. Calculated from "Statement of Assets and Liabilities of the Church, July, 1898."

105. Statement of George Q. Cannon, *Deseret News,* October 20, 1891; and JH, April 27, 1898.

106. Diary of Wilford Woodruff, July 20, August 10, 16, 1893; *Marriner Wood Merrill and His Family,* p. 169.

107. Diary of Wilford Woodruff, September 4, 1893; JH, March 29, 1899.

108. Diary of Wilford Woodruff, January 9, 10, 1894.

109. Cowley, ed., *Wilford Woodruff,* p. 573; Diary of Wilford Woodruff, August 9, November 1, 1894.

110. Incorporation papers, Office of the County Clerk, Salt Lake City; JH, November 28, December 2, 23, 1898, April 24, 27, 1899; "Statement of Assets and Liabilities of the Church, July 1898"; *Deseret Weekly,* September 14, 1895.

111. Cannon and O'Higgins, *Under the Prophet in Utah,* p. 215; Diary of Wilford Woodruff, December 20, 1894, January 15, 1895.

112. Compiled from "Statement of Assets and Liabilities of the Church, July 1898."

113. Cannon and O'Higgins, *Under the Prophet in Utah,* p. 209; JH, July 29, September 13, November 22, 1898; Smith, *Life of Joseph F. Smith,* pp. 303–304.

114. JH, November 23, 1898; *Deseret News,* December 15, 1898.

115. JH, November 25, December 1, 1898; *Deseret News,* December 15, 1898. See description in JH, January 1, 1899.

116. B. H. Roberts, *A Comprehensive History of the Church . . .* (6 vols.; Salt Lake City, 1930), VI, 357, 419; *Deseret News,* January 3, 4, 1899; JH, January 4, 1899.

117. JH, October 22, December 25, 1903; Roberts, *Comprehensive History,* V, 419–421; Smith, *Life of Joseph F. Smith,* p. 431.

118. See Romney, *Life of Lorenzo Snow,* pp. 430–444.

119. This paragraph is based upon R. Davis Bitton, "The B. H. Roberts Case of 1898–1900," *Utah Historical Quarterly,* XXV (1957), 27–46.

120. James Wilford Garner, "The Case of Senator Smoot and the Mormon Church," *North American Review,* CLXXXIV (1907), 46.

121. Smoot Proceedings, III, 285.

122. Many articles on this theme can be found by consulting the *Readers' Guide to Periodical Literature* for the period 1900 to 1915.

123. Ruth and Reginald W. Kauffman, *The Latter Day Saints* (London, 1912), p. 272.

124. *Deseret Evening News,* June 14, 1905; "An Address . . . to the World," *Proceedings of the Seventy-Seventh Annual Conference of the Church . . .* (Salt Lake City, 1907), supp. p. 8.

125. Thomas Kearns, *Congressional Record,* 58th Cong., vol. 39, part iv, pp. 3608–3613.

126. JH, June 8, 1899.

127. JH, January 27, 1900.

128. JH, February 20, April 4, 1900.

129. *Deseret Evening News,* March 5, 1902. Some 50,000 shares of stock were said to have been in the company's treasury.

130. *Ibid.*

131. Incorporation papers, Office of the County Clerk, Salt Lake City.

132. Testimony of T. R. Cutler before Federal Trade Commission, *Salt Lake Tribune,* April 6, 1920.

133. Testimony of Joseph Geoghegan, Smoot Proceedings, IV, 374ff.

134. *Deseret News,* December 25, 1906; Cannon and O'Higgins, *Under the Prophet in Utah,* pp. 264–265.

135. *Deseret Evening News,* May 17, 18, 1906.

136. JH, October 25, November 13, December 2, 1899.

137. Incorporation papers, Utah Iron Mining Company and Utah Iron Company, Office of the Secretary of State; JH, November 9, 18, December 8, 18, 30, 1899, January 13, 1900, April 18, 1902, September 24, 1903.

138. The "business empire" of the Mormon Church in 1957 is described in "Change Comes to Zion's Empire," *Business Week,* November 23, 1957, pp. 108–116; and "Mormon Merchants," *The Wall Street Journal,* December 20, 1956.

Index